Fidel

Fidelity and Honour

The Indian Army from the Seventeenth to the Twenty-first Century

Lt. General S.L. Menezes (retd.)

Foreword by General S.F. Rodrigues,
PVSM, VSM, ADC (retd.)

OXFORD
UNIVERSITY PRESS

OXFORD
UNIVERSITY PRESS

YMCA Library Building, Jai Singh Road, New Delhi 110001

Oxford University Press is a department of the University of Oxford. It furthers the
University's objective of excellence in research, scholarship, and education
by publishing worldwide in

Oxford   New York

Athens   Auckland   Bangkok   Bogota   Buenos Aires   Calcutta
Cape Town   Chennai   Dar es Salaam   Delhi   Florence   Hong Kong   Istanbul
Karachi   Kuala Lumpur   Madrid   Melbourne   Mexico City   Mumbai
Nairobi   Paris   Sao Paolo   Shanghai   Singapore   Taipei   Tokyo   Toronto   Warsaw

with associated companies in   Berlin   Ibadan

Oxford is a registered trade mark of Oxford University Press
in the UK and in certain other countries

Published in India
By Oxford University Press, New Delhi

© Oxford University Press, 1999

The moral rights of the author have been asserted
Database right Oxford University Press (maker)
First published in VIKING by Penguin Books India (P) Ltd 1993
Oxford India Paperbacks 1999
Second impression 2001

ISBN 0 19 565047 6

Typeset in Times Roman
Printed in India at Rashtriya Printers, Delhi 110032
and published by Manzar Khan, Oxford University Press
YMCA Library Building, Jai Singh Road, New Delhi 110001

To
The Soldier of the Indian Army,
Better than the Best in the World

Contents

Acknowledgements

I am very considerably indebted to the following for permission to quote from the publications indicated, or for the research facilities extended, as applicable, without which this book would not have been possible (every effort has been made to seek written permission):

- The Director, National Archives of India (NAI), New Delhi;
- The Director, Ministry of Defence Historical Section (MDHS), New Delhi ; and the Director, Public Relations (DPR), for the photographs reproduced;
- The Director, National Army Museum (NAM), London;
- The Director, Nehru Memorial Museum and Library (NMML), New Delhi;
- The Director, United Service Institution of India (USI), New Delhi;
- The Director, Royal United Services Institute for Defence Studies (RUSI), London;
- The Royal Commonwealth Society (RCS), London; and the Indian Army Association, London;
- The Director, Public Record Office, Kew;
- Her Majesty's Stationery Office (HMSO) for, *The Transfer of Power*, eds. N. Mansergh and Sir Penderel Moon, London, Vols. XI & XII, 1981-83;
- The Deputy Director, British Library (Oriental and India Office Collections) (BL [OIC]): Martin Moir's *General Guide to the India Office Records* (London, 1988), and the very considerable archival material held in the BL[OIC];
- The Director, Imperial War Museum (IWM), London, to reproduce a 1915 photograph; and the Director, International Institute for Strategic Studies (IISS) to quote from *The Military Balance;*
- Gerald Duckworth and Co. for Sir Penderel Moon's *The British Conquest and Dominion of India* (London, 1989);
- Leo Cooper for, W.Moore's *The Thin Yellow Line*, London, 1956; and the Maharaja of Jaipur's *The Indian State Forces*, Leo Cooper, 1961;

- Curtis Brown and John Farquharson for, Patrick Macrory's *Signal Catastrophe,* Jonathan Cape, London, 1966; and Russell Braddon's *The Siege,* Jonathan Cape, London, 1969;
- Random Century Group for, Norman Dixon's *On The Psychology of Military Incompetence,* Jonathan Cape, London, 1976;
- Philip Mason, ICS (Retd.) for, *A Matter of Honour,* Penguin Books, London, 1974 and for his Foreword to Hugh Toye's *The Springing Tiger,* Cassell, London, 1959;
- Professor Judith M. Brown for, *Modern India,The Origins of an Asian Democracy,* Oxford University Press, New Delhi, 1984;
- George Philip Ltd for, G.H. Corr's *The War of the Springing Tigers,* Osprey, London, 1975;
- F.W. Perry for, *The Commonwealth Armies: Manpower and Organisation in Two World Wars,* Manchester University, 1988;
- John Pemble for, *The Invasion of Nepal,* Clarendon Press, Oxford, 1971; and *The Raj, the Indian Mutiny, and the Kingdom of Oudh, 1801-1859,* Harvester Press, Hassocks, Surrey, 1977;
- John Murray (Publishers) Ltd for, Sir Philip Magnus' *Kitchener, Portrait of an Imperialist,* London, 1958;
- Sidgwick and Jackson for Peter King's *A Viceroy's Fall: How Kitchener Destroyed Curzon,* London, 1986;
- The Macdonald Group for, John Smyth's *Percival and the Tragedy of Singapore,* London, 1971; and Louis Allen's *Sittang, the Last Battle,* London, 1973;
- The Oxford University Press for, Stephen Cohen's *The Indian Army : Its Contribution to the Development of a Nation,* Delhi, 1990; Burton Stein's *Thomas Munro,* 1989; and G. Pandey's *The Construction of Communalism in Colonial North India,* 1990;
- William Trousdale for, *War in Afghanistan, 1879-80: The Personal Diary of Major General Sir Charles MacGregor,* Wayne State University Press, Detroit, 1985;
- Major Alexander Greenwood for, *Field Marshal Auchinleck,* Pentland Press, Durham, 1990;
- Khushwant Singh for, *The History of the Sikhs,* Oxford University Press, New Delhi, 1991;
- Lt. Gen. S.K. Sinha for, *Operation Rescue: Military Operations in Jammu and Kashmir, 1947-48,* Vision Books, New Delhi,

1977;
- Lt. Gen. S.D. Verma for, *To Serve with Honour*, Natraj, Dehra Dun, 1989;
- Lt. Gen. Harbakhsh Singh for, *War Despatches, Indo-Pak Conflict, 1965*, Lancer, New Delhi, 1991;
- Virgin Publishing for, Pierce G. Fredericks' *The Sepoy and the Cossack*, London: W.H. Allen, 1971;
- Brian Robson for, *The Eden Commission and the Reform of the Indian Army, 1879-95*, JSAHR, London, 1982;
- D.C. Ellinwood and S.D. Pradhan eds. for, *India and World War I*, South Asia Books, Columbia, 1978;
- Dr Ian Beckett for, *The Singapore Mutiny*, JSAHR, London, 1984;
- Thames and Hudson for, C. Chenevix-Trench's *The Indian Army and the Queen's Enemies: 1900-47*, London, 1989;
- Penguin India for, Leonard Gordon's *Brothers Against the Raj*, New Delhi, 1990;
- Dr T.R. Sareen for, *Japan and the Indian National Army,* Agam Prakashan, New Delhi, 1986; and *Select Documents on Indian National Army*, Agam Prakashan, New Delhi, 1988;
- Maj. Gen. D.K. Palit for, *War in High Himalaya : Indian Army in Crisis, 1962*, Lancer, New Delhi, 1991;
- Longman Group UK for, V.P. Menon's *The Story of the Integration of the Indian States*, Longman Group, UK, 1956;
- Gillian Kaye for, Lieutenant General Sir Francis Tuker's *While Memory Serves,* Cassell, London, 1950; and *Gorkha: The Story of the Gurkhas of Nepal,* Constable, London, 1975;
- Firma KLM for, Amiya Barat's *The Bengal Native Infantry, 1796-1852,* Firma KLM, Calcutta, 1962;
- Sumitra Choudhury for, R.C. Majumdar's *The Sepoy Mutiny and the Revolt of 1857,* Firma KLM, Calcutta, 1974;
- A. Campbell-Johnson for *Mission with Mountbatten*, Robert Hale, London,1951;
- Hugh Tinker ed. for *Indian Armed Forces,* Madras: *Indo-British Review,* Vol. XVI, No. 1, March 1989;
- J. Grey for *Commonwealth Armies and the Korean War,* Manchester University, 1988;

- Inderjeet Gopal Singh for, Dr Gopal Singh's *History of the Sikh People,* World Book Centre, Delhi, 1978;
- Colonel Hugh Toye for, *The Springing Tiger,* Cassell, London, 1959;
- T.A. Heathcote for, *The Indian Army, 1822-1922,* David and Charles, London, 1974;
- Army Educational Stores, Chandigarh, for, Mohan Singh's *Soldiers' Contribution to Indian Independence,* Delhi: Army Educational Stores, 1974;
- Harcourt, Brace, Jovanovich for, Welles Hangen's *After Nehru, Who?,* Rupert Hart Davis, London, 1963;
- H.V. Hodson for, *The Great Divide, Britain-India-Pakistan,* OUP, Karachi, 1985;
- Oxford University Press, Oxford for, Penderel Moon's ed., *Wavell:The Viceroy's Journal,* London, OUP, 1973;
- Deirdre Mosley for, Leonard Mosley's *The Last Days of the Raj,* Weidenfeld and Nicolson, London, 1961;
- L. James for, *Mutiny in the British and Commonwealth Forces, 1757-1956,* Buchan and Enright, London, 1987;
- Harper Collins for, Barbara English's *John Company's Last War,* Collins, London, 1971;
- B.T. Batsford for, Geoffrey Evans' *Slim,* Batsford, London,1969;
- P.J.O. Taylor for, *Chronicles of the Mutiny and other Historical Sketches,* Harper Collins India, Delhi, 1992;
- Crecy Books for permission to reproduce A.C. Lovett's paintings from Major G.F. MacMunn's *The Armies of India,* A. and C. Black, London, 1910 [reprinted by Cathedral Publishing, 1985].

Finally, I am indebted to Dr R.M. Llewellyn-Jones for help rendered, and inevitably my publisher, David Davidar, for suggesting this work.

Foreword

The Indian soldier has always had a reputation for courage, a sense of duty and honour. The Indian Army has proved its mettle in different situations and environments and has always acquitted itself with distinction. However, for a variety of reasons, there has never been an effort to analyse, in their entirety, the different factors that went into the Indian Army's evolution, and the Army's gradual development, over the years, into the magnificent organization it is today. This book fills that vacuum admirably.

The problem, earlier, was that there was a distressing lack of objective accounts that could cover the early formative years dispassionately recording the events and personalities that formed the matrix on which the Indian Army grew. Stephen Cohen, in his book, *The Indian Army,* tackled this problem on a macro level and succeeded admirably in setting out the parameters within which the Army developed. This history goes into these areas in greater detail and I am particularly glad that the author has not confined himself to merely recounting different events, but has sought, where possible, to objectively examine the issues raised and share with us his views on the course of action that could be taken. Within his pragmatic assessment the Army leadership does not emerge entirely unscathed.

In the first thirteen chapters, the author's analysis takes the readers from the early beginning of the Presidency Armies, through the initial tentative use of troops in aid of civil power and the variety of uprisings and mutinies in the Presidency Armies prior to 1857. He has analysed the 1857 Uprising in a refreshingly different way and has propounded the thesis that the uprising was a spontaneous outburst by a poorly managed Bengal Army and not a preconceived, much less a well-planned, mutiny. He suggests that the uprising failed primarily because it was not a coordinated action, and also because of poor leadership.

The evolution of the Indian Army after the Uprising of 1857, its gradual expansion and enlarged scope of deployment, in furtherance of the grand designs of the British, have also been dealt with in considerable detail. I particularly enjoyed the author's treatment of the martial races theory, which he has convincingly refuted, with extensive quotes from historical records of battles. There is a beautiful quote from Field Marshal Auchinleck: '...but the fault was not that of the Madras soldier...the best material in the world will not make good soldiers, unless it has good officers.' So very true, today as well!

The author has analysed, in detail, the process of Indianization, starting with Lord Curzon's creation of the Imperial Cadet Corps in 1901 and his announcement of the King's Commission in the year 1903. The commission was stillborn because of opposition from Lord Roberts. Montagu and Chelmsford were ultimately able to institute over fifty temporary commissions between 1917 and 1919 and the author lists the trials and tribulations faced by those far-sighted functionaries who sought to Indianize the Army. All these endeavours culminated in the establishment of the Indian Military Academy (IMA) in 1932.

The war years (1939-1945) make very interesting reading. The Indian National Army (INA) has been researched comprehensively and this particular analysis provides valuable insight into the INA itself-its leaders, the various Indo-Japanese and Indo-German protocols covering its role and, finally, a summary of its achievements and failures.

The formative years of the post-independence Indian Army have been covered well. The latter chapters, dealing with the contemporary period, include a very frank analysis of certain landmark events that occurred. The unhappy decision of dividing the Indian Army at the time of Partition, and the trauma suffered by many affected units, makes poignant reading.

The treatment of the post-independence Nehru years includes the controversial political involvement in the affairs of the Army and the subsequent 1962 debacle. The penultimate chapter is devoted to an analysis of the performance of the Indian Army in important events.

Though the author has rightly chosen not to narrate the detailed story of the 1965 and 1971 wars, he has analysed them in adequate detail. The compulsions under which the Indian Army undertook Operation Bluestar and Operation Pawan have been elaborated upon.

In this book, the author, with the benefit of his exhaustive research, has very imaginatively brought the Indian Army into focus. He has extensively used quotes from reliable sources to authenticate his views.

This book breathes life into a wonderful organization that I have had the privilege to belong to and explains what is, after all, a very individual tradition, the formation of which our predecessors have contributed to substantially.

New Delhi   *General S. F. Rodrigues*
31 October 1992

Prologue

It has not been a light task to write the story of the Indian Army in a compact and concise form, within the length suggested by the publisher, owing to the very considerable literature on various facets, both official and unofficial, in Calcutta, Delhi and London. That has meant leaving out far more than it has been possible to include. The task is doubly difficult when this story is intended for readers with varied attitudes on the subject. It is hardly an exaggeration to say that every reader will have an Indian Army conception of his own, some viewpoints being diametrically opposite. On the one hand, we have laudatory accounts; on the other, deprecatory—the latter postulating that until independence in 1947 it was a mercenary army. While this book is not meant to glorify war, whether under the British or after independence (for I am one with General William Tecumseh Sherman, who said in 1879, 'Its glory is all moonshine. It is those who have neither fired a shot nor heard the shrieks and groans of the wounded, who cry aloud for blood, more vengeance, more desolation. War is hell.'); it must nevertheless be appreciated that courage must be recognized, irrespective of the motivation. In the event, any army's identity is rooted in the consciousness of its history. The concept of Indian nationalism that exists today did not subsist when the East India Company raised the three Presidency Armies of Bengal, Madras and Bombay, which were later unified into the present day Indian Army. There has been in it, by and large, an apparently superb bonding between the leader and the led, which was never quite possible to explain. Or as Sardar Baldev Singh, the first Indian Defence Minister, put it, 'The discipline inculcated by association with British officers has been a cementing force of no small value.' My aim has been to present the story, warts and all, in its continuing process of evolution to this day. Some may feel I have reverted to *a priori* reconstruction. It is not so. It is just that hindsight is the more perfect vision. The story falls naturally into three periods. The first is the story of the armies of the Bengal, Madras and Bombay Presidencies, initially under the East India Company up to 1857, and then under the Crown; the second is the story of the unified Indian Army from 1895 to independence in 1947; and the third is the story of the "partitioned" Indian Army to date. It is to be noted that, if, in the words of the poet, 'the noblest study of mankind is man,' then in this story much material is to be found to that end, for, from its inception over three hundred years ago, it has always consisted of volunteers—often hereditary soldiers following generation after generation in the same regiments and corps; in some cases, eight generations up to today.

The process was initially a slow one, for, while in the latter half of the eighteenth and early nineteenth centuries, in India, trade may have followed the flag, in the late seventeenth and first half of the eighteenth centuries the Indian soldier followed the British trader. Gradually, and inevitably, the three Presidency Armies took shape and evolved from what were local levies into more modern armies—organized, armed and clothed after the fashion of the European armies of the time. Here it needs to be mentioned that putting the Indian soldier into the unsuitable and uncomfortable scarlet coat was not egalitarianism nor paternalism, but economics, for the East India Company recorded, 'to give a more martial appearance and to take off a very considerable quantity of woollen goods.' These armies carried the rule of the Company throughout India, and even abroad.

After the unification of 1895, though there was no prior operational planning or commitment for Indian troops to serve in France, against a "first-class" enemy, nevertheless, equipment-wise, "second-class" Indian divisions arrived in 1914 just in time, in the words of Field Marshal Sir Claude Auchinleck, 'to stem the German onslaught,' on the Allied line, which could not have been possible without them. 'The Turkish attack on the Suez Canal in 1915 was thrown back almost entirely by Indian troops.' The victories against the Turks in Mesopotamia and Palestine were achieved largely by 675,000 troops from India, not forgetting the campaign against the Germans and their efficient African soldiers in East Africa. Over a million rations for Indian troops abroad were supplied daily from India during much of the First World War. On the onset of the Second World War, the authorities in Britain again doubted whether the Indian Army, 'could be trusted to face the German war machine—then the most highly trained and equipped of any army in the world.' As, 'the pressure of the German armies grew, and as the Allies fell back or were overrun,' recourse was again had to the Indian Army, despite no operational planning in this regard, as had happened in 1914, and indeed by Britain 'on many a previous occasion.' During the most critical period of the Second World War in Africa, 'when Rommel threatened to break through into Asia, six of the fourteen infantry divisions under the Commander-in-Chief of the Middle East were divisions of the Indian Army.' Before this, some of these Indian divisions had eliminated the Italians from Eritrea and Abyssinia, and later three of these Indian divisions were foremost in pushing the Germans out of Italy, half the British force. At the same time, 'the 14th Army, predominantly Indian, was bringing about the total defeat of the Japanese in Assam and Burma, inflicting many more casualties on them than did the Americans in the whole of their Pacific campaign.' Space has not permitted going into all the details of the campaigns of the First and Second World Wars, or post-independence; these are well-known and covered in the official accounts, or other numerous contemporary publications. Nor have I sought to describe any individual battle, taking my cue from the Duke of Wellington, who epitomized the dilemma in his retort to an author who sought his help in writing an account of Waterloo: 'Write the history of a battle, Sir? You might as well write the history of a ball.'

It was Prince Otto von Bismarck who said, 'Were the British Empire to disappear, its work in India would remain one of its lasting monuments.' The Indian Army is one of those monuments. Many British in 1947, however, said it was the beginning of the end; actually it was the end of the beginning. Whereas, numerically, the Indian Army was at its zenith in the Second World War, it is good to be able to say, without doubt or hesitation, that the Indian soldier of today is better than he ever was under the British, a high standard indeed. Still invoking Field Marshal Auchinleck, he has always been, 'second to none in soldierly spirit and pride of profession.' Today he has these qualities in much greater degree, because to his perpetual loyalty to his regiment, has been added a paramount loyalty to his country as is abundantly manifest from his devotion and sacrifice in the three conflicts with Pakistan and one with China, as also during the multiple peacekeeping tasks abroad, apart from the multiplicity of occasions that aid to the civil authorities has been rendered. Today the Indian soldier, 'knows and feels that the army he serves is his

Army,' truly a great Army, still 'a remarkable Army unlike any other'—the paradigm of its times. There is an old Persian proverb, 'History is a mirror of the past, and a lesson for the present.' Comparison between historical events need not be taken too far, but nevertheless all past events in the Indian Army have lessons for today—and tomorrow. This book is therefore a small tribute from one who served it for over thirty-seven years.

New Delhi   *Lt. Gen. S.L. Menezes*
31 October 1992

List of Abbreviations

BL[OIC]—British Library (Oriental and India Office Collection), London.
CIGS—Chief of the Imperial General Staff.
CO—Commanding Officer.
DSO—Distinguished Service Order.
ECO—Emergency Commissioned Officer.
GOC—General Officer Commanding.
GOC-in-C—General Officer Commanding-in-Chief.
HMSO—Her/His Majesty's Stationery Office.
IAF—Indian Air Force.
ICO—Indian Commissioned Officer.
ICS —Indian Civil Service.
IECO—Indian Emergency Commissioned Officer.
INA—'Indian National Army'.
ISLR—Indian Self-Loading Rifle.
IWM—Imperial War Museum, London.
JCO--Junior Commissioned Officer.
JSAHR—*Journal of the Society for Army Historical Research,* London.
KCIO—King's Commissioned Indian Officer.
MC—Military Cross.
MDHS—Ministry of Defence Historical Section, New Delhi.
MGO—Master General of the Ordnance.
MVC—Maha Vir Chakra.
NAI—National Archives of India, New Delhi.
NAM—National Army Museum, London.
NCO—Non-Commissioned Officer.
NMML—Nehru Memorial Museum and Library, New Delhi.
NWFP—North West Frontier Province.
Orme Mss—Orme Manuscripts in the BL[OIC].
PVC—Param Vir Chakra.
PW—Prisoner of War.
RAF—Royal Air Force.
RIAF—Royal Indian Air Force.
RIN—Royal Indian Navy.
SEAC—South East Asia Command.
VC—Victoria Cross.
VCO—Viceroy's Commissioned Officer.

ONE

Early Beginnings

THE FIRST Englishman reportedly to have visited India was Bishop Sighelmus of Sherborne in AD 883. According to the *Anglo Saxon Chronicle,* King Alfred sent him on a pilgrimage to Mylapore, then a small village on India's eastern coast and the reputed site of St.Thomas' tomb.[1] It was nearly 700 years after the return of Sighelmus before another Englishman came to India, in 1579. He was the Jesuit, Thomas Stephens, the first Englishman known to have settled in India, and whose descriptive letters to his father, a wealthy London merchant, are believed to have been the unwitting motivation for English commercial interest in India.[2]

On 31 December 1600, Queen Elizabeth I granted a charter to an association, the Governor and Company of Merchants of London trading into the East Indies, having assessed the prospects of advantageous trade. This company, more commonly known as the English East India Company, was granted exclusive rights to trade across the world, 'beyond of the Cape of Bona Esperanza (Good Hope) to the Straits of Magellan.'[3] The Portuguese and Dutch had preceded the English, and the French followed. Much of the history of this Company, during the seventeenth and early eighteenth centuries was a struggle to assert these conferred rights, using arms when required. As described by Martin Moir: 'The struggle involved a peculiar

1

pattern of trade and settlement in the East, a pattern ...of conflicts with other European trading rivals, and with Asian powers.'[4]

The Company's initial efforts to develop direct trade with the Spice Islands and the Malay Archipelago encountered the growing strength of the Dutch East India Company. Moir adds: 'Thus the Amboyna Massacre of 1623, in which a group of English merchants and their servants was killed on the orders of the Dutch Governor, was followed in 1628 by the English Company's withdrawal from Batavia to Bantam in Java.... Thereafter, although the Company's trade in the Archipelago still continued...controlled first from the Presidency at Bantam till 1682, and from 1684 from Bencoolen (Fort Marlborough) in Sumatra...the Company's endeavours shifted from this region by the middle years of the seventeenth century...Earlier attempts to open up trade with Japan through the Hirado factory (1613-23), and with Thailand, at Ayutthaya and Patani, had also failed by the 1630s, and it was therefore to the Indian sub-continent that this Company turned for a way out of its commercial difficulties.'[5]

In January 1613, Emperor Jahangir's firman, permitting an English factory or trading post at Surat, was delivered to Captain Thomas Best, the Company's senior representative at the time at Surat. Thereafter, in 1615, Sir Thomas Roe, India's first English Ambassador, arrived at Agra. Roe wisely noted before his departure in 1619: 'A war and traffic are incompatible...let this be received as a rule that if you will profit, seek it at sea and in quiet trade, for, without controversy, it is an error to effect garrisons and land wars in India.'[6]

The Company's trade in India, which commenced with the establishment of the factory at Surat in 1613, 'was primarily directed during the seventeenth century towards the purchase of cotton piece-goods for import to England, for profitable re-export to Europe, and also for use in the country-trade with other parts of Asia. Other Indian commodities...also became of growing value to the Company during this period,' notes Moir. By the middle of the seventeenth century the Company's Indian trade was organized into three main areas—the Western Coast, controlled from the Surat Presidency; the Coromandel (now Cholamandalam) Coast; and Bengal and Orissa. Again according to Moir: 'On the western side, the importance of the

Surat Presidency gained through the opening up of the Company's trade with Iran from the 1620s, and from the cessation of English hostilities with the Portuguese from 1635 onwards. During the 1630s, factories subordinate to Surat were set up elsewhere in western India—at Tatta, Broach (now Bharuch) and Ahmedabad—and later in the 1640s at Basra in the Gulf, and in the Red Sea at Mocha and Suakin. The Surat factory remained the headquarters of the Company's western Indian trade until 1687, when it was succeeded by Bombay.[7] The Company's Surat establishment continued as only a factory.

In 1661, despite Roe's advice, the Company was given the authority by King Charles II to send armed ships and men to make war against non-Christians, 'in the place of their trade.' In a later renewal of the charter this became against any "heathen nations" of Asia, Africa and America. In 1662, the island of Bombay became the property of the English King, ceded to him by Portugal as a portion of the marriage settlement of his Queen, Catherine of Braganza. It had been ceded to the Portuguese by the ruler of Gujarat in 1534. It was the English Company's first territorial acquisition in India. A detachment of the King's troops, subsequently augmented by a few Europeans of various nationalities and 150 "Deccanis", was its garrison in 1667. But, to the King, the maintenance of this property proved a burden. Moreover, the relations between Sir Gervase Lucas, the King's Governor of the island, and the Company's President at Surat became strained over precedence. The former, as an officer of the King, claimed precedence over the latter, the Company's representative. The violent disputes over precedence, combined with the then-perceived poor financial prospects of his property, induced King Charles to offer Bombay to the Company.

The island was handed over in March 1668 on a yearly rental of ten pounds in gold, and was placed under the Company's President at Surat, while a Deputy Governor was appointed at Bombay. At the same time, the King's troops in Bombay were offered service under the Company, with all ranks and pay retained, and those who declined were granted free passage back to England. Reportedly, most of the troops accepted service under the Company, and, thus, the King's troops were converted to the service of the Company, a conversion which was reversed when after 1857, the Europeans in

3

the Company's forces were converted to the service of the Crown. Certain increases were made in the Bombay garrison, in 1683, when it was supplemented by two companies of Rajputs (variously referred to as "Rashpouts" or "Raja Poots"), each company consisting of one hundred men, commanded by their own Rajput officers. Recourse was had to Rajputs, and not Marathas, as Bombay, at the time, was under pressure by the Maratha forces. This small force, auxiliaries to the Bombay-European troops, though not the first Indian soldiers of the English, may be regarded, in the opinion of Sir Patrick Cadell, as the beginnings of the Indian Army, for, as *The Imperial Gazetteer of India* (1909) rightly records: 'The Indian Army sprang from very small beginnings.'[8] Here it must be noted that some of the Indian State Forces (ISF), merged into the Indian Army after independence, date their raisings to much before 1683, which is covered in a subsequent chapter in relation to their mergers.

Some of these Rajputs were detailed from Bombay to guard the Surat factory, and were granted an extra allowance *(batta)* for being detailed on detached duty. Subsequent years were marked by economic constraints, one of these leading to the withdrawal of the *batta* from the detachment at Surat. Though no reaction is recorded to this withdrawal, subsequent periodic withdrawals of the *batta* from the Bengal and Madras Armies led to protests, which were deemed by the British as mutinies. Separately, the English interference at sea, with the pilgrim traffic to Mecca, led to their expulsion in December 1688 from western India, excluding Bombay, as such interference was, in effect, war against the Mughal Emperor. Bruce Lenman narrates their return: 'A contemptuous Imperial firman or decree of the Emperor Aurangzeb in February 1690 readmitted the East India Company to trade in his dominions as before the war, in exchange for a grovelling admission of guilt and a stiff fine of 150,000 rupees (at the time about 15,000 pounds). To Aurangzeb, the Company was still a mere flea on the back of his Imperial elephant.'[9]

Though the Company had started to trade on the Coromandel Coast virtually at the same time as on the Western Coast—a trading post being established in 1625 at Masulipatam (now Machilipatnam), later moved to Armagon (now Dugarajapatnam) on the same coast, where fortifications were erected—it was through acquiring from the Nayak of Wandiwash (now Vandavasi) on very favourable terms the concession of Madras in 1639, christened Fort St. George in 1640, that it secured a suitable base for the expansion of its trade. Moir states: "By 1684, Madras was formally raised to the level of a Presidency, with responsibility for several factories on the coast— Porto Novo (Parangippetai), Cuddalore (Fort St. David) and Vizagapatam (Visakhapatnam), as well as for factories...in Bengal.'

In 1634, a firman of the Emperor Shah Jahan gave the Company permission to establish factories, initially at Hugli and Balasore, with a fort at Pipli. In 1686, several further factories were maintained at Hariharpur, Cossimbazar, Patna, Dacca (now Dhaka) and Malda. Because of frequent disputes with the local Mughal authorities, and the English, in 1686, sending an expedition of ten ships and 600 men to attack the Nawab of Bengal, these factories, between 1686 and 1690, were liable to complete closure. The establishment of a permanent settlement at Calcutta in 1690, and the construction of the first Fort William there, in 1696, on the approximate site of the present General Post Office, resulted in the governor and president of Fort William being recognized in 1700, 'as the controlling Company authority in Bengal, independent of Madras,' according to Moir.

Thus, by the beginning of the eighteenth century, the East India Company had succeeded in establishing itself commercially on the subcontinent. 'Beyond the confines of India...the Company had also created a profitable trading empire from the Red Sea to the China Sea,' and this, sequentially, later led to Indian troops being employed there.[10] Guards were inevitably enrolled for the protection of the factories and trading posts established. These guards were meant to add to the dignity of the chief officials or factories, as well as serve a protective purpose, and were, mainly, poorly-equipped chowkidars. As time went on, their military character became more marked. In Calcutta, the guards or peons recruited were colloquially referred to as "Buxaries", as such men were being recruited from the area about Buxar, the Shahabad district, which, up to 1857, was the great recruiting ground for the Bengal Army. Today, this same area makes up the Bhojpur and Rohtas districts.

In 1698, a further Company of English Merchants received its charter. It was known as the English Company, in contradistinction to the existing London Company the two Companies becoming bitter rivals in India. Both Companies were eventually united, under the title of the United Company of Merchants of England trading to the East Indies. 'This united East India Company, which emerged in 1709, was a much stronger body than its predecessors. The complex overall development of this Company, during the next century and a half, included phases of unparalleled wealth and territorial power, major transformations in its central objectives, and, eventually, increasing subordination to British government control.'[11]

One of the measures taken was the reconfirmation of the three Presidencies. The president of each was also the nominal commander-in-chief of the exiguous military forces of each Presidency, and was responsible only to the Company's directors in England. Communications by sea or land being tedious, the forces of the three Presidencies became distinct and separate from each other. Thus a Presidency Army system was established of small military units, composed of Europeans recruited from England, or locally, and of Indian auxiliaries. The latter were then armed with their own weapons, wore their own dress and were commanded by their own officers, or, as W.J. Wilson described in his *History of the Madras Army:* 'They had no discipline, nor any idea that discipline was required. They were armed with matchlocks, bows and arrows, spears, swords, bucklers, daggers, or any other weapons they could get.' In the Bombay Presidency, three companies were disbanded in 1706 for seeming neglect of duty, even though their pay had been in arrears for four years!

At the beginning of the eighteenth century, the strength of the Presidency forces was still so exiguous as not to tempt the presidents to undertake any adventure with the neighbouring Indian rulers. The Company of Merchants was, for the time being, being what its name implied. But circumstances beyond the control of the directors in London supervened to convert its servants in India into organizers of conquest, for nothing was to interfere with what Sir John Malcolm has described as, 'that spirit of plunder and that passion for the rapid accumulation of wealth which actuated all ranks.' Already, by 1768, twenty Britons, who had made fortunes in India, were Members of Parliament in England. The Company had an important place in the life of Britain, selling annually 2,000,000 pounds worth of imported goods, and making large loans to the British Government. Ministers

6

and politicians were interested in its stock and the patronage of its directors.

The Company's activities, at this juncture, may be divided into two periods, from 1709 to 1765, when the Company was still primarily a commercial body, and from 1765 to 1857, when it became involved in governance. During part of the first period, from the Treaty of Utrecht in 1713 to the outbreak of war with France in 1744, the Company's trade expanded steadily as a result of the virtual ending of its conflict with the Dutch, the maintenance till then of moderately peaceful relations with France, and the decreasing authority of the Mughals. Further east, the Company's commerce at Canton became established. 'The outbreak of war with France in India in 1744 (War of Austrian Succession 1742-1748) brought this largely peaceful commercial phase to an end, and initiated a period of change in the Company's affairs. The French capture of Madras in 1746 led to a prolonged military and diplomatic conflict in which the English and the French vied to gain the upper hand in the Carnatic* and Hyderabad by intervening or taking opposing sides in local dynastic rivalry. From this conflict the English Company eventually emerged the victors after the capture of the French centre of Pondicherry (now Puduchcheri) in 1761, which was returned to France after the Treaty of Paris in 1763.'[12]

Of this period, Penderel Moon said, 'Both parties, with their eyes fixed on limited and immediate objectives, were, for some years, unaware of the high stakes for which they were playing. They thought they were fighting each other for the trading advantages that influence over local rulers might secure for them; but, the real issue, as it turned out, was which of them should succeed the Mughals as the masters of all India.'[13]

The Madras Presidency authorities received a shock when, in 1748, Captain Stringer Lawrence, promoted to Major by the King only in the territories of the East India Company, and subsequently deemed by the English as "the father of the Indian Army", arrived at Fort St. David since Madras at the time was occupied by the French, and took up his appointment as 'Major of the Garrison at Fort

---

* The Carnatic was the stretch of country below the Eastern Ghats between the Kistna (Krishna), and the Cauvery (Kaveri).

St. George (Madras).' Captured by the French shortly after, he was released in 1749, and, in 1752, was the first army officer to be appointed Commander-in-Chief of all the Company's forces in India*.

The Presidency forces began to improve their organization, and promotion was by seniority. This rule could not be departed from, unless sanctioned by the governors of the respective Presidencies. The Indian elements were a little superior to an armed police force, commanded by their own officers who were individuals of position in the respective Indian communities from which the soldiers were recruited. The capture of Madras by the French Company in 1746, had obliged the English Company to commence the formation of a military establishment. Stringer Lawrence's appointment constitutes the first link. This action was taken by the English, to counter French efforts, for, as early as 1676, Francois Martin, Governor of Pondicherry, had enrolled 300 Indians as soldiers to supplement his scanty force of Europeans. The French used the word *cypayes,* from the Persian *sipahi* (soldier). In 1740, Benoit Dumas, his successor, formed a force comprising Europeans and 4,000 to 5,000 Indians, armed·in the European fashion. The war with France temporarily ceased with the Treaty of Aix-la-Chapelle in 1748, both sides having more Europeans in their forces than had ever existed in India. Neither side could increase these forces, as all available troops were required for future operations in the main European theatre of war.

The contending armies in India of these two European powers could only be augmented by the employment of Indian troops, whose value began to be appreciated. This had earlier been the practice adopted by others, like Alexander, who enlisted into his army the local people of conquered territories. Though the Indian soldier of those days, through a lack of proper armament, was inferior to his better-armed European counterpart, it became apparent that victory would be with the side which best succeeded in raising and suitably arming its Indian forces (the French first using *cypayes* at Mahe in 1721-29). The brilliant Swiss officer, Louis Paradis, who served the French, widely used *cypayes* in the short period before he was killed in 1748. In the same year, before the

---

* See Appendix 1 for the succession of Army Chiefs.

temporary cessation of hostilities, the Indian company at Tellicherry was feared, to be planning to defect from the English and join the French. The company commander, who was a Subedar, Bhikam Khan, and ten others, were banished to St. Helena in the Atlantic. He appears to have escaped, however, being rearrested at Tellicherry in 1756.

War with France again broke out, and the Madras Government, in May 1754, appealed to the Bombay Government for help. Before the resumption of hostilities, however, Captain Alexander Delavaux, the Engineer of the Madras Presidency, had already deserted to the French. The Madras appeal was answered, and a force of 750 men was despatched from Bombay—three Indian companies and 450 men of the Bombay-European regiment, comprising 200 British, one hundred Swiss and 150 "topasses". The despatch of this Bombay force to Madras established the readiness of one Presidency to help another despite the distance involved. It also manifested the limited strength of the Presidency Armies till 1754. Apart from the companies of Swiss mercenaries, the French Rangers, formed from French and Franco-Irish regiments after the capture of Pondicherry (and later Hanoverian mercenaries), supplemented the Company's European infantry after 1761.

The year 1754 marks the last occasion on which "topasses" are mentioned. They were Eurasians, probably given the name "topas" by locals because of the European headgear they wore. It is not certain when this designation in the Company's forces was specifically abolished, though the designation "topas" continued for many years for a certain category of personnel employed by shipping companies plying between India and Britain. The year 1754 also saw the arrival in India of the English King's troops, for the first time since 1668, until when the island of Bombay was garrisoned by the King's troops before being ceded to the Company.

Meanwhile, in Bengal, the Company had got entangled in local politics resulting, in 1756, in the Nawab Siraj-ud-Daula's seizure of Calcutta and Company factories in other places, and the counteraction by the relief force from Madras led by Robert Clive, which culminated in the Nawab's defeat at Plassey (now Palasi) in June 1757. 'What had started, in part, as an effort to secure for the Company trading privileges in Bengal, ended with the Company holding *de jure* control over the whole province. Initially, this control was sought to be exercised indirectly, through a succession of puppet nawabs, until, in 1765, under Clive's direction, a measure of legality was conferred by the Mughal Emperor's formal grant of the *diwani* (revenue authority) of Bengal, Bihar and Orissa to the Company, and the subsequent reduction of the Nawab's position by the Company to one of titular dignity.'[14]

Paradis' successes on behalf of the French, led the English to follow the French example. Consequently, before the battle of Plassey, in June 1757, Clive had commenced to reorganize the Indian troops in his command by forming them into a regular battalion with a few European officers. He armed and dressed them like the Europeans, so that, in battle, and from a distance, they were indistinguishable from the Europeans; thus, the concept of equipping them in the local style was displaced. Purbias, Bhojpuris, Awadhis and Rohillas were ready to enlist with the British in Bengal; they, earlier, used to enlist in the Nawab's service. The first battalion thus organized in Bengal by Clive was nicknamed the "Lal Paltan" because of the troops' red coats. The English word "platoon" is derived from the French word *peloton* (troop), and both, or either one, may be considered to be the origin of the Indian word *paltan*, which, by usage, has come to be considered to mean "battalion". The establishment of the "Lal Paltan" was:

- Indian—one Indian commandant, one Indian adjutant, ten subedars, thirty jemadars, 820 rank and file; and
- British—one captain, two subalterns, one sergeant-major and ten sergeants.

The Lal Paltan consisted of ten companies, including two grenadier companies. The ten companies included all the Indians, except the Indian commandant and the Indian adjutant. These two Indian officers formed, as we would call it now, the "battalion headquarters". The Indian commandant on parade took position along with the Hindustani-speaking British captain, and was followed by the Indian adjutant. The other British officers and non-commissioned officers formed the "staff" of the battalion. As J.Williams then

10

recorded: 'Dressed and drilled in the European style, each company had its distinctive colour, which also carried the emblem of its subedar. The grenadiers, as a mark of distinction, had a Union Jack in the upper corner of their flag.'[15]

Up to this date, Indian troops had been organized only in companies, generally under their own officers. Clive decided that, for a battalion organization, some British element was necessary, but he also sought to adhere to the previous system. There was an Indian commandant, and the proportion of Indian to British officers was moderately high. T. Rice Holmes stated: 'The early English rulers believed that they would secure the attachment as well as the obedience of...natives of good family to enter their service as officers, and giving them the ample authority in which their birth and habits of command fitted them to wield. The native commandant was indeed under the supervision of an English officer, but he was occasionally seen in command of a detachment of which European soldiers formed a part to undertake the responsibility and to win the glory of some distant enterprise.'[16]

The introduction of British non-commissioned officers into Indian units is also a point to be noted, as it remained a general rule, up to 1857, in Indian infantry battalions, when some British non-commissioned officers in the latter joined the mutinous Indian troops of the Bengal Army. After 1858, some British non-commissioned officers continued for varying periods in the Indian Sappers and Miners, and later in the Indian Signal Corps, as also some military administrative services, but not in the Indian infantry and cavalry. (In the latter, at least one British non-commissioned officer opted to serve on in the same regiment, as a risaldar.) By a quirk of fate, with this Indian military organization, the French designs, of Joseph-Francois Dupleix and others, had been achieved by the British.

The Company's military successes caused an augmentation of the Indian units in the three Presidencies. Of this development, E.W.Sheppard has said in *A Short History of the British Army* (1959): 'An army was built up from the people of India themselves, which in the end brought its own country under the sway of its foreign masters.' Immediately after the battle of Plassey, a second Indian battalion was raised in Bengal. In 1759, in Madras, six Indian battalions were raised on Clive's organization. In Bombay, Indians,

11

Arabs and Africans, mainly from Abyssinia, but some also from Madagascar, then formed an auxiliary element within the battalion of Europeans. Indians were organized into independent companies in 1760, and then into battalions in 1767.

The years following Plassey witnessed the extension of the Company's rule, and Indian battalions, which had been supervised by a small complement of three British officers, but were commanded by Indian commandants and Indian company commanders, were now battalions with British commandants and British company commanders. A policy that opposed the acquisition of territory, and remonstrations to that effect from the directors in England were of little avail. The viceroys of the Mughal Emperor and their subordinates were scrambling for power after the death of Aurangzeb in 1707, and, with the death of Asaf Jah at Hyderabad in 1748, the British and French were provided with one such occasion for intervening in local politics.

Sequentially, the balance of military power became unstable, with the strength of the Marathas now asserting itself. The European traders, for some years peaceful, in order to amass wealth, employed their Indian soldiers on various sides, according to the relative commercial gains likely to result. But, at no stage did they forget that other facet of warfare—Machiavellian intrigue, in which good faith was the most frequent casualty. After the recall of Dupleix to France, in 1754, the French position in India weakened. Had Dupleix, the greatest French colonial governor in India, not been recalled due to the machinations against him, including those by the British, it is possible that the French, rather than the British, may have prevailed, and India could have been Francophone today. But, as Clive put it to Robert Orme, in September 1765: 'Fortune seems determined to accompany me to the last—every object, every sanguine wish is upon the point of being completely fulfilled, and I am arrived at the pinnacle of all I covet, by affirming the Company shall, in spite of all envy, malice, faction and resentment, acknowledge they are become the most opulent company in the world by the battle of Plassey.'[17]

Militarily, Plassey was a skirmish on an undistinguished battlefield, according to John Terraine, and yet, 'from the opening of the 18th century, the Western World had been big with ideas, and the most world-changing was that of the use of steampower.... All that was lacking was the gold to fertilize it, and it was Clive who undammed the Yellow Stream.'[18] Seen in this light, 'Plassey appears as the midwife of the Industrial Revolution. And it was on this that the power of the British Empire itself rested for nearly two centuries,'[19] said Terraine.

Two years after Plassey, the Dutch were overpowered at Chinsura, and, in 1764, the Nawab of Oudh (Awadh) was defeated at the battle of Buxar, with the English using, in the main, Indian troops. The emergence of a more settled form of government in Bengal thereafter, combined with the appointment of Warren Hastings as Governor-General (1773-1785), who was entrusted with powers over the other two Presidencies and relied on the prowess of Indian troops, made it possible for the Bengal and Bombay Armies to provide aid to the Madras Army during its struggle with Hyder Ali (who described the British as 'the most faithless and usurping of all mankind'), as also during renewed hostilities with the French in South India during 1778-83. The temporary peace with France, Tipu Sultan and the Marathas in 1783-84, 'from the point of view of historical hindsight marked the consolidation of the Company's newly gained territories, and the beginning of a further, even if deemed intermittent, phase of imperialist expansion, relying largely on Indian troops, leading to British domination of the entire subcontinent with the augmented Presidency armies.'[20]

In 1765, the Indian battalions were formed into brigades, each having a proper staff. At this time, the British officers of the Indian troops were selected from among the officers of the European regiments, and were chosen from the point of view of their suitability to serve with Indian troops. Such officers enjoyed many advantages, but had no relative precedence, with the result that they continually found themselves in subordinate positions to the younger officers of the King's troops. The inferiority was resented, and these British officers began to demand equal treatment. The result of this agitation was the reorganization of the Presidency Armies, in 1796. At this time, the Europeans in the military in India (the King's and the Company's) numbered about 13,000, while the number of Indian troops in the three Presidency Armies was 57,000 (Bengal 24,000; Madras 24,000; Bombay 9,000).

Before going into the 1796 reorganization, whereby the overall strength of the Indian component was reduced, it is necessary to consider, first, the characteristics of the Indian forces of the Company during this period, and the characteristics of their adversaries. Fighting was a profession for several hundred thousands. Many people found their way to Bengal, and, whereas previously they used to join the Nawab's forces, now they enrolled in the Company's forces, attracted by the promise of more regular pay. Thus Pathans, Afghans, Jats and others from the Punjab also enlisted themselves under the British, though the Bengal Army gradually drew persons largely from Oudh and Rohilkhand. From 1776 till 1857, the Bengal Army was almost entirely recruited from the tract between the Ganga and the Gogra (now Ghagara), the men being described as Purbias, and, till 1857, were viewed as, 'a brave and manly race of people,' and were mostly Brahmins and Rajputs. The Madras and Bombay Armies, however, contained a majority from the respective hinterlands, in contrast, thus, to the Bengal Army—the first Bengali unit as such being the 49th Bengal Regiment, raised during the First World War. Though it is not possible to say how many, some Pathans, Rohillas, Rajputs, Arabs and Abyssinians, always a minority, were enrolled in Bombay and even in Madras.

Discipline and training were superior to that of their opponents. Marching, manoeuvring in formation and concentrating fire enabled smaller bodies of the Company's soldiers to overcome their adversaries. Allowing for exaggeration in estimating the numbers of a defeated enemy, the princely armies of those days dragged, in their train, ten times the number of fighting men in the shape of followers, and constituted a moving township. In a Mughal army, for example, the emperor would be accompanied by fifteen or sixteen rajas, each of whom could bring into the field 25,000 horsemen. The Jesuit, F. Catrou, estimated, in 1707, Aurangzeb's army to be 300,000 cavalry and 600,000 foot soldiers. This is not to presuppose that the British-Indian forces did not have large baggage trains and a considerable number of camp followers. They increasingly did, as they learnt, to their cost, or rather, at the cost of the unfortunate Indian camp followers, both men and women, particularly in the First Anglo-Afghan War, 1839-1842.

Thousands of freelances were also employed, adventurers ready to bid for any service which offered some pay, and, even more, plunder. There were inevitably exceptions like the loyal Afghan bodyguard of the Rani of Jhansi in 1857-1858. Courage was displayed both by individuals and bodies of troops, but panic could as easily occur, as evidenced in the Nawab's forces at Plassey after Mir Madan's death. The safety of the zenana could often be of greater concern than the security of the army. In this context it is relevant to mention that families did not accompany the Purbia troops of the Bengal Army, but remained, instead, in their respective villages. Militarily, this was, in the Bengal Army, an administrative advantage, till comparisons began being made with the practices in the Madras and Bombay Armies. G.A. Grierson, in his *Bihari Folk Songs,* in the *Journal of the Royal Asiatic Society* (1884), evocatively mentions in this context:

My Lord, in what month wilt thou return?
My beloved has gone away and entered naukari,
Leaving me alone in the house.
He took two or four days chhutti, *and came,*
And went away at dawn.

After the French forces had been dispersed, there were still, for many years, French officers training and directing the local princes' armies. Sometimes they would even be employed on opposite sides, as when Michel Raymond, remembered to this day on his death anniversary in Hyderabad, was with Nizam Ali, and Pierre Cuillier Perron with Mahadji Scindia. But these freelance officers were neither numerous, nor had they the advantage of continuous employment, while their troops were often not regularly paid by their princely masters. *En masse* desertions from one service to another were frequent, some not always successful. James Skinner and William Gardner crossed over to the British in 1803 from the Maratha service, but some others were killed by Holkar. Earlier, Walter Reinhardt, with his disciplined battalions, had changed masters frequently, from Mir Kasim to the Nawab of Oudh, and, eventually, to Begum Somroo, Reinhardt's wife. What is not generally remembered is that there were also formed bodies of the

15

Company's troops, seeking to sell their services to the opposing prince, one further instance being that of Captain Coulson of the Madras Army, and the garrison at Chittapet (now Chittampatt) in 1761 joining Hyder Ali. This followed on from an earlier case, in 1694, when Dr Blackwall sought to defect from the British at Fort St. David, provided he was made the governor. An outstanding exception to the general run of forces trained by freelances was Scindia's force, the Deccan Invincibles, which had been trained by de Boigne. This force would have become a formidable power against the British-Indian forces had de Boigne not left India on account of ill-health, and had Mahadji Scindia lived longer, as evidenced by the gallantry of the de Boigne-trained Purbias at Laswari, which followed the battle of Delhi, both in 1803. G.B. Malleson records: 'Here they were unaided by the presence of European officers (in fact, they had been basely deserted), though trained in a European school; they were left solely to their own resources; and though superior in numbers the superiority was not strongly marked. Yet, here they fought with a gallantry, a resolution, an energy, that would have done honour to any troops in the world.'[21]

General Gerard Lake the Commander-in-Chief, —later Lord Lake of "mind your fighting, damn your writing" fame—paid the following tribute in his "Despatch after Laswari" to Scindia's Purbia soldiers: 'All the sepoys of the enemy behaved well, and if they had been commanded by their French officers, the event would have been extremely doubtful. I never was in so serious a business in my life, nor anything like it. Their gunners stood to their guns until killed by the bayonet. These fellows fought like devils, or rather heroes.'[22] Scindia's Purbia soldiers rightly deserve these British encomiums, except that Britons generally omit to mention that they were Purbias, or, that the attacking Indian soldiers of the Bengal Army, in the main, were also Purbias.

Also, in 1803, General Arthur Wellesley, later the Duke of Wellington, defeated other Purbia infantry battalions of Scindia at Assaye. Years later, long after Waterloo, Wellington was asked what was 'the best thing he had ever done in the way of fighting.' He replied with one word, 'Assaye'. Nevertheless, after 1858, Purbias largely ceased to be recruited in to the Bengal Army, being no longer deemed martial. The contrast in the subsequent British economic development of the Punjab vis-a-vis the eastern United Provinces (in today's Uttar Pradesh) is stark. Past developmental deprivation in the latter region is today a predisposing cause for violence. Conversely, the South Indian classes of the Madras Army and the Mahars, who then formed the major component of the Bombay Army, despite having stood by the British in 1857, and having earlier conquered South India and the Deccan for the British, were thereafter, progressively deemed non-martial, in the pursuit of Grecian features and "grenadierdom". This myth of the martial races will be reviewed in a subsequent chapter.

Reverting to the details of the 1796 reorganization of the Presidency Armies, the major changes were the great increase in the number of British officers in Indian units, and the consequent diminution, in responsibility or trust, in the Indian officers; the creation of artillery battalions (European gunners, and Indian lascars and syces); and the formation of double-battalion Indian regiments from the independent battalions then in existence. Each Bengal cavalry regiment now consisted of one officer of field rank in command (major or lieutenant colonel), fifteen British officers and four British non-commissioned officers, twelve Indian officers, actually sub-officers, and 465 Indian rank and file. The cavalry officers were separated from the infantry, and placed on a general cavalry list, apart from a major general being appointed to command the cavalry brigades.

The double-battalion Bengal regiments were formed by linking existing battalions and amalgamating half-battalions of reduced regiments with these. Thus, the new 12th Regiment consisted of two battalions—the first comprising the old 12th Battalion and the right wing of the 21st, and the second the old 17th Battalion and the left wing of the 21st. The conversion was haphazard, and, in the instance given, resulted in the oldest battalion of the Bengal Army, raised by Clive in 1757, becoming the second battalion of the junior regiment in the list. The British element in the establishment of each regiment of two battalions was one colonel commandant, two lieutenant colonels, two majors, eight captains, twenty-two subalterns, ten ensigns and two British non-commissioned officers. The Indian element consisted of forty Indian officers (sub-officers, equivalent to today's junior commissioned officers), 200 non-commissioned

17

officers, forty drummers and fifers (then usually Eurasians, the sons of the European troops in India, such Eurasians not being then eligible to serve as combatants), and 1,600 soldiers. Each battalion had ten companies (including two grenadier companies).

Up to this time, the officers had been on a general list for promotion. Under the new arrangement, the officers, up to the rank of major, were on regimental lists for promotion, the lieutenant colonels and colonels being placed on separate lists for each Presidency, and an establishment of general officers was instituted. Furlough regulations were introduced and improvements made in the interior economy of regiments, though, the individual Bengal Army soldiers continued to cook their own food. The artillery battalions had five gun companies and fifteen companies of lascars (ammunition carriers). In the Madras and Bombay Armies, similar changes were made to those effected in Bengal, with marginal variations in the number of personnel. In the renumbering of units within their respective Presidency Armies, little regard was paid to continuity of tradition.

This reorganization, not completed till 1804, improved the prospects of the British officer, yet, the dignity and authority of the Indian sub-officers, which had already been decreased by Clive's introduction of the British element into the battalion organization in 1757, were now still further diminished. T. Rice Holmes comments: 'But the very successes which the sepoys helped their masters to gain paved the way for their own depression. As soon as the English ventured to acknowledge to themselves the fact of their supremacy, the same self assertion which led to the substitution of their own for native administration in Bengal, showed itself in their growing tendency to add to the number of their officers with each battalion and to concentrate all real power in their hands...the English officers who, thus, superceded the natives, were picked men who knew how to maintain their authority. But, in 1796, a further change took place...the increase in the number of European officers still further lowered the already fallen position of their native comrades. Thenceforward, there was nothing to stimulate the ambition of a sepoy. Though he might give signs of the military genius of a Hyder, he knew that he could never attain the pay of an English subaltern, and the rank that he might attain after some thirty years of faithful service (subedar; pay Rs. 74 per month), would not protect him from the insolent dictation of an ensign (pay Rs.180 per month) fresh from England. But, for a few years, nothing occurred to show the authors of these changes how disastrous they were to prove.... It was not until the excitement of conquest, which had diverted his mind, subsided, that they began to brood over their grievances.'[23]

The regimental system, as introduced for the first time into the Indian infantry, was not wholly satisfactory. The colonel commandant's control, instead of being exercised only in matters which affected the regiment as a whole, was applied to details which affected battalions individually, and battalion commanders were, therefore, deprived of the initiative which they should have been allowed to exercise. They chafed at obtaining their superior's sanction in such matters as the promotion of non-commissioned officers, acceptance of recruits and the granting of leave. Moreover, the two battalions, which now formed a regiment, were separate units. Though theoretically linked together, they had no mutual bonds except their exasperation at the colonel commandant's unnecessary interference in the domestic affairs of the battalions.

The years up to 1857 saw changes, which, sequentially, were reflected in the Presidency Armies. Apart from raising regular units, it also became necessary to raise irregular corps (they were less expensive), as also local contingents, for the same reason. The principal stages in British expansion during the remaining years of Company control have been summarized by Martin Moir:

- 1792-1801: Extension of the Madras Presidency's control over districts formerly belonging to the rulers of Mysore, Tanjore (now Thanjavur), Hyderabad and the Carnatic.
- 1800-1803: Large parts of Oudh, Agra and the districts around Delhi taken from the Nawab of Oudh and the Marathas, respectively, by the Bengal Presidency, which also assumed responsibility for the administration of Orissa (1803).
- 1816-1820: Garhwal, Kumaon (1816), Saugor (now Sagar) and Narbada (now Narmada) territories (1817), and Ajmer and Merwara added to the Bengal Presidency. Also, a number of districts in Western India,

previously subject to the Marathas, annexed to the
Bombay Presidency (1817-18).
- 1826: Arakan, Tenasserim and parts of Assam ceded to
the Bengal Presidency by the Burmese.[24]
- 'Thereafter, the main annexations during the Company
period included Coorg (1834), Sind (1843), the Punjab
(1849), Lower Burma (1852), Nagpur (1853) and Oudh
(1856). Apart from these directly annexed and administered territories, the Company's government, especially by Governors-General from Wellesley (1798-
1805) to Dalhousie (1848-1856), also gradually established a series of protected states across the subcontinent, notably in Rajputana, Punjab, Kashmir, Central
and Western India, Hyderabad, Mysore and
Travancore. Essentially, the rulers of such states were
allowed to retain responsibility for their internal government, but were compelled to accept the presence of
British residents or agents,' who advised, and, on occasion, intervened; the rulers could also be made to keep
a subsidiary force, this force being paid for (subsidized)
by the concerned rulers.[25] These were euphemisms for
vassalage to the Company. Such events resulted in large
increases to the Presidency Armies. The Indian strength
of 57,000 in 1796 was, thus, by circumstance, only temporary, for, when the Anglo-Maratha War of 1803-05
terminated, the strength of the Presidency Armies was
already:

	Indian	British	Total
Bengal Army	57,000	7,000	64,000
Madras Army	53,000	11,000	64,000
Bombay Army	20,000	6,500	26,500
Total	130,000	24,500	154,500

By 1824, the unsatisfactory nature of the 1796 reorganization
was acknowledged, and the infantry organization which had been
current before 1796, was restored. The Indian infantry regiments of
two battalions each, which had been formed only some thirty years

before, were broken up again into single battalion regiments. This necessitated the redesignation of the units affected, and the regiments of Indian infantry were renumbered by Presidencies, according to the date on which they had originally been raised. One of the defects of the 1796 reorganization was, however, allowed to continue—that is, the high proportion of British officers to Indian officers (today's junior commissioned officers) was retained. The number of British officers of regular Indian cavalry and infantry (single battalion) regiments was fixed at twenty-two.

After the 1824 reorganization, the Bengal Army consisted of three brigades of horse artillery (nine European and three Indian troops), five battalions of foot artillery (twenty European companies with an equivalent number of gun lascar companies attached), a corps of engineers of forty-seven British officers, a corps of Indian sappers and miners, a corps of Indian pioneers, eight regiments of regular Indian cavalry, five regiments of irregular Indian cavalry, sixty-eight battalions of Indian infantry, and two regiments of European infantry. The Bengal Army also consisted of local and provincial corps, such as the Ramgarh Local Battalion, the Cuttack Legion and many others. The Madras Army consisted of two brigades of horse artillery (one European and one Indian), three battalions of foot artillery (each of four European companies, with four companies of gun lascars attached), eight regiments of Indian cavalry of four squadrons each, two battalions of Indian pioneers, two regiments of European infantry, fifty-two battalions of Indian infantry, and three extra and local battalions. The Bombay Army comprised four European troops of horse artillery, eight European companies of foot artillery, a corps of Indian sappers and miners, a corps of Indian pioneers, three regiments of regular Indian cavalry, two regiments of irregular Indian cavalry, two regiments of European infantry, and twenty-four battalions of Indian infantry.

As irregular cavalry regiments and local infantry units are more frequently mentioned, it is desirable to touch on both of these augmentations. The enrolment of irregular cavalry was but following the example of the local rulers. These horsemen were not clothed or armed by the state, but were on the "silladar" system ("silladar" meaning "bearer of weapons"), each man furnishing his own horse and equipment (later, other than his rifle) while the horse supply was kept up by means of a "chanda fund" (supported by monthly subscriptions). There were also two or three European officers with each of these irregular units. By keeping the establishment of British officers to the minimum, one of the chief defects of the 1796 reorganization was avoided. In origin, this was a yeomanry system, the "silladar" soldiers receiving a higher rate of pay than the "non-silladar" soldiers whose needs were, to an extent, furnished by the government. The more influential "silladars" were also allowed to enlist kinsmen, or clansmen, who were too poor to provide their own horses and equipment. The men so enlisted were known as "bargirs", and were maintained and equipped at the expense of their more fortunate patrons, who, in turn, drew a recognized proportion of the pay of their "bargirs". (The "silladar" system in the Indian cavalry was finally only abolished in 1921.)

As territorial expansion took place, local corps were raised for the particular part of the country to which it was desired to afford protection. Mention has already been made in the 1824 reorganization of such units as the Ramgarh Local Battalion and the Cuttack Legion. In 1846 a frontier brigade was raised in the Sutlej States for police and general purposes, and the Corps of Guides was also formed; in 1849, the Punjab Irregular Force, which afterwards became the Punjab Frontier Force, was enrolled for duty on the frontier. In 1851, the additional establishment of this new force was fixed at three light field batteries, five regiments of cavalry, and five of infantry. The force was originally under the provincial administration, and was not placed under the Commander-in-Chief until many decades later. A garrison company was added in 1852, a further infantry regiment formed from the Sind Camel Corps in 1853, one mountain battery in 1856, and a second in 1862. (The three light field batteries were converted into mountain batteries in 1876.) Another local force was raised on the annexation of Nagpur in 1854, and the Oudh Irregular Force in 1856, after Oudh was annexed. The latter force disintegrated in 1857, while the former was broken up a few years later.

Separately, by a treaty of 1800, the Nizam of Hyderabad had maintained a contingent of 9,000 horse and 6,000 foot, which was officered by the English Company, after the French had been displaced. In 1853, a new treaty was concluded with the Nizam, the latter assigning Berar to the Company for the payment of this contingent, the force thus ceasing to be a part of the Nizam's army. It was, notionally, to be maintained for his use, but available for service elsewhere. It consisted of four regiments of cavalry, four field batteries, and six battalions of infantry, commanded by a brigadier general under the civil authority of the British Resident at Hyderabad. Besides this contingent, which was, thus, practically incorporated into the Company's army, many other Indian princely states were required to maintain contingents of troops representing the military aid which they were supposed to render to the British. These latter forces, at the time aggregating 30,000 to 40,000 men, were then generally deemed by the British to be, 'of no military value, being poorly disciplined mercenaries, without loyalty to the State they served or to the British government.' In the event, however, recourse was had to some of these State Force units in 1857.

One cannot leave this facet of the progressive augmentation of the Presidency Armies, and the raising of local forces and contingents, without quoting William Howitt, who wrote of the period before 1857: 'A fatal friendship indeed, has that of the English been to all those princes that were allured by it. It 'has pulled them everyone from their thrones, or has left them there the contemptible puppets of a power that works its arbitrary will through them. But friendship or enmity, the result has been the same for them.'[26]

Before concluding this chapter on the early beginnings of the Indian Army up to 1857, it would be pertinent to note a few British opinions as to the state of the Presidency Armies, particularly Bengal, much before the uprising actually occurred. Sir Henry Russell, who had served as the British Resident at Hyderabad for eleven years, and after whom two infantry units of the Hyderabad Contingent were named as "Russell's Infantry", in his evidence in 1832 before the Parliamentary "Select Committee on the Affairs of the East India Company" (copy in the British Library) emphasized: 'The chief cause of discontent of native officers is that once they have attained the rank of Subedar, they have nothing more to look to; having got all that they can get, they have no further inducement to exert themselves; they become first indolent, and then dissatisfied. There ought to be some higher object kept in their view to which by

23

diligence and fidelity they may still attain. There was a native officer of the Madras establishment of the name of Mohammed Yusuf, who was entrusted in the early British operations with a considerable independent command, of which he discharged the duties with judgement and fidelity; and if we raise the natives to higher offices in the civil department, it will be difficult to maintain the exclusion of them in the army.' Before the Select Committee's report, the appointment of subedar major was created in each unit as a sop, but status-wise this was in no way comparable to the extinct appointment of Indian (or native) commandant held by Mohammed Yusuf and others.

The gifted British statesman, Sir John Malcolm, emphasized the need for trust in the same Select Committee's deliberations in 1832: 'That a certain proportion of European troops should always be in India is fully admitted; but there is no error more common than that of considering the latter as a check upon the native armies. They never have and never will provide such. Long experience has rendered my opinion upon this subject the same as those of Sir Thomas Munro. The necessity of check implies distrust that degrades. It is by complete confidence alone that the Native Army of India can be preserved in efficiency and attached to the Government it serves.' He added presciently that this army, 'is our safety and danger.' How the Bengal Army soldiers were antagonized and their goodwill lost even prior to 1857, will be reviewed in a subsequent chapter, but suffice it to say that the lack of trust in purely Indian infantry brigades continued till well on into the Second World War, latterly Gurkha battalions being allotted as the third battalion in Indian infantry brigades, when a British battalion was not available to serve as a check.

An essential condition for retaining the goodwill of the Bengal Army soldier was to respect his caste and religious feelings. Colonel Gervase Pennington in his evidence before the 1832 Select Committee observed: 'The native Army of Bengal is essentially Hindu, having only a slight mixture of Muslims among them. The Rajputs, the flower of that army, are born soldiers, and pride themselves on being so considered. Treated justly, you may rely on their fidelity; treated kindly, you may rest assured of their devoted attachment, but you must not interfere in their religion, nor in their prejudices regarding caste. Any wrong done to them on these points cannot be atoned for by apologies or expressions of regret.' The wrongs that had been done in relation to these caste feelings prior to 1857 will also be mentioned in a subsequent chapter. How strong these caste feelings were is clear from the fact that every soldier in the Bengal Army had his own separate cooking pots and *lota*. The system was certainly inconvenient, but caste feelings could sometimes have been assuaged more tactfully in the light of subsequent events.

In one of his essays first published in 1844, Sir Henry Lawrence struck a note of warning, despite the sop of the creation of the appointment of subedar major and risaldar major: 'There are many commandants in the Maratta (sic) and Seikh (sic) service, who were privates in our army. General Dhokul Singh, now at Lahore, was a drill naik in one of our Sepoy Corps; and Raja Buktawar Singh, one of the richest and most powerful men at Oude (sic), was a Havildar in our Cavalry. But is it not absurd that the rank of Subedar and Russaldar (sic) Major is the highest that a native can attain in a native army of nearly three hundred thousand men, in a land too that above all others has been accustomed to see its military merit rewarded and to witness the successive rise of families from the lowest conditions, owing to gallantry in the field?...The grandsons of the Gauls, who opposed Caesar, were senators of Rome and the Jye Singhs and Jeswant Singhs led the Mughal armies, but it cannot be said that it was to any such liberality the empire of either Rome or Delhi owed its fall.'

When his advice was ignored, Sir Henry wrote another essay in 1856, in which he reiterated: 'The minds of Subedars and Rissaldars, Sepoys and Sowars, can no more with safety be forever cramped, trammelled and restricted as at present, than can a twenty-foot embankment restrain the Atlantic. It is simply a question of time. The question is only whether justice is to be gracefully conceded or violently seized. Ten or twenty years must settle the point.' Prescient words but by a tragic irony of fate, the Indophile Sir Henry was a year later to be killed by an artillery shell splinter during the siege of the Lucknow Residency in 1857, while his younger brother, John (later Lord) Lawrence was to go from strength to strength in the British hierarchy from 1857 onwards till he became Governor-General and was extolled for his toughness; the same younger brother, with whom the then Governor-General, James Dalhousie, had sided against Sir Henry in the working of the Punjab Board of Administration in 1852, and to whom Sir Henry wrote in a farewell letter on 20 January 1853: 'As this is my last day at Lahore, I venture to offer you a few words of advice, which I hope you will take in the spirit it is given in, that you will believe that, if you preserve the peace of the country, and make the people high and low happy, I shall have no regrets that I vacated the field for you.... I would simply do to them as I would be done by.'

In an 1856 letter to Lord Stanley in London he wrote: 'We act contrary to common sense and in neglect of the lessons of history, in considering that the present system can end in anything but a convulsion. We are lucky in its having lasted so long...' Before the news of his death had reached them, the directors of the East India Company in London, had, on 22 July 1857, unanimously proposed to appoint Sir Henry Lawrence, 'provisionally to succeed to the office of Governor General upon the death, resignation or coming away of Viscount Canning, pending the arrival of a successor from England.'

On the eve of the 1857 Uprising the strength of the armies under the Company in India was about 313,500 Indian and 38,000 European.

Two

The Presidency Armies In War Before 1857

THERE IS little doubt that the British conquered India on the basis of the prowess of the Presidency Armies, but, objectively, it is as well to remember that the assessed performance in battle of these armies progressively diminished, particularly that of the Bengal Army as the calibre of the enemy confronting them correspondingly increased. There was an overconfidence developing among the British officers, engendered by past successes, against successive Asian enemies, and an increasing lack of a bond between some of the newer British officers and their Indian troops in the nineteenth century compared to the previous century. This resulted in serious reverses particularly in the First Anglo-Afghan War and the Anglo-Sikh Wars.

The 940 Madras soldiers who had arrived with Robert Clive in December 1756 in Bengal, proved themselves, as they had done earlier in South India. They marched from Fulta (now Falta) and recaptured Calcutta in January 1757[1]. (Before this, in Bengal, only a few local Indian levies had been raised, apart from European militia and gunners. Both largely deserted on the second night of Nawab Siraj-ud-Daula's attack on Calcutta in June 1756.) The Madras soldiers and the First Bengal Infantry (the Lal Paltan) raised by Clive, equipped with European arms, were used in the capture of Chandernagore (now Chandannagar) from the French in March 1757, and, as is known, in the defeat, thereafter, at Plassey of Nawab Siraj-ud-Daula. At Plassey, Clive had 2,100 Indian troops and 950 Europeans.

The proportion of Indian troops to Europeans was now higher than what Clive had in September 1751. He had seized Arcot with 300 Indian and 200 European soldiers. When the siege ended, he had 120 Indians and eighty Europeans. These were the same South Indians that the English, initially, had felt could not be made into disciplined soldiers. Before Plassey, there had been some doubt expressed whether the South Indian troops would be a match for the Nawab's soldiers from the North (the Lal Paltan was North Indian in composition with some Indian sub-officers and non-commissioned officers from Madras), but they astonished their North Indian opponents by their steadiness under fire, the effectiveness of their own fire, and their ability to use the bayonet. After Plassey, by October 1757, the original European infantry component of Clive's force had been reduced to 150, due to deaths, according to A. Broome, from, 'every description of debauchery,'[2] and the effects of the climate.

Until additional European troops were provided, Clive raised the Second Bengal Infantry in August 1757 from mixed North Indian classes, like the Lal Paltan. Had the fortification of the first Fort William not been improved without Nawab Siraj-ud-Daula's permission, causing him to seize Calcutta in June 1756, there would have been no Black Hole incident, and no sequential battle of Plassey in June 1757, and possibly no British-Indian Empire of the eventual magnitude of 1849. The Black Hole incident was one of negligence rather than cruelty. The prisoners had actually first been allowed their freedom, but were only confined when some of the British soldiers became drunk and abusive. Thereafter 143 prisoners were allegedly confined in a room usually referred to as the "Black Hole" in the then Fort William, which was already used by the British for their own prisoners. The room was said to be so small that only twenty-three came out alive the next day. Though Arcot had been the first British military victory in India, they could not have created an empire from South India. As described by Amiya Barat, although the Bengal Native Infantry, as it was called, 'was the latest born, it came to surpass the others (the infantry of the Bombay and Madras Armies) in rate of growth and in ultimate size—by 1852 it became over 50,000 strong—called as it was to execute a task undreamt of at its foundation: the conquest for the Company of all North India.'[3]

When it was reported that Raja Ram Narain, the Governor of Bihar, had allied himself with the Nawab of Oudh and declared himself independent of the "subahdari" of Bengal, even though eventually no battle was fought, Clive raised the 3rd Bengal Infantry from Bhojpur. When towards the end of 1758, news reached Bengal from Madras, of the capture by the French of Fort St. David, attributed to the defection of three Indian companies (such defections to the other side being current among European troops as well), Clive wrote to Governor George Pigot at Madras, 'Were our enemies supplied with wings to fly into the place?' Thereafter, Clive sent part of his troops by sea to Vizagapatam, for employment in the Northern Circars, under Colonel Francis Forde, to meet the possible peril posed to Bengal by the French in South India in general, and Masulipatam in particular. With Forde were 500 Europeans, some of the Madras soldiers who had come to Bengal with Clive and two Bengal Infantry battalions. As to this sea voyage, 'the Bengal sepoys, later to be described as so very prejudiced against crossing the sea, embarked on this occasion without a murmur.'[4]

Some Bengal Army soldiers embarked again for Madras in 1768, with a call at Vizagapatam. At the latter, they were so distressed by the want of provisions and water on board, and by overcrowding, that they refused to go further by sea, and marched instead from Vizagapatam. In 1770, on their way back, two companies were lost at sea. In view of their subsequent reluctance to embark in later years as complete units, other than as volunteers, it can validly be assumed that they were not initially aware of the vicissitudes of sea voyages, such as ships being lost at sea, apart from the administrative problems of water storage and cooking on board, conjoined with the prohibitory cost for Hindus of the purificatory religious ceremony to be performed on their return after a sea voyage. As to the 1759 military operations, Forde reported: 'I attacked Masulipatam, and after a very sharp conflict, had the good fortune to get possession of it. I have taken near 500 European prisoners...my whole force consisted of 315 rank and file....' He omits in this total his Indian troops, apparently viewing them as mere auxiliaries to his European troops. Forde continued in his report, 'My 1,500 sepoys behaved well;...they mounted the ramparts with the Europeans and behaved with great humanity after they got in.' Of this sophistry, Philip Mason wryly commented: 'He does not here mention that the troops for the main attack were divided into three divisions, one mixed, one entirely of Europeans, and one entirely of sepoys. It was the second of these, the Europeans, who faltered and almost lost the day.'[5]

Forde's expedition has been described by Broome as, 'one of the most successful and important expeditions ever undertaken by the Bengal Army,'[6] and in May 1759 a treaty was concluded whereby Nizam Salabat Jung ceded a considerable area around Masulipatam, and also undertook to expel the French. Clive was now called upon for help by Nawab Mir Jafar, whom the English had elevated in place of Siraj-ud-Daula, when the Shahzada, later Shah Alam II, the eldest son of the Mughal Emperor Alamgir II, fled from Delhi, and set out to capture Bihar, Orissa and Bengal in order to establish his claim to the throne. At that time, G.B. Malleson recounts: 'Mir Jafar was in all external affairs, but a pageant ruler.'[7] With two of his Bengal Infantry battalions in the Northern Circars, Clive raised the 4th and 5th Battalions. The Company's and Nawab's forces defeated those of the Shahzada at Patna after a brief battle.

Returning to Calcutta in June 1759, Clive found the Dutch chagrined or as Malleson put it: 'The English, in virtue of the consequences of Plassey, were prospering to an extraordinary degree; the Dutch, in virtue of the same consequences were declining in influence and wealth.' Mir Jafar contemplated using the Dutch as a counterpoise to English ascendancy: he, 'was anxious to substitute, for a foreign master, a foreign ally.'[8] Holland was then one of the five great maritime powers of that century. In October 1759 a Dutch fleet of seven armed ships, carrying 700 Europeans and 800 Malay soldiers, arrived in the Hugli, Mir Jafar informing Clive that he 'had granted them certain indulgence as regards their trade, and they had agreed to send away the ships,'[9] as soon as the season would permit.

The Dutch did not depart, and reportedly began recruiting soldiers at Chinsura, Cossimbazar and Patna. (The Dutch agency at Chinsura, twenty miles north of Calcutta, had been founded as early as 1646.) Though Holland was at peace with England at the time, the Dutch seized English ships on the Hugli, and attacked English factories such as Fulta. After some skirmishes the Dutch were defeated by Forde at Bhadara, halfway between Chinsura and Chandernagore (probably today's Bhadreshwar, according to S.C. Hill). Forde, who had just returned from the Northern Circars, used some European soldiers, but mainly the 5th Bengal Infantry. The British were now paramount in Bengal, and H.H. Dodwell recorded: 'The subahdar was of their making; their troops formed the only effective force in the province.'[10] When Clive first left India in January 1760, each Bengal Infantry battalion had its full complement of three British officers, each of the five battalions having 1,000 soldiers. There had been some reluctance on the part of British subalterns to join these Bengal Infantry battalions according to J.Williams, for an additional two rupees per day was added to the pay of the subalterns as drill money.[11] Of this period, Penderel Moon narrated: 'The Company's servants, who gained for their masters political power in Bengal, at first viewed that acquisition in the buccaneering spirit of Elizabethan seamen. Bengal was a rich and valuable prize that could yield fortunes to individuals and pay tribute to England; and they feathered their own nests with little regard to anything else.'[12]

Separately, the directors in London were complaining that their Bengal representatives were 'so thoroughly possessed of military ideas as to forget their employers (were) merchants and trade was their principal object....Were we to adopt your several plans for fortifying, half of our capital would be buried in stone walls.'[13] The directors in April 1760 emphasized 'the unmurmuring generosity of the proprietors in consenting to reduce their dividend 25 percent...the burden would be too great for us to bear much longer...the fixed garrison at Calcutta should not be more than 1,500 Europeans (the blacks at your discretion).'[14] Thus, gracelessly, the directors disposed of the Bengal Infantry, their sword arm in the north till 1857.

After Clive's departure, Henry Vansittart, the Company's new Governor at Calcutta selected by Clive, on his arrival from Madras, was informed that Nawab Mir Jafar was unable to produce the arrears of the payments to the Company promised after Plassey, his treasury being empty. 'In vain did Mir Jafar struggle against the yoke he had imposed upon himself. He could not shake it off. To purchase English aid, he had mortgaged the resources of the State.'[15] His vacillations, for his own survival, occasioned chagrin to the Calcutta Council. His palace was now surrounded by the Company's European troops and his son-in-law's European adventurer-led troops. Under pressure from the Council, Mir Jafar reluctantly, in September 1760, abdicated in favour of Mir Kasim, his son-in-law, the latter having already agreed to pay the ostensible arrears due to the Company, from Mir Jafar, and thereafter 200,000 pounds in cash as a gesture of gratitude personally to the Company's Calcutta Council members, as also ceding the three districts of Burdwan, Midnapore and Chittagong to the Company for the maintenance of its troops in his ostensible support. 'Admitted to the deliberations of the English Councillors, Mir Kasim soon came to the conclusion that there was not one amongst them who could not be bought. His father-in-law had bought their predecessors; he would ascertain their price and buy them.'[16]

Vansittart received 50,000 pounds (Rs 500,000), J.Z. Holwell 30,000 pounds, and the others over 14,000 pounds each. A little earlier in 1759, on his father Alamgir II's death, Shah Alam II had declared himself Emperor, and had sought the acknowledgement of his title by the provincial rulers. The Nawab of Bengal, and, concomitantly, the English Company, refused to do so. Shah Alam II and the Nawab Wazir Shuja-ud-Daula of Oudh invaded Bengal, the conflict continuing till March 1761, when the Company's forces prevailed. The Emperor now invested Mir Kasim as the Nawab of Bengal. Of this period James Mill said: 'The conduct of the Company's servants upon this occasion furnishes one of the most remarkable instances upon record of the power of interest to extinguish all sense of justice, and even of shame.' Mir Kasim had met all his commitments; he had been an effective Nawab, but had received insults and further demands. Thus, just when peace was established with the Emperor, the Calcutta Council came into conflict with Mir Kasim in June 1763 on account of its own venality, and war broke out, contrived by the English. 'Mir Kasim was a man of a stamp very different to that of his father-in-law...he had from the very first resolved to be a master in his own house. He had used the English to procure him power, but he never trusted them as Mir Jafar had trusted them. In a short time, he came to hate them....'[17] Malleson added: 'The annals of no nation contain records of conduct more unworthy, more mean, and more disgraceful than that which characterized the English government of Calcutta, during the three years which followed the (earlier) removal of Mir Jafar...that conduct is attributable to one cause—the desire for personal gain by any means and at any cost.'

Mir Kasim was not responsible for the start of the war. This was due to William Ellis, the arrogant chief of the Company's factory at Patna. On 24 June, a brigade of Mir Kasim's troops, under an Armenian commander, Markar Johannes (or Margar), left Monghyr (now Munger) for Patna, which was part of his territory. Ellis, with three Bengal Infantry battalions and 300 Europeans, had seized most of the city, and begun plundering it. While they were busy doing so, Markar's brigade recaptured the city. Only about 1,500 Indian soldiers and 200 Europeans were able to get away, and sought to escape towards Oudh. They were pursued by two brigades of Mir Kasim's troops, Markar's and Walter Reinhardt's. (The latter was also known as "Somro".) On the deaths of their commanding officers, the Company's troops surrendered; most of the Europeans, who were not British, joined Mir Kasim's forces, as did some of the Indians. Mir Kasim took 150 to 200 Britons hostage at Patna. Three Bengal Infantry battalions had thus disintegrated at or near Patna, and the Calcutta Council declared war on Mir Kasim. Mir Jafar at the time was already wasting away, reportedly from leprosy, and was only too ready to agree to the exorbitant demands of the Council.

Mir Jafar was restored in July 1763, and the Bengal Council sought help from the Madras and Bombay Presidencies, while the raising of seven further battalions of Bengal Infantry was completed, thus making fourteen battalions, two more having been raised in 1762, and three having disintegrated at Patna. The Madras Government regretted its inability to help as it was busy with the alleged rebellion by its native commandant, Mohammed Yusuf Khan, during 1763-1764.* Bombay helped with two European and two Indian companies of infantry, and one artillery company. The Company's forces, under Major Thomas Adams, particularly in the capture of Monghyr and Patna, prevailed over Mir Kasim's, on account of disunity amongst the latter's commanders. 'Indeed it may be affirmed that few things have more contributed to the success of the English than the action of jealousy of one another of the native princes and leaders of India.'[18] After the fall of Monghyr, Mir Kasim ordered his Armenian Commander-in-Chief, Gregory Arathoon (also known as Gorgin Khan), to be assassinated, and then most of the 150 to 200 British prisoners at Patna to be killed by Reinhardt.

Towards the end of 1764, Mir Kasim fled to Oudh, and effected an alliance with Nawab Shuja-ud-Daula, and Emperor Shah Alam II, and as Malleson recounts rightly charging the Calcutta Council 'that, after having made with him a treaty, "to which they had pledged the name of Jesus Christ" by virtue of which he had made over to them three districts for the avowed purpose of paying the expenses of an army that should support him...they had used that force for his destruction.' The Company thereafter raised four further battalions of Bengal Infantry in early 1764. On 5 March 1764, Major John Carnac became Commander-in-Chief near Sasaram in Bihar, on the death of Adams, and his second-in-command, Captain Ronald Knox. Both had broken down from the rigours of the campaign which had contributed more to the consolidation of the British than Plassey. Carnac was not a good Army Chief, a phenomenon to be observed often later. 'He possessed few of the qualities required in a General. Careful of his own comfort, absorbed by a love of the acquisition of money, then very prevalent amongst the high officials in India, he displayed neither energy nor enterprise. With far greater means at his disposal, he accomplished much less. He paid but little attention to the comfort of his troops who however, disliked him less on that account than for the distrust he evinced on many occasions of their capacity to beat the enemy. The immense dislike felt towards him by his officers and men, which can be traced in all the correspondence of this time, was increased by the semi-regal state with which, while

* For more details, see chapter, "Some Alleged Mutinies In The Three Presidency Armies Before 1857".

careless for others, he shrouded himself. It was his delight to pitch his camp at some distance in the rear of that of his army, and whilst living in a life of luxury and ease, to leave the details of his command to subordinates.'[19]

Carnac had a force of 6,000, supported by Mir Jafar's 12,000. His men's hopes were, however, belied for military incompetence has its own psychology. Though Carnac knew that the Nawab of Oudh and Mir Kasim had moved from Allahabad and were endeavouring to cross the Ganga at Benares (now Varanasi), Carnac moved leisurely. He received orders from the Calcutta Council to act, instead he called a Council of War. A Council of War normally never fights, though by a quirk of circumstance it eventually did at Plassey. Carnac's Council of War decided to retreat to Patna, and Dinapur (now Danapur) was reached on 13 April, and six days later, Carnac's 'tent, pitched as usual some distance from the camp, was threatened by a detachment of cavalry, and he himself was roused from the occupation of a game of whist to run for refuge amongst his own sepahis.'[20]

For secret service money, attendants and table money, Carnac drew some Rs 11,000 per mensem, a sum exceeding that drawn by his predecessor or successor for these purposes. The mere approach of the opposing force was enough for Carnac to fall back on Patna. Before that he had put out a force to lure the opposing troops into an ambush. He cancelled the ambush, but forgot to inform the force that was to lure the enemy. His force then took up an entrenched position at Patna, part of which was already occupied by Mir Jafar. 'It was the largest force ever till then, put into the field against an enemy (in Bengal and Bihar); it was certainly the first that had allowed itself to be beleaguered.'[21] The next day the armies of Emperor Shah Alam II, the Nawab of Oudh and Mir Kasim, about 40,000, took up a position confronting Carnac and Mir Jafar, and attacked. 'The soldiers of the Nawab Wazir displayed, notwithstanding, prodigies of valour. They did not retire until the battle had gone irretrievably against them. Beaten but not disgraced...,' the Nawab Wazir fell back to Buxar. The Company's troops were anxious to pursue him, but were withheld by Carnac. Possibly this was due to the fact that, while at Patna, he was carrying on negotiations with the Emperor and the Nawab Wazir, as the result showed a year later. (On 28 June,

Carnac was removed for earlier opposition to Governor Vansittart.) In 1765, back again as the head of the Bengal Army, Carnac wrung from the indigent Emperor a donation, for himself individually of two lakh rupees.

Carnac's removal in 1764 had no connection with his conduct (or lack of it) of the campaign. It, nevertheless, satisfied the members of the Calcutta Council, and was a relief to his officers and men. His successor from 13 August 1764 was Major Hector Munro, 'Not a great tactician.... He disdained the ceremonious pomp and stately ceremony in which Carnac had delighted.'[22] Munro advanced on 6 October, with nine Bengal Infantry battalions, 1,000 Bengal cavalry, and 900 Europeans—both artillery and infantry. After the failure to capture Patna, the Nawab of Oudh had lost faith in Mir Kasim. The Emperor was only a figurehead. The Nawab Wazir was thus the head of the opposing contingent of 40,000, for he had bought over Mir Kasim's European brigades. 'The day after (23 October) the appearance of the English force at Buxar, (Mir Kasim) was placed on a lame elephant, and dismissed as one who brought bad luck to any cause.' (This story is told in detail in *Seir-ul-Mutaqherin.*) Mir Kasim found his way to Rohilkhand, where he became a pensioner of the upright Najib-ud-Daula. Left by his death without a protector, he eventually died in 1777 in Delhi in extreme poverty, his only shawl being sold to pay for his funeral sheet.

Earlier in 1763, at Gheria (now Giria), Mir Kasim's army, leaving its strong entrenchments, had unwisely marched into the open to meet the Company's forces. At Buxar, Nawab Shuja-ud-Daula ill-advisedly pursued the same course. The Nawab Wazir fought with resolution, despite the mistakes of his subordinate commanders which led to his defeat. His men fought bravely, but the steadiness of the Company's forces under attack brought them victory. At Plassey, about 2,100 of Clive's force of three thousand were Indian soldiers. At Buxar, the Indian proportion was higher, 6,200 (including cavalry) out of 7,200. The casualties of the Company's forces killed and wounded were 746 Indians and 101 Europeans. The losses in the Nawab Wazir's contingent were more, very many from drowning, during the retreat. According to Malleson, 'Buxar takes rank amongst the most decisive battles ever fought. Not only did the victory of the English save Bengal, not only did it advance the British frontier to Allahabad, but it bound the rulers of Oudh to the conqueror by ties of admiration, of gratitude, of absolute reliance and trust, ties which made them, for the ninety-four years that followed, the friends of his friends and the enemies of his enemies. For that constancy of friendship, England repaid them in 1855-56 (by annexation)!'[23]

Buxar supplemented Plassey by strengthening the English hold over Bengal and Bihar. The grant of the "diwani" of Bengal, Bihar and Orissa to the English Company by the hapless Shah Alam II, who was being 'driven from pillar to post and post to pillar'[24] followed as a sequel. By February 1765, the English had subdued as far as Allahabad, including Benares, and Chunar, and in March had overrun Oudh, occupying Faizabad and Lucknow. The Emperor Shah Alam II, representing that he had been a state prisoner of the Nawab of Oudh at Benares now sought British protection. Munro, thereupon, marched on Benares, of which Clive was later to write to the directors on 30 September 1765, after his return to India in May 1765, and an early visit to that city: 'How much must the expectations of your army be raised, when they are suffered without control, to take possession, for themselves, of the whole booty and donation money, and plunder on the capture of a city. This I can assure you, happened at Benaras.'

Nawab Shuja-ud-Daula made his last stand at Kora (now Kara) on 3 May 1765, so that when Clive returned that month for his second Governorship of Bengal, ostensibly to restore the situation resulting from the war with Mir Kasim, he found the Bengal Army victors. The Bengal Council contemplated granting Oudh to the Emperor, thus becoming the power behind the Mughal throne, and marching on Delhi to instal him there. Clive, however, restored Oudh to Nawab Shuja-ud-Daula, less Kora and Allahabad, upon the payment of a war indemnity of fifty lakh rupees. (The Nawabs of Oudh thus mortgaged their independence. Within the space of thirty years they had to give up half their territories to pay for British protection.)

The Emperor was given Kora and Allahabad with an annual tribute of twenty-six lakhs (Allahabad was held by the British nominally for the Emperor till 1771, when they sold it to the Nawab of Oudh for fifty lakhs. They continued, nevertheless, to garrison it, when eventually it was transferred to them at their insistence in 1798). As is known, in return the Company had secured the "diwani" of Bengal, Bihar and Orissa. (It quickly stopped paying pecuniary tribute to the Emperor in 1770, and eventually in 1835 replaced the Emperor's image on its coinage with that of the British monarch.) Penderel Moon described the charade gone through on 10 August 1765 in Clive's tent at Allahabad. The Emperor was 'ceremoniously seated on a throne—a draped armchair positioned on top of a dining-table, and delivered Clive the imperial firman granting the diwani of Bengal to the Company. It was essentially a fraud...'[25]

Mir Jafar died in January 1765, and his successor, Najm-ud-Daula, was only recognized by the Company on condition that he appointed the British nominee as his executive deputy. The Company now controlled the whole administration of Bengal. Through the victory of the Bengal Army, in which more than nine-tenths were Indian, at Buxar, 'the Company became "Nabobs" in fact, if not in name, perhaps totally so, without disguise.'[26]

Since the acquisition of the diwani involved revenue collection, which needed the backing of force, Clive, to retain some military efficiency, despite having to disperse his troops, and yet maximize revenue collection divided the Bengal Army into three brigades at Monghyr (300 miles from Calcutta), Bankipore (near Patna) and Allahabad. The unit commanders now answered to the brigade commanders, instead of to the Commander-in-Chief direct. In the context of internal security Clive further advised, though not fully implemented in his time, that the Indian element of each battalion should be composed of an equal number of 'Gentoos (Hindus) and Mussalmans.' This was the first policy direction as to class composition in a Presidency Army. The Company's Committee of Secrecy in London approved Clive's suggestion, and commented that: 'If it were only on the principle of "divide et impera", the Moormen and Gentoos should be separated into distinct companies. Besides the obvious reasons, other advantages might result from it, by detaching all Mussalmans or all Gentoos into a particular country, as might be expedient in war or to conciliate their affection by rendering it more satisfactory to the inhabitants in times of peace.'[27]

Clive left India finally in January 1767, the Indian element of the Bengal Army being deemed efficient, and the European element having been disciplined. Colonel Richard Smith recorded to the historian Robert Orme at the time, 'some of our sepoy battalions would astonish the King of Prussia and they astonish me.'[28] In 1762, a Madras Army contingent had even been employed in the Philippines to invest Manila, in the war against Spain. In 1768, the Court of Directors, however, felt it necessary to advise the Bengal Council to decrease the number of Indian troops since 'an establishment of fifteen thousand sepoys would be far superior to any country force...brought against the provinces...' and 'would be best answered by your paying them regularly, using them with humanity....'[29] The first direction was not implemented as the Bengal Presidency had to send troops to the other two Presidencies on account of the First Anglo-Mysore War with Hyder Ali, which was of the Madras Council's making, and the operations against the Marathas. As to the second direction at the time, humaneness, in the treatment of, or in the arrangements for, Indian troops was often non-existent. The despatch of Bengal troops by sea to Madras in 1767, earlier mentioned, was one such example, the Court of Directors later recording of the then mismanagement, '...from the horrid inconsiderate, cruel management of the last embarkation to the Deccan not a Gentoo (will) ever venture on board a ship again.'[30] This, in the event, was what was to happen.

The First Anglo-Mysore War lasted from 1767 to 1769. Hyder Ali, a Punjabi, had risen from the ranks in the Mysore Army to become its commander, and then the ruler of the kingdom of Mysore. He was a brave soldier. When Nizam Ali, having displaced his brother, Salabat Jung, at Hyderabad, obtained British assistance with a view to attacking Hyder Ali, and capturing Bangalore, he also expected help from the Marathas. Hyder Ali divided his enemies. He bought off the Marathas, and entered into parleys with Nizam Ali. Colonel Joseph Smith recommended a withdrawal from Bangalore, but the Madras Council overruled him. The gallant Smith, now facing the superior conjoined forces of Hyder and Nizam Ali, perforce retreated with his 5,000 Indian soldiers, 800 Europeans and 1,000 Arcot cavalry. Repeatedly attacked, this small force marched over twenty miles without rest or food. After a few weeks, Smith, with his mainly Indian force, attacked, killing 4,000 and capturing sixty-four guns. Earlier Tipu had infiltrated into Madras, to the very bungalows of the members of the Madras Council, but withdrew on learning of his father's reverse. In 1768 Nizam Ali negotiated a separate treaty with the British. A similar offer by Hyder Ali was rejected against Smith's advice.

The members of the Madras Council decided to continue the war and appointed two of their members to accompany Smith in the field to ensure that all money made in procuring supplies was shared with the Madras Council. Hyder again sought to negotiate offering some territory and ten lakh of rupees though it was not he who had started the war. The Madras Council rejected his offer and appointed the pliable Colonel Wood to replace Smith. As soon as he learned that Smith had left, Hyder attacked Wood, captured the Madras Army's baggage, and almost succeeded in capturing the whole force. Wood was relieved, and Smith reinstated, but Hyder had already advanced on Madras, covering 130 miles in three days; Smith, by circumstance, following. When Hyder was five miles from Madras, the Madras Council agreed to discuss terms, which Hyder had all along been prepared to do. The Treaty of Madras was concluded in 1769. All territory was restored, and each side undertook to assist the other in the event of being attacked. When later attacked by the Marathas Hyder invoked the treaty, but the British disowned it. Hyder Ali, thereafter, never forgave the British for breaking this alliance. When hostilities were resumed in 1780 in the Second Anglo-Mysore War, and the Madras Council sought troops from Bengal, five Bengal Infantry battalions marched from Bengal in January 1781 and only reached the Madras Presidency in July, losing half their number *en route* through sickness and death as well as concomitant desertions. (By 1780, there were thirty-five battalions of the Bengal Infantry of 1,000 soldiers each, compared to twenty-one battalions in 1777.) At the time, no solution was attempted for the reluctance of the Hindus of the Bengal Army to embark on a sea voyage, by including general service terms at the time of enrolment, as was done in the Madras and Bombay Armies, nor of enrolling more Muslims into the Bengal Army, as the English felt 'the Moors (were) bound by no ties of gratitude, and every day's experience (convinced) us that Mussulmans remain firm to the engagements no longer than while they (were) actuated by principles of fear, always ripe for a change whenever there (was) the smallest prospect of success.'[31]

Now occurred the First Anglo-Maratha War of 1778-1782. Earlier, in 1773, when Peshwa Narayan Rao was assassinated, his uncle, Raghunath Rao, became the Peshwa for a short while, though he was suspected of being behind Narayan Rao's death. When Narayan Rao's wife gave birth to a posthumous son, Nana Phadnavis, the Chief Minister of the Maratha Confederacy, in effect, proclaimed the latter as the Peshwa, and Raghunath Rao took refuge with the British at Bombay. In 1777, there were reports of French offers to the Marathas of armament, and assistance in training. Consequently in 1778, Warren Hastings ordered six Bengal Infantry battalions and some cavalry to march right across India and reinforce the small Bombay Army. The commander, Colonel Matthew Leslie, in five months barely covered 120 miles in Bundelkhand. On news reaching in July 1778 that the French had declared war, Hastings ordered Colonel Thomas Goddard to replace Leslie, who, however, had died. Owing to the delay by Leslie, the Bombay Council though advised by Hastings to await Goddard's arrival, nevertheless despatched an expedition of 4,000 men of the Bombay Army, supported by 19,000 baggage bullock-carts, moving at two miles a day. A committee accompanied the expedition, and when confronted by a force of 50,000 Marathas, sixteen miles from Poona (now Pune), decided to retreat, abandoning all guns and most of its stores. Despite the Bombay Infantry rearguard under Captain James Hartley effectively holding back the Marathas, much to the admiration of Mahadji Scindia, the committee decided to surrender at Wadgaon.

Under the convention the British were to hand over all territories seized from the Marathas after 1775, as also Raghunath Rao, and to return Goddard's force to Bengal. The Bombay Council, though this reverse was its creation, decided on an all-out war against the Maratha Confederacy. Goddard was first to negotiate for the restoration of the *status quo ante* to the Wadgaon surrender. Meanwhile, Raghunath Rao escaped from Scindia, and sought refuge with Goddard. Nana Phadnavis now sought Raghunath Rao's return, as also that of Salsette, seized by the British in 1774. Goddard thereupon broke off negotiations as he learnt that the Marathas, the Nizam and Hyder Ali were forging an alliance against the British. Goddard made an alliance with the Gaekwar of Baroda, seized Ahmedabad and Gujarat from Scindia and Holkar. On Goddard's suggestion,

Hastings sent 2,000 Bengal Infantrymen under Captain William Popham to strike at Gwalior. Without any prearranged training or equipment, or any artillery, this force effected a brilliant escalade of the sixteen-foot escarpment and thirty-two-foot wall of Gwalior fort. Scindia hurried back from Gujarat, and came upon a delayed reinforcement for Popham of the Bengal Infantry under Major Jacob Camac. The latter, feeling he was being encircled, retreated, but then attacked. Scindia's army withdrew, and the Treaty of Salbai was signed in May 1782. The Marathas gave Raghunath Rao a pension, and the British retained Salsette.

Thereafter in 1782, the Court of Directors criticized the frequent organizational changes made 'according to the whim and caprice of different Governors and Commanders,' on the ostensible plea of economy, which was never achieved. The directors expressed the view in favour of the battalion as the basic unit, as opposed to the regiment, since thereby only captains and lieutenants would be needed, and not majors commanding regiments, thus initiating a thrust towards downgradation in order to counter any possible upgradation.[32]

Following from the British operations against their colonies in North America, the French had declared war against the British. Hyder Ali had cautioned that the French settlement of Mahe was under his protection, but despite this the British captured it after the outbreak of war with France, leading to the Second Anglo-Mysore War of 1780-84. Nawab Mohammed Ali of Arcot, a vassal of the British, informed them that Hyder Ali had since received a large consignment of French armaments and was about to invade the Carnatic. Among his cavalry were 5,000 horsemen, whom the British had trained, but whom Mohammed Ali had not paid, and who had then deserted the latter.

Hector Munro, last mentioned at Buxar, now Commander-in-Chief at Madras, discounted Mohammed Ali's fears and, till 17 July 1780, reportedly made no preparations, apart from ordering Colonel William Baillie with a force of 3,000 to cross the Kistna southwards. Munro's actions were, thereafter, inept, while Hyder's forces of 90,000 men were the most effective of any Indian ruler at the time. Hyder, a capable leader, in four days moved against Arcot, Mohammed Ali's capital. Baillie, though only twenty-five miles

42

away from Madras, was ordered by Munro to link up at Conjeveram (now Kanchipuram), forty miles away, against the advice of the latter's staff who had suggested the link-up be at Madras. Hyder moved against Munro with his main force and detached Tipu, with a force of 11,000 against Baillie. Baillie repulsed Tipu's attack, but sent word he was not strong enough to break through to Conjeveram.

Baillie's force was augmented to 3,800 and resumed its advance, but he halted, when he came up against Tipu ten miles from Conjeveram, where Munro awaited him not moving. Hyder now threw his whole army against Baillie's force, mainly of the Madras Infantry, which fought bravely, but after repeated attacks, being all wounded— including Baillie— or killed, it was overwhelmed. Baillie surrendered with about 200 wounded Europeans. Munro had moved towards the sound of firing but lost his way, and returned to Conjeveram, when some Indian survivors of Baillie's force reached him. Leaving his stores and heavy guns, Munro retreated to Madras. Hyder captured Arcot. The destruction of 'Baillie's force was the severest military defeat the British or any other European power had so far suffered at the hands of a purely Indian army.'[33] According to Sir John Fortescue's *History of the British Army*, Baillie's defeat was due entirely to the 'obstinate and unwise (civilian) council (of Madras) directing operations with the delightful confidence of irresponsible strategists designing a campaign with imperfect maps of an unexplored country,' a phenomenon also observable later.

Warren Hastings then moved Eyre Coote, Commander-in-Chief in Bengal, to Madras by sea in October 1780 with some 550 Europeans, mainly artillery, and the five battalions of Bengal Infantry, already mentioned, to march on foot from Midnapore. Coote found a Madras Army of 7,000 only on his arrival; he, hence, awaited the marching column from Bengal. For three years Coote marched up and down seeking to bring Hyder to battle. There were three engagements, which were deemed victories for the Madras Army, particularly the ones at Porto Novo and Sholinghur. Coote was not defeating Hyder by marching and counter-marching, but urged his force was too small. Coote now had a stroke, but after a few hours resumed operations carried in a palanquin. Meanwhile a Madras Army force of 1,700 under Colonel John Braithwaite was surprised by Tipu at Tanjore, and surrendered. Separately, a force of 1,000 from Britain under Colonel Thomas Humberstone, destined for Madras, landed at Calicut (now Kozhikode) instead, due to the presence of a strong French fleet *en route.* Though unfamiliar with the terrain, he marched towards Mysore, but, after some initial successes, was halted by Tipu.

Meanwhile, in the latter half of 1782, Lord George Macartney, the new Governor of Madras, sought to conduct some operations himself, and asked for troops. Coote refused, so Macartney used Munro, who was doing nothing since Coote's arrival. The Dutch port of Negapatam (now Nagappatinam) was captured by Munro, as also Trincomalee from the French in Ceylon, using an ad hoc force of the Madras Army and an element of the Bengal Army. (Trincomalee was later recaptured by the French.) Coote complained to Calcutta, while Macartney complained to London, 'In God's name, how could you send such a man as old Coote here?' Coote left for Calcutta to recuperate, and Hyder Ali died in December 1782. About this time, Mathews, the Commander-in-Chief, Bombay Army, was sailing down the coast to reinforce Humberstone, when he was advised by the Bombay Council to seize Mangalore. Tipu invested Mangalore. Coote sailed for Madras again, stating, 'I have one foot in the grave, and one on the edge of it.' During the sea voyage, he had another stroke, and died three days later at Madras. After a year's siege, Mangalore fell in January 1784, and a treaty in March concluded the war. Peace prevailing in Europe and India, the directors instructed the Presidencies to reduce their military expenditure, an exhortation repeatedly urged on the conclusion of any hostilities.

When in succession to Warren Hastings, Earl Charles Cornwallis reached Calcutta in 1786, he was both Governor-General and Commander-in-Chief, his surrender to George Washington at Yorktown in 1783 not being held against him professionally. He had initially declined the Governor-Generalship in 1785, but accepted in 1786 when the offer was conjoined with his being Commander-in-Chief. Thus with Cornwallis at Calcutta, Major General Sir William Medows at Madras, and Major General Sir Robert Abercromby at Bombay, all three Presidencies were thus governed by general officers, Cornwallis believing that 'military officers are the best of all governors.' The army in India at this time numbered about 70,000, 60,000 being Indian soldiers, 5,000 Europeans (including the Swiss Regiment de Meuron) of the Company, and 5,000 troops of the King paid for by the Company. In Cornwallis' opinion, his Indian soldiers 'would not in size disgrace the Prussian ranks.' He wrote to the Commander-in-Chief in Britain, the Duke of York, 'A brigade of our sepoys would easily make anybody emperor of Hindustan.' This is what Indian soldiers made the English Company in the next few decades.

At this time, Tipu was militarily the strongest ruler, even though his war with the Peshwa and the Nizam had ended in 1787 without any advantages to him. Cornwallis did not desire any clash with Tipu, but, in the event, Tipu had already sent an embassy to Paris, seeking aid. Earlier, Hyder Ali, after gaining control of Malabar, had made the Raja of Cochin his tributary, but had failed to bring under his suzerainty the Raja of Travancore, an ally of the British. Putting down a rebellion in Malabar in December 1789, he turned to Travancore, and brought up a siege train. On Cornwallis protesting, Tipu said the attack on Travancore had been unintended. Cornwallis commenced negotiations for a triple alliance with the Peshwa and the Nizam, and deputed Medows to commence hostilities against Tipu. As the Madras Army was not ready for operations till May 1790, Tipu overwhelmed the Travancore defences, and hurried back. Tipu outmanoeuvred Medows, for every Madras Infantry officer of the rank of captain and above, according to James Rennell, took with him on the campaign half-a-dozen servants, large bed, tables, chairs, 'his stock of linens (24 suits), some dozens of wine, brandy and gin; tea, sugar and biscuits, a hamper of live poultry and his milch goat'[34] (almost similar impedimenta being observable in the nineteenth and twentieth centuries also). Coimbatore was somehow captured. Cornwallis moved from Calcutta to South India in order to do better than Medows. Tipu was confronted with the three Presidency Armies, the Peshwa and the Nizam, about 100,000 under the overall command of Cornwallis. The latter captured Bangalore in March 1781, but Tipu recaptured Coimbatore. Cornwallis then attacked Seringapatam (Srirangapatnam) in February 1792, and Tipu sought peace. Here Medows, though still Governor of Madras, had commanded the right hand column which went astray through no fault of his. He thereafter attempted suicide. Cornwallis was criticized for not deposing Tipu. Tipu paid about rupees three crores as

45

indemnity, surrendered half his territory, released all prisoners taken by him or Hyder Ali, and gave two of his three eldest sons as hostages. Cornwallis' defeat of Tipu, then militarily the most formidable Indian ruler, has not been given full recognition, because by his humaneness he permitted Tipu to be in a position to fight again later. Cornwallis was also a humane commander. He issued remedial instructions when he found no provision for wounded Indian soldiers, but only for European soldiers. He hanged British soldiers for looting and burning Indian property, and sought to stop the maltreatment of Indians by Europeans. He censured a court-martial that had dealt leniently with an officer who had beaten an Indian. Both he and Medows refused prize money, as also their share of the gratuity distributed from the indemnity paid by Tipu. The final defeat of Tipu in 1799 in the Governor-Generalship of Wellesley was rendered easier as a result of the lessons learnt during Cornwallis' campaign, even though Edward Thornton in his *History of the British Empire in India* has described Cornwallis' capability as 'the highest order of commonplace.'

Thereafter in 1798, the French Governor of Mauritius, issued a proclamation calling for volunteers 'to serve under the banner of Tippoo,' who 'only awaits the moment when the French shall come to his assistance to declare war against the English, whom he ardently desires to expel from India.' Before this, a French privateer had put in at Mangalore in 1797. Its captain, M. Ripaud, falsely claimed to be an envoy to Tipu to discuss the expulsion of the British with French help. Tipu's minister, Purnaiah, felt he was an impostor, but Tipu sent two envoys with Ripaud to Mauritius. The French Governor referred Tipu's request to Paris, but nevertheless called for volunteers to fight for Tipu against the British, whom Tipu had described as 'those oppressors of the human race.' The arrival of a hundred French and Creole volunteers at Mangalore made Richard Wellesley, then Governor-General, decide to go to war against Tipu. The Madras Council was instructed accordingly, and Arthur Wellesley, the Governor-General's brother and the future Duke of Wellington, then commanding a King's regiment in Bengal, was moved to Madras, along with his regiment.

Both the Madras Commander-in-Chief, General George Harris, and Arthur Wellesley advised that Tipu's comments should first be obtained, but the Governor-General decided on completing the preparations, before addressing Tipu. Had the Governor-General acted on his brother's and Harris' advice in June 1798, war could have been avoided. He sought the cooperation of the Marathas and the Nizam against Tipu. The Peshwa was hesitant, but the Nizam reacted by disbanding the French-led force he had maintained against the Marathas and the British. This force flew the French Tricolour. The death in 1798 of its commander, Michel Raymond, facilitated his doing so, as he was not happy with the next senior French officer, Pirron. As stated earlier, Raymond is remembered to this day in Hyderabad, but not Pirron. A British-led force replaced the French-led force. Meanwhile, a letter from Napoleon to 'Citizen' Tipu was intercepted by the British, which, *inter alia*, stated: 'You have already been informed of my arrival on the border of the Red Sea with an innumerable and invincible Army full of the desire of delivering you from the iron yoke of England.' Nelson also cautioned that Napoleon planned an attack 'in concert with Tippoo Saib.' On completing his preparations for war, in November 1798 Richard Wellesley wrote to Tipu.

Tipu exclaimed it was better 'to die like a soldier, than to live a miserable dependant of the infidels.' Harris was in overall command of 40,000 troops, with 20,000 of the Madras Army, including 4,000 Europeans; 6,000 of the Bombay Army, including 1,600 Europeans; six "subsidized" battalions from Hyderabad led by the Company's officers; four battalions from the French-led force but now commanded by the British; and 10,000 of the Nizam's cavalry, also led by British officers. Arthur Wellesley and his regiment, the 33rd Foot, were with the Nizam's forces. Tipu mustered 37,000, and resorted to a scorched-earth policy to halt the 100,000 bullocks with the Company's forces. Harris reached Seringapatam in April 1799. Tipu sought to discuss terms, but was asked to surrender half his territory, pay rupees two crores indemnity, and give four of his sons and most of his commanders as hostages. He refused. Seringapatam fell on 4 May 1799, and looting commenced. Tipu was found dead, with three bayonet wounds, shot through the head. Of the Indian rulers that the British defeated, Tipu was the most formidable. He saw that the British were a threat to Mughal or Muslim rule in India. Arthur Wellesley was brought in on 5 May to control the looting. He wrote, 'Nothing can have exceeded what was done on the night of the 4th.' The distribution of prize money followed. Harris took 143,000 pounds, and offered the Governor-General 100,000 pounds. He declined, recording 'The dreadful fate of Tipu Sultan cannot be contemplated without emotions of pain and regret.'

Towards the end of 1800, the Governor-General assembled forces at Trincomalee, mainly from the Madras Army, for an expedition against the Isles of France (Bourbon and Mauritius), under the command of Arthur Wellesley; French privateers operating from these islands had inflicted two million pounds worth of damage on British shipping. The British naval commander, however, refused to participate as he had received no orders from Britain. (These islands were eventually captured in 1810.) The Governor-General then planned to use this Trincomalee force to capture Batavia, but instructions were received in 1801 to send a force from India to Egypt, to assist in operations against a French Army abandoned there by Napoleon. (In the event, Amboyna and Batavia were captured in 1810 and 1811 respectively.) By the time this mainly Bombay Army force of 7,000 made its way with some difficulty overland to the Nile, the French had been defeated. This expedition was the first occasion Indian troops had been deployed on the Mediterranean. After Tipu's defeat, the Maratha Confederacy could have been the power that defeated the Company, and succeeded the Mughals. The Marathas were, however, divided. The able Nana Phadnavis had for many years wisely guided the Peshwa, and been able to control Scindia, Holkar, the Gaekwar, and the Bhonsle of Berar. The Peshwa had joined the British in the Third Anglo-Mysore War against Tipu, but had rebuffed the British in the final Fourth Anglo-Mysore War. In 1800, Nana Phadnavis died at Poona, and, according to Colonel William Palmer, the British Resident, thus 'departed all the wisdom and moderation of the Maratha Government.'

Though Nana Phadnavis had always advised against it, the Peshwa, Baji Rao II, now accepted a subsidiary force from the Company, because of Holkar advancing on Poona in October 1802. He became a "subsidized" vassal, a force of five battalions being positioned in his territory. The Peshwa thus had joined Richard Wellesley's 'system of defensive alliances and mutual guarantees.'

James Mill wryly observed: 'The direction of the Governor General therefore was that in this manner everyone of the Mahratta states would become dependent upon the English Government; those that accepted the alliance, by the alliance; those who did not accept it, by being deprived of it; the same happy effect, in two opposite, cases, by the same ingenious combination of means.'[35]

Scindia and Berar did not accept the Treaty of Bassein, and concentrated their forces in May 1803 in order to march on Poona. Asked by the British to withdraw, they refused, and war was declared in August 1803. In Orissa, Puri and Balasore were captured from the Raja of Berar, thus linking the Bengal and Madras Presidencies, through the Northern Circars. In Gujarat, Scindia's territories like Broach were captured. In the north, the Bengal Army under Lord Lake, the Commander-in-Chief, was directed to eradicate 'the French state...on the banks of the Jumna, together with all its military resources,' the Governor-General's description of Scindia's forces commanded by Perron and a number of French officers. Before the commencement of operations, Perron and a number of European and Eurasian officers of Scindia's crossed over to the British, generous pensions being offered. Lake won victories at Aligarh in August 1893, Delhi (Patparganj) in September, and Agra and Laswari in October, conforming to the Governor-General's direction for 'the extension of the Company's frontier to the Jumna,' and 'the possession of the nominal authority of the Mughals.' The pay of his regular and irregular Indian troops was five months in arrears.

Arthur Wellesley's five-month campaign in the Deccan, mainly with the Madras Army, included the victory at Assaye in September, deemed by him the closest victory of his career, even closer than Waterloo. After Assaye, Arthur Wellesley wrote, 'The (Madras Army) sepoys astonished me.' After the fall of Asirgarh, Scindia sought a truce. Arthur Wellesley now turned against the Raja of Berar, defeating the latter's forces, using mainly the Madras Army, at Argaum in November, and Gavilgarh in December. The British succeeded due to giving the opposing forces no respite, one of Wellesley's columns covering sixty miles in thirty hours. Arthur Wellesley and some others held that Scindia had weakened his army by training his forces in European style, and that he should have relied on Shivaji's latter pattern of irregular warfare, relying in the main on irregular horsemen. On 18 November 1803, General Wellesley wrote to the Secretary to the Governor-General: 'Whether (the) power...of the Maratha nation would not have been more formidable...if they had never had an European...in their service, and had carried on their operations in the manner of the original Marathas only by means of cavalry. I have no doubt whatever, but that the military spirit of the nation has been destroyed by the establishment of infantry and artillery.' The Second Anglo-Maratha War ended only on the Beas in 1805, where Lake had pursued Holkar.

In 1814-1816 occurred the Anglo-Gurkha War. Border disputes with Nepal had been occurring for years. With the outbreak of the monsoon in 1814, the Bengal Army troops withdrew from the border pockets in which they were deployed, and the Nepalese troops moved in, killing some of the Indian police left there. Kathmandu was informed by Lord Hastings that this was a hostile action, and four Bengal Army columns were launched at Nepalese or Nepalese-held territories. Sir David Ochterlony, who commanded the only successful column, the western-most, launched at Malaun from Ludhiana, without any British troops, commented that the war was 'the most impolitic measure we have ever attempted—setting aside the physical difficulties.' The column on his right flank was commanded by the ageing but still rash Major General Robert Rollo Gillespie, mentioned at Vellore in 1806, who was now killed while rallying his troops for a third assault on Kalunga, a Gurkha stockade, a few miles north of Dehra Dun, marked today by two monuments at Nalapani, one to Gillespie and the British and Indian troops, and the other erected by the British to the opposing troops, including Garhwalis and Kumaonis, whose women and children fought alongside them. All three of Gillespie's attacks were piecemeal. The British and Indian casualties in the three abortive attacks exceeded the defender's strength of 600. The stockade was abandoned, the Gurkha commander, Bal Bahadur, and seventy survivors escaping to take up service with Maharaja Ranjit Singh. Major General Gabriel Martindell, who had failed in punitive operations at Rewa in 1813, was appointed to succeed Gillespie, the Governor-General reasoning that his previous failure 'would have stimulated him to exert himself in regaining the ground he had lost in the public estimation on that occasion.'[36] It had no such effect.

Against Nepal proper, two Bengal Army columns were launched under the aged Major Generals John Wood and Bennet Marley respectively. Wood bumped into a stockade near Butwal. The Gurkhas started to withdraw, but so did Wood. Wood withdrew against a force half his strength; Marley, to cover his concentration, put out three strong posts of five hundred men each, two out of supporting distance. The latter were wiped out. Marley stepped back. The Governor-General sent him reinforcements. Marley marched energetically out of range of the opposing force. Sir Francis Tuker narrated: 'Before long, however, he found the responsibility of this operation altogether too much for him so, without telling a soul, or arranging for anyone to act for him, he quietly rode away by night into self-imposed retirement. On being acquainted of this, the Governor General placed this officer on the invalid or non-effective establishment a merciful end.'[37]

This was, however, apparently not the end of Marley's career, as assumed by Tuker. He was later allowed to hold further command, dying in 1842, curiously a full General, according to Moon.[38] Unknown to Marley, however, there were some difficulties on the Nepalese side as well. The Gurkha commander, Bhagat Singh, who had approached Marley's front with a few hundred men, was given orders to attack a force ten times his own. He demurred and was court-martialled. He was thereafter directed to attend open durbars dressed in petticoats.[39]

In between Gillespie in the west and Marley and Wood in the east, the Governor-General had launched Colonel William Gardner and his brother-in-law, Major Hyder Hearsey, with two irregular parallel forces composed mainly of Rohillas, into Kumaon. Both were irregular officers, till 1803 in the Maratha service. Hearsey was defeated and captured, but Gardner captured Almora, and cut the Nepalese communications to Garhwal and Kangra. During the operations in 1814, Ochterlony had recommended the enrolment of former Nepalese troops in the Company's Army, as each position was taken. In 1815, orders were issued for the formation of two Nasiri (friendly) battalions at Subathu, a Sirmoor battalion, and a

Kumaon Levy. Many of these men were Garhwalis and Kumaonis, and not strictly Gurkhas. Treaty negotiations now broke down over whether a large part of the Terai should pass into British hands, and a British Resident be located in Kathmandu. A British-Indian force was consequently assembled at Dinapur. The capable Ochterlony was given command. In January 1816, he marched from Saran in command of 14,000 regulars and 4,000 irregulars, and turned the formidable Gurkha fort of Makwanpur *en route* to Kathmandu. Lieutenant John Shipp of the 87th Regiment (the Royal Irish Fusiliers) gave a description in his memoirs: 'Our gallant general walked every yard of this critical approach with his men, encouraging them as he went, and that sort of thing works wonders.'[40] On 28 February, the Gurkhas sued for peace, and on 4 March 1816 signed the Treaty of Sagauli with Ochterlony, whereby a British Resident was appointed at Kathmandu. Nepal ceded the Terai, as also those districts which are today Kumaon, Garhwal and the Simla Hills, and quit those parts of Sikkim seized from the latter's Raja.

Earlier, about the middle of the eighteenth century, the ruling Burmese dynasty had commenced a series of progressive conquests, the capital being at Ava. After seizing the Irrawaddy (Irawati) delta and the Tenasserim coast, the Arakan, bordering the Company's territory, was also occupied, Arakanese refugees (Rohingyas) settling in Chittagong. Manipur was seized in 1813, and in 1818, a Burmese-selected Ahom prince was made the ruler in Assam. Demands, for the making over to the Burmese of all the Arakanese refugees, were rejected by the Company. In 1811, the refugees very temporarily regained control of the Arakan. In 1824, the Burmese advanced towards Cachar, but were driven back. Maha Bandula, their Commander-in-Chief, orally threatened to capture Chittagong and Dacca, and even Calcutta, and declaimed. 'They (the British) contrive to conquer and govern black foreigners, the people of castes, who have puny forms and no courage. They have never fought with so strong and proud a people as the Burmas, skilled in the use of sword and spear.' In May 1824, Maha Bandula, with 8,000 troops, advanced on Ramu, near Chittagong, garrisoned by 300 Bengal Army troops and local levies. The latter fled, and the former disintegrated, after most of the officers were killed. Many were sent as prisoners to Ava, Maha Bandula orating that he had prepared golden fetters for the British Governor-General.

Of the Company's sequential sea-borne assault, the army component was 11,000 personnel, half from the Madras Army, and half European troops, owing to Bengal Army objections to sea voyages. The ships from Madras and Calcutta reached Rangoon (now Yangon) in May 1824, but did not find the expected supplies and country-craft in order to proceed to Ava in June up the Irrawaddy. Maha Bandula, having delayed in capturing Chittagong, was foiled by the monsoon. He, with 60,000, now turned against the British-Indian force of 4,000 at Rangoon. He was repelled, the British naval squadron seizing the Tenasserim coast. Ava, to be captured after four to six weeks, had not been approached after eight months. Thereupon overland columns were launched, one of 7,000 from Cachar, and the other of 11,000 from Chittagong. The former lost hundreds of camels, elephants and bullocks without much progress, though Raja Gambhir Singh with 500 Manipuri troops was able to reoccupy Manipur. The Arakan force with naval support did better; though Arakan town was recaptured in March 1825, this force did not succeed in penetrating into Burma (now Myanmar) proper, as a quarter of the force died, and half of the remainder fell ill. Eventually, an advance commenced from Rangoon in February 1825, hundreds of bullocks having arrived from Calcutta. Maha Bandula was fortuitously killed by a rocket, and a peace treaty was signed at Yandobo, fifty miles from Ava, in February 1826.

Thereafter, in 1840 occurred the First Anglo-Chinese War. This expeditionary force to China, partly from the Madras Army, was not connected with the interests of India. It was really intended to further British trade in opium; 20,283 chests of opium, imported by British traders for sale in China, had been seized in 1839, the Chinese Emperor's son having died of an overdose. The British in turn seized the island of Chusan in 1840. No progress being ostensibly made in negotiations, Canton was captured in May. Though bad administration caused more casualties than the fighting, after a year Nanking was taken. The Chinese agreed to cede Hong Kong and opened Chinese ports to British trade. (The Chinese Governor of Canton, Yeh, was later to be in custody in Fort William in 1858 in the Second

Anglo-Chinese War.) The Madras Army was thus not available for the First Anglo-Afghan War of 1839-42, the British retreat in which from Kabul has been described by Field Marshal Sir Gerald Templer as, 'the most disgraceful and humiliating episode in our history of war against an Asian enemy up to that time.'

In 1837, Lord George Auckland, the Governor-General, set out on a tour, accompanied by his sisters, Fanny and Emily Eden. During his two-and-a-half years' absence from Calcutta, his Council carried on. From Auckland's two summers in Simla resulted the First Anglo-Afghan War of 1839-1842. Kaye, wrote later in 1857, in *The History of the War in Afghanistan:* '... That pleasant hill Sanatorium, where our Governors-General surrounded by irresponsible advisers, settle the destinies of empires without the aid of their legitimate fellow-counsellors, and which has been the cradle of more political insanity than any place within the limits of Hindustan.'

All Auckland's advisers at Simla were infected with Russophobia. Having lost Kashmir, Peshawar and Multan to Maharaja Ranjit Singh, Afghanistan was deemed dangerous if it came under Russian influence. The Sadozai clan of Ahmad Shah Abdali no longer ruled at Kabul, his grandsons, Shah Shuja and the blinded Shah Zaman, having sought asylum with the British at Ludhiana in 1816. From Ludhiana, Shuja had sought to regain the throne, but had been defeated. Dost Mohammed, a Barakzai, was then the Amir, and was reported to be corresponding with the Tsar at St. Petersburg, which he had every right to do. This correspondence the Russians denied. A young Bengal Army subaltern, Alexander Burnes, later as Lieutenant Colonel Sir Alexander Burnes, to be killed at Kabul by a mob in 1841, had in 1835, travelling ostensibly to seek openings for British goods, reported, 'It was now a neck and neck race between Russia and us.'

Separately, since November 1837, the Shah of Persia, with Russian advisers and engineers, had been investing Herat in Western Afghanistan with Dost Mohammed's concurrence, as it was still ruled by a Sadozai, and where a Bombay Army subaltern, Eldred Pottinger, happened to be travelling on leave disguised as a Kutchi horse-dealer. Herat, then termed by the British as "the key to India", was expected to fall, and Pottinger assisted in its defence. The

Persians, with their Russian advisers, were expected to advance to Kandahar, and thus bring the Russian presence to the Company's Indian border. Auckland referred to Herat, 1,000 miles from the Indus, as 'the western frontier of India.' He was prevailed upon by his political advisers for Shuja to make a further attempt to regain the Afghan throne. The fighting was to be done by Shuja and Ranjit Singh, the British to provide money to both, as also British officers to train the former's forces during their raising. Without consulting Shuja, Ranjit Singh was approached. The latter had doubts, and the former did not wish to create the impression that he was being restored with Sikh help. It was then devised that he would advance through the Bolan Pass to Kandahar, and some Sikh Army troops through the Khyber to Jalalabad. So far no participation of a British-Indian force had been contemplated, nor was the relief of Herat. The Commander-in-Chief in India, Sir Henry Fane, was averse to this militarily, opining that 'every advance you might make beyond the Sutlej to the northwest...adds to your military weakness.' Wellington warned that an advance into Afghanistan would end up as 'a perennial march into that country.' Auckland was prevailed upon by his political advisers, headed by Sir William MacNaghten, who had no experience of Afghanistan, into an inane invasion. A *Blue Book* was published in 1839 to justify the invasion, portraying Dost Mohammed in an unfavourable light, and omitting Burnes' earlier reports on him, such as: 'He is a man of undoubted ability, and has at heart a high opinion of the British nation; and if half you do for others were done for him, and offers made which he could see contributed to his own interest, he would abandon Russia and Persia tomorrow.' Burnes was pacified with a knighthood at the age of thirty-two. If truth is the first casualty in war then logic is the next.

There were doubts about the success of the invasion, both in India and Britain, the Governor-General's Council protesting it had not been consulted at all. While the regiments of the Bengal and Bombay Armies were assembling at Ferozepur and Bombay respectively for the invasion, the Persians withdrew from Herat. Thus the pseudo-imperative for going into Afghanistan no longer existed. The Bengal and Bombay Armies now expected the invasion to be cancelled. Instead Auckland, pressurized by his political advisers, only partially reduced it, thereby enabling Fane to hand over command to Sir John Keane, Commander-in-Chief of the Bombay Army. Fane resigned shortly after, but died while awaiting passage. MacNaghten, the architect of the invasion, was to be the British envoy to Kabul, and Burnes his political assistant. By the end of 1838, the "Army of the Indus" was ready to move through Baluchistan on what Auckland's political advisers hopefully described as 'a grand military promenade.' The only happy person appeared to have been Ranjit Singh, happy that the British were now the main component of the invasion, and not the Sikhs, but he died in January 1839. In March 1839, an observer of the Indian scene recorded:

Oh, blind to the future, if drum and sword
Be all that your vision contemplate!
May the warning voice not remain unheard
Till the warning voice shall be heard too late?

Before the departure of the invasion force, Burnes had received a letter from Mountstuart Elphinstone, a former Governor of Bombay, now in retirement in Britain, who had led a delegation to Afghanistan in 1807 for a treaty against the French: '...I have no doubt you will take Candehar and Cabul and set up Soojah but for maintaining him in a poor, cold, strange and remote country, among a people like the Afghans, I own it seems to me to be hopeless. If you succeed, I fear you will weaken the (Afghan) position against Russia. The Afghans were neutral, and would have received your aid against invaders with Gratitude; they will now be disaffected, and glad to join any invader to drive you out.'

The Sikh Army contingent of 5,000 concentrated at Peshawar, consisted mainly of Punjabi Mussalmans. Shuja's force of 6,000 consisted of some Afghans and Gurkhas, but mainly of Indians, under Sir Willoughby Cotton. The Bengal Army's contingent consisted of 9,500 men; 30,000 camp followers, both men and women; 30,000 baggage camels, and large herds of sheep and goats for consumption. Keane, to keep his mind clear, was carried behind the cavalry advance-guard in a palanquin to Afghanistan, borne by relays of Indian bearers, across plains, deserts and mountains, followed by a groom leading his charger. The rest of the force stretched for forty miles behind him. Permission had not been obtained from the Amirs for the passage through Sind of the Bombay Army contingent, though they eventually relented.

A suitable atmosphere was sought to be created for the advance by bribing the tribal chiefs *en route*. This bribery was a facet of British policy throughout. The Bengal Army Division was on the verge of mutiny for want of food during the march, having been put on half rations, the followers on quarter rations. The Bombay Army contingent had to rest for two months at Kandahar in order to recover, and for replacement of its supplies, Burnes giving a champagne and claret breakfast to all officers at Kandahar. Keane's success at Ghazni was in doubt, the heavier artillery having been left behind by him at Kandahar, but the defection of a nephew of Dost Mohammed's, bribed by Burnes' assistant, Mohan Lal, with five hundred rupees, enabled Ghazni to be stormed on 21 July 1839. Dost Mohammed fled to the north of the Hindu Kush, and Shuja was installed at Kabul. A shower of honours and awards followed, some deserving, many undeserving, as is often the case. Auckland was made an Earl, and Keane a Baron, the latter being then described as 'perhaps the most undeserved peerage for military honours in British history.' Auckland had said the British-Indian force would be withdrawn when Shuja had been "secured in power". He was not secure, as he was deemed to have been installed by infidels. It was thereupon decided in January 1840 to retain the Bengal Division as a garrison at Kabul and Kandahar, and for the Bombay Army contingent plus some Bengal Army units to return to India through the Khyber with Keane, who confided to a junior officer, '...for mark my words, it will not be long before there is some signal catastrophe.' His staff officer, Henry Havelock, later recorded of Keane, that he 'hardly deserved the name of general.'

The unwise decision to retain a British-Indian garrison at Kabul was due to the belief that without a pro-British ruler, Afghanistan, and then India, would be lost to Russia. Lord Henry Palmerston, the then British Foreign Minister, had in 1838 before the onset of this war declared, 'We have long declined to meddle with the Afghans, and have purposely left them independent but if the Russians try to make them Russian we must take care that they become British.' According to Pierce Fredericks he was better known for his interest in ladies than foreign affairs; *The Times* referred to him as "Lord Cupid", for, at one point, both the Russian Ambassador's wife and the British Prime Minister's sister were his mistresses, while the two ladies corresponded in friendly terms with each other. Palmerston now recorded in 1840: 'It seems pretty certain that sooner or later the Cossak (sic) and the Sepoy...will meet in the centre of Asia. It should be our business to take care that the meeting should be as far off from our Indian possessions as may be convenient and advantageous to us. But the meeting will not be avoided by our staying at home to receive the visit.'

Keane got through the Khyber in time. A snakes and ladders situation now developed. An Afghan force raised by Shuja in order to replace his Indian and Gurkha troops, all deserted along with their commandant. The 2nd Bengal Cavalry broke when charged by Dost Mohammed and eighty-six companions north of Kabul. It was ordered to be disbanded for misconduct. His honour vindicated, Dost Mohammed surrendered on 4 November 1840, and was exiled to Ludhiana as a British pensioner. A new cantonment was built in 1840 outside Kabul for the Bengal Division, shortly to be under the command of Major General William Elphinstone (a cousin of Mountstuart Elphinstone), as Shuja, *inter alia*, needed the Bala Hissar Fort for his expanded harem of several hundred women. The vacation of the Bala Hissar by the British-Indian force was ordered by MacNaghten. Lieutenant (later Major General Sir Vincent) Eyre then remarked, 'It must always remain a wonder that any government, or any officer or set of officers...should, in a half-conquered country, fix their forces in so extraordinary and injudicious a military position,' in low-lying swampy ground. The choice of Elphinstone, who was only fit to be invalided out of the service, as the new commander of the Bengal Division in Afghanistan, is deemed by Kaye as 'inexplicable by any reference to intelligible human motives.' An elderly genial gentleman, his only qualification for the appointment had been that he had gone grouse shooting with influential persons in Britain including Auckland. He had never served in India before, till he arrived in 1839, having been on half-pay since Waterloo in 1815, his elevation being due to the integrity of the roster. Emily Eden, Lord Auckland's sister saw him and wrote in February 1840, 'He is in a shocking state of gout, poor man—one arm in a sling and very lame—but is otherwise a young-looking general for India.' Sequentially, he was designated Commander-in-Chief in Afghanistan, being then described as 'the most incompetent soldier that was to be found among the officers of the requisite rank.'

Auckland was fully conscious of Elphinstone's physical disabilities, and had been fearful that Elphinstone may consequently turn down the appointment urging his infirmities. There were much better Company officers available, notably Major General William Nott already at Kandahar, but then Nott was too frank, and professionally effective too. He had disagreed with the British policy in Baluchistan and Afghanistan. Nott wrote to his daughter after Elphinstone's appointment that: 'The officers of the Indian Army are a set of helots, and bear kicks like asses.'

Both British and Indians, desirous of doing so, were allowed to bring their families. The British officers spent their time racing, shooting, fishing, jackal-hunting and ice-skating. The new cantonment and the arrival of the families gave the semblance of permanent occupation, aggravated by the libertine behaviour of many of the British personnel with Afghan women, though the odd marriage did occur. On arrival, Elphinstone was appalled by the siting of the cantonment, and by his irascible one-armed second-in-command, Brigadier John Shelton, who thoroughly disliked Indian troops. He could do nothing about either. Meanwhile, Shuja was only in power by the use of British and Indian troops against the rebellious tribes, particularly in the period May to September 1841, when one tribal chief was ordered to be blown from a gun, a punishment Shuja was having recourse to, from Ghazni onwards. On 2 November 1841, the libertine Burnes, who lived in the city and was to succeed MacNaghten, when the latter departed to be Governor of Bombay, was killed by a mob, along with his brother and another officer, as well as his guard of Indian soldiers, his Indian servants and their families. His assistant, Mohan Lal, who lived in an adjacent house, survived. Mohan

Lal had warned Burnes of the impending attack on him and the British, but Burnes had chosen not to heed Mohan Lal's warning, even though some British officers had already been killed while walking in Kabul bazaar. Burnes had only a little earlier recorded of MacNaghten, 'A man whose eyes are always on the horizon, and apt to miss what is under his nose.' The British treasury in Kabul was also looted. The bribe money now ran out, 1,200,000 pounds a year being required to keep Shuja on the throne. Positive action by Elphinstone that day may have saved the situation, but he vacillated, his fall from a horse the day before adding to his problems. Shelton was not much help, being argumentative. Elphinstone, thereupon, consulted even junior subalterns. During Elphinstone's conferences, Shelton lay on the floor, pretending to be asleep. Only Shuja sent his troops to rescue Burnes, but they ill-advisedly sought to take the direct route through the attacking mob, instead of from the rear. On 3 November tribesmen poured into Kabul.

The new cantonment had not been designed for defence, by Elphinstone's predecessor, Willoughby Cotton, and the supplies and magazine were outside the cantonment. The latter were thus lost on 4 November. All the decisions in the developing situation continued to be militarily inept. They did not immediately move into the defensible Bala Hissar, Shelton opposing such a move, nor did they promptly move out to Jalalabad, where, by circumstance, there was a weak British-Indian brigade under Sir Robert Sale. A Gurkha battalion of Shuja's force, under MacNaghten's political assistant, Eldred Pottinger, sent out to Kohistan, north of Kabul, earlier to suppress rebellious chiefs, was itself annihilated. Pottinger, though badly wounded, just managed to escape, most of the British officers of the Gurkha battalion being killed. The only British unit, the 44th Foot, on 27 November refused to follow their officers in order to evict some Afghans. The 37th Bengal Infantry thereafter refused to operate with the 44th Foot. On 10 December news reached that a brigade from Kandahar could not get through on account of the snow. Terms were then agreed upon with Akbar Khan, the exiled Dost Mohammed's son. The British would be allowed to withdraw unmolested, being supplied provisions on payment, and would return Amir Dost Mohammed unharmed. Shuja could return to

Ludhiana, or stay on as an Afghan pensioner.

By 23 December, the British had still not been able to withdraw, MacNaghten in the interim trying to buy off the marauding tribesmen. This led to his own death. Eventually, on 6 January 1842, about 4,500 troops, the families, and 12,000 camp followers marched out, all guns except six, all spare muskets, and all coin having been surrendered. Elphinstone left behind six officer hostages, the sick and wounded officers, and these British officers' families. Patrick Macrory commented: 'No one supposed for a moment that he was referring to any but the British wives and children, nor was any plea put in for the far more numerous wives and children of the sepoys and camp followers...these were native and expendable.'[41]

Elphinstone's concern did not even extend to wounded British other ranks. Elphinstone's seeming lack of compassion is recorded by Macrory: '...from mid-December onwards the ground was inches deep in snow. The Indian troops suffered particularly from the cold, but although there was a complete winter stock of firing, fires were not allowed...the miserable troops sank deeper into apathy and numbed despair. Pottinger...now urged that old horse blankets should be cut into strips which the troops could roll puttee-fashion round their feet and legs...nothing was done, and the troops were left to the misery of their hard leather boots. Within a few hours of the start of the march the frost had done its work and hundreds were suffering the agony of frost-bitten feet...Pottinger and (George) Lawrence still hoped against hope that at the eleventh hour Elphinstone would come to his senses and order the army to march straight in and occupy that formidable stronghold (of Bala Hissar) before the Afghans could rally to prevent them. But Elphinstone was not the man to be capable of such an audacious change of plan. The cross-roads were reached, the advance guard turned left towards Jalalabad, and the Bala Hissar died away in the winter dusk behind them.'[42]

This was the promenade as to which a veteran India-watcher had observed earlier, 'In India, every war is more or less popular, and there had not been a good one in years.' The rear guard was immediately attacked, losing fifty per cent of its strength and two guns. During the late night and early morning of 6 and 7 January, the

Afghans plundered the rear. On 8 January, the main column was ambushed in the Khurd Kabul Pass, about 3,000 being killed. On 9 January, the remaining British women and children were handed over to Akbar Khan for protection, along with their husbands. On 10 January the rear guard observed: 'The road was strewn with the mangled corpses of their comrades and the stench of death was in the air. All along the route they had been passing little groups of (Indian) camp followers, starving, frost-bitten, and many of them in a state of gibbering idiocy. The Afghans...had simply stripped them and left the cold to do its work, and now the poor wretches were huddling together naked in the snow, striving hopelessly to keep warm by the heat of their own bodies. There were women and little children among them, who piteously stretched out their hands for succour. Later the Afghans were to report with relish that the unhappy fugitives...had been reduced to eating the corpses of their companions. But they all died in the end'. They died in the Khurd Kabul pass.[43] The total disintegration of the British-Indian Kabul garrison was complete when a sole horseman, the wounded Dr William Brydon, rode into Jalalabad on a maimed horse which then died. The horse had been given up to him by a wounded subedar the day earlier.

When the then Commander-in-Chief, Sir Jasper Nicolls of the British Army, heard of the catastrophe, he chose as the Commander of the relief force, Major General James Lumley, also of the British Army. Like Elphinstone, Lumley made up in deportment what he lacked in professionalism. Fortunately, he was so decrepit that the doctors advised that he could not possibly assume the appointment, which they should have done for Elphinstone as well. Hence the efficient Major General George Pollock, a Company officer and a saddler's son, was chosen. He was 'not the first Major General on the roll, nor the oldest alive in the Army List, nor him who had the most grandfathers in England, but for once—this terrible once—the man best suited to the service at hand.' Macrory provided one epitaph on this war: 'Pollock's force was marching back along the line of Elphinstone's disastrous retreat; at every point they came upon ghastly evidence of the fate of the Kabul force. Rotting corpses and skeletons picked clean by carrion met them at every turn. At Tezeen they found a pile of fifteen hundred corpses of Elphinstone's sepoys and camp followers, who had been stripped naked by the Afghans and left to die in the snow.'[44] In the Khurd Kabul Pass an eye-witness wrote: 'The sight of the remains of the unfortunate Caubul force was heart-rending. They lay in heaps of fifties and hundreds, our gun wheels passing over and crushing the skulls and bones of our late comrades at almost every yard.'

Henry Lawrence, who accompanied Pollock, at the time provided a terser epitaph: 'Our Caubul army perished, sacrificed to the incompetence, feebleness, and want of skill and resolution of their military leaders.' Later in 1846 he was to write: 'At Caubul, we lost an army, and we lost some character with the surrounding states. But I find that by far our worse loss was in the confidence of our Native soldiery. Better had it been if our harassed troops had rushed on the enemy, and perished to a man, than that surviving sepoys should be able to tell the tales they can of what they saw at Caubul...when it is not the Hindustani (most exposed to cold, and least able to bear it) who clamours for retreat and capitulation, but the cry is raised by the men (British) he has been accustomed to look up to and to lean upon.'

Norman Dixon summarized in his *On the Psychology of Military Incompetence,* 'When news of the disaster reached India and London, much mental energy was devoted to the discovery of scapegoats. The two favourites for this role were Shah Soojah, accused by his critics of treachery, and Elphinstone's Indian sepoys. In neither case were the accusations justified. Soojah had in fact remained loyal to the last. As for the sepoys, though dragged from the warmth of their native India to fight another man's war in the freezing climate of Afghanistan, they, if anything, fought more bravely and endured what were for them particularly adverse conditions more stoically than any other unit of Elphinstone's army.'

There are always penalties in war for incompetence. The British conduct of the unnecessary First Anglo-Afghan War was so fatuous, that one wonders how a nation capable of such fatuity should have been able to create a British-Indian Empire, and retain it thereafter for almost a century. There was even indecision on the part of Auckland as to whether a relief force should be sent to recover the British hostages, and the British sick and wounded. Both he and Nicolls felt that the garrisons at Jalalabad, Ghazni and Kandahar should first be withdrawn, and the recovery of the hostages dealt with later. But the Company's officers like Nott at Kandahar, James Outram in Baluchistan, and Henry Lawrence in Peshawar felt that Burnes' and others' deaths must first be avenged; the hostages, and sick and wounded, released.

Pollock reached Peshawar in February 1842, but before he could force the Khyber, the garrison at Ghazni was compelled to surrender, after its water supply was cut. Again terms were negotiated with the Afghans, and again there was a breach of faith. The Indian soldiers were attacked after surrendering, enslaved and converted, as also had those who had survived the slaughter in the march from Kabul towards Jalalabad in January 1842. Meanwhile, Sale, the brigade commander at Jalalabad, was also in favour of surrender but his Council of War, described as "jackdaws", was opposed to it. In April, Shuja was murdered at Kabul. The besieging Afghans at Jalalabad fired a gun salute in celebration. This was interpreted by the Jalalabad garrison as a celebration of Pollock being repulsed. The garrison sallied out, in a last effort, and the Afghans fled. The Jalalabad garrison unwittingly thus found itself relieved, and marched out to meet Pollock. Sale became a hero, and gun salutes were fired all over India.

Edward Ellenborough, the new Governor-General, now put the political officers in Afghanistan under the military. It had become standard practice in Afghanistan for the military to blame the political officers, but the subsequent military fiascos were really due to military ineptitude. Thucydides had said in 500 BC that wars start on a triviality, but are not, thereafter, fought on trivial issues. But then Thucydides was not aware of the First Anglo-Afghan War. Overall there is little doubt that the misadventure was embarked on by the political officers like MacNaghten. Ellenborough now ordered Pollock at Jalalabad and Nott at Kandahar to withdraw to India. Both represented, and there was a concomitant outcry in India and Britain at leaving the hostages and others in Afghan hands, Ellenborough complaining in June 1842 to the British Prime Minister that 'Major Generals Nott and Pollock have not a grain of military talent,' in contradistinction to the laudatory terms he had described them in April 1842 after the relief of Jalalabad. Nott recorded to his daughter at about this time, 'I have now several times seen European troops under fire with sepoys alongside of them, and, believe me, the more I see of sepoys, the more I like them; properly managed, they are the best troops in the world. Some John Bulls would hang me for saying this.' In deference to the clamour against the withdrawal from Afghanistan without the hostages and others being rescued, Nott was given the option on 4 July of "retiring" to India via Ghazni and Kabul, instead of direct to Quetta. If Nott opted to "retire" via Kabul, then Pollock should link up with him, and both should 'retire to India via Kabul.' Call it what you will, sophistry or semantics, but Ellenborough, though a civilian, had had unfulfilled military aspirations. Of him, it had been said, 'a soldier, as a soldier is a thing he worships.' When originally appointed Governor-General, he had sought to be designated as "Captain General".

Pollock and Nott victoriously "retired" via Kabul, blowing up the Kabul bazaar as a punitive measure, having so received instructions. The mutilated remains, of the British officers killed, had been displayed there. An eye-witness, Captain McKinnon, recorded: 'To punish the unfortunate houseowners of the bazaars (many a guiltless and friendly Hindu) was not distinguished retaliation for our losses.' Most of the British sick and wounded, the British hostages, the British families, and the few prisoners taken by the Afghans, were brought back to India, including Shelton, except, according to Peter Hopkirk, one British sergeant's wife, who eloped with her Afghan guard at Bamian. Some had died in captivity, including Elphinstone. Nicolls now congratulated himself for appointing Pollock, whom he had not originally recommended. Pollock deserves commendation for this tactical achievement. He refused to be hurried, and retained balance in all his actions through the Khyber to Kabul and back. His force was the only one to have effected a successful passage of the Khyber against opposition, without suffering major casualties, a fact not achieved even by Akbar and Aurangzeb. (Timur and Nadir Shah had paid for safe passage through the Khyber.) A monument at Dum Dum commemorates his "victorious withdrawal" from Kabul (he was a Bengal Artillery officer). Shuja's family and the blind Shah Zaman took up residence at Ludhiana again. Dost Mohammed returned from Ludhiana to Kabul as Amir, making his son Akbar, his Wazir. Dost Mohammed reigned for twenty years. He later recorded in his autobiography, 'What I cannot understand is why the rulers of an Empire so vast and flourishing should have gone across the Indus to deprive me of my poor and barren country.' Shelton, for his part, died in Dublin in 1845 after a fall from his horse. On hearing the news, his regiment (the 44th) gave three cheers.

After an expenditure of fifteen million pounds over the four years, 1839-1842, borne by Indian revenues, it was a case of reversion to the *status quo ante,* apart from the very many thousands of Indian, and hundreds of British casualties. Though the British were now back on the Sutlej, psychologically the Bengal Army was never the same. Several hundred frost-bitten Indian soldiers returned from Afghanistan with the relief force, rescued from slavery; most had been forcibly converted and so had lost their caste. They gave eye-witness accounts that the British had been found wanting in leadership and courage. This memory of the First Anglo-Afghan War contributed to the 1857 Uprising—most of the Bengal Army units that had served in Afghanistan mutinying. There are some military commanders even today, who say or do nothing, so that they ostensibly do nothing wrong. In this inept campaign, some one hundred-and-fifty years ago, the courteous Elphinstone, who sought to do nothing nevertheless did everything wrong. Field Marshal Templer, in his Preface to Macrory's *Signal Catastrophe,* summed up: 'The mounting of this campaign reads like a mad-hatter's tea party. As has so often been proved in war, if the wrong man is chosen to carry out a difficult task, trouble, if not tragedy, must inevitably result...leadership today is an unpopular word.'

Sequentially, in 1843, Sind was annexed by Major General Sir Charles Napier. He had arrived in India for the first time in 1841, at the age of sixty to command a division of the Bombay Army at Poona. (He was to come out again in 1849 as Commander-in-Chief.) A much-wounded Peninsular War veteran, he yearned to command an army in battle. Taking with him a contingent of the Bombay Army in 1842 to Sind, Napier was curiously made the supreme civil and military authority there by Ellenborough. But first as to how the Indus was covertly surveyed. In 1830, Ellenborough was President of the Board of Control for India, and a member of Wellington's Cabinet. Ranjit Singh had recently presented the King of England with some valuable Kashmiri shawls. What was William IV to send in return? Earlier it had been the British traveller William Moorcroft's dream, before he died near Balkh in 1825, to see the River Indus used to transport British goods northwards to the fringes of Central Asia, whence they could be carried by caravans to the markets of the old Silk Road. *The Times* in November 1842 now urged to 'extend our manufactures throughout the whole of central and northern Asia.' British-India was thus always looking for a place where the British flag might be set, in order that British trade might follow it. High on the list of Ranjit Singh's hobbies was horses. Ranjit Singh was thus to be presented with the largest horses seen in Asia, five massive English dray horses (he had recently sent a Sikh envoy to the Russian court). On account of their size and the unsuitability of the climate, it was urged that they could not travel 700 miles overland to Lahore, and therefore had to go by boat up the Indus. The officer chosen to lead this espionage-cum-survey mission had been Alexander Burnes of the Bombay Army, later to be killed by a mob at Kabul. Sir Charles Metcalfe, who had had a Punjabi wife and was then a member of the Supreme Council at Calcutta, and later to be Governor-General of Canada, was the only one to protest, recording: 'The scheme of surveying the Indus, under the pretence of sending a present to Raja Runjeet Singh, is a trick,...unworthy of our Government.' The Amirs of Sind objected to the passage of the vessel with its equine cargo, but, threatened with the consequences if they held up Ranjit Singh's gift, they reluctantly agreed to allow Burnes to proceed. The Amirs had subsequently against their will been compelled to accept and pay for a subsidiary force of the Company's troops. Their territories had been made the line of communication for the British-Indian forces to and from Afghanistan, and certain strategic points, Karachi, Tatta, Sukkur, Rohri and the island of Bukkur, had been occupied by the British, ostensibly temporarily. Napier now confided to his diary, 'We have no right to seize Scinde yet we shall do so, and a very advantageous, useful humane piece of rascality it will be.'

Ostensibly, Napier had been sent to ensure the safety of the British-Indian force withdrawing from Kandahar, through Baluchistan and Sind, but which force was capable of ensuring its own safety. The Amirs would have signed a new treaty without coercion. There was, however, the contingency planning for Napier to strike at the Punjab through Sind, while other British-Indian forces moved forward from Ferozepur. Ferozepur State had been annexed in 1835, on Sardarni Lachman Kaur dying without a male heir, for just such a purpose. Outram, who had been the envoy to the Amirs, before being ordered to revert to regimental duty in the Bombay Army, had twenty years' service in India, compared to Napier's four months, then recorded: 'Until we entered Sind, I verily believe all classes in the country were as happy as those under any Government in Asia.' The opportunity, which Napier had manoeuvred, now occurred, at Miani on 16/17 February 1843, of commanding an army in the field, even though it was only 3,000 men with twelve guns, against reportedly over 18,000 armed only with matchlocks, and in Napier's words, 'gorgeous as a field of flowers,' presumably waiting to be plucked. Much of his force, including three of the four battalions of Indian infantry, was from the Bombay Army. Among the cavalry was the Scinde Irregular Horse, under John Jacob, who had already earned a reputation. Against sixty-two killed of the British-Indian force the Amirs lost 5,000 killed. Sind was annexed. Napier's prize money was almost rupees seven lakhs. Ellenborough now ordered the Amirs to be shipped to Mecca. However, Sir Robert Peel, the Prime Minister, wrote to him, 'I wish I could say to you with truth that I felt perfectly at ease about the affairs of Scinde.' It was not Napier who sent the signal "Peccavi" (I have Sind), but an anonymous contributor to *Punch*, punning that Napier had "sinned". Mountstuart Elphinstone then opined that the conduct of the Sind campaign was analogous to the behaviour of the bully, who, worsted in the street (Afghanistan), returns home (Sind), and beats his wife.

Thereafter, the First Anglo-Sikh War was fought in 1845-1846. The Sikh leaders were aware that, since the death of Ranjit Singh in 1839, the partition or annexation of their territory was contemplated by the British. Many thought of making them allies of the Sikh kingdom, but the latter seemed likely to break up as a result of political assassinations. The competing Sikh factions offered inducements of higher pay to the Sikh Army in order to gain its support. Some of the Sikh Army plundered bazaars, and murdered strict officers and unpopular paymasters. Most of the Europeans in the

Sikh Army, mainly French, fled, after two Britons in Sikh employ were murdered. The British felt it was their duty to intervene in the situation in the Punjab, but Ellenborough was not desirous of doing so, as there was a mutinous spirit in the Bengal Army. The British were finding it difficult to garrison Sind, once the extra allowances had been withdrawn after its annexation, apart from the fact that the Lahore Durbar was encouraging desertions from the Bengal Army, with offers of nearly twice the Company's pay and allowances. By this time, the Sikh Army was run by regimental panchayats or committees, an organizational pattern that was to be adopted also in the concerned Bengal Army units in the 1857 Uprising. These regimental panchayats were throwing their support, first behind one leader, then behind another. The Sikh leaders, for their part, felt that Auckland had invaded Afghanistan in 1839, Ellenborough Sind in 1842, and now Henry Hardinge, the new Governor-General, would invade the Trans-Sutlej Punjab in 1844. At this time, the Sikh Army numbered 69, 500 infantry, 27, 575 cavalry and 4, 130 artillerymen. Hardinge wrote to the former Governor-General, his brother-in-law, Ellenborough, 'How are we to justify the seizure of our friends' territory, who in adversity (the First Anglo-Afghan War) assisted us to retrieve our affairs...?' In the spring and summer of 1845, he increased the forces in the Cis-Sutlej Punjab from 13,500 to 32,500, and assembled a large number of boats for the bridging of the Sutlej, seemingly for defensive purposes.

Many Sikh Durbar leaders, including Gulab Singh of Jammu, made secret contacts with the British, so that they would retain their land-holdings. The Sikh troops were better than their leaders, questioned the British pseudo-defensive intentions in assembling boats on the Sutlej, and decided to defend Trans-Sutlej Punjab, commencing deployment along the Sutlej in November 1845. The Commander-in Chief, Sir Hugh Gough, thereupon moved up forces from Meerut and Ambala to link up with those at Ferozepur. The Sikh Army, presumably ultimately to prevent this link up, crossed into a Cis-Sutlej Sikh enclave in December 1845, legally not so far having intruded into British-controlled territory. Many among the British thought the Sikh Army a rabble, and so Hardinge declared war, proclaiming all Sikh territory south of the Sutlej to be now under the

British. Hardinge placed himself under Gough's command, waiving his status as supreme commander. The Sikh Durbar felt that war with the British could not be left to the regimental panchayats, and sequentially appointed Lal Singh, the paramour of Rani Jindan, the mother of the young Maharaja Dalip Singh, as Wazir, and Tej Singh as Commander-in-Chief. Both, independently, were secretly in touch with the British. Tej Singh, an Hindustani from Meerut, could have overrun Sir John Littler at Ferozepur, before Gough could link up, but deliberately refrained from doing so, being so advised by the British political officer at Ferozepur. Separately, Lal Singh, having entrenched the main Sikh Army at Ferozeshah, pushed on with a small force to Mudki, to prevent Gough linking up with Littler at Ferozepur. Both forces were equal with a strength of 11,000, and the British found that the Sikhs were not the rabble they thought they were. John Lawrence commented at the time, 'We began the campaign as we have begun every campaign in India before and since, by despising our foes.' Casualties on 18 December 1845 at Mudki were heavy on both sides; Sale, the defender of Jalalabad being among the dead. Gough sent for reinforcements from Meerut and Ambala, deciding, on Hardinge's advice, to attack at Ferozeshah, only after Littler had linked up.

Littler linked up at midday 21 December. Without proper reconnaissance, Gough, seventy and probably already senile, resorted to his "Tipperary tactics" and immediately attacked Lal Singh, before Tej Singh could rejoin. The lighter British artillery was comparatively ineffective against the heavier entrenched Sikh artillery. Defeat confronted the British-Indian force, many proposing withdrawal to Ferozepur. Gough and Hardinge decided to attack again at first light 22 December, before Tej Singh could link up, and were successful, Lal Singh having ensured that his gunners ran out of ammunition. The irresolute or treacherous Tej Singh, after a couple of indecisive attacks, withdrew. Overawed by the hitherto invincibility of the Sikh Army, the Bengal Army did not distinguish itself at Mudki or Ferozeshah. At Mudki, most Bengal Infantry units fired into the air, and at Ferozeshah had lain down on the ground during the attack. Gough was of the opinion that the Bengal Army had not yet recovered its morale after the disaster of the First Anglo-

Afghan War. As it so happened, all the Bengal Army units that suffered heavy casualties in the Sikh wars mutinied in 1857.

After Ferozeshah, Hardinge wrote, 'Another such victory, and we are undone.' As to Gough's performance, he wrote to the British Prime Minister that he had 'no capacity for order and administration', and 'ought not to be entrusted with the conduct of war.' Wellington felt Gough was 'inclined to use bayonets, where guns would have done better.' After Ferozeshah, the aura of the Sikh Army's invincibility having been demolished, the Bengal Army did better, for the Sikh Army had lost over 2,000 dead and suffered over 20,000 wounded. The Sikh Army now developed a strong position at Sobraon on the south bank, but keeping the main body and the artillery on the north bank, a boat-bridge connecting Sobraon with the north bank. A force of about 8,000 was also directed at Ludhiana, burning a part of Ludhiana cantonment. After Lal Singh had provided a rough sketch of the Sikh defences at Sobraon, the British attacked on 10 February 1846. Tej Singh fled at the initial attack. Part of the Sikh boat-bridge collapsed. Hardinge's ADC, his son, recorded, 'Few escaped; none, it may be said, surrendered. The Sikhs met their fate with that resignation which distinguished them.' About 10,000 of the Sikh Army at Sobraon were killed or drowned. The tragedy for the Sikh soldier was to have to fight a war for a government which hoped for its own defeat, and with leaders who did not believe in their cause against the British.

It was decided to reduce the Sikh infantry to 20,000, the cavalry to 12,000; all the Cis-Sutlej territory to be ceded, as also the Jullundur Doab; to pay the British a war indemnity of 1,500,000 pounds, and that the Sikh Durbar should cede all the hill territory between the Beas and the Indus, including Hazara and Kashmir. The British decided to sell the latter to Raja Gulab Singh, who had remained neutral during the war, for 750,000 pounds, after payment of which he would be made Maharaja. Though also offered Hazara on payment, he was not desirous of buying it. The Sikh Durbar requested that a British-Indian garrison be maintained at Lahore for its protection from its own army. A British Resident was later also positioned at Lahore. In order to comply with the directors' demands for economy after the expenses of the First Anglo-Afghan War and the First Anglo-Sikh War, Hardinge reduced the Presidency Armies by 50,000 (two hundred from each infantry battalion and cavalry regiment), thereby effecting a saving of one million pounds annually. The Second Anglo-Sikh War, however, occurred during 1848-1849. When it commenced and these cuts had to be restored, Wellington exclaimed 'I never could understand why he was in such a damned hurry,' by which time Hardinge had left India. In May 1848, a conspiracy to suborn the Bengal Army units at Lahore had been revealed, in which Rani Jindan seemed to be involved. When she was moved to Benares, the Sikh Army became distressed. Had Henry Lawrence been in Lahore at the time, this war may not have occurred. He was on sick leave in Britain. Then during the subsequent rebellion at Multan of Dewan Mulraj against the Sikh Durbar, two British officials, Patrick Vans Agnew and Lieutenant William Anderson, were perchance killed. Mulraj, though confirmed as Dewan on his father's death, had had to resign as he was unable to pay the enhanced succession fee. Thereupon a Sikh Army contingent of 7,000, under Sher Singh Attariwala, left Lahore in July, and joined a British-Indian force at Multan. In September, Sher Singh Attariwala and his force joined Mulraj, Sher Singh issuing a proclamation for war against the British, and their expulsion from the Punjab. A British-Indian force of 20,000 was assembled at Ferozepur under Gough, then over seventy and still the Commander-in-Chief. He was, however, courageous, even though bull-headed.

Sher Singh Attariwala, after a disagreement with Mulraj, moved first to the Chenab, and then to Chillianwallah on the Jhelum. Gough had planned to attack on the morning of 14 January 1849 after an artillery bombardment, but, as was often his wont, precipitately did so on the afternoon of 13 January after an inadequate artillery bombardment, explaining, 'Indeed I had not intended to attack today, but the impudent rascals fired on me. They put my British blood up and I attacked them.' The British-Indian force suffered considerable casualties, nearly three thousand officers and men, but captured twelve Sikh guns for the loss of four of their own, during the flight of the British cavalry. (The Dogras and Rohillas of the Sikh Army had crossed over to the British, during the battle.) Both Gough and the Sikhs claimed a victory, the latter firing a twenty-one gun victory salute. The brigade commander of the British cavalry was so elderly, that he could not mount his horse without assistance. It was possibly for this reason that he had been promoted. He was so near-sighted, he could not see in which direction his brigade was facing. He had never commanded a cavalry brigade before, even in peace. The flight of the British cavalry was stopped by their chaplain, armed with his pistol. Gough sought to promote him on the battlefield to brevet bishop. James Dalhousie, now the Governor-General, at this stage said of Gough, '...utterly lost any power of memory, which he...may have ever possessed.' The official policy at the time however, was that 'Command should be...essentially...a final reward for zealous services, and as a means of enabling old officers, each in his turn, to gather from it the wherewithal to pass...their old age in pecuniary ease and comfort...'

It is interesting to note that the site of the desperate battle of Chillianwallah, between the Sikh Army, many of them the descendants of the very men who fought for or against Alexander the Great, and Gough's British-Indian force, was practically the same as the battle of the Hydaspes between Alexander and Porus. This historical parallel was apparently well-known, for the British sang at Chillianwallah:

Sabres drawn and bayonets fixed
Fight where fought Alexander.
O'Paddy Gough's a cross betwixt
Bulldog and salamander.

In view of the heavy casualties at Chillianwallah, a decision was taken in London to replace Gough, Wellington selecting Sir Charles Napier, and informing him, 'If you don't go, I must.' (Wellington was now eighty.)

Meanwhile, at Multan, Mulraj surrendered to the British-Indian force under Major General William Whish. The latter was immediately ordered to join Gough, as Sher Singh had been reinforced by his father, Chattar Singh, from Peshawar, along with 1,500 horsemen provided by Amir Dost Mohammed, who was to be given back Peshawar, if the Sikh Army defeated the British. On 21 February, much before Napier could arrive, Gough, having been joined by Whish, attacked the Sikh Army at Gujrat. Gough used his artillery, and the Sikhs suffered terrible casualties. After a short intense battle, the Sikhs withdrew. Followed up, they surrendered on 13 March. The Sikh kingdom created by Ranjit Singh thus ended, all its residual territory, after the First Anglo-Sikh War, now being absorbed into British-India. The Koh-i-noor diamond was seized and presented to Queen Victoria. It had been part of the Peacock Throne, carried off from Delhi in 1739 by Nadir Shah. Thereafter, it had passed to the Afghan ruler at Kabul. When Shah Shuja had fled to the Punjab, Maharaja Ranjit Singh had prevailed upon him to present it to the latter. The young Maharaja Dalip Singh was first moved to Fatehgarh. In 1853 he temporarily became a Christian, and resided in Britain, and later France. He died a Sikh in 1883, having been joined for a few years in Europe by Rani Jindan. An attempted return to India in between to regain his inheritance proved abortive.

The new Commander-in-Chief, Sir Charles Napier, arrived in May 1849. Dalhousie had been disconcerted by the appointment, for, though he had been distressed by Gough's conduct of the battle of Chillianwallah, he had the powers to appoint a commander-in-chief in an emergency from among the general officers serving in India. Charles Napier, dubbed the "Conqueror of Sind", within six months of taking over had court-martialled forty-six officers. Before leaving Britain, he had sought to be designated Dalhousie's successor. In accepting the appointment, he had expected the Second Anglo-Sikh War would still be on. He then expected to be the Governor of the Punjab, but Dalhousie instead appointed a Board of Three to administer the Punjab. Napier now had ideas of conquering Afghanistan and the adjacent provinces of China in order to distribute them as *jangi inams* (rewards for war service) to his Indian soldiers. In his opinion, Nepal should have become British territory, and he confided in his diary, 'No Indian prince should exist. The Nizam should no more be heard of. Nepal should be ours. Would that I were King of India. I would make Moscow and Peking shake.' Dalhousie reported Napier to the Board in London, whose Deputy Chairman replied: '...We have had two Commanders-in-Chief recalled for conduct much less objectionable, and much less dangerous. But it would seem that this family is exempt from the rules applied to the rest of the world...' At their first interview, Dalhousie, half his age, had told him, 'I have been warned not to allow you to encroach on my authority, and I will take damned good care that you do not.' And that is what happened.

Indian soldiers were entitled to a compensatory allowance when food and other articles of daily utility were excessive in price, there being no government ration supply for Indian soldiers at the time. New instructions were now issued, less favourable than the previous ones for troops in the Punjab. The Divisional Commander at Wazirabad, Brigadier General John Hearsey, in view of the sequential discontent in the Bengal Army in the Punjab, recommended deferment of implementation till some justification could be put over to the troops for their pecuniary loss. Napier agreed, and directed the old instructions would continue in the Punjab until the rationale for the change could be ascertained from Calcutta. Dalhousie could not overrule Napier in view of the effect on the Indian troops' morale in the Punjab. It was suggested to Napier that he should have first referred the matter to Calcutta for clarification. Napier urged that time did not permit such a prior reference, in view of the virtual mutinous state of the Bengal Army. He refused to withdraw his order, said he would do it again in similar circumstances and resigned, leaving India after a tenure of eighteen months.

Separately, after the two Anglo-Sikh Wars, certain Sikh units were raised by the British. For the defence of the western border against the tribesmen of the Trans-Indus territories a large force was needed. The "Corps of Guides", of 190 men that had been raised in 1846 by Henry Lawrence after the First Anglo-Sikh War, was now increased to regimental strength of 840 men, and ten additional "irregular" regiments, five cavalry and five infantry, were raised for the Punjab, not by the Army, but by the Board of Three, constituted by Dalhousie to administer the Punjab. At Henry Lawrence's insistence, in order to give Indians more authority there were only three British officers in these regiments. Four battalions had originally been raised as the 1st, 2nd, 3rd and 4th Sikh Infantry, in 1846 for policing the Doaba between the Beas and the Ravi, the term "Sikh Infantry" meaning, in effect, Sikh, Dogra and Punjabi Mussalman troops formerly in the Sikh service. After the Second Anglo-Sikh War, this Punjab Irregular Force, later named the Frontier Force, had the 1st to 4th Sikh Infantry, and the 1st to 5th Punjab Infantry. The rationale for this difference in designation was that the former were practically former Sikh Army regiments, whereas the latter were regiments raised from former Sikh Army soldiers. In the Bengal Army, also, certain Sikh regiments were raised. It had been the practice of the Presidency Armies to raise regiments from those they had defeated, often from the prisoners of war. They had done so from French and Dutch prisoners of war in South India and the Dutch East Indies respectively, when they had been captured by units of the Madras Army. The first four Gurkha regiments were thus raised during and after the Anglo-Gurkha War. After the First Anglo-Sikh War of 1845-1846, two local Sikh regiments were also raised, the Regiments of Ferozepore and of Ludhiana. Some nine years later, a military police battalion (in today's terminology, an armed police battalion), was raised for service in the Santhal area after the Santhal uprising. This unit known as "Rattray's Sikhs", today's 3rd Battalion The Sikh Regiment, along with the Ferozepore and Ludhiana Regiments, were taken into the Bengal Army after 1858. Another interesting facet is that after the annexation of the Punjab every Bengal Infantry regiment was ordered to recruit at least a hundred Sikhs. By 1856, most Bengal Infantry regiments had some, if not the full, complement of one hundred Sikhs, and when these Bengal Infantry regiments outside the Punjab in 1857 broke up, most of the Sikh element worked their way to the British lines. At Lucknow, they were part of the defence of the Residency under Henry Lawrence. In the Punjab, John Lawrence withdrew them from existing Bengal Army regiments to form new regiments, when the former were disarmed. (After the Second Anglo-Afghan War more Sikh battalions were raised.) In 1857, the Ludhiana Regiment, in the garrison at Benares, reportedly mutinied, but it was then urged that this was due to the badly handled disarming of the Benares garrison by the later notorious Colonel James Neill.

Napier was succeeded as Commander-in-Chief by Sir William Gomm, also of the British Army. He was described as an antique, who 'ought not to have been selected for such a command at the age of 70, and with no recent military experience.' Another war with Burma now occurred over two British merchant ships' captains having been fined by the Burmese authorities an aggregate of 171 pounds, it is to be noted not on Burmese complaints, but on complaints by British-Indian nationals to the Burmese authorities. This war led to the annexation of another large slice of Burmese territory, which fortuitously included the Pegu gold mines. Like the war over Jenkins' ear, as can be seen, this war started over a triviality, but was not waged for an ultimate triviality. Dalhousie sent a "Cromwellian Ambassador", Commodore Lambert of the British Navy to Rangoon to demand reparation of 920 pounds for ill-usage of the two captains, otherwise to forward the Governor-General's letter of complaint to the King at Ava. Lambert was apparently interviewed by the Governor of Rangoon in his dirtiest clothes. Lambert complained to Ava, and a new Governor was promptly appointed. The new Governor agreed to accept a communication, but had not granted an interview to any deputation. Lambert sent a British deputation with the communication, which was accepted. The British deputation complained that it was not granted an interview (none had been agreed to). Lambert seized the King of Burma's personal sloop; despite entreaties by the Governor, he refused to return it, and was naturally fired on when he sailed away with it to Calcutta. The fire was returned, and the Burmese battery silenced. Dalhousie commented, 'These commodores are too combustible for negotiation,' but never answered John Lawrence's query why he had ever sent a naval commodore if he wanted peace, when there was a perfectly good commissioner of Tenasserim, through whom all procedural correspondence had been conducted with the Burmese authorities after the First Anglo-Burmese War.

Dalhousie now decided on compensation of 100,000 pounds for Lambert's expedition, not allowing sufficient time for the King of Burma to answer Lambert's communication. War was then declared, the King's polite reply arriving a week after Dalhousie's proclamation of war. Gomm, now over sixty-nine, had no desire to take the field in person, so chose, as the commander, his friend General H.Godwin, also aged sixty-nine. They had been subalterns together, and the argument was urged that Godwin had served in the

First Anglo-Burmese War, twenty-five years earlier. The land forces numbered 6,000, and apart from three British regiments, was equally provided by the Bengal and Madras Armies. The expedition arrived off Rangoon in April 1852, and after the whole coastline of Burma had been seized by bombardment, an advance was made to Prome, still 400 miles from Ava. Rather than risk advancing further, Pegu was annexed in December 1852, creating a contiguous British territory, along with Arakan and Tenasserim annexed in the First Anglo-Burmese War. The naval component of this expeditionary force was under Rear Admiral Charles Austen, aged seventy-three, who died during the expedition, Godwin dying shortly after at his friend Gomm's residence at Simla. There had been no *casus belli* whatsoever for this war as recorded by the statesman Richard Cobden at the time, in his pamphlet, "How wars are got up in India", wherein he stated: 'It must be borne in mind that all the parties to these suits were British subjects; the Governor of Rangoon had not been adjudicating in matters in which Burmese interests, as opposed to those of foreigners, were at stake....These wars are carried on at the expense of the people of India...what exclusive interest had the half-naked peasant of Bengal in the settlement of the claims of Captains Shepherd and Lewis, that he should alone be made to bear the expense of the war which grew out of them?'

The Second Anglo-Burmese War was the last war fought by the East India Company resulting in the augmentation of its territory, but it was not the Company's last war, for that was the Anglo-Persian War of 1856. Under instructions from London, war was declared by the new Governor-General, Charles Canning, on 1 November 1856, against Persia, in the name of the East India Company, in the words of Barbara English in *John Company's Last War,* 'a trading company which had founded an empire, and now considered it owned a continent.' This war, though brief and ostensibly successful, was as unnecessary as most others before it. It was seemingly caused by the Persian infiltrations, allegedly with Russian advisers, into Herat, "the key to India", which had reportedly alarmed Amir Dost Mohammed of Afghanistan, now an ally of the British. The British were again suffering from a recurrent bout of Russophobia. Earlier, in 1800, a delegation of 500, under Lieutenant Colonel Sir John

Malcolm, had been sent from India to Persia to negotiate a treaty against the French and Russians. He had bribed so heavily that the Persians were still under the impression that the Indian Government had promised him a three per cent commission on the money he gave away. Though a member of the British Cabinet, the Duke of Argyll, doubted any danger to the British-Indian Empire through Persia, it was decided to exert military pressure on Persia. While the Bombay Army was preparing for the war, before the formal declaration of war by the Governor-General, a curious situation arose at Bushire, where the British Resident in the Persian Gulf resided. A steamer had been sent to Bushire with a despatch box said to contain an ultimatum to be delivered to the Shah of Persia. When the despatch box was formally opened, it was empty, so the steamer had to be sent to Bombay to find the missing ultimatum to the Shah. Someone in Bombay thought someone else in Bombay would put it into the despatch box, allowing for the mitigating fact that the someone responsible for putting the despatch box on the steamer did not forget, even though the box was empty. Separately, on 27 September a Company steamer had dropped anchor at Bushire Roads, and two Commissariat officers and one Quartermaster General's Branch staff officer disembarked and unhurriedly collected logistical information from the locals for the intended invasion of Persia through Bushire.

Immediately after the invasion fleet sailed from Bombay on 1 November 1856, the Bombay Government published a general order thanking all the officers for organizing the loading of the expedition, giving full information of the composition of the expedition, regiments, strengths, armaments, animals etc. This was undoubtedly a mistake wrote the Governor of Bombay later apologetically to Canning, but then they had assumed the Persians knew everything already. A small force from the Bombay Army under Major General Foster Stalker captured Bushire on 1 December 1856, and Outram and Havelock landed with 5,000 more troops at the end of January 1857. In Barbara English's view, 'At this time, the expedition had hardly managed to find any Persians to fight: a nineteenth century Parkinson's law coming into operation ensuring that the army continued to grow in numbers ... all wars are noxious, especially to India, which can't raise the money to pay for them.'[45] The Persian

Army was defeated, and hostilities ceased in April, the British and Persian commissioners having reached an agreement in Paris. The Shah gave up all claims to Herat, and undertook to accept the decision of the Government of India in the event of any future dispute with Afghanistan. By this time, Stalker had committed suicide, partly due to being replaced by Outram, and partly due to having suffered losses at the Bombay races while campaigning in Persia. His suicide was followed by that of Commodore Richard Ethersey of the British Naval Persian Gulf Squadron, partly due to extended service in the Gulf. In a way anticipating 1858, when the British Government took over the administration of India from the Company, Barbara English records the situation in 1856, 'In practice, the cuckoo had grown so much too large for its foster-parents, that the British Government was obliged to interfere from time to time.'[46]

Although it was later alleged in 1857 at the Emperor of Delhi's trial that he had conspired with the Shah of Persia, this was not proved. If the Shah had been involved in a plot to throw out the British from India, he would scarcely have made peace in May 1857, the month the British felt they were in the gravest danger of being driven out of India. While the Anglo-Persian War was on, Persia was alleged, at the time, to have sent letters to the Muslim princely states in India, to rise against the British. These alleged letters are now not traceable, and so, historically, the then response of the Indian Muslim states is unknown. In June 1857, however, Persia curiously formally offered Britain 30,000 troops to put down the 1857 Uprising. This was not mentioned at the trial.

In the book which he wrote while imprisoned by the British from 1942-1945, *Discovery of India,* Pandit Jawaharlal Nehru discussed the campaigns by which the British became masters of India, and commented: 'Looking back over this period, it almost seems that the British succeeded in dominating India by a succession of fortuitous circumstances and flukes. With remarkably little effort, considering the glittering prize, they won a great empire and enormous wealth. It seems easy for a slight turn in events to have taken place which would have dashed their hopes and ended their ambitions.' After which he adds: 'And yet a closer scrutiny reveals, in the circumstances then existing, a certain inevitability in what happened.'

THREE

Some Alleged Mutinies In The Three Presidency Armies Before 1857

IN RELATION to the development of the Bengal Army, eventually the largest Presidency Army, Dr S.N. Sen, the author of the Government of India publication, *Eighteen Fifty Seven,* has recorded in his Foreword to Amiya Barat's *The Bengal Native Infantry 1796-1852:* 'The white element was from the very beginning mutinous, and their mutinies generally yielded success, i.e. their grievances, mostly financial, were remedied. So these mutinies could not but have effect on the sepoys. Financial grievances are not necessarily venal, nor can the sepoys be condemned for not throwing over their (religious) scruples against sea voyages for money...'[1]

Barat adds: 'During its career, the Bengal sepoy army accumulated unavoidable testimonials to its valour and fidelity, and a multitude of honours. Yet, from 1824 onwards, that same army showed itself to be an increasingly unreliable instrument in the hands of the Government...until the evidence of unrest being ignored, it rose in 1857 in a mutiny which first shook the British power in India, and then destroyed the (Bengal) Army itself.'[2]

Before the 1857 Uprising of the Bengal Army is described, it is necessary to review some cases of alleged collective insubordination, both European and Indian, in chronological sequence, in the

81

three Presidencies; and also what can be termed as attempted European coups against a Presidency governor, and to discern the causes of these outbreaks. Philip Mason postulates, 'the classic ingredients of every Indian mutiny—ineffective officers, disruptive influence from outside, a military grievance.'[3] It is desirable to keep these postulated ingredients in mind, including when subsequently reviewing the post-1858 mutinies, as also the post-1947 mutinies, for there have been mutinies after independence as well. From every mutiny some lessons can be drawn, but it is as well to remember that many of the mutinies so deemed by the British, were, for the Indian soldiers, the normal process of bargaining with an employer. In addition, as some of the European mutinies in India—admittedly not all—had ripple effects on Indian units, it is desirable to mention them as well for greater comprehensiveness, since the threat of using Indian troops against European mutineers was often invoked.

The first recorded mutiny in the forces of the English Company in India was a European mutiny at Bombay in 1674. Fifty to sixty English soldiers, in a company that had originally arrived at Bombay, in 1671, under Captain John Shaxton, protested against the prevailing high prices, and the cut in their salaries which was effected to defray the cost of their uniform. The directors "new to the business of government" often issued instructions divorced from the realities of the circumstances in which the Company was operating in Bombay. An alleged ringleader was executed, though Shaxton, himself the Deputy Governor and a member of the Presidency Council, was suspected of fomenting the mutiny among his own subordinates, against his superior, Governor Gerald Aungier, at Surat, a phenomenon which was repeated later. Thereafter, in 1683, as a result of a wrangle between Richard Keigwin, the Captain of the Bombay Garrison, and Charles Ward, the then Deputy Governor, a mutiny occurred. Ward was said to care nothing for Bombay, and was busy feathering his own nest. The military at Bombay resented civilian bungling in the management of Bombay's defences and finances. Keigwin, a naval captain, took control of Bombay from the Company, declared himself Governor, and stated he was acting in the higher interest of the King. He ensured Bombay's neutrality in local politics, the first time this was so in many years since the taking over of Bombay by the Company. John Child, the Governor at Surat, sought to maintain an uneasy peace by moving to Bombay, but Keigwin alleged that 5,000 pounds, collected to build a church, had been misappropriated, and that Child from Bombay was said to have sent an Indian agent to Surat to poison a former member of his own Council. Curiously, Child was Shaxton's son-in-law.

Keigwin so improved the finances of the then minor port of Bombay, that when his rebellion against the Company ended in 1684, after more than eleven months, there was much more money in the local treasury than when the "Keigwin Rebellion" began. Keigwin's action raised several issues which are pertinent. 'Did a King's officer serving under the Company owe allegiance to the Company, or a higher allegiance to the Crown—that is, was Keigwin justified in disobeying his immediate superiors in order to carry out his duty to their superior?'[4] queries Stephen Cohen. Keigwin and his fellow-mutineers deemed their loyalty to the Crown as paramount, over and above their loyalty to the Company. The legality of Keigwin's and his fellow-mutineers' actions seemed to have been upheld by the British Government, for they were granted complete pardon. Keigwin was given a bag of gold as his reward, reassigned to his ship, later being killed in action.[5] The Company dubbed Keigwin "a new Cromwell", "the Oliver of the Rebels" and "Protector of Bombay". To pre-empt future Keigwins, the Company obtained the approval to appoint their own sea-going officers on their ships rather than having to depend on British naval deputationists like Keigwin, and also obtained the power to impose martial law at sea.[6] Keigwin had referred to the, 'intolerable extortions, oppressions and injust impositions that had been, for these five years past, most rigorously exacted,' and charged the Company with 'maliciously ruining His Majesties' subjects.'

In the years 1753-1754, due to prevailing necessity, 'An Act for punishing Mutiny and Desertion of Officers and soldiers in the Service of the United Company of Merchants of England trading to the East Indies, and for the punishment of offences committed in the East Indies, or at the Island of St. Helena,' was enacted. Apart from desertions to the French, like Captain Alexander Delavaux's in 1749, or the planned desertion to the French of the Indian company at Tellicherry in 1748*, the Company's Council had had difficulty over the past two years in maintaining discipline in the Madras Army.[7] The Council had, two years earlier, sent back mutinous officers to Britain, for, when it had tried to court-martial some officers for various mutinous representations about *batta,* others banded together with the accused so that the latter could evade punishment.[8] One of the original three accused died, one deserted to Pondicherry, and one was pardoned. This enactment, however, did not prevent the desertion to the besieging French of three Indian companies from Fort St. David in 1758, or of the "White Mutiny" of Madras Army officers in 1809. The Company did not have much luck with its "engineer-generals". A predecessor of Delavaux, Captain von Werhinhoffe, was dismissed as constituting, 'a great charge to the Company to no purpose.' Captain John Brohier, the initial engineer of the present Fort William at Calcutta, deserted to the Dutch in Ceylon in 1760.

After Plassey in 1757, at the time of Nawab Siraj-ud-Daula's capture in Bihar, a French force of 200 soldiers, was reported to be marching to his assistance. Robert Clive despatched Eyre Coote with 500 Indian soldiers, mostly from Madras, and 220 European troops, who were a mixed lot—French deserters, French prisoners, Swiss and German mercenaries, as well as British troops. The advanced guard of two Indian companies was commanded by a subedar. The latter arrested a disguised person who proved to be a Swiss deserter from the British service. While in custody he wrote a letter to the French to attack. The Swiss was tried by a court-martial, convicted of being a French spy and hanged. His Indian guard, who had apparently been bribed, was tried by an Indian court-martial, sentenced to 500 lashes, with the cat o'nine tails, the first recorded case in the Bengal Army, and dismissal after the flogging.[9]

Coote's pursuit was the first time the Company's troops had reached the border of Bihar and Oudh. Both European and Indian troops became mutinous, first the Europeans, then the Indians. The Europeans asked for an extra field allowance and refused to march any further for want of boots and arrack, urging their officers wanted them dead for their prize money. Coote went on to Patna with the

---

* For more details, see chapter, "Early Beginnings".

Indian troops. Later at Patna, Coote had thirty Europeans tried by a court-martial, and flogged before the whole force.[10] The Indian troops now decided to proceed no further; those from Madras, were told, before sailing, that they would only be in Calcutta for three months, but had now been nine months in Bengal, and were daily marching further away from Calcutta. Coote persuaded them to return to duty, hinting at loss of prize money.

In 1763-1764, there was the rebellion by Native Commandant Mohammed Yusuf Khan, who was described by Sir John Malcolm, in 1826, as 'the bravest and ablest of all the native soldiers that ever served the English in India.' He had enrolled under Clive in 1752, and distinguished himself in operations in South India repeatedly thereafter. In 1754, he, along with a subedar, was awarded a gold chain and a custom-made gold medal, as a reward for services against the French in the neighbourhood of Trichinopoly (Tiruchirapalli), and made Native Commandant of all the Company's Indian soldiers in the Madras Presidency. Stringer Lawrence recorded of him, in March 1754: 'Besides his intelligence and capacity, I cannot too much praise his zeal and alacrity for service.' Robert Orme was also laudatory to Mohammed Yusuf: 'Brave and resolute...but cool and wary in action, and capable of stratagem.' In 1757 he had defeated Hyder Ali in an action at the Nattam Pass. In 1758 he did excellent service against the French, and, in 1759, in opposition to the wishes of Mohammed Ali, the Nawab of Arcot, the Madras Government allowed him to "rent" the districts of Madurai and Tirunelveli. At the end of 1762, he commenced hostilities against the Raja of Travancore and seized several villages. The Madras Government ordered him back to Madras, but, instead, he apparently strengthened his forces and hoisted the French Tricolour on the instigation of 200 French troops, who had earlier defected to the English and were put under Mohammed Yusuf's command.

At the time of his insurrection, he had, at Madurai, 200 French troops, 5,000 Indian soldiers, 1,700 horses and 7,000 irregulars; and at other locations under his command 5,000 Indian soldiers and 8,000 irregulars, aggregating 26,900. In October 1763, Madurai was besieged by the British, but to little effect as Mohammed Yusuf's artillery was superior. In early 1764, he promised the Madras Government obedience in the future. He was asked to surrender all his forts and forces. This he declined to do. He was repeatedly attacked for seven months, but held out. Owing to the hardship of the siege and resultant discontent, he was seized by the French troops, forty-two of whom had earlier left him and joined the besieging English force. They, then, surrendered Madurai on 13 October 1764. He was hanged by the Nawab on 15 October without reference to the Madras Government, dying only on the fourth attempt. Colonel W. Fullarton, one of the ablest officers in the Madras Army at the time, recorded: 'While he ruled...his whole administration denoted vigour and effect: his justice was unquestioned....I found that wisdom, vigour and integrity were never more conspicuous in any person of whatsoever climate or complexion.'

Phythian-Adams commented: 'Doubts have been expressed as to whether Mohammed Yusuf was driven into rebellion by circumstances beyond his control or whether he had all along intended to make himself independent, with the successful example of Hyder Ali before him. But whichever point of view is accepted the fact remains that his death not only deprived the Company of the services of one of the finest soldiers Madras has produced, but also had the unfortunate result of relegating Indian officers in future to subordinate positions on the abolition of the rank of Indian Commandant.'[11] S.C. Hill emphasized that Mohammed Yusuf's execution, 'closed for many years all opportunity of a high career to the natives of Madras who entered into the military service of the Company.'

In December 1763, on the departure of Major Thomas Adams and Captain Ronald Knox, both worn out by campaigning—and who were to die within a short while of each other—command of the Company's forces on the border of Bihar and Oudh had temporarily devolved on Captain Jennings, the senior captain present, till the arrival of Major John Carnac, who was a vacillating and lethargic officer, but, on Adams' death, the only major in Bengal. The Company's forces, six Indian battalions and one European, had been camped near the border for about two months, when, in January 1764, disaffection showed itself among the European troops. These now included German and Polish mercenaries and four French companies which had surrendered at Pondicherry, three of which were initially sent to the Philippines in 1762; also present were French and Dutch defectors recruited in Bengal to make up British casualties.

Thus less than half the European troops in the Company's forces in Bengal were British. The four French companies included one company under Lieutenant Claude Martin, later the endower of the La Martiniere schools at Lucknow, Calcutta and Lyon. The other three French companies had been formed from the French companies that had returned from the 1762 Madras Army operation in the Philippines. The French companies' departure from Manila had to be expedited in view of their possible defection there to Spain.

Though the high cost of provisions was the initial cause of dis content, the main cause was the non-payment to the troops of Mir Jafar's donation to them after the conclusion of the campaign against Mir Kasim, even though Mir Jafar, on his second installation, had paid the amount to the Company's Council at Calcutta. The greedy Council members had prevented the money from being paid to the troops. Mir Kasim's emissaries now offered higher pay and promotion to those who deserted the Company and joined him, but this was unknown to Jennings, who gave his personal assurance that Mir Jafar's donation would be distributed as soon as received. As a precautionary measure, he deployed the two most disaffected European companies along the River Karamnasa, the actual border, with two Indian battalions. A few days later, in February, the rest of the European battalion fell in and marched off to join the other two European companies, having appointed an English sergeant, named Jack Straw, as its Commanding Officer and promoting him to Major.[12]

When Jennings sought to arrest Straw, these European troops came at Jennings, with their bayonets fixed. Their overt aim was to march on Calcutta and represent their grievances but the covert intention was to join Mir Kasim's European contingents under Walter Reinhardt (Somroo) and Medoc, and, according to G.B. Malleson, 'make themselves masters of the whole country.' The latter was conveyed to Jennings by the former French officer, Claude Martin, who later became a local Major General in the English Company's service in Oudh. Having, on his own initiative, now obtained a lakh of rupees directly from Mir Jafar, who was camped nearby, Jennings was able to announce the distribution of the first instalment of the donation, till such time as he was able, if possible, to extract the amount withheld by the corrupt Council at

Calcutta. Straw and most of the non-French elements relented, but about 170 European—mainly French, but also three British—and one hundred Indian soldiers crossed the river, and joined Mir Kasim's forces. The Indian battalions now decided to mutiny when they learnt that under Jennings' distribution a European private was to get forty rupees as the first instalment, whereas the Indian equivalent was to get only six rupees. Jennings had been showing great presence of mind, for, as a captain, he was commanding a force normally commanded by a general officer.

The European units, both officers and men, irked at the Indian battalions seeking to emulate the Europeans in the latter's collective insubordination, sought to fire at the Indian soldiers, both with muskets and artillery. With great personal heroism, Jennings avoided a conflict and proportionately increased the distribution to the Indian rank and file by contributing, along with the British officers of the Indian battalions, from personal resources, the lowest Indian rank now getting eighteen rupees instead of six rupees. Carnac took over from Jennings in March 1764, by which time the second instalment from Mir Jafar was distributed, but the disaffection among the Indian troops continued on account of the considerable disparity between the amounts paid to Indians vis-a-vis Europeans. A subedar, accused of inciting his men to desert to Mir Kasim, was tried and blown from a gun.

This form of execution had been employed by the Mughals, and was often adopted by the French and the British for punishing Indian soldiers, but rarely European soldiers. It was semantically argued that death was instantaneous, even though it was meant to frighten those required to witness it, as parts of the human anatomy were hurled among the spectators. Major Hector Munro of the Bombay Army succeeded Carnac in mid-1764. There was still grumbling, among the Indian troops, about the proportion in which the donation money had been distributed, and they also sought increased pay and allowances as the war with Mir Kasim was not over, but continued beyond the border, the River Karamnasa. Munro said there was no further donation money. On 8 September 1764, the Lal Paltan, then the oldest battalion of the Bengal Army, mutinied at Manji and imprisoned its officers. Whilst the mutineers were asleep, however, the men were arrested by the 6th Bengal Infantry and disarmed.

Twenty-four were tried by an Indian court-martial, found guilty, and sentenced to be blown from guns. The first four were tied to the guns and were about to be blown away, when four grenadiers claimed it as their right to be executed first. Munro granted the request. They were blown away, there being not a single dry eye among the assembled Europeans.[13] There was much murmuring among the Indian troops, but Munro directed the artillery against them, as also so directing the European troops. Four more were then executed. Here accounts differ. Malleson states that twenty were executed that day in front of Munro and four sent to another station, while H.H. Dodwell states eight were executed that day in front of Munro, and that another sixteen were sent to different stations for execution. In this 1764 mutiny, not a single European was blown from a gun.

In 1766, Clive, after his return in May 1765, had to quell a mutiny by the European officers of the Bengal Army. This problem arose out of the discontinuance of the ostensible field allowances known as *batta*, half-*batta* and double-*batta*, which had been a cause for discontent not only in the Bengal Army, but also in the Madras Army. Both, Nawab Mohammed Ali in the Carnatic and Nawab Mir Jafar in Bengal, had provided funds for paying an extra allowance (double-*batta*) to Europeans who fought for them. After the revenues of certain districts were assigned to the Company to defray military expenses, the continued payment of this *batta* fell on the Company, which endeavoured to reduce it in the interests of its own profits. To add to the discontent in the Madras Army, the *batta* was being paid at a higher rate in Bengal, and in Bengal it amounted to more than an officer's basic pay, it being argued by the European officers there that Bengal was more expensive than Madras. When the Bengal Company Council proposed a reduction, there was opposition. The matter was referred to the directors in London. Their orders confirming the reduction were received at the time of the outbreak of hostilities with Mir Kasim, so action on this direction was deferred. On a reminder being received from London, action on this measure was postponed till Clive returned, as it was known he was being sent back to India by the directors to implement this and other unpopular economies.

Clive drew up fresh regulations regarding *batta*, based on the rates prevailing at Madras, effective 1 January 1766. The officers complained, but Clive insisted that the orders from London must be carried out. Separately, with five lakh rupees bequeathed to him by Mir Jafar on his death in February 1765, he started a fund for the benefit of European officers and men disabled by wounds or illness (no such fund being envisaged for incapacitated Indian personnel). The Bengal Army had recently been divided by Clive into three brigades, each of seven Indian battalions, one European regiment, and one Indian cavalry regiment, at Monghyr, Patna and Allahabad, under Sir Robert Fletcher, Sir Robert Barker and Colonel Richard Smith, respectively. Fletcher had earlier been dismissed for insolence in the Madras Army, but had been reinstated through patronage. The other two were reliable, Smith and Barker later becoming Commanders-in-Chief after Clive. Reverting to Fletcher, on reinstatement he had returned as a Major in the Madras Army, promoted to Lieutenant Colonel and knighted. A corrupt officer, he indulged in nefarious activities, including taking a commission on the sale of illicit arrack to his troops.

In April 1766, Clive received a report from Fletcher that officers below the rank of major planned to resign their commissions unless double-*batta*, which under the new regulations had been abolished, except for service outside Bengal, was restored. Clive treated this as a mutiny. A large Maratha force was, at the time, one hundred miles from Allahabad. The concerned officers thought that hostilities were imminent, and, that, as in 1763, the orders would not be implemented. Clive, however, wrote to Madras to send all available officers to Bengal, and instructed the three brigade commanders to arrest the ringleaders and court-martial them, as also to ensure the loyalty of all Indian personnel. Clive left for Monghyr, sending four staff officers ahead of him, who found that forty-two officers at Monghyr had resigned. The day before Clive's arrival, one of these staff officers learned that the European troops were assembled on parade but were refusing to obey orders, in sympathy with the European officers who had resigned, and were themselves about to mutiny. This officer assembled two Bengal Infantry battalions, with loaded muskets and fixed bayonets, against these European troops, who then dispersed. Clive arrived the next day, and rewarded the Indian troops with two months' double pay. Clive ordered the officers who had resigned to leave for Calcutta, deputing a Bengal Infantry battalion to escort them. These officers now repented; Clive's attitude and the proposed use of Indian troops against them broke their will. Some revealed that Fletcher had been the instigator of the conspiracy. It collapsed at Patna, Barker having acted firmly and having already sent the ringleaders to Calcutta, where, however, according to Penderel Moon, the British citizens of Calcutta raised a defence fund of 16,000 pounds for these officers. The rest, on Clive's arrival at Patna, asked for a pardon. At Allahabad, all the Indian battalions were one hundred miles away, facing the Marathas. As the disaffected officers there were expected to instigate the European battalions to mutiny, one Indian battalion was recalled to Allahabad, marching 104 miles in fifty-four hours. The concerned officers were then told they would be shot by the Indian troops if they sought to disaffect European troops.[14]

The mutiny collapsed at Allahabad as well, and the ringleaders were sent to Patna under an Indian escort. These ringleaders, including Fletcher, were tried by a court-martial. Clive had wanted the foremost among them, including Fletcher, to be shot, but he was, ostensibly, advised that this would not be legal, as it was, essentially, a conspiracy, and not a mutiny. Fletcher and his fellow-conspirators were only cashiered, unlike the Indian soldiers Munro had blown from guns. The cashiered officers were then deported back to Britain, in some cases being forcibly carried on board ship by Indian troops. (On returning to Britain, Fletcher became a Member of Parliament, thus, joining, at the time, nineteen other Members of Parliament who had served in India and made their fortunes.) Clive, shortly after, suffered a nervous breakdown, and left for Britain, where, though exonerated of the financial allegations made against him, he committed suicide in 1774. For his part, Fletcher, whom Clive had wanted shot by a firing squad, came to India for the third time, on this occasion as Commander-in-Chief of the Madras Army.

Now occurred what could be termed as a coup against the Madras Government. After the conclusion of the war with Hyder Ali in 1769, the Company's servants at Madras, under the guidance of an engineer in the employ of the Company, named Paul Benfield, continued 'to feather their nests,' according to Penderel Moon, as ostensible creditors of Nawab Mohammed Ali of the Carnatic.[15] He was supposedly paying off his debt to the Company for keeping him in power and waging war with Hyder Ali on his behalf, but, in reality, he was only notionally doing so, by having to borrow from the Company's servants at exorbitant rates of interest, so that his indebtedness, far from diminishing, was actually getting greater. The so-called lenders received from him assignments of land revenue. A large number of the Company's servants at Madras had shares in these loans, some of which were fictitious. Their management was in the hands of Benfield, who had come out to Madras in 1764 on a salary of a couple of hundred pounds a year (but, by 1786, had amassed a fortune of half-a-million pounds). He had, at his disposal, the savings of most of the Europeans in Madras, and paid them interest at two per cent a month, lending these sums at a much higher rate to Mohammed Ali, who, then, with these amounts repaid the Company for retaining him as Nawab, and from which Company's servants he was in effect borrowing in order to do so.[16]

Mohammed Ali had never forsaken the idea of adding Tanjore, purportedly his dependency, whose Maratha Raja was a descendant of Shivaji, to his dominions. In 1773, he requested the Company for help to capture Tanjore, as the Raja had seemingly defaulted in payments to Mohammed Ali, and was, according to Mohammed Ali, negotiating with the Marathas and Hyder Ali against Mohammed Ali, and, thus, against the Company. The amount due to Mohammed Ali was only ten lakh rupees which the Raja could have paid, but, the Madras Government, under the influence of the Benfield group, ordered the Madras Army to capture Tanjore, imprison the Raja and his family, and hand over the whole of the Tanjore territory to Mohammed Ali. Within two years, according to Penderel Moon, Benfield obtained assignments of over 200,000 pounds on the revenues of Tanjore from Mohammed Ali.[17] With communications taking almost a year each way, finally, on learning of it, the directors in London disapproved of the capture of Tanjore by the Company's troops, and ordered its restoration to the Raja, on condition he paid for the maintenance of a company of the Company's troops for garrisoning the Tanjore fort. George Pigot (of French Huguenot descent), the averred hero of the defence of Madras in 1759 against the French, and who had left Madras in 1763 with a fortune of over 400,000 pounds, now returned for a second tenure as Governor with a view to implementing the return of Tanjore. He had saved Tanjore from Mohammed Ali in 1762, and was now keen to restore it to the Raja. At the time of his return in 1775, Pigot (now Lord Pigot) found the corrupt Fletcher, instigator of the "White Mutiny" of 1766 in the Bengal Army, ensconced as Commander-in-Chief of the Madras Army. The Raja was restored in 1776, thus becoming a dependant of the Company, rather than of Mohammed Ali. The latter could not understand how the Company gave him Tanjore in 1773, and, in 1776, took it away.

Meanwhile, Paul Benfield sought assurances that the so-called assignments, made to him of over 200,000 pounds on the Tanjore revenues by Mohammed Ali, would be honoured by the Raja of Tanjore. In Penderel Moon's opinion, it would appear that Mohammed Ali, in collusion with Benfield, had falsely enhanced the assignments, much in excess of what Benfield had loaned him, in order to be able to extract revenue from Tanjore through Benfield. Pigot did not agree with Benfield, but Fletcher, and the other members of the Madras Council, supported Benfield, being party to the transactions. Pigot did not bow to the majority of his Council, and ordered Fletcher to be arrested and tried by a court-martial. Fletcher, using the authority of the corrupt majority of the Council, ordered the Madras Army, in his capacity as Commander-in-Chief, to arrest and imprison Pigot. Mohammed Ali distributed several lakhs of rupees for prayers to be said for Pigot's death, and he did die, in May 1777, after eight months of confinement.[18] A Madras jury recorded a verdict of wilful murder by reason of his confinement, though it was apparently a natural death. Fletcher took sick leave and died at sea. Brigadier General James Stuart, who played a prominent part in the coup against Pigot, and had personally arrested him, was acquitted by a court-martial and shortly became Commander-in-Chief of the Madras Army. He was unlikely to show respect to any Governor. When Lord Macartney was Governor of Madras in 1783, he ordered Stuart's arrest and expulsion from Madras. Stuart was dismissed for disobedience, and sent to London under arrest. The next senior King's officer, Sir John Burgoyne, refused to take Stuart's place. Stuart's friends in London were able to put government pressure on Macartney to resign. In 1786, when Macartney had returned to Britain, they fought a duel in Hyde Park, and Macartney was severely wounded.[19] He later became Governor of the Cape Colony.

In the words of Warren Hastings, the then Governor-General, in 1777 there was now 'a convulsion of four days, which might have shaken the very foundations of the national power and interests in India.'[20] To go back to 1774, as Moon describes it, Warren Hastings and his old colleague in the Council, Richard Barwell, 'were yoked by three councillors brought out from England—General John Clavering, Colonel George Monson and Philip Francis—who were unconnected with the Company, owed their positions not to the Directorate but to the Ministry, and knew nothing of Bengal.' There were no considerations of merit in the appointments of Clavering and Monson. Clavering was a choleric, old soldier with not much intelligence. He was a friend of the King's and had been appointed by the British Prime Minister, Lord North, overlooking more suitable candidates. He was given the position of Second-in-Council, with the right of succession should the appointment of Governor-General fall vacant, and was also appointed Commander-in-Chief. There was some confusion in London as to whether Hastings intended to resign after over thirty years in India. North, in order to please the King, wanted him to, so that Clavering could be appointed Governor-General. Hastings had still not decided when, in June 1777, Clavering decided to assume the position of Governor-General, convened a Council meeting and asked Hastings to hand over the keys of the Treasury and Fort William. Clavering's action was referred to the Supreme Court, which declared that Hastings was neither dead, nor of unsound mind, nor had he resigned. Hastings now told North that he had no intention to resign. Two months later Clavering died of dysentery in Calcutta, going down in history as "Governor-General of India for a Day".

Then, in 1780, owing to a much-delayed relief by Bombay Army troops, two Madras companies mutinied at Tellicherry. One mutineer was blown from a gun, and two were administered 1,000 lashes. The first recorded mutiny in which the Company's Indian troops killed some Europeans now occurred. In October 1780, companies of the Circar Infantry of the Madras Army at Vizagapatam resented the move by sea to Madras, as they had apparently been enrolled only for local service, and considered themselves "armed peons", not trained to fight Hyder Ali. They fired at Europeans from their ships, killing three.[21] Led by a Muslim subedar, some then marched off to Hyderabad, while others went home.

A 1781 example will suffice as an illustration of the pernicious effect on the discipline in army units because of cliquism among British officers. Early, in 1781, an expeditionary force of five infantry battalions of the Bengal Army had marched out from Bengal to serve under Coote in the Madras Presidency. *En route* the units were stricken with dysentery, as many as 1,800 being sick at one time during the 1,200-mile march. Desertions followed, and some of those apprehended were blown from guns. Amidst this trauma for the men, two captains of the 2nd/24th Bengal Infantry, Sandford and Scott, became antagonistic towards their Commanding Officer, Major Samuel Kilpatric, and accused him of misappropriating the men's money, collected when the unit was raised in 1778. The force commander exonerated Kilpatric, but the two captains now got a havildar to make the same allegation. Kilpatric demanded an open inquiry, and the force commander paraded the whole unit, requiring anyone, other than the concerned havildar, to make their complaints. No one made any complaint, but testified to Kilpatric's kindness, and the personnel's happiness at serving under him. Though Sandford was tried and reprimanded, he, in September 1781, nevertheless, challenged Kilpatric to a duel as a result of which the latter died.

In 1784, a Crown regiment mutinied at Arcot owing to a sudden change in the arrangements for victualling. When the latter was restored, the mutiny subsided, no action being thereafter taken. When, however, some Madras Army infantry and artillery men at Arcot found themselves starving, due to arrears of pay, also in 1784, and threatened to seize the guns, two Indian troops were blown from a gun. In the same year, the Madras Government decided to form a regular cavalry arm in the Madras Army, as the reverses suffered by it against Hyder Ali were ascribed to the lack of cavalry. On 21 April 1784, a resolution was passed to continue in the Company's service the four regiments of the Nawab of Arcot's cavalry, 'temporarily taken into the Company's service in 1780, and paid and mounted by the Company during the war against Hyder Ali.' On 30 April all the four regiments at Arni mutinied, confined their officers and threatened to kill them should any troops march against them. They said there were large arrears of pay owed to them, and their families were starving. On 15 May, some European troops arrived. They found the 3rd Regiment drawn up, defending their European officers, so that the other three regiments could not take them away. These three regiments then surrendered, but to make an example a subedar and a sowar were blown from a gun. Orders were issued to disband the 1st, 2nd and 4th Regiments, to raise a new regiment (to be designated the 2nd Regiment of the Madras Cavalry, today's 7th Cavalry) from selected personnel of the three disbanded regiments, and to redesignate the 3rd Regiment (as the 1st Regiment of the Madras Cavalry, today's 16th Cavalry).

This mutiny by these former regiments of Mohammed Ali was due to apprehensions about their future. They had aggregated arrears of almost a year's pay due to them from the Company, plus outstanding claims against the Nawab dating prior to 1780 when they were taken over by the Company, ostensibly on a temporary basis. It was a common practice in the princely armies, including that of the Nawab of Arcot, to demand arrears of pay by refusing to carry out orders. There had been several such mutinies in 1776-1778, and a number had been executed on the Nawab's orders. The reason for the mutiny was the feeling that, as a result of their new status, all past claims against the Nawab would be repudiated.[22] Then, in January 1785, a Crown unit mutinied, along with its officers, at Poonamalee on account of full *batta* being discontinued. The mutiny was resolved after five days, when Indian and other European troops were brought in, but no one was blown from a gun. Thereafter, also in 1785, the Madras Presidency was unable to pay its army, due to a lack of funds being generated within the Presidency. Bengal dragged its feet in assisting. Fourteen infantry battalions were ordered to be disbanded, yet the resources were still insufficient. Owing to the delay in clearing their arrears of pay, three battalions near Trichinopoly mutinied, as other units had been paid proportionately more. The matter was resolved by paying the arrears as for the others.[23]

In 1794, collective discontent among European officers, amounting to a near mutiny, confronted Sir John Shore, later Lord Teignmouth, as soon as he took over as Governor-General from Earl Cornwallis, the latter having been both Governor-General and Commander-in-Chief. It had earlier been announced, in London in 1790, that

General Sir William Medows, the Governor of Madras, should become the Governor-General (he having already earlier been Governor of Bombay), 'upon the death, removal or resignation of Earl Cornwallis.' In 1791, Medows, not being desirous of being Governor-General, formally declined the elevation, but his subsequent attempted suicide during operations would probably have prevented his being so elevated. He later explained that, 'Mr. Medows had had a misunderstanding with General Medows that had terminated in a duel, in which matters had been amicably adjusted.'[24]

Shortly before Cornwallis' departure, Robert Abercromby was brought in as Commander-in-Chief, since Sir John Shore, a Company civil servant, was to be Governor-General. At this time operations were carried out successfully by the Madras Army against the Dutch in Ceylon and in the Spice Islands. The European officers of the Bengal Army were, however, in 1794, discontented. As described by Penderel Moon, Shore had little confidence in Abercromby, deeming him, 'totally inadequate to the status of Commander-in-Chief,' and writing to London of, 'a great fund of dissatisfaction in the Army,' and, 'the absolute importance of an early and attentive consideration of this subject.' One of the grievances was the discrimination against the Company's officers in favour of the King's officers, a Company's officer in command of a battalion being ranked only as equivalent to a King's officer in command of a company, and no Company's officer permitted to rise to the rank of general officer. (According to W. Badenach, writing in 1826: 'In 1786, the Court of Directors had expressed their dissatisfaction at...the rank of captain (being conferred) to the officer commanding a battalion, as they thought the duty could well be done...by a lieutenant.') There were, then, 1,000 British officers in the Bengal Infantry alone, with only fifty-two appointments of major and above, it being argued that captains commanding Bengal Infantry battalions had considerable other opportunities for adding to their official pay. Cornwallis was aware of the latter problem, for he had made it clear when he took over as Governor-General and Commander-in-Chief in 1786, that as bad as the civil administration was in Bengal, the abuses in the Bengal Army were greater. For instance, British officers in Oudh had received large sums of money from the

Nawab to pay personnel in the ostensible Company's units in Oudh, many of which, in fact, did not exist, within the knowledge of the previous Commander-in-Chief, General Robert Sloper, as his son was one of the officers involved.[25]

In Penderel Moon's opinion, it was also, then, quite common to embezzle some of the funds meant for the upkeep of Indian soldiers. The more palpable frauds of major magnitude were stopped by Cornwallis before he left for Britain in 1793, but, owing to his preoccupation with the war against Tipu Sultan, and the necessity for his presence in South India for the purpose, he had been unable to tackle all the abuses before he left for Britain, nor the main grievance, poor pay and poor prospects for promotion. On his voyage back to Britain, Cornwallis prepared proposals transferring all the Company's military forces to the Crown, but suggested that the European officers of the Company form a separate service to the existing British service. Cornwallis' proposals were rejected after several months, but the new regulations providing for better promotion, pay and conditions of service only reached Bengal in May 1796. In the meantime, the European officers of the Bengal Army were on the verge of mutinying, having learnt of Cornwallis' proposals, and not wanting the Company's military forces to be merged with those of the Crown.[26] The senior officers of the Bengal Army were unable to discipline their juniors, as the latter knew all about the former's graft.

The latter now formed an executive committee to negotiate with the Bengal Government, and, if necessary, to arrest the Governor-General and Commander-in-Chief, take control of the Bengal Government, and oppose the landings of any further Crown regiments that may be sent out from Britain to curb their agitation. Shore, however, put the Crown regiments at Madras on stand-by for Bengal, asked the British naval squadron at Madras to also stand-by to sail to Calcutta, and contemplated using Indian troops against their own officers, as Clive had done. The new regulations, when received from Britain, revived rather than abated the threat of mutiny, for they were, in Shore's opinion, "a mess of confusion", and he felt that, if implemented, he would have to use force, which he wished to avoid. Abercromby suggested that the new regulations received from Britain be modified in Calcutta, in order to make them more acceptable, and a number of further concessions were granted. This had the desired effect, Shore recorded: 'I think the wisest mode has been followed, and that severity might have occasioned the absolute disorganization of the Army, whose expectations have been too much trifled with.' Shore added that Abercromby's abilities were, 'far more respectable than I was led to believe from the reports of others.' Robert Dundas, the President of the Board of Control in London, felt that stern action should have been taken against the disaffected officers and that Shore should be recalled. Cornwallis was persuaded to agree to go to Bengal again for twelve months to resolve the grievances, and was sworn in in London as Governor-General in February 1797. Dundas, however, now became fearful of a mutiny and granted some further concessions. Cornwallis thereafter declined to go, and the plan to recall Shore was dropped.

The Company's European artillery at the Mount in Madras now mutinied in January 1798. Their demands were regular payment on the 1st of each month, that arrack be served to them in the barracks, and pay not be cut for off-duty attire. They seized guns and loaded them. After trial, one was blown from a gun, and three hanged. Two to be shot had their sentences commuted. All the demands were conceded.[27] Just before this European mutiny, the 27th Madras Infantry had mutinied at Guntur for non-payment of the allowance promised when it moved there. To circumvent payment, the unit was then being moved back south. The ostensible ringleader was blown from a gun.

In 1806, a mutiny by Indian troops occurred at Vellore. As some historians have referred to this incident as "The First War of Indian Independence", it is recounted in some detail. The fortress at Vellore in which the sons of Tipu resided with their families, was, at the time, garrisoned by 1,500 Indian and 370 European soldiers. At 3 a.m., on 10 July 1806, the Indian soldiers of the garrison suddenly attacked the Europeans, opening fire on them while they slept in their barracks; over one hundred Europeans were killed, many more wounded, and over a dozen British officers were shot down as they emerged from their houses to see what was going on. The European survivors made their way to a bastion above the main gateway, where they barricaded themselves, while the mutinous soldiers looted. News of the outbreak reached Arcot, sixteen miles away, early in the morning, through a European officer outside the fort at the time. Among the troops at Arcot were a British cavalry regiment and some Madras cavalry. Within fifteen minutes, the Commanding Officer of the British regiment, the 19th Dragoons, Colonel Rollo Gillespie, had galloped off to Vellore with one troop; the rest of the Dragoons, the Madras cavalry squadron and some galloper guns (later to be known as horse artillery) followed. Gillespie reached Vellore at about 8 a.m. The outer gates of the fort were open, as the mutinous soldiers were still looting, but the inner gate was shut. The mutineers had made no attempt to man the ramparts. Gillespie was hauled up onto the ramparts by a rope let down by the European survivors, and he immediately assumed command, awaiting the arrival of the galloper guns. They arrived at 10 a.m., the inner gates were blown in, Gillespie led a charge, and the fortress was again in British hands.

About 350 Indian soldiers were killed in the fighting, many were made prisoners, and those who escaped by jumping from the ramparts were later rounded up. A few were tried and executed, six being blown from guns, five shot, eight hanged and five transported.[28] Most were discharged; the three affected regiments (1st/1st, 2nd/1st, and 2nd/3rd) of the Madras Infantry were disbanded. The folly of the Madras Army Headquarters and the Madras Government was the basic cause of this episode. The Madras Army Commander-in-Chief, the evangelical Sir John Cradock of the British Army, decided to smarten up the Madras Army. As the commission of inquiry had brought out, a new set of dress regulations was issued with the approval of the Madras Government and the Governor, Lord William Bentinck, then aged thirty-two. The Indian soldiers of the Madras Army were now required to remove all caste marks, earrings and beards, and keep moustaches only according to a regulation pattern, and to wear a new type of headgear, called a "turban", but resembling that worn by Europeans and Eurasians, with a leather cockade, and leather stocks as well. Both Hindus and Muslims were upset, and the new measures were deemed a calculated attack on their respective religions. The first signs of disaffection were discerned in May 1806, when the 2nd/4th Madras Infantry, then at Vellore, respectfully declined to wear the new "turban". Their representations were cursorily treated by their commanding officer, twenty-one men were arrested and sent to Madras for a court-martial, where two were sentenced to 900 lashes each, and the rest to 500 each. The two sentences of 900 lashes were carried out, but the remainder apologized and were pardoned.

The 2nd/4th Madras Infantry was then moved from Vellore to Madras. Reports of objections to the new "turban" now came in from several other stations. Cradock sought to withdraw the orders, but Bentinck and his Council were averse, since a Brahmin and a Syed had been ostensibly consulted before issuing the new dress regulations. A warning of the imminence of the mutiny at Vellore had been given on 17 June 1806 by a soldier, Mustafa Beg, to his commanding officer. His report was referred to a committee of Indian officers for investigation, who declared it false. Mustafa Beg was imprisoned as insane. He escaped from his cell during the mutiny, but later returned. He was given a reward of 2,000 pagodas (Rs 7,500 at the time), and a subedar's pension. The British officers were apparently out of touch with their men, for, in the normal military context, greater attention should have been paid to Mustafa Beg's report, and, when the mutiny did occur, they should not have been taken completely by surprise, which, in fact, they were.

In order to cover up their errors, some of the Madras Army Headquarters' authorities urged that the mutiny was instigated by Tipu's sons as part of an extensive plot to restore Muslim rule in Mysore, one of the affected regiments being largely Muslim, formerly in Tipu's service. The other two regiments were mainly Hindu. There was no evidence of any such plot, and the involvement of Tipu's sons was not established. They were moved to Calcutta, and Bentinck and Cradock recalled to Britain (the former later to return as Governor-General). The most experienced British official in South India at the time, Major General Sir Thomas Munro, wrote to Bentinck that the mutiny was not political. 'However strange it may appear to Europeans, I know that the general opinion of the most intelligent natives in this part of the country is that it was intended to make the sepoys Christian,' a fear that was to reoccur in 1857 in the context of the tallow used to grease the new cartridges. Cradock and Bentinck claimed they were not aware of the religious susceptibilities in such matters, not having served in India before. Nevertheless, the matter of changing the pattern of the Madras Army soldier's headdress had been debated eight years before, in 1797, by a military board, which gave it, 'every consideration which a subject of that delicate and important nature required,' without any change being then introduced. (Curiously, Vellore fort was again to be the scene of some bloodshed, in January 1991, when some Sri Lankan Tamil extremists, confined there, attempted to break out.)

Vellore was the first major Indian mutiny of the British period where much British blood had been shed. The impugned dress regulations were cancelled on 17 July, and on 24 September 1806 a general order was published by which, 'interference with the native soldiery in regard to their national observances, was strictly prohibited.' Thereafter, Charles Grant and Edward Parry, two powerful Directors in London, wrote in 1807 to Robert Dundas, Chairman of the Board of Control, that one factor in the mutiny at Vellore was the degradation of the authority of the Company's officers in the eyes of their Indian troops, and the sequential dangerous alienation of the European officers in the Company's service. It was urged this resulted from the preference shown to officers with King's commissions, and that the Company's military officers with long careers in India, were regularly passed over for the most important appointments, including that of Commander-in-Chief of the Madras Army.[29]

Added to these resentments, there were other grievances that were to agitate the officers of the Madras Army in 1809. The first was the decision by the Court of Directors not to appoint Lieutenant General Hay MacDowell, Commander-in-Chief of the Madras Army, after the recall of Cradock, to the Governor's Council, as had been the practice previously. The directors' reason for doing so was that Cradock's errors of judgement caused the Vellore mutiny. MacDowell appealed the decision, both his status and emoluments being thus lowered, claiming that it was a slight to the entire Madras Army. As the directors deliberated his appeal, another perceived insult was made upon the honour of the Madras Army's officers. This was seen as the work of Sir George Barlow who had replaced Bentinck as Governor of Madras after the Vellore affair. Seeking to reduce military spending in response to a demand to the effect from London, Barlow ended the financial perquisite of commanders of the field units of the Madras Army, called the "tent contract" allowance, a monthly allowance given to every such commander for ostensibly equipping their Madras Army soldiers for service in the field, even when in cantonments. The economy exercise had actually been started during Cradock's and Bentinck's tenures in Madras, but the discontinuance had been approved by Barlow as officiating Governor-General, before moving to Madras. Barlow's order was seen, in Burton Stein's words, as a further slur by suggesting, 'a possible conflict between the private advantages that might accrue to such officers and their public duty.'[30]

Barlow's decision resulted in a diminution of the officers' profit. MacDowell, already angry over his exclusion from the Madras Council, was prevailed upon by other officers to arrest and court-martial the Madras Army's Quartermaster General for carrying out Barlow's order. Barlow countermanded his action by releasing that officer. This, along with information from London that the directors had refused to alter their decision as to his membership in the Madras Council, caused MacDowell to resign and sail for Britain. However, just before his departure from aboard his ship that was shortly to be lost at sea, he issued a general order to the Madras Army, wherein he said that his imminent departure alone prevented him from opposing the Governor and rearresting the Quartermaster General, Lieutenant Colonel John Munro, for contempt of military authority. In his general order, MacDowell reprimanded the officer. Barlow retaliated by dismissing the Deputy Adjutant General who had acted lawfully under MacDowell's instructions in signing the impugned order, and, then, ill-advisedly also suspended a dozen Madras Army officers in different stations who represented against Barlow's treatment of the concerned staff officer, Major Thomas Boles. (The Adjutant General of the Madras Army was also dismissed by Barlow, along with the Deputy Adjutant General, who had actually signed MacDowell's last Madras Army order; but the former was no longer in Madras, having sailed for Britain along with MacDowell, both being drowned at sea when their ship went down.)

Soon after the Company's military officers mutinied, first at Masulipatam, then at Hyderabad, Seringapatam and other garrisons. At the former, the fort was seized. At Seringapatam, some of the British officers involved their Indian troops in the mutiny, apart from the actual seizure of the fort. A planned unified march on Madras by the garrison at Masulipatam and Hyderabad was averted by the persuasiveness of two respected Madras Army officers, then on political assignments. Colonel (later Sir) Barry Close, British Resident at Poona, hastened to Hyderabad and stalled the plans of the Company's officers there to march to Madras—he, 'allegedly organized the opposition of sepoy troops against their own officers.'[31] The other was Lieutenant Colonel (later Sir) John Malcolm, who though himself sympathetic to the mutinous officers, almost immediately upon returning from a diplomatic mission to Persia sought bravely to defuse the situation at Masulipatam. At most Madras Army stations, seditious toasts were drunk. Barlow now decided to use Indian troops against the mutinous officers. This "White Mutiny" collapsed without the support of the Indian troops. The European officers were not prepared for civil war. Some were cashiered, most were pardoned.

Both these mutinies in the Madras Army, that of Indian troops at Vellore in 1806 and that of European officers at several stations in 1809, were naturally seen as dangerous by some of the directors in London. Having earlier shifted the blame for the 1806 Vellore mutiny from evangelicalism, 'to the inherently bad policies of the previous Madras governments,' Grant and a majority of the directors conveyed full support for Barlow in the action taken by him in the 1809 officer mutiny.[32] When, however, in 1810 Grant and others in his group finished their terms as directors, a majority of anti-Barlow directors was able to bring about his recall from Madras in 1812, as also curiously re-instate most of the officers dismissed/cashiered in Barlow's tenure, some thereafter rising to general officer rank.[33] Barlow's successor as Governor was a military officer. His humiliation was complete.

In May 1812, another planned mutiny was revealed in the Madras Army. Apparently, the ex-Dewan of Travancore had suborned some personnel of the 2nd/14th Regiment at Quilon, for the battalion to help him in seizing the throne of Travancore. Jemadar Sheikh Hasan and Sepoy Salabat Khan, the alleged ringleaders, were blown from a gun, the former apparently having been led to believe that he would be the new dewan of Travancore. Twenty-seven others were executed later. In 1815, after Java was taken, including by a volunteer contingent of the Bengal Army, a mutiny occurred in a

Bengal Army unit, as the troops' return had been ostensibly delayed after the capture, much beyond the period they had specifically volunteered for. Captain W. Badenach, whose book on the Bengal Army came out in 1826, however adds another facet, the posting of British sergeant-majors and sergeants to each Indian infantry battalion: '...and strange as it may appear, up to the present period, the most important point connected with their duty has never been sufficiently, defined...it has sometime been productive of very serious consequences, and created discontent among the native officers, as in the case of a jemadar who was the chief instigator of the mutiny in Java with the intent to get himself appointed to the command of the island...the real or imaginary degradation he had received at the hands of the sergeant major rankled in his mind.'[34]

This mutiny is not mentioned much in the official accounts of this expedition. The person referred to as a jemadar by Badenach was, at the time of the mutiny, a subedar. He had, before this expedition, been dismissed for not taking orders from a British sergeant-major when he was a jemadar. He had appealed to the directors in London, and been restored to duty. He had proceeded to Java in 1811 as a subedar, and had become friendly with the Surakarta Court. This mutiny has been researched by P.B.R. Carey, partly from Dutch records in Indonesia and the Netherlands, as the British had not then wished to publicize it. In 1814, it had been decided to return the island to the Dutch. The British troops had started returning to India. The impression gained thereafter was that this Bengal Army unit would be transferred to the Dutch for a lump sum payable to the British, to help the Dutch control the island. The local Javanese were very frightened of the Bengal Army contingent (though the unit itself had become familiar with the members of the Surakarta Court, as a result of doing guard duty on the palace). In 1815 Subedar "Dhaugkal" (presumably Dhonkal) Singh of the Bengal Light Infantry, in collusion with the Surakarta Court, conspired to take over the island, whereupon he would be appointed the Governor of Java. The site, where the Governor's residence was to be constructed, had been selected. The initial date fixed to take over the island was delayed by two days, to enable more members of the battalion to join the "rebellion". During this delay of two days, the plot was revealed to the sergeant-major by the latter's orderly. The subedar and others were tried and executed. Seventeen were shot, and fifty put into irons for transportation. For four years in Java, money deposited by the men had not yet been remitted to their families. In the event, one hundred Bengal cavalrymen were transferred to the Dutch in 1816. P.B.R. Carey, thereafter, summed up this mutiny: 'The 1815 plot should thus be seen initially rather as a desperate attempt on the part of the Indian soldiers to take the law into their own hands in order to prevent their abandonment by the British, rather than as a carefully organized conspiracy to topple the British administration in Java.'[35]

At this juncture the state of discipline in the Bengal Army needs mentioning. John Pemble records in *The Invasion of Nepal:* 'The sepoys, finding it increasingly difficult to obtain the leaves of absence on which they depended for settlement of their domestic and legal concerns, had been applying for discharges, and, when unsuccessful, deserting in large numbers.'[36] Separately, in Hyderabad, in 1812, two mutinies occurred in quick succession in the Nizam's army which was officered by British officers, providing Henry Russell, the Resident, justification to disband these units so that the Company could then raise a Hyderabad Contingent, to be paid for by the Nizam, but totally controlled by the British. The first case occurred at Hyderabad, where a battalion of the Nizam's troops tied the British commandant, who was endeavouring to carry out reforms, to a gun to blow him away. He was rescued, and the ringleaders were executed. The second mutiny occurred at Indur, and thus the first two battalions of Russell's Brigade came to be raised in lieu.

Next came the Barrackpore mutiny of 1824. Horrendous memories regarding the suppression of this mutiny were still prevalent in 1857, this, in a way, apparently providing the rationale to kill the British in the 1857 Uprising. In October 1824, three Bengal Army regiments, the 26th, 47th and 62nd, were ordered to march to Chittagong to take part, thereafter, in the Arakan campaign of the First Anglo-Burmese War of 1824. They had already just marched to Barrackpore from Muttra (now Mathura). To go back a bit further as to the vicissitudes of the 47th, between 1807 and 1811 alone there were four changes of location. In 1814, it marched 500 miles from Barrackpore to Benares; in 1816, 300 miles to Dinapur; and in 1818, 500 miles to Agra. In each march, the soldiers themselves paid for their bullock-baggage transport. The decision to march to Chittagong was taken because most Bengal Army regiments were, at that time, averse to a sea voyage. In 1758 and 1768 they had done so, but, thereafter, their attitude hardened, except as volunteers, for instance to Macao in 1808. In the latter half of the eighteenth century, Crown regiments had also been mutinying in Britain when ordered to embark for India. None of the regiments were keen to go, as news of a Burmese success at Ramu in the Arakan had also been accompanied by reports of the Burmese torturing the 250 Bengal Army personnel taken prisoner there, and of mutilating the bodies of the dead.

Added to these psychological concerns was the administrative problem. The higher caste Hindu soldiers of the Bengal Army used to wrap up their brass drinking and cooking vessels in their beddings. Since it was difficult for them to carry this awkward load, already overloaded with their knapsack, arms and ammunition, it was customary for them to hire bullocks with their own money to carry these vessels. Owing to all the available bullocks having already been bought in Bengal for the sea-borne force, partly from the Madras Army, which had landed at Rangoon in May 1824, no fit bullocks could be found for these marching regiments at reasonable rates of hire. The request for an additional allowance for the Burmese war, or for the government to provide the bullocks, was not sympathetically answered. At the same time, the Muslim subedar major of the 47th may have threatened the Hindus, who were in the majority, that they would be sent by sea if they created further problems. Their officers were mostly new to the regiment, being suddenly posted in on account of the 1824 reorganization. The commanding officer was also considered to be in the subedar major's pocket. The suspicion implanted by the subedar major that they were to be sent by sea caused rancour, though their officers, including the commanding officer, assured them to the contrary and officers contributed from private (regimental) funds towards partly paying for the bullocks, despite the exorbitant charges.

Finally, on 1 November 1824, when the 47th was due to march, they assembled on the parade ground, but did not formally fall in; they complained that their knapsacks were old and torn, and would not carry them. Though a deduction had already been levied two months earlier, new knapsacks had not yet been provided. The commanding officer had earlier informed the Commander-in-Chief, General Edward Paget of the British Army, about the mutiny; Paget had no previous experience of India or Indian troops. He ordered two European regiments, some European artillery and some Indian cavalry, to cordon off the parade ground on 2 November 1824. According to the subsequent court of inquiry proceedings (in the British Library, London), the 47th, joined by some men of the 26th and 62nd Regiments, stood there, 'in stupid desperation, resolved not to yield, but making no preparation to resist.' The court of inquiry added that the so-called 'mutiny was an ebullition of despair at being compelled to march without the means of doing so.' In a petition to the Commander-in-Chief on the parade ground, they begged that they feared they were being sent by sea, and requested their discharge, in order not to lose their caste, and that the subedar major, and his unpopular relative the havildar major, be both shot. Paget replied that they were not being sent by sea, and that he was not prepared to listen any further, unless they first ground their arms. This they declined to do and requested a discharge. Their officers were told that they must march to Chittagong, or ground their arms. The troops again declined, requesting a discharge. Paget galloped off the parade ground, and, as previously arranged, the artillery opened fire. No prior warning that the artillery would fire was given. J.W. Kaye adds that it was even doubtful that they knew the guns were there. The troops flung down their muskets and tried to flee. At least sixty were killed by the artillery and several were sabred; some were drowned.

The next day, a court-martial sentenced forty-one to death. Twelve were hanged, but the sentences of twenty-nine were commuted to fourteen years' imprisonment with hard labour. Others, apprehended later, were similarly sentenced. The Indian officers were dismissed, and the regiment disbanded. Paget's handling of the situation was severely criticized both in India and Britain, because none of the men's muskets were found to be loaded. According to Kaye, he had no knowledge of the Bengal Army, and bitter prejudice against it, 'even though this same Bengal Army had won for Britain, most of its then Indian Empire.' If a senior Bengal Army officer, like David Ochterlony, had been present at Barrackpore, discontent would not have been deemed a mutiny. The artillery-firing and cavalry-sabreing of the 47th could certainly have been avoided. The directors were not happy with the way Paget handled the situation, and contemplated recalling William Amherst, the Governor-General. He had made no comment when forwarding the inquiry proceedings, deeming it entirely a military matter. The directors however felt he could have taken an interest in the situation, instead of leaving it entirely to Paget to handle. The sentences of imprisonment were remitted. The philosopher Herbert Spencer later described it as, 'a despotism under which...a regiment of sepoys was deliberately massacred...'

For many in the Bengal Army, possibly, unknown to some of its British officers, those dying on 2 November 1824 became martyrs, for the Calcutta *Englishman* records, on 30 May 1857, after the outbreaks at Meerut and Delhi: 'A circumstance has come to our knowledge which, unless it had been fully authenticated, we could scarcely have believed to be possible, much less true. When the mutiny at Barrackpore broke out in 1824, the ringleader, a Brahmin of the 47th Regiment Native Infantry, was hanged on the edge of the tank where a large tree now stands, and which was planted on the spot to commemorate the fact. This tree, a sacred banyan, is pointed to by the Brahmins and others to this day, as the spot where an unholy deed was performed, a Brahmin hanged. This man was, at the time, considered in the light of a martyr, and his brass "pootah" or worshipping utensils, consisting of small trays, incense-holders, and other brass articles used by Brahmins during their prayers, were carefully preserved and lodged in the quarter-guard of the (Barrackpore) regiments, where they remain to this day, they being at this moment in the quarter-guard of the 43rd Light Infantry at Barrackpore. These relics, worshipped by the sepoys, have been, for thirty-two years, in the safe keeping of regiments, having, by the operation of the daily relief of the quarter-guard, passed through the hands of 233,600 men, and have served to keep alive, in the breasts of many, the recollection of a period of trouble, the scene of a Mutiny and its accompanying swift and terrible punishment, which, had these utensils not been present to their sight as confirmation, would probably have been looked upon as fables, or, at the most, as very doubtful stories.'

Such bloody memories were, undoubtedly, an important factor in the unfortunate bloodshed that occurred in 1857-1858. Philip Mason, thereafter, quoted an old Indian officer as saying, 'They are your own men whom you have been destroying.' Mason added: 'He could not trust himself to say more...(Paget) could surely have avoided that sudden and brutal act which, like Dyer's at Amritsar a hundred years later, suggests a man using power to vent a deep dislike which had perhaps grown stronger for being long suppressed. These two cases, Vellore and Barrackpore, set the pattern of mutiny. They were a warning to which few paid attention.'[37] There were, however, to be further mutinies, or near mutinies, before 1857. About a year after the Barrackpore mutiny, in the 46th Regiment on 14 October 1825, a company in Assam refused to march to the border with Burma on account of total emaciation due to extended service in that area. When the four leaders were seized, all the others insisted that they, too, should be confined with them. The leaders were sentenced to death—the sentence was later commuted, and the others were discharged. Medically, it was established at the inquiry: 'They did not appear to be able to support the weight of their own muskets and bayonets,' the Brown Bess being almost twice the weight of a Second World War Number 4, Mark 1 rifle.

Writing after the 1824 Barrackpore incident, and viewing the discipline of the Bengal Army from its inception to 1826, Badenach, who had served for twenty years in the Bengal Army, recorded: 'In writing the following pages...my attention was turned entirely to suggesting practical improvements in a system, which, in many of its important branches, is vicious...[38] After careful investigation of the conduct of the native troops in the Bengal side of India, from that time up to the present period, I am happy to be able to say that I have not discovered a single instance of their having shown insubordination or any disposition to mutiny, unless when improperly treated...'[39]

He adds that, to his personal knowledge, in the whole history of the Bengal Army (up to 1826), only one European officer had been killed by a Bengal Army soldier, and, in this case, the Indian officer in question was immediately cut down by the battalion's own Indian officers.

When, in 1827, Charles Metcalfe (later Lord Metcalfe), left Delhi, where he had been the British Resident, to become a member of the Governor-General's Council at Calcutta, he believed that the Company's government was unpopular, but the only possible threat to it was a mutiny in the army. So long as the army remained faithful, and money was available to pay for it, Metcalfe wrote, in 1828: 'We can keep India in order by its instrumentality, but if the instrument should turn against us, where would be the British power? Echo answers, Where?'

When Bentinck came out as Governor-General, from the start he was required to effect economy. His predecessor, Amherst, had left a deficit, mainly as a result of the First Anglo-Burmese War. Consequently, the directors had specifically enjoined on Bentinck a reduction in military expenditure, particularly specifying that the *batta* drawn by British officers, even when not on active service, should be reduced by half. A saving of nearly one million pounds was effected by reductions in the Presidency Armies alone. Thereafter, the halving of *batta* for officers brought Bentinck unpopularity, since the officers had come to regard it as part of their pay. Bentinck's predecessors had protested against the proposed reduction, and had not implemented it, but Bentinck did not wish to displease the directors, for, earlier, they had recalled him, when he was Governor of Madras, on account of the Vellore mutiny. Protests came in from every station, including from the Commander-in-Chief, Lord Stapleton Combermere. The directors adhered to their decision, even though this saving was a comparatively small one, 20,000 pounds per annum. Thereafter, army officers declined all Bentinck's invitations, and boycotted him whenever they could.

From November 1838 onwards there occurred a series of mutinies and incipient mutinies due to non-payment of the full *batta*. From early on, there had been examples of units being employed by one Presidency Army in what could be regarded as the sphere of action of another Presidency Army, but the liability was only accepted in time of war. During hostilities the Indian soldier was ready to serve in a territory outside his own Presidency, but, when such a foreign territory had been pacified/annexed, he resented the withdrawal of the allowances, and insisted that these concessions were stilll due to him during peace time, as he still was in what appeared to him to be a foreign territory. The result was that service outside his own Presidency during peace caused serious discontent. The government faced a problem in deciding which troops, without being paid the extra allowances, were to occupy the new territories. Such a territory had to be garrisoned by the troops of one or other of the Presidency Armies—the administration of a mixed Presidency force during a time of peace would have presented difficulty. This difficulty was complicated by the idiosyncracies of the Presidency Armies themselves. In the Bengal Army, no provision was made for the men's families, and the men were accustomed to visiting their families at regular intervals. The further away they were from their homes, the more difficult this became. In the Bombay Army, a certain percentage of families was permitted, but in the Madras Army, on the other hand, all the men's families, if desirous, could accompany the unit to wherever it moved. The higher caste men of the Bengal Army had a major religious objection to being moved across the sea to Burma, but the Madras Army had no similar objection. This accounted for the fact that the Indian portion of the force that took part in the First Anglo-Burmese War was from the Madras Army, and that, thereafter, Burma thus became one of the stations for the Madras Army. In due course, after a few years, this commitment of the Madras Army began being questioned by the personnel of the latter. They looked askance as to why a greater share of this commitment could not be borne by the Bengal Army.

The first of a series of incipient mutinies, owing to the non-payment of *batta*, commenced in 1838-1841 at Sholapur,[40] Secunderabad, Hyderabad, Malegaon and Kotah within some Madras Army units; the Madras Army was required to take over certain garrison stations from the Bombay and Bengal Armies, as the latter moved northwards to Sind, Baluchistan and the Punjab, prior to entering Afghanistan. At Sholapur, for example, in 1838, one in ten men was sentenced to two years' imprisonment. Incidents, thereafter, took place in January 1842 in the Bengal Army brigade assembled at Peshawar. Brigadier Wild was under pressure to aid the beleaguered Bengal Army brigade at Jalalabad. The Sikh Army's contingent of 5,000, deputed to cooperate with Wild in the passage of the Khyber, was already mutinous. On 10 January, the 64th Bengal Infantry refused to accept its pay, or to advance into the Khyber and Afghanistan, until increased allowances and warm clothing were issued. Wild now wanted to use the other Bengal Infantry battalions against the 64th, which would have been catastrophic as all the Bengal Infantry at Peshawar were similarly inclined, apart from the adverse effect on the Sikh Army troops *vis-a-vis* the Bengal Army brigade. After a full night's effort, Wild was dissuaded from doing so by Henry Lawrence, then the British Political Agent at Peshawar. The following day, the 64th Regiment accepted its pay.

In October 1843, the 6th Light Cavalry of the Madras Army was suddenly required to proceed on field service from Kamptee to Bundelkhand, the regiment having previously been informed that, on the completion of its tenure at Kamptee, it was being moved to its home station of Arcot. Subsequent orders, however, required the regiment to move to Jubbulpore (now Jabalpur), to form part of the Bengal Division at Saugor. This order and counter-order appears to have occasioned disorder in the regiment, aggravated on 1 December by the announcement that field *batta* was being discontinued, as for the Bengal Division, an erroneous promulgation for this Madras Army unit at Jubbulpore by the Army Department. A large proportion of the men, that same evening, resolved not to do any further duty. Moreover, how were they to feed their families so far from home with the withdrawal of *batta*, when expenses at Jubbulpore were so much more for rice-eaters? The next day they delayed carrying out their duties, and were warned against a recurrence. They proceeded to the residence of the second-in-command, and stated they were not prepared to serve under their commanding officer, who had shown them no sympathy. On 7 December they were addressed by the station commander. The erroneous withdrawal of the *batta* was cancelled, but they sought to change their commanding officer. The latter did not consider the regiment fit for field service now, and it was moved to Arcot, reaching there in July 1844. A court of inquiry was held, and seventeen were brought to trial before a court-martial, and sentenced to death. Lieutenant General Lord George Tweeddale, Commander-in-Chief of the Madras Army, limited the death sentence to two—'privates Mohammed Bordu and Abdul Rehman,' the two who, reportedly, actually administered the oath to not perform their duty to the others on 1 December.[41] Separately, in October 1843, there were renewed indications of disaffection in the 64th Bengal Infantry at Ludhiana, the same regiment that had refused pay at Peshawar in 1842. It appeared that the success of the Sikh Army in obtaining from the Sikh Durbar an increased basic pay of twelve rupees per mensem was having an effect on the Bengal Army in the Punjab, then paid eight-and-a-half rupees a month (basic seven rupees). Separately, the Sikh Durbar's emissaries were encouraging desertions and defections from the Company's troops by offering promotions and more pay. At the beginning of February 1844, the 34th Bengal Infantry, the 7th Bengal Light Cavalry, and an Indian company of the Bengal Artillery, refused to leave for Sind to relieve Bombay Army troops due for a turnover, unless they were paid the allowance since discontinued, when Sind was an operational area till 1843. It was then contemplated to make Sind the Bengal Army's responsibility, in order to give the Bombay Army some relief because of its smaller size. The 34th Bengal Infantry was disbanded in front of the whole Meerut garrison. About 300 men from other units were also discharged. But the disbanding of the 34th Bengal Infantry did not prevent the spreading disaffection. The 4th and 69th Bengal Infantry now became mutinous; 191 and ninety personnel were discharged from each, rather than disband two further regiments so soon after the 34th. The other affected units agreed to march to Sind, on various expectations that the discontinued allowances would be restored. Among these units was the 64th Bengal Infantry, which had been so assured by its commanding officer. When, some months later, the restoration did not occur, the 64th again mutinied, its commanding officer being cashiered. Six personnel were executed, seven imprisoned for life and twenty-five sentenced to various terms of imprisonment. A large number was dismissed. The 64th had just been seven months at Ludhiana, after coming out of Afghanistan before being ordered to Sind. Many of those discharged from the 34th and 64th Bengal Infantry, and other concerned Bengal Army units, took service with the Sikh Army, and opposed the Bengal Army in the First and Second Anglo-Sikh Wars. In the 64th, it was discovered that seventy-one were ex-convicts, convicted and jailed in other units. The divisional commander then recorded that the Indian soldier did not, 'understand mutiny in anything like the same light (as) our idea of the matter.' Philip Mason describes this series of mutinies as, 'the crop of mutinies arising from financial pedantry and the annexation of Sind.' He quotes a Bengal Army soldier as saying: 'I suppose there will be an order joining London to Calcutta.'[42]

After the refusal of the Bengal Army units to go to Sind without the restoration of the previous Sind allowance, two Madras Army regiments, the 7th Madras Cavalry and the 47th Madras Infantry, earmarked for Burma, were induced to go now to Sind on the guarantee of the Governor of Madras, that they would be entitled to the same allowance as for Madras Army units in Burma. They made family allotments accordingly. When they reached they learnt the allowances promised by the Governor could not be sanctioned for Sind, as it was contrary to the then regulations of the Bengal Army. When they received their next pay, after a deduction of the family allotments, some received no pay, and some were in debit. The Madras soldiers protested forcibly; several were court-martialled and punished. S.N. Sen succinctly summed up this collective insub-ordination in Sind in 1844: 'During the First Afghan War, General Pollock had paid his troops a special *batta* when they crossed the Indus. This was treated as a precedent, and the sepoy expected similar inducements when he was called upon to undergo the hardship of trans-Indus employment. But in 1843 Sind had been annexed, and became an integral part of the British Indian empire. The sepoy could not now legally claim any special compensation for serving in an Indian province, however distant it might be from his usual station. This was a piece of legal casuistry he could not understand. The Indus was still there, life in Sind was as hard as it had been in 1842, and, if his claim was legitimate in 1842, how could it lose its validity in 1844?'[43]

In 1845-1846, when, in the course of the First Anglo-Sikh War, the British were faced with a grave situation in the Punjab, a plan was discovered in Bihar to suborn the Indian troops and uproot British authority. On 18 December 1845, the commanding officer of the 1st Bengal Infantry was informed by a jemadar of the same regiment at Dinapur that the Regimental Munshi, Peer Buksh, was in league with some rich Wahabis at Patna and had been distributing money to excite the religious prejudices of the Indian officers and soldiers, and tamper with their allegiance. To test the veracity of this information, the commanding officer asked the jemadar and another Indian officer to accept the money. This was done and Peer Buksh arrested. The fundamental cause for this conspiracy was the discontent at the various innovations being introduced by the government—the resumption of lands endowed to religious institutions; the spread of English education, at the expense of Islamic education; the introduction of female education, as also the introduction of the common messing system in jails. For the successful execution of the conspiracy, the cooperation, or at least the acquiescence, of the Indian soldiers was considered necessary. Apart from Dinapur, suborning efforts had also been made at Sagauli, Hazaribagh and Doranda, and recruitment for an armed force had apparently begun at Jagdishpur, under Raja Kunwar Singh, with the possible intention of assisting the Sikhs in the Anglo-Sikh Wars, when the alleged plot was discovered. A similar endeavour to tamper with the 4th Bengal Infantry at Rawalpindi was allegedly made by the Wahabis in 1852, the conspiracy apparently originating from the Wahabis at Patna.

As in Sind, in 1843, following the annexation of the Punjab in 1849, the extra allowance given to Indian soldiers in the Punjab when it was deemed a foreign territory was now discontinued, since the Punjab had become a British territory. No one seemed to have learnt from the Sind experience of 1844. In July 1849, the two Bengal Infantry regiments, the 13th, and seven companies of the 22nd, at Rawalpindi, refused to take their pay. The press was sympathetic to the Indian soldiers; *The Mofussilite* of 2 August 1849 stated: 'The folly of the Government in a little matter led to the disaffection of probably good men and excellent soldiers.' Costs of foodstuffs went up and yet allowances were withdrawn, while the pay of Indian soldiers had remained constant at seven rupees a month since 1796, out of which he had to provide hutting for himself at each location, pay for bullock transport for each move, feed himself, and remit money home. The pay of the British soldier however progressively increased, with additional amenities and comforts.

The refusal of pay caused concern since many discharged Sikh Army personnel were roaming around disgruntled, not having been absorbed gainfully. The regiments eventually accepted their pay, the ostensible ringleaders being dismissed. Another Bengal Infantry regiment, now ordered to march from Delhi to a Trans-Sutlej location, initially refused to accept pay, though it eventually did. Thereafter, the 32nd Bengal Infantry at Wazirabad did the same in January 1850 (after learning that two other regiments were still receiving Sind *batta*), but was prevailed upon by the divisional commander, General John Hearsey, to accept its pay after four ringleaders were first sentenced to fourteen years' imprisonment. On revision being ordered, they were sentenced to death, later commuted to transportation for life.[44] When originally sentenced to fourteen years' imprisonment, they were to be manacled and set to work in the cantonment in the presence of other troops, on road construction as "chain gangs", a practice recently introduced in the Punjab. At this juncture, in 1849, Henry Lawrence sagely observed: '...after a hundred years experience of Indian warfare, the East India Company was still nearer the ABC than the Z of a sound, practical, military administration.'[45]

Thereafter, in February 1850, the 66th Bengal Infantry at Gobindgarh Fort, near Amritsar, tried to seize the fort, when learning, after arrival at the fort, of their not getting *batta*. As recorded at the subsequent court of inquiry: 'Besides the political importance of the fort, the fort contained ten lakhs of treasure, innumerable quantities of arms and ammunition of war, which had, lately, been taken from the enemy, and also a month's supply for 1,800 men.' A Bengal Cavalry regiment was brought in, and the 66th ordered to be disbanded. The 66th had marched from Lucknow in November 1849, and was formally told of the withdrawal of fixed *batta* when it reached Gobindgarh at the end of January 1850. At Lucknow, the

British sergeant-major informed the pay havildars, but the officiating commanding officer did not tell the men formally. (The permanent commanding officer was on furlough, and, in all, eight out of twenty-two officers authorized were absent on deputation or temporary duty.) He had, later, at 10 p.m. on 31 January, agreed to see four men from each company, who explained that they had moved further from their homes, but were now getting less pay at the same location than the regiment just relieved. Ninety-seven personnel were tried by a court-martial including two subedars and one jemadar. Forty-two were sentenced to various terms of imprisonment with hard labour from fourteen to seven years, including the jemadar. Two subedars and forty-seven others were dismissed, and six acquitted.[46] The men to be lodged in Amritsar Jail were put in irons, and marched through their own regiment on parade to the jail. Those to be dismissed were taken on foot to Ludhiana for the purpose, and given two annas a day subsistence allowance for the Amritsar-Ludhiana journey. The regiment itself was now marched to Ambala, then marched through the cantonment 'in the presence of the troops paraded on this occasion,' and the men left on the Saharanpur road. *The Athenaeum* recorded on 9 March 1850: 'Had the 66th once closed the gates on its officers, the mere circumstances would have rendered them desperate and the first flag of revolt in the Punjab...would, in that case, have been hoisted by our own troops.' In Vellore, in 1806, the mutinying troops had failed to close the outer gates, and, in both cases, Indian cavalry had helped to put down mutinying Indian infantry. Sir Charles Napier, the then Commander-in-Chief, felt that the officiating commanding officer was to blame for not himself originally explaining the discontinuance of the allowance at Lucknow, adding that such laxity was enough to destroy the best army in the world. He was court-martialled, reprimanded and went on to command a Nasiri (Gurkha) battalion. Napier also felt it necessary to emphasize, in a general order, that young officers must associate more with the Indian officers, and keep in direct contact with the men. He found that interpreters were still required in every unit.

In 1852 another mutiny occurred in the Bengal Army on account of the Second Anglo-Burmese War. As their enrolment was for general service, even overseas, Madras Army soldiers had no major inhibitions about sea voyages, despite unfortunate experiences, like that of a contingent of 300 Madras soldiers that sailed from Manila in September 1764 and reached Madras in August 1767, having changed ships some five times, and lost a third of its strength. Under the terms of their enrolment, most of the Brahmin and Rajput soldiers of the Bengal Army were not obliged to serve overseas, and there was some difficulty in making up the required number of Bengal Infantry regiments for Burma. From the commanding officer's initial report, it was believed from the pay havildars that the 38th Infantry Regiment at Barrackpore, recently returned from Afghanistan, would volunteer for Burma. At the time only six out of the seventy-four regiments of the Bengal Army were "special general service regiments" with a liability to serve anywhere. When later asked whether they would embark for Rangoon or the Arakan, the men of the 38th replied they would march anywhere, but would never embark. It was then decided they would march to the Arakan, but some now feared they would be embarked *en route*. In a curious anomaly at this juncture, in March 1852, the Commander-in-Chief was in Kangra while his headquarters moved from Calcutta to Simla, his Adjutant General was in Simla, and the Judge Advocate General was in Sind. The incident was thus, in effect, handled by the Governor-General at Calcutta. Dalhousie did not want another 1824 Barrackpore scenario, and recorded: 'I could not fail to remember the melancholy incident in the same station of Barrackpore on the same occasion of a march of troops for a Burmese war, when, from some misunderstanding and want of justice and temperate handling, the native troops were, at length, massacred as mutineers. Bearing that sad scene in mind, I felt that while I should never advise the Government to permit open disobedience of its orders, to truckle to its sepoys, or in any the slightest degree to compromise its own authority; yet, if it were practicable to modify existing orders, so as to avert an occasion which stupidity or error might make use of for a manifestation of discontent, or even of open mutiny, it would be a wise act for Government to avoid such occasion for misapprehension, and so as to preserve them from the certain consequences of their own folly.' In view of the regiment's fears, it was now to march to Dacca, and there relieve a general service regiment.[47]

Dalhousie's succinct minute does contain undertones that all was not well in the Bengal Army. For one, eleven of the twenty-two officers of the unit were away at the time. At the court of inquiry, the commanding officer placed on record, 'in 1840, the 38th had manifested an insubordinate spirit to avoid going to Kandahar; that prompt and decisive measures adopted by me in bringing to trial eighty-six men saved the regiment.' In 1852, eight men were dismissed, though the commanding officer had recommended 400 for discharge, saying they were of the lower castes. The annexation of further territory in Burma in December 1852 created the sequential problem of finding troops to garrison it. Owing to the majority of the Bengal Army regiments being averse to sailing by ship, it would still be a difficult march for them to Burma, with part of the track being impassable to bullock-carts. On a temporary basis, the Madras Army was prepared to provide the additional units, but objected to the total commitment being a permanent one for the Madras Army, whose soldiers did not enjoy service in Burma *per se*. Further, a tour of duty in Burma would come round so frequently for regiments of the Madras Army, that service in that army could become increasingly unpopular. Resultantly, by 1856, all future recruitment in the Bengal Army was to be with a general service liability, but this had its own repercussions in 1857. Separately, however, trouble did take place as a result of this Burma commitment in the Madras Army. A Madras Army regiment was later to refuse to embark for Bengal, having earlier done a tour of duty in Burma.

In 1855 a murderous attack occurred on Brigadier General Colin Mackenzie, Commander of the Company's Hyderabad Contingent at Bolarum. Through a combination of staff ignorance and inefficiency, the dates of Moharrum were initially confused, and a garrison order apparently prohibited on that Sunday any procession on the route past Mackenzie's house. That year Moharrum fell on a Sunday, the day most important to Shia Muslims. Much of the 3rd Cavalry of the Hyderabad Contingent was from Oudh. They chose to take the now-authorized procession on an unauthorized route. Mackenzie went out to remonstrate as the procession with *tazias* passed his house, and is alleged, though accounts differ, to have snatched one or two of the standards being carried by the processionists. A crowd of troops, both Shia and Sunni, followed him back, and assaulted him. He barely survived, having been left for dead. All the Muslim officers of the 3rd Cavalry were dismissed, except two, and two Hindu officers of Mackenzie's guard were similarly punished for not sufficiently resisting the processionists. Dalhousie recorded that Mackenzie had been indiscreet, the 'order was not only unusual, but objectionable in that it put forward the Moharrum in direct conflict with the Christian Sabbath, and so introduced a religious element into the prohibition.' There was the feeling that the attack had been preplanned when the route was adopted. The inquiry report stated that the troops that assaulted Mackenzie were, 'opium eaters to a man.' Philip Mason commented, 'No one thought this had more than local significance. But it was not long before there came just the spark that was needed to ignite the whole lowering sulphurous mass of unease and distrust.' This incident was another indication of the bad state of the Company's Army. After the inquiry, Mackenzie was transferred as a Major to Murshidabad, and appointed Agent to the Governor-General. He eventually retired as a Lieutenant General.

A retired British officer was constrained to write in 1857: 'Almost all the mutinies in India, whether in Bengal or elsewhere, have been more or less produced, or at least have had in some sort the initiative, from ourselves. There has usually been some departure from contract, some disregard of the feelings, health or convenience of the native soldiers, when at the same moment the utmost care was lavished on a European regiment; some interference with their pay or rights, or what they supposed to be their right.'[48]

He added: 'The entire army of India amounts to 315,520 men costing 9,802,235 pounds. Out of this sum no less than 5,668,110 pounds are expended on 51,316 European officers and soldiers.'[49] Moreover, 'The European Corps takes no share in the rough ordinary duties of the service.... They are lodged, fed and paid in a manner unknown to other soldiers.'[50]

By way of conclusion to this chapter, T. Rice Holmes' encapsulation is very apt: '...these isolated acts of insubordination did not (then) ripen into a general revolt, but though they were checked at the time, partly by concession, partly by the punishment of the ringleaders, no decided steps were taken to make their recurrence impossible. Nothing but a radical reform of the relations between officer and sepoy, an unmistakeable resolve to treat the latter both firmly and generously, could have healed his discontent. But the authorities were satisfied with applying a palliative when they should have wrought a cure; and they could have felt no satisfaction in punishing offenders whom their own injustice had provoked to sin.'[51]

A correspondent of the *Delhi Gazette* of 27 March 1852 went even further. He was of the opinion that not only in almost every instance of mutiny in the Indian regiments was the government to blame, but also that it would, 'most assuredly turn itself out of the country at no very distant period by its own repeated acts of gross mismanagement and of bad faith to its own native troops.'

Whereas the discipline of Indian troops was overall vastly better than that of European troops in India, for offences like that of rape, murder, alcoholism and so on, Indian troops were alleged to be conversant with the offence that the British emotively labelled as mutiny, but which, generally, Indian troops viewed only as an assertion of their rights, an attitude which culminated in the uprising of 1857. Much of the *batta* authorization problem was due to the Presidency Army system, which caused many of the ostensible mutinies, but it would be incorrect to impute all the events of 1857 to the Presidency system. There were many other contributory causes to the 1857 Uprising, but as a result of the parochialism it fostered, the Presidency Army system must bear a share of the responsibility for some of the events of 1857 in the Bengal Army. So frequently were units disbanded at short notice in the Presidency Armies that there was much percipience in J. Malcolm's urging in 1826 that the Indian soldier, 'should be taught to look to meritorious services in the army as a road to employment under the civil administration.'[52] Allowing for his seeming remoteness in the British hierarchy from the Indian soldier, there was, nevertheless, percipience also in Governor-General Dalhousie's observation before he handed over to Lord Canning in March 1856: 'The sepoy is a child in simplicity and biddableness, if you make him understand his orders, if you treat him justly, and don't pet him over-much.'

Almost a century later, in November 1946, James Callaghan, then a Member of Parliament, and, later, a Prime Minister of Britain, stated to an audience: 'There is no reason why servicemen who have a collective grievance or a collective request should not represent it collectively.' But this was not the view a century earlier, for then the British thought any mutiny could lead to India being wrested from them, as the Haitians had wrested Haiti from the French in 1804. The British adopted the posture of the Dutch against the Guyanese mutineers in Surinam in 1772. Amiya Barat added a piquant corollary, apart from the fact of the absence of a considerable portion of the officers from regiments in which mutinies occurred, 'one particularly striking coincidence, if it was coincidence, was that the (permanent) colonel commanding was in no case present (physically) with his regiment when it (actually) mutinied.'[53]

FOUR

Civil Disturbances And The Use Of Troops In Aid Of The Civil Power Before 1857

OF THE period before 1857, Vincent Smith, in *The Oxford History of India,* recorded: 'It is equally certain that the minds of the civil population of all classes and ranks, Hindus and Mohammedans, princes and people, were agitated and disturbed by feelings of uneasiness and vague apprehension. The disturbance of sentiment was not manifested by insurrections, as the discontent of the army had been signalled by mutinies.'[1]

Smith was not quite correct as to the alleged non-manifestation of civil disturbances, for, as S.B. Chaudhuri, in *Civil Disturbances during the British Rule in India 1765-1857,* stated: 'Very seldom in the years from 1757 to 1857 was the country free from either civil or military disturbances.'[2] Like the discontent in the Bengal Army, the discontent of the civil population before 1857 was manifested by a long series of disturbances, most necessitating the use of troops, indeed too many to be encompassed in one chapter.

The word "disturbances", thus, is used to apply to every form of civil disaffection or discontent, whether religious, communal, political, agrarian, or cases of disputed succession. That the British had to contend almost throughout with some form of civil disturbance is known, but the facet of the army being called upon so frequently before 1857 to aid the civil power, is not so well known. Even communal disturbances, or those arising from a local grievance, often took on a political complexion, entailing the calling out of troops as we shall later see at Benares in 1809, and Bareilly in 1816. From the historical point of view, an example of a requisition of that period to use troops to aid the civil authority is a letter from the Magistrate of Bhagalpur to the Judicial Secretary of the Bengal Government, dated 5 March 1803: 'To issue a proclamation requiring this armed force to disperse and notifying that any person firing upon or resisting the officers of government will be treated as rebels...that in the event of disobedience to the above requisition the Magistrate despatch a Military force...to reduce them to obedience and support the Court and Collector, and for that purpose the Detachment be instructed to fire upon the Insurgents if opposed.'

The imposition by the British of Mir Jafar was widely detested, first by Ramram Singh of Midnapore, then by the people of Burdwan. At Burdwan, the Bengal Army company commander was initially compelled to report: 'I am sorry to say we have been greatly worsted.' Thereafter, Mir Kasim's authority was overtly challenged by Asad Zaman Khan, Raja of Birbhum, in October 1760, but, covertly, it was directed against the British in conjunction with the Raja of Burdwan. A Bengal Army contingent failed to overcome the disturbance in January 1761. Only when this force was augmented was Asad Zaman Khan compelled to pay an indemnity. When Mir Kasim was deposed in 1763, and Mir Jafar restored, Rangpur district held out for Mir Kasim. Four companies of Bengal Army troops had to be deployed to resolve the situation. According to G.B. Malleson, Mir Jafar, now, for the British, had become, 'a golden sack into which they could dip their hands at leisure.'

The "Sanyasi Rebellion" from 1763 onwards, was one of the most formidable that the Bengal Army, at almost its very inception, had to face. The movement consisted of the activities of two different groups—Hindu sanyasis and Muslim fakirs—who gained support from the dispossessed zamindars and disbanded soldiers of the Nawab of Bengal. After the great famine of 1770, economic distress drove people in large numbers to join the Sanyasi Rebellion. By the end of 1773, according to Dr R.C. Majumdar, there was an, 'upsurge to the Sanyasis in the wild belt of country from Rangpur to Dacca...(and they) threatened to sweep away the English power completely.'[3] Their fighting potential was not insignificant. In 1772, they defeated a Bengal Infantry company sent against them, and killed its British commander. Encouraged by this success, bands of sanyasis, each comprising 5,000 to 7,000 men, overran Bogra and Mymensingh districts in Bengal. In 1773, another Bengal Infantry contingent was sent against them. It attempted to pursue a band of 300 sanyasis, but was defeated. Only twelve Indian soldiers survived. Extirpation of the British had been the motive for these annual incursions of this religious grouping, but from 1773 they gradually ceased under the pressure of the military operations against them. It was during these operations that Warren Hastings raised a body of cavalry in September 1773, known today as the President's Bodyguard. Similarly, in the years 1770-1800, there were uprisings among the Chuars, a tribe inhabiting the hills between Ghatsila and Birbhum in today's Bihar. Operations by the Bengal Army, in aid of the civil authority, had to be conducted after they completely surprised a military force in 1770, killed and wounded a considerable number of men, and overwhelmed several picquets.

By 1781, the strain on the Bengal Presidency's finances was serious after two years of war with the Marathas (the Madras Presidency also needing funds for the war with Hyder Ali). Bengal Government loans were floated in Calcutta, but the response was inadequate to carry on the Anglo-Mysore War. Two courses were considered by the Governor-General, Warren Hastings—for the Nawab of Oudh, Asaf-ud-Daula, to reduce his ostensible large debt owed to the Company for the maintenance of two brigades of the Company's troops in Oudh; and for the rich Raja Chait Singh of Benares to give a loan to the Company for the purpose. In July 1781, Hastings set out from Calcutta with an escort of 500 Indian troops. Earlier, Chait Singh's zamindari had been detached from Oudh and was placed directly under the Company, Chait Singh having won over a majority in Hastings' Council, which consisted of Philip Francis, General Clavering, the Commander-in-Chief in India, and Colonel Monson; Hastings, though, himself opposed the move. Chait Singh's annual payment for his zamindari was twenty-two-and-a-half lakh rupees, which he had fixed with Philip Francis, but which Hastings considered low. The Company had given an undertaking that the demand would not be increased 'on any pretence whatsoever.'[4] Chait Singh had already been asked to pay an extra contribution of five lakh rupees annually towards the war with the French, which he paid, with reservations, for two years. Discerning that there had been a reconciliation between Hastings and Francis, Chait Singh sent Hastings a personal bribe of two lakh rupees, which he, at first, refused, but then paid into the Government treasury as a contribution by himself to the war expenditure against the Marathas.[5] Hastings now demanded a further war subsidy of five lakh rupees annually for the Company, and, on the suggestion of Eyre Coote, who was by now Commander-in-Chief, a provision of 2,000 horsemen, later reduced to 1,000. Chait Singh provided 500 horsemen, and 500 matchlockmen.

Some months before Hastings set out, the British Resident at Benares had reported that Chait Singh had started augmenting his fortifications, and had cached munitions obtained from the French. On hearing of Hastings' proposed departure for Benares, Chait Singh offered the Company twenty lakh rupees more, but Hastings rejected this amount as he expected to extract forty to fifty lakh rupees for the Company's war expenditure. If Chait Singh, in the event, refused to pay, he proposed reverting the zamindari to the Nawab of Oudh, and destroying the fort. On arrival, Hastings turned down Chait Singh's request for an interview, and sent a letter to him asking for an explanation for non-payment of the annual war subsidy of five lakh rupees and the non-provision of 500 horsemen. Hastings, according to Penderel Moon, against the advice of the Resident, did not deem the reply satisfactory, and sent the Resident and two Bengal Infantry companies from his escort to arrest Chait Singh. Chait Singh was confined to his house near the river in August 1781. His armed retainers, across the river, came in boats to rescue him. The Bengal Infantry guard of two companies was now found to be without ammunition. A third company, ordered to carry ammunition to them, could not get through owing to the crowds outside. The two companies, still without any ammunition, were all killed or wounded.

Chait Singh was let down to the river from the house, and crossed to the Ramnagar fortress. His retainers were in a position to have over-whelmed Hastings and his weakened escort at the Residency, but, instead, they departed with Chait Singh. Hastings sought assistance from the Chunar cantonment fifteen miles away. The captain commanding the Bengal Infantry battalion ordered to render assistance to Hastings first chose to attack Ramnagar fort *en route,* but was beaten back with heavy losses. The severed heads of all the deceased British officers were paraded through the villages of the zamindari, which were, by now, in total revolt against the British. Hastings sought refuge in Chunar, till troops from other stations arrived.[6] A satirical ditty sung locally at the time in the area was:

> *Ghore par howdah, hathi par zeen*
> *Jaldi chalagaya Warren Hasteen.*[7]

Separately, in Bengal the rumour spread rapidly that Hastings had been killed, and anti-British disturbances broke out in several districts. With the arrival of additional troops, the disturbance was put down, but the Bengal Infantry troops could discern that Chait Singh's threat to the Company's authority only passed off because of their assistance. As a reward, a sum of twenty-three lakh rupees was distributed among the troops; the money came from Chait Singh's treasure captured at Bijaygarh fortress. Chait Singh was deposed, and his nephew, a minor, was installed; the land revenue was enhanced to forty lakh rupees annually. Had Hastings accepted Chait Singh's letter of apology, as advised by the Resident, he would have been able to extract thirty to forty lakh rupees towards the war subsidy. It was partly on account of the hostility he displayed towards Chait Singh that the House of Commons, some four years later, decided to impeach Hastings. Chait Singh's insurrection also had repercussions among some zamindars of Gorakhpur and Bihar, who rose against the British, and had to be put down, also by using troops. Some were imprisoned, like Rani Sarbeswari of Sultanabad, who died in Bhagalpur jail on 6 May 1807.[8] Even the Begums of Oudh were suspected by Hastings of helping Chait Singh.[9] They had apparently offered Rs 1,000 per severed British head.

In January 1799, a murderous attack by Wazir Ali occurred on G.P. Cherry, the British Resident at Benares.[10] Wazir Ali (sometimes spelt Vizier Ali) was the disputed son of the late Nawab Asaf-ud-Daula of Oudh. Wazir Ali, though acknowledged by the late Asaf-ud-Daula's mother, who, earlier, had him installed by the British as Nawab, was apparently not his son. He was, allegedly, the son of a servant in the zenana, whom Asaf-ud-Daula had bought and acknowledged as his son to spite his brother, Saadat Ali, who was in exile at Benares after being implicated in the murder of one of Asaf-ud-Daula's favourites. Eventually, Saadat Ali was installed in 1798 as Nawab by the British after a show of force, by deploying the Company's troops. Wazir Ali moved to Benares, on a pension of one-and-a-half lakh rupees annually. Owing to his intriguing from Benares against Saadat Ali, and sending an emissary to Kabul against the British, the Governor-General had ordered him, in the future, to reside at Calcutta, far from Oudh. Whereupon, after the murder of Cherry (whom Wazir Ali unjustly blamed for his deposition) and several other Englishmen at Benares during a breakfast, he fled and collected several thousand armed men. Some of the Nawab's troops, sent to deal with the insurrection, joined Wazir Ali instead. A strong contingent of Bengal Infantry had to be brought in to resolve the matter. Wazir Ali was captured in December 1799, and moved to Fort William, Calcutta, where he died a prisoner in May 1817, being reportedly confined in 'a sort of iron cage.' On his funeral seventy rupees was spent, whereas his marriage had cost thirty lakh rupees. Some reports say he died at Vellore, it always being feared that he would flee to Afghanistan and coordinate an invasion by Zaman Shah.[11] Wazir Ali had allies in Bihar and Dacca, and links with Daulat Rao Scindia and Tipu Sultan. Separately, also in 1799, Aga Mohammad Reza, an Iranian adventurer, entered Cachar from Sylhet, and overcame the local ruler with the help of the Kukis. He, 'gave out that he was the twelfth Imam, destined to deliver India,' from the British, according to James Mill. He and 1,200 of his followers were defeated with the use of Bengal Army troops.

In 1800, after the defeat of Tipu Sultan, and the installation of the boy-Maharaja of Mysore—Krishna Wodeyar, a descendant of the original ruling family—the Madras Army had to be employed against Dhundia Wagh, a Maratha, who had been converted to Islam by Tipu and given military employment. At the time of the fall of Seringapatam, he was in prison in irons. He escaped from jail, recruited a number of discharged soldiers of the Mysore Army, assumed the title of "King of the Two Worlds", and appointed nawabs in the territory he was operating in.[12] He conducted guerrilla operations against the new British-appointed administration in Mysore State. The operations by the Madras Army against Dhundia Wagh gave Arthur Wellesley his first opportunity for independent military command. Ultimately, Wagh was defeated and killed, Arthur Wellesley exclaiming in relation to his Madras Army forces, 'We have now proved (a perfect novelty in India) that we can put down the lightest-footed and most rapid forces, as well as ... destroy heavy troops and storm strong fortifications.'[13]

The British held the view that Dhundia Wagh was seeking to be a second Hyder Ali. A series of "poligar" risings also followed in South India, from 1800 to 1806, in Tirunelveli district, the Ceded districts, and north Arcot, which were put down with the use of Madras Army troops. The poligars were subordinate feudal chiefs occupying tracts of land, more or less wild at the time—the word being derived from the Tamil *palaiyakkaran,* the holder of a feudal estate. In the attacks on the poligar fort at Tirunelveli alone fifteen British officers were killed.

Similarly, in Bundelkhand, a local zamindar, Gopal Singh, who had lost out in a succession dispute with Raja Bakht Singh, conducted operations for four years from 1808, and, as James Mill says: 'The marauding attacks of Gopal and his levies, carried out intermittently, ultimately tired out the resources of his powerful antagonist...and are worthy of record as an instance of success,' of such operations 'which can flow from personal activity, resolution and devoted adherence of a faithful band of followers imbued with political purpose.'[14] The Bengal Army, for its part, again felt itself indispensable in containing this rising against the British. Thereafter, it was a rising by the Jats of Bhiwani in 1809 and 1824. In the former alone, nineteen of the military force sent against them were killed and 114 wounded. Separately, from 1794 onwards in Vizagapatam district, and from 1798 in Ganjam district, there were recurring uprisings necessitating the use of the Company's troops. Though suppressed at the time they re-occurred up to 1834 periodically. The causes were enhanced land rent and the non-payment of arrears.

Meanwhile, there was trouble again in South India. After Tipu's defeat, the rulers of Travancore and Cochin had become the Company's vassals. Cochin paid a regular tribute, and Travancore undertook to give assistance whenever required, in return for protection, and undertaking, from 1805, to pay for a subsidiary force of four battalions. The Raja's payments for the latter fell into arrears, and he pleaded that he was unable to pay, the treaty having been forced on him. He was advised to disband his own State force, known as the Carnatic brigade, correspondingly to cover the costs of the subsidiary force. This he was unwilling to do, as an earlier economy suggested by the British, to reduce his State force's allowances, had resulted in 1804 in the revolt by 10,000 of his Nair troops. James Mill observed: 'To impose upon him (the Raja) the maintenance of a force infinitely more numerous than was necessary for the defence of the country...and to urge the exaction with unrelenting vigour were unworthy of the character of the British nation.'[15]

The British now sought the dismissal of the Dewan, Velu Tampi. The latter was thereupon alleged to have arranged for the Residency to be attacked at night by a force of 20,000. The Resident got away to a ship in the harbour carrying Bombay Army troops. Military action followed, troops like the 3rd Kafri (African) Regiment being brought in from Ceylon. Velu Tampi committed suicide in the temple of Bhagavati. His body was publicly exposed on a gibbet. His brother was hanged without trial for being his alleged accomplice in the commission of atrocities. H.H.Wilson has described these actions at Travancore as, 'among the least justifiable of the many questionable transactions by which the British power in India has been acquired or preserved.'[16] Velu Tampi, to this day, is a hero in southern Kerala. At various times he was alleged by the British to have been in touch with the French, Dutch and Americans. Preceding these major operations in Travancore, over 4,000 troops had been deployed in the Wynaad against an insurrection by the Pyche raja from 1796 to 1805.

From 1809 onwards the "grave" Benares riots began, in which, reportedly, according to the *District Gazetteer of Benares,* several persons were killed. There had been major communal riots before this in which troops had been deployed, for example, at Jaunpur 1776; Sylhet 1782; Surat 1795; Maunath Bhanjan (Mau) 1806, and Gorakhpur 1808, but the ones at Benares in 1809 were ostensibly of greater magnitude. The *District Gazetteer of Benares* compiled in 1907, comments, *inter alia:* 'The only disturbance of the public peace (in Benares in the first half of the nineteenth century) occurred in 1809 and the following year, when the city experienced one of those convulsions which had so frequently occurred in the past...the trouble subsided with the partial reorganization of the city police in October 1810; but before peace had been restored fresh riots arose with the introduction of the house tax...and it was again found necessary to station troops throughout the city to repress the popular disorder till the withdrawal of the obnoxious measure in the ensuing year.'[17]

The Bengal Criminal Judicial Proceedings for 1809 and 1810 in the Oriental and India Office Collections of the British Library refer to the "most culpable neglect of duty" and "highly criminal conduct" of the police, 'both Hindus and Mohammedans conjoining in...exerting themselves to inflame passions, and that the military alone preserved order.' The casualties of the communal portion of this riot were then put at twenty-nine to thirty killed and over a hundred wounded.[18] James Mill, who had access to records on the subject, stated: 'The sipahis, although of both persuasions discharged their duties with perfect impartiality and military steadiness; the police, equally mixed, had earlier taken part in the conflict according to their respective creeds.'[19] In October 1809, the behaviour of the police had rendered their name, in the acting magistrate's words, 'generally obnoxious but particularly to the sepoys, whose meritorious conduct entitled them in a manner to feel contempt for the cowardice of the police.'

As Gyanendra Pandey thereafter records: 'The military sepoys luckily held firm, but there was considerable anxiety amongst civil and military officers in Benares at the time as to which way the wind would blow. For about twenty days in October and November 1809 the sepoys were not allowed time off to bathe, dress or prepare their food.'[20] Pandey further says: 'When the military guard was finally withdrawn in 1809 and the police restored to their normal functions in Benares, sepoys going into the city reportedly poked fun at the police. Some of them also persistently defied a magisterial order against the carrying of arms in the streets of Benares. The incidence of disputes between military and police personnel on account of these pinpricks increased in August and September 1810. As the season of melas associated with the Dussehra celebration approached, the civil authorities were understandably perturbed about the possible consequences of such quarrels between the two arms of the law and the state...'[21] There was a communal disturbance again at Benares in 1813; there were communal riots also at Mubarakpur in Azamgarh district in 1813, 1834 and 1842, requiring the deployment of troops.

In 1810, at Mandvi, near Surat, a group, mostly Bohras, seized the raja and his minister, killing the latter. At nearby Surat several Hindus were killed. The Bombay Cavalry and Bombay Infantry were requisitioned and several hundred rioters were sequentially killed. A further major communal outbreak in which twenty-one were at least killed occurred at Bareilly in 1816. After this had been put down, a hartal by both communities followed against the imposition of a house tax for maintaining the municipal police, which was realized with some harshness by the latter. A Mufti then took up the case of the affected people. The new cause of the disturbance, after the hartal had been observed for two weeks, was the injury allegedly inflicted on a woman by the police while collecting the tax. In an attack that ensued on the Treasury, some rioters were killed in firing by the military treasury guard, and the Mufti himself received a slight injury. From a hartal by both communities, according to R.C. Majumdar, the issue now became the defence of Islam. Numbers of armed Muslims from Pilibhit, Shahjahanpur and Rampur rushed to the Mufti. Estimates vary from 5,000 to 15,000, armed with matchlocks and swords. On 21 April 1816, they murdered the son of William Leycester, the Circuit Judge, and surrounded the local Bengal Infantry detachment. This military force being inadequate, a battalion of Bengal Infantry from

133

Moradabad was rushed to Bareilly. Both Hindu and Muslim troops conducted themselves impartially. After some setbacks, the rioters were overcome at their entrenchment adjacent to a burial ground. More than 300 of them were killed, and a greater number wounded and taken prisoner. In the Bengal Infantry, twenty-one were killed and sixty-two wounded.[22] The Governor-General, Lord Hastings, now felt it necessary to warn the directors in London of 'the possibility of convulsions in the Empire.'

There were communal clashes again, requiring the use of troops at Bareilly in 1837; Bundelkhand in 1826 and 1841; Bhiwandi in 1837; Lucknow in 1843, 1853, and 1856; Allahabad 1852; Moradabad 1853; Bara Banki 1853, and Faizabad (Ayodhya) in 1856.

The difficulties experienced by the British during the war with Nepal (1814-1816) produced disturbances almost throughout India. Thus, unlike the essentially petty earlier Rohilla War of 1774, in 1817-1818 there occurred what the British refer to as the Pindari War. The Pindaris were actually gangs whose numbers had been swollen by the break-up of the Maratha armies after their defeat in 1805. One of the principal Pindaris, Amir Khan, was virtually an independent chief, maintaining a regular army and seizing much of Holkar's territory after Yeshwant Rao's insanity and death. There were also lesser chiefs like Sheikh Dulla and Kitu, but irrespective of the names of the lesser leaders, Pindari bands roamed Rajputana, Malwa, the territories of the Nizam, the Peshwa, the Bhonsle, Oudh and the Company. Lord Hastings felt the restoration of law and order in Central India was necessary, as it was in chaos. In this he was facilitated by being both Governor-General and Commander-in-Chief, like Lord Cornwallis earlier. Dealing with these fast moving gangs, which dispersed on the approach of a regular military corps and took shelter in Scindia's and Holkar's territories or in fortresses of their own, became a major military operation. Action had eventually been precipitated by large Pindari incursions occurring in Guntur and Ganjam districts. According to Penderel Moon, several hundred villages were plundered, young girls carried off, and burning ashes smeared on the faces of those believed to be concealing their wealth. Many thus committed suicide. As a prelude to the operation in 1817, the Nawab of Bhopal was taken under British protection in 1816. An enveloping movement was launched by 120,000 regular troops to trap 30,000 Pindaris. The northern pincer was under the personal command of Hastings, and the southern under Sir Thomas Hislop, Commander-in-Chief at Madras. Amir Khan at this juncture agreed to become a territorial ruler, and on 9 November 1817 was made the Nawab of Tonk; he agreed to disband his army. Operations were conducted against the others who were defeated, except Sheikh Dulla who escaped but was later killed in 1828.

Also serious in extent was a disturbance in Cuttack in 1817[23] The land revenue had been fixed at too high a level, and the price of salt, the Company's monopoly, had also been increased. The new judicial arrangements introduced were incomprehensible to the poor. The extortions of the subordinate officials inducted from Bengal provoked a protest led by Jagabandhu Mahapatra, the former commander of the army of the local Raja of Khurda. The Collector's office at Khurda was burnt down and Puri plundered; over one hundred police and others were killed, compelling the Collector and his Treasury Guard of Indian troops to withdraw to Cuttack where martial law had to be declared. Order was restored with the arrival of Bengal Infantry reinforcements at the request of the civil authorities. Jagabandhu eventually surrendered in 1825, and was allowed to reside at Cuttack with a pension.

Simultaneously, the landholders in the district of Aligarh were also a recurrent problem to the British. The zamindars converted their residences into fortresses of much strength, and in 1814 regular troops had been first used against them as they were then allegedly harbouring gangs of Mewati marauders. By 1817, the most formidable zamindar was Daya Ram of Hathras. His fort had walls of great height and thickness with guns on top; it was surrounded by a deep ditch. The garrison was about 8,000, of which 3,500 were horsed[24]. Daya Ram objected to police arresting an alleged murderer in his zamindari without his permission, and had then apparently detained the District Magistrate when he came to protest. He was issued a notice to disband his forces and demolish his fortress, but before he had replied, a whole Bengal Army Division was sent against him. He resisted from 12 February to 2 April 1817. Daya Ram's fort was considered to be a 'second Bharatpur,' according to James Mill, and there was the 'most powerful assemblage of artillery hitherto witnessed in India.' Forty-two mortars and three gun batteries went into action against him. Daya Ram fought stubbornly but his defences were eventually breached.

After the Sanyasi Rebellion, the next ostensibly anti-British religious movement in Bengal was the Faraidi (or Ferazi) reform movement, which was founded by Haji Shariat-ullah in 1804. From religious reformation, he turned towards political aims, and declared the country to be "Dar-ul-Harb", where a true Muslim could not live. His son, Dudhu Mian, was even more politically inclined, appointing "Khalifas". There was the feeling that the real aim of the movement now was the restoration of the Muslim power[25]. Dudhu Mian became a terror for nearly two decades to the zamindars and indigo planters, and troops had to be deployed on account of his group's acts of lawlessness, culminating in a major riot in 1838. The Faraidi movement, in its way, was the precursor in Bengal of the Wahabi movement, initiated in India by Saiyid Ahmad at Rai Bareilly in 1820-1821, but which also spread all over India. Initially he preached religious reform, like the Wahabis in Southern Arabia, but gradually his movement took a political turn. A crusade was invoked against the British, and military training imparted. (He was a former Pindari.) For reasons of security, the headquarters of the movement, the Hindustani Mujahidin, was moved to Sittana, near Malakand, on the North-West Frontier. There, in 1827, he declared war against the Sikh government, but was killed in a pitched battle a few years later. The movement, however, continued and created communal disturbances and alarm in Bengal, particularly from 1830 onwards. Three thousand to 4,000 strong, under one Titu Mian or Mir Nasir Ali, committed violent outrages in three districts, and overwhelmed the militia deployed against them, most of which perished, only having blank ammunition. At the request of the civil authorities, a Bengal Infantry contingent was then called in, a fierce battle fought in 1831, and Titu and one hundred others were killed.

After the reverse at Ramu in 1824 in the First Anglo-Burmese War, disaffection manifested itself in all the districts of the Upper

Provinces, and even as far away as Kutch. Mill recorded: 'The eager credulity with which the inhabitants of the British provinces received every rumour of discomfiture...showed how little sympathy unites the subject and the sovereign.' In the Gujar rising alone, in 1824, near Roorkee, over 200 were killed. Then, in Bengal, in 1833, another religious sect, the Pagla Panthi, led by one Tipu, who had given himself royal powers, started an insurrection. Founded by a Pathan, Karam Shah, in 1775 in northern Mymensingh district, Tipu was his second son. In 1825, he indulged in plunder and rapine and gave the movement a political bent. By 1833 he had a following of over 3,000. A large-scale military operation had to be launched against him at the request of the civil authorities.

Separately, in 1825 Bengal Army troops had to be used at Bharatpur in a dispute over succession. The Raja died in February having passed the succession onto his six-year-old son with the approval of David Ochterlony, then the British Resident at Delhi. The young Raja's mother acted as regent, and her brother as the young Raja's guardian. In March 1825, Durjan Sal, the late Raja's nephew, killed the guardian, imprisoned the regent, and began ruling notionally in the young Raja's name, but, in effect, in his own name. The late Raja had had a premonition of this when he had asked Ochterlony to ensure his son's succession. Ochterlony was determined that his word to the late Raja be honoured, if necessary by military force. He was, however, over-ruled by the new Governor-General, William Amherst. Ochterlony resigned in protest at the dishonouring of a British commitment given by him to the late Raja (and died of a broken heart shortly after at Meerut). The new Resident at Delhi, Charles Metcalfe, was eventually able to prevail on Amherst that Ochterlony had been right, necessitating now a major military operation by 27,000 troops under the Commander-in-Chief, Lord Combermere, during December-January, for, in the intervening months, Durjan Sal had augmented the defences of Bharatpur. Lord Lake had failed to take Bharatpur in 1805 in the Anglo-Maratha War, after suffering 31,000 killed and wounded. Durjan Sal now claimed that the augmented defences, like the Fatehburj, had been built with the bones of the British-Indian force killed in 1805. Combermere was in no hurry, as there was no war or threat elsewhere to engage him. Bharatpur fell after a siege of over two months, and the succession dispute was resolved. Ten months earlier, Ochterlony would have ensured the rightful succession with a fraction of the number of troops required ten months later had Amherst not dithered. Without going into the details of the siege, one facet needs mentioning in this narrative. The 2nd/15th Bengal Infantry had brought back their riddled colours from Bharatpur in 1805. Though they had planted the colours on top of the ramparts in the fourth assault, they could not be reinforced, and had had to make their way down again with the now tattered colours. It had then been recorded that Lake had been 'blasted out of the headlines to the footnotes....' After 1805, when new colours were presented to the battalion to replace the riddled ones, orders were issued for the old tattered colours to be burnt. They were, however, found missing. The same battalion was part of the successful assault force in 1826. When the new colours were unfurled on the ramparts of Bharatpur, pieces of the old colours were found tied to the new ones. This had been done by the descendants of the men killed and wounded in 1805. Where the pieces were so flimsy and could not be attached to the new colours in 1826, the injunction of the elders was for their descendants to carry them on their persons to the top of the self-same ramparts the elders had been ordered to withdraw from in 1805. In another succession dispute in Gwalior in 1843, forces were launched both from the north and the south, actions taking place at Maharajpur and Panniar. Here again the maharaja was a minor. An ex-minister had deposed the regent. The northern force was 7,000 strong, under Hugh Gough, the Commander-in-Chief, accompanied by Lord Edward Ellenborough. The ex-minister, Dada Khasgiwala, withdrew. Thereafter, the Gwalior Army had to be dealt with.

Reverting chronologically to the Wahabis, even after Saiyid Ahmad's death the movement continued at Sittana, obtaining money and adherents from all over India. In 1839, at the time of the First Anglo-Afghan War, Moobarz-ud-Daula, the brother of the late Nizam, formed a Wahabi conspiracy to overthrow the then Nizam, as also the British. Socially and economically the Wahabis were on the side of the peasantry. They were well-knit drawing recruits from the whole country, from Dacca to Peshawar. From 1850 a jihad was declared against the British, and during the next seven years, sixteen expeditions, aggregating 33,000 troops, were sent out against Sittana and other adjacent areas, at the request of the civil authorities at Peshawar, as, in some cases, the Wahabis had enlisted the sympathy of some of the Frontier tribes. The Wahabi headquarters generally kept aloof from the 1857 Uprising, presumably favouring purely Islamic movements.[26] Some individual Wahabis did join the uprising at Poona and Belgaum, Patna and Delhi, the latter publishing a fatwa against the British, but, numerically, their contribution to the 1857 movement was marginal. A few years after 1858, they resumed their operations from Sittana against the British, necessitating further expeditions.

At the end of 1828, after the Treaty of Yandabo had been concluded with the Burmese in 1826, whereby Assam was now British, a rebellion under Gadhadhar Singh, an Ahom prince, had to be put down by using troops. The old Ahom ruling dynasty had expected to be reinstated, after the eviction of the Burmese. Gadhadhar Singh and his supporters were thereafter imprisoned. In 1830 there was a second rebellion in Assam, which was crushed, again by using troops, while, simultaneously, insurrections by the Khasi and Singpho tribes were also being put down. This time the Assamese had set up Kumar Rupchand as their Raja. Two of their ringleaders were, on this occasion, hanged, and Kumar Rupchand and three others sentenced to fourteen years' imprisonment in Bengal, and all their property confiscated. The Khasi insurrection, led by Raja Tirat Singh, had started with two British lieutenants and one official being killed in 1829, and took some years of military operations before Tirat Singh surrendered in 1833, on the assurance that his life would be spared. He died a state prisoner at Dacca in 1841.[27] There had been earlier Khasi insurrections in 1783, 1787-1789, 1795 and 1825. Each time hundreds were killed, the troops also suffering many casualties. Another insurrection of Singphos occurred at Sadiya in 1839. Colonel Adam White, the Political Agent, was killed and eight other officials were killed or wounded. Then, in 1849, the Nagas rose, necessitating further operations.

Meanwhile, in South India in 1834, the Raja of Coorg (now Kodagu) had begun indulging in insane bouts of murder, putting to death his relatives, his ministers, his officials and his chieftains. After the defeat of Tipu, the Raja of Coorg had accepted the British as his suzerain. Some people now approached the British for his deposition, but it was found that he had killed off every possible heir or relative who could have succeeded him. Four divisions of the Madras and Bombay Armies were deployed against him. After some fighting, he surrendered and retired to Benares on a pension[28]. A rising in Delhi in 1835 followed the murder of William Fraser, the British Political Agent at Delhi. The murder was more for personal revenge than political reasons, but nevertheless developed political undertones, necessitating the deployment of troops against a local nawab. Fraser had decreed in favour of the nawab's half-brother in a property dispute. The Nawab Shamsuddin had Fraser assassinated. The Nawab and the assassin were later hanged; the Nawab became a martyr for the Muslims of Delhi and his tomb a place of pilgrimage. Fraser's grave was sequentially desecrated in 1857 [29].

When Nasir-ud-din Haidar, the King of Oudh, died in July 1838, without a recognized male heir, the rightful heir, according to Islamic law, was the deceased's uncle, Mohammed Ali Shah, and Colonel John Low, the British Resident at Lucknow, began the arrangements for placing him on the throne. Meanwhile, the Padsha Begum, the late King's adoptive mother, had begun the enthronement ceremonies of a purported son of Nasir-ud-din, whom the latter had disowned. Low demanded that the Begum withdraw her candidate. After some parleying with the Begum's representatives, the Resident gave her time to surrender. On her refusing to do so, the Company's subsidiary force, from the Bengal Army, blew in the palace gate, and the Bengal Infantry stormed its way in killing or wounding about one hundred of the Begum's supporters. She and her nominee were made prisoners and Mohammed Ali was installed, his protection being ensured by the Company's troops.

By 1838 Lord Auckland was constrained to convene a committee to investigate the state of the Bengal Presidency police, as it was found to be disaffected and still could not be relied upon to deal with communal disturbances, even after the lessons of Benares and Bareilly. The report, submitted on 18 August 1838, emphasized that the individuals of whom the Bengal Presidency Police was composed were influenced by 'the feelings of the populace.' Later, in

April 1848, after the risings of the Bhils in Khandesh (1818-1831), the Kittur Desais near Belgaum (1824-1829), the Ramoosis near Kolhapur (1826-1829), the Gadkaris of Kolhapur (1844), the Sawant Desais (1844-1850 and 1858-1859), and the Kolis in the Konkan and Gujarat (1828-1830 and 1844-1848), Sir George Clerk, the Governor of Bombay, recorded of the Bombay Presidency Police: '...Yet it would seem that whenever anything resembling rebellion does occur in this presidency (as to) speedy detection... the police is lamentably deficient.' Martial law was invoked in most of these risings. Shortly after Ellenborough's arrival as Governor-General in April 1842, when the position in Afghanistan was still critical, there were uprisings in Saugor district and part of Bundelkhand. They were suppressed with the use of troops, and were at first attributed to disaffection due to the effects of the Afghan reverses on Indian opinion. Ellenborough appointed a commission of inquiry under Colonel William Sleeman, who had previously served in the area. Sleeman attributed the uprisings to maladministration and reported: 'The European officers no longer show that courtesy towards the middle and higher classes, and that kindness towards the humble, which characterized the officers of the day; and the native officials rather imitate, or take advantage of, this. The outbreak in Saugor originated in the insolence of office.'[30]

Thereafter, Ellenborough, in an endeavour to extirpate corruption, favoured military men for civil departments. Kaye then commented, that the civil service, 'fattened upon the golden eggs and scattered feathers only for the military.' Another reason that influenced Ellenborough in proposing military men was his desire to have public servants who were friendly towards Indians. He believed that military officers, who had shared hardships and dangers with Indian soldiers, had 'acquired a kindly disposition towards the natives,' whereas the 'civil servants in the Cutcherry (Court House) only see the worst part of native character.'[31] In mockery, the Governor-General used to call civil officials, 'Cutcherry Hussars', because many of them, though not soldiers, kept moustaches.

In 1849, the Moplahs or Mapillas, partly of Arab descent, desecrated the Hindu temple at Manjeri in Malabar, the same temple they had burnt down in 1774 in Tipu's reign. In 1774, they had to be defeated by a large body of Tipu's troops. Troops had again to be deployed against them. The years between 1836 and 1857 were the peak years of the Moplah explosions—no fewer than twenty-two outbreaks, apart from abortive attempts; in all, thirty-eight occurrences in the period. In 1855 the Collector of Malabar, Henry Connolly, was killed while reading on the veranda to his wife on a Sunday. (One brother had been earlier treacherously killed by the Amir at Bokhara in 1841, and two in the First Anglo-Afghan War.) The culprits were finally rounded up. (The worst outbreak of Moplah violence was yet to occur, in 1921.) About this time, 1855-56, the Santhal uprising was continuing in Bengal. Raniganj was just saved, by troops being moved by rail from Barrackpore to Raniganj. The disturbance was put down after several months of military operations, many being killed and several being executed. An inquiry revealed that they had been oppressed by the Bengal police and revenue officials, and harrassed by landlords and moneylenders. Representations to deputy commissioners and commissioners had elicited the advice that they should seek redress in the civil courts. The Santhals killed the Indian officials first, and then the British, when the latter sought to protect the former. Similar disturbances, necessitating the use of troops, had taken place in 1831-32 in parts of Bihar and Orissa due to the protracted discontent of the tribes, Kols, Dangas and Chuars, living in their forested areas, some under Company rule, some under local Rajput chiefs who were tributaries of the Company. One cause of disaffection was the influx of settlers from Bengal and Bihar who, being better agriculturists, ousted the tribals from the land with the encouragement of the local chiefs, as they were able to pay higher rents. The disturbed districts had to be handed over to the military, and a regular campaign had to be conducted. Over one thousand were killed. Some battalions fell back under tribal pressure, and one column was even defeated. In August 1855 the insurgents exceeded 30,000, armed with axes and poisoned arrows. Operations continued till February 1856 when the tribal leaders were arrested.[32] Thereafter use was made of the tribal headmen for police and revenue purposes.

Many Britons in India, like Sir John Shore, who had been Governor-General from 1793 to 1798, felt that a disaster was impending. Shore recorded: 'I have lived long enough among the people of India to witness their sufferings, and to become acquainted in some measure with their feelings...and I am convinced that a crisis is not far distant.'[33] He elaborated: 'The real cause is our own short-sighted policy and cupidity and the consequent extortion and mis-government....'

But as we shall later discern in relation to the disturbances after independence in which troops have been used, that it would be too simplistic to dub all the civil disturbances chronicled in this chapter as products of the British period and British policies. It would also be a mistake to regard the aggregated causes of these disturbances at the time as outweighing many of the benefits of the British connection. Nor would it be correct to assume that there were civil distur-bances only in India at the time and not in adjacent Ceylon, Malacca, and Burma. The Madras and Bengal Armies were employed in Ceylon in 1819 in dealing with civil disturbances there, and the Madras Army in Malacca in 1831-32, and in Burma in 1829-31, 1852, 1853 and 1854 to 1857.

FIVE

The 1857 Uprising And Its Prelude

FROM MAY 1857 onwards, a spontaneous uprising swept across parts of northern India. Referred to by the British as the Indian Mutiny, because it started in the Bengal Army, it should more appropriately be referred to as the Indian Uprising of 1857, as segments of the civil population were also involved. From the point of view of hindsight, the 1857 Uprising, coming as it did a century after Plassey, should not have been a surprise to the British. Perceptive administrators like Henry Lawrence had repeatedly been warning the overambitious Lord Dalhousie, 'in administrative and social reform one of the greatest, in understanding of others' feelings or institutions one of the most deficient of British Viceroys, a great Victorian, energetic, progressive and calamitous,'[1] in the words of H.V.Hodson. It is only surprising that the Bengal Army had not self-destructed earlier.

The poor identification latterly with their troops on the part of some British officers; the senility of many who were seventy years of age, the evangelicalism of others; the inertia of the senior Indian sub-officers on account of the lack of avenues for promotion after over forty and nigh on fifty years' service, conjoined with the discontent among the rank and file due to the varying orders as to the authorization of *batta*, were all portents for those with a modicum of insight. As to evangelicalism, Penderel Moon postulated: 'In England, by the middle of the nineteenth century, it had become almost an article of faith that British rule was a blessing for India— a blessing ordained by Providence, and designed, as some believed, for the express purpose of converting Indians to the Christian faith. This belief proved to be an illusion.'[2] Nevertheless, Palmerston had then pontificated, 'Perhaps it might be our lot to confer on the countless millions of India a higher and holier gift than any mere human knowledge.' Moon added, 'Christian missionaries were, however, less successful in making converts than their Muslim predecessors, and the Mutiny put an end to the idle dream that the people of India would embrace Christianity.'[3]

The system of promoting officers through sheer seniority, along with the extensive denuding of the better officers from regiments for staff and political appointments, and the concomitant induction of less efficient officers with no identification with their men, had so eroded the leadership of the Bengal Army, that a cataclysm was inevitable. The symbiotic relationship of the late eighteenth and early nineteenth centuries between the British and Indians in the Bengal Army had ironically been vitiated by the many victories in past campaigns, for these very victories had engendered an over-bearing arrogance in some of the more recently arrived British, and a feeling of deprivation and anguish among the Indians of the Presidency Armies, particularly the Bengal Army. As the extent of the Company's territory expanded, the Bengal Army was employed on increasingly distant and difficult campaigns in Afghanistan, Sind, and the Punjab, without corresponding improved prospects for the Indian sub-officers or enhanced emoluments for the Indian ranks serving so far from Oudh and Bihar, the main recruitment areas for the Bengal Army. The soldiers of the latter now deemed they were indispensable to the future success of the Company's forces, whereas many of the British officers correspondingly arrogated to themselves an overwhelming intellectual superiority *vis-a-vis* the alleged intrinsic ineptitude of Asians, whether soldiering under them or opposing them. Sequentially, the Bengal Army soldier was chagrined because, whereas the British traders had been made rulers by the Bengal Army in North India, the Indian soldier in that Army remained comparatively unrewarded. Dalhousie had even stopped the free postage facility to his home.

On 27 November 1849, Sir Charles Napier, the Commander-in-Chief, resigning in protest at Dalhousie's withdrawal of certain benefits from the Bengal Army units on the annexation of the Punjab, recorded to the Duke of Wellington: 'Our troops are faithful to a proverb. I have studied Indian troops for nearly eight years constantly as the head of Bengal and Bombay sepoys, and I can see nothing to fear from them except when ill-used, and even then they are less dangerous than British troops would be in similar circumstances.' On his return to Britain, he wrote: 'He (the sepoy) is devoted to us as yet but we take no pains to preserve his attachment. It is no concern of mine... shall be dead before what I foresee will take place but it will take place.'

Henry Lawrence was positively clairvoyant before the 1857 occurrences as to the declining image of the British officers in the eyes of their Indian soldiers, particularly in the Bengal Army, when he, *inter alia*, iterated: 'Strange that after we have conquered all round, we should have lost weight with our own people...the many (British) are usually provided for, but honours and rewards, present and future, are still wanted for the few (Indians)...it behoves us therefore now more than ever to give legitimate rewards and, as far as practical, employment to the energetic few, to that leaven that may serve our Empire or may disturb, nay, even destroy it.'

During the last weeks of his life in Lucknow, after his earlier removal by Dalhousie from the Punjab, for his moral stance, Henry Lawrence witnessed his premonitions becoming reality in 1857, resulting in the loss of his own life from an artillery shell splinter. Events moved too fast for the Indophile Henry Lawrence to do much. The story in Oudh for the British would have been different if he had been moved to Lucknow initially, instead of Coverley Jackson officiating as Commissioner. One of the Company's more perceptive civil servants, F.J. Shore, son of Sir John Shore, devoted two volumes of "Notes on Indian Affairs" to laying bare at considerable length in 1837 the defects of the Company's government, which he recorded had no foundation in the affection of the people, and had 'hitherto been one of the most tyrrannical in practice (however benevolent and philanthropical may have been its professed intentions) that has ever existed.'

The three Presidency Armies, without central direction, had developed different patterns of recruitment. In the Madras and Bombay Armies all castes of troops were mixed together in companies and platoons, whereas the Bengal Army emphasized the higher castes, causing John Jacob to comment in his *Tracts on the Native Army of India:* 'While in Madras and Bombay the troops become half European through their association with the military, in Bengal the officers become half Hindoo, and become so preoccupied with matters of caste and status, that they lose their professional sense of soldiership.'[4] Dalhousie failed to discern the feeling of resentment among the Bengal Army soldiers in the Punjab and Sind, resulting in decisions which only emphasized the anguish of their deprivation, by insisting on only the basic pay for Indian soldiers throughout the Company's Indian territories, and thus doing away with the extra allowance hitherto paid to the Bengal Army soldiers serving in Sind and the Punjab, and the Madras and Bombay Army soldiers serving outside their Presidencies.

Several princely states were treated as having lapsed by Dalhousie. His annexations were later believed by the British themselves to have contributed to the 1857 Uprising. As to the annexation of Satara in 1850, General Sir John Low, earlier Resident at Oudh and Malwa, stated, in 1853, when he was later serving as a member of Dalhousie's Council, 'The confidence of our native allies was a good deal shaken by the annexation of Satara...it is remarkable that every native who ever spoke to me (in 1850) respecting the annexation of Satara asked precisely the same question, "What crime did the late Raja commit that his country should be seized by the Company?"' In Moon's opinion, Apa Sahib, a descendant of Shivaji, had been faithful to the Company. Earlier, his brother, Raja Pratap Singh, though competent, had been deposed as the ruler of Satara by the Bombay Government in 1839 for allegedly trying to spread disaffection amongst the Company's soldiers, despite George Auckland not finding the evidence convincing. Most Indians and many British officials criticized the Bombay Government's decision. Apa Sahib's only omission had been his failure to beget a male heir, though he adopted one on his deathbed. The Satara family sent a legal agent to Britain, who spent several years in London trying to get the State restored. In 1857, he allegedly instigated an uprising in Satara, but it failed. He fled, but a number of people, including one of his sons, as will be recounted later in this chapter, was blown from guns.

In 1853, the Raja of Nagpur, Raghuji Bhonsle, died without a male heir. This did not debar his eldest widow from adopting an heir. Dalhousie deemed Nagpur as lapsed. The only dissenting voice in the Governor-General's Council was that of Low, even though he knew he would be overruled: 'In one respect, the natives of India are exactly like the inhabitants of all parts of the known world; they like their own habits and customs better than those of foreigners.'

Jhansi was also annexed at about the same time, when, towards the end of 1853, the Raja of Jhansi died without a natural heir, adopting a son the day before his death. Dalhousie declared the State as lapsed since there was no natural heir, against the advice of the Deputy Commissioner, and later the Commissioner, arguing that this would benefit the people of Jhansi. In 1857, the people of Jhansi indicated that they did not appreciate the decision. The Raja's widow, Rani Laxmibai, sent a counsel, John Lang to London to fight her case. He did so, convinced of the justice of her cause, as were most British officials in India, but in vain. She became a heroine in 1857-58, 'the bravest and best military leader,' in the words of General Sir Hugh Rose, the opposing commander.

The doctrine of lapse was also applied to titles. Dalhousie abolished their titles when the Nawab of the Carnatic and the Raja of

Tanjore died without natural heirs (they had earlier lost their territories in Wellesley's time, who had also unjustly pensioned off the Nawab of Surat). In Delhi, in 1849, the Emperor Bahadur Shah's heir, Dara Bakht, had died. Dalhousie urged that the Mughal line should be terminated, as the next in line had not been born when Bahadur Shah had ceased to rule, and that the Red Fort should be vacated by his family on the Emperor's death. The directors approved the discontinuance of the title on the Emperor's death, Dalhousie separately getting the heir next in line to agree to vacate the Red Fort when his father died. In 1856 this heir, Fakhir-ud-din, also died.

Baji Rao II, the last Peshwa, had lived on an annual pension of eight lakh rupees from the British for thirty years at Bithur, near Cawnpore (Kanpur). He died in 1854 without a male heir, but had adopted a boy named Dhondu Pant, the future Nana Sahib. The latter petitioned that the pension should be paid to him, but Dalhousie did not agree, as it had already been paid for thirty years. The jagir of Bithur was, however, continued. The Nana sent Dr Azimullah Khan to London to plead his case, but also in vain. The latter was three years abroad, visiting the Crimean war front and the siege of Sebastopol, and was impressed by the Russians, causing Henry Lawrence to exclaim, 'Many sensible natives of India think every Russian is eight feet high, and that Bombay and Calcutta are threatened by a Russian fleet, while an army is coming down the Khyber. Many Englishmen are hardly less absurd.' In fact, the latter were more so as to the Russian bogey, even well into the twentieth century.

The annexation of Oudh in 1856 was, according to H.V. Hodson, 'A sickening blow to Muslim pride throughout India, and one of the chief proximate causes of the war known in Britain as the Indian Mutiny.'[5] Done on the specious plea of maladministration, it exacerbated the prevailing resentment. The rulers of Oudh had been the most faithful allies of the British, to abrogate Wajid Ali Shah's sovereignty shocked all his subjects. This annexation aggravated the discontent in the Bengal Army, both because it was illegal, and because it ended the privilege by which the Company's soldiers from Oudh could submit petitions for legal redress through the British Resident. In effect, the Company's soldiers caused most of the Resident's work, for which purpose there was a full-time Assistant Resident. The other two Presidency Armies also had some soldiers from Oudh who had offered themselves there for enrolment, Bombay more than Madras. Up to 1857, while personnel from Oudh made up two-thirds of the Bengal Army, one in ten of Oudh's Brahmins and Rajputs served as soldiers elsewhere in the subcontinent. These Oudh men in the Company's service, and after the 1840s those who had been deputed from the Company's armies to the service of the protected princes, some 60,000 in all, could submit petitions, usually on land disputes, to the Resident. About one hundred such petitions were received every month. This system also resulted in abuses. The soldiers used the threat of an appeal to the Resident to frighten their opponents, and, on occasion, gave the use of their names to relatives and neighbours. Annexation turned the Resident into a Chief Commissioner, and the population of Oudh became equal subjects of the Company. The Company's Oudh soldiers were no longer a privileged group. This deprivation of their seeming rights induced frustration directed at the British for, before annexation, their petitions had received the highest attention. Dalhousie had taken the loyalty of the Oudh soldier for granted.

W.H. Sleeman, the Resident before annexation, and one of the few like Henry Lawrence, who deprecated the policy of annexation, expressed his views categorically: 'The system of annexing and absorbing native states—so popular with our Indian services— might some day render us too visibly dependent on our native army...The native states I consider to be breakwaters, and, when they are all swept away, we shall be left to the mercy of our native army, which may not be always sufficiently under our control.' Separately, the army of 80,000 which the King of Oudh maintained, in addition to the subsidiary force for which he paid the Company, was often itself on the verge of mutiny, or actually mutinying, on account of non-payment of their arrears. About half of these personnel were never present and their pay was the perquisite of the commanding officers, some of whom were British on deputation. An instance of a mutiny, for arrears of pay, in the King of Oudh's service was that of Captain Barlow's regiment at Faizabad in 1853. Barlow spent more time at the races in Cawnpore than in his regiment. Sleeman recommended, not annexation, but that the British should assume the administration, as trustees for the Oudh royal family and its people, spending the entire revenues for their benefit. He iterated that annexation would 'accelerate the crisis which the doctrine of the absorbing school must sooner or later bring upon us.'

In 1854, Sleeman proceeded on leave to Britain due to ill-health, and died during the voyage. Dalhousie said he was not recommending annexation, but it was annexation that was approved. 'I have received orders to do Oude,' wrote Dalhousie. *Punch* countered at the time:

'*Peccavi. I've Scinde.*'
Cried Lord Ellen so proud.
Dalhousie, more modest, said,
'*Vovi, I've Oude.*'

(I have vowed.)

He now stated, 'So our gracious Queen had five million more subjects and 1,300,000 pounds more revenue than she had yesterday.'[6] Thus, the King of Oudh was also pensioned off. Wajid Ali Shah and some of his family members were sent to Calcutta. His 60,000 subjects in the Company's and subsidiary forces could not understand why their King had been removed, who had been faithful to the British. He had not been a cruel king, like some in Europe, but only harmlessly sybaritic. They thought the Company had taken over Oudh solely for gain. Their perplexity continued till the 1857 Uprising.

Ironically, the British, within a few months, had created a situation the opposite of what they had envisaged. Many thousands, nearly all related to the men in the Bengal Army, lost their service as a result of the disbandment of the old royal army of 80,000, as also the disbandment of the armed guards of the Oudh taluqdars. The British accommodated 15,000 in the newly-raised Oudh Irregular Force and Military Police. The rest were released with a gratuity equal to a few months' pay. Most carried their resentment to their villages, but many remained agitated in Lucknow. John Pemble records that as early as 'May 1856, the Commissioner Baraich reported that discharged soldiers from Lucknow were abroad, spreading rumours to the effect that the deposed monarch was to be restored which unsettled men's minds, prevented institutions from taking root, and inspired doubts about the permanency of British rule.'[7] A year later these were concretized in the uprising of the units of the Bengal Army, who were joined in Oudh by the disaffected discharged soldiers of the former King, as well as by the Oudh Irregular Force raised from those who had been retained.

Dalhousie's successor was Lord Charles Canning, later to be satirically dubbed by the British in India as "Clemency" Canning for his role in 1857-58. In accepting the post of Governor-General, he had no conception of any conflagration that may occur, but in a speech at a banquet in August 1855, given before his departure, he made a perceptive generalized observation: 'We must not forget that in the sky of India, serene as it is, a cloud may arise, at first no bigger than a man's hand, but which growing bigger and bigger may at last threaten to overwhelm us with ruin.' His immediate problem on arrival in March 1856 was the administration of Oudh. James Outram, the Chief Commissioner immediately after Sleeman, also had had a breakdown in health, and had to proceed to Britain on leave, Coverley Jackson, one of the Commissioners, had been asked by Calcutta to officiate temporarily. An unsympathetic person, he quarrelled with his colleagues. He delayed payments to the discharged Oudh soldiers, treated the ex-King's complaints with scant courtesy, appropriated a palace meant for the begums, made revenue assessments that were too heavy, and dealt harshly with those who represented. By the end of 1856, Oudh, the homeland of so many of the Company's soldiers, was thoroughly discontented. In January 1857, Jackson was replaced by Henry Lawrence, but by then it was too late; the obituary of this Bengal Artillery officer who was killed during the siege of Lucknow was apt, 'It was not so much what he did, as what he was.'

The faithfulness of the Company's Indian troops prior to 1857 had been an established fact. Offered, on many occasions, inducements to defect, whether by the French, Hyder Ali, Tipu Sultan, the Marathas, or the Sikhs, the Indian soldiers had, in the main, stood firmly by the English Company. However, by now the fidelity of the Company's troops was taken for granted. Major General Sir Thomas Munro, Governor of Madras 1820-27, had, at that time itself, felt that once Indian troops had 'lost their present high respect for their officers and the European character...they will rise against us.' These doubts had increased since the disaster of the First Anglo-Afghan War, which had shaken the troops' confidence in British officers and soldiers. In the initial battles of the Anglo-Sikh wars, the Bengal Army regiments thus had not shown much combat spirit, and, as it so happened, they were the regiments that were disaffected in 1857. After the First Anglo-Afghan War and the two Anglo-Sikh wars, dissatisfaction with the state of the Bengal Army was expressed often. Dalhousie told the President of the Board of Control that the discipline of the three Presidency Armies, officers and men, was virtually non-existent, particularly that of the Bengal Army. Of the incompetent officers in the Bengal Army, Dalhousie had written in 1851: 'Commanding officers are inefficient, brigadiers are no better; divisional commanders are worse than either, because older and more done; and on top of all they send out commanders-in-chief seventy years old.'

General William Gomm, soldiering in his seventieth year, could not overlook the claims of others, also seventy years old. Dalhousie abolished the ineffective Military Board, three of its five members being appointed on the basis of being the longest surviving officers in the Bengal Army, and consequently mentally incompetent due to senility. This board had considerable responsibilities, all mismanaged—the Commissariat, Ordnance, Stud Farms and Public Works. The board was broken up, and a military officer placed at the head of each department—a Commissary General, an Inspector General of Ordnance, and a Superintendent of Studs. A separate Department of Public Works, staffed by officers of the Corps of Engineers and Artillery, was set up, civil engineers were now taken in. Dalhousie also abolished other boards like the Medical Board replacing these boards with Directors-General. The Medical Board, for instance, had consisted of the three longest surviving medical officers. Dalhousie also began moving the important headquarters of the Bengal Army away from Calcutta to northern India. A case in point was the headquarters of the Bengal Artillery being moved from Dum Dum to Meerut. It was, however, impossible for Dalhousie to get consistent advice from a commander-in-chief. On the one hand he had had the peripatetic Charles Napier, and on the other the antediluvian William Gomm.

The officering of the Presidency Armies was also the subject of controversy at the time. In the early days, an Indian regiment had only three European officers, but they were all selected. There had also been scope for Indians to be "native commandants". Though, in irregular regiments, the scale of having three European officers continued, in regular regiments the establishment of European officers progressively increased over the years. The scope for Indian officers correspondingly decreased. Twenty years before 1857, Lord William Bentinck was right when he reiterated that the Presidency Armies had never been better than when there were only three European officers to a regular regiment, as was still the case in the irregular regiments. 'The connection between European and native officers was much closer, their dependence on each other greater, a more cordial intimacy existed between all ranks.' Two decades after Bentinck, but before 1857, John Jacob and Henry Lawrence were both proponents of the irregular system, the latter recording: 'We ought either to disband our army, or open our posts of honour and emolument to its aspiring members. We act contrary to common sense and in neglect of the lessons of history, in considering that the present system can lead to anything but a convulsion. We are lucky in its having lasted so long.' As the majority took a different view, the system, latterly current, of twenty-two European officers in a regiment continued.

Seniority also had become the bane of the service not only among Europeans, but also among Indians. Promotion by seniority for the latter was, however, deemed by many Britons to be the main means of ensuring Indian contentment. All allegedly had the scope of rising to the rank of jemadar as platoon commanders (today's designation, naib subedar), if they lived long enough and served for about forty years. Sequentially Henry Lawrence, James Outram and John Jacob, all, similarly, postulated before 1857 that the rank of subedar (company seconds-in-command) was now filled with 'poor old wretches, feeble in body and imbecile in mind,' with no influence in their regiments. This was more pronounced in the Bengal Army which largely mutinied, and less so in the Madras and Bombay Armies, where promotion on merit was possible. The European officers were not much better. The better officers had left for civil or political appointments where greater scope existed, compared to the then stultifying regimental environment. Consequently, some regimental commanders were ineffective elderly men in their sixties, many having been at regimental duty continuously for over thirty years, holding their appointments by sheer seniority rather than any merit. Many officers did not even know the names of the men in their companies, and there was the general complaint that, compared to the previous century, officers had little contact with their Indian soldiers.

Captain Albert Hervey of the Madras Army recorded, in 1850: 'I regret very much to say that it is too often the case that...young officers on first commencing their military career talk about those "horrible black nigger sepoys"...they look down on them as brute beasts....This is why we hear of misunderstandings, mutinies, courts martial....Treat the sepoys well—and they will die for you. But abuse them and they are very devils.'[8] Sleeman, while still the Resident, had recorded of the Bengal Army recruited largely from Oudh, 'The

Army think we want them more than they want us.' Earlier, a Russian observer had written of the Indian soldiers serving the British, that they were 'like cats, more attached to the house than the master.' As to the class composition of the Bengal Army, many now favoured class regiments (Gurkhas, Sikhs), some favoured class-company regiments (Sikhs, Dogras, Punjabi Mussalmans). Dalhousie had urged in 1856 that the number of Punjabis and Gurkhas in the Bengal Army should be increased at the expense of the original classes, arguing, 'We must be strong, not against the enemy only, but against our population, and even against possible contingencies connected with our native army.' Dalhousie's proposal must have become known to those from Oudh, thus adding to their apprehensions.

One major change in the Bengal Army, that Dalhousie approved but left for Canning to issue the order on, was the introduction of a general service liability including for overseas service, as in the Madras and Bombay Armies. Apart from six general service regiments in the Bengal Army, the other sixty-eight regiments consequently claimed exemption from serving across the "Kalapani", apart from volunteering when asked to do so, in 1808 for Macao, in 1811 for Java, and even in 1857-58 for China. A Bombay Army company had merely been detailed to proceed to Macao as early as 1785-86 without the necessity of asking for volunteers, as had been the Madras Army expedition to Manila in 1762. Personnel from Oudh and the contiguous areas, serving in the Madras and Bombay Armies, already undertook to serve overseas. Canning issued the order in July 1856 that any new recruit in the Bengal Army had to agree to serve overseas, as the requirement from the Bengal Army for garrisoning Burma emphasized the urgency, in view of the burden borne by the Madras Army for the past few decades. Canning had not expected any resentment, as no right of the existing personnel was being withdrawn. This was not to be, as service in the Bengal Army had become an extended family affair—sons, brothers, nephews, cousins, all serving in the same company, let alone regiment; often as many as eight from the same family. Canning had also been briefed to effect a reduction in the Bengal Army, which was considered bloated. According to Moon, he had therefore, intended, 'at a suitable occasion to make the general service liability universal, discharging those who did not opt for it, thereby effecting the reduction sought by the directors.'

Thus, as Michael Edwardes puts it: 'The causes of the Mutiny were complex. From English history they would seem to be little more than the affair of the greased cartridges. But these were merely a blast of wind to a fire ignited long before, and which was to burn its way to the twentieth century.'[9]

At the time the army in India was as follows:

- Bengal Army   137,500   Local contingents 40,000
- Madras Army   49,000   Military police   39,000
- Bombay Army   48,000

- Total Indian   313,500   Total British   38,000

As to whether there was any prior plan, Sir Syed Ahmed Khan recorded in 1860, 'The manner in which the rebellion spread, first here, then there, now breaking out in this place, and now in that, is alone good proof that there existed no widespread conspiracy.'[10] As outlined, the causes were deep-seated, and a situation existed where any incident in 1857 could create a convergence, and set off a conflagration among the same placid people, whom Warren Hastings in 1813 had described to one of his successors, the Marquess of Hastings as: 'Our Indian subjects...are as exempt from the worst propensities of human nature as any people on the face of the earth, ourselves not excepted. They are gentle, benevolent, more susceptible of gratitude for kindness shown them than prompt to vengeance for wrongs sustained, abhorrent of bloodshed, faithful and affectionate in service, and submissive to legal authority.'

The uprising of 1857, in effect, began in February and March in Berhampore and Barrackpore. Soldiers refused to handle the cartridges issued for use with the new Enfield rifle. The feeling initially current was that animal substances had been used to grease them. Soon, all cartridges, including those that had been in use for years, became suspect. The events at these places are linked. In February, the 19th Bengal Infantry was at Berhampore, and the 34th at Barrackpore. As we have seen earlier, the latter had been disbanded in 1844 after two alleged mutinies, one at Peshawar in 1842 when ordered to advance through the Khyber, and one in the Punjab in 1843 when ordered to proceed to Sind. Two years later a new regiment was raised, to fill a need, with the same number. The headquarters and seven companies of the 34th were at Barrackpore, and three at Chittagong. A company of the 34th arrived on escort duty at Berhampore, bringing details of the supposed attempt to destroy the soldiers' caste by the use of cartridges greased with beef tallow thereby converting them to Christianity. The commanding officer of the 19th, Lieutenant Colonel M.W.Mitchell, was an ardent evangelical, and considered it his duty to try to convert his regiment by regular Sunday sermons. In this he had not succeeded. Lady Canning recorded he was 'terribly given to preach,' and Canning later said Mitchell was 'not fit to be trusted with a regiment.' On 26 February he ordered a parade for the following day for a firing exercise with blank ammunition, the percussion caps being issued on 26 February for the 27th. The soldiers refused to accept them in the fear that the next day's cartridges would be polluted. Mitchell called in the 11th Irregular Cavalry against his regiment, and threatened to send it to Burma or China. Eventually, Mitchell withdrew the cavalry, and his regiment returned to the lines. Next morning matters were back to normal with the regiment, but Fort William had already decided to disarm it near Barrackpore, with a British regiment present—which had to be brought from Burma—and then to disband it. The 19th reached on 30 March, and was apparently advised by the 34th to kill the British officers. This the 19th refused to do, and was disbanded with due ceremony, uniforms being allowed to be retained.

On 29 March, however, the first attack on a British officer in 1857 had already occurred in the 34th. Sepoy Mangal Pandey, one of the quarter-guard, called upon his unit to rise in rebellion. The adjutant and sergeant-major attempted to disarm him, but he severely wounded both. One soldier grappled with him, but the others from the guard struck the two wounded British, and one fired at them. After a court-martial, Mangal Pandey was hanged. His name thereafter became a generic one for the British for all the rebels of 1857-58—they were called "Pandies". (In 1957 a memorial was erected to Sepoy Mangal Pandey at Barrackpore and in the former Dalhousie Square, Calcutta.) The 34th, less the Chittagong companies, was disbanded. At the time, the class structure of the ten companies of the 34th was: 335 Brahmins, 237 Rajputs, 231 Hindus of other castes, 200 Muslims, seventy-four Sikhs, and twelve Eurasian drummers. The men were stripped of their uniforms and their medals, and some, in due course, joined the Nana Sahib. Jemadar Ishwari Pershad, the guard commander, was also hanged. As it so happened, his execution had been just read out at a parade in the then cantonment in north Delhi, a murmur running through all Indian ranks, while the 3rd Bengal Cavalry from Meerut was crossing the boat-bridge into Delhi.

Before one moves on to the events at Meerut, the fate of the three companies of the 34th at Chittagong can be narrated. They first, apparently, forwarded a memorandum that disapproved of Mangal Pandey's action, but in November they plundered the treasury, loaded three elephants, released the prisoners from the jail, and marched off into Tripura. The Raja of Tripura stopped them; they then moved off towards Manipur. They were pursued by the Sylhet Light Infantry of the Bengal Army, and those who survived entered Manipur, where a discontented Manipur prince joined them with his followers. They were again attacked and defeated by the Sylhet Light Infantry. By now 206 had been killed, the rest mostly perished in the jungles. Some, however, reappeared in a subsequent rising in Manipur in 1890; one as a Manipur general, when some British civil and military officials were assassinated.

In the early part of 1857, the 36th Bengal Infantry was stationed at Jullundur (now Jalandhar), but had a detachment at Ambala to receive instruction on the new cartridge at the Musketry Depot. When a detachment of the 36th was escorting the Commander-in-Chief, General George Anson, to Simla, two non-commissioned officers from the depot detachment went to greet their friends in the escort. A subedar treated them as outcastes for having handled the new cartridges, though they had not yet done so. They were denied the use of the escort's hookahs or water from the escort's *lotas*. The depot commander appreciated the gravity of the situation, and begged that official investigations be immediately made. The seriousness was to a great extent discounted. No official investigation was made at Ambala, only instruction being suspended till Anson's decision was made known. Kaye said of Anson in *A History of the Sepoy War*, that, going on seventy, he had had two advantages over others for selection as Commander-in-Chief; he could at least both hear and see. On 16 April, his decision was made known—the soldiers were to use the suspect cartridges. Incendiary fires followed nightly at Ambala. (The 36th mutinied at Jullundur on 7 June.)

The trouble spread to Meerut and Lucknow by the last week of April. At Lucknow the regimental doctor's quarters of the 48th Bengal Infantry were burnt, as there was a grievance that the Indian soldiers were being polluted by the doctor. (He had allegedly drunk directly from a bottle of medicine, and then dispensed the same medicine to the troops.) On 2 May, a battalion of Oudh Irregular Infantry, at Lucknow refused to use the newly-issued ammunition. The following day, Henry Lawrence discreetly disarmed them, then sought to restore confidence by restricting punishments to a few discharges, announcing some promotions, and thereafter rearming about 200 personnel, but soon the news from Meerut and Delhi came in. Militarily, there possibly would have been no "Indian Mutiny" if Colonel G.M. Carmichael Smyth had not held the unnecessary parade at Meerut, and if either Major General William Hewett or Brigadier General Archdale Wilson had ordered the immediate pursuit of the sowars of the 3rd Bengal Cavalry who were heading for Delhi. John Lawrence said of these and similar British commanders, 'I do assure you that some of our commanders are worse enemies than the mutineers themselves.'

As to the actual events at Meerut, Carmichael Smyth is said to have been, according to the official records, 'a hard and unpopular officer',[11] never having gained the confidence of either the officers or the men. Similar personality traits recurrently occur in commanding officers in many of the subsequent mutinies or major disciplinary cases. He was quick in detecting faults, and lacking in balance. Well aware of the disaffection on this issue in the Bengal Army, even though he had just returned from leave, but presumably with the ill-conceived aim of testing his regiment, he ordered a parade of ninety skirmishers on 24 April, despite the advice of his adjutant. The alleged purpose was instruction in the modification of the loading drill, by which the end of the cartridge was to be torn off instead of bitten off. Eighty-five refused to touch the cartridges offered to them, as all cartridges were by now suspect, though it was urged at a subsequent court of inquiry that they were similar to those previously used. Hewett, the General Officer Commanding of the Meerut Division, told Carmichael Smyth that he would rather the latter had done nothing at the time, but could not now avoid convening a court of inquiry under pressure from Carmichael Smyth and others. The proceedings were submitted to Anson at Simla who directed that the eighty-five be tried by a court-martial. The court sentenced all to ten years' penal servitude, reduced in eleven cases to five years by Hewett. On 9 May, sixteen days after Carmichael Smyth's regimental parade, the whole Meerut garrison was assembled to witness the fettering of the prisoners. Considerable time was taken in riveting the leg irons. During the process, the convicted persons, many of whom had fine records of service, pleaded for mercy, and cursed their colonel in particular. The spectacle tried the Indian troops, but they were faced by British artillery, cavalry and infantry. The 'sowars and sepoys were for the time powerless.'[12] On the evening of the following day, Sunday, 10 May, the outbreak occurred. At the time, as the 60th Rifles, a British unit, was assembling for the Sunday evening church parade, a cry was raised that the intention of the British was to descend on the Indian troops, disarm and chain them. 'A panic spread, and the outbreak was precipitated.' Some troopers galloped to the jail and released their imprisoned comrades. The whole 3rd Light Cavalry then joined the Indian infantry, and, as G.H.D. Gimlette recounted: 'The evildoers of the bazaar, among whom the Mohammedan butchers were conspicuous in the indiscriminate murder of all the Europeans and Eurasians they could come across, and in plunder and destruction....Houses were set on fire in all directions. None of the officers of the 3rd Light Cavalry were murdered by their own men...their own men guarded them and their families and brought them to safety.'[13] Among the 1,500 strong mob were the malefactors released from jail. Gimlette continued: 'The story had many times been told...how the maddened mutineers and yelling mob were allowed to continue their work of massacre and destruction through the night with impunity, and the troops to clear off unmolested to Delhi. Old General Hewett, over seventy, corpulent and helpless, was as if mentally paralysed; incapable of doing anything himself he allowed Brigadier Archdale Wilson to act for him. The proceedings of the latter were however merely futile.'

The same Archdale Wilson whom Brigadier General John Nicholson, while on his deathbed, vowed to kill for alleged military pusillanimity outside Delhi, before the latter himself died, exclaiming, 'Thank God, I still have enough strength to shoot that man.' What Gimlette does not recount, nor, for that matter, do most British writers, was the killing by the British themselves of a British woman, known to history as "Mees Dolly", the widow of a British sergeant. Captain (later Field Marshal) Henry Norman merely recorded: 'By the way, I must mention that a European woman was hung at Meerut, being implicated in the arrangements for the first outbreak,' on 10 May. Though Norman does not say so, she was hanged without trial, for 'egging on the mutineers.'

The bulk of the 3rd Light Cavalry, mainly Muslim, made off for Delhi in order to meet Emperor Bahadur Shah II; some started for their homes in Oudh, and some seventy to eighty remained on duty at Meerut. On 15 May, some Bengal Sappers and Miners marched into Meerut, in the normal course from Roorkee. On the following day, when the unit magazine was ordered to be taken away from them, they were seized with an "incomprehensible panic", and one of them shot their commanding officer. Thinking themselves compromised, they scattered, fifty seeking shelter in a grove, where the artillery destroyed them. Meanwhile, at Delhi, the Bengal Army garrison joined the 3rd Cavalry on arrival, the sowars displaying the marks of the fetters which riveted them in Meerut, and killing any Europeans they came across, particularly a group of fifty European and Eurasian men, women and children at Daryaganj on 16 May. Separately at faraway Hoti Maidan, by 24 May, the 55th Bengal Infantry was suspected, and was to be disarmed. Most of the regiment fled on seeing the force approaching to disarm them. In despair, the commanding officer, Lieutenant Colonel A.C. Spottiswoode, shot himself. The regiment was pursued, 120 being killed in the pursuit. Of the 150 captured, forty were blown from guns on 10 June. Of 500 who escaped, many were circumcised and converted by the tribesmen, and sold as slaves. One-hundred-and-twenty-four later gave themselves up, and were executed.

Meanwhile, at Cawnpore, the garrison included the 2nd Light Cavalry. The original 2nd Light Cavalry had been disbanded with ignominy, after it had broken up in disorder at Parwandarrah in Afghanistan on 2 November 1840, when surprised by a handful of Amir Dost Mohammed's horsemen. As we have seen earlier, he himself surrendered shortly after. Another regiment, the 11th Cavalry, was raised to replace the 2nd Cavalry, and the British officers of the 2nd were transferred *en bloc* to the 11th. The latter distinguished itself at Multan in 1849, and in 1850 was renumbered as the 2nd, curiously, with all the battle honours of the original regiment. An occurrence which was said to have precipitated the outbreak at Cawnpore is described by Colonel S.Williams, Military Secretary to the Government of the North-West Provinces: 'Again, the unfortunate incident of a cashiered officer, named Cox, firing on a patrol of the 2nd Cavalry on the night of 2nd June, and his acquittal the next day after trial on the plea of being unconscious at the time from intoxication, caused much dissatisfaction, the mutinously inclined cavalry declaring openly that perhaps their firearms might be discharged by accident some day.'[14] The latter is what happened on 4 June at Cawnpore. Even then, the 53rd Regiment was not joining in, but the aged Major General Hugh Wheeler, in an inexplicable error, ordered the artillery to open fire on it. Excepting eighty personnel, the 53rd broke, and became bloodthirsty as a result.

The cavalry and infantry at Cawnpore decided to march to Delhi. No European had so far been killed. Emissaries of the Nana, presumably briefed by Azimullah, prevailed upon them to return. On 11 June, about 120 British men, women and children from Fatehgarh, who had sought refuge at Cawnpore, were killed. Then followed the massacre, after Wheeler's capitulation of his entrenchment, despite the Nana Sahib's ostensible guarantee. William Howard Russell, the London *Times'* correspondent, was of the opinion that the defence of this entrenchment into which Wheeler had moved the European and Eurasian population was 'one of the minor epics of avoidable heroism which spatter the pages of British Indian history.' It is on record 'that a sowar...carried off from the river one of the general's daughters who never returned to her own people.'[15] Gimlette does not, however, tell the full story. Many exaggerated versions were depicted of her defending her honour at Cawnpore in newspapers, magazines, paintings and stage plays in Britain; such narrations were sought to provide the justification for some of the atrocities committed by the British on Indians at the time. In all these portrayals, when she is hopelessly compromised, she kills her abductor and his family before allegedly killing herself. In fact, she was not abducted but rescued, became a Muslim, married her rescuer, and lived to a considerable age in the Cawnpore bazaar, never betraying her husband. A Highland regiment, however, had reported recovering her body, counting the hairs on her head, and distributing the hairs equally among the regiment, so that each man killed that number of "Pandies". She was the daughter by Wheeler's Indian wife (a Brahmin).

Before passing on from Cawnpore, a few words on the Nana, and his role, if any, in the atrocities there. Philip Woodruff (Philip Mason) describes him as "an amiable non-entity". Writing contemporaneously, F.C. Maude, in his *Memories of the Mutiny* states: '...of his individual influence there seems no trace throughout. We know something of what Azimoolah did...but the stolid discontented figure of the Nana himself remains in the background...inanimate, incapable of original ideas, and more elated, perhaps, with the present glory of the hundred guns fired in his honour than with any distinct idea of future dominion...' It is doubtful if it was the Nana who organized the massacres of the Europeans at Cawnpore; his counsellors' brains were active in devising outrages. As an instance of the latter, some of the 6th Bengal Infantry formed the guard on the Bibighar, and when orders, ostensibly, in the name of the Nana were sent to them, to kill the British women and children prisoners, 'they went so far as to fire their muskets through the windows without doing very much harm, but refused to enter the house and cut the victims down with swords.'[16] Russell recorded: 'The writing on the wall (of the Bibighar), alleged to be the work of the (British women) prisoners (before their deaths), was added after the recapture of Cawnpore, and was used in India to inflame British troops...as justification for reprisals of great savagery. There seems no doubt that the massacre was the work of palace servants, possibly finally to compromise the Nana Sahib. No rebel troops took part in the affair.'[17]

He was certainly no soldier. The only occasions he took the field—both unsuccessfully—were on 16 July at Cawnpore, and 16 August at Bithur. Begum Hazrat Mahal blamed him for much of the woes of the uprising, for it was the killing of the British women and children that she deemed responsible for the ill-fortune of the uprising. Gimlette states, 'The Nana and his remaining followers crossed the frontier into Nepal; two of our spies reported them as a collection of 12,000 to 15,000 people, living without shelter in the jungle, half-starved and in great distress. The most poverty-stricken and dejected of all were some troopers of the 2nd Light Cavalry.

Nothing further is recorded of them.'[18]

Sir Syed Ahmed Khan's generalization as to the Indian atrocities would be, to a major extent, valid for those at Cawnpore as well, '...*Badmaashes* treacherously violated the most solemn promises they made to those unfortunates who fell into their hands.' Within weeks the collective disaffection spread through most of the North-West Provinces and Oudh, the British there were dead or beleaguered, having not been allowed to flee. Martin Gubbins, the Commissioner of Lucknow, describes the situation in Oudh in early June: 'When the troops at the capital had set the example, all the rest soon followed, and the fabric of civil government fell to pieces like a house made of cards...the people were left to themselves as we retreated.'

In Moon's opinion, in many places, the British precautionary measures were inevitably interpreted as preparations for an attack on the concerned units, as had happened before at Barrackpore in 1824. The units in question broke up in panic, overwhelmed by the instinct of self-preservation. Many, perforce, fought to the end, but many also went to their homes, and there awaited the conclusion of the uprising. It was the soldiers of the Bengal Army who kept the uprising going, just as it had been they who began it. The men from those regiments, whose officers had been killed, were never offered the amnesty that was extended to all others. John Russell Colvin, Lieutenant Governor of the North-West Provinces, sought to do so in May 1858, but his proclamation was overruled by Canning due to a misunderstanding of the intent. He died shortly after, and is buried in the Agra Fort. He was a man like Henry Lawrence, who did much for the British image among Indians, but, sadly, died before he could do more. Those not covered by Canning's amnesty felt that their lives were only assured as long as they eluded the British. T. Rice Holmes iterated: 'It was not the inconsistency of their character that drove the same sepoys who had risked their lives on the field of battle to protect their officers, and watched by their bedsides when they were wounded, to murder them when the Mutiny broke out; it was the inconsistency with which they were treated.'[19]

166

Beyond the Gangetic plain and parts of Central India, there was little or no disturbance in 1857-58. There was generally quiet in Bengal, Madras and most of the Bombay Presidency. An attempt to suborn the sentries of Fort William was allegedly reported at Calcutta, and attributed to the entourage of Wajid Ali Shah. He was, thereafter, confined in Fort William. (Curiously, a violent agitation of indigo cultivators swept Bengal in 1859-60, where, scarcely a year earlier, the 1857-58 Uprising had the least response.) Thus those areas where the British presence was the longest established, and where English education was prevalent, remained unmoved, whereas those areas in the Gangetic plain, where British authority was most threatened, were backward educationally and opportunity-wise. The more recently annexed Punjab became a base for military reinforcements, and from where the Sikh princes personally led their forces for the reimposition of British authority in Delhi and areas to the east. As to the civil disturbance, Judith M. Brown narrated: '(It) was complex in origin. It was essentially elitist—not initiated or supported by the really poor or landless, but by some of the dominant castes and notables in the countryside. Those at the base of society were caught up in a conflict which they neither chose nor understood; in which they were victims or only followed their traditional masters and patrons.'[20]

Russell noted compassionately, 'What a life must be that of the Oudh peasant? Whichever side wins, he is sure to lose; and in the operations which determine the conquest, he is harassed and maltreated by both sides.' On the whole, as observed by Dr Tara Chand in *The History of the Freedom Movement in India:* 'The uprising was an attempt—the last attempt of the medieval order—to halt the process of dissolution and recover its lost status.... No leader of the requisite organizing ability arose to guide the movement.'[21] Karl Marx, who along with Frederick Engels, extensively covered the events of 1857-1858, sought to anticipate events in 1853 when he wrote: 'England has to fulfil a double role in India, one destructive and the other regenerating: the annihilation of an old Asian society, and the laying of the material foundations of Western society in

Asia.'

Many of the regiments which mutinied remained together, and fought as units or in brigades. They went into action with bands playing the same airs, often the attackers and defenders playing the same tune; bugles sounding the same calls, mess nights being observed, and the British-bestowed colours flying. Among the brigades, the most prominent were the Gwalior Contingent, the Indore Brigade, the Neemuch Brigade, the Rohilkhand or Bareilly Brigade, and "The Fighting Regiments", as the Dinapur Brigade called itself. Gimlette stated: 'Everywhere the native cavalry was the first to strike, and the most murderous of the rebels.'[22] The most notable Indian officer leader was Bakht Khan, an artillery subedar, upon whom the Emperor Bahadur Shah conferred the rank of General, and appointment of Commander-in-Chief, when he arrived at Delhi with the Rohilkhand Brigade and at least one British non-commissioned officer accompanying, namely Sergeant Major Gordon of the 28th Bengal Infantry. Bakht Khan was then described by his former commanding officer in the Bengal Horse Artillery as, 'Sixty years of age;...served the Company for forty years; height 5 feet, 10 inches; 44 inches round the chest; family of Hindu extraction...clever and good at (gun) drill.'[23] On the fall of Delhi in September 1857, he moved to Farrukhabad, but was not well received. On 25 December, the Nawab ordered the taluqdar of Allahganj to plunder Bakht Khan, believed to be in possession of several lakhs of rupees from Delhi. He was in nominal command of the forces in Oudh during 1858, and was killed in an action at Nawabganj.

The Gwalior Contingent or Subsidiary Force, 8,000 strong, mostly from Oudh, was in sympathy with the other Purbia regiments. It was considered an alien force by the Marathas of the Gwalior State Force. The infantry of the contingent on 14 June killed seven British officers, six warrant and non-commissioned officers, and three women and children, the survivors fleeing to Agra. In September the infantry joined the Rani of Jhansi, and in November accepted Tantia Tope as their commander. They formed the bulk of Tantia's army in the attack on Cawnpore, when Charles Windham was defeated, but were later defeated at Cawnpore by Sir Colin Campbell and at Swarajpur by Brigadier Hope Grant. Five or six regiments of this contingent rallied to Tantia at Kalsi, and formed the bulk of his reconstituted army, with which he marched to the relief of Jhansi. They were defeated by Hugh Rose, retreated to Gwalior, and in June 1858 dispersed at Morar.

The troops at Mhow, on 1 July, killed three officers, then amalgamated at Indore with Holkar's infantry, and were known as the Mhow and Indore Brigade. In October they surprised a British column outside Agra. The British recovered, and the Indore Brigade was dispersed. At Nasirabad, the troops were all Bengal Army, except the 1st Bombay Lancers. The latter, though discontented, did not mutiny; the others did on 28 May, reaching Delhi on 18 June. On the 19th, this brigade posed a threat to the British, behind what was then known as the Ochterlony Gardens, where David Ochterlony had resided till he resigned in 1825, and which was part of the area today known as Shalimar Bagh. Severe fighting followed, the British flank being nearly turned. Along with the Neemuch Brigade, the Nasirabad Brigade attacked certain batteries on 5 August. After the fall of Delhi, the Nasirabad Brigade marched off into Oudh, and is mentioned as putting up a determined fight at Sultanpur, before being defeated. This brigade held together along the Nepal border till April 1859, when it finally dispersed.

The Neemuch Brigade on 3 June killed several Europeans, and marched off for Delhi via Agra. At Shahganj, near Agra, this brigade inflicted a reverse on the Agra garrison, under Brigadier T. Polwhele, but instead of following up its success at Agra, marched to Delhi, where it fought through the siege till 24 August, when it was broken up, along with the Kotah Contingent, by Nicholson at Najafgarh on 25 August. The regiments from Dinapur kept together in Bihar, Oudh and Bundelkhand under Raja Kanwar Singh, who possibly has not received the attention he deserves from Indian historians, compared to that bestowed on other leaders of the time. After his death, this brigade held together, till 1859.

As in the case of the 55th at Hoti Maidan, one of the main causes of certain units allegedly mutinying was panic as to British disarmament policy, *"dar ke mare"*. Further tragic examples are those at Multan and Peshawar. Taking Multan first, a horse artillery troop was used to disarm two Bengal Infantry regiments, and then itself disarmed. As guarding them with British troops became a burden, it was resolved to send them off home on foot in small batches from Multan, at varying intervals. They at first acquiesced, but then a rumour started that they were to be massacred *en route* home. On 31 August, they armed themselves with clubs, and attacked the European and Sikh troops, killing some of the latter and the adjutant of the former. No mercy was shown to these disarmed troops, and of the 1,300 disarmed at Multan very few escaped death. Now to Peshawar. The 51st Bengal Infantry had been disarmed on 22 May. Desertions soon commenced. Rewards were offered for their apprehension, and the Afridi and Mohmand tribesmen were encouraged to bring them in, which they willingly did after circumcising the Hindu fugitives. On 29 May the subedar major and others of the 51st were hanged in the presence of the assembled troops*. On 28 August, the remnants of the 51st were searched, as it was believed they were secretly buying arms. They bolted towards a field, where concealed arms were allegedly later found. The European troops and newly-raised 18th Punjab Infantry had been readied for this contingency, and fifty of the 51st fell at the first volley, and numbers were bayoneted in the lines. Some were made prisoner, some attempted to flee and were cut up by the European troops. Those who tried to seize arms and ammunition were repulsed. Most of those who got away were followed up and annihilated. Those captured were tried by a drumhead court-martial, and executed on the same and following day. The official record stated: 'Of the 870 men who, on the morning of the 28th, composed the 51st Bengal Native Infantry, within eight and forty hours, not the odd 70 survived, and a few days after it was

---

* See Appendix 2 for the address that was read out at this representative execution parade of that period.

reported that only nineteen famished fugitives lingered on in the neighbouring hills.' Four or five got to the Khyber, where the tribesmen said they would let them go to Kabul as Mohammedans, but not as Hindus. They were converted on the spot. Thus ended the 51st Bengal Infantry.

At Dinapur on 25 July it was decided not to disarm the three regiments, but to remove the percussion caps in their possession. The men fired on their officers, and marched off towards Arrah, where they joined Raja Kanwar Singh. At Arrah, fifteen Europeans and Eurasians took shelter in the house of the civil engineer, with a guard of forty-five personnel of Rattray's Sikhs, then a military police battalion. This guard, from 27 July, held out against the three regiments. An attempt on 29 July to relieve this house, with a column of over 400 from Dinapur, failed, with very heavy casualties as the result of an ambush. Arrah was however relieved on 2-3 August by an ad hoc column of about 200 under Major Vincent Eyre, who has been mentioned earlier in the narration of the First Anglo-Afghan War. He had been sailing up the river to Allahabad, when he heard of the Arrah situation. Without waiting for sanction he disembarked, and effected the relief. On 11 August, he marched against Kanwar Singh and defeated him at Jagdishpur. The uprising in Bihar was thus broken. From a military point of view, Eyre had been both intrepid and skilful. The incident is mentioned on account of its curious sequel in relation to how militarily deserving persons do not sometimes receive awards. Strategically, had the house at Arrah fallen, the whole of Bihar would have risen, and Bengal cut off from the North-West Provinces. Eyre went on to distinguish himself in the relief of Lucknow, but was not given any further opportunity to shine, though he did become a major-general. 'Perhaps the fact that he had done what he did (at Arrah), entirely on his own initiative annoyed his superiors,'[24] is the opinion of P.J. O. Taylor. Many years later, now retired, Eyre accidentally met Lord Strathnairn (Sir Hugh Rose of the Central India Campaign in 1858-59). Rose asked Eyre conversationally, 'How is Lady Eyre?' 'Who is that?' replied Eyre. 'Why, your wife,' said Rose. To which Eyre answered, 'Mrs Eyre is well, thank you.' Rose promptly had the omission rectified, and Eyre was knighted. In this context, P.J.O. Taylor invokes the old saying, 'It isn't what you know that matters; its who you know that counts.'

Taylor also sheds light on an interesting facet pertaining to Kanwar Singh. Long before 1857, he had asked the government to manage his estates, as he was considerably in debt. The Commissioner of Patna, William Tayler, effectively did so for some years, and the quantum of the debt burden was reduced. When Lieutenant Governor Halliday overruled Tayler, the latter's assistance to Kanwar Singh ceased and the old man lapsed into further debt again. Kanwar Singh was desperate. Tayler pleaded for him, but without success. After Kanwar Singh revolted in July, Tayler recorded the old Raja, over eighty, had been driven to rebel by the government's lack of sympathy. For this, Tayler was suspended for several months without pay for his independent views, and then demoted. He eventually resigned, and took up practice at Patna, mainly taking cases against the government.

Now occurred the destruction of the 26th Bengal Infantry. Disarmed at Mian Mir (Lahore) along with three other regiments, the 26th was, in July, to draw off the British troops while the other three regiments escaped. After the killing of their commanding officer, the 26th was pursued. One-hundred-and-fifty drowned in the River Ravi, when chased by villagers, the remainder sheltering on an island. The Deputy Commissioner, Frederick Cooper, now arrived. A further forty or fifty drowned while trying to escape, but 282 were arrested and brought to Ajnala, where they were mainly lodged in the police station, but sixty-six were lodged in a round tower or bastion. Cooper, on the plea that he did not have the resources to escort them to Lahore, decided to put them all to death. They were led out in batches of ten, and shot by Sikh levies. When the bastion was opened, forty-five were found dead, Cooper exulting that the Black Hole of Calcutta had been avenged. The remaining twenty-one were also shot. Forty stragglers from the regiment were brought to Lahore, and blown from guns. Thus within forty-eight hours, the 26th Regiment had been destroyed. Cooper was assailed in the British

Parliament, but supported by the local authorities. Gimlette related, 'Cooper brought discredit upon himself by his exulting in describing his acts, both in his official report and subsequent book, *The Crisis in the Punjab.*' [25]

Meanwhile, at Benares, on 4 June, the 37th Regiment was ordered to be disarmed. Also at Benares was the Ludhiana Regiment of Sikhs. (The latter had a detachment at Jaunpur.) Thereafter, T. Rice Holmes narrated, 'They (the 37th) were quietly obeying when suddenly the European troops were seen coming...and a panic seized the whole regiment. Those who had laid down their muskets ran to take them up again, and...began to fire on the British...the artillery...poured in a shower of grape among the mutineers.... At this moment the Sikhs, who were reluctantly advancing from behind to support the Europeans, were startled by the noise of firing in their rear...the Sikhs...confused and apprehensive of treachery, rushed wildly against the artillerymen...the Sikhs, staggering under a fearful discharge of grape, broke and fled after the 37th; and Neill promptly pursuing them completed the victory...the first sight that met their eyes when they awoke was a row of gallows, on which Neill was busily hanging batches of mutineers as fast as they were brought in. Soon afterwards he received a message from the Government, ordering him to hurry on to Allahabad. Instantly he telegraphed back: "Can't move: wanted here."...the story of the slaughter at Benares drove another detachment of the Sikhs at Jaunpur to rebel...and stimulated the villagers to fling off...every vestige of British authority....The Governor General had already issued an order placing...Benares under martial law. Some of the officers used their authority with indiscriminate ferocity. Lads, who had been guilty of nothing worse than waving rebel colours and beating tom-toms, were summarily executed. Gentlemen volunteered to serve as hangmen, and gloried in the skill with which they disposed of their victims. But mere executions, however severe, were not enough to restore British authority...but let it be recorded that to him (Neill) the infliction of punishment was not a delight, but an awful duty.'

Kaye, however, rightly felt that the evangelical James Neill hanged 'with as little compunction, as though they had been pariah dogs or jackals or vermins of a baser kind.' Neill's indiscriminate hangings had a disturbing effect on the troops at Allahabad as well, where the same "grand guignol" was performed; Neill sanctimoniously writing, 'God grant I may have acted with justice. I know I have with severity, but under all the circumstances I trust for forgiveness.' The Ludhiana Sikhs went on to take part in the siege of the Lucknow Residency. From those at Benares who did not flee with the 37th, the 15th Sikhs was reconstituted. Separately, twenty-one Sikhs of the 28th Bengal Infantry were hanged at Ludhiana in 1858 for alleged crimes committed at Jhansi the previous year.

Reverting now to the 39th Bengal Infantry, when it had been disarmed at Dera Ismail Khan, on 20 July it was discovered that a number of Malwa Sikhs of the 10th Punjab Infantry had planned to kill their officers, seize the fort, re-equip the 39th, and march on Delhi. The ringleaders were arrested. The 39th was moved to Sialkot, where it was disbanded. Then at Saugor, the 42nd Regiment had mutinied. On 7 July, the 31st, the bulk of which had not mutinied, was attacked by the 42nd, though, as a precautionary measure, all British officers of the 31st had been withdrawn. There were many casualties on both sides, the engagement lasting all day. The 31st drove the 42nd out of Saugor. When after 1858, the Bengal Army was reorganized, the 31st became the 2nd Bengal Infantry. At Mirzapur occurred the curious developments in the 47th Regiment. The commanding officer, by censoring the troops' mail, discovered the possibility of mutiny. He hanged some after a summary court-martial, on the basis of the letters they had written, and sent off the majority, on furlough. On 9 September he reported that the regiment had volunteered for service in China, where it was shortly sent, along with the 70th Bengal Infantry, to be employed in the Second Anglo-Chinese War (1858-60).

In September 1857 at Jubbulpore, it was reportedly discovered that Shankar Shah, a local Gond Raja, his son and some adherents were inciting the 52nd Regiment. The Raja and his son were blown from guns on 18 September in the presence of the 52nd. That night the 52nd deserted *en masse*, except for a havildar major and a few soldiers. *En route* a detachment commander, Lieutenant F. Macgregor, was made captive. A message was sent to the commanding officer offering to release Macgregor, if the havildar major and soldiers, who had not joined the mass desertion, were sent to the 52nd under escort. It was stated that, if the latter were not sent to the regiment, Macgregor would be taken to Delhi. In the event, the commanding officer could not send the havildar major and the concerned soldiers to their deaths, and though the divisional commissioner offered 8,000 rupees for Macgregor's release, he was killed and not taken to Delhi.

By the time the 1857-58 Uprising had been put down, there were 15,000 disarmed Bengal Army soldiers in the Punjab, and 13,000 in other parts of the Bengal Presidency. The plan adopted in the Punjab was to despatch them in batches. Twenty men a day from each station, under an armed police guard, were sent off to their own areas, three different routes being chosen. The 13,000 disarmed in the Bengal Presidency were similarly despatched. The 33rd, whose commanding officer, Brevet Colonel R.T. Sandeman, had burst into tears, when ordered to disarm it in June 1857 at Phillaur after thirty-two years' continuous service in it, had its arms eventually restored on parade with full ceremony. So also did the 58th, disarmed at Rawalpindi; the 59th, disarmed at Amritsar; and the right wing of the 4th Regiment disarmed at Nurpur.

Some other memorabilia of the events of 1857 pertaining to the Bengal Army deserve mention. The 9th Irregular Cavalry, being suspect, was ordered to move from Delhi to Bannu, in detachments. One such detachment, under Risaldar Wazir Khan, mutinied at Kalabagh on the Indus in September. It was pursued by a detachment of the 17th Irregular Cavalry, and was about to be attacked, when Wazir Khan, a brave man, stepped forward and challenged Risaldar Ali Wardi Khan of the 17th to single combat. The rest watched. Wazir Khan was killed, and Ali Wardi Khan severely wounded. The detachment of the 17th, mostly Purbias, now attacked and killed all of the detachment of the 9th.[26]

As to Europeans on the side of the mutineers, Sir Syed Ahmed Khan observed generally, 'It is no secret that during the mutiny some Christian captives offered to become Mohammedans if their lives were spared, and did in fact embrace our faith, but the rebels treacherously murdered them notwithstanding.' One British deserter from Meerut certainly died fighting the British at Badli ki Serai, outside Delhi on 8 June. A European, in the uniform of a Russian cavalry officer, was seen leading a successful sortie against the British at Chinhut (now Chinnahat) on 29 June, eight miles from Lucknow. When Brigadier Adrian Hope was killed in the unsuccessful attack on Ruiya fort in April 1858 it was believed the person who did so was a European (the taunting slang and voice were allegedly unmistakably British). Surgeon W.W. Ireland, writing in 1861, was, however, critical of those British who were 'ready to attribute a strenuous resistance (by Indians) to the aid of men of their own (British) race,' commenting that 'no one who knew how much of the work in India was really done by the native wondered at the practical skill they now showed.' Another example is the Rotton family of Lucknow. The founder of the family, William Rotton, was an Englishman, originally in the Maratha service. One of his sons, though aged sixty, fought against the British for three months, and three grandsons were killed fighting the British. Excuses were made that they had Indian mothers and that the son was supposed to be a Muslim. The fact remains that the whole family fought against the British. An intriguing aspect in their indictment mentions some other 'renegade Christians who were living in Lucknow,' and were seen in European uniform during the siege.

There was also a belief in the British camp at Delhi that a European "renegade" was directing the artillery. It was supposed this man had formerly been in the Company's artillery and that he was the sergeant-major of the 28th Bengal Infantry, who had accompanied Bakht Khan to Delhi.[27] In the British records of the time (in the National Archives of India) his name is given as Gordon, and he is formally listed as "abducted". (This would discount one oral version that he had killed the adjutant, and, therefore, defected.) At

176

Delhi, a British non-commissioned officer, was reportedly converted to Islam, given the name Sheikh Abdullah Beg and was observed directing artillery fire against the British.[28] Presumably, Gordon was Sheikh Abdullah Beg. Thereafter, accounts differ. Major Kendall Coghill wrote to his brother from Delhi on 22 September 1857: 'Hodson pursued the princes; (he) had only 100 men and they had 10,000, but they gave up their arms—the three princes, the band of Christian (Eurasian) drummers of 28th NI, and the English sergeant-major of 28th NI who was formerly an artilleryman, and during the siege pointed the enemy's guns on us, calling himself Sheikh Abdoolah and dressing like a sepoy. The (Christian) band were all killed on the spot, but the three princes were brought with the sergeant-major to an open spot where the princes had commenced the slaughter and violated our ladies themselves, and they were mercilessly killed and stripped and laid flat on the open ground till the dogs and jackals walked off with them. The sergeant-major is still in our guard in irons, and going to be blown away from a gun in the presence of the force.'[29] (The alleged violation of European women by the Mughal princes was hearsay.)

G. MacMunn, however, in the *Cornhill* magazine, 1930, quotes Captain F.C. Maisey of the Judge Advocate General's Department at Delhi: 'It was proposed to bring him to trial for aiding and abetting the rebels....But on quiet examination, the evidence proved quite worthless....So the poor wretch got off trial. He was not, however, released, but the matter was reported to the C-in-C, and what the final result was I do not know.'

After the initial events at Meerut and Delhi, a siege-train had been ordered to be assembled at Phillaur. It was to be escorted by the Nasiri Gurkhas, then at Sabathu, from Phillaur to Ambala. The Nasiri Gurkhas complained that, while they had been ordered to undertake a distant service, their pay had been allowed to fall into arrears. They, thereupon, mutinied, and looted the treasury at Sabathu. The British inhabitants of Simla, fearing the same fate as at Meerut and Delhi, fled from that station. The Gurkhas returned to duty as soon as their demands were met.[30] Mention needs to be made here of the assistance sought by the British from Nepal in 1857. The assistance was readily forthcoming; Maharaja Jang Bahadur Rana himself crossing into India at the head of his army, assisting the British in Oudh for a year. The scenario thereafter is best described by Sir Francis Tuker: 'Jang's Gurkhas had never in all their lives set eyes upon such wealth as there was in Oudh and, especially, in Lucknow....By the time that they were due to leave India for their own country, they possessed a baggage train of several thousand bullock-carts, all loaded well above the Plimsoll Line with the plunder of their year's campaigning. It soon became apparent that the Nepalese Army was but a baggage guard to its own transport for, once on the move, it had no troops to spare to go out and fight....The next problem which presented itself to the Nepalese Government was that of dealing with the big influx of mutineers escaping from British retribution. Some 50,000, many of them armed and organized in their original regiments, crossed the border into Nepal. The first thing was to disarm them. By October, Jang had collected a force of eleven regiments of infantry and a regiment of artillery....They surrendered their arms to his force, as well as eighteen English hostages, all non-combatants, whom they had brought with them as counters for a bargain in which their very lives would be at stake.'[31]

Before going on to the Bombay and Madras Armies in 1857, mention needs also to be made of the defence of Lucknow from June to November 1857. It suffices to quote the notification of 8 December 1857 of the Governor-General: 'Of the native officers and men of the 13th, 48th and 71st Regiments of Native Infantry, who have been amongst the defenders of the Residency, it is difficult to speak too highly. Their courageous constancy under the severest trials is worthy of all honour.' This was followed by a general order, 'Every native commissioned and non-commissioned officer and soldier who had formed part of the garrison shall receive the (Indian) Order of Merit, with the increase of pay attached thereto, and shall be permitted to count three years of additional service. The soldiers of the 13th, 48th and 71st Regiments of Native Infantry, who had been part of the garrison, shall be formed into a regiment of the line to be called "The Regiment of Lucknow".' One-hundred-and-eighty-two Victoria Crosses (VCs) were awarded to British personnel in 1857-58, the same number as for the whole of the Second World War to all the Commonwealth forces. Of the 182, twenty-four were awarded on 16 November 1857 in the second relief of Lucknow. Though the uprising could not have been dealt with except by the use of Indian troops of all the three Presidency Armies, as British troops alone could not have done so, nevertheless Indians were not eligible for this award till shortly before the First World War. Till then it was urged that there was a separate series of gallantry awards for Indian troops, the highest being the Indian Order of Merit (IOM) Class One.

Some facets need mentioning as to the award of the VC in 1857-58 to British personnel. There was then provision for "elections" for this award in each British unit after an action, and the award seems to have been made for lesser deeds than subsequently insisted upon for First World War awards. Five of the VCs awarded on 16 November at Lucknow were by election. Civilians were also then made eligible, two awards, one to a European and one to an Anglo-Indian, occurring in 1857, when "under the orders of a general officer in the field". There was also criticism by the new Commander-in-Chief, Colin Campbell, of Brigadier General Henry Havelock recommending a deserved VC for his son, then his ADC. Campbell wrote to the British Commander-in-Chief, the Duke of Cambridge, advising against the award, as young staff officers 'by their reckless and flamboyant behaviour, frequently steal the glory from their regimental colleagues.' Young Havelock did not get the award. For his part, the royal Duke did not favour brains or initiative. He complimented friends, 'Gad, Sir, I know you have no brains.'

Now to the Bombay Army in 1857. The Governor of Bombay at the time was Lord John Elphinstone. The news of the outbreak at Meerut reached him on 14 May. He had previously been Governor of Madras. When he had arrived at Madras, an official commented, 'We want a Governor, and they send us a guardsman; we want a statesman, and they send us a dancer.'[32] He had matured since, but initially assumed that the Bombay Presidency and Bombay Army would pass unscathed through 1857. The first outbreak was in Satara. In this recently annexed State, there was still a strong feeling in favour of the adopted son of the late Raja's brother. Moreover, the chiefs of the region, who, with only one exception, had no male issue, knowing that their adopted sons would not be allowed to succeed to their estates, were personally anxious for the overthrow of the British. On 12 June, the magistrate at Satara reportedly learnt that Rangaji Bapaji, who had argued against the annexation in London, planned to attack the cantonment and release the prisoners from the jail. One of the co-conspirators was arrested, but Rangaji Bapaji escaped. Seventeen alleged conspirators were convicted and executed, including Bapaji's son. The initial call to rise at Satara came not from a Maratha, but from a "Hindustani" peon, who was the first to be hanged there for trying to subvert the 22nd Bombay Infantry.

Next were Kolhapur, Belgaum and Dharwar, each with a garrison of a Bombay Army regiment having a high percentage of *"pardesis"* from Oudh. In this region also, many chiefs had been denied the privilege of adopting heirs to their estates, and they were backed by the sympathies of their people. In Kolhapur and neighbouring Sawantwadi, there had already been civil disaffection. In 1842, the Raja of Kolhapur had died, leaving two infant sons. The State was studded with forts garrisoned by hereditary defenders, "gadkaris". These hereditary defenders were removed by the British administrator, without any prospect of alternative employment. This measure was resented, and in 1844 a revolt had broken out. This resentment had been exacerbated by the States of Kolhapur and Sawantwadi being forced to pay the expenses of suppressing this 1844 revolt, and was rekindled with the news of the Nana Sahib's declaration that he was the Peshwa. Meanwhile, the *"pardesis"* of the three Bombay Army regiments (27th, 28th, 29th) at Kolhapur, Belgaum and Dharwar were in touch with each other. On 31 July, the Indian adjutant of the regiment at Kolhapur was able to warn the British officers. The *"pardesi"* soldiers plundered the treasury and the station, and the majority made for the Sawantwadi jungles. On this news, most European women and children at Bombay were put on board ships and two detachments of European troops were sent by sea to Goa, destined for Kolhapur and Belgaum respectively. (Goa had last seen British troops when it was captured by the British in 1808.) By the time they reached Kolhapur, order had already been restored. With the European detachment now present, it was decided to disarm the 27th Bombay Infantry. Next day, twenty-one were convicted, two were hanged, eleven shot, and eight blown from guns.[33] Correspondence was apparently discovered between the *"pardesis"* of the regiment, and their relatives in the Bengal Army, as also correspondence between the Wahabi high-priest of Poona and his disciples in the Kolhapur and Belgaum area.

At Belgaum, the Collector having discovered the identity of the prospective ringleader of the contemplated mutiny by the 29th Bombay Infantry, sent him out on temporary duty. In his absence, on 10 August, a number of suspects were arrested, and correspondence allegedly found of an organized Muslim conspiracy. The writer and one of his associates were tried and executed.[34] Meanwhile, at Bombay, which had a garrison of three Bombay Army regiments, Moharrum was approaching. The Superintendent of Police was of the opinion that the Muslim residents of Bombay would not participate in any stir, unless the troops set the example. He, therefore, watched the troops more and the townsfolk less. The mutiny was postponed to Diwali in October, by when eight were arrested. Two were executed, and six transported for life.[35] In September, two alleged attempts to mutiny in the regiments at Hyderabad (Sind) and Ahmedabad were detected, and, at Karachi, a mutiny actually took place, all among the Purbias of the concerned regiments.[36] Now Kolhapur was reported to be disaffected again, when a group seized the town and shut the gates. The gates were blown, and thirty-six were tried and executed.[37] Some months earlier, the Sawant Desais had plundered villages in the region below the Western Ghats. The dense forests afforded them protection, and they were able to evade the punitive columns. By the end of 1858, however, they were subdued with the aid of the Portuguese Government in Goa.

Though it is generally believed that there were no incidents in the Madras Army, this is not quite so. The actual South Indian troops now stood by the British, unlike 1806, but the *"pardesi"* elements, mainly of the Madras Cavalry, and about five to ten per cent of the Madras Infantry, had their sympathies with the Bengal Army, and some overt acts of disaffection were committed within the limits of the Presidency. The 8th Madras Cavalry refused to embark for Bengal and was disbanded. Outside the Presidency, at Raipur on 22 January 1858, seventeen other ranks were hanged for a mutiny during which a sergeant-major was killed—two sowars from the 3rd Madras Cavalry, and one non-commissioned officer and fourteen other ranks from the Madras Artillery. According to papers presently available, the actual killer of the sergeant-major would not appear to have been captured.

At Nagpur, the 1st Cavalry of the Nagpur Subsidiary Force was suspected of being about to mutiny in an hour's time. The regiment was disarmed, with the assistance of the 4th Madras Light Cavalry, and on 29 June 1857 three ostensible ringleaders were hanged.[38] Meanwhile, at Hyderabad (Deccan), where, according to T. Rice Holmes, 'The Wahabis were labouring zealously to keep up the fire of their disciples' fanaticism, and there was danger of the troops yielding to the pressure of their co-religionists,' the opening of fire by the Madras Horse Artillery, with the approval of the Nizam and Nawab Salar Jung, stopped the insurrection at Hyderabad from developing.[39] The aim, apparently, was to make Hyderabad State into a 'second Oudh of the Deccan,' and 'Hyderabad (city) into a Lucknow.' Fears of the 1st Madras Infantry mutinying at Hyderabad, however, continued for some time till December 1857 (it then had a higher percentage of troops from Oudh by circumstance of its location, compared to other Madras Infantry units located in southern India, and had refused to move on relief).

By way of conclusion to this chapter, one had seen how the 1857 Uprising originated, gained in momentum and ran its course. Was it a spontaneous outburst or a premeditated revolt? Cracroft Wilson, the Commissioner appointed to go into this question, was convinced that a date and time (31 May 1857) had been fixed for a simultaneous rising at all the military stations of India, but adduced no evidence in support of his conclusion.[40] The observed events also contradict his hypothesis. The rising at Meerut was, manifestly, not premeditated—it was precipitated by Lieutenant Colonel Carmichael Smyth's ill-advised parade. At Lucknow one Oudh regiment refused to bite the cartridge early in May 1857 (why it should have been asked to do so at that stage was not satisfactorily explained), but the uprising in Oudh took place at the end of the month, the police in Oudh rising still later. There was a lull for a fortnight after the events at Meerut and Delhi. Different regiments behaved differently. Nowhere did the soldiers' conduct conform to a common pattern, and the obvious deduction is that they had no pre-concerted plan. The disarming measures drove units to rebel in self-defence. Could such units not have been shown the same consideration as that shown to the Nasiri Gurkhas at Sabathu? At Neemuch and Nasirabad, at Jhelum and Sialkot, at Allahabad and Fatehpur, at Benares and Bareilly, it was the approach of European troops that started the alarm. As John Lawrence later pointed out, disarming and dismounting caused panic, and panic caused revolt. When asked why some of the units did not mutiny till September or October, an anonymous Indian writer had recorded in *The Thoughts of a Native of Northern India on the Rebellion, its Causes and Remedies:* 'I told you it was not a concerted plan. Many of them had till late hopes that the government would feel fully satisfied by disbanding the regiments already gone, but now they are daily convinced that the Government only awaits the arrival of the European soldiers to annihilate and get rid of the Bengal Army by disarming them or blowing them up by cannons.'[41]

Sir Syed Ahmed accepts some correspondence must have been going on about the greased cartridge, but there was no common plan of resistance. They were all waiting to see what others would do. The deliberate indiscretion of Lieutenant Colonel Carmichael Smyth caused the outbreak. Whereas it was later argued that 'no cartridges greased with the fat of cows or swine were destined to be issued to the sepoys,' but Lord Roberts had stated, 'When the sepoys complained that to bite them would destroy their caste, they were solemnly assured by their officers that they had been greased with a perfectly unobjectionable mixture. But nothing was easier than for the men belonging to the regiments quartered near Calcutta to ascertain from the low caste native workmen...at the Fort William arsenal, that the assurances of their officers were not in accordance with the facts.'[42] Lieutenant M.E. Currie, Commissary of Ordnance, of the Bengal Army is on record as saying that, 'No inquiry is made as to the fat of what animal is used,' for greasing the cartridges, as also Colonel Augustus Abbott, Inspector of Ordnance, that 'the tallow might or might not have contained the fat of cows or other animals.'[43] Kaye tells us that in 1856 and in January 1857 cartridges greased with tallow partly composed of beef fat (though not of lard) were manufactured at Calcutta and Meerut.[44] It is also true that, according to Captain (afterwards Major General) Boxer, the Enfield rifle cartridges that were sent out from England to India were greased with beef fat, and it is most probable that the cartridges manufactured in India, till the outcry, were greased with the same substance.[45] Currie admitted that it was, 'not the intention of Government that all grease used in any preparation in the magazine is to be made of goats and sheeps' fat only.' Neither Currie nor Abbott could curiously ascertain what kind of tallow had been used in greasing the new cartridges, till the outcry occurred.[46] It was subsequently posited as, 'not true that any cartridges greased either with beef fat or with lard were ever issued to any sepoys, save only to one Gurkha regiment, at their own request.[47] There was no collusion with any foreign power. Persia had already been excluded, as we have seen earlier. There is no evidence that the uprising was inspired by Russia, even if someone in a Russian cavalry officer's uniform was allegedly seen leading the successful sortie against the British at Chinhut. The only foreign power that the rebels approached was Nepal, and that was for seeking refuge, and not before the uprising. As Dr S.N. Sen recorded: 'The bulk of the (Bengal) Army came to harm by the persistent policy of rendering them harmless...it should be noted that the army as a whole did not join the revolt but a considerable section actively fought on the side of the Government. Its actual strength is not easy to compute. Every disarmed regiment was not necessarily disloyal, and every deserter was not a mutineer.'[48]

About 30,000 of the Bengal Army served the British to the end; a like number was either disarmed or deserted; an aggregate of 70,000 of the Bengal Army joined the uprising at various times. Indian soldiers fought with as much valour against the British as they did for them in 1857-58, but European methodology proved superior, as the Indians opposing the British lacked institutionalized leadership, subedars becoming generals overnight. That there was some consciousness as to this leadership void is apparent from an offer made to two officers by the mutinous 9th Light Cavalry, to lead the unit on higher pay with leave to the hills every summer. Despite all the heroism no central organization could, however, be set up against the British. If the whole Bengal Army had simultaneously risen, the history of the British in India would have been different. The rebels came from every section of the population in the affected areas. If there were Sikhs on the Ridge with the British outside Delhi, there were Sikhs inside the city. If there were Sikhs inside the Residency at Lucknow, there were also Sikhs outside it. The Gujars were not interested in the political situation, and robbed both sides with equal vigour, even setting up rajas in different areas. The Banjaras of Saharanpur decided to set up a king of their own, rather than continue with Bahadur Shah. Queen Zinat Mahal was reportedly in the pay of the British, and William Hodson had reportedly been given a large bribe by her not to kill the Emperor.

As to the alleged indignities suffered by British women, stories of which were used to justify British atrocities, Edward Leckey controverts most of them in his book, *Fictions connected with the Indian outbreak of 1857 exposed,* published in 1859. The false rumour pertaining to the alleged indignities inflicted on Miss Wheeler at Cawnpore has already been controverted earlier in this chapter, by way of illustration of the falsity of many such canards. Sir William Muir, the then head of the Intelligence Department, has categorically recorded that nothing, 'has come to my knowledge which would in the smallest degree support any of the tales of dishonour.' Russell, for his part, records that Indian women were often "ill-used".

How did the British deal with the prisoners taken? We have already seen what Rice Holmes has recorded as to Colonel Neill. Captain Jeremiah Brasyer, throughout the Commanding Officer of the Regiment of Ferozepore (Brasyer's Sikhs), in Oudh, recorded, 'a "pandy" deserter, caught redhanded, had little mercy shown to him. Death by rope from the nearest tree or at the cannon's mouth was certain.' MacMunn to justify the latter, narrated, 'So recently as the great mutiny of the Bengal Army in 1857, this penalty was imposed to a considerable extent on soldiers...this mode of punishment is instantaneous and far more humane than that of impromptu tree hanging, which is a process of slow strangulation. The former is not only instantaneous and, therefore, painless, but has the great advantage that should form the motive of all serious punishment, that it acts as a terrifying deterrent. There are many extant accounts by eye-witnesses of such executions in which, indeed, one of the outstanding features is the fortitude with which the condemned accepted their fate, recognizing its instantaneous method of despatch from one sphere to another, which in the East is, in itself, never dreaded.'[49] Separately, *The Regimental History of the 3rd Gurkha Rifles* states, '...after the Mutiny of 1857, many rebels fled to the Himalayas and twelve of them were captured (near Almora)...the orders of the government were "capital punishment on the spot". The Commissioner did not like this task at all. The men were placed along the edge of the precipice over hanging a river and were shot one by one.'[50] Obviously without the benefit of any trial a la Neill and others.

Queen Victoria issued a proclamation in November 1858 taking over the Government of India from the East India Company. Thus ended a strange dyarchy, or, as Macaulay put it, 'The strangest of all governments designed for the strangest of all empires,' an Empire created by a trading company 'in a fit of absent mind.' On her part,

Begum Hazrat Mahal issued a counter-proclamation in the absence of her husband, Wajid Ali Shah, the former King of Oudh, then confined in Fort William, Calcutta*. After independence, Queen Victoria's statue was removed at Lucknow and Begum Hazrat Mahal's proclamation inscribed on the pedestal.

Maulana Abul Kalam Azad's Foreword to the Government of India publication, *Eighteen Fifty Seven*, is authoritative: '...There would have been no revolt in India in 1857 had not the initiative been taken by the disaffected sepoys...yet the crisis might have been avoidable had not the Government bungled in the administration of the army...the Mutiny, I'm inclined to hold, was not inevitable.' He adds: 'The leaders were mutually jealous and continuously intrigued against one another.'

Haraprasad Chattopadhyaya perceptively recorded, that the British saw the suppression of the 1857 Uprising as 'the completion of the work initiated by the battles of Plassey and Buxar.'[53]

In 1922 a British historian, F.W. Buckler in a paper presented to the Royal Historical Society, took the legal view that it was the Company, the "Dewan" of the Mughal Emperor, that had, in effect, "mutinied," against Emperor Bahadur Shah.

---

* In view of its evocative historicity, this proclamation is reproduced as Appendix 3 by way of an epilogue to the events of 1857-58, for Begum Hazrat Mahal showed more sense and courage 'than all her generals together.'

SIX

The Presidency Armies Under The Crown And Their Unification (1858-1895)

THE MUTINY of the Bengal Army had been shattering. Reforms were inevitable; the reconstruction of the Bengal Army in particular, and the reorganization of the three Presidency Armies in general, as also the status of the European units of the late East India Company's army. The then Secretary of State for India, Sir Charles Wood, told Lord Canning in 1859, 'I never wish to see again a great Army, very much the same in its feelings and prejudices and convictions, confident in its strength, and so disposed to unite in rebellion together. If one regiment mutinies, I should like to see the next regiment so alien, that it would be ready to fire into it.'

The Royal, or Peel, Commission, appointed in July 1858, and presided over by Major General Jonathan Peel, then Secretary of State for War, had evidence before it of the mistrust of certain classes of Indian troops, but to garrison India with only British troops was impossible. Apart from cost, it would not be possible to recruit the numbers required. The proposal that British troops in India should be supplemented by colonial troops from the East Indies etc., received little support. As to troops for India being again recruited from Africa, an anonymous British writer, presumably a serving or retired

188

Presidency Army officer, cautioned as to, 'putting in the hands of the most untameable and treacherous beings upon the earth the arms which we dare not trust in the hands of our own Asiatic subjects.' Bartle Frere, later Governor of Bombay, argued that if the British needed a foreign army to hold India, then they should leave altogether, for, if India was to be held at all, then it must be by trusting Indians. The Royal Commission, in March 1859, recorded that the army in India must be composed mainly of Indian troops, but recommended that the proportion of Indian to British troops should not exceed three to one for the Madras and Bombay Armies, and that the artillery should all be in European hands. (As to the latter, an exception came to be made as to mountain batteries.) Before 1857, the artillery had had a proportion of Indian gunners under European officers, and all the European gunners had been troops of the Company, and not of the Crown. The commission envisaged an army of a maximum of 190,000 Indian and 80,000 British troops, as opposed to 313,500 Indian and 38,000 British troops in 1857. After the reorganization was completed in 1863, the actual numbers were 135,000 Indian and 62,000 British troops. Owing to the fear of a Russian invasion in the 1880s, there was an increase of 30,000 in the total, the proportion remaining the same till the First World War.

A certain number of the old Bengal Infantry regiments were reformed, but in the rebuilding of the Bengal Army the old recruiting areas of Oudh, the North-West Provinces and Bihar, from where the Brahmins and Rajputs of the Bengal Army had been recruited, were, to an extent, abandoned. Curiously, the irregular cavalry regiments of the Bengal Army, recruited from the same areas as the regular regiments that all mutinied, largely remained loyal to the British. An example was the two regiments of the Scinde Irregular Horse, which only had an aggregate of five British officers, and not a man deserted. The elimination of doddering subedars and British commanding officers of seventy years of age, and promotion by merit instead of seniority, were now enforced.

A local European army was proposed by Canning, and others, because they considered it would be fully at the disposal of the Government of India, and more economical, compared to any Crown troops in India; also that the European officers and men of a local

189

European army would identify themselves with India and its inhabitants, providing a source from which both officers and men could be drawn for various civil employments. At this time, the Company's European troops in 1860 numbered 15,000. On the other hand, it was urged by the War Office that the British armed element in India should be at all times imperial, and ought not to be divided, serving different masters; that the tradition of British units could be preserved only by the rotatory return of European regiments to Britain; and that a local European armed force would be more liable to disaffection than one which was relieved by units from Britain. The advocates of a local European armed force were shortly to be stunned, by what has since been known as the "White Mutiny". The Company's European troops objected to being transferred to the Crown, 'as though they were livestock,' without their wishes being consulted and without any bounty. (Lord Canning was afraid Indian troops would also claim such a bounty.)

After much covert disaffection and open insubordination, 10,000 Europeans took their discharge. At Meerut, highly inflammatory writings had been reported; at Berhampore the European regiment gave, 'three cheers for the Company, and three groans for the Queen'; and at Allahabad the disarming of the European regiment by Indian troops was contemplated as in 1766. It was thereafter decided that the European units of the three Presidency Armies should be transferred to the Crown. The distinction between the "Royal troops" and "the Company's European troops", which had existed, now disappeared. The European infantry units in the three Presidency Armies became British Army regiments, and the Bengal, Madras and Bombay European artillery were amalgamated with the Royal Artillery. The cost of 10,000 free passages to Britain for the Europeans taking their discharge was 250,000 pounds. It would have been cheaper for Canning to have agreed to a small bounty and avoided the mass discharge. (Some 2,000 odd returned to India.) While in India, the British troops were to be lent to and paid for by the Indian Government, the Company having always been liable for the cost of the Royal troops serving in India. The commission also recommended that Indian regiments should be formed by a general mixture of all classes and castes. The "general mixture" system in

Indian regiments was never wholly adopted, and largely ceased to exist altogether till the Second World War.

In 1860, by when the 1857 Uprising had ceased, the government had the task of reorganizing the Bengal Army. The Madras and Bombay Armies, the Hyderabad Contingent and the Punjab Frontier Force did not need reconstruction *per se,* but reorganization was general. In 1861 the reorganization of the cavalry and infantry was announced. Many regiments of irregular horse were disbanded or incorporated with others. Some regiments and levies of infantry were broken up, others were transferred to the newly-organized civil police force, which took over various duties, such as the escort of money and the guarding of civil treasuries, hitherto performed by the army. All Indian artillery was abolished, except the batteries of the Punjab Frontier Force, the Bombay mountain batteries and the field batteries of the Hyderabad Contingent. All the cavalry was now organized on the "silladar" system, except the three regiments of the Madras Army, and the establishment of British officers of regular cavalry and infantry regiments was reduced to six per unit. This reorganization took some years, and, on its completion in 1865, the order of battle of Indian units was as follows:

	Cavalry Regiments	Artillery Batteries	Corps of Sappers and Miners	Infantry Regiments of single battalions
● Bengal Army	19		1	49
● Madras Army	4		1	40
● Bombay Army	7	2	1	30
● Punjab Frontier Force	6	5		12
● Hyderabad Contingent	4	4		6
● Other local troops	2			5
● Total:	42	11	3	142

The other local troops were the two regiments of the Central India Horse, the infantry of the Deoli and Erinpura Irregular Forces, the Malwa and Mewar Bhil Corps, and the Bhopal Levy. At this time the Merwara Battalion had been temporarily converted into Military (armed) Police. The Indian cavalry regiments now consisted of 420 troopers, organized in six troops, with six British officers, the commandant, second-in-command, two squadron commanders, an adjutant and a general duty officer. The Indian infantry regiments were reduced to a strength of 600 soldiers in eight companies, with six British officers, the commandant, two wing commanders, an adjutant, a quartermaster and a general duty officer. With six British officers each, cavalry and infantry regiments had double the number of European officers in the old irregular corps, but only about a fourth of the latterly authorized British officer establishment of the earlier regular regiments.

The officering of the reorganized Presidency Armies was resolved by the institution in 1861 of a Staff Corps for each of the three Presidency Armies, every appointment of a British officer to an Indian regiment being deemed a staff appointment, carrying with it a staff allowance, in addition to the pay of rank. In the earlier Presidency Armies, British officers belonged to regimental cadres, and in practice it was found, particularly in 1857, that these regimental cadres were insufficient to bear the strain caused by the absence of officers in civil employ or on the staffs of various headquarters. Moreover, officers had a right to promotion in regimental succession, but officers of one regiment had no claim to equality of promotion with officers of another. Thus promotion in one regiment might be faster than in another, and the officers of the first could, through no merit, obtain seniority over those of the second. Thus, there had been disparity in the promotion within the various regiments, and within the various Presidency Armies.

The institution of the three Staff Corps sought to establish corps of officers in each Presidency of sufficient strength to ensure that regimental establishments would be maintained, in spite of the departure of officers on extra-regimental duties, including civil employment. Promotion to higher rank was now governed by length of service. Officers, after twelve years of service (subsequently

192

reduced to eleven), were to become captains; after twenty years, majors; and after twenty-six years lieutenant colonels; five years in this latter rank gave the brevet rank of colonel. (But it did not remove the inequality in the rank of officers holding the same appointments in different corps. Thus, a major in one regiment might be a company commander, whereas, in another, a captain might be a company commander. The equalizing of rank and appointments remained difficult until the introduction of the regimental system into the Indian Infantry in 1922.) As already recorded, possibly by a tradition handed on since the time Robert Clive organized regimental "staffs" for his newly-formed Indian battalions, officers held "staff" appointments in the combat units in which they were serving, though they were actually commanders.

These Staff Corps were now open to British Army as well as former East India Company officers, and the Company's military college at Addiscombe was closed down. Thereafter, all fresh appointments to the Presidency Armies in India were to be made from the British Army. In later years cadets passing out from Sandhurst were posted direct to an unattached Indian list, and, after a year's duty with a British regiment in India, were appointed to Indian regiments. Officers had the option of joining the Staff Corps or remaining on the old conditions. There was also a large number of surplus officers arising from the post-1860 disbandments. At the same time, the "cadres" of the old regiments were retained, resulting in the rapid promotion of those who had not joined the Staff Corps, and in their sequential early attainment of "colonel's allowances" (which had now been granted to every lieutenant colonel after twelve years' service in that rank), carrying with it emoluments then amounting to 1,124 pounds per annum. These allowances were termed "off reckonings", and were a survival of the days when the colonels of regiments retained a proportion of the contract allowances for the clothing of their men, a custom obtaining in the British and Indian services alike. For many years, the result was a long list of officers drawing "colonel's allowances", and a still unsatisfactory state of Staff Corps as contrasted with regimental promotions.

Between 1860 and 1878, the Presidency Armies were not engaged in any major campaign. There were many expeditions on the

North-West Frontier, the China War of 1858-60, various expeditions to the eastern and north-eastern frontiers, the Abyssinian War of 1867-68, the expedition to Perak, and the despatch of an Indian contingent to Malta in 1878. Of the North-West Frontier expeditions, Sir William Hunter, ICS, observed then in his book, *Our Indian Mussalmans:* 'British India could have been spared the Frontier War of 1863...a few well timed arrests (of Wahabis) would have saved us nearly the thousand killed or wounded in the Ambeyla Pass. We should probably have been spared the campaign on the Black Mountain in 1868.' Various trials of such Wahabis took place between 1864 and 1872. Hunter also states that, 'the Army contractors (as revealed) in the trial of 1864 carried on a profitable business,' with both sides. There were also several other demands for troops. Some instances were a major communal riot in Bombay in 1861; in 1872, in aid to the civil power, against the reformist Sikh sect, the Kookas (Namdharis), where eighty-two were ordered to be blown from a gun by the Deputy Commissioner; in 1878 operations against the guerrilla bands of Wasudeo Balwant Phadke who was looting treasuries and post offices and was exiled to Aden; and in 1879-80 what was termed the Rampa "rebellion" in the Godavari valley, near Bhadrachalam, involving thousands of tribals. Much was done to consolidate the reorganized Presidency Armies in this period, but the war in Bhutan, starting in 1864, requires mention.

The Bhutanese were given to descending from Bhutan to carry out depredations in the foothills of Assam and north Bengal. The Bhutanese were also not well-disposed to the Company's missions, or the latter's endeavour to establish trade relations with Tibet. In 1773, the Tashi Lama had explained to the British, at the time of the then depredations into Cooch Behar, that the Bhutanese "fully deserved punishment", but suggested that further military action be foregone. In 1837, however, the Company sent a further mission to Bhutan to persuade the Bhutanese to desist from raiding Assam. Thereafter, as recorded in the Parliamentary Papers for "Bootan" for 1865, when Ashley Eden in 1863 led another mission to Bhutan to negotiate a treaty, 'The Penlow took up a large piece of wet dough, rubbed my face with it, pulled my hair, slapped me on the back, and generally committed other acts of very great insolence.' Eden signed

194

a convention, recording "under compulsion", on 29 March 1864. Thereupon, the war followed, the British muskets and guns versus the Bhutanese arrows and boulders, the British losing as many men of the Bengal Army as if the Bhutanese had been armed with muskets. The campaign continued into 1866, the eventual treaty satisfying neither the British nor the Bhutanese.[1]

Though strictly not pertaining to the Indian Army, there was a curious episode in 1869 in the Andaman Islands, where five VCs were awarded, seemingly too easily, set against standards for Indians in the world war awards. Seven British soldiers were landed to try and trace a party of British sailors who were missing, feared killed at the hands of the local tribes. There was a heavy sea running. The rescue party was soon in danger itself, its boat being swamped. A fresh rescue party was sent, and made three successful trips. None of the hostile tribes was in sight, so the awards were not 'in the presence of the Enemy.'

The establishment of the three Presidency Armies remained practically the same, but changes took place in dress, equipment and armament; in 1874 the first issue of the Snider rifle was made. The Imperial Assemblage was held in 1877 at Delhi, proclaiming Queen Victoria the Queen Empress. The Governor-General had hoped to announce an Indian Privy Council and an Indian peerage (analogous to the Irish peerage). Whitehall vetoed both. Baroda's artillery received special attention at this Assemblage. The guns were of gold and the wheels of silver, and vice-versa. Though the Viceroy introduced a medal to commemorate the occasion, the War Office did not permit it to be worn in uniform.

Now, in 1877, Colonel (later Field Marshal Lord) Frederick Roberts, Quartermaster General, was a leading proponent of the Forward Policy in Afghanistan. Roberts and his group had awaited a suitable opportunity to press their case; this arrived when Lord Edward Lytton became Governor-General, in succession to Lord Thomas Northbrook. Lytton came to India in 1876 with instructions to deal with Afghanistan in accordance with the Forward Policy: 'The maintenance in Afghanistan of a strong and friendly power has at all times been the object of British policy. The attainment of this object is now to be considered with due reference to the situation created by the recent and rapid advance of the Russian army in central Asia towards the northern frontiers of British India... Her Majesty's Government cannot view with complete indifference the probable influence of that situation upon the uncertain character of an Oriental chief...,' for had not Napoleon and Tsar Nicholas plotted an invasion by that route in 1807? Salisbury, the Foreign Secretary, however cautioned Lytton, '...You should never trust experts. If you believe the doctors, nothing is wholesome; if you believe the theologians, nothing is innocent; if you believe the soldiers, nothing is safe.' Before his departure for India, he learned that his Council at Calcutta was, however, opposed to the Forward Policy. Meanwhile the Dean of St. Paul's, London, was preaching, '...those who sow the wind of aggressive ambition, must look to reap the whirlwind of disaster.'

Some, like John Lawrence, had appreciated the folly of despatching William Elphinstone's army forty years earlier. The situation had not now so changed as to expect a different result, but those who recommended consolidation of the British-Indian Empire, without further northward expansion to meet the supposed Russian threat, were derided by the Forward Policy proponents. The only debatable point for the latter was where the border should be drawn supposedly to stop the Tsar. The concept of a "Scientific Frontier" was now conceived, well within the territory of Amir Sher Ali of Afghanistan. This was, however, only an interim device to annex the southern half of Afghanistan, pending the later annexation of the whole, including Herat, Roberts writing in 1877, 'To save Afghanistan from Russians it is absolutely necessary for India to be in possession of Herat.' For his part, a Russian writer in 1875, M.A. Terentyeff, was urging Russian help in a second "Bengal mutiny".

When, during the Russo-Turkish War of 1878, the Russians were at the gates of Constantinople, war seemed certain between Britain and Russia. The Russian General Constantine Kaufman had reportedly assembled a force variously estimated at 30,000 to 35,000 to strike at India through Afghanistan. In the event, the Tsar backed down, the British, however, by then having already sent 8,000 Indian troops to Malta, and then Cyprus, on a contingency basis, if in the event it was necessary to employ them in Turkey against the

Russians. While Kaufman's alleged invasion was called off, Sher Ali sought to turn a Russian mission back, but Kaufman insisted it was too late to do so. When St. Petersburg was queried by the British Foreign Office as to the purpose of the Russian missions to Kabul, the former apparently denied all official knowledge of it; Lytton was incensed at Sher Ali, alleging a welcome to a Russian mission, while having earlier twice refused entry to a British mission. Lytton did not appreciate Sher Ali's problems, his favourite son having just died, and Kaufman both refusing to withdraw his mission and also threatening to replace Sher Ali by his nephew, Abdur Rahman, then a Russian pensioner in their territory. Sher Ali yielded very reluctantly, the Russians promising him 30,000 troops against the British, but simultaneously issuing a caveat against any British missions being received in Kabul.

On 14 August 1878, Lytton wrote to Sher Ali to accept a British mission, consisting of General Sir Neville Chamberlain and Major Louis Cavagnari. Like Lytton and Roberts, Cavagnari favoured the breaking up of Afghanistan into several small petty states. Chamberlain commented on the ultimatum that Sher Ali was scarcely, 'to be expected to turn Christian and apply for a bishopric.' Receiving no reply, Cavagnari rode to the nearest Afghan post beyond the Khyber for permission to enter. This was refused, the Russians in the meantime having clarified to the British that their mission to Kabul was only a courtesy one. The Amir was given a final ultimatum to reply by 20 November, both apologizing for his conduct and accepting a British mission. No reply being received by that date, three British columns entered Afghanistan the following day. The Amir's reply was received ten days later, accepting the British mission, but by then the British considered the Second Anglo-Afghan War to have commenced, not deeming the Amir's reply apologetic enough. Lytton sought to teach Sher Ali an unnecessary lesson. The 35,000 British-Indian force, after some engagements, seized the Khyber, Jalalabad and Kandahar. Sher Ali now sought from Kaufman the 30,000 Russian troops, which he had been assured. Kaufman said this was not possible in mid-winter. Sher Ali set out for St. Petersburg to intercede with the Tsar, having appointed his eldest son, Yakub Khan as Regent, whom he had just released from custody. At the frontier, the Russians denied him entry. Sher Ali died at Balkh in February 1879, broken-hearted, having refused both food and medication. Yakub Khan informed the British of his father's death, and Cavagnari offered certain harsh terms—all Afghan policy to be controlled by the British, British missions to be located in Afghanistan, and certain territories near the Indian border, including the Khyber, to be ceded. After some negotiations, Yakub Khan accepted these terms, being guaranteed protection against the Russians and Persians, and an annual payment of 60,000 pounds. An unsympathetic British official versified at the time:

> *And yet when I think of Sher Ali as he lies in his*
> *sepulchre now,*
> *How he died betrayed, heartbroken, 'twixt infidel friend*
> *and foe,*
> *Driven from his throne by the English, and scorned by*
> *the Russians, his guest,*
> *I am well content with vengeance, and I see God works*
> *for the best.*

The Second Anglo-Afghan War of 1870-80 was, until the Russian intervention in Afghanistan in 1979, the last major conflict in Afghan territory with a foreign power (the Third Anglo-Afghan War of 1919 was, by and large, in British-Indian territory). It was an unnecessary war, like the First Anglo-Afghan War had been. It was said of the Hapsburgs (and Bourbons), that they learnt nothing, and forgot nothing. It could well be said of the British in the 1870s, in relation to Afghanistan, that they had learnt nothing, and had forgotten everything; Lord Salisbury, then Secretary of State for India, was not however one of these. In a speech in the House of Lords in June 1877, he stated that, 'in discussions of this kind a great deal of misapprehension arises from the popular use of maps on a small scale.' A career officer, Lieutenant Colonel R.D. Osborne, resigned in protest at the war, and John Lawrence in London described it as, 'high-handed aggression aggravated by duplicity.'

Major General Sir Samuel Browne, VC, commanded the Khyber Line Force in the first phase of the war, November 1878-

May 1880. His force suffered greatly from inadequate transport, and some considered Browne responsible for this, though the official history of the war records: 'The Peshawar Valley Force was assembling when General Browne arrived there on the 9th November... The greatest difficulty encountered was that of equipping it... for....Peshawar had already been drained by the Kurram Column (Roberts'), and that little remained for the Khyber Line Force, which, although destined to be first in the field, was the last whose organization received the sanction of Government.'[2] It was from Roberts' Kurram Field Force on 1-2 December that one jemadar and nineteen other ranks, all Pathans from the 29th Punjab Infantry, were accused of treachery (one soldier fired to warn the Afghans of the attack). Later, one was hanged and the rest sentenced to various terms of transportation. Fourteen other Pathans deserted with weapons from the 1st Punjab Infantry, necessitating a predominance of non-Mohammedan troops in the composition of the force.

The Treaty of Gandamak was signed on 26 May 1879 by Amir Yakub Khan and Cavagnari, to the anger of most Afghans, at the village of Gandamak, between Kabul and Jalalabad, where some forty years earlier the remnants of the ill-fated Kabul garrison in the First Anglo-Afghan War had made a last stand against the Afghans. Under the treaty, Cavagnari, the son of one of Napoleon's generals, described by William Trousdale as, 'part Italian, part French, part Irish, and all British,'[3] was to proceed to Kabul as the first British Resident there since the deaths of Sir Alexander Burnes and Sir William MacNaghten in the winter of 1841-42. A continuation of hostilities was a foregone conclusion, as the British did not withdraw from much of the territory seized, but not to be ceded.

Lytton, however, on the assumption that the war was conclusively over with Cavagnari's departure for Kabul, had convened in July 1879, even before Cavagnari reached Kabul, a commission for the reform of the Presidency Armies. It was to be presided over by Ashley Eden, now Lieutenant Governor of Bengal. According to Brian Robson, it was heavily weighted in favour of the Bengal Army, Roberts being a member, having returned from the Kurram. This was part of Lytton's plan. Some weaknesses had inevitably been revealed in what was the first campaign of the Second Anglo-Afghan

199

War, but General Frederick Haines, then Commander-in-Chief in India, did not feel a commission was necessary, and questioned the motives. According to Robson, there were deeper motives, Lytton chortling, 'I intend to open up on the two presidency governments the batteries preparing for their demolition,' (after the other two Presidency Armies had been got rid of). Haines had been Commander-in-Chief in Madras before becoming Commander-in-Chief in India, but 'The almost unbelievable Byzantine bureaucracy of the Indian Army was (now) at work.'[4] (Roberts' Chief of Staff, Charles MacGregor, and many of the Bengal Army members, had to leave Simla again for Afghanistan after Cavagnari's death, but the Eden Commission, however, proceeded in their absence.)

The Kabul Mission, which was, in the event, composed of about eighty-three personnel (accounts vary slightly), entered Kabul on 24 July 1879, and occupied the Residency provided within the Bala Hissar: Envoy and Minister Plenipotentiary, Major Sir Pierre Louis Napoleon Cavagnari, Bengal Staff Corps; William Jenkyns, his Political Secretary, and Ambrose Kelly, his medical officer; and a military escort of seventy-five men from the Corps of Guides under Lieutenant Walter Hamilton, VC. All died in the attack on the Residency in September 1879, except for nine grass-cutters and a few others outside the Bala Hissar at the time of the attack. Cavagnari's body was never recovered, but his pug-dog was found wandering around Kabul, and later sent to Lady Cavagnari. The Kabul Memorial at Mardan, the Guides' headquarters, gives the names of sixty-nine other than Hamilton (twenty-one cavalry, forty-eight infantry). Hamilton had earlier been recommended for the award of the VC for an action on 2 April 1879; the Duke of Cambridge, then Commander-in-Chief in Britain, since 1855 (till 1895), dithered about it, till news came of his death on 3 September. The VC could not then be awarded to a dead person, so the Secretary of State for War now helpfully antedated his endorsement to 1 September, to enable Hamilton to get his VC posthumously *ex post facto*. Cavagnari apparently had not taken any precautions. Roberts, for one, had felt, in relation to the Treaty of Gandamak, that, 'the Afghans had not had the sense of defeat sufficiently driven into them.' In William Trousdale's view, Lytton and his friends knew that the whole Indian army would scarcely suffice to keep a British envoy alive in Kabul.[5] Cavagnari had, in August, reported, 'They can kill the three or four of us here, and our deaths will be readily avenged.' On 2 September he had reported 'all well' and on the next day he was dead. The proponents of the Forward Policy had prevailed and the war was resumed—Roberts advancing to Kabul. By the time it concluded in September 1880, the British had again withdrawn from Afghanistan. Cavagnari, before his death, had recorded, 'If my death places the red line on the Hindu Kush, I don't mind.'

The British Government was askance on learning of Cavagnari's death and Roberts' advance. Prime Minister Benjamin Disraeli (Lord Beaconsfield) recorded, 'We may be only five days' march from Kabul, but that could be as bad as the Great Desert, if we have no transport and inadequate commissariat....I remember with alarm 50 or 60 thousand camels have already been wasted. What alarms me is the state of the Indian Army as revealed in a letter from Lytton...before the catastrophe. (It was for those reasons Lytton had assembled the Eden Commission in 1879.) Except Roberts, who he believes is gifted, and who is certainly a strategist, there seems no one much to rely on; Stewart respectable, Massy promising; but all the persons, with slight exceptions, to whom we have voted parliamentary thanks, and on whom the Queen had conferred honours, utterly worthless. As for General Sam Browne, according to Lytton, he ought to have been tried by a court martial, and he goes through them all with analogous remarks. And these are the men whom, only a few weeks ago, he recommended for all these distinctions! I begin to think he ought to be tried by a court martial himself....' Disraeli added 'When V'Roys and Comms-in-Chief disobey orders, they ought to be sure of success in their mutiny.'

Roberts later maintained that only those of proven complicity in the massacre of the Residency staff were executed at Kabul. A plot was never proven, and the evidence upon which the majority were executed was tenuous, H.B. Hanna recording, 'The difficulty with regard to evidence was got over by permitting Mohammed Hyat, the Indian civilian, to whom in the absence of Pushtu-speaking British officers, the task of beating up witnesses was assigned, to examine informers in secret, the commission accepting his report of their depositions instead of insisting on their appearing before it in person; a procedure which left the accused in ignorance of their accusers, and deprived them of the chance of proving their innocence by the production of rebutting testimony.'[6] Eighty-nine were tried, and forty-nine executed. MacGregor, Roberts' Chief of Staff, said the British court consisted of, 'two idiots and one lazy man.' Trousdale records of the Kabul hangings, 'Though, in some cases, arbitrary to be sure, these (Kabul) executions seem to have been conducted with greater dignity and respect for the victim (if such words are appropriate to execution) than many summary executions during the first phase,'[7] of this war. Trousdale quotes William Simpson, the special artist of the *Illustrated London News* present during the war, that to discourage fanatical "ghazi" attacks, the British hanged some in pigskin hoods so that they would be defiled at death, and not be received in paradise. Cavagnari himself had presided over the execution of a Muslim and the subsequent burning of the body, a practice considered by Muslims as an indignity. The Afghans, for their part, consistently mutilated the dead, and there is even a record of their having exploded gunpowder in the mouth of a British private.

On account of certain occurrences at Kabul in December 1879, Army Headquarters, Simla, now ordered Sir Donald Stewart to march from Kandahar to Kabul. On 19 April 1880, Stewart's division, marching from Kandahar to Kabul, encountered an Afghan force of approximately 1,000 horse, and 13,000 foot at Ahmed Khel, twenty-three miles south of Ghazni. Stewart's troops numbered 4,000, both infantry and cavalry. Stewart's force defeated the Afghans. Upon his arrival at Kabul, as the senior military officer, Stewart, who was later to be Commander-in-Chief in India, also assumed command of the forces under Roberts. A critic of Roberts has stated that, 'he consistently reported more men ahead than were really there,' and that the strengths at Kabul on 11 December 1879 were exaggerated. At Peiwar Kotal earlier Roberts had said there were 18,000 Afghans when actually there were 4,000.[8]

One of the much publicized reverses, which occurred during the severe fighting around Kabul on 11 December 1879, was General

W. Dunham Massy's alleged abandonment of some guns on the battlefield. (The abandoned guns were recovered by MacGregor.) Massy believed this event of 11 December had been played up by Roberts to provide an excuse for removing him, and took his case to the press. It was more a case of faulty decisions. Roberts had been in charge of a war that was bogged down, a war he and his friends had favoured. Fortuitously, the battle of Maiwand was in the offing on 27 July 1880. The village of Maiwand lay about forty-five miles from Kandahar. Brigadier General G.R.S. Burrows, with his force of 2,500, gave battle to Ayub Khan of Herat on 29 July 1880, and suffered a defeat losing half his men, and most of his transport and baggage animals. It was fashionable after the battle to blame the Bombay Army regiments. The Jacob's Rifles did falter, but the concerned two companies were not from the Bombay Presidency proper.

The usual picture of Roberts' Kabul-Kandahar march is one of efficiency, but differs with that portrayed in the diary of his Chief of Staff, MacGregor: 'The march of this force is that of a disorganized rabble; an Afghan seeing it, said we were like an Afghan army.' The swift march of 320 miles in twenty-three days succeeded because the new Amir, Abdur Rahman, wanted it to succeed. The Afghans had shown in the past what they could do to such an army, if they wanted so to do. Roberts' reputation was enhanced by contrast with Burrows' disaster at Maiwand, and James Primrose's near Kandahar. The ultimate victor at Kandahar was Abdur Rahman, who was saved the necessity of defeating Ayub Khan. Whether there were Russian artillery officers at Maiwand has been questioned by many writers, mainly on the basis that the Afghan artillery at Maiwand was brought to bear upon the British with an accuracy thought impossible for Afghan artillery crews. There was no proof that there were any Russian officers present, and the likelihood is that there were none. It is more likely that the Afghans had been trained by gunners of the Bengal Army, who had fled to Afghanistan in 1857.

While the great baggage trains and thousands of camp followers were still part of such army expeditions in and from India, the numerous wives, children and civilian servants, who had accompanied the Army of the Indus in 1838 on its promenade, were no longer impedimenta to the same extent in 1878-80 in the Second Anglo-Afghan War. The British did not now have that degree of overconfidence as in the First Anglo-Afghan War. This was a campaign in which the British learned, in the words of Pierce Fredericks, that, 'the hardest part of a punitive expedition is getting out after the work is done.'[9] Like the Sino-Indian conflict of 1962, it destroyed more political and military careers than it made. It also established the limits of the British-Indian Empire, seemingly expanding till then, and marked the end of the Forward Policy. Rudyard Kipling's Kim, the orphan boy of Lahore, later said, 'When everyone is dead, the Great Game is over, not before.' (After 1947, the Americans and Russians continued it, and now, in 1992, Chinese, Turks, Iranians and Pakistanis.) Many men lost their lives in this war, because of the folly of a few. Lytton had the last word: 'Our Commander-in-Chief and his whole staff are a coagulation of mediocrities, and inveterately obstinate stupidities, and they have weighed upon me and upon India like a horrible incubus throughout the war.'

The former Governor-General, John Lawrence's policy of "masterly inactivity" had been scorned by the Forward Policy proponents, of whom Roberts was one; nevertheless this Second Anglo-Afghan War was the last time British-India would actually fight a war across its North-West Frontier, despite the various contingencies that had been envisaged. The shorter Third Anglo-Afghan War of 1919, again forty years later than the previous one, was hardly noticed by many, except by the Waziristan Militia who deserted *en masse*. In the Second Anglo-Afghan War, there was no Sir Alexander Burnes trysting in the zenanas of Kabul and paying the price for his idiocy. The war did produce many memoirs, including the diary of Sir Charles MacGregor, Chief of Staff to Roberts and then to Stewart.[10]

Charles Metcalfe MacGregor, the founder of the United Service Institution of India, and in memory of whom the MacGregor Medal is still awarded, had two goals—to win the Victoria Cross, and to be the Amir of Afghanistan. He failed to achieve either, but in his diary called Roberts, the victor of Kandahar and the ostensible redeemer of the honour of the British-Indian Army, 'a cruel blood-thirsty little brute,' 'the most selfish little brute in creation,' 'a third-rate man,' 'very crooked,' and so on. MacGregor went on to write his own unbalanced Forward Policy paper of 359 pages on "The Defence of India: a Strategical Study" in 1884, in which he declared, 'I solemnly assert my belief that there can never be a real settlement of the Russo-India question till Russia is driven out of the Caucasus and Turkistan. ...I propose, by a timely exhibition of boldness and energy, to seize Herat with as little as possible by a coup de main... the Khanate should be raised in insurrection and a Chinese army under British direction should advance westward beyond Kashgar.'

The Second Anglo-Afghan War involved miscalculations in the actual cost of the war as well. Sir John Strachey, the Finance Member of the Viceroy's Council, reported on 24 February 1880 that the cost of the war for the years 1878-79 and 1879-80 had totalled 3,892,000 pounds, a sum that occasioned much satisfaction. Upon further calculation the cost was 19,574,000 pounds, a differential of 15,682,000 pounds which, even allowing for habitual cost overruns, was excessive. The Indian public was able to perceive that India had been made to pay heavily for British imperial nervousness, or, as the punster put it, "Mervousness", after the nearby Russian city of Merv. Pierce Fredericks aptly sums up this war as, 'a war started to forestall Russian influence at Kabul was now to be settled by the installation of a Russian pensioner in the same location.'[11] Abdur Rahman remained securely on the throne of Afghanistan for twenty years.

Before moving on from this war, three events, cited by Trousdale, need mentioning. The Reverend James Williams Adams, Bengal Ecclesiastical Department, was the only cleric ever to be awarded the Victoria Cross, for saving the lives of several lancers during the hostilities around Kabul on 11 December 1879. Roberts' Arab charger, Vonolel (1877-1896) was decorated by special permission of the Queen with the Afghan War Medal with four clasps (Peiwar Kotal, Charasia, Kabul, Kandahar) and the Kabul-Kandahar Star. Khushdil Khan, who had been a member of Cavagnari's escort in 1879, and survived by being away from the Kabul Residency at the time, curiously went over to Ayub Khan at Herat and held a military command under him against the British in 1880 at Maiwand and Kandahar. He fled with Ayub Khan to Herat, remaining in his service for many years, even in India. Eventually, returning to Afghanistan in 1904, he became first Governor of Kabul, and later of Kandahar, proclaiming Amanullah Amir in 1919, the latter then launching the Third Anglo-Afghan War. As an epilogue to this war, in 1886, Roberts, then Commander-in-Chief, had a conversation with F. Villiers, the London *Graphic* artist in India, about a campaign beyond the North-West Frontier. Roberts invited Villiers to accompany him: 'You are very kind, General...with whom will the fighting be?' 'Why, with Russia of course,' he replied.[12]

Meanwhile, the Russians had been following the war closely, Major General L.N. Soboleff producing three volumes on it in 1880, 1881 and 1882 respectively. Of the first campaign itself he validly recorded: '...the absence of a seriously considered plan of operations, the inability to combine caution with decision, the utter helplessness shown in securing the lines of communication, the miserable condition of the intelligence and scouting services, the inability to arrange the regular despatch of transport trains, the want of tact shown to the native population, the subjection of military operations to political considerations.' Soboleff concluded that the war clearly demonstrated the weakness of the British position in India.

The Anglo-Afghan War of 1878-80, which had thus involved the employment of a considerable army from India and a strain upon the military resources of India, produced lessons in every branch of army organization in India. Many shortcomings had been observed in the first campaign itself, and the Army Organization (Eden) Commission of 1879 had been assembled by Lytton as already mentioned, not only to devise means for the reduction of military expenditure, but to test how far the existing system had been found adapted to the requirements of active service. The Indian troops at this time numbered about 135,000. The commission's inquiry eventually resulted in many reforms, but the immediate outcome was the reduction in 1881 of four regiments of Indian cavalry and eighteen of Indian infantry, and an addition of one British officer to each of the remaining regiments. The strength of each Indian regiment was, at the same time, increased from 499 to 550 all ranks in the cavalry— except in the Madras Army, whose cavalry regiments were pegged at 387 all ranks—and from 712 to 832 in the infantry. This gave the same total strength of the three Presidency Armies as existed prior to the 1861 reduction, the commission being satisfied that increased efficiency would be gained, as well as improved fighting power, despite the reduction in the number of combat units. The unit reductions were distributed as follows:

	Indian Cavalry	Indian Infantry
● Bengal Army	2	5
● Madras Army	-	8
● Bombay Army	1	4
● Punjab Frontier Force	1	1

Meanwhile, the way was prepared for the larger reform proposed by the commission, to abolish the three Presidency Armies, but which had not so far been accepted by the Secretary of State for India. In 1864 the three Presidency departments of Military Accounts and Audit had been consolidated into one, under an Accountant General attached to the Military Department of the Government of India. In 1876 the general management of the three Remount departments of the Presidencies had been placed under one head. In 1884 the three Ordnance departments, which had hitherto been entirely separate, were amalgamated under one head and placed under the Government of India. A partial reorganization of the Transport Service was also carried out, and Commissariat Regulations were compiled for all the three Presidencies. The enrolment of certain ostensibly low-caste classes (wrongly dubbed "non-martial"), whose military efficiency had not been deemed satisfactory, was prohibited. (This facet is examined in a subsequent chapter.) The endeavour was initiated to carry out "class" segregation by eliminating Punjabis from Hindustani regiments and vice-versa, while the mixed troops and companies of the Punjab Frontier Force were replaced by "class" troops and companies. Pioneer corps were instituted for the Madras Army, and Army Hospital Corps were raised for all three Presidency Armies. After the evacuation of Afghanistan, there was an expedition against the Mahsud Wazirs on the North-West Frontier, and some active service in the Egyptian Campaign of 1882, and at Suakin in the Sudan in 1885.

The year 1885 witnessed three major events: the preparation of a large force for the defence of the North-West Frontier, the recommencement of an increase in the number of Indian units, and the Third Anglo-Burmese War. The first was necessary on account of the clash between Russian and Afghan troops in the disputed Panjdeh valley on their respective border, where the Afghan troops who suffered heavy losses, were expelled by the Russians. An Indian force over.5,000 strong, including State Force units, with 168 guns, was mobilized, and a considerable quantity of supplies and transport was collected. Of the 1885 Panjdeh crisis, Pierce Fredericks records, 'The spectre of nearly a century—the cossack and the sepoy meeting in Central Asia—was about to become a reality but in the event there would only bé a few hundred of these escorting General Sir Peter Lumsden appearing for Britain and General Zelenoi appearing for Russia (on a joint boundary commission to stop further Russian advances). Only a very few foresaw that before the matter was settled, the two nations would be on the verge of war over a speck on the map, Panjdeh, a place notable for nothing whatsoever except that in the opinion of at least one British officer its carpet weaving was rather above the neighbourhood average.'[13] The Russians had demanded in 1884 that the British make the Afghans withdraw; the British demanded that the Russians withdraw. A Calcutta paper urged London to address the Russians in the words of Dalhousie, 'If you will have war, then, by God, you shall have it, and let it be war to the knife the world over.' The British Ambassador in Moscow had reported that a Russian politician had admitted to him that once you let a general loose in Central Asia, it was extremely difficult to know where he was going to stop. The Afghans lost 800 men, and the Russians had forty killed or wounded. At the time of the clash, Viceroy Frederick Dufferin and Amir Abdur Rahman were meeting in Rawalpindi, where the latter had been greeted with a guard of honour, and a military band playing the Gilbert and Sullivan air, "For he might have been a Russian, a Frenchie, or Turk or Proosian or perhaps Italian! But in spite of all temptation he remains an Englishman." Abdur Rahman was not unduly worried by the clash, stating that he had, 'lots of generals in Afghanistan.' The Indian Army did get the go-ahead for its railway to Quetta, but was told to call it "road-building".

Fortuitously peace was maintained, but it was felt that the army in India was no longer strong enough for the task which might be imposed on it. After 1857, the accepted policy had been the reduction of the number of Indian units to a strength sufficient for internal security and the local defence of the border. The possibility of a war with a great European power now seemingly rendered it necessary to increase the number of troops in India. The Indian units were increased in the following manner: three new cavalry regiments, two in the Bengal Army and one in the Bombay Army; a fourth squadron was to be added to all the Bengal and Bombay cavalry regiments, while the Madras cavalry were now to have a regimental strength of 489 in place of 387 all ranks. The Indian mountain batteries were each to have six instead of five guns. The infantry in the Bengal Army was to be increased by nine battalions, notably five of Gurkhas, two of Sikhs, one of Dogras, with one of Mazhabi Sikhs as pioneers, while every battalion was to be 912 instead of 832 strong. These increases, which were completed in 1887, brought the aggregate of Indian troops to 153,092. Of the financial position in 1887, Brian Robson comments, 'The cost of the increase had effectively wiped out all the savings postulated by the Eden Commission. Such is the fate of most proposals for military economy.' The Third Anglo-Burmese War in 1885-86 followed the alleged growing influence of the French in Upper Burma by King Thibaw granting them commercial privileges, including a railway concession and the right to manage the royal monopolies of teak and petroleum. He had every right to do so. The whole of Burma was now annexed, and Thibaw exiled to India. Thereafter, protracted operations against guerrilla bands and dacoits continued till 1896, the latter having been augmented by Thibaw's disbanded army, so that the increased garrison, which was thereby necessitated, absorbed a considerable portion of the augmentation referred to above. A lesson should have also been learnt that conventional armies do not normally win unconventional wars.

In April 1886, a case of collective disorderliness was reported in the 3rd Gurkha Rifles at Almora, before the District Commander. The removal of the then commanding officer was sought, as, on an audit objection, he had reduced the dearness allowance for rice to twelve annas per month from Rs 2.8 annas. They wanted pay and rations like the *"gora log"*. In 1886 the Indian battalions were linked together in groups of three, or sometimes two, battalions each, on the lines of the 1872 Cardwell scheme in the British Army (of two linked British battalions, one was to serve in Britain and one abroad by rotation). The linked battalions could thus supply trained men to battalions in the field, whereas, under the single battalion system previously in existence, battalions in the field could only be strengthened by volunteers from other regiments or by recruits. Recruits, for the first time, were now enrolled for a group, and, although a recruit might be trained and serve with one particular battalion, he was liable to be called upon to transfer to any other battalion of the group. In 1888 depots were fixed for these groups, and were placed at such stations as it would be obligatory to garrison in case of large-scale mobilization. It was then intended that, in peace, one battalion should always be at the depot, so that the men might periodically return to the neighbourhood that they had been recruited from. These groups of linked battalions were in no sense regiments, but the common depot, and the dependence on each other for assistance, formed a certain bond.

Another military measure, instituted at the same time as the linking of battalions, in 1886-87 was the formation of a reserve for Indian units. Previously, military pensioners seem to have been regarded as a potential reserve in case of need, but reliance could not be placed on them, since pension was then only earned after forty years' service. Two such reserves were formed, the Active and the Garrison Reserve. The latter was to comprise men pensioned after twenty-one years' colour service, or twenty-one years' colour and reserve service combined, but this reserve was allowed to die out as, since no periodic reservist training was prescribed, the men were found to be ineffective when called up. The Active Reserve introduced was to consist of men who might be allowed to pass to the Reserve with not less than five (later reduced to three) or more than twelve years' colour service (later fixed at a thirty-two years' age limit). The numbers were originally limited to 218 for an infantry battalion in the Bengal Army and Punjab Frontier Force, 160 for those of the then Madras and Bombay Armies, 300 for the Sappers and Miners. This Reserve system was later on progressively extended to other arms and services, commencing with the Indian mountain batteries. Arms and accoutrements were kept in arsenals and issued at the periods of training, kits were stored at the regimental depots. Reservists were, at first, called up annually for one month's training, but later for a two months' period every two years. Opportunity was at the same time taken to revise the pension rules, an ordinary pension being given to all soldiers on completion of twenty-one years' service. As early as 1874, the then Commander-in-Chief, Lord Napier of Magdala, had advocated a graduated scale of service for pension ranging from twenty to forty years, but this had not then been agreed to. Reservists obtained a pension of three rupees or Rs 3.50 per month after twenty-five years' total colour and reserve service. The Reserve system worked well in north Indian units, fairly so in Bombay units, but reportedly not so well in Madras units. (By 1904, the Reserve amounted to about 25,000 men, and it was then decided to increase its strength gradually to 50,000 men, reducing the reserve pay from three rupees to two rupees a month as an off-setting measure, and also to extend the Reserve system to "silladar" cavalry regiments.)

Two other measures were sequential to the Third Anglo-Burmese War of 1885. In March 1886, levies and military armed police, composed of Hindustanis, Punjabis and Gurkhas, were raised for service in Burma. Battalions were increased in number, until all the levies aggregated 18,500 men. Later about 16,000 of these men constituted the Burma Military Police. The second measure did not come into force until 1893 when, ostensibly, in order to improve the material of the Madras Army for service in Burma, local battalions were formed for the Madras Army, mainly of Sikhs, Punjabi Mussalmans and Gurkhas, and in the course of a few years eight battalions of the Madras Army were thus reconstituted. Some of the occurrences in Burma used against South Indian soldiers were the alleged disinclination of the 12th Madras Infantry to advance at Minhla in 1887, the alleged inadequate performance of the 10th

Madras Infantry in the Chin Hills in 1889, and the reluctance at Shwebo of the 25th Madras Infantry to do duty during Dussehra*. In the Second Anglo-Afghan War of 1878-80, contingents from some of the princely states of the Punjab had served in the Kurram valley between Thal and Parachinar, so when war seemed imminent with Russia in 1885, the princes of India placed the resources of their states at the disposal of the Government of India. From this offer rose, in 1889, the "Imperial Service Troops", which were under the control of the princes furnishing them and commanded by State Force officers, but subject to the supervision of British inspecting officers.

The execution and supervision of military works, which had formerly been carried out by the Department of Civil Public Works, was, between 1882 and 1890, transferred to a separate Military Works Department, and this in 1899 was completely militarized as the Military Works Services. The first step in the amalgamation of the Presidency Commissariat departments was made in 1885, when a Commissary-General-in-Chief was appointed. In 1886 a plan of mobilization was prepared for the first time, and this year saw the transfer of the Punjab Frontier Force from the control of the Punjab Government to that of the commander-in-chief. In 1890 the three Presidency Staff Corps were amalgamated into one "Indian Staff Corps". In 1895 the pay of all non-commissioned officers and men in the Indian artillery, sappers and miners and infantry was raised by two rupees per mensem, the pay of the soldier becoming nine rupees instead of seven rupees, a figure at which it had remained for over a century.

In 1891, recruiting depots for the various classes of which the Bengal Army was composed were established, and placed under district recruiting officers, a system subsequently applied to the Madras and Bombay Armies. The Bombay Army, like the Madras Army in Burma, decided to recruit ostensibly "better material", two regiments being reconstituted as Baluchistan frontier regiments, composed of Hazaras, Baluchis and Dogra Brahmins, Punjabi Mussalmans and Sikhs. A little later, allegedly undesirable classes,

---

* This animus against the Madras Army will be covered in the chapter, "The Myth Of The Martial Race Dogma".

like Mahars, were unjustly eliminated from the Bombay Army, and the "class company" system introduced in lieu of the "general mixture" organization. A similar reconstitution, after prolonged discussion, was applied to the Madras Army.

In 1891-93 the Indian infantry were armed with the Martini-Henry rifle, the Lee-Mitford magazine rifle having been issued to the British troops in India. In the latter half of the 1885-95 decade, assistance was given to the British Government by the employment of Indian soldiers in Central Africa, East Africa, Uganda, and also in West Africa. In 1893 the sixteen Hindustani regiments of the Bengal Army became "class" (instead of class company) regiments, of Brahmins, Rajputs, Hindustani Mussalmans, Jats and Gurkhas. This change was introduced because, Roberts felt, it would appear mistakenly, that the class system attracted better men; regiments it was thought would be more contented, a competitive spirit would be created, and the separation of classes was thought to be more consonant with the prevailing thinking than mixing, for example, of Brahmins and Rajputs in one unit. In the same year, the Intelligence branch, still part of the Quartermaster General's Department at Army Headquarters, was strengthened. During this period, Indian troops were engaged in military operations in Burma for several years, and on the eastern and north-eastern frontier against the Chins and Lushais (1890-93), in Naga Hills and Manipur (1891), and against the Abors (1894). The operations in Manipur were consequent to the Political Agent in Manipur being speared, and then the Chief Commissioner of Assam and three military officers accompanying him for a parley at the palace being beheaded by the faction that had ousted the Maharaja. (1991 was recently observed as the centenary year of the Manipur War of Independence.) The North-West Frontier was the scene of the Black Mountain expedition in 1888, of the two Miranzai expeditions in 1891, and of the Hunza Nagar fighting in the same year. Fighting in Waziristan in 1894-95 was followed by the defence and relief of Chitral in 1895, and the Swat campaign of 1896. Winston Churchill, who was a war correspondent for several newspapers, including *The Pioneer*, Lucknow, during the Swat campaign, recorded, at its end, after some stolen weapons had been handed back, 'Perhaps these firearms had cost more in blood and treasure than any others ever made. To extort those few had taken a month, had cost many lives, and thousands of pounds. It had been as bad a bargain as was ever made.' In 1893 the British Parliament passed the Madras and Bombay Armies Act, abolishing the offices of Commander-in-Chief in those Armies, and withdrawing the power of military control hitherto exercised by the governments of those two Presidencies. This measure which took effect in April 1895 after much discussion, brought to a conclusion the changes which took place in the Presidency Armies after 1857, the Army Organization Commission of 1879 having earlier recommended the abolition of the Presidency Army system, and the division of the unified Indian Army into four territorial army corps under one authority. It had become an anachronism that the Central Government should have little authority, and the Commander-in-Chief none over the Presidency Armies of Madras and Bombay, which were moreover largely stationed outside these Presidencies. The shortcomings of this state of affairs were many. The Bengal Army, responsible for an area of vast extent, had become unwieldy for a single command. It was, accordingly, felt that the division of the unified Indian Army into four territorial commands, Punjab, Bengal, Bombay and Madras, would best serve the purpose.

Various measures, such as the unification of various military departments, had been gradually carried out before the Madras and Bombay Armies Act was passed. Speaking generally as to these four 1895 commands, the Punjab Command encompassed the Punjab and the North-West Frontier Province (NWFP); the Bengal Command included Assam, Bengal, the United Provinces and parts of the Central Provinces and Central India; the Madras Command comprised the Madras Presidency, the garrisons in Hyderabad and Mysore, and Burma; while the Bombay Command embraced the Bombay Presidency (including Sind), Aden, Baluchistan, Rajputana, and parts of Central India and the Central Provinces. Each command was placed under a lieutenant general, whose headquarters was given power to transact a certain amount of business which had formerly been dealt with by Army Headquarters or the

Military Department.

One of the reasons for discarding a proposal in 1892 for three armies or commands was that, if adopted, an undue disparity in strength would exist between the Army of the North and the strengths respectively of the Armies of the West and South, a fear of the preponderance of a particular army analogous to that of the Bengal Army in 1857. The principle was insisted on that the forces in the new commands should conform to each other as nearly as possible in numerical strength. Stress was laid on the separation of the former Madras and Bombay Armies from each other and from the Bengal Army. The forces in the various commands were in fact to be localized for service in those commands, it being pointed out that the troops of the former Bengal Army, serving in the Bengal Presidency proper, would ordinarily be kept apart from those serving in the Punjab. The new organization brought all the forces under the direct control of one commander-in-chief, but the four commands were still as separate from each other as the old Presidency Armies had been. Further measures were required to complete effectively the unification of the Indian Army. These will be dealt with in the next chapter when Lord Horatio Herbert Kitchener took up his appointment as Commander-in-Chief on 28 November 1902.

To conclude this chapter, the events of 1895-1902 are briefly recorded. Between 1895-98, further campaigns on the North-West Frontier engaged a large number of troops. The years 1899-1900 saw the despatch to South Africa of large quantities of stores of all kinds for the operations against the Boers, and the location of Boer prisoners of war in India and Ceylon. In 1900-01, an expedition to China against the Boxers took place, and in 1901-02 further operations in Waziristan. In 1902, certain local corps hitherto under the Foreign Department, that is, the two regiments of the Central India Horse, the Bhopal Battalion, the Deoli and Erinpura Irregular Forces and the Merwara Battalion, were brought under the commander-in-chief, and allotted to commands according to their geographical location. (The Malwa and Mewar Bhil Corps were not then transferred to the Indian Army, as they were to be converted into police.

In 1903, the Hyderabad Contingent was broken up, in consequence of the arrangement concluded with the Nizam in respect to Berar. By breaking up the 3rd Lancers, Hyderabad Contingent, its cavalry was formed into three regiments of four squadrons, instead of four regiments of three squadrons, and transferred to the Bombay Command; the artillery batteries were abolished, and the six battalions of infantry were transferred to the Madras Command.)

In 1898-1902, two Indian mountain batteries and five infantry battalions were added to the Punjab and Bengal Commands. The five infantry battalions were raised to replace those lent to the British Government for service as colonial garrisons, such as Mauritius, Ceylon and Singapore. Indian troops were first employed as colonial garrisons in 1898, and, thereafter, Indian troops for such garrisons were deemed a permanent arrangement. But before that Indians had been recruited into the various colonial forces, for instance, one hundred Jat Sikhs in 1895 in the Central African Protectorate, today's Malawi: even before Africans were recruited there. Other changes were the reconstitution of four regiments of the Bengal portion of the army, three as Hindustani Mussalmans and Mussalman Rajputs (Ranghars) from the East Punjab, and one as a pioneer regiment of Labana Sikhs and Jats, and the incorporation of the Punjab Frontier Force as an integral part of the Punjab Command. At this time, a case of a collective complaint was averred in the 17th Bengal Infantry at Agra, one of the units being reconstituted with Hindustani Mussalmans and Ranghars. It was alleged that they displayed a "mutinous spirit" at not having any Ranghar sub-officers and few Ranghar non-commissioned officers. They squatted outside the quarter-guard in protest. Thirty-seven were court-martialled. (A similar "squat-in" was again to take place in April 1943 outside its cookhouse on a Sunday by the Rajputana Mussalman/Mussalman Rajput company of the 3rd/4th Bombay Grenadiers, on it being unnecessarily replaced by a Punjabi Mussalman company. Though entirely peaceful, the sentences awarded were savage.)

The former Madras Army underwent considerable change. In 1895, Telugus were eliminated, and the remaining personnel ostensibly gradually "improved". Between 1902 and 1904, two infantry battalions were reconstituted from Moplahs, one battalion was converted to Gurkhas, while nine others were transformed into battalions of Punjabis, leaving the locally recruited Madras battalions at thirteen, from the fifty existing in 1857. The personnel of a regiment of Madras Cavalry were also replaced by a large infusion of men from Rajputana and the Punjab. The personnel of the former Bombay Army were also ostensibly gradually "improved" by the progressive elimination of the allegedly less efficient elements. The preference was for "Grecian" features.

In 1896, the three Presidency medical services were amalgamated under a director-general. The military factories were placed under the direct administration of the Director-General of Ordnance, followed in 1900-01 by the establishment of a Cordite factory at Aruvankadu in the Nilgiris. In 1899, it was decided to withdraw regular troops from the Khyber, and from the Kurram, Tochi and Shahur valleys, and to garrison these outlying positions by militia. In 1900, a change took place in the battalion organization of the Indian infantry, by the introduction of the "double company" organization in place of wings or half-battalions; it linked the eight companies of a battalion in four pairs of double companies, each in command of a British officer, the aim being to give more definite responsibility to the British officers in the battalion and to create a more manageable sub-unit than the "wing" of four companies. In 1900 also, the reorganization of the transport service was finally authorized. The idea was to substitute organized units and cadres of camel, mule and cart transport, commanded by British officers, in place of the unorganized ad hoc transport allotted to regiments and depots, and, by means of "enumeration officers" to ascertain the animal resources of the country so that it might be possible to expand the peace-time animal transport to meet the exigencies of war. The title of the Commissariat was now changed to the "Supply and Transport Corps". In 1900-01, the .303 magazine rifle was introduced for the Indian Army, and the re-armament of regular troops was completed in 1902-03.

The year 1900-01 also saw the inception of mounted infantry schools. In every battalion of British infantry, and in the majority of Indian infantry battalions, not less than 160 men were to be trained in mounted infantry duties, so that, on mobilization, two mounted infantry battalions (one British and one Indian) of four companies each would be available for each division. A new mountain gun was introduced and a large number of machine-guns released. In 1901, the ranks of captain and major were now attainable in nine and eighteen years instead of in eleven and twenty years. In 1902-03 the scattered ambulance establishment was organized into an Army Bearer Corps, and various improvements were made in the Army Hospital Corps and in the nursing service. Coast defences were developed, as also a plan for mobilization. A military railway company was added to the Army, and a second company raised thereafter. In 1903, Burma was separated from the Madras Command, and constituted an independent military charge, practically a fifth command. The commands were subdivided into military districts, but they were not, in any way, organized army corps, nor were the troops in the military districts organized into divisions and brigades. On 1 January 1903, the designation "Indian Staff Corps" was abolished. The former title was a misnomer, because the bulk of the appointments held by the British officers were regimental, not staff appointments. From that time, the British officers, as well as the rank and file of Indian units, belonged to "the Indian Army". Judith M. Brown succinctly encapsulates the British view as to the Indian Army at the end of the nineteenth century. 'At no cost to the British taxpayers (except when employed overseas), it was a large force which could be widely deployed to protect imperial interests; and its presence in the subcontinent helped to safeguard imperial trade and communications between Europe and Australasia. The value of this "English Barrack in the Oriental Seas", as it was called (by Salisbury) in Parliament in 1867, was indicated by the areas in which India's army was used in the second half of the nineteenth century— China, Persia, Ethiopia, Singapore, Hong Kong, Afghanistan, Egypt, Burma, Nyasa, Sudan and Uganda. Its potential manpower was also great in times of great emergency.'[14]

Separately, Lord Curzon had become Viceroy in 1899. Curzon's ambition to become Viceroy had first occurred, according to Peter King, 'when Curzon was Secretary of the Eton Literary Society, and Sir James Stephen "told us" Curzon wrote later, "that there was in the Asian continent an empire more populous, more amazing and more beneficent than that of Rome. Ever since that day...the fascination, and, if I may say so, the sacredness of India have grown upon me.'[15] He immediately made an impact on the military in India and London. After meeting the then Military Member of the Viceroy's Executive Council, Curzon was constrained to observe, '...an absolute amiable old footler, the concentrated quintessence of a quarter of a century of official life.' And as to the British Army officers' attitude in relation to crimes against Indians and Burmans, he wrote to Roberts, then Commander-in-Chief in Britain: 'The argument seems to be that a native's life does not count; and that any crime ought to be concealed, rather than bring discredit on the Army. I have set my face like flint against such iniquity.' To a War Office requirement of 20,000 coolies for the South African war, he had retorted, '...in practice it means for Indians a full share of the battles and burdens of Empire, but uncommon little of the privileges and rights.' More was to follow, as narrated in the next chapter, for Queen Victoria had conveyed to Curzon a warning of the "red tapeism" in India.

SEVEN

The Kitchener Era And The Kitchener-Curzon Dispute

IN 1832, the new Commander-in-Chief in India, General Sir Edward Barnes, had not seen eye to eye with Governor-General William Bentinck. According to the latter, Barnes was liable, 'to see every thing from the point of view of the Horse Guards.'[1] It was impossible for him to play a subordinate role to the Governor-General. The British Government agreed that, 'It is absolutely necessary to keep down that strange spirit of insane pride and self-exaltation which seems to affect some of our military men in India.' Whereas, in 1833, in the Bentinck-Barnes controversy, it was the Commander-in-Chief who was recalled, in the Curzon-Kitchener controversy of 1903-05, it was the Viceroy who eventually resigned. General Lord Horatio Herbert Kitchener knew nothing about India, but nevertheless pressed for the Indian Command, and not the War Office, London. On 3 November 1900, he therefore telegraphed, from South Africa, the Secretary of State for War, St. John Brodrick. Brodrick, *inter alia* replied, 'I can assure you that so far as I can assist to secure your wishes I will try to do so. (The) Indian Army is suffering from constant changes (in Commanders-in-Chief)—hiatus between (Sir George) White and (Sir William) Lockhart—

Lockhart's illness! (Sir Power) Palmer as *locum tenens*—covering altogether three years.'[2] Lockhart died shortly after. Lord Henry Lansdowne, a former Viceroy and Brodrick's predecessor, had earlier been of the opinion that Kitchener had become "too Zabardastic" (sic).

On 3 December Kitchener wrote to Brodrick, 'I fear from it (Brodrick's letter) my chance of the Indian Command is small, and I fully recognize that my lack of experience of India renders it difficult, if not impossible to place me at the head of military affairs there. Still some Indian (Army) officers have told me that they considered it would be an excellent thing for the Indian Army to have someone who was not used to the Indian routine, and could look at (Indian) military matters from a larger view than India alone—I fear it was somewhat presumptuous on my part to look forward to the Indian Command. After Lord Roberts' recommendation I certainly did hope for it, and it is rather a bitter pill to give up all hope...'[3] As regards the War Office, for which he was then wanted, he added, 'I am not the man for the place.... I should be of little use and that I should be a certain failure that is my personal conviction.' Brodrick asked Kitchener to reconsider in the context of prevailing Indian conditions, 'where management without previous experience may try the power of a man whatever his military talent.' Ultimately with the influence of his friends, Kitchener achieved his aim, even though before her death Queen Victoria had sworn, 'that nothing should ever induce her to consent to Kitchener becoming Commander-in-Chief (in India),' as his manners were 'too ferocious' for Indians.[4] Earlier in Egypt, according to Trevor Royle, when Kitchener had been appointed the Commander-in-Chief he was viewed as, 'a toady, who gained power by cultivating friendships...in high places.'

The appointment had been made, 'not without some heartburning...about the possible consequences of setting two natural autocrats to work together in a distant continent.'[5] George Curzon wrote to Kitchener on 31 March 1901 that he was awaiting his arrival, that he intended to be supreme in civil and military affairs, and adding as to the Frontier problem: 'I take its management exclusively into my own charge.'[6] As to the Indian Army, he recorded, 'I see absurd and uncontrolled expenditure. I observe a lack of method and system. I detect slackness and jobbery. And in some respects, I lament a want of fibre and tone.' Kitchener arrived in India on 28 November 1902 convinced that a Russian invasion was imminent and therefore to take immediate steps to meet the Russian threat (the British then believing that Russia would be allied with France, in the event of a European war). The early disasters of the South African war had exposed the British Army. Kitchener believed the Indian Army was in a worse state. According to Sir Philips Magnus, Curzon, 'who was nine years younger than Kitchener, and ambitious that his viceroyalty should be the most memorable...was in urgent need of an efficient instrument for effecting military reforms. The Viceroy's personal relations with the Army had been unhappy, partly on account of the ineffectiveness of Kitchener's immediate predecessor, Sir Power Palmer...shortly before Kitchener's arrival Curzon had imposed collective punishments, for reasons which the Army considered inadequate, upon two (British) regiments.'[7] The Army Headquarters felt Curzon was, 'giving the natives too much rope.' In 1899, when a European jury had acquitted some men of the Royal West Kent Regiment of the gang rape of a Burmese woman (Burma then being under the Government of India), after the men's officers had withheld evidence likely to lead to their conviction, Curzon discharged the men from the army, removed the commanding officer, reduced the sergeant-major to the ranks, censured their officers, moved the regiment to Aden (the most unpleasant station available to the Government of India), and cancelled all leave of the battalion.[8] Racial violence must be checked, he felt, lest it boil over into rebellion, and the time came when, 'the English may be in danger of losing their command of India, because they have not learnt to command themselves.'[9] Shocked by the indifference of the military authorities to incidents in which Indians were ill-treated and killed, as the *'punkah* coolie' in the Scots Fusiliers, or killed by carelessly discharged rifles, he had imposed punishments on the units in question. Peter King opines that, 'from the documents it is quite clear that Curzon acted correctly and moderately.' Lady Curzon, an American, was separately reported to have said, 'The two ugliest things in India were the water buffalo and the British private soldier.' In the midst of the pageantry of the Coronation Durbar in 1903, he had to endure the cheering by the British guests of the 9th Lancers, one of the regiments he had punished for beating an Indian cook, who later died of his injuries, and suspected of also killing another Indian.

A feud had thus already developed between the Viceroy and the Army Headquarters. Kitchener, however, intended to command in the same dominant manner he had done in the Sudan and South Africa. In the Sudan, according to Peter King, 'the (Mahdi's) head was brought to him, just as General Gordon's head had been carried to the Mahdi, and Kitchener planned to have the skull polished as a decoration...but instead kept it in an old kerosene tin...'Queen Victoria was outraged. In South Africa, a "kick-back" benefited Kitchener. For his part, Curzon was as impatient as Kitchener. His partitioning of Bengal, described by some Indian nationalists as the biggest blunder since Plassey, had nearly caused a revolt. His attempt to make Indian university education more "purposeful", by controlling the number of candidates for university degrees, had caused ill-feeling, being construed as an endeavour to stop the growth of an intellectual elite. For his times, however, Curzon was a friend of India, in relation to all that he achieved in his term of office—a forward-looking health policy, a reduction in salt duty, forward planning for famine relief, further canal and railway construction, encouragement of Hindi, preservation of monuments, and the introduction of Indian Standard Time (IST). Even the latter was opposed in India. All his measures were well-intentioned. He would have preferred the purchase of stores for the Indian Army from within India, rather than Britain, thereby encouraging indigenization, but was overruled by the Secretary of State.

He also constituted an Imperial Cadet Corps, with the sanction of the King. The corps, according to Lovat Fraser, then editor of the *Times of India*, 'consisted of cadets of princely and noble houses, and was formed to give young men of rank an opportunity of training in their hereditary profession of arms, and of obtaining commissions in the Army.' Several of the younger ruling chiefs joined the corps. The course of instruction lasted two years. Those desirous of a commission in the "Native Indian Land Forces", as distinct from their own State forces, were required to undergo an additional year's training. Some of the cadets, on commissioning, were appointed to the personal staff of general officers. Through this scheme Curzon, in a way, opened the door for the admission of Indians of princely families to the officer ranks of the Indian Army, though only on a limited basis, due to the opposition of the War Office. These officers did not have any power of command over British personnel. However, on Curzon's departure, the corps did not receive the attention it deserved, and finally, in 1914, with the start of the First World War, the corps was disbanded. When started in 1901, the Imperial Cadet Corps was established temporarily in Meerut, and then in Dehra Dun. (In the same campus today stands the Rashtriya Indian Military College which was inaugurated in 1922.) During this period (1901-1914), seventy-eight cadets from various Indian states were trained.

Kitchener was, like Curzon, a conservative politically, and before he left England, he had made Lady Cranborne his unofficial contact with the conservative political establishment. (Lady Cranborne's husband, who was first cousin to the British Prime Minister, A.J.Balfour, succeeded as Lord Salisbury in August 1903.) Kitchener had a long friendship with her influential family, which felt that it had a personal responsibility to the British Empire. Many of these friends distrusted the policy which the Viceroy, suspecting Russian intentions in these areas, was pursuing in Afghanistan and Tibet (the latter through Francis Younghusband) at the same time; the policy was finally disapproved by the British Government. In effect, there had been two foreign policies for some time, from Whitehall and from Simla respectively. To Lady Salisbury, Kitchener communicated his plans weekly from India in order to keep his friends informed. Arrangements were made by Kitchener's Military Secretary, Hubert Hamilton, for top secret documents and plans to be delivered personally by Hamilton's lawyer to Lady Salisbury "under the guise of legal documents", as, in the event, Hamilton forwarded to her on 6 August 1903, a copy of Kitchener's complete plan for the defence of India against a Russian invasion, only abridged copies being sent to Curzon and Roberts. An officer was sent to England to explain the plan privately to Lady Salisbury, and to the Prime Minister, if so arranged.

As soon as Kitchener, a bachelor, reached India, on 28 November 1902, Lady Curzon had written a 'friendly little line' from Dehra Dun on 9 December 1902: 'Do please take the Army and all the military straight into your heart! It will be a wonderful load off George ... I suppose you know that the prayer of the soldiers has been that the two giants would fall out, and it will be a great grief for them to see you work in harmony, and to know the intense satisfaction it is to George to know that you are here at last ... there is a sort of traditional and iron-bound isolation which encircles you and us. So we shall drag you out of your solitude—we hope very often and see you often when there is no society ... please don't answer this.'[10]

Curzon wrote, 'How are you going to sign, while you are in India?' The Viceroy explained that he always signed "Curzon" and not "Curzon of Kedleston". 'For the additional labour, with the thousands of signatures I have to write, would be prodigious. I hope, therefore, unless you have strong views to the contrary, that you will sign "Kitchener" and will instruct the Department to the effect,' the Viceroy added. Curzon did not desire the name 'Kitchener of Khartoum' (Power Palmer, Kitchener's predecessor, referred to him as "Kitchener of Chaos") circulating more than the truncated "Curzon". Kitchener complied with Curzon's request.

The higher military organization that Curzon had inherited vested control of the Indian Army in two separate authorities. The Commander-in-Chief was responsible for its fighting efficiency; the Government of India, through a less senior soldier known as the Military Member of the Viceroy's Council, was responsible for its administration. At the time Curzon had conveyed to Kitchener that both the organization and administration of the Indian Army (not meaning the higher military system) were in need of immediate reform. 'The idea that pervades everyone in India,' Kitchener wrote to Lady Salisbury on 30 December 1902, 'is that the Army is intended to hold India against the Indians ... I think this is a wrong policy.' He explained that the Indian Army's main task was not to support the civil power in the districts, but to guard the frontiers against external aggression. He found the Indian Army, as he wrote on 16 July 1903, 'all higgledy-piggledy over the country, without any system or reason whatever.' The units were not collected in field formations for annual collective training, but were scattered usually in units of one battalion, for internal security, or in consequence of the Government's reluctance to build barracks at the required cantonments. No one knew how these battalions would be brigaded in war, or which general officers would command the field force divisions on mobilization. Kitchener's plans for remedying these conditions were not original. He reduced garrisons to the minimum compatible with internal security, closing down thirty-four smaller military stations, and saved enough units and manpower to form nine field divisions instead of four.

He stressed that general officers should lead in war the field formations they had trained in peace. Kitchener divided the nine divisions, the "teeth" component of each consisting of approximately ten thousand bayonets, between two army commands. The northern army of five divisions was deployed to guard the Frontier based on Peshawar, along with the Kohat, Bannu and Derajat Brigades; a southern army of four divisions was disposed southwards, with divisions at Mhow, Poona and Secunderabad, and a forward division at Quetta, as also the Burma Division and the Aden Brigade, under command. At the head of each army was a lieutenant general, who was responsible for command, inspection and training, but had no administrative functions and consequently no administrative staff. The ten divisions, including Burma, constituting the two armies were directly subordinate to the Army Headquarters for administrative purposes. This reorganization was an improvement. Divisional and brigade commanders were told what their precise roles were in war, and assumed greater responsibility in peace than hitherto. The lieutenant generals commanding each army were ordered to devote their energy to training.

Kitchener, in October 1903, ordered a renumbering and redesignation, based on a sequential methodology, of the regiments of the Indian Army. All units were renumbered according to their original Presidencies and seniority, regiments like the 1st Punjab and 2nd Punjab thus gaining precedence even though at the time they had no Madras (South Indian) classes; nevertheless they claimed the battle honours of the concerned earlier Madras Infantry units. Gurkha regiments, however, were numbered separately. All mention of the original Presidency Armies was sought to be omitted. Some anomalies came about in the renumbering of Indian cavalry regiments. The three cavalry regiments, which had formed part of the Madras Army in the past, were actually the oldest surviving Indian cavalry regiments. Yet the oldest, *inter se*, of these three Madras cavalry regiments, was now renumbered the 16th Light Cavalry.

Most of Kitchener's letters between 1903 and 1905 were now concerned with the controversy between the Viceroy and the Commander-in-Chief. Kitchener found that he was not able to command solely as he had done in the Sudan and South Africa. Instead, he had to share many functions of his Indian Command with, and to leave supply, transport and ordnance services entirely in the hands of, a junior officer, Major General Sir Edmund Elles, who was the Military Member of the Viceroy's Council. As a staff officer, Elles had a good reputation, but Kitchener was determined to be supremo. He decided to do away with the Military Department which Elles controlled. The Military Department was responsible for all noncombatant administrative services, and also maintained a watching brief over army expenditure. Its head served as the channel of communication between the Viceroy and the Commander-in-Chief, and was expected to advise the civilian Viceroy on broad aspects of military policy. The Military Member of the Viceroy's Council was thus entitled to criticize the proposals of the Commander-in-Chief, and Elles, by circumstance, used that privilege. He attended all meetings of the Viceroy's Council, while Kitchener, who ranked second to the Viceroy in precedence, was required to attend, as Extraordinary Member, only when invited, or for matters with which he was closely concerned. This system known as "dual control" was repugnant to Kitchener. It had come into existence in 1833 due to conditions of active warfare on the expanding frontier, and inadequate communications between the Commander-in-Chief in the field, and the Viceroy at Calcutta or Simla, which conditions had, in the event, for a long time ceased to exist.

The prevailing system, Kitchener felt, caused duplication if not duplicity. It had worked when Roberts was Commander-in-Chief, because the Viceroy, the Commander-in-Chief and the Military Member had been friendly. Before Kitchener arrived, Curzon's desire for reform had made him look into military detail. Kitchener's predecessor, Power Palmer, had allowed Elles to encroach, so that friction had supervened between the two staffs, that of the Military Department and Army Headquarters respectively, not talking to each other, though under the same roof. The Military Member, who was always a military officer, began to appear to Kitchener like the Commander-in-Chief's rival. Early in 1903, Sir Walter Lawrence, Curzon's private secretary, was asked to breakfast by Kitchener in Fort William, Calcutta, and shown a note proposing the abolition of the Military Department. Kitchener would not let him take it away to read, and said all he wanted to know was whether Curzon would accept his proposal. Lawrence told Kitchener that since the latter, 'had not yet seen the (North-West) Frontier, had not really seen anything of the (Indian) Army or the work of the Military Department, the obvious criticism would be that the proposal was founded on ideas formed before he reached India.'[11] Kitchener put the note in his pocket, and said he would wait for a year. Kitchener became paranoid about the Military Department much before that, pulping the files, referred to him, into papier-mache for the renovation of the ceiling of his house in Simla.

On 25 January 1903, he wrote to Lady Salisbury, 'Curzon is all that one could wish and as kind as possible, but the system by which a Member of the Council is made responsible for the administration of the (Indian) Army independent of the Commander-in-Chief, while the latter has only executive functions, is extraordinary. What it comes to is this; a machine is handed over to the Commander-in-Chief for him to work by turning the handle, but he must not interfere in any way with the defects in the complicated machinery. I asked Curzon why he liked to keep up such a farce, and his answer was, if the Commander-in-Chief had anything to do with the machinery, he would become too powerful, so to keep him down we take his power away, and run another man as well. Between the two, civil elements get control. I am astonished at the satisfaction expressed. ... I am sorry to say under the present system I find initiative for good in the administration of the Indian Army is so choked that it ceases to be workable.'[12] In another letter to her, he wrote that the Russians would be rapping at the door, and if nothing had been done in the meanwhile about the duality in control, 'we shall deservedly go to the wall.' These letters were copied by her and sent to Balfour.[13]

In February 1903, Kitchener disapproved of an order drafted in his name by Elles without consultation. He called for the resignation of Elles and the abolition of the Military Department, Curzon recording that it was harder to govern Kitchener than to govern India. To Brodrick, now Secretary of State for India, Kitchener wrote on 21 September 1903: 'The baboo department will not and cannot be made to move.... Life is hardly worth living with all the worries caused by the Military Department.'[14] Such letters to Lady Salisbury, or to Brodrick direct, without Curzon's knowledge, were not frowned upon in Britain, for Brodrick, his mind working in a convoluted way, now wrote to Kitchener on 29 April 1904, 'I have not written to you practically since you went to India, partly because I believe it is forbidden by practice for us to communicate with anyone except the Viceroy, and partly because I know you have been very busy. But I want to break through the rule for once on the principle that when the cat's away, the mice will play! (Curzon had just left India on home leave.) And because I think we have got to a point where it is absolutely essential that you and the Home

Government understand each other. On the other hand I want you to lock this letter up and not to let it be known to others that I have written it .... I hope you will reply this letter "sub rosa". I shall keep your communications entirely to myself.'[15] Of this period, John Maynard Keynes, who then worked at the India Office, wrote of the India Council in London 'as Government by dotardry. At least half those present showed... signs of senile decay.'

By then, Balfour had made up his mind, Kitchener's friends having played their role, for he had already written to Kitchener in December 1903: 'I have not touched on questions of Indian Army administration, but my personal conviction is (at best as at present advised) that the existing division of attributes between the Commander-in-Chief and the Military Member in Council is quite indefensible.'[16] Thus, when Curzon reached England on leave in May 1904, the issue had virtually been decided. Consequently, Curzon's later complaint of conspiracy between Kitchener and the British Cabinet had some basis. In the meantime, Kitchener had come into conflict with the Governor of Madras, Lord Oliver Ampthill, aged thirty-five, who became acting Viceroy during Curzon's absence on leave. Elles had objected to an unimportant order issued by Kitchener. Ampthill asked Kitchener to withdraw the order. Kitchener tendered his resignation on 26 September 1904. Separately on 4 August 1904, Kitchener had written to Lady Salisbury, 'Poor Army! It is the happy or unhappy playground of politicians, who have to leave their mark; and what a mark they leave!' Ultimately, in November 1904, Balfour informed Curzon that he and Brodrick were convinced that Kitchener's resignation would have a disastrous effect upon British public opinion, and that they had both reached the conclusion that the system of dual control would have to be altered. Balfour urged Curzon to find some method of reaching an accommodation with Kitchener.[17] Curzon returned to India on 13 December 1904, having earlier accepted a second tenure. It would have been better if he had not accepted an extension in his Viceroyalty.

On 22 December 1904, Kitchener informed Lady Salisbury that

he was, 'writing his final denunciation of the system of dual control.' His hatred of Elles had become psychopathic. On 5 January 1905, he told her that he had warned Curzon that he would resign unless his views were upheld by the British Cabinet, and that Curzon had accepted that, 'as the natural consequence.'[18] He sent a copy of his paper to her on 16 February in which letter he referred to a series of "secret" telegrams which he had recently received from a former member of his staff, Major R.J. Marker, who had left India, after his suit had been turned down by Lady Curzon's sister, Daisy Leiter. (She in 1903 married Curzon's former ADC, the Earl of Suffolk.) Marker had been appointed private secretary to the new Secretary for War. Kitchener described that appointment as, 'very lucky...as through him anything can be safely transmitted to me. I pay for all telegrams, so they are private and absolutely safe.' Kitchener had forgotten that Curzon had the power to require the Telegraph Department to produce for his perusal copies of all telegrams, private or secret, which power a subordinate officer had apparently already invoked as to Kitchener's incoming and outgoing telegrams. Curzon, however, declined to peruse them at the time.

All positive work was at a standstill at the Army Headquarters. Kitchener canvassed all senior military officers in India of the rank of major general and above, except Elles. Kitchener obtained assurances of support from all, except one, whose reply was ambivalent. Curzon considered Kitchener's canvassing an act of disloyalty. Kitchener's proposal to abolish the Military Department was considered in Council on 10 March. (The Viceroy's Council at that period was still exclusively British.) Curzon's comments on Kitchener's proposal stressed the good which Kitchener had managed to accomplish under the existing system, and added, 'Administrative systems are not constructed to test exceptional men, but to be worked by average men....I believe that the combined duties which Lord Kitchener desires to vest in the head of the Army are beyond the capacity of any one man, of whatever energy or powers.' Curzon pointed out that Kitchener's proposal would have the effect of depriving the Viceroy of an adequate military adviser when the

Commander-in-Chief took the field on the outbreak of a major war, and accused Kitchener of an ambition to subvert the civil supremacy in India, and to substitute a military dictatorship. Elles defended himself, but Kitchener said nothing. He knew his limitations, and that he would be outvoted—he had no gift for debate. Peter King opines, 'Kitchener believed, like Talleyrand, that the gift of speech was given in order to enable us to conceal our thoughts.'[19] Though Lord Cromer, who had worked with Kitchener in Egypt was of the view that, 'it is sometimes difficult to extract the whole truth from him,' Kitchener found himself in a minority of one. After that Curzon wrote to Brodrick on 23 March, wherein he emphasized that Kitchener's proposal would have the effect of establishing, 'a military despotism,' which would, 'dethrone the Government of India from (its) constitutional control of the Indian Army.' He denied that the duplication of military advisers caused inefficiency. Kitchener dissented from the Viceroy's views, and the dispute was then referred to the British Cabinet. Curzon's determination to maintain the dual system was doomed, by the superior public prestige of Kitchener. In reporting to Lady Salisbury (14 March), Kitchener, *inter alia*, mentioned that Curzon had sent for him in order to complain that, 'it was very mean of me to let it be known at home that I would resign if the dual control were continued, as it would coerce the government my way, and they were thus unable to judge the case on its merits.' Kitchener said that he replied that he had done, 'the straight thing.'[20]

A few months earlier, in October 1904, war between the British and Russians had seemed likely after the Russian Baltic Fleet, on its way to the war in the Far East against Japan, had fired, off the Dogger Bank, on a British trawling-fleet which it mistook for torpedo boats. The Russian-Japanese War was still in progress, and it was inconceivable that Kitchener would be permitted to resign when military changes were in progress in India. The British Cabinet communicated its decision through Brodrick on 31 May. The decision was presented as a compromise which gave Kitchener about two-thirds of what he had sought. The Military Department was retained, as a result of strong representations by Roberts and by three ex-Viceroys, including Lansdowne, then Foreign Secretary, but it was shorn of most of its power to interfere with the Commander-in-Chief. The Military Member, who was in future to be known as the Military Supply Member, and to wear plain clothes in order to emphasize his civilian character, was to be relieved of all strictly military work. He was to retain control of only supplies and transport, but was empowered to advise the Viceroy on the financial and political aspect of any defence matter which came before the Council for discussion, though a separate Military Finance Department was now created under a "joint financial secretary". Hamilton, Kitchener's Military Secretary, wrote to Marker in London: 'It is a decision for the soldier against the civilian; one which recognized for the first time the paramountcy of the soldier in military matters.'

The Viceroy and the Commander-in-Chief were instructed for the future to communicate direct, instead of through the Military Supply Member. Separately, Lord Frederick Roberts wrote to Kitchener on 1 June that although the Military Supply Member was to be, 'disassociated from all strictly military work,' he and Lansdowne had insisted that the Viceroy's Council should not be deprived of the assistance of 'a colleague to whom they could look for advice on all the delicate and difficult questions which often arise in regard to the native army.' (Like Roberts latterly, Kitchener was of the British Service, but Kitchener had never served in India before becoming Commander-in-Chief, whereas Roberts served forty-one years in India in all, including as Commander-in-Chief, having originally been in the Bengal Artillery, till it was disbanded in 1858.) Kitchener told Roberts that he was 'a good deal surprised' by his letter. Lansdowne informed the House of Lords on 1 August that, 'we decided against Lord Kitchener,' but Curzon did not conceal his chagrin. Curzon and Brodrick both failed to heed Dalhousie's dictum of 28 June 1854, 'that men who correspond over a space of 10,000 miles, should watch their pens, for ink comes to burn like caustic when it crosses the sea.' Curzon wrote on 21 June that, 'a disembowelled military member has been left to prevent me from resigning.'[21] Kitchener, on his part, inferred that the British Cabinet wished to avert Curzon's resignation. On 25 June, when Curzon threatened to resign unless Kitchener wrote to Brodrick to accept certain modifications of the new arrangements, Kitchener, as they were matters of detail, agreed. The discussion then grew heated when Curzon said he would resign within the hour unless Kitchener would ask Brodrick to consent that the Military Supply Member should revert to his former title of Military Member, and that he should always be a soldier. Curzon then allegedly dropped onto a sofa, and appeared to burst into tears. Kitchener stated he gave way, and wrote on 26 June to Sir Edward Stedman, the Military Secretary at the India Office: 'I hope Mr Brodrick will approve of my attitude in this matter. I have done everything possible (perhaps too much) to conciliate the Viceroy and prevent a crisis. I have had a pistol held to my head which I really believe was loaded, as he is very much upset at the terms of the despatch and his loss of prestige.'[22] Kitchener preserved an undated copy of a letter he had sent at the time to Stanley (later Lord Derby), Financial Secretary to the War Office, 'The only tip I had was yours, to let him down easy....Even before I got downstairs I felt I had made a mistake....Had he gone, on the despatch, he would have had much sympathy, both here and at home, and might have done a good deal of harm. No report about his conduct in Tibet and Afghanistan would have been possible, as these had been condoned, and it would have widened the discussion to a considerable extent. He would have appeared as a martyr to the cause of constitutional government.'[23]

On 18 July, in a speech to the Legislative Assembly, Curzon observed that the Government of India had received 'with regret' the British Government's instructions to introduce a new form of military administration, 'contrary to the advice which they had all but unanimously tendered to His Majesty's government,' and that, 'we have converted the position of the Military Supply Member into one of greater utility and efficiency. We have very considerably strengthened the guarantees for civil supervision and control.' Curzon claimed the right, as previously, to nominate the new

Military Member in succession to Elles. Brodrick refused to appoint Curzon's nominee, Major General Sir Edmund Barrow, because he knew that Kitchener would object. Brodrick insisted at the same time that the term "Supply" should be restored to the title of Elles' successor. Curzon represented but Brodrick reiterated his refusal to appoint Barrow, and required Curzon to, 'consult Lord Kitchener as to who in his opinion is the best man for the post, and let me know his views.'[24]

Curzon resigned, and the announcements of his resignation and of the appointment of Lord Gilbert Minto as Viceroy were both made on 21 August 1905. The *Times of India* recorded on 22 August: 'The sardonic and sinister figure of Lord Kitchener now bestrides India; we dislike his brutal and domineering methods.' The quarrel with Kitchener became personal as a result of Curzon's interpretation of Kitchener's views on the role of the new Military Supply Member. After reading Kitchener's minute which set forth the modalities for implementing the new scheme, Curzon told Brodrick that the new Member would be left with less than two hours' work a day, and that the post would be a sinecure. Kitchener repudiated that suggestion. An acrimonious correspondence ensued between the Viceroy and the Commander-in-Chief. On 30 August, Kitchener wrote to Lady Salisbury, 'Curzon had rather surpassed himself, I think, by writing me the last letter of the enclosed correspondence. In old days I suppose I should have called him out on it and shot him like a dog for his grossly insulting letter. All I can do now is to have nothing more to do with him....Every one knows I never saw the paper in question—not through any carelessness of mine, but because it was hid away in a big file which was referred to me on a different question (which I answered), without any reference to this paper having been placed at the bottom of the file. It all seems to me so low and disgusting.'[25] On 31 August, Winston Churchill wrote to his mother, 'The Military Member in India is really in the same position as the Secretary of State for War in England. What has happened is that the Commander-in-Chief had not merely swallowed up his own War Minister, but the Viceroy as well.'

Kitchener had been let down by his staff. Curzon retired, writing to Ampthill, Governor of Madras, 'It may even be said that I made a...mistake, for I trusted K whom I have now found to be without truth or honour.' Kitchener proposed that his correspondence with Curzon should be published in the press, along with a White Paper on the telegrams which had passed between Curzon and Brodrick. The *Times of India* commented on 28 August that such a, 'lamentable spectacle ought to have been impossible,' and it censured Kitchener and Curzon for, 'an offence against the public interest.' In response to an appeal by Lady Curzon, who was mortally ill, dying shortly after in 1906, Kitchener agreed to shake hands with Curzon at a farewell ceremony on the lawns of the Viceregal Lodge at Simla. Kitchener wrote to Lady Salisbury on 26 October 1905 that he had consented, 'only to stop people talking although it was not very pleasant to shake hands with a man who had called you a liar. However, I consoled myself by the consideration that it was the Viceroy to whom I was saying good-bye, not Curzon.' According to Peter King, after Lady Curzon's death, 'Curzon was to write a note which he placed amongst her papers between the letters from Kitchener,[26] "This was the man who was half in love with Mary".' Kitchener told Lady Salisbury on 2 November that he suspected that Curzon had used his security powers, 'to see my private telegrams, all of which I personally paid for and thought safe....I looked upon these telegrams exactly the same as private letters.' Kitchener added that he had reason to believe that Curzon was thinking of publishing the telegrams which he had exchanged with Marker, private secretary to the Secretary for War. They were never published. In their clash, Kitchener and Curzon were both inspired by a sense of duty. As to the controversy from which their quarrel sprang, in March 1907, the Viceroy's Council voted in favour of the new system of military administration. However, in pursuance of his policy of economy, John Morley, the new Liberal Secretary of State for India, asked Minto in July 1907 whether it was necessary to retain the new Military Supply Department. Kitchener advised Lord Minto to make no change, because he felt the system was working well, but

Morley saw no reason to continue to pay a salary to any official, whose appointment was regarded as redundant. Morley was determined to cut military appropriations, as also to curtail excursions beyond India's frontiers. In his opinion, 'the Government of India is always Jingo,' adding, 'the Jingo is the Devil Incarnate.' The appointment of the Military Supply Member was accordingly abolished on 1 April 1909. Kitchener thereafter assumed personal control of this department, while retaining its separate identity. Roberts sent Kitchener a friendly warning on 17 June 1909 that his method of command was becoming very impersonal, 'It is for this reason that I have been unable to agree altogether with the changes that have been made in the military administration of the Indian Army. Few men can get through the amount of work that you can, and no soldier that I know had your power of organization; and my fear is that future C-in-Cs will not have time to attend to the Council work, and look after the Army at the same time.' The system of military administration, which Kitchener sought to reorganize, was antiquated. It is, nevertheless, true that he centralized all power in himself. It was earlier said of him in Egypt, 'He was not only Commander-in-Chief, but Chief Staff Officer as well. He scarcely ever issued a written order, and confined himself to curt telegrams, the forms for which he carried in his hat....He had practically no staff, and did everything himself.' His less competent successors were thus confused. War remains the ultimate test of any military system, and, in this context, the report of the Royal Commission, on the ill-conceived Indian Expeditionary Force in the First World War to Mesopotamia, stated, in July 1917, that: 'The combination of the duties of Commander-in-Chief in India and the military member of Council cannot adequately be performed by any one man in time of war.' This report let down too gently the commanders of the expedition to Mesopotamia, which facet will be examined in the next chapter as to the Indian Army in the First World War. However, William Birdwood, later to be Commander-in-Chief and Field Marshal, disagreed with the commission on this point. He had been on Kitchener's staff in India.

Kitchener's proposed military system, though not perfect, must be deemed superior to the one it proposed to displace. It was better adapted to the then needs, but was never fully implemented due to the financial stringency imposed by the Liberal government. Kitchener effected a number of useful measures in improved training, equipment and armaments, though his reorganization did nothing about many other prevalent shortcomings. A Staff College was established, first at Deolali, then at Quetta, in September 1906. The Indian Army was supplied better rations, sport was encouraged, and regimental institutes for Indian troops established. Additional ordnance factories were built to try to make the Indian Army as self-supporting in war as the then Imperial policy permitted. The establishment of further military dairy farms was encouraged. Most of the measures had not, however, fructified at the onset of the First World War.

Throughout his extended stay in India (1907-1909), Kitchener was grooming himself as the next Viceroy, and often expressed concern as to what he described as sedition. He wrote to Lady Salisbury on 6 June 1907 that it was, 'pretty strong underneath the surface. The principal agitators are the more or less educated lawyer class. They are doing all they can to get at the loyalty of the Army. They preach another mutiny, to drive us out of the country. It will require careful handling.'[27] Kitchener irrationally opposed Minto's suggestion that the situation might be improved if an Indian was appointed a member of the Viceroy's Council, thus echoing Curzon who had told Prime Minister Balfour in 1901, 'It is often said, why not make some prominent Native a member of the Executive Council? The answer is that in the whole continent there is not an Indian fit for the post.' Minto appointed an Indian member and said of Kitchener, 'With whom constitutional reforms, Indian members and the like go somewhat against the grain.' Kitchener told Minto that it was "unrealistic" to worry about terrorist incidents occurring in Bengal, and that he was more concerned about terrorist occurrences in the Punjab, because the Punjabis, 'are the fighting classes from which we draw our army.' Morley, however, refused to countenance any augmentation of forces to offset the, 'extension of native rights.' At a 1909 Viceroy's Executive Council meeting, Sir Guy Fleetwood Wilson, the Finance Member, was to observe that all the other twenty-one members had fallen asleep while he was speaking. He attributed his own reserves of strength to his 'good friends, the Simla monkeys whose entertaining companionship stemmed many a wave of overwhelming depression.'

When he relinquished command in September 1909, Kitchener took long leave, calculating that those additional months of leave would bring him very near the time when Minto's term as Viceroy would be expiring, Kitchener expecting to come back to India as Viceroy.[28] On 1 June 1910, however, Morley informed Minto that he had warned Herbert Henry Asquith, the Prime Minister, to expect his resignation if the British Cabinet was to insist upon sending Kitchener to India as Viceroy. Morley then wrote, 'To put our biggest soldier in the post of GG would be to set up the sword as the symbol of our rule over India, and the basis of it.' Asquith, who pressed Kitchener's case, was unwilling to permit Morley to resign on this issue, and Sir Charles (later Lord) Hardinge was appointed to succeed Minto, Morley writing to Kitchener on 9 June 1910 : '...a decision has been reached about the Indian Viceroyalty...we are not going to invite you to go back in a new capacity....The sole difficulty arises from misgivings as to the impressions which would be likely to arise in India from a military appointment.' As Sir Shane Leslie aptly commented, 'Curzon had intended to point Kitchener like a howitzer against the Amir (of Afghanistan) but Kitchener had turned into a blunderbuss and exploded in his hand.'[29] Lloyd George was to describe Kitchener as, 'One of those revolving lighthouses which radiate momentary gleams of revolving light far out into the surrounding gloom, and, then, suddenly relapse into complete darkness.'

General Sir Ian Hamilton, who was Kitchener's second-in-command in South Africa, later succinctly recorded: '...history has now revealed to us what is the absolutely stark truth, he (Kitchener) hated organizations; he smashed organizations if they were ever imposed or inherited by him.' Bishop J.E.C. Welldon, who had been Bishop of Calcutta for part of Curzon's tenure, and had resigned after differences with Curzon, though on a more amicable plane than Kitchener, erected an evocative tablet to Curzon: 'He preferred able men who went his way to stupid men who also went his way; but he preferred, I think, an inferior man who would follow him to a superior man who would resist him.'[30] The best summation of Curzon is possibly that of the Indian leader, Gopal Krishna Gokhale: '...he (Curzon) belonged to the galaxy of spirits, who live for lofty ends, and make a religion of all their work.'[31] Bipin Chandra Pal's assessment of Curzon's regime is balanced: 'Throughout his seven years' viceroyalty in India (Curzon) tried persistently to put down the pretentious, as he believed them to be, of the English-educated classes in this country, on the one hand, and on the other, to win the goodwill of the toiling masses in every walk of life, whether in the ministerial services of the government or in the Indian Army, or among the general population of the country.'[32]

The controversy between the Mulki Lat Sahib and the Jungi Lat Sahib weakened forever the position of the Viceroy in India.[33] The clash had been unnecessary, and was the last major civil-military dispute in British-India. It was, however, predictable, for Curzon had written to Brodrick on 16 March 1902: 'I wonder if you feel as I do that, from the business point of view, soldiers with rare exceptions, are the most impossible men. They seem to me to be congenitally stupid. Their writing is atrocious....I have a few good men, but the majority fill me with despair. And, as for a military committee—I would as soon remit a question of state to a meeting of Eton Masters.'[34]

There were, of course, lesser subsequent civil-military disputes, but they were restricted to within the government, till the advent of the Krishna Menon era. Morley, who initiated the Morley-Minto Reforms, and thwarted Kitchener becoming Viceroy, deserves India's gratitude. In the words of Stephen Koss: 'If Morley failed to dismantle the Empire of Swagger, he nonetheless managed to impede its forward march.'[35]

EIGHT

The Indian Army In The First World War

IN *The Viceroy's Fall—How Kitchener Destroyed Curzon*, Peter King recounts: 'When Kitchener left India and "his system" behind him in 1909, he chose as successor one of his divisional commanders, Sir O'Moore Creagh (V.C.), known as "No more K". Kitchener had concentrated his efforts on the (Viceroy's) Council rather than the Army, preparing the way, so he thought, to succeed Minto as Viceroy. The new Commander-in-Chief, alas, lacked "administrative ability", and so many reforms proceeded at a slow pace. When he, in turn, left India in 1913, the succession was "fixed" by his former Chief on a routine visit to Balmoral to see his old friend George V. It was to be none other than Kitchener's aide, Duff, the man who had designed the system "that never was."'[1]

Such "fixing" is mentioned not to carp, but merely to reiterate the saying, 'It isn't what you know that matters, but who you know that counts.' By 1909, as commented on by Lord Frederick Roberts in the previous chapter, Lord Horatio Herbert Kitchener had become less visible to the troops, increasingly leaving the implementation of

241

the system of "tests" for units, and attendance at these "tests", to his subordinates. (The "test" was a fifteen-mile forced march for each battalion, followed by an advance to contact to a specified objective, all on a hard scale of rations.) His leadership was totally impersonal, for even earlier in Egypt, an officer recorded, 'I never saw him look at or speak to a private soldier, or take the slightest trouble to ingratiate himself with his troops.'

In 1911, the possibility of Indian troops reinforcing a British Expeditionary Force in France was mentioned at a meeting of the Committee of Imperial Defence, but no decision was taken. Consequently no planning was conducted. There had been continuing reluctance in London to employ Indian troops against Europeans, except inevitably Russians, who were, in any case, viewed as Asians with their shirt-tails tucked in, for which reason no Indian troops had been sent to South Africa in the earlier Anglo-Boer War. (Only some British officers from India, and some Indian cavalry personnel, in a non-combatant remount role, had been sent. George Curzon had refused to send the 20,000 Indian "coolies" asked for.) The same attitude now prevailed in 1911, as to not employing Indian troops against the Germans in Europe. The signing of the Anglo-Russian Convention of 1907, and sequential changes in the external Indian situation, had led to the appointment in 1912 of an Army in India Committee, under the chairmanship of Field Marshal Lord William Nicholson, former Chief of the Imperial General Staff, to report on the strength to be maintained to meet India's military obligations, as may be envisaged by the committee, and whether any reduction in military expenditure was feasible. The priorities were the maintenance of internal security, dealing with hostile tribesmen on the North-West Frontier, and to defend India from an invasion, still presumably Russian, pending the arrival of troops from Britain. As to Indian troops being sent overseas, while the Indian Army was not to be maintained with a view to meeting external Imperial obligations, it should be capable, when the Frontier situation allowed, of cooperating in overseas theatres.

Before any formal action could be taken on the

recommendations, the First World War broke out in August 1914, and rendered them nugatory, though by 1911 the first four divisional signal companies of the future Indian Signal Corps had been raised, followed by further augmentation in 1914. The majority favoured a field force of seven divisions and five cavalry brigades. The committee's report was that the Indian Army should be organized and equipped solely for Frontier warfare. It was not for the Government of India to maintain forces out of Indian revenues to serve overseas, beyond those required for self-defence on a line Kandahar-Jalalabad.

On 23 October 1913, Sir Edmund Barrow, Curzon's proposed Military Supply Member, whom Kitchener had not favoured and Brodrick had not approved, had written to Curzon, 'Lord Nicholson told me in Simla he considers the present organization quite unworkable, and most unsatisfactory....I know Nicholson had in mind a modification of the present scheme...which would have probably saved K's face.'[2] (Kitchener, however, had not favoured Nicholson as his successor in India in 1907, when the latter sought the post!) When O'Moore Creagh retired in 1913, Kitchener arranged for his former Adjutant General, Sir Beauchamp Duff, to be the new Commander-in-Chief. He had prepared Kitchener's reorganization proposals. Barrow added, 'Although Duff has never commanded a regiment, a brigade, a division or an army (like myself), his connection with K and his pliant character would commend itself to Ministers.' Lovat Fraser, editor of the *Times of India* till 1907, and who published a biography of Curzon in 1913, described Duff as, 'an office clerk,' and told Curzon in 1913, 'I don't venture on prophecy, but I firmly believe that the terrible mistake of appointing two unsuitable C-in-Cs in succession will have disastrous effects.'[3] Roberts told Curzon, 'I was much concerned, though I cannot say I was astonished at Duff's appointment....It is very unfortunate for the Indian Army. Kitchener does not care for the (Indian) Army and Duff is not a soldier at heart.' In his view, 'Kitchener had neglected the Indian Army, and O'Moore Creagh the Council.'

Kitchener's premise had been that the troops would be

concentrated in their respective divisional district areas. This had been dependent on the construction of accommodation in the larger cantonments proposed by Kitchener in 1904. On financial grounds, additional construction had been found impracticable. Consequently, troops allotted to field force divisions, due to internal security, were still outside their respective divisional district areas. On account of the incomplete implementation of Kitchener's proposals, training for war had not been carried out by the time of the First World War, owing to the ostensible dispersion of troops. A defect in the system was that Army Headquarters, administratively dealing direct with divisions, was burdened with minor details, no administrative staff having been given to the two army commands. Divisional commanders were similarly burdened, there being no intermediate administrative staff between them and Army Headquarters.

On account of financial constraints, no provision had been made to command the internal security troops after the departure of the field formations. On mobilization, therefore, no machinery existed to ensure continuity of normal military administration in India, apart from the Army Headquarters. In accordance with the Liberal government's policy under William Gladstone since 1907, there had been a continuous run-down of establishments. F.J. Moberley recounts that, 'The Army Council enquired as to what assistance India could provide in the event of war in Europe. The Government of India replied on 30 July 1914 that two divisions and a cavalry brigade could be sent, and that this could be increased by another division at some risk to India. The reply was not received until after the war had started.'[4] The First World War revealed even greater defects in the Indian Army than had been perceived, and grave defects also in its equipping. In August 1914, the Indian Army consisted of thirty-nine horsed cavalry regiments and 138 infantry battalions, including twenty Gurkha battalions. Eight battalions were on colonial garrison duties. The Indian Artillery was confined to twelve mountain batteries, all other divisional artillery being British. The strength was over two hundred thousand, but including 45,000 non-combatants. The ancillary services were either non-existent, or undeveloped. Seven of the nominal nine Indian divisions were actually capable of immediate mobilization. It had earlier been suggested that the British troops should be brigaded separately in each division, since this would simplify supply procedures, but the suggestion was again rejected, a British unit remaining in each brigade, till well into the Second World War. Peace establishments were so inadequate that, in order to effect the mobilization of the field force divisions, units earmarked for internal security were largely depleted. Administrative and technical personnel required on mobilization had to be "milked" from the peace establishment of existing combat units. The standard of equipment in the pre-First World War Indian Army was low, which the Indian Army formations discovered when they found themselves fighting opposite troops equipped on a more modern basis.

No mechanical transport service yet existed, while equipments were generally out of date; as to machine-guns, artillery, hospital equipment (and even medical establishments), the Indian Army was inferior to European armies. The divisional artillery was inadequate in relation to the then requirements, and the so-called medium or heavier artillery was obsolete. The requisite chain for reinforcements was lacking. The ceiling fixed for the Indian Army Reserve of approximately thirty-five thousand was, on mobilization, discovered to be unsound. The creation of effective reserves had been found to be difficult; enrolment was for twenty-one years, with the option of serving for another four to qualify for pension. There was no organization to cope with the emergent recruitment of large numbers of fresh personnel, nor with their training, on the scale required to permit of large-scale expansion and to meet heavy war wastage. India's indigenous resources had still not been sufficiently developed, and the Indian Army was, therefore, largely dependent on outside sources for the munitions of war. Kitchener, now Secretary of State for War, however, deemed in 1914, that the Indian Army could participate effectively overseas, though there had been no contingency planning for overseas expeditions as he well knew, having been Commander-in-Chief. He encouraged the despatch of expeditions beyond the Government of India's assurance of 30 July 1914. In August 1914, the Indian Army was asked to provide two divisions for Egypt. Two divisions and one cavalry brigade were mobilized, conforming to the assurance of 30 July 1914. The speed of this mobilization was creditable, but even before this expeditionary force could embark for Egypt, its destination had been changed to Marseilles. Another brigade was now sought for Egypt, also a force to attack Tanga in East Africa, augmentation of the expedition sent to France, and calls for Indian units to relieve British colonial garrisons. Tension with Turkey resulted in a brigade being sent initially to defend the oil installations at Abadan. Battalions were to mobilize at a strength of 753 all ranks, and were to embark with ten per cent reinforcements. According to F.W. Perry, the requirement of 830 all ranks proved beyond most units, and demands had to be made on the linked units from the very outset. When the depleted linked unit was itself ordered shortly thereafter to mobilize for another expeditionary force, it in turn placed its demand on another linked unit, by when there was no undepleted linked unit fit for field service. They were now only fit for internal security. Such was the case with the 5th, 8th and 9th Divisions. Thus, to despatch the six expeditionary forces proved a gigantic task.

As an illustration, 82nd Punjabis sent off 686 all ranks as reinforcements, before itself mobilizing for Mesopotamia ('The Land of Two Rivers') in 1916.[5] On mobilization, each unit formed its own small depot to train recruits, but the replacement of casualties was to be very difficult during a protracted war. Similarly, the Indian Cavalry had its own problems. Except for the Madras Cavalry regiments, enrolment was under the "silladar" system. It was not a system that could ensure the efficient replacement of men and horses in war. No recruit training directives were issued. Training was rudimentary. When internal security units were required in 1916, to replace those sent overseas, ten battalions were obtained from the Nepal Army from January 1916 to March 1920. (This arrangement was again invoked in the Second World War, and shortly after independence.) The role of the Indian Army was now as an Imperial

Reserve for the whole globe.

In France, when the 3rd and 7th Divisions arrived in September and October 1914, they had to be re-equipped, and a transport service improvised before they could proceed to the front. Then in September 1914, the 6th Division and 1st Cavalry Division were mobilized for France, but the 6th Division was diverted to Mesopotamia. Thereupon, additional cavalry brigades were mobilized to make up the 2nd Cavalry Division, which was sent to France in lieu of the 6th Division. The two cavalry divisions arrived towards the end of 1914. The muddles of the Somme and Mons are synonymous with the war in France. Censored letters of the Indian troops in France available in the British Library, London, reveal the extent of the military ineptitude prevalent. The conditions were appalling. For the British, having overcome their objection to using Indian troops against an European enemy, the arrival of the Indian troops was invaluable, but tragic for the Indian troops concerned. Once the Indian Corps moved up to try to stem the German advance till Kitchener's "New Armies" from Britain became available, enormous battle casualties occurred—including those from gas warfare and inadequate warm clothing for a winter campaign in Europe. The Indian Army officers' wives in Britain were hurriedly knitting and making woollen clothes for their husbands' units in France. Of the 5,250 (inadequate numerically) reinforcements received by the Indian Corps in January 1916 analysed by Perry, 876 were found unfit for service. Of a batch of 331 of these, eighty-five per cent were unfit due to old age, poor physique and similar grounds, all discernible before despatch.

At this very early stage the reserve system had already collapsed, and to relieve depleted battalions in France, battalions were drawn from all over, even from Hong Kong and North China. Drafts were found by denuding units in India, but were often not of the same classes required by the depleted units. Perry illustrates this situation after the receipt of reinforcements in May 1915 in the 9th Bhopal Infantry (later the 16th Punjab Regiment), which originally had two companies each of Sikhs, Punjabi Mussalmans, Rajputs and Brahmins:

- Sikhs from the original unit, and from the 21st Punjabis.
- Mussalmans from the original units and from the 19th Punjabis and 17th and 18th Infantry.
- Rajputs from the 4th, 11th and 16th Rajputs.
- Brahmins from the 1st Brahmins and 89th Punjabis.
- Other classes from the 8th Rajputs, 89th Punjabis, and 96th Infantry.[6]

How drafts were found for France is indicated by the case of the 39th Garhwal Rifles, an infantry unit, which received a draft of about one hundred from the Tehri Garhwal Field Company, a State Force Sappers and Miners unit, and 240 from the Burma Military Police, a para-military force. Thereafter complete sub-units from India were often drafted, but generally not of the requisite class, making the rebuilding of an effective unit difficult. By the end of 1915, it was consequently decided to withdraw the Indian Corps from France to Egypt to reorganize, but the situation in Mesopotamia involved moving them there, where conditions were more chaotic. But more about that later, yet even here two Indian battalions from France were felt to be too Muslim for employment against the Turks in Mesopotamia, and were sent instead to East Africa. The two Indian cavalry divisions in France, by the nature of their organization, were committed in the front line to a comparatively lesser extent than the infantry divisions had been, and consequently with comparably lesser casualty replacement problems, remained in France till March 1918, when they were reformed as the 4th and 5th Cavalry Divisions for the final advance in Palestine.

Two infantry brigades and ancillary units had been mobilized for service in East Africa, and were launched in an abortive sea-borne attack on the port of Tanga in November 1914. After the reverse at Tanga when the expedition sought to disembark at Mombasa, the customs authorities there wanted to charge *ad valorem* duty of five per cent. The expedition's Intelligence Staff officer, Major Richard Meinertzhagen, had summed up this Indian Army expedition *ab initio* at Bombay: 'The senior officers are nearer

248

to fossils than active energetic leaders.' Built up to divisional strength, to protect Zanzibar and the Mombasa-Nairobi rail link, despite many heroic actions they were a waste of resources, suffering from illness, and unable to defeat totally the brilliant German, Von Lettow Vorbeck, and his force of "askaris" and German civilians. Von Lettow, despite no reinforcements, remained almost undefeated by a larger force till after the 1918 Armistice. With the Indian Expeditionary Force embarking for Egypt being despatched to France, other forces from India had to be mobilized for Egypt. By mid-November 1914, there were, in Egypt, one regular Indian brigade mentioned earlier, two State Force brigades, three improvised Indian brigades, the Bikaner Camel Corps and eight unbrigaded battalions. These were formed into the 10th and 11th Divisions. With the repulse of the Turkish attack on the Suez Canal, a brigade went to Mesopotamia in March 1915, another to Gallipoli in April 1915, and a third to Aden, before eventually ending up in Mesopotamia. In the Gallipoli brigade, two battalions were found too Muslim to be tested against the Turks, and were therefore sent to France, being replaced by two Gurkha battalions from there. One of the other difficulties was the provision of officers, primarily to replace wastage, but partly also for expansion requirements. Recourse was not had to commissioning Indians, apart already of several hundred for the medical services, one in the British Army and four for the Royal Flying Corps, except for a few temporary commissions from late 1917 onwards, and another exiguous number commissioned earlier through the Imperial Cadet Corps, Dehra Dun. (These had no powers of command over British personnel.) Officer training institutions (cadet colleges) were opened at Quetta and Wellington (Nilgiris) for members of the British community in India and for British other ranks, the Staff College at Quetta being temporarily closed. Of the 9,493 Indian Army commissions granted in India in the First World War, two-thirds were from the British community in India.[7]

On 28 March 1917, the Secretary of State telegraphed enquiring what additional effort India could make towards the campaigns of

1918, mentioning the relieving of British troops in India, Egypt and Mesopotamia, and the possible further employment of Indian infantry in France. On 11 April, 'the Viceroy said India would raise twenty-three new battalions, modifying this on 8 May to the raising of two new divisions.'[8] Enhanced recruitment was needed. At the end of 1916, rates of pay and service conditions were therefore improved, the latter by granting free rations. Currently, Indian troops were providing rations for themselves when not on active service. The civil authorities had to be brought into a joint Central Recruiting Board, with subordinate provincial boards. A revision of attitudes was necessitated as to what were or were not "martial" classes. Apart from the 111th Mahar, the 49th Bengal Regiment and the 71st Punjabis, a Christian battalion, were also raised, and 63,000 Punjabi Mussalmans were recruited out of a fit male population of 145,000, and 43,000 out of 112,000 Sikhs, by the middle of 1917. The expansion was through the formation of second battalions of existing units, though it was often not possible to duplicate in the second the classes of the parent unit. As illustrated by Perry, the 9th Bhopal Infantry, now with a company each of Sikhs, Brahmins, Rajputs and Punjabi Mussalmans, had a second battalion of Ahirs, Gujars, Jats and Hindustani Mussalmans. The third and fourth battalions were again different. The First World War's recruitment shows forty different classes plus 38,000 recruits referred to as "other Hindus", and 4,000 as "other Muslims".[9]

The entry of Turkey also created certain problems, other than the operational ones. The Sultan of Turkey was the Khalifa of Islam, the successor to the Prophet. On 14 November 1914, the Sultan had proclaimed a Holy War on all making war on Turkey and her allies. Desertions occurred among Muslim soldiers, mainly from the trans-Frontier tribes. Desertions occurred on the Suez Canal and in Mesopotamia. Desertions also took place in France. These will be reverted to in the next chapter. Two major mutiny cases occurred in Muslim units away from the operational theatres. Four companies of 130th Baluchis were deemed to have mutinied at Rangoon in December 1914, and in February 1915 four companies (one wing) of the 5th Light Infantry mutinied at Singapore. These mutinies will be dealt with also in the next chapter, on account of the political undertones. There was a mutiny by a platoon in China from the all-Muslim 18th Infantry in June 1918, but this was not deemed to be political. Since the campaign in Mesopotamia was conducted directly by the Army Headquarters in India, till February 1916, from Simla in summer and Delhi in winter, and was an even bigger muddle compared to that in France, and absorbed the largest force of Indian troops, it is covered in some detail, for the lessons stand out.

Oil had earlier been discovered in Mesopotamia, and three quarters of the British Navy's oil supply came from the Middle East. The German *Drang nach Osten* (Drive to the East) had been put in motion, the Kaiser implying he was a direct descendant of the Prophet's sister, and announcing he had become a Muslim, with a view to Turkey coming into the war. German advisers controlled the Turkish Army, and the Turks were deemed to be threatening Egypt. In September 1914, Barrow, now the Military Secretary at the India Office, had prepared a paper titled, "The Role of India in a Turkish War", proposing the occupation of Basra by the Indian Army in order to protect the refinery at Abadan, thirty miles away. Later, Barrow was to say of the campaign in Mesopotamia, 'It was believed to be a sideshow, and "No Man's Child."' The Army Headquarters in India had not *per se* wanted to send troops to either France or Mesopotamia, concerning itself with the North-West Frontier, but had been overruled by Whitehall. Five thousand men—one brigade group—embarked from Bombay on 16 October 1914 in order to occupy Abadan. Britain declared war against Turkey shortly after a gunboat incident in the Sea of Marmara, and the so-called demonstration in strength was almost immediately engaged in a full-fledged war without any conceptual plan. The Expeditionary Force occupied Basra and then, augmented, received orders from the Indian Army Headquarters to proceed to Baghdad, 300 miles away; apparently Army Headquarters liked the resonance of the word "Baghdad". In the absence of road communications, for such a large-scale riverine support operation up the Tigris there had been no prior planning. The force was built up to divisional strength, Major General Sir Charles Townshend of the British Army, one of the defenders of Chitral against the tribesmen in 1895, being the general officer commanding 6th Indian Division. As Norman Dixon succinctly puts it in *On The Psychology of Military Incompetence*: 'If the degree of military incompetence is indicated by the ratio of achievement to cost, then the activities of Expeditionary Force "D"...merit examination. Firstly, there was a 250-mile discrepancy between what it was designed to do, and what it tried to do. Secondly, the cost of this discrepancy was large. To reach Kut (el Amara, 190 miles from Basra), cost Townshend 7,000 casualties; during the ensuing siege a further 1,600 died; attempts to relieve his force accounted for another 23,000 casualties; when he eventually surrendered to the Turks, 13,000 of his troops went into captivity and of these 7,000 died while still prisoners of war. All this went-for nothing, not one inch of ground or any political advantage; nothing, that is, beyond corpses, suffering and ruined reputations...under pressure from London, the Viceroy Lord Hardinge and the Commander-in-Chief, India, Sir Beauchamp Duff increased the Mesopotamia force to divisional strength (6th Division). Thanks to the machinations of four men—Hardinge; Duff; the Mesopotamia Army Commander (General Sir John) Nixon; and the leader of the freshly constituted Expeditionary Force, Townshend—this modest venture led to a British military disaster so total yet unnecessary, so futile yet expensive; that its like did not occur again until the Fall of Singapore in 1942.'[10] The last three variously through military stupidity and/or ambition caused the deaths of thousands. The crux was the difference between the aim prescribed by Whitehall and what Army Headquarters actually did.

Whereas Whitehall's aim was specifically to protect the refinery and the pipeline, the Indian Army was unnecessarily engaged now in trying to capture Baghdad. The force Whitehall had asked for to protect the oil installations was one division, but the force required to capture and hold Baghdad would be at least two corps, of more than 30,000 men each, facing four enemies: the Turks, raiding

Arabs, the terrain and the climate. As Dixon adds, 'Nixon, who made up in ambition for what he lacked in intelligence, ordered Townshend to capture Amara, a township on the Tigris some hundred miles north of Basra...(Amara means "The Garden of Tears", supposedly where Adam and Eve left the garden of Eden.)...As well as occupying Amara, Townshend struck westwards and took Nasirya. Nixon's appetite for glory was whetted by these easy victories; with no thought to the risks, he pressed Townshend to continue his advance a further ninety miles to Kut (el Amara). In this he was backed by Duff, who had never visited Mesopotamia and had no idea of the conditions prevailing there. But Townshend had. He wrote to General Sir James Wolf Murray in England, "The question is where are we going to stop in Mesopotamia. We have certainly not good enough troops to make certain of taking Baghdad....I consider we ought to hold what we have got....All these offensive operations in secondary theatres are dreadful errors in strategy; the Dardanelles, Egypt, Mesopotamia, East Africa—I wonder and wonder at such expeditions being permitted in violation of all the great fundamental principles of war, especially that of Economy of Force. Such violation is always punished in history.' In the event, Duff never did visit Mesopotamia. Of this letter, Russell Braddon notes, 'The letter was completely in character. It revealed a gift for strategic appreciation amounting almost to prescience....'[11] Dixon further adds, 'For all its strategic prescience it bore little relationship to Townshend's subsequent behaviour. Though he clearly realized that he was being asked to undertake a major campaign with the logistics of a subsidiary defensive operation, he said nothing of this to his superior.'[12] Thereafter, Townshend willingly implemented Nixon's order that he should advance to Kut, but on his own initiative talked of going on to Ctesiphon, 190 miles away, and even beyond that to Baghdad. 'As to why he did so, there is no evidence at all—except his character. Indisputably, he was a man ambitious to the point of egomania: a man whom the lure of promotion had goaded throughout his career to such incessant intriguing and importunate letter writing...'[13]

Kut was captured, but the Turkish Army escaped to fight again another day. Townshend's force suffered twelve per cent casualties, against an estimated six; the casualty evacuation chain totally collapsing on an extended line of communication, as portrayed by Braddon, 'The wounded suffered frightfully. Untended, they lay freezing all night—some to be stripped and murdered by Arabs—and, when day light came, were placed on supply carts, unsprung, iron slatted, and drawn across a cruelly uneven surface to the river bank. There, in fierce sun, they languished until they could be crammed on to the decks of iron barges and towed very shortly downstream to Amara. What little water they were given was impure. What little treatment they could be given was ineffective. Their wounds went gangrenous...and they lay in a morass of their own blood and excreta, assailed by millions of flies. Quite unnecessarily, many of them died.'[14] Nixon and Duff were obsessed with the capture of Baghdad, and were unconcerned with the number of casualties and the plight of the wounded. A.J. Barker writes, in *Townshend of Kut,* '...for all the utterly inadequate arrangements made for the transport and treatment of the wounded and for their hideous sufferings, the Indian Government must be regarded as primarily responsible.'[15]

It was clear to Townshend that to advance beyond Kut would be foolhardy, but he was, 'loath to relinquish his own dream of becoming Lieutenant General Sir Charles Townshend, Lord of Baghdad,'[16] for the Turks were but Asians, not officered by Europeans. He marched towards Baghdad, but did not reach it, for at Ctesiphon there were 3,000 Turks, with 30,000 Turks reportedly moving towards it. Nixon, in his ambition, discounted the latter report operationally, but chose nevertheless to move himself and his headquarters back to Basra's safety. Townshend's force suffered 4,000 casualties at Ctesiphon and was counter-attacked by the very Turkish force Nixon had declared imaginary. Townshend harked back to his Chitral days as a captain, when he had been lauded as a hero for withstanding a forty-six days' siege by tribesmen. The defence of Kut was now Townshend's fixation, instead of a withdrawal to Amara, forgetting the Turkish Army were not tribesmen. The latter course would have shortened his communications, whereas Kut, a collection of mud huts, was tactically worthless. Nevertheless he still imagined he could take Baghdad, if non-existent reinforcements arrived from Britain, as shown by him '...identifying himself, as the occasion demanded, with such great captains as Hannibal, Napoleon and Wellington; there was nothing he liked better than to quote the precepts of famous military commanders.'[17]

Townshend persuaded Nixon, by fiddling his figures, that he had only rations for thirty days for his British troops, but no relieving force was able to reach him, for the Turks had established themselves north of Amara. Townshend surrendered after 147 days, for the relieving force, the 3rd and 7th Divisions, under Lieutenant General Fenton Aylmer, VC, had neither the strength (few battalions had more than 400 men, some less) nor the supplies to break through the Turkish force at Amara, nor did Townshend try to assist in a link up. Aylmer had arrived direct from the Army Headquarters, India, where he had been Adjutant General for three years. He had been awarded a VC on the Frontier in 1892, but had never commanded any field formation till sent to Mesopotamia. His generalship was murderous. The ostensible relief force suffered 23,000 casualties, approximately twice those of the besieged. Those who were killed were fortunate, for the wounded suffered in the Mesopotamian winter, dying gradually from exposure and maggots. Viceroy Charles Hardinge, Commander-in-Chief Duff, and Theatre Commander Nixon were culpable. The first lied to Whitehall that the medical arrangements were sound, the second was inept, and the third misrepresented facts to the Secretary of State, Joseph Chamberlain: 'Wounded satisfactorily disposed of, many likely to recover....'[18] The disposal was death, and the recovery was that of corpses.

In addition to fudging his supplies position to emphasize the need for urgent relief, Townshend minimized the Turkish strengths opposing the relieving force, resulting in Aylmer attacking an enemy stronger than he was led to believe. Townshend's signallers were required to send numerous private messages to his friends in Britain and India, but none for his troops' families. Aircraft dropped "pullthroughs" for cleaning rifles, but no mail for his troops throughout the siege. He repeatedly requested for promotion, and sought permission for himself to escape to fight again another day, by abandoning his division. He also sent unctuous communications to the Turkish commander opposing him. After the surrender, when supplies eventually ran out after 147 days, he abandoned his division of 13,000 men on 19 April 1916 to death from starvation and disease as prisoners, without doing anything to better his troops' lot, during their 1,200-mile march, while he luxuriated in the comforts provided by his Turkish captors, first at Baghdad, then Constantinople, and, finally, at a villa on the fashionable island of Halki in the Sea of Marmara, having informed his troops he was only leaving them to procure their repatriation. Fifty per cent of the Indian troops and seventy per cent of the British troops died in captivity, for '...in the building the Turks called a hospital, (Townshend's troops)...were being allowed by their captors to die in agony. There was no treatment for them and very little food, and those who fouled their beds were given an injection of brandy-coloured fluid, after which they stopped fouling their beds because they were dead.'[19]

Braddon emphasizes that of all the senior officers in Townshend's force, only one shared the fate of his men in captivity—Major General C.J. Melliss, VC, Indian Army, who evidenced a genuine concern for his men and endeavoured to improve the conditions for some of the prisoners. 'Though rough-tongued and blisteringly outspoken, Melliss nursed a great compassion for his men.'[20] Conversely, when 345 British and Indian prisoners were exchanged for an equal number of Turkish prisoners (all that the Expeditionary Force had captured), Duff forbade the returning prisoners from publicizing the suffering of those that were still in captivity, and thus no international pressure was possible for the amelioration of the conditions of their captivity. Dixon comments, 'In the mismanagement of the Mesopotamian campaign sheer stupidity played a relatively minor role. Certainly Duff was no genius and Nixon was unintelligent, but Townshend was not. Men's fates were decided for them not so much by "idiots" as by commanders with marked psychopathic traits. Stupidity and ignorance there may have been, but it was the ambitious striving of disturbed personalities which accounted for the loss of Townshend's force.' Townshend arranged with the Turkish commander for his pet dog to be sent to Basra. The dog, Spot, therefore was better off than the 7,000 British and Indian prisoners who died, for he was transported to Britain, rejoining his master when the latter was repatriated. Dixon wryly adds, 'Townshend could not understand that...a speech in which he referred to himself as having been "the honoured guest of the Turks", would hardly endear him to the friends and relatives of the 7,000 who had died in captivity.'[21]

Braddon avers, 'To have been members of the garrison of Kut, and to have survived the captivity which followed its fall, became a source of justifiable pride to Townshend's officers and men. They had fought and won some remarkable battles; they had beaten their enemy at Ctesiphon and only withdrawn from the field when he had returned in greater numbers than ever; and they had themselves been defeated, after the longest siege in history, only by hunger. Remarkably, none of them bore a grudge against the Turks,...and that those who murdered on the march were not Turks, but Kurds and Arabs.'[22] Braddon continues, 'Kut el Amara was the most humiliating disaster to have befallen a British expeditionary force since 1842 when, in a lunatic retreat from Kabul, sixteen thousand men died because of the decision of one half-witted general. It was to remain the most humiliating disaster until Singapore fell in 1942, because of the decisions of a series of half-witted military planners. In 1916, however, Kabul had been forgotten. Singapore was inconceivable and Kut seemed an unprecedented defeat at the hands of the despised Oriental.'[23] It was decided to retire Duff, and he was succeeded as Commander-in-Chief by General Sir Charles Monro.

In July 1917, the Government of India commenced the raising of a further twenty-one battalions. By August, the two new divisions proposed in May 1917, began assembly in Mesopotamia, and by

December another new division was contemplated.[24] On 4 December an Indian division was moved from Mesopotamia to Egypt in order to relieve a British division for France, on account of the increasing crisis in France. At the same time, Britain asked for Indian units to replace British units in the British divisions in Egypt. A decision was also now taken that Palestine would be the main theatre in the war against Turkey, and not Mesopotamia. A further Indian division was thus ordered from Mesopotamia to Egypt. The German successes in France of March 1918 necessitated expediting the "Indianization" process of British formations elsewhere, less Salonika. The twenty-one new battalions which had been sanctioned in July 1917 were not yet ready for this purpose, so recourse was had to raising twenty-two battalions overseas by taking a company or half-company from Indian units in Egypt and Mesopotamia, the despatching units being completed by drafts from India. As an example, a new battalion, the 1/150th Infantry, was formed with a company each from the 2nd, 4th, 8th and 13th Rajputs. Other such infantry amalgamations were the 131st, 133rd, 140th to 145th, 151st to 156th Infantry all disbanded in 1919. When in September 1918 it was decided to "Indianize" the British division in Salonika also, the units were found by reducing the Indian divisions in Mesopotamia from twelve to nine battalions each. By the time they were arriving in Salonika, the war was ending in November 1918. From the point of view of the Indian Army this was supposed to be an intermediate stage, for India contemplated raising another sixty-seven battalions to complete the "Indianization" at Salonika, and to reform the single British division in Mesopotamia.[25]

Between the beginning of 1917 and the end of the war alone, the Indian Army had doubled, but the quality of the army was causing concern. An example was the shooting of thirty-three Hill Brahmins (from Garhwal and Kumaon) who had been allotted to the 38th Dogras Depot at Jhelum for recruit training. They wanted non-commissioned officers of their own class to train them. Three hundred demonstrated, and thirty-three were killed when they stoned the escorting troops. In addition, there was the facet of the considerable number of Indian non-combatants (unenrolled), colloquially referred to as followers. To illustrate the situation in Mesopotamia alone on 19 October 1918, the ration strength was over 414,000, but only 217,000 in combat and field administrative support units. Of the differential, 71,000 were in the Labour Corps, and 42,000 in Inland Water Transport. The majority from the non-combatants (unenrolled) were Indians, but, in addition to local people, there were also men from China, Mauritius, Cape Coloureds and the West Indies. The list of units on that date also shows 'Detachment, Madras Gardeners'. The principal Indian non-combatant units were in the Labour, Porter and Syce Corps. Individuals were recruited for these non-combatant corps variously for six, nine and twelve months, so there was much transit of such persons.[26] By the end of the First World War, 1,105,000 Indian personnel in all had been sent overseas—France 138,000; Mesopotamia 657,000; Egypt and Palestine, 144,000; and smaller contingents to Aden, East Africa, Gallipoli and Salonika. In addition, over 170,000 animals for employment overseas, and 3,700,000 tons of supplies and stores were despatched.[27] In the past the Indian princes had often offered their State forces for service to the Indian Government, and the system was institutionalized in the Imperial Service Troops scheme of 1889. In 1914, the strength of the Imperial Service Troops had been 22,613. By November 1914, there were 48,806 Imperial Service Troops, of whom 26,099 were overseas.[28] Twenty mounted units and thirteen battalions in all had been ultimately employed overseas from the Imperial Service Troops.

To summarize this chapter, the role of the Indian Army from 1914 to 1918 became that of an Imperial strategic reserve, a role for which it was unprepared either by way of equipment or preparedness. In addition to providing Indian formations to various theatres to meet Imperial commitments, the Army Headquarters in India found itself conducting a major campaign in Mesopotamia for nigh on two years, a campaign for which it was neither perspectively nor conceptually prepared. The First World War clearly established that the Indian Army did not have efficient reserve, mobilization and recruit training systems to meet an emergency. To meet the requirements of wartime expansion, it almost destroyed itself in order to maintain the formations overseas at subsistence level. Manpower shortage was not the problem. In notional recruitable population terms, India could have produced 219 divisions in the First World War, but was called upon to produce seventeen.[29] The extension of recruiting to new classes was not a lesson fully assimilated, and had to be reassimilated in the Second World War. As Perry validly narrates, 'What the war of 1914-18 did was to underline the ambiguous status of the Indian Army and, indeed, of India itself. Neither fully independent nor fully subordinate to London, India and the Army followed policies partly originating in India, partly in London, and with no clear responsibility or control of events. The climax of this divided policy control was witnessed in the events in and around Kut in 1916.'[30] As to Townshend's or "Charlie of Chitral's" psychology, it would be appropriate to quote Dixon: 'It would seem that senior commanders fell into two groups, those primarily concerned with improving their professional ability and those primarily concerned with self-betterment. Critics of this theory may well object that professional excellence and the protection of self-esteem are not mutually exclusive incentives, that far from being different in motivational make-up, Montgomery of Alamein and Townshend of Kut were two of a kind. Both were conceited, vainglorious showmen with an eye to their personal advancement, both had charismatic personalities and were popular with their men. If there was any difference, according to this argument, it was in their luck. Had Montgomery been at Kut, and Townshend at Alamein their subsequent reputations would have been reversed...let us see how they (critics) may be answered....On several occasions Montgomery risked his own career by sacrificing popularity with those on whom his promotion might depend, for the sake of what he felt was the right course of action in terms of military efficiency....This sort of personal risk-taking for the sake of larger issues was not a feature of Townshend's make-up. For him it was always self first, and Army second....Montgomery would never have abandoned ten thousand of his men to a lingering death in the desert.'[31]

To conclude, what Field Marshal Erich Ludendorf said of the British troops in France in 1914-1918, that they were lions often led by donkeys, can also be validly said for the Indian troops. They then saved the British Empire, at a cost of 60,000 dead Indians, earning over 9,200 decorations, including eleven VCs. Never before had the Indian Army had to accept such casualties. It was later to be officially recorded, 'They did all that flesh and blood could do.' This was the first conflict in which Indians had been eligible for the latter award, but in the award process there were ironies, as there usually are. The London *Times* published on 24 November 1914 that Havildar Gagna Singh, a Dogra of the 57th Rifles, was the first Indian to be recommended for the VC. He had received five bullet wounds in a German attack. In the event, he received the Indian Order of Merit, the first VC formally being announced in the name of Sepoy Khudadad Khan, 129th Baluchis. From the war diary of the 129th Baluchis, the circumstances surrounding the award are not clear. The diary, with numbered pages, has the relevant pages missing.[32] All that can now be said for Gagna Singh's "missed" VC, and numerous others, is to quote Bridgadier P.H. Hansen, VC, DSO, MC: 'The important thing is to have a C.O. who can write a citation, with sufficient gift of persuasion to attract serious attention from higher authority.'[33] As to officer VCs, like Lieutenant General Aylmer and his "murderous" attacks, it would be appropriate to quote Colonel Harry Greenwood, VC, DSO, OBE, MC: 'VCs have a proven absence of cowardice, but not many have the imagination or compassion required for high command, and many are promoted because of their decoration and for no other very good reason.'[34]

Ironically, had what was then described as the "Alexandretta Project" been launched in February 1915, there would have been no disaster in Mesopotamia or at Gallipoli. Kitchener had issued orders for a force from Egypt under General William Birdwood of the Indian Army to be landed in the Gulf of Alexandretta in the

Mediterranean, to cut the Baghdad Railway. However on 16 February, on Winston Churchill's insistence, as First Lord of the Admiralty, this force was ordered to land at Gallipoli, in order to support the British naval operation against the Dardanelles, Churchill's unfortunate brainchild. Churchill was later to comment, 'I should say that nothing in war ever goes right, except by accident.'

NINE

Political Movements And The Indian Army In The First World War

ON THE eve of the war, M.A. Jinnah was in London at the head of a prestigious Indian National Congress deputation. To quote his biographer, Stanley Wolpert, this deputation had been sent to lobby the Secretary of State for India, Lord Robert Crewe, and Members of Parliament,' to open the Council of India to at least three (one-third of its total composition) non-official Indians elected by members of British India's Imperial and Provincial Legislative Councils....Though this young Bombay Muslim was only thirty-seven, he...may thus be said to have ventured to London in 1914, not simply at the helm of another political deputation but as potential heir to the Dadabhai (Naoroji)-Pherozeshah (Mehta)-Gokhale mantle of Western-Indian National Congress leadership....Jinnah was certainly Western India's most brilliant young barrister and shrewdest parliamentarian-diplomat, "the best talker of the pack," as Lord Crewe so crudely put it....M.K. Gandhi, at this time was forty-five....had no leadership status in the National Congress. The almost equal yet opposite force that the First World War was to exert upon the political fortunes of

263

Jinnah and Gandhi was not immediately apparent...at the start of the holocaust while Jinnah was still smarting from the...rejection...of his Congress deputation's demands, Gandhi urged resident Indians in England to "think imperially", and was instrumental in organizing a field ambulance training corps in London...however Gandhi soon...resigned from the service.'[1]

For understanding the impact of the various political movements on the Indian Army in the First World War, one must go back at least to 1905. In that year, the Japanese had defeated the Russians in a war over Korea. R.P. Dua records, 'In India particular interest was shown over the outcome of this war, not so much because of the fight over Korea, but because it was a victory of the so-called barbarians and uncivilized Asians over a major European power.'[2] Many Indians now felt that they had an Asian example, for, 'Japan had demonstrated that the technical and organizational pre-requisites of nationhood were not confined to Caucasians,'[3] according to Stephen Cohen. Separately, the partition of Bengal, also in 1905, dividing the Muslim majority area from the Hindu majority area (including Calcutta), aggravated matters. Implicitly, Lord Curzon's desire was to stem the tide of Indian nationalism in Bengal, strive to insulate the Muslims against it and thereby seemingly to assuage any incipient pan-Islamic movement in India. The Germans were then already inducing Turkey to stir up a pan-Islamic agitation throughout the Muslim world, especially directed against Britain, under the overt guise of a German port in the Persian Gulf as a terminus for the Berlin-Baghdad railway. Indian revolutionaries already had an active propaganda centre in Berlin apart from Paris and London. During a brief crisis in British relations with Turkey, when it had seemed possible hostilities would occur, British apprehensions had been expressed as to the possible effect on Indian Muslims. In the Indian National Congress, those termed moderates, like Mahadev Govind Ranade, Gopala Krishna Gokhale and Dadabhai Naoroji were now under pressure from more radical Congressmen, like Lokmanya Tilak and Lala Lajpat Rai. The Congress remained remarkably moderate and non-revolutionary throughout the First

World War, in no way tampering with the Indian Army.

Meanwhile, by this time 16,000 Indians had settled in California, and 4,000 in Canada, very many being Sikh ex-servicemen. This had come about partly due to the famine areas of East Punjab being comparatively neglected since 1887, the main emphasis being on the development of canal colonies in the Muslim West Punjab; and the US Government encouraging migration from the Punjab, impressed by the industry of the Punjabis as farmhands, on a then daily US wage of one to one-and-a-half dollars (three rupees to Rs 4.50). In India now Dr Gopal Singh opined, 'The Punjab, which was the last to fall to the British was also the first to rise against them in full fury.'[4] Riots started in 1907 at Lahore and Rawalpindi in protest at the Colonization Act, increasing land revenue and water rates in the canal irrigated areas. The leaders of the protest were Lajpat Rai of Lahore and Sardar Ajit Singh of Lyallpur. Lajpat Rai made his entry into politics earlier at a time when the annual sessions of the Congress began with resolutions of 'loyal homage to the King Emperor,' the same National Congress that Curzon had hoped to see into its grave.

Newspaper stories appeared in the Punjab that Lajpat Rai was about to attack the Lahore Fort with a force of 100,000 on 10 May 1907, the 50th anniversary of the 1857 Uprising. Exaggerated newspaper reports in Britain alleged that a conspiracy to instal him as Maharaja of the Punjab had been unearthed.[5] He and Ajit Singh were arrested and deported without trial to Burma. When John Morley, the Secretary of State, heard the news, he exclaimed, 'I can't stand that, I will not have that.'[6] Lajpat Rai's deportation without trial convulsed the country, and he and Ajit Singh were released in November 1907. The Viceroy, Lord Minto, later wrote to Morley, 'I cannot say that I look upon the performance of the Punjab Government at that time with any admiration. Lajpat Rai is undoubtedly a man of high character, and very much respected by his fellow countrymen and if, when I was asked to deport him, had I known what I do now, I should have required much more evidence before agreeing.'[7] On his return from Burma when the split came at the Surat session of the Congress,

Lajpat Rai urged the extremists, 'not to be impatient.' Ajit Singh however went abroad in 1909, and aligned himself in 1914 with the Ghadr (Revolutionary) Party, originally the Hindu Association of the Pacific Coast founded in 1913, amongst whose members were Hardayal, the philosopher and litterateur of St. Stephen's, Delhi; Maulvi Barkatullah, from Bhopal; and Ramchandra Peshawari.

Lajpat Rai happened to be in England when the First World War broke out in August 1914. The response in India to the British call for help was generally overwhelming, though the Germans had hoped that the outbreak of war would result in a general revolt, including in the Indian Army. German agents had been at work, some later shot in India, and had gathered an incorrect impression of Indian feeling, including in the Indian Army. As early as 1911, General Count F. von Bernhardi in his book, *Germany and the Next War,* had projected that a combination of the pan-Islamists and the revolution- aries of Bengal would shake the entire British position. Tilak, for his part, even though just released from jail, declared, 'Our sense of loyalty...is inherent and unswerving.' Lajpat Rai decided to go to the US, where he stayed till the end of 1919, before proceeding to Japan. He maintained a diary of his stay in the US and Japan, available in the National Archives of India. Though the British had been unjust in deporting him, he nevertheless still believed in British justice. He was wary of foreign agents being allowed to infiltrate the Indian Army, and discouraged wild speculation of subverting the Indian Army by the Indian expatriate revolutionaries in the US. The latter nevertheless continued to write to relatives in the Indian Army in order to disaffect them.

At a reception in San Francisco in October 1914, Lajpat Rai an- nounced, 'I am an Indian patriot and I wish freedom for my country. I have no sympathy with the Germans, nor I have anything against them. Considering all present circumstances, (we) would rather stay in the British Empire as a self-governing part of the latter than...be organized by another nation.' A German agent present broke a clay figure of John Bull into pieces to signify the disintegration of the British Empire. Lajpat Rai disassociated himself from such sentiments. Barkatullah told him that, 'a big rising was expected (in the Indian Army)..., that a date had been fixed and India would be free in three months,' with arms bought by Germany, and supplied through Afghanistan, Siam and China, and by sea (the German Foreign Minister, Arthur von Zimmerman, had issued instructions to this effect to the German Consuls General in San Francisco—Franz von Papen—Shanghai and Bangkok and to the embassy in Kabul). Lajpat Rai thought, 'the man was...a kind of fool. Even if India succeeded in turning out the British he did not want either the Afghan Amirs' or German rule in India.' He felt that, 'liberty with foreign help was not worth having.' When Haramba Lal Gupta, a member of the Berlin-India Committee, told him that the Germans were eager to have him on their side he refused to be taken in, and opposed a proclamation (*Ilan-i-Jang*) inviting Indian troops overseas to rebel. He was of the opinion that the Germans would only grab India and denude her. When the subject of such a proclamation to subvert Indian troops was later raised again by Gupta and Ramchandra Peshawari, the Ghadr Party leader, he dismissed it. The latter, though he had acquired control of the Ghadr Party, had little rapport with the 10,000 Sikhs in it. Lajpat Rai met Gupta in 1919 again in Japan and recorded, 'I have lost all faith in secret work and in secret organizations.'

However, the Ghadr Party, headquartered in San Francisco, had gone ahead with an armed revolution to end British rule in India with arms and explosives from abroad. Apart from the US and Canada, there were now Ghadr Party branches in Shanghai, Hong Kong, Panama, Siam and the Philippines. In May-July 1914 just before the outbreak of the First World War, the *"Kamagata Maru"* incident occurred. This chartered ship carried 376 immigrants to Canada, mainly Sikhs, but with some Muslims as well. Though complying with all Canadian regulations, they were not allowed to land even after two months in Canadian waters, mainly under British pressure. Incensed, the Ghadr Party provided the returning emigrants with 270 pistols at Yokohama. By the time the ship docked at Budge Budge near Calcutta, the First World War had broken out, and the government decided to search the ship and send the emigrants back to the Punjab by a special train, under a Punjab Police escort. Most of the pistols were seized, but over 300 Sikhs refused the order to entrain against their will in their own country, and took out a procession with the Guru Granth Sahib. The police fired and eighteen processionists were killed as well as three policemen. Those arrested were tried and sentenced to various terms of imprisonment.[8]

The outbreak of war had, in effect, occurred four years earlier than conceived by the Ghadrites. 'The increasing disputes (sometimes violent) between American and Indian workers also led to a reappraisal of their (the latter's) attitude.'[9] Some Sikh ex-servicemen emigrants, who had destroyed their medals and torn up their discharge certificates/papers, now returned to India to subvert Sikh subunits by way of preparation for an uprising, joined by some of the *Kamagatu* emigrants. Separately, in Bengal, terrorist attacks on the pattern of the previous few decades continued, increasing from fourteen in 1914 to thirty-six in 1915. In the Punjab, 15 November 1914 was the first date fixed by the Ghadr Party for the uprising. After the success of the revolution in the Punjab, the next phase was to be a "Free State of Kashmir" liberated from its ruler. The arms, however, did not arrive in time, so the dates kept on changing. 'What would have happened if the *SS Maverick* had arrived at the estuary on the Raimangal (now in Bangladesh) with 8,080 rifles, 2,400 carbines, 400 repeating rifles, 500 revolvers and 4,000 cartridges in all, and the rebel Ho Kuo Chuen (National Protection Party) of South China had agreed to hand over...across the Himalayas arms worth $5 million?'[10]

The Ghadrites, before departing for India, had been exhorted, according to an approver's later evidence, 'arms will be provided for you on arrival in India. Failing this, you must ransack the police stations.'[11] They continued arriving in batches, Khushwant Singh recording, 'On their way to India they approached Indian troops abroad.'[12] At Hong Kong contact was made with the 26th Punjabis; at Singapore with the Sikhs of the battery of Malay States Guides, and with the 5th Light Infantry, a Muslim unit which mutinied shortly after (dealt with later in this chapter); and at Penang with the Sikhs of the main body of the Malay States Guides. The government intelligence had information of the Ghadrite plans, through informers and censorship of mail. The ringleaders were arrested at Calcutta, but from the southern ports like Colombo some were able to reach the Punjab. 'The Ghadrites discovered to their chagrin that the atmosphere in India was far from conducive to revolution. Leaders of the National Congress were sympathetic to the British cause. Mahatma Gandhi had volunteered for medical service, and even radicals such as B.G. Tilak expressed strong disapproval of those who wished to exploit the situation. The Punjab was sending the flower of its manhood to the front. The only significant Sikh political party, the Chief Khalsa Diwan had reiterated its loyalty to the Crown, and priests of several important Sikh shrines denounced the Ghadrites as renegades or thugs...the Ghadrites made desperate efforts to secure a footing amongst the peasantry. They went to religious festivals at Amritsar, Nankana Sahib and Tarn Taran, and openly exhorted the people to revolt. There was little response, and the revolutionaries had to fall back on their own resources. They held meetings and made plans to raid arsenals and government treasuries, but all they succeeded in doing by the end of 1914 was to commit a few dacoities and kill a police constable (actually a sub-inspector) and a village official.'[13]

According to Sir Michael O'Dwyer, the Lieutenant Governor of the Punjab, 'No less than 45 serious outrages had been committed up to February 1915 by the revolutionaries.'[14] But it could also be said, though O'Dwyer does not say so, that many more of the Ghadrite forays failed in the Punjab, because of someone's absence at the required moment or because a key man was missing. In January 1915, Rash Behari Bose, who had been part of the group that had unsuccessfully tried to assassinate the Viceroy, Lord Charles Hardinge, when riding on an elephant in a procession in Delhi, in 1912, arrived in the Punjab from Bengal and took over the Ghadr Party revolution against "the British vampire". He was accompanied by N.G. Pingle, a Maharashtrian, who had returned to India from the

269

US with the Ghadr Party revolutionaries. Most of the Sikh troops in the 23rd Cavalry squadron at Mian Mir (Lahore), 26th Punjabis at Ferozepur (recently returned from the Far East) and 12th Cavalry at Meerut, to mention a few, were expected to mutiny. Ghadr Party agents had even been sent to several other cantonments which had Sikh troops—Agra, Allahabad, Ambala, Benares, Cawnpore, Faizabad, Jhelum, Kohat, Lucknow, Mardan, Multan, Peshawar, Rawalpindi and Sialkot. At this juncture, there were only about 15,000 British troops in India of whom eight battalions were committed to the Frontier. On receiving encouraging reports, Rash Behari fixed 21 February 1915 for the uprising by Indian troops in different cantonments. Bomb-making, which had so far been done in the French enclaves in India, was now also started in the Punjab. Copies of the Declaration of War (*Ilan-i-Jang*) were prepared, and tricolour flags made. Instruments to cut telephone and telegraph wires, and implements to damage railway lines were issued. When the proposed date of the uprising was revealed by a captured revolutionary, Rash Behari advanced it to 19 February, but this was also divulged by an informer who had infiltrated his inner circle. The regiments concerned were searched and disarmed. At Lahore alone 180 in all were arrested, at Benares fourteen, and even at Aden from amongst the Labana Sikhs of the 12th Pioneers, and at Mandalay seventeen from among the Sikhs in the Burma Military Police. Many were executed after a court-martial—twelve from the 23rd Cavalry—and most sentenced to transportation for life. Some were given lesser terms of imprisonment, and had their properties confiscated. Separately at Mandi, five were arrested, tried and sentenced to various terms of imprisonment.[15] In cooperation with the US authorities, thirty-nine were arrested in that country of whom eighteen were Germans and Americans, all of whom were convicted and sentenced for waging war on US soil against the British in India.

Rash Behari Bose left the Punjab, and settled in Japan, where he married. He is mentioned again subsequently in a later chapter in relation to the formation by the Japanese of the 'Indian National Army' (INA) in 1941-1942. Pingle was arrested in the 12th Cavalry

Lines at Meerut, tried and hanged. Of the 8th Cavalry at Jhansi, MacMunn records, 'Further down country, another cavalry regiment was in trouble, killing its commanding officer and wounding others.'[16] Of the period April to August 1915, O'Dwyer went on to record, 'For the revolutionaries, being now desperate...resorted more freely than ever to cowardly assassination of those who were helping the government. In April a loyal Sikh sirdar was murdered in Hoshiarpur. In June a Sikh magnate of Amritsar was murdered...on 11 June they rushed the (military) picquet (on an important railway bridge near Amritsar), killed two of the sentries, and carried off four rifles and some ammunition...by August 1915, that is after nine months of the first outbreak, we had crushed the Ghadr rebellion.'[17] O'Dwyer was eventually himself killed in 1940 in London by Udham Singh, a Ghadr Party member. (Earlier, Madan Lal Dhingra had killed Sir William Curzon-Wylie in 1909 in London.) According to O'Dwyer, in all 8,000 Ghadr Party revolutionaries returned to India, though Hardinge put it at 7,000, and the CID records mention a lower figure of 5,000.[18]

Some of the returning ex-servicemen emigrants, who had not been arrested, but had been restricted to their villages, now sought re-enrolment in the Indian Army. Army Headquarters was not prepared to take the risk of recruiting these ex-servicemen, some of whom might have been aiming, 'to corrupt their comrades, as happened...at the beginning of the Ghadr campaign.'[19] Why did the Ghadr Party uprising fail? Gopal Singh ventures an answer: '...they made an honest and determined effort to liberate their country, however, innocent they were in their study of world history and the forces at work against them at that time...the majority of them had seen army life before and knew key men in the armed forces (in their former regiments). The contact men in various centres of the army either changed their minds, or contact could not be established with them at the given time, as at the Mian Mir (Lahore) cantonment, to provide leadership. The leadership was too loud-mouthed and their activities were mostly an open book known to the police. Informers had been planted among them by the Government. Disaffection was sought to be created in various centres, but their efforts were not co-ordinated.'[20] In the same context, A.C. Bose opines, 'When...German gold began flowing, all sorts of adventurers joined the movement, some for easy money, some for a comfortable life in enemy countries...in fact, British intelligence was far too efficient for them and thanks to the help they (the British) received from their wartime allies in most cases the former had prior information about the plans and movements of the Indians. The latter actually lacked the two essentials of revolution, secrecy and surprise and they carried on their operations as if on a well lit stage.'[21]

While the Ghadr Party activities were current in India, Sultan Abdul Hamid and Khedive Enver Pasha of Turkey continued their pan-Islamic efforts. The rural Muslims in India and their rural leaders at that time took little interest in any but local politics. Some of the urban Muslims had however been imbued with pan-Islamic aspirations. The neutral attitude of Britain in the Turco-Italian and Balkan wars of 1911-1913 had caused resentment The views of the pan-Islamic movement in India were reflected in the publication, *Zamindar* edited by Zafar Ali at Lahore, and *Comrade* at Delhi by the Ali brothers, Mohammed Ali and Shaukat Ali. Collections were made for the Turkish Red Crescent Society, and appeals to the Muslim troops of the Indian Army either to mutiny or desert. Mutinies took place at Rangoon amongst some of the Pathans in the 130th Baluch, and at Singapore amongst the Mussalman Rajputs (Ranghars) of the 5th Light Infantry, which was an entirely Muslim unit.

Before dealing with these mutinies overseas, mention must be made of the several Muslim troop desertions in groups with and without arms, that occurred both in India and overseas in the Indian Army, once Turkey came into the war in November 1914 against the Allies, and which continued well on into 1917. The groups that deserted with arms in India, often headed for Afghanistan, where an army of over 100,000 under Enver Pasha was thought by them to be assembling against the British in India. According to Sir Louis Dane, the former Foreign Secretary of the Government of India, 'northern

India must have been lost for the time,' if the Afghans had attacked, 'as there were serious signs of mutiny in some regiments.'[22] Similarly, Muslim troops that deserted in France to the Germans, or in Mesopotamia to the Turks, were sent to Afghanistan to foment trouble in the militia and among the Muslim troops of the Indian Army deployed on the border. For example, Jemadar Mir Mast and fourteen of his platoon deserted in France in March 1915 from the 58th Rifles. He was lionized by the Germans and presented with the Iron Cross by the Kaiser. In April 1915, his brother, Jemadar Mir Dast with the 57th Rifles, was presented the VC by King George V to match the Iron Cross presented to his brother.[23] In Mesopotamia attack plans were divulged to the Turks by some Muslim troops deserting, before the latter were sent on to Afghanistan. In February 1915, groups of Muslim students had disappeared from Lahore, Rawalpindi and Peshawar. With the assistance of the Wahabi "Hindustani Mujahidin" mentioned earlier, they were taken to Kabul. Here a provisional Indian Government had been set up, with German help, Raja Mahendra Pratap being the President, and Barkatullah the Prime Minister. The latter has earlier been mentioned as a Ghadr Party office holder. Before that he had been a professor in Tokyo from 1909 to 1914, but on account of the consistent anti-British views in his publication, *Islamic Fraternity* it was suppressed and he lost his academic appointment on British representation. Raja Mahendra Pratap was a wealthy UP landowner, who had gone to Europe on the outbreak of the First World War, where he had met Hardayal, already mentioned as a Ghadr Party office holder. Mahendra Pratap only returned to India after independence. (After the First World War, Hardayal settled in Sweden, and became an apologist for British rule in India.) Both Mahendra Pratap and Barkatullah had met the Kaiser, who had given them individual leather-bound letters to each Indian princely ruler. Communications were also addressed by them to the Indian prisoners of war in Germany, who, though well-treated, were, for indoctrination purposes, kept separately from those who deserted. *En route* to Kabul, they had also had interviews with the Sultan of

273

Turkey and the Khedive Enver Pasha.

Dr Mathra Singh, a Sikh revolutionary, joined them at Kabul. A Turco-German mission was also established in Kabul at the same time. Mathra Singh was later handed over by the Russians to the British authorities, while he was trying to cross into Persia. Brought back to India, he was hanged for his earlier participation in the Ghadr Party subversion of Sikhs in Indian Army units in the Punjab. Also handed over with him to the British in Persia by the Russians were three of the Lahore students. One was tried for treason by the British in Persia, and shot. Two sons of an ex-serviceman, were brought back to India and granted a conditional pardon by O'Dwyer. They gave out details in August 1916 of the "Silk Letter Plot".[24] These letters were written on silk, concealed in the linings of coats, by two maulvis formerly of the Deoband (Darul Uloom School of Theology), and then in Kabul, for a general Muslim troop uprising in India, conjoined with the Frontier tribes and the Wahabi "Hindustani Mujahidin", allied with the remaining Ghadr Party revolutionaries in India, against the British. Amir Habibullah of Afghanistan, however, adhered to his treaty with the British right through the First World War, thus aborting most of the hostile activities against and subversion of the Indian Army on the Frontier. 'He...is reported to have said to the Turco-German mission that when they could show him an army of 100,000 at Herat, he would begin to think they meant business. It was at this stage that the Germans left Kabul in disgust.'[25]

There were thus incipient collective disciplinary problems among the Muslim troops, particularly in the 15th Lancers by that time in Mesopotamia. By now certain precautions had started being taken. Two Jat squadrons were inducted in lieu of Multani Pathan squadrons in the 15th Lancers. Two battalions, largely Muslim, had been replaced at Gallipoli, opposite the Turks, by Gurkha battalions, but retaining the 14th Sikhs, who performed courageously. When the two Indian divisions were withdrawn from France for Mesopotamia in 1915, two largely Muslim units as a precaution were sent to East Africa rather than risk deploying them opposite the Turks. Before going on to political developments in 1917, at this stage it is necessary to revert to the mutinies in the 130th Baluch at Rangoon, and the 5th Light Infantry at Singapore in 1915, with a view to discerning their political undertones. This is not to suggest that there were not mutinies in other armies in the First World War. For example, sixty out of sixty-eight French divisions were affected by mutiny in 1917; the British mutiny at Etaples in 1917, as also that of the British West Indies Regiment in Italy in 1918, apart from that of the British Marine Battalion in north Russia in 1919. In the 130th Baluch, the collective insubordination and disaffection was limited to certain Pathans' (actually four companies out of eight) reluctance to fight the Turks, in response to the appeal to this effect by the Sultan of Turkey. The same battalion, earlier *en route* to East Africa, had bayoneted a British officer while embarking from India initially having been warned for Mesopotamia. The unit was immediately re-routed to Rangoon. A Shropshire Light Infantry battalion was used for disarming the four companies at Rangoon.[26] Over one hundred-and-ninety personnel were court-martialled, one VCO and one havildar being shot, and the remaining sentenced to transportation for life or lesser terms in the Andamans, where curiously the non-mutinous companies of the unit had been doing duty earlier at the time of the disaffection in Rangoon. As thirty-seven Indian Army personnel were publicly shot in mass executions on account of the mutiny in the 5th Light Infantry, it needs to be gone into in some detail.

In March 1922, the War Office had published "The Statistics of the Military Effort of the British Empire during the Great War" in Part XXIII *Discipline*. The statistics of the courts-martial resulting in 346 executions are recorded for the British Imperial Forces (including Indian), as well as non-combatants unenrolled. I have not been able to glean the detailed actual figures of the total executions of Indian Army personnel as they are not given in the Government of India publications, and the actual court-martial execution proceedings at the British Public Records Office are closed for one hundred years (some Indians and Gurkhas figure among those executed in various overseas theatres where they were a major component, for instance in France, according to the unit war diaries in the British Public Record Office, though the majority executed overall was British). The breakdown by theatres was:-

- France   322
- East Africa   5
- Mesopotamia   4
- Constantinople   4
- Gallipoli   3

- Salonika   3
- Egypt   2
- Italy   1
- Palestine   1
- Serbia   1

Three of those shot by firing squads were British officers — two for desertion, and one for murder, all of the British Army. Desertion in the face of the enemy was officially the offence for which the greatest number paid the penalty (the figures were compiled from 1 October to 30 September of the following year):

Offence	1915	1916	1917	1918	1919	1920[27]
Desertion	40	62	78	77	6	-
Murder	1	6	3	10	8	8
Cowardice	5	6	5	2	-	-
Quitting post	2	2	2	1	-	-
Striking superior	-	1	2	3	-	-
Disobeying orders	-	4	-	1	-	-
Mutiny	-	-	2	1	-	-
Sleeping on duty	-	-	2	-	-	-
Casting away arms	-	-	2	-	-	-
Total	48	81	96	95	14	8

291 were Imperial (including Indian) troops. Five colonial troops, five camp followers, ten Chinese and four coloured labourers were also in the figure of 346. It is necessary to retail these figures

as according to William Moore, 'the figures (of executions) were forty-seven men short of the truth — all of them were Indians (of the 5th Light Infantry.')[28] Actually thirty-seven of the 5th Light Infantry were executed, ten having their death sentences commuted. The discrepancy could well be more overall in relation to Indian personnel executed, as presumably Singapore and Rangoon were not considered theatres of war when the aforesaid War Office publication was compiled. One is, however, grateful to William Moore for pointing out the discrepancy.

The mutiny in the 5th Light Infantry, till then known as the Loyal 5th, is by now well documented, there being several printed accounts, particularly by Ian Beckett (including the Court of Inquiry proceedings in the British Library), as also various unpublished eye-witness accounts as at the time wartime secrecy was in force in relation to these occurrences.[29] (Certain records in the British Public Record Office will only be released round about 2015.) The battalion, the only one in Singapore at the time, was organized in two wings of four companies each, one of Hindustani Mussalmans and one of Mussalman Rajputs (Ranghars), with an Indian strength of 818. There were certain promotion problems between these two classes, and one current VCO vacancy was first being allotted to the latter by the CO but the decision was then countermanded under pressure from the officers and VCOs of the other wing. This had happened for the second time to the same NCO, Havildar Imtiaz Ali. In addition, the personnel had been subjected to pan-Islamist propaganda not to fight the Turks by a civilian, Kasim Ismail Mansur, who kept a tea shop frequented by the unit's personnel, as also Ghadr Party propaganda not to fight for the British, by Ghadrites passing through Singapore, particularly one Jagat Singh. There is no documentary evidence of the latter, though locally in Singapore there was little doubt as to Ghadrite influence. Further, the British officers were in two camps, one with the commanding officer, or neutral towards him, and one against him. According to Beckett, the present CO, when previously second-in-command, had been considered 'a sleepy easy going officer' by the previous CO. He had been posted out for a three months' special report, but had since returned as CO. On becoming CO, he had initiated adverse reports on two of the officers, whom he felt had been working against him in the previous CO's tenure. As a result, some of the men began seeing the CO over the heads of their wing commanders and wing officers.

The battalion, under orders to move on 16 February 1915, did not wish to fight the Turks, nor go to France on account of the slaughter there. Unknown to the unit, Kitchener had already declared it 'too Mussalman' for deployment against the Turks, and it was in fact going to Hong Kong. For security reasons this had not so far been communicated to the personnel by the CO, as ships were still being torpedoed in the adjacent seas. The GOC in his farewell address (in English) had not mentioned Hong Kong as the destination but had said, 'although it is not their good fortune to go to Europe they are going where there is need of their service.' The CO's imperfect translation on the farewell parade did not help the troops' understanding. On the afternoon of 15 February 1915, the disgruntled and mutinous Ranghar wing, moved out of the unit lines with its weapons, having seized 30,000 rounds of ammunition; it formed three groups. One group with Havildar Imtiaz Ali sought to attack the CO's house where the Subedar Major, the second-in-command and his wife, and two other officers had taken shelter. On hearing the sound of firing, a detachment of the Malay States Volunteer Rifles had come to their assistance. A second group went to the internment camp for about 300 Germans, issuing them arms and stating that they were now the allies of the Germans. (The unit had previously been on guard duty on this camp before the unit's impending move.) The local volunteer corps on duty was overpowered, fourteen being killed including the commandant, as also, accidentally, a German internee. The Germans were informed that they were now being released. They were taken aback and only seventeen availed of the opportunity to escape (six being later recaptured). Unknown to the British some of these seventeen had already been tunnelling with a view to escaping. That the internees were unwilling to escape disproved the local British theory of the

Germans' collusion in the mutiny. A third group sought to establish a stop on the main road from Singapore to prevent reinforcements from arriving. Apart from those at the internment camp the mutineers also killed all Europeans they encountered. Twenty other Europeans were thus killed including an Englishwoman and two of the unit's British officers. As that day was a holiday on account of it being the Chinese New Year's Day, firing by the mutineers was thus assumed by many to be the sound of Chinese crackers.

An ad hoc force was progressively put together from the local artillery garrison, a British sloop, French, Russian and Japanese cruisers, Johore State Forces and other local volunteers and the mutineers rounded up, from 16 February onwards, some casualties occurring in rescuing the CO. (At the outbreak of the mutiny, some personnel from the non-mutinous wing had come to protect the CO's house, but, apart from being without any ammunition, he considered it "precarious" to accept their help.) Before being rounded up, the mutineers, on 15 February, had prevailed on eleven Sikhs of the Malay States Guides Battery to join them. (Earlier, the Malay States Guides, comprising mainly Indians, had apparently sought to serve in the war, but when ordered to move to East Africa in December 1914, the unit had a change of mind.)

It was apparent that the mutinous wing had no coherent plan, apart from seeking to free the interned Germans and to conjoin them in further action. Once the Germans had shown no major interest in escaping, then any impetus the mutineers had, petered out. In the rounding up by 18 February forty-six mutineers were killed or drowned, and 422 were rounded up, by which time a total of thirty-two Europeans had been killed. When he first reported the incident to the Secretary of State, Lord Crewe, the Governor of the Straits Settlements described it as "an emeute", while Crewe described it as more of 'a regimental riot than...anything which could possibly be described as a mutiny.' Nevertheless, martial law was declared by evening ,15 February, and all European women and children were put aboard ships on 16 February. Kasim Ismail Mansur, later to be hanged, had already been arrested earlier for the Malay States

Guides' refusal to proceed overseas. A letter from him to the Turkish Consul in Rangoon had also been intercepted, wherein he requested a Turkish ship to take the Muslim troops from Singapore to Turkey. A detachment of the 36th Sikhs, *en route* from Tsingtao in China to India, though without arms, also came under suspicion for collusion in the mutiny, because the unit had mutinied on the Frontier at Dargai before the First World War. However, nothing was found against it.

In addition to the eleven men of the Malay States Guides, 202 men of the 5th Light Infantry were tried by summary general courts-martial. Thirty-seven were publicly shot, and eighty-nine actually imprisoned for varying terms up to transportation for life. Each firing party was to be detailed from units that suffered casualties from the mutineers in the proportion of five to fire to one to be executed. The first two to be publicly executed were two VCOs who were shot by ten men of the Malay States Volunteer Rifles, commanded by Lieutenant M.B. Shelley, who had left a manuscript account. He could not find anyone in the whole of Singapore to brief him as to how to conduct the firing party. In the event, two volleys were required to execute one of the VCOs. The largest execution was of twenty-one by a firing party of 105. The proceedings dragged out as the biodata, offences and sentences of each of the accused were read out in the four languages of the large gathering of the public present for the spectacle. A ragged first volley failed to kill all the accused and was followed by an even more ragged second volley for which the firing party stepped forward. Even then warders had to walk along the line with pistols in order to finish the proceedings. Ironically in a subsequent debate on the death sentence in Britain, quoted by William Moore, Brigadier F.P. Crozier wrote to the *Daily Express* in May 1928 in the light of his experience of carrying out executions in East Africa, South Africa and France, that in this age of automation such executions should be carried out with automatic weapons (machine-guns). The moral of this, or any other mutiny, is, as Sir Charles Egerton of the Colonial Office expressed it at the time, pick the right commanding officer to lead a battalion. For its part the 5th Light Infantry had Ahirs inducted in lieu of Ranghars, and eventually moved to Africa. It was disbanded in the 1922 reorganization.

Meanwhile, on the political plane, at Poona, in 1917, B.G. Tilak, in a recruiting speech, was emphasizing that the opportunity afforded by the First World War should be seized: 'If you want Home Rule be prepared to defend your Home. Had it not been for my age I would have been the first to volunteer. You cannot reasonably say that the ruling will be done by you and the fighting for you—by Europeans or Japanese, in the matter of Home Defence. Show...that you are willing to take advantage of the opportunity offered to you by the Viceroy to enlist in an Indian Citizen Army. When you do this, your claim for having the commissioned ranks opened to you will acquire double weight.'[30] The 1917 Calcutta session of the Congress went further, J.N. Roy of Bengal proposing, 'I happen to be one of those that think we would do little with responsible government in this country if we had not military training at the same time. In fact speaking for myself, had I a choice between responsible government and military training I would unhesitatingly choose military training.'[31] As a result of Bengal's support for the war effort, the 49th Bengal Regiment was raised in 1917 at Karachi, and for the first time comprised Bengalis (the number forty-nine was an existing blank in the renumbering of Bengal Army units by Kitchener in 1903). Subhas Chandra Bose sought to be enrolled for this battalion, but was rejected on medical grounds (weak eyesight). After a spell on the Frontier, the unit was sent to Mesopotamia for line-of-communication duties. Here promotion rivalries broke out between the Bengali Brahmins and the Kayasthas; in 1918 two VCOs were murdered, including the popular subedar major, and a third was wounded. There were absolutely no revolutionary influences at work in this disciplinary situation, either of the Dacca Anushilan Samiti or the Yugantar group. The assailants were executed. Most of the British officers, particularly the CO, had not been happy about being posted to this new regiment. The CO promptly again recommended disbandment, having done so earlier when asked for a progress report as to the battalion's efficiency one year after its raising. So ended the brief existence of the 49th Bengal Regiment. (A similar endeavour in the Second World War, in the form of an embodied Bengali coast artillery battery, ended in a major case of collective indiscipline at Diamond Harbour, near Calcutta.)

The First World War not only saw the end of the German empire, but also started the process that weakened the imperial bonds between Britain and India. In August 1917, the Secretary of State, Edwin Montagu, announced, 'the increasing association of Indians in every branch of the administration, and the gradual development of self-governing institutions with a view to the progressive realization of responsible government in India as an integral part of the British Empire.' As the cumulative result of consistent pressure by nationalists in India over the thirty years since the founding of the National Congress, within a few days of this announcement, nine officers in the "Native Indian Land Forces" (ex-Curzon's Imperial Cadet Corps) were granted temporary King's commissions in the Indian Army, pending the subsequent granting of commissions to others through the Daly College, Indore, and Sandhurst. This will be dealt with in a subsequent chapter. Honorary commissions were also now given for the first time on the active list to selected VCOs. As Judith M. Brown records, 'In other centuries war had served to build rather than to break Europe's overseas empires; the British Raj in India was a case in point...whatever the complexities of the colonial relationship, the years of the First World War witnessed a remarkable change in Britain's connection with India.'[32]

From November 1917, Montagu toured India, along with the new Viceroy, Lord Thesiger Chelmsford, for five months, to gauge public opinion for himself, even though the war was still on. By July 1918 their report had been placed before the British Parliament. The outcome was the Government of India Act of 1919, which embodied their proposals and came to be known as the "Montford" reforms. Montagu also published his perceptive observations during the five months' tour as *An Indian Diary*, wherein he recorded the view that less damage would have been done to the Indian Army, if Kitchener had wanted Duff promoted, for the latter to have been the Army

Chief in 1910, instead of O'Moore Creagh; thereby enabling someone more professionally qualified to have become the Army Chief in 1914. India owes a great deal to Montagu's initiative generally, and in particular in relation to the Indianization of the officer cadre, which, till then, had been consistently opposed by the British Cabinet, under pressure from the War Office. Concomitantly, steps to increase the number of recruits were taken in consultation with nationalist politicians. A War Conference was convened at Delhi in April 1918. M.K. Gandhi was among those attending. The aim of the conference was to invite the cooperation of all in bringing about a cessation of political propaganda against the British Government, and in concerting measures for the successful prosecution of the war. Gandhi, thereafter, in 1918, visited Gujarat and sought to recruit soldiers, but not with much success. By now the Congress' leadership roles of M.A. Jinnah and Gandhi at the start of the First World War were getting reversed, Gandhi's power increasing and Jinnah's influence diminishing. Nevertheless, both had supported the British war effort as a means leading to greater control of the government, a *quid pro quo* acknowledged by the British by inviting India to the Imperial War Conference in London.

To conclude this chapter, the First World War, with a greater recruit intake into the Indian Army, provided the rural population scope for greater upward mobility, as also, scope to search for opportunities outside the ancestral village. A splendid literary trilogy in this context is Mulk Raj Anand's novels, *The Village, Across the Black Water* and *The Sword and the Sickle*. These portray a Punjabi villager enrolling in the First World War to escape problems in his village, and, after the large-scale demobilization, inevitably becoming a revolutionary, for the First World War proved to be, as the Second World War was to prove later, both an engine and catalyst for social change, particularly for the millions who served in the Indian Army. However, while the minority gained honours and awards for wartime service, the majority was unhappy at summarily being released from comparatively well-paid employment, and thus not receiving any reward. Turbulence in the Punjab surfaced; as an example one can consider the Akali agitation in the 1920s, in which, as to the control of the gurdwaras, ex-servicemen, as also servicemen on leave, played a considerable part. Thus, apart from the impact on the Indian Army, at the macro level, the First World War broke the political impasse in India, and, in the event, the Second World War, as we shall later see, accelerated these political developments.

However, the Indian soldier in the First World War was, by and large, still not politically-minded. There was some political consciousness, notably among the Ghadrite Sikh ex-servicemen, and also some religious consciousness among certain classes of Muslim troops. As we shall see, in a subsequent chapter on martial and non-martial classes, the demands of the war were such that many had to be recruited from the latter classes, which had been allowed to provide few, if any, soldiers in pre-First World War years. Despite the tradition-orientation in the Indian Army, service overseas had exposed them to the more open attitudes of the French. Algerian and Senegalese officers, admittedly in most cases carrying out the same duties as VCOs in the Indian Army but classified as officers, were equivalent to French officers and not in the category of sub-officers. This point was often made by the Indian Muslim League office in London from 1915 onwards, both personally and in writing to the Secretary of State. Similarly, the Turks, fellow-Asians, were commanded and led into action by their own officers, and not by Europeans employed for the purpose, though German advisers may have been present at the battalion level just as a British officer was present as an adviser to Indian State Force units overseas. The Russians also, as Indian troops discerned, when they met Russian units in northern Mesopotamia or Persia, had Central Asians as officers and not sub-officers. There are First World War letters on record from retired VCOs and honorary commissioned (on retirement) officers (one of the latter was Captain Ajab Khan, a member of the Viceroy's Advisory Council) that their sons, after serving in the First World War, deserved better than what the British had offered their fathers.

The Indian Army at the end of the First World War was, thus, not the same as that of 1914. While tradition was still strong, change was also in the air. Of the nationalist political scenario at the end of the First World War, which eventually set the scene for Partition, Stanley Wolpert writes: 'Proper British barrister that he was, Jinnah had groomed himself to be the perfect Indian Viceroy...were it not for the war this Muslim Gokhale might well have succeeded to a national leadership over Congress as well as the League....By greatly accelerating the timetable of Indian political expectations...the war offered Gandhi his historic opportunity to muster mass support for the programme of revolutionary action he had coincidentally developed at this opportune hour.'[33]

From now onwards, the problem for the British in India was not military or administrative, but essentially political, though not sufficiently recognized as such. The reality in this regard was often obscured right up to the outbreak of the Second World War.

TEN

The Myth Of The Martial Race Dogma

THE MYTH of the martial races was exploded during the First World War. At the outbreak, recruitment was based on the dogma of the martial races, a concept which did not exist in any other modern army. Recruitment-wise, in relation to the past pattern, the most adversely affected people, in the main, had been the South Indian classes and Mahars. As the progressive bias against the enrolment of South Indians emerged earlier, this facet is dealt with first. In his book, *Ten Years in India,* published in London in 1850, Albert Hervey was identified as late of the 40th Madras Infantry.[1] His beloved regiment had been disbanded in 1882, after Hervey had died, having attained the rank of Major General. As the invalid formulation of the martial race dogma by Lord Frederick Roberts, Commander-in-Chief of the Madras Army 1881-1885, had led to the progressive reduction in that army, it would be appropriate to quote from Hervey's reminiscences by way of initial rebuttal. 'Recent occurrences (presumably meaning the First Anglo-Afghan War) partly adding lustre to the arms of our country, and partly deteriorating therefrom, have combined to render our interest in India greater than heretofore. The Bengal and Bombay Presidencies are those on which the attention of Europe have been fixed as playing the most distinguished part in the tragical drama which has been lately enacted, whilst the sister Presidency of Madras has apparently sunk into insignificance, and been termed by the would-be witty, the benighted Presidency, whether justly so or not is another thing. But the Madras Army has been, as it were, resting and looking on at the deeds enacted in the north-west...they have already conquered, and are ready to conquer again and again. Give them the opportunity, and they are second to none in the deadly charge, the skirmish or the escalade; and it is because these great troops are left in the background that the other two armies have been brought conspicuously before the world, that the former glorious deeds of the benighted are thrust into the shade as a secondary consideration...but no, such is not the case. Military ardour and heroic chivalry are at the present period as bright in the breasts of our noble "sipahis" as they were wont to be in the days of Clive...there is no army in the whole of Europe in which military discipline is better maintained. There are no troops better clad and appointed; there are no soldiers more faithful, more brave, or more strongly attached to their colours and officers than are those of the Madras Army. I have the honour to belong to this army and I am proud of it....I can safely say that a more manly set of fellows I could never desire to command. The great secret is to treat them as men should be treated, and a more tractable race of beings I would never wish to see...and I think I am not far wrong in saying, that he is in point of moral courage second to none in the world. Behold the (Madras) sepoy in the field, on the line of march, in the siege, on board a ship—in any position, he is still the soldier. How patient under privation! How enduring of fatigue! How meek and submissive under control, or correction! How fiery in action! How bold in enterprise! How zealous in the performance of his duty! How faithful in his trust! How devotedly attached to his officers and colours!' It cannot be said that Hervey had gone to press, as it were, to forestall reduction in the Madras Army, for reduction was not then contemplated in 1850.

Yet, Roberts, of his spell as Commander-in-Chief at Madras,

only three decades after Hervey's book was published, recorded: 'Each cold season I made long tours in order to acquaint myself with the needs and capabilities of the men of the Madras Army. I tried hard to discover in them those fighting qualities which had distinguished their forefathers during the wars of the last and the beginning of the present century. But long years of peace, and the security and prosperity attending it, had evidently had upon them, as they always seem to have on Asiatics, a softening and deteriorating effect; and I was forced to the conclusion that the ancient military spirit had died in them, as it had died in the ordinary Hindustani of (the) Bengal (Army) and the Mahratta of (the) Bombay (Army) and that they could no longer with safety be pitted against warlike races, or employed outside the limits of southern India. It was with extreme reluctance that I formed this opinion with regard to the successors of the old Coast Army, for which I had always entertained a great admiration....Madrassis as a rule are more intelligent and better educated than the fighting races of northern India . . . the Sappers and Miners were a brilliant exception to the rest of the Madras Army, being indeed a most useful efficient body of men but as no increase in that branch was considered necessary, I obtained permission to convert two Infantry regiments into pioneers on the model of the Pioneer corps of the Bengal Army.'[2] Roberts did not try to explain why the Madras Sappers, who were raised from the Madras Infantry and recruited from the same classes, should have been an exception. The difference, manifestly, was in the quality of the officers latterly posted to the Madras Infantry, for the Madras Sapper officers were selected officers deputed from the British service, whereas the Madras Infantry officers were not so selected.

Roberts became Commander-in-Chief in India from 1885-1893, and went on to postulate, 'From the time I became Commander-in-Chief, Madras, (1881) until I left India (1893) the question of how to render the army in that country as perfect a fighting machine as it is possible to make it, was the one which caused me the most anxious thought, and to which solution my most earnest efforts had been at all times directed. The first step to be taken towards this end, was, it seemed to me, to substitute men of the more warlike and hardy races for the Hindustani sepoys of (the) Bengal (Army), the Tamils and Telegus of Madras, and the so-called Mahrattas of Bombay...it had become essential to have in the ranks of our Native Army, men who might confidently be trusted to take their share of fighting against a European foe (Russia was meant). In the British Army, superiority of one regiment over another was mainly a matter of training; the same courage and military instinct are inherent in the English, Scots and Irish alike, but no comparison can be made between the martial value of a regiment recruited amongst the Gurkhas of Nepal, or the warlike races of northern India, and of one recruited from the effeminate peoples of the south...several companies and regiments composed of doubtful material were disbanded, and men of well known fighting classes entertained instead....'[3] (According to Geoffrey Moorhouse, Roberts' maternal grandmother was a Rajput.)

Though Roberts does not say so, two of the cases invoked by him against the Madras Infantry's performance in Burma were those of the 12th Regiment at Minhla in November 1885 during the Third Anglo-Burmese War, and that of the 10th Regiment during the Chin Hills insurrection in 1888-89. In the former case, the regiment had been allegedly reported as "disinclined to advance". The official records show that the commanding officer and most of the other officers had been posted in just before induction into Burma, and the battalion, thereupon, had been dispersed in detachments. In addition, 'several of the commanding and other officers of the Madras regiments...were physically unfit for active service. They were unable to walk or get about the country with their men. No chargers were permitted to be taken from India, and several of these officers found the small Burma pony quite unable to carry them.' The Madras Army officers, however, implied that adverse publicity was being given to the Madras Infantry by the "Bengal press" correspondents (there were no Madras press correspondents in Burma), at the instigation of some Bengal Army officers, in order that the "superiority" of the Bengal Army was publicized through the press.

(Even today, some officers and regiments resort to the media more than others.) There were eight other Madras Infantry regiments in Burma at the time, apart from the Bengal Army regiments. It was ensured that no aspersions were cast on the latter in order to perpetuate the martial race dogma, when it was well-known that all the Bengal Army regiments did not perform equally efficiently.

Curiously, the Madras Army officers were correct in their suspicions. It was only in mid-1886 that the then Burma Force Commander, Major General G.S. White, had recorded in the 12th Madras Infantry's annual inspection report that, 'the regiment is clean and orderly, but it is not composed of fighting material.' The report reached Army Headquarters, Simla, which asked for the comments of the previous Burma Force Commander, Lieutenant General H.N.D. Prendergast, VC, and of the Commander-in-Chief at Madras, Lieutenant General H.T. Macpherson, VC. Prendergast truthfully admitted that, when handing over, he had told White, 'It is right that you should know that there were some ugly rumours of the conduct of the 12th Regiment at Minhla,' and that this may have misled White. When writing his despatch on the operation, however, he had gone into the matter, before his departure from Burma, and ascertained 'that, not every sepoy was a hero, but fault could not justly be found with the 12th Regiment....I reported the conduct of the corps was very good.' The latter was possibly not known to White. He also recorded that six Madras Infantry regiments had done "excellent work", and the detachments of two others had shown "conspicuous gallantry under fire".

The Commander-in-Chief at Madras was inevitably caustic of White's attempt to give a dog a bad name in order to hang him. He felt that it was, 'to be regretted that a searching inquiry,' had not been instituted immediately 'if the behaviour of the men had been so discreditable.' He added that, 'in deciding on any measure with regard to this regiment, it is as well to bear in mind that there have been other occasions in recent times when the conduct of troops other than those of the Madras Army has been most unfavourably commented on, and yet no official action on those cases has been

made public....Taking into consideration this fact and the length of
time (almost two years) that has elapsed since the occurrences have
been inquired into, His Excellency thinks further action is to be
deprecated.'[4] As to the 10th Regiment, much of the problem was
found to stem from a second-in-command who had proved unfit and
been posted out, thereafter being posted back to the same unit as
second-in-command, where he had been found unfit.[5] Both the
commanding officer and second-in-command were retired. In addition, some blame could be attached to the concerned assistant
political officer in the Chin Hills, a problem that even occurred
initially in dealing with counter-insurgency situations in our own
North-East. Notwithstanding all this, the 12th was "Punjabized" in
1890, having been recommended for disbandment; and the 10th
disbanded in 1891. The former became the 72nd Punjabis, and the
latter's place was taken by what is today the 10th Gurkha Rifles.
Unfortunately, for the Madras Infantry, White was to succeed
Roberts as Commander-in-Chief in India in 1893.

The martial race dogma thus had been, progressively, a development from the martial classes concept. First, men had been sought
after because of their height and build, but later for their colour and
complexion, a form of racial or colour prejudice, leading to a
recruiting proclivity for North Indians, who were deemed more
martial, and had been described by J.W. Kaye as 'the tallest, best
formed and of the noblest presence.' Meanwhile, the Mahars had
been sequentially excluded from service because they belonged to
too low a social caste. The officers of the 2nd/1st Bombay Infantry,
once it had been bestowed the honour "Grenadiers", sought after the
battle of Koregaon in 1818, to be associated with the concept of
"grenadierdom", and progressively discharged all lower caste men,
the Mahars or Pariwars, and the ostensibly non-martial Bene Israel
Jews and Christians, when it was these classes in the main that had
earned for the regiment this particular honour as the memorial at
Koregaon on the Poona-Ahmednagar road establishes. The courage
in battle of these classes, against 25,000 of the Peshwa's troops,
mainly Arabs, had led to their being declared non-martial, and to the

extinction for them of an opportunity for service. Roberts, however, was not the only proponent. The dogma was advanced by the majority of British officers that only about ten per cent of India's male population would make good soldiers—and from which the army must be recruited—and that the rest of the population was militarily worthless. He, however, by virtue of the positions he held, institutionalized the dogma, which was totally opposed by one of his predecessors who had also been Commander-in-Chief at Madras before becoming Commander-in-Chief in India, General Sir Frederick Haines. By circumstance, the latter retired in 1881.

The dogma, in fact, began being formally asserted by various British military authorities in 1858, at the time of the Royal (Peel) Commission, and was proclaimed as an axiom by it without substantive proof. It then, ostensibly, stemmed from the premise that, since the proportion of Indian troops was to be reduced, owing to the specialization of social functions in the country created by the caste system, fighting was the business only of certain classes of the population, and there was no use in enrolling soldiers from the entire recruitable male population on the concept of a national army. What the British, in effect, began doing after the 1857 Uprising was to increase the recruitment from the Punjab, representing the Punjab as the main fighting base of India, which it had actually been for them in 1857-58. What was the "Punjabization" of the Indian Army, was portrayed as the result of social evolution, a form of social Darwinism. What was forgotten was that it was the British, in order to justify their policy, who had changed the historical pattern of military activity in India for their own convenience. One illustration was the shifting of the focus of recruitment from the Gangetic plain to the Punjab. Before 1857, the Bengal Army was indeed recruited from the so-called martial classes, but the classes at that time were from the Gangetic plain and comprised the yeoman Brahmins and Rajputs of that region, whereas, after 1857, as a result of deliberate policy, the recruiting was predominantly in the Punjab, and the so-called martial races were now assumed to exist more or less exclusively in that province, and no longer to any major extent as heretofore in the Gangetic plain. During the latter half of the nineteenth century the dogma of martial races was thereafter rigidly maintained in defiance of the historical facts of the earlier victories of the Madras and Bombay Armies, and their general steadfastness on behalf of the British in 1857-58.

Thus one of the sorry developments of the late nineteenth and early twentieth century was the progressive elimination of men of South India from the Infantry. By 1928, from fifty-seven Madras Infantry battalions and the Madras Sappers and Miners in 1857, there remained the 1st Madras Pioneers and the Madras Sappers and Miners. Then, only the latter remained, even though Edmund Candler, writing in 1919 after the First World War, stated: 'The war has proved that all men are brave, that the humblest follower is capable of sacrifice and devotion....These revelations have meant a general levelling in the Indian Army and the uplift of classes hitherto undeservedly obscure.'[6]

He also recorded, but apparently to no purpose: 'It is difficult, too, to write of the Madrassi-Hindu, Mussalman or Christian—as an entity apart. All I know of him is that...when he is measured with other classes, his British officers speak of him as equal to the rest.'[7]

Chenevix-Trench recounts an opposed river-crossing in Mesopotamia, 'In the last (boat) afloat (of the ostensible second wave), the rowers (Madras Sappers) were reduced to two. One was killed, and his oar drifted away. The last rower paddled on until his oar was smashed. He then tied a line round his waist, jumped overboard and tried to tow the boat by swimming. For a while his head was seen among the bullet splashes, then it disappeared. If ever a deed deserved the VC, it was his: but there was no survivor to tell his name. He was just an anonymous little, blackish, low caste Madrassi.'[8]

The Madras Infantry had had all three religions mixed down to section level, with no communal problems, almost right up to the end of the nineteenth century. Visiting German delegations, then, from their point of view, had more than once said that only in the Madras Army had they seen what they considered "regular soldiers" on parade in India. Thereafter, in the 1890s, in order to model themselves on North Indian class-company battalions, a Madras Infantry battalion could be organized also on a class-company basis, if so recommended by the concerned commanding officer—four companies Hindu and four companies Muslim, the Christians being progressively reduced from such a reorganized battalion. Of the latter, even G.F. MacMunn was poignantly constrained to record in *The Martial Races of India* that: 'One of the most gallant soldiers the writer had ever known was an ordinary Indian Christian, of the 23rd Wallajabad Light Infantry, one Naik Anthony, who was mortally wounded in a sortie from a beleaguered post on the Chinese frontier of Upper Burma. It has always been a matter of regret that he was too late to read the funeral service over him.'

One such class-company reorganized unit, the 25th Madras Infantry, had problems within a year at Shwebo in Burma in 1894. The Hindu subedar major having proceeded on retirement, it was now the turn of a Muslim to be the subedar major, instead of the appointment being from a common seniority roster. Whereas previously all communities had observed each other's festivals together, now the Hindus were told to observe Dussehra in a separate area, the Hindu being also described by the subedar major as *murda khanewala*. Inevitably what was alleged to be a mutiny occurred. The subedar major accepted he had uttered the expression in question, but it was not deemed sufficient aggravation by the Commanding Officer. When the Hindus sought to see him collectively, he confined the four companies to the lines. The officiating District Commander, after a visit, released them from confinement. This was deemed condonation, debarring disciplinary action. Various personnel were administratively dismissed or discharged. The CO went on to 'urge that, had the men in the companies been mixed,' the incident would not have occurred (the officiating incumbent in his absence on furlough, had apparently obtained the Commander-in-Chief Madras' sanction for the class company reorganization). He added, 'I also urge that while caste regiments are wise, caste companies I consider an error.'[9] The battalion was initially

recommended for disbandment, but was later converted to a class
unit, the 2nd, later the 78th, Moplah Rifles, along with the 17th
Madras Infantry as the 77th Moplah Rifles. Both these class battalions were declared inefficient in 1907 and disbanded. Had the 25th
been left on a mixed basis, there would have been less reorganiza-
tional pains, though eventually its fate would also have been disbandment, for the slightest excuse was availed of for disbanding a
Madras Infantry battalion or to "Punjabize" it. In 1864 the treasure
chest of the 18th Madras Infantry was found missing at night. It was
immediately selected for disbandment. In 1898 the men suspected a
post-mortem was being carried out in the 27th Madras Infantry, a
Muslim soldier having collapsed and died during a punishment pack
drill. Some of the co-religionists in his company demonstrated.
Despite the criticism of the 'injudicious action of the medical officer
in shutting himself up in the mortuary with a hospital assistant and
the corpse,' in due course it became the 87th Punjabis. But then
"Punjabization" did not necessarily guarantee good discipline as we
have seen in the previous chapter. Should the Punjab units reconstituted from the Madras Infantry (or those reconstituted from the
Bombay Infantry) have been allowed to retain the battle honours of
the original units, battle honours that none of the new classes had
earned?

When the cult of Grecian features spread in the other two
Presidency Armies, it was subjectively argued that stout-heartedness
had ceased in the south. Actually, the better British officer wanted to
be near the Frontier where the action was, and the garrison stations
of South India were deemed too far off for quick mobilization, as was
required, for instance, in the Panjdeh crisis in Afghanistan in 1885.
Every regiment or battalion, even today, despite improved selection
procedures, carries three or more officers less good than the others,
but the spirit of the regiment or battalion carries them along. There
was, however, a tendency for more than the normal proportion of the
less efficient British officers to gravitate to the comparative ease of
the "downcountry life" of the South Indian garrison stations. It was,
therefore, not the Madras Infantryman who had become less martial,

but the British officer posted to command him, who was less martial than hitherto.

As stated earlier, Roberts, a former Bengal Artillery officer, was still biased in favour of the Bengal Army. He had consolidated his reputation by his march to the relief of Kandahar in the Second Anglo-Afghan War, where the survivors of the battle of Maiwand were besieged throughout August 1880. According to T.A. Heathcote, 'Roberts' account of the dejected state of the Bombay Army garrison at Kandahar was coloured, almost certainly unconsciously, maybe to make the performance of his own force stand out more boldly.... That the troops defeated at Maiwand and shut up in Kandahar belonged to the Bombay Army, led Roberts and many Bengal Army officers (still smarting under the humiliation of their army by the loyal Bombay troops during the Mutiny) to use this as proof that the Bombay soldiers were no longer of real military value!'[10] Roberts admits in *Forty-one years in India* that before he started for Kandahar from Kabul (where his father had been a brigadier for a short while in command of Shah Shuja's forces in 1841), he knew nothing of the other Presidency Armies, 'except that, as belonging to the Bombay Army, they could not be composed of the best fighting races.' In a similar subjective way the alleged inadequate performance of some Madras Army units, during the Third Anglo-Burmese War and the subsequent annexation, had been deemed by him to establish that South Indians were of little use as fighting men and that they should no longer be recruited into the infantry, forgetting that the infantry component in the First and Second Anglo-Burmese Wars and the intervening garrisons of Burma were almost exclusively from the Madras Army on account of the reluctance of the majority of the Bengal Army units to undertake sea voyages. The Madras Infantry had moved to Burma without mutinying. Some of the Bengal Army units in the earlier Anglo-Burmese Wars had performed even more inadequately than the later Madras Army units. What Roberts should have realized was that if there was any weakness in the Madras and Bombay Armies, it was the officers who were weak in their leadership and tactics.

Roberts would not appear to have read at Madras the minutes of Sir Thomas Munro, the Governor of Madras in 1824 at the time of the First Anglo-Burmese War. When Rangoon fell to the British in June 1824, Munro recorded his 'appreciation of the reliability and bravery of Madras sepoys in a campaign made difficult by the need to provision by sea, by disease, and by the unanticipated resistance of the Burmese. He spoke proudly of how Madras sepoys on leave when the war began made strenuous efforts to join their comrades' departure for Burma, and how some...marched twenty-four miles a day for two weeks to join the expedition. He did not say what any reader of his minute then would have known, that this devotion by ordinary (Madras) sepoys contrasted with the refusal of many Bengal sepoys to undertake service in Burma, thus placing major responsibility upon Madras and Munro for conducting the war.'[11]

Munro also recorded what confronted the Madras soldier in Burma: 'In the present war there are difficulties of a nature which we have never experienced before...from our ignorance of the country and the people, the obstacles opposed to an invasion by land, by mountains, rivers, and unhealthy jungles, and the hindrance caused to operations of every kind by the long continuance of the rainy season. In all our Indian wars we had the advantage of a long previous establishment in the country, and a perfect knowledge of the people. We had a station that was our own from whence to extend ourselves, and we acted in alliance with some native chief, and by supporting his title and authority we secured the submission of the people and obtained aid as we advanced, from the resources of the country. The people were not hostile to us, but as willing to be the subjects of our government, or of our ally, as of their former princes. In Ava we have none of these advantages...'[12]

The injustice done to the Madras Infantryman from 1864 to 1928 was sought to be corrected in 1941 when the Madras Regiment was re-raised in the Second World War. This was abundantly recognized by Field Marshal Sir Claude Auchinleck, who has recorded, in Phythian-Adams' tribute to the Madras soldier: 'But the fault was not that of the Madras soldier...the best material in the world will not make good soldiers unless it has good officers.'[13] Sir Arthur Hope, the then Governor of Madras, added, 'The Madras Infantryman could be relied upon to hold out to the last against desperate odds as in Baillie's defeat at Perambakkam in 1780, to fight with dash and daring at the battle of Assaye in 1803, and to cope undismayed with all the strangeness of jungle warfare in Burma (in three Anglo-Burmese wars). These splendid services were rendered under hard conditions with pay several years in arrears, and supply frequently wanting and generally precarious.'[14]

As to his aspersions on the Bombay Army, Roberts should have discerned that, of the four Bombay Army regiments involved at Maiwand in July 1880, three at this time were recruited from Baluchistan, the Punjab and beyond, including Pathans, and it was the Bombay Grenadiers recruited from the Bombay Presidency proper, who behaved most creditably. Of the Bombay Grenadiers, Leigh Maxwell in *My God Maiwand* records, in refutation of Roberts' erroneous opinion: 'They had done magnificently. Ordered up by (Brigadier General) Burrows, they had advanced as steadily as on parade and would have gone on right into the Herati lines if need be. After they had been called to a halt because of the furious Afghan defensive cannonade, they fired their volleys with devastating effect into the counter attacking Afghan regular infantry, driving them from the battlefield, delivering a significant blow to their morale. They responded still to their orders, but thirst and fatigue were playing their part....Anderson (the commanding officer) knew that he must form company squares, the expedient which had saved the day at (the earlier battle of) Ahmed Khel, but in the heat of the crisis his adjutant shouted the (wrong) orders for making a regimental square; and the native officers followed suit with the correct drill book orders for forming a square from line...this resulted in the most hopeless confusion....'

Maxwell goes on: 'There, on the plain of stone and sand, deserted by their comrades and without artillery support, they fought on until their limited supply of ammunition ran out, holding the ghazis at a distance, until the already heavily punished Herati infantry came to pour volleys into the Grenadier ranks and Afghan artillery once more commenced its deadly thunder. Thereafter two thirds lay dead or seriously wounded, it could be that the last forty charged out with the bayonet...horsemen charged among them; there was no ammunition left to make the tribesmen keep their distance. Dispersed and scattered, they were cut down or shot as easy prey.'[15] Notwithstanding this, Roberts' incorrect postulation as to Marathas, as a class, allegedly stemmed from the battle of Maiwand.

Henry Lawrence, in his *Essays Military and Political, Written in India,* collated and published in 1859 after his death, was of the opinion that lower castes and non-warlike classes would be good soldiers: 'Courage goes much by opinion; and many a man behaves as a hero or a coward, according as he considers he is expected to behave.' Army Headquarters only acted on this perception in the First World War. One of the developments early on in the war was the collapse of the formulation that recruitment be confined only to the so-called martial races. Whereas they performed bravely, so also did the other classes hitherto deemed non-martial for purposes of recruitment. Recruitment of only the martial classes provided too small a base despite inducements, monetary and otherwise, as also threats. Though 136,000 Punjabi Mussalmans, 88,000 Sikhs, 62,000 Rajputs, 55,000 Gurkhas, 55,000 Jats, 41,000 South Indians, 36,000 Hindustani Mussalmans, 28,000 Pathans, 23,000 Dogras, 19,000 Ahirs, 18,000 Gujars, and 14,000 Rajputana Mussalmans were recruited, among others, the numbers were still insufficient, and seventy-five other classes had to be perforce recruited, like the Mahars whose long and distinguished military history had been sought to be extinguished.[16] As early as 1892 a staff officer of the Adjutant General's Branch had predicted that, 'Recruiting for the native armies was practically breaking down towards the end of the Second Afghan War, and although at present a sufficient supply of men is forthcoming, I am of the opinion that it will again break down when stress is put on it.' The Nicholson Committee, appointed in 1912, had found that in the context of a serious war, Sikh recruitment might have to be reduced, and that classes such as Telugus and Nagas would have to be recruited. The First World War broke out before the Nicholson Committee's report could be formally acted upon. 'At the outbreak of the war, it was found that the Punjab supplied about half of the soldiers in the Indian Army. In 1914, of the total of 1,096 infantry companies, 431 companies were wholly Punjabi, and 221 were partly Punjabi. In the cavalry, out of the total of 155 squadrons, 95 1/2 were wholly Punjabi, and 47 1/2 were partly Punjabi.'[17]

After the British drastically changed the pattern of recruitment in the light of some of Roberts' postulations, the Mahars also were not recruited. At the turn of the century they were again recruited, only to be once again discontinued before the First World War. Recruited again in the First World War in limited numbers, their recruitment was once more discontinued after the First World War, till the Mahar Regiment was raised in the Second World War, and which regiment continues valiantly to this day. The recruiting vicissitudes, endured by the Mahars as a so-called non-martial race, also merit comment. They were a sizeable portion of Shivaji's army, served as hereditary village policemen, and were thus to all intents and purposes deemed a traditional martial class. Till the fad of grenadierdom, that is the recruitment of taller and fairer soldiers, afflicted the Bombay Army, Mahars constituted latterly at least one quarter if not more of the Bombay Infantry. The father of Dr B.R. Ambedkar, the drafter of India's Constitution, served in the Bombay Army as a subedar, and Dr Ambedkar was brought up in Bombay Army cantonments. By the year 1900 only a few Mahars were still serving, and by 1914 virtually none. The Mahars continuously suffered the anguish of deprivation of the means of livelihood by these developments, and in 1910 had petitioned the Secretary of State: 'We, the Mahar inhabitants of India, residing in the Bombay Presidency,...do not aspire to high political privileges and position, since we are not educationally qualified for them, but humbly seek employment in the lowest grades of the public service, in the ranks of police sepoys, and of soldiers in the Indian Army. We are making no new demands; we do not claim employment in services in which we have not been engaged before. Indeed, some few of our people still hold positions in the police force...so also have our people been employed in the Indian Army from the very commencement of the British Raj in our country, and they have risen to the highest positions by their valour and conduct. But the present changes in the Indian Army have been most prejudicial to the interests of our people. We have been excluded from military service entirely, for reasons not known to us.'[18]

The Mahars rightly urged they were not essentially inferior to other Indians, and offered to serve in class company regiments if not permitted to serve in Maratha battalions, or even in Muslim regiments if higher caste Hindus, like the Marathas, objected to serving with them. Alternatively, they sought enrolment as mule drivers, or as non-combatants enrolled like mess servants if they could not be recruited as infantrymen.[19] By the circumstance of the First World War occurring, the Mahars were again recruited, first in the labour battalions, then as infantrymen in 1917, initially as one company each in two Madras battalions, and, later as, the 111th Mahars, only to be wasted out again after the First World War. In the pre-First World War perspectives, the Marathas were also to be eliminated after the Mahars, in view of Roberts' observations, and were no longer to be deemed martial. Various disciplinary cases were urged against the Konkani Marathas. One was a clash with the Bombay Police in 1887 for the latter standing by and doing nothing, when passing Moharrum processionists stoned the unit lines of the 17th Bombay Infantry, and a soldier was injured. Again the same unit had a problem at Bhuj in 1897 when some recently arrived transferees did not agree to the new order on company messing. It was urged that, though they cooked in a particular company area themselves, there should be no objection to their eating their own food, paid for by themselves, in the company messes of their friends and relatives in other companies. In the same year, at Bareilly, in the 14th Bombay Infantry, a lance havildar (a cobbler by caste) abused a Maratha, questioning his origins. Some men were not happy at the Commanding Officer's handling of the case in the orderly room, and wished to see him. The Sikh jemadar adjutant ordered one of them to be placed in the quarter guard, whereupon the rest of the company threw their belts at the jemadar adjutant, and sat down in passive resistance at the quarter guard.[20] The performance of Maratha battalions in the First World War, however, apparently surprised the Army Headquarters' dogmatists of the Roberts' school of thought. Candler wryly commented in 1919: 'I saw it stated in a newspaper that one of the surprises of the war has been the Mahratta....That his emergence should be a surprise was illogical....The Mahrattas proved their worth at Maiwand.'[21] In fact, their performance in Mesopotamia alone "out-martialled" most other classes recruited in the infantry.

Now, to an ostensible non-martial race in the Punjab. The *chuhras* traditionally had not been permitted to join earlier military organizations, and later the Indian Army, except as sweepers, though former *chuhras*, who had converted to Sikhism, had a valiant military history as Mazhabi Sikhs. Yet in the final two years of the First World War, when there was considerable pressure for further recruitment from the Punjab, Sir Michael O'Dwyer, the Lieutenant Governor, attempted to seek further Jat Sikh recruitment by the taunt that even Bengal had provided a unit (49th Bengal Regiment), and pointed also to the rise in Mazhabi recruitment, '...if regard be had to the available numbers, the Mazhabi Sikhs have far surpassed the Jats...do the Jats view the cavalry of the Mazhabis with equanimity?' However, having served their purpose during the First World War, the Mazhabi Sikhs also were progressively wasted out, the last Sikh Pioneers' unit being disbanded in 1932, till taken in again as the Sikh Light Infantry in 1941. The regiment has maintained as splendid a record, as that of the old Sikh Pioneers before the latter's disbandment. Candler recorded of the latter, 'Their courage amounted to utter recklessness of life.'

Before one can conclude this chapter, the irony of the Brahmin Infantry needs to be mentioned. The ranks of the Bengal Infantry had been largely recruited from the agricultural Brahmins of Oudh. Thus regiments of the Bengal Infantry that went to countries as far apart as Afghanistan and China contained many Brahmins, stalwart young yeomen who were then classified as martial. Their ceremonial and

302

other inhibitions as regarding food, water and sea voyages created problems. The then obligation to strip to eat made the Afghan winter, for instance, a sad trial. The question of water and sick attendants, when wounded, in any campaign caused complications. After 1857-58 their numbers in the Bengal Infantry were greatly reduced, for in order to be accepted as "martial", one had also to be accepted as totally loyal. In every war that they had participated in till then, the Brahmin soldiers of the Bengal Infantry had gained distinction and renown. However, by the time of the First World War, the UP Brahmins in the infantry, other than the Hill Brahmins, were all concentrated in two battalions, on the premise that pride of caste would be enhanced and sense of scrupulosity thus diminished. As two impressive battalions they were sent into the field, but unexpectedly declined to abrogate their cooking and feeding requirements on active service. Some chose to starve in preference, and thus were deemed to have reduced their military utility. The details of the 3rd Brahmins are available. Employed on the lines of communication in Mesopotamia, as their individual cooking, hitherto, had prevented their deployment forward in the fighting line, in April 1917 the group system of cooking was introduced. This had been done as the formation commander had sought their relief, as the impression had gained currency that the individual system of cooking was being insisted on to avoid serving at the front. Their relief from Mesopotamia on this score would have created the wrong precedent. Though there had been prior consultation with the platoon commanders before the introduction of group messing (approval of cooks etc), two havildars and eighty other ranks evidenced mutinous conduct. One sepoy was sentenced to death, and others variously to transportation for life and imprisonment up to five years. The sentences were commuted, and eighty-two were sentenced to four years' imprisonment. The battalion was moved to Muscat. Sequentially, after the First World War, these originally fine battalions were disbanded, the UP agricultural Brahmins thus having become non-martial.[22]

To conclude this chapter, of the seventy-five ostensible

non-martial classes recruited in the First World War, many had been formerly recruited like the Mahars, Telugus, Moplahs, and Bhils, but also now new classes like the Punjabi Christians from whom the 71st Punjabis were raised. All were again eliminated after the First World War, the 49th Bengal Regiment and the 71st Punjabis being disbanded. By and large, these non-martial classes performed as well as the martial classes, allowing for the type of units and theatre they were employed in. Mark Twain once wrote: 'Courage is the resistance to fear, mastery of fear—not the absence of fear.' Or as Candler put it in 1919, 'The Afridi, who is outwardly the nearest thing to an impersonation of Mars, yields nothing in courage to the Madrassi Christian....'[23] Despite this, the system of recruiting the ostensible martial classes only again persisted up to the Second World War, for in the run down after the First World War it was the so-called non-martial classes, who had served their martial purpose during the war, who were now eliminated, no thought being given to an Indian Army with an all-India base of recruitment in its combatant arms. The condescending British views in the early 1930s were reflected by MacMunn, 'India, unlike almost any other country, has a vast mass of unwarlike people, whose hand has never kept the head. In this class must be mustered those who have the brains and aptitude to assimilate Western education far more rapidly than the more virile races. But it is these virile races that have dominated India in the past, and as the Simon Report (1930) has stated would do so again if British control was removed. It is moreover in these forceful classes that the real future of India for good must lie whether it be peaceful or otherwise...we do not speak of the martial races of Britain as distinct from the non-martial, nor of Germany nor of France. But in India we speak of the martial races as a thing apart and because the mass of the people have neither martial aptitude nor physical courage...the courage that we should talk of colloquially as guts...the gentle yet merciless race of hereditary moneylenders from which Lala Gandhi springs, only kept within bounds by an occasional flaying and roasting, have never been able to, or even tried to protect their hoards.'[24]

The Second World War had to occur before the lessons of the First World War were to be learnt by the British, but even at independence, after the post-war demobilization, thirty per cent of the population was still supplying eighty-seven per cent of the Indian Army. It had again been assumed at the commencement of the Second World War that the martial classes could produce adequate numbers, but, as in 1914-18, this proved incorrect. During the inter-war years there had been an ingrained reluctance as postulated by MacMunn to reintroduce classes that had been recruited before, or to introduce any new classes. Apart from the re-raising by Auchinleck of the Madras Regiment, the Sikh Light Infantry and the Mahar Regiment after the commencement of the Second World War, other ostensible non-martial class regiments, also raised by Auchinleck, encompassed the Rawats, Minas and Katats in the Ajmer Regiment; Adivasis in the Bihar Regiment; Assamese, Nagas, Lushais (Mizos), Kukis and other North-Eastern tribes in the Assam Regiment; the Chamar Regiment; and the Lingayat Battalion. Post-Second World War, the Assam, Bihar, and Mahar Regiments, and the Sikh Light Infantry were retained, and have rendered sterling service, whereas the Chamar and Ajmer Regiments, as also the Lingayat Battalion, were disbanded in 1946 in the post-war rundown.

S.D. Pradhan thus rightly describes the position at the end of the First World War, a 'distinctive feature...was the mixing of some of the castes in a unit. Though some of the soldiers might have resented it, yet it became instrumental in bringing them closer. The soldiers of one caste got opportunities to mix with the soldiers of other castes.' The Indian Army, 'in this way worked as a catalyst for the growth of nationalism...soldiers became agents for social change....'[25]

ELEVEN

Indianization And The Indian Army Between The World Wars

IN LAYING the foundation stone of the War Memorial (where today's Amar Jawan Jyoti is also located), in New Delhi on 20 February 1921, the Duke of Connaught said, 'On this spot in the Central Vista of the capital of India, there will stand a memorial archway designed to keep present in the thoughts of the generations that follow after, the glorious sacrifice of the officers and men of the Indian Army, who fought and fell in the Great War....Today we know that more than a million Indians left these shores to serve abroad, of whom nearly 60,000...gave up their lives....In this hour of crowding memories, let us...recapture once again that thrill that passed through us all when we first heard in those far off days of 1914 that the Indian troops had landed at Marseilles and were pressing towards our thinly. held battle lines in France and Flanders....'[1]

By the time of the Duke of Connaught's visit to the Punjab, 420,000 acres of land had been distributed among 5,902 VCOs, over 14,000 persons had been given *jangi inams*—special pensions—for two "lives", 200 specially selected VCOs had been given jagirs, and 200 VCOs granted honorary commissions.[2] By 1 January 1923, 371

306

honorary commissions had been bestowed. Such honorary commissions now carried both pay and pensionary benefits, which had not been so previously. The economic and social impact in the Punjab was intended to be considerable. The Duke made no mention in his speeches of Indianization of the military officer cadre. (The designation VCO is used for easier understanding, even though it was formally only introduced in the early 1930s.)

The British were tardy in introducing Indian King's Commissioned Officers into the positions of British officers, even though some among them had been conscious that the structure of the Presidency Armies, and later the Indian Army, produced certain strains, unless the recruited classes were placated by providing some advancement. Initially, for a few years from 1757, the British had allowed "native commandants" in battalions, even though the real power for operations rested with a Hindustani-speaking captain. This concept gave an opportunity for ambitious Indian soldiers in the initial Presidency Armies to achieve promotion to the level of "native commandant", even though control in the more important functions rested with the British captain. When the appointment of "native commandant" was discontinued in the 1760s after Mohammed Yusuf's "rebellion", the problem of accommodating Indian aspirations remained, and these were sought to be met by introducing the appointment of subedar major in 1820. As early as the 1840s, Sir Henry Lawrence of the Bengal Army had urged further avenues for promotion for Indians*. He, for his times, had been a prophet crying in the wilderness.

After 1857, however, few Britons were desirous of positioning Indians as officers, as distinct from sub-officers, certainly not Lord Frederick Roberts, who from 1885 onwards, consistently differed on this with Major General Sir George Chesney, the Military Member of the Viceroy's Council. Roberts recorded, 'Indian soldiers, like soldiers of every nationality, require to be led; and history and experience teach us that eastern races (fortunately for us), however brave

---

* For more details, see chapter, "Early Beginnings".

and accustomed to war, do not possess the qualities that go to make leaders of men, and that native officers in this respect can never take the place of British officers. I have known natives, whose gallantry and devotion could not be surpassed, but I have never known one who would not have looked to the youngest British officer for support in time of difficulty and danger.'[3]

Sir Theodore Morrison, Principal of the Mohammedan Anglo-Oriental College, Aligarh, today's Aligarh Muslim University, in 1899, in his book, *Imperial Rule in India*, had nevertheless urged, presumably to counter the opposition as represented by Roberts: 'The natives have just cause for complaint against us that we do not admit them to posts of military command....Every other suggestion that has from time to time been made for establishing natives (as officers) into the regular army, bristles with difficulties, but the same objections cannot be made to their admission as a special corps....I venture to think that the Empress herself might devise a practical solution of the problem, by raising a corps of Imperial Guards, to be officered by the aristocracy of India....It would perhaps not consist of more than three regiments...successful candidates would then proceed to Sandhurst....When the first English commandants' term had expired, the regiments should be left within the charge of the native officers....They should be given liberal opportunities of seeing service, that the others might have a chance of seeing whether...the native leaders of Indian society have in them the stuff of which rulers are made....'[4]

Curiously, the first very small step for some form of Indianization of the officer cadre, as mentioned earlier, came from Lord Curzon in his "Memorandum on Commissions for Indians" of 4 June 1900, possibly prompted by Morrison. Curzon's arguments for doing so were, however, incongruent. Against much opposition, in 1901 he had nevertheless established the Imperial Cadet Corps, first in Meerut, then in Dehra Dun. On 4 July 1905 four graduates of the Imperial Cadet Corps were granted a modified form of commission in "His Majesty's Native Indian Land Forces". One more was commissioned in July 1906, three in January 1907 and one in

September 1911, the approximately seventy others trained either dropping the idea of a military career or going to their respective State Forces. This commission was only for "gentlemen", and not for all civilians, or those sub-officers, later known as VCOs. Curzon had seen in this modified form of commission, a military career for those, 'whose pride of birth or surrounding prevents them from embracing a civil profession, whose interests lie naturally on the side of the British Government, but whose sympathies are in danger of being eliminated, and their energies dulled by the absence of any field for their natural ambitions.' These aspirants were to be, as already indicated, from princely or feudal families, and not from, 'the newer aristocracy who, if the criteria were one of wealth or education or precocity in European manners, would flood us with a stream of applications supported by every sort of examination test, but resulting in the very last type of young officers we should desire to procure.'[5] These officers were, however, in effect posted to "supernumerary" appointments, in order to avoid their commanding British personnel in any way. At regimental duty in the Indian Army, they were only to be squadron/company officers. They could, however, command Imperial Service (State Force) Troops. In 1903, Curzon did apparently announce that Indians would be made eligible for full King's commissions, but Roberts was totally opposed. (Even after ceasing to be the Commander-in-Chief in Britain, Roberts was, till his death in 1915, a forceful member of the India Council in London, and continued his opposition.)

O'Moore Creagh, Lord Horatio Herbert Kitchener's successor in India in 1910, however, ventilated the matter in 1918, after he had retired, writing in his *Indian Studies*: 'In 1903 Lord Curzon publicly announced that Indians would be made eligible for King's commissions. The matter was let drop till 1910 when I put forward a scheme for complying with the promise made so long before. It is no use discussing it now, because the proposal was rejected. It was a great pity this was done...this change had to be made sooner or later, for a Governor General's official promise must be kept, but it was delayed for politicians love handing over contentious questions to their successors, and this moral cowardice has necessitated a somewhat difficult problem...being left for solution during this war.'[6]

He had apparently recommended irregular regiments for such Indian officers. He had hoped that a favourable decision would be announced during King George V's visit in 1911-12. But he also saw fit, despite having served in the Deoli Irregular Force and the 44th Merwara Infantry, to emphasize the necessity for cultivating the "warlike castes". The latter, in his view, would resent being commanded by the "unwarlike castes", whose 'only weapon is the tongue,' thus "creating discontent". Meanwhile, Curzon having earlier departed, interest in the Imperial Cadet Corps was negligible, for even a modicum of Indianization was, by and large, considered an affront by the majority of British officers who were rigid in their complex as to Indians. In fairness to Lord Minto, the Viceroy in early 1910, he did suggest, in the context of O'Moore Creagh's proposal, that the Imperial Cadet Corps' establishment at Dehra Dun be converted to an Indian "Sandhurst", but any such connotation was then anathema to the War Office, as advised by Roberts.

Notionally, Indianization of the military officer cadre had been possible after the Charter Act of 1833, and Queen Victoria's proclamation of 1858, but none had been taken into the civil service till 1870; by 1871 four had been taken in. After 1879 a statutory Civil Service was created and the number of Indians entering by examination progressively increased to sixty-three by 1915, five per cent of the total. In the Indian Army, the requirement to be met was far greater. At the meagre rate of ten vacancies annually at Sandhurst allotted in 1918, it would have taken a century to have a substantial proportion of Indian officers, and without armed forces officered by Indians, India could not attain self-government or Dominion Status. In fact, it has never been clear as to how the mystic figure of ten was arrived at. Prince Victor Albert Duleep Singh, son of Maharaja Dalip Singh, did pass out from Sandhurst in the 1890s, but was commissioned in the Household Cavalry of the British Army, and not into the Indian Army. Similarly, Mahaduv Singhji, the nephew of the cricketer Ranji, was commissioned in the British Army in the First World War and transferred to the Indian Army in 1918.

Sir Michael O'Dywer, the Lieutenant Governor of the Punjab during the First World War, had toured from district to district exhorting the martial races to come forward. Even the threat of conscription was used, but the promise of commissions as officers was more effective in recruiting in the Punjab than the district quotas and threats, for on 4 May 1918 he iterated, 'As regards the further grant of King's commissions the Government of India have already made their proposals before the Home Government and we may be sure they will receive early and sympathetic consideration. Meanwhile, eleven representatives of leading martial tribes have received commissions in the King's Indian Forces within the last few months, but the number to be granted will naturally depend in a great measure on a response to the call for recruits. We have often been told by those who claim to understand the Indian mind that the one thing wanted to open the floodgates to recruiting is the grant of King's commissions. The next few months should show whether that view is correct. '[7]

Many in Britain and India had viewed the start of the Indianization of the officer cadre as a British response to the assistance that India had given in the war, but Curzon, by now Foreign Secretary, chose to refute the idea that this amounted in any way to a reward, observing, 'The (educated) classes to whom it is now proposed to offer additional concessions have no right to claim them on the ground of war service, for they have rendered no such service. On the other hand, those who have helped us most in the war neither asked for nor want...the concession,' under discussion. There were, thus, mixed motives behind these promises. As mentioned by O'Dwyer, eleven VCOs had been given King's commissions for past services by the martial races, and also as further inducement for future faithful service by them. By 1923 the aggregate of such commissions that had been bestowed was twenty.[8] These commissions meant little in effective terms, for the persons concerned were already advanced in age and could not aspire to much promotion. Thus despite the August 1917 announcement by Edwin Montagu, 'of the increasing association of Indians in every branch of the administration,' nowhere was implementation more dilatory than in the Indianization of the military officer cadre, for the need for increased Indian assistance had diminished with the termination of the First World War. Even the ten annual vacancies reserved at the Royal Military College, Sandhurst, were sought to be limited to 'selected representatives of familiies of fighting classes which have rendered valuable services to the State during the war.'

Montagu was opposed at every step, and snidely debunked because he was a Jew, but he had the courage to reiterate, 'It is not merely enough to observe a principle, we must act on it. The services of the Indian Army in the war and the great increase in its numbers make it necessary that a considerable number of commissions should be given. Race should no more debar him (the Indian) for promotion in the Army than it does in the Civil Service.' The mental block for the British was that Indianization meant not only the substitution of Indians into some of the positions held by British officers, but that, eventually, Indianization must also postulate that Indian officers if fit should be eligible for higher command alongside and over Europeans. It was also sequentially argued that the number of British Sandhurst graduates volunteering for the Indian Army would be affected. By a quirk of circumstance, after Montagu, Indianization was again in the doldrums, but Rufus Isaacs, Lord Reading, another Jew, succeeded Thesiger Chelmsford as Viceroy, and was to argue valiantly in favour of Indianization.

Indianization should, of course, have been tried in the Indian Army much before the First World War, when partial Indianization was introduced in the civil and medical departments and other similar services. In fact it was the King's intention, he being sympathetic to O'Moore Creagh's proposal, to announce it in 1911 as a concession by him at the time of his visit to India. Roberts in particular advised against it, urging that the other services of the Government of India were not parallel to the Indian Army, in that the "cheek by jowl" mess life and the close daily association in the army made the proposition different, with the result that it was announced in 1917, only after his and Kitchener's deaths, on a limited basis, on account of representations received during the First World War. The credit for overcoming the opposition of the War Office must go to Montagu. Out of the over 9,000 officers granted temporary commissions through the cadet schools at Quetta and Wellington, none were Indians. When Charles Hardinge, the Viceroy till 1916, did make a suggestion for the grant of temporary commissions to Indians, the answer came that Whitehall had no objection to an aggregate of 200 being commissioned in the "Native Indian Land Forces", through the Imperial Cadet Corps. Nothing seems to have happened on this, partly because the establishment at Dehra Dun had been run down by the circumstance of the war, and partly presumably on account of the limited employability of this type of commission. By the delay in the decision, however, as to the grant of temporary commissions to Indians, valuable experience as officers in the First World War was thus lost for the concerned Indian aspirants, though some served in the ranks of the British Army, like A.A. Rudra and K.A.D. Naoroji, Dadabhai's grandson, awaiting a favourable decision as to their being eligible for temporary commissions. They were only commissioned in 1919 after Montagu's announcement, through a course of instruction at the Daly College, Indore. On the other hand, four qualified Indians were commissioned in the Royal Flying Corps during the war, but only after H.S. Malik threatened to join the French Air Corps, on account of the delay in the decision as to Indians being commissioned in the Royal Flying Corps.[9]

Montagu, during his visit, had wanted to establish immediately an Indian "Sandhurst", with entry being open to any qualified Indian, but Monro, the then Commander-in-Chief, while himself not totally opposed to Indianization, insisted that preference should be given to the sons of servicemen, thus limiting the number of more educated Indians, who fared better in written examinations. While the selection process was underway for the first Indian entry to Sandhurst, a shorter course had been in progress at the Daly College, Indore, concluding in 1919. Apart from the servicemen from the traditional

313

classes, the civilian cadets represented most of the communities and most of the religions in India. The thirty-nine passing out were first granted temporary commissions, over the opposition of the War Office, who argued there was no need now to commission them, as the emergency was over; thirty-two were later granted permanent commissions.[10] Also granted permanent commissions were those nine ex-Imperial Cadet Corps officers, who had earlier been granted temporary commissions in 1917. Among the Daly College entry was Field Marshal K.M. Cariappa, OBE. These officers joined the Indian Army in the status of British officers, and, in the initial years, joined any unit exactly as a young Briton would do, as a company officer. Both in 1917 and in 1919, when temporary commissions were granted, preferences were expressed for regiments with the same class composition as of those who were being commissioned. The initial decision was that as far as possible this should be avoided in principle, the same parameters to be followed as for British officers on their first posting. For instance, all the nine ex-Imperial Cadet Corps were posted to classes other than their own. From the files in the British Library (Oriental and India Office Collections), the failure rate at Sandhurst was high, the majority of Indian cadets then sent there not being granted commissions. The reasons for this were manifold, faulty selection being the main cause. Another was the inability of their parents to continue to pay for them in Britain. The first Indian from the Sandhurst entry to be the Chief of the Army Staff was General M.S. Rajendrasinhji, DSO.

Meanwhile, in 1919, a committee, presided over by Lord Reginald Esher, had been appointed, to inquire into the organization and administration of the army in India, with a majority of British civilian and military members, but also with two Indian members. In retrospect, in relation to its report submitted in 1920, one wonders as to what purpose the committee served, with a presiding officer from Britain. (In 1905, Kitchener had been of the view that, 'Esher is an, outsider, who knows little or nothing of the Army.') Whether as to Indianization or any other facet of importance, like broader based recruitment, the committee was cautious; *status quo ante* seemed to be the philosophy of the majority, except for one of the Indian members, Sir Krishna Gupta, who was opposed, however, on every point by the traditionalist Sir Umar Hayat Khan. This latter difference was construed as Indians not being able to agree even on Indianization. However, the committee did suggest changes in the command system, better balance between the "teeth" arms and services, improvement in equipment, the requirements for expansion in war, and the eventual removal of British battalions from Indian brigades in order to simplify the ration supply problem. (The latter was not a new proposal, but was again not agreed to, in order to maintain a check on Indian battalions in a brigade.) The Esher Committee was also of the view that the Indian Army was part of the Imperial forces.[11] This view was later to be disputed by the new Central Legislative Assembly in 1921.

Then, on 13 April 1919, the military firing at Jallianwala Bagh occurred, which the historian Alfred Draper has described, in his book *Amritsar, The Massacre That Ended The Raj.* Earlier that month there had been an outbreak of violence in Amritsar. The District Magistrate already had forebodings about the situation and had reported, 'The soil is prepared for discontent by a number of causes. The poor are hit by high prices, the rich by a severe Income Tax assessment and the Excess Profits Tax. Mohammedans are irritated about the fate of Turkey. From one cause or another the people are restless and ripe for the revolutionists.' The outbreak of violence at Amritsar that occurred thus had many causes, the most recent of which was the passing of new legislation, known as the Rowlatt Acts, against Indian opposition. These acts were the outcome of the report of a Sedition Committee appointed in 1917, under the chairmanship of Justice Sydney Rowlatt, to consider what special provisions of criminal law would be required to deal with terrorism and other seditious movements when the Defence of India Act lapsed six months after the end of the war. Some of the provisions for placing restrictions on suspects had helped in combating terrorism in Bengal, and the committee, of which two Indian lawyers were members, recommended unanimously certain provisions to be applied by notification in specified areas, for restricting the movement and activities of suspects, and for detaining them without trial.[12]

The report did not excite major comment when it was published, but when the bill to give effect to this recommendation was moved in the Central Legislative Council in February 1919 it was opposed by all the non-official members. The Government of India persisted with the bill and got it passed in March by the votes of the official majority. M.A. Jinnah and Madan Mohan Malaviya resigned. Had the government waited for the new expanded Legislative Assembly to be in session, the bill would not have been passed. The influenza epidemic that had ravaged India at the end of 1918 and which officially had taken a toll of six million, but probably sixteen million, had also added to the general malaise of the population. Mahatma Gandhi now called for satyagraha against the legislation, and the observance of a general hartal. There already had been military firing at Delhi on 30 March, and police firing at certain other towns like Bombay. Meanwhile, disturbances were taking place in the urban areas of the Punjab, the worst being that at Amritsar, the commercial capital of the province.[13]

Earlier, in April, Dr Saifuddin Kitchlew, a lawyer, and Dr Satyapal, a doctor, who had proclaimed the impending collapse of British rule, were ordered to be arrested at Amritsar by O'Dwyer. Violence followed in which some Europeans were killed and injured, and some government buildings set on fire. Brigadier General Reginald Dyer was moved from Jullundur on 11 April, and the next day issued orders forbidding any assembly, proclaiming by beat of drum that disobedience would be met by force. When he learnt on Sunday, 13 April, that, a meeting was to be held at the Jallianwala Bagh, Dyer proceeded there with ninety troops of the Indian Army and two armoured cars. Without further warning he ordered his troops to open fire, and the unarmed peaceful crowd, mainly pilgrims from the countryside who were probably unaware of Dyer's order and observing Baisakhi, in the Bagh, being unable to disperse quickly, since Dyer's troops occupied the one proper exit, was mown down. The firing continued for ten minutes, 1,650 rounds officially killing 379, and wounding over 1,200. The Bagh was popular among pilgrims.

There was a difference between the official British casualty figures and the unofficial Indian figures. A post-independence inscription records, 'This place is saturated with the blood of about 2,000 Hindu, Sikh and Muslim patriots who were martyred in a non-violent struggle to free India from British domination.' (Udham Singh, who later killed O'Dwyer in London in 1940, was probably among the wounded.) Dyer belonged to the family that had founded the brewery firm of Dyer Meakin (today's Mohan Meakin). Ill-health had kept him out of the First World War; he was a case of arteriosclerosis. A chain-smoker, he was a man with a short temper, likely to overreact when under pressure. Apart from the firing, he also ordered members of the public to crawl on all fours when moving down the street where the missionary, Marcia Sherwood had been left for dead. Six youths were whipped in public for the attack, without there being any certainty that they were involved. Criticized by the Hunter Committee that was set up to probe the firing, he was later retired. On return to Britain, the public set up a fund for "the man who saved India", over 27,000 pounds being collected. He was not, however, restored to duty after his retirement, dying in 1972. (His medals recently fetched over 7,000 pounds at an auction, and are on permanent display at the National Army Museum, London.) Gandhi returned his Zulu War Medal and Kaisar-i-Hind Medal, terminating 'co-operation in any shape or form with this satanic government.' Rabindranath Tagore returned his knighthood, and Vladimir Ilich Lenin wrote a letter to the *Amrita Bazar Patrika* conveying his shock and sympathy.

Thereafter the Third Anglo-Afghan War occurred. Throughout the First World War there had been fears of an Afghan invasion, but it had not come about, due mainly to Amir Habibullah not succumbing to the blandishments of the German Mission in Kabul. In February 1919, Habibullah was murdered. One of his younger sons, Amanullah, whose supporters may perhaps have been responsible for the murder, eventually succeeded him, one of Habibullah's brothers, Nasrullah, initially seizing the throne. Amanullah felt that he might strengthen his position by launching an attack on the British in India, as many in Afghanistan had urged his father to do, when the British were preoccupied with the First World War, particularly at the time of the reverses at the hands of the Turks at Gallipoli and in Mesopotamia. He was encouraged in believing that British rule in India was collapsing, possibly by the Indians who had fled to Kabul during the First World War, thus providing him an opportunity for retaking Peshawar. Then in the Jallianwala firing some Muslims were also killed, enabling him to declare "jihad" against the British. Probably he had also learnt of what Lawrence James describes as, 'much grumbling, obstruction, and even strikes, amongst the (British) men from garrisons in Mesopotamia and India who found that their demobilization was held back in 1919.... None had any objection to frontier defence, but they thought it of secondary importance to the obtainment of jobs in Britain.'[14]

Early, in May 1919, Afghan troops crossed into Indian territory through the Khyber, and Amanullah called on the Frontier tribes to rise. There was some response, an Afghan force advancing into Waziristan being joined by Wazirs and Mahsuds in large numbers, the Waziristan militia virtually deserting *en masse* with their weapons. (On account of the latter, even after the Afghan regulars had been driven back, the British were faced with a Frontier war harder than they had so far experienced, the Derajat Column alone suffering 639 dead and 1,683 wounded during 1919-21.) There was often friction between the military and political officers, the latter feeling they understood the tribesmen better. A story is often recounted of a British political officer, disappearing during a skirmish from the column, and rejoining in the evening to enquire, 'And what were your casualties today? Our chaps lost two.' The Afghan force advancing from Afghanistan was repulsed by an Indian brigade in the Khyber. The Afghan frontier town of Dakka was occupied by the brigade, and bombs were dropped on Jalalabad and Kabul by a single Handley Page, this latter recourse being considered more cost effective by the Committee of Imperial Defence, than having the Indian Army advancing once again to Kabul. The ground support Bristol fighter aircraft, however, was so decrepit, that a pilot experienced the novelty of being fired down upon by the tribesmen in the hills above the aircraft. Another Afghan force had been launched under Nadir Khan (the future Nadir Shah) directed at Thal in Kurram, which was invested. Dyer and his brigade were moved from Jullundur (he had not yet been retired), and were able to lift the siege of Thal. Amanullah suspended hostilities, realizing that if his country was invaded he would be toppled. A treaty was signed after protracted negotiations at Rawalpindi in 1921, before concluding which Amanullah had sought, not very successfully, also to negotiate with the Bolshevik Government in Russia. The treaty conditions were that the subsidy to the Amir be withdrawn, a British legation at last to be established in Kabul, and the British claim to control Afghanistan's foreign relations dropped. As a result of this war unsettling the Frontier tribes, Curzon's policy of holding the tribal areas only with tribal militia was reviewed, and the key forts at Razmak and Wana were now occupied by regular Indian and British troops. The Waziristan militias were disbanded, and in their place were raised the Tochi Scouts and South Waziristan Scouts.

These Frontier hostilities occurred at the time of some Muslim unrest in India occasioned by the Khilafat Movement. At the end of 1919 the Ali brothers, Mohammed and Shaukat, who had been interned during the war, were released. They threw themselves into what is known as the Khilafat (Caliphate) agitation. The Sultan of Turkey was recognized to some extent as the Khalifa (Caliph) of Islam. As a result of Turkey's defeat in the war, the curtailment of his temporal power, particularly in sovereignty over Mecca and Medina, was represented as a vicious assault on Islam. Mohammed Ali met the British Prime Minister, David Lloyd George, in March 1920, but was told that Turkey would not be allowed to control non-Turkish lands (the British were committed to freeing Arabia from Turkish rule). The Khilafat leader thereafter encouraged 30,000 poor Indian Muslims to sell their property and migrate to

Afghanistan in order to avoid living under the British, the enemies of Islam. After some weeks the Afghan government closed the border to prevent a further influx, and most of the 30,000 drifted back to India in groups. The Muslim troops of the Indian Army, as distinct from the Waziristan militia, by and large, had resisted the Afghan appeals to join the invaders, as also several pressures of the Khilafat leaders to join the movement, and were not essentially deflected from their duties at the time of the Third Anglo-Afghan War; however, Muslim units, as far as possible, were not deployed, though some incidents did occur. Then, in July 1921, at a Khilafat conference at Karachi, the Ali brothers supported a resolution declaring India *haram* (forbidden by religion), and that Muslims should not serve in the Indian Army any further. On the advice of Lord George Rawlinson, the Commander-in-Chief, they and their associates were prosecuted and sentenced to two years' imprisonment. The Sultan of Turkey eventually fled from Constantinople in November 1922, and the succeeding government headed by Mustapha Kemal (Kemal Ataturk) abolished the Khilafat. The Khilafat Movement's endeavour to subvert Muslim troops in the Indian Army thereupon ended, having achieved only nominal success. Separately, in Malabar, the Moplahs' agitation for the survival of a distant Caliph ended as a backlash against the non-Muslims. M.A. Jinnah had not gone along with the Khilafat Movement, but Gandhi had, withdrawing in 1921 after the massacre of policemen at Chauri Chaura in the UP. Sir George Lloyd, Governor of Bombay, had earlier written to Montagu in 1920, 'All the value and goodwill that one hoped from your reforms is being rapidly submerged on account of the actions of these two or three men, and feeling has never been worse than at present since the Mutiny.'[15] Stanley Wolpert describes this period as, 'Jinnah's moment of rude historic awakening to the harsh realization that his dream of attaining national leadership over an Indian Dominion was irrevocably shattered. Were that so, he would have no options other than to abandon public life entirely, or try to find perhaps at "the brink of a precipice"—another nation to call his own.'[16]

Meanwhile, mutiny had broken out in June 1920, first at Jullundur, and then in a company at Solan, among the Connaught Rangers, an Irish regiment, whose Irish nationalism was aroused, they being used in suppressing Indian nationalist agitations. The men peacefully refused to parade until Ireland had been given her freedom, and the repression and atrocities by the British Army in Ireland were put to an end. It was an Indian unit that was initially ordered to cordon off the Connaught Rangers, and to deal with them, by force, if necessary, till British troops arrived. Five months later with the minimum of publicity a statement was issued by Army Headquarters, 'His Excellency the Commander-in-Chief regrets to announce that a serious case of mutiny occurred in the First Battalion, The Connaught Rangers, between 28 June and 2 July 1920 at Jullundur and Solan, in consequence of which sixty-nine non-commissioned officers and men were brought to trial on charges of varying degrees of mutiny. Of these sixty-one were found guilty and eight were acquitted. Of those found guilty, fourteen were sentenced to death by being shot. In the case of one private the sentence of death was carried into execution at daybreak on 2 November 1920. In the case of the remainder the death sentence was commuted to penal servitude for life and less.' Private James Daly, the ostensible ringleader, who was buried in the Dagshai cemetery, was thus one of the last British soldiers to be executed for mutiny in peacetime.[17] His remains have since been moved to the Republic of Ireland. The case is mentioned as Indian troops were initially ordered to be deployed against the Connaught Rangers.

In 1921, a terrorist group, partly composed of ex-servicemen and serving soldiers on leave, was detected. Known as the Babbar (Lion) Akalis, it was an offshoot of the Akali movement for the control of the gurdwaras being taken over by elected committees of management, and out of the hands of mahants. On 20 February 1921, the "Nankana Holocaust" had occurred, when Mahant Narain Das had organized the killing of 130 Sikhs and the burning of their bodies. It was largely recruited from ex-Ghadrites. As in the case of the Ghadr conspiracy of 1915, the group had been infiltrated by the

Punjab Police, and by the end of 1923 most of the members of the group had been rounded up, and a number hanged or imprisoned for long periods. Because of the participation of servicemen and ex-servicemen in this agitation, the proportion of Sikhs in the army was reduced to thirteen per cent in 1930 from twenty per cent in 1914, and that of Punjabi Mussalmans and Pathans raised to thirty-four per cent from twenty-six per cent in 1914. Separately, at this time, an Indian Military School had been set up by the Russians at Tashkent for the political and military training of Indian Communists, the Comintern having convened a meeting of Indian Army Muslim deserters at Baku in 1917.

Also, in 1921, the passing of the Indian Territorial Force (ITF) Act was to re-formalize a second line of defence to supplement the Indian Army. This was, in effect, meant to be a more wide-based successor to the Indian wing of the Indian Defence Force of 1917. The ITF was intended for those Indians for whom military service had not been a tradition. Enrolment was for six years, extendable by another four. Initial training was of one month, with annual training of one month, later increased to two. The seventeen provincial battalions seem to have had little difficulty in making up their strength, the 11th Battalion of the concerned regiments being the ITF battalion generally, but the four urban battalions did (a fifth exclusively Parsi urban battalion at Bombay had a short life). The ITF only had a liability in India. Separately, the volunteer units, which had been part of the European wing of the Indian Defence Force in the war, now became the Auxiliary Force (India), as before open only to Europeans and Anglo-Indians.

As it so happened, the first Legislative Assembly, after the Montagu-Chelmsford reforms had become legislation, sat in early 1921, just when the Esher Committee report of 1920 had been published. Sir P.S. Sivaswamy Aiyer moved fifteen resolutions on the report. One suggested that twenty-five per cent of the number to be commissioned annually should be reserved for Indians; some others that the Indian Army existed for Indian defence, and not the furtherance of Imperial policy; the necessity for reduction in

Defence expenditure; and the substitution of a civilian member for the Commander-in-Chief in the Viceroy's Executive Council. By circumstance of the resolutions being moved at the end of the session, the government did not at that moment have a majority present in the House. The resolutions, in the event, had to be accepted almost in their entirety, much to the chagrin of official circles in Delhi and London, for many years. The operative resolutions, insofar as Indianization was concerned, were, first, the eligibility of all qualified Indians, subject to the modification (carried by one vote) moved by the government with the help of the representatives of the traditional classes, 'that the large majority of the selections should be from the communities which furnish recruits to the army, and, as far as possible, in proportion to the numbers in which they furnish such recruits'; second, the establishment of an Indian "Sandhurst", and the establishment of an institution to prepare Indians for Sandhurst.

Rawlinson, thereafter, immediately in 1921 itself, convened a Military Requirements Committee, presided over by himself, in order to implement the operative resolutions. With commendable courage, the Rawlinson Committee proposed the formal postulation of the eventual replacement of British by Indian officers, indigenous self-sufficiency, and the broadening of the base of all recruitment, including that of officers. Apart from twenty-five per cent being reserved for Indians in the annual commissioning into the Indian Army through Sandhurst, there should also be an annual increase of two-and-a-half per cent.[18] These formulations were not acceptable to Whitehall, and alternative proposals were prepared by the Military Secretary in the India Office, Lieutenant General Sir Alexander Cobbe, VC. These were forwarded by the Secretary of State. Cobbe reiterated all the past arguments against Indianization, repeating what Roberts had stated earlier. He then went on to suggest that an Indian Dominion Army should be formed consisting of reservists, with Indians as officers and British higher commanders, distinct from the Indian Army which would only have British officers, and continue with its Imperial role, till such time as the Indian Dominion

Army was built up over several decades, and progressively took over responsibility for internal security and frontier defence. Viceroy Reading was distressed, replying, that Indianization of the existing Indian Army was, 'the crucial test of our sincerity in the policy of fitting India to advance towards the goal of self-government.'

Rawlinson convened another committee in 1922 under Lieutenant General Sir John Shea to go into Cobbe's proposals, and formulate a scheme for the progressive Indianization of the Indian Army. The Shea Committee disagreed with the Legislative Assembly resolution as to a fixed percentage of Indians to be commissioned annually. It also disagreed with the Rawlinson Committee as to fixing an annual percentage increase, and with Cobbe as to a separate Indian Dominion Army. Instead it postulated that complete Indianization (except for Gurkha units) should be carried out in three phases of fourteen years each. If the first phase was successful, then the second could be reduced to nine years. If not, the second phase would be fourteen years also. Similarly, the third phase could be seven years. From the second phase, British officers would cease to be commissioned into the Indian Army, any requirement being met by deputation from the British Army. Indian officers would progress upwards by length of service, initially replacing VCOs, and ultimately there would be no VCOs. The Shea Committee felt an Indian Military College was necessary, and that an Indian Commissioned Officer (ICO) should have a lesser rate of pay than a KCO serving in India, since the latter's pay included an overseas service element. Thus, conceptually, the Indian Army could be Indianized within thirty years, commencing in 1925.[18]

Lord Reading wished to place the Shea report before the Legislative Assembly, as an earnest of the government's intentions in relation to Indianization, but differences developed with Viscount Peel, the Secretary of State. The latter described the Shea Committee's recommendations as lending, 'colour to the dangerous belief in a policy of retreat,' and that the British Government would decide the stages towards self-government, and not the Government of India. Against Shea's proposal to Indianize twenty infantry battalions, seven cavalry regiments, and six pioneer battalions, in the first phase, forty battalions and seven regiments in the second phase, and the rest in the third, Peel said only four units could be Indianized. Whitehall eventually agreed to six battalions and two cavalry regiments being Indianized. Meanwhile, Rawlinson had proceeded with opening a pre-Sandhurst institution in the old campus of the Imperial Cadet Corps, with a capacity of seventy cadets. The Prince of Wales, later King Edward VIII, formally inaugurated the College on 13 March 1922, it being designated the Prince of Wales Royal Indian Military College (RIMC), today's Rashtriya Indian Military College. The full duration of education was normally to be six years; sons of VCOs could be nominated on payment of half the normal fees of Rs 1,500 per annum, or a total waiver in special cases. This institution did help in reducing the Indian failure rate at Sandhurst.

Separately, internal reorganizations were being carried out simultaneously, partly on the Esher Committee's recommendations. The nine divisional organizations were replaced by districts and brigades. Four of the districts were equivalent to divisions, but no field force was contemplated, as no overseas operations were envisaged. From 1922 infantry battalions were grouped into regiments and redesignated. The smaller regiments were grouped with larger regiments so that one joint training battalion could serve at least five battalions, an active battalion being converted into a training unit. The class composition in each of the regiment's battalions had to be the same. Cavalry regiments were reduced from thirty-nine to twenty-one, none now being silladar. The first Indian artillery regiment was raised in 1935, the first Indian officers being posted to "A" Field Brigade, today the 1st Field Regiment (Self-propelled). The Field Artillery Training Centre was then set up at Muttra. (By the end of the Second World War, the Royal Indian Artillery had sixty-one operational units, as opposed to only one in 1935. Today there are three hundred.) Three cavalry regiments were given the training role in 1937. Shorter enrolment was introduced from 1923, variously from four to seven years, depending on the arm or service. Extension was permissible to complete fifteen years' service for pension. Those not extending their colour service were placed on the Reserve. State forces were now to be placed in three classes, Class A being deemed equivalent to the Regular Army. Aid was correlated to the classification.

In 1923 the Lee Commission was given the task of laying down the emoluments and rate of Indianization of the Secretary of State's services. The effect of the recommendations was to reduce to a trickle British recruitment to all Class 1 services, except the Indian Civil Service (ICS) and the Indian Police (IP) (the Indian Army was not included in the terms of reference of this committee, which had four Indian and four British members). For the ICS, it was proposed that recruitment should be so adjusted that it would be half-Indian in fifteen years, and the IP after twenty-five years. The proposals were implemented. Rawlinson, thereupon, in 1923, convened a Progress of Indianization Committee, presided over by General Claude Jacob, with seven other British members. This committee came out against Indianization, rather than gauging progress, urging: 'The tendency will be for the Indian officer to gravitate towards men of his own class, impartiality will be exceptional, and is, in fact, impossible owing to the caste system and the difference in races. Consequently, only a few of these officers will ever really command the respect and obedience of the men serving under them...the tendency of the Oriental in the army is to look to somebody else for orders.' The committee went on to the performance of the Imperial Service Troops in the late war, where twelve per cent British officers had to be posted in eventually, adding, 'It is doubtful whether any general officers in command of operations would trust a regiment officered entirely by Indians....' [19]

This committee then questioned whether India, with a population then of 320 million, was in fact "a nation" as the nationalist leaders were urging, and gratuitously added, 'Japan is a nation in the true sense of the word, India is not.' Thereupon the committee turned to the nationalist comparison with the French attitude towards the Algerian soldier. In this context the committee urged that the Algerians were part of the French metropolitan army, and not the

French colonial army, and no Algerian, so far, had progressed beyond captain; and thereafter advised against any further Indianization till the success of the "eight unit" scheme could be discerned, coming out with one of the more memorable non-sequiturs of the British period: '....with the tradition of hundreds of years of injustice and corruption on the part of Indians in authority, he (the Indian soldier) is prejudiced against his own race...we may anticipate a rooted objection on the part of the Indian soldier to go to an Indianized unit,' arguing that recruitment to the regiments concerned would thereby be affected. The committee while endorsing the concept of Indian officers for the "eight units" being trained at Sandhurst, re-emphasized the high wastage rate of Indian cadets.

Sequentially, Army Headquarters came to the mistaken conclusion that the Indian-educated classes, except, perhaps, the Khattri and Kashmiri would never make efficient officers, most of the benefits of education having apparently ill-advisedly passed to the clever "unmanly" classes, and that the only source on which to draw reliable 'Brindians', the term colloquially applied by the British to the Indian King's Commissioned Officers (KCIO), must be from the traditional classes that then furnished the VCOs, and that the sons of the VCOs, if the VCOs themselves were not trainable, would be more trainable material if caught young, rather than the educated "unmanly" classes. King George's Schools, for their basic education, were therefore started for these boys, as also the Kitchener College, Nowgong, prior to selection for a commission. But even the selection of some Bengalis, Khattris and Kashmiris for Sandhurst led to an article in *The Army Quarterly* by Jewan Singh (obviously a pseudonym), inveighing against them: ' Instances could be given of the cowardly—or, to say the least of it, utterly unofficer-like and unsoldier-like behaviour of Bengalis and Khattris of the Punjab in the department (medical) which has been open to them as commissioned officers for a long period back: two from my own personal experience, and others on thoroughly reliable evidence. The Kashmiris of the Valley of Kashmir—often big powerful men—have always had the reputation of being useless as fighting men....'[20]

Owing to the Third Anglo-Afghan War, problems on the Frontier, and the continued need for Indian troops to garrison places like Mesopotamia, there had been a delay in the post-war reduction, for which the Legislative Assembly was pressing in order to reduce the Army Budget. Rawlinson very commendably was able to reduce the Indian Army from 159,000 in 1921 to 140,000 in 1925, the British troops in India from 75,000 to 57,000, and the military expenditure from eighty-two crores to fifty-six crores annually. As nationalist pressure was increasing for an Indian "Sandhurst", an Indian Sandhurst Committee was convened in 1926, presided over by Lieutenant General Sir Andrew Skeen, later the author of the well-known book, *Passing It On*. Except for one other British member, twelve members were Indian, and included M.A. Jinnah and Motilal Nehru. Owing to other preoccupations, the latter later resigned, as he did not have the time to visit all the similar training institutions in the Dominions. (In 1927, he did, however prepare a report on Defence policy for the Congress party, known as the Nehru Report.) The committee found that since 1918, for eighty-three vacancies at Sandhurst, 243 had competed in India, and sixteen in Britain. Forty-four had passed out successfully. The figures were improving with boys from the RIMC also now competing. Skeen took a very positive view, noting that the four Indians in the Royal Flying Corps in the war had done well—two being killed, one being awarded the Distinguished Flying Cross.[21]

The recommendations, briefly, were twenty vacancies annually at Sandhurst, increased annually by four till the Indian "Sandhurst" was established by 1933; the capacity to be one hundred, with an annual intake of thirty-three for a three-year course of training; if Indian boys, like those studying in Britain, still wished to go to Sandhurst, then twenty vacancies were to continue annually, increasing by twelve every three years; assuming all were successful at Sandhurst and the Indian "Sandhurst", then by 1945 half the commissioned intake would be Indian, and by 1952 half the total officer cadre would be Indian; Indians should also be admitted to the Royal Military Academy, Woolwich, till corresponding arrangements could be made in India, for eventual commissioning in the Artillery, Engineers and Signals; and the "eight unit" scheme to be done away with as British officers of other units were apt to look down on these units. Field Marshal Birdwood, the Commander-in-Chief in 1928, an Indian Army officer himself, however, did not agree with doing away with the "eight unit" scheme, the then Secretary, Army Department arguing that it was the most rapid method of laying the foundation of a national army. Nor did Birdwood agree to a military college in India. He agreed to six vacancies at Woolwich. The Indian representatives reopened the matter of the Indian Military College at the Round Table Conference in 1930, and it was, thereafter, opened at Dehra Dun in 1932. Three from the first course became Chiefs of their respective armies—Field Marshal S.H.F.J. Manekshaw in India, General Mohammed Musa in Pakistan, and General Smith Dun in Burma. As a compensatory gesture to doing away with the "eight unit" scheme in accordance with Skeen's recommendation, a "fifteen unit" scheme was now conceded after the Round Table Conference, equivalent to a divisional strength. The Mhow District or Division was so nominated, though the 'Indianized' units were located all over India. Sequentially, the opponents of Indianization now argued that one division of the Indian Army's operational capability had been rendered ineffective.

Separately, in 1928, a Statutory Commission on Communal Disorders had reported, 'The numerous instances in which military assistance...has had to be sought has indicated that in the larger towns the task of preventing breaches of the peace at times of communal excitement is apt to be beyond the powers of the civil police. Since 1926 (to 1928) on the occasions of communal riots troops have been required to restore order in Calcutta, Delhi, Rawalpindi, Lahore, Multan and other places...while also some outbreaks have been prevented only by the military preparation to be in readiness....' During 1922-27 there were 112 major communal disturbances requiring the army to be deployed or to stand by.

At this point of time, a Russian threat through Afghanistan continued to be perceived, and the Defence Plan of 1927-28 projected a requirement of 250,000 reinforcements from Britain and the other Dominions. The concerned British Cabinet Committee had defined the threat as, 'an attack by a great power upon India, or upon the Empire through India.' (In the Second World War, it became a German threat.) Curzon earlier had combined the reform of Frontier defence policy with an administrative change, withdrawal of control of the Frontier from the Punjab Government, and the creation of a new North-West Frontier Province (NWFP). It had been mooted by Edward Lytton and favoured by Henry Lansdowne, but implemented by George Curzon. The new province included all the trans-Indus territory, except the district of Dera Ghazi Khan adjoining Baluchistan, as also the cis-Indus district of Hazara, populated mainly by Pathans. When Gandhi started his civil disobedience campaign in March 1930, the predominantly Muslim NWFP was expected to remain calm, but there was a good deal of latent disaffection. This civil background is being given, for now occurred what has been incorrectly referred to as the 2/18th Garhwal Rifles "mutiny". The NWFP's separation from the Punjab had deprived it of several advantages. Being a Frontier province, political reforms extended to the Punjab were not applicable to the NWFP. Its inhabitants were not eligible any longer for the benefits of land in the Punjab canal colonies, as also the district administration under the Punjab had been more efficient than in the NWFP now. Meanwhile, Khan Abdul Ghaffar Khan, a very great man, morally and intellectually, who was abandoned to his fate at Partition, had come to be known as the "Frontier Gandhi", and had initiated a movement for the Punjab's political reforms to be extended to the NWFP, as also for certain social changes. To help him in social work, he had organized a group of volunteers, the "Khudai Khidmatgars" (the Servants of God).

Though he and his volunteers had not started so far any civil disobedience in Peshawar in response to Gandhi's call, he was

1st and 3rd Brahmins in 1910. The former reorganized as 4th/1st Punjab, and the latter was disbanded after the First World War

43rd Erinpura Regiment, 44th Merwara Infantry, and 108th Infantry in 1910. All progressively disbanded in the rundown after the First World War. (108th Infantry re-raised as the 3rd/4th Bombay Grenadiers in the Second World War, today's 3rd Battalion, The Grenadiers)

Execution in 1915 of a batch of 21 mutineers of 5th Light Infantry (after the first volley)

Italian prisoners of war captured by Indian divisions in Abyssinia in 1941

Before the execution of Indian prisoners of war by the Japanese in Malaya in 1942
(photographs found on the recapture of Singapore in 1945)

The execution of Indian prisoners of war by the Japanese in 1942

Bayoneting by the Japanese of the executed Indian prisoners of war in 1942

A captured position being searched in 1944 for further Japanese

A mountain battery on the move in Burma during the advance in 1945

The Sittang bridge built by Indian Sappers in 1945 after the second battle of the Sittang

The Supreme Commander, Lord Louis Mountbatten, inspecting an Indian guard of honour before formally accepting the Japanese surrender at Singapore

Lieutenant Colonel (later Brigadier) Mohammed Usman presenting a captured Japanese sword to the Commander-in-Chief. (In the 1948 Jammu and Kashmir operations, the gallant Brigadier Usman was killed by Pakistani shelling)

Field Marshals Bernard Montgomery, Archibald Wavell and Claude Auchinleck at the Viceroy's House in 1946

A 3.7 inch howitzer engages the invader in Kashmir in 1947

After the link-up with the besieged town of Poonch, the Indian Army assists in the evacuation of civilians by the Indian Air Force in 1948

Senior officers at Army Headquarters, New Delhi, 1950. Seated: Major General Sant Singh, Master General of the Ordnance; Major General S.P.P. Thorat, DSO, Chief of the General Staff; General K.M. Cariappa, OBE, Chief of the Army Staff and Commander-in-Chief; Major General H.L. Atal, Adjutant General; Major General S.B.S. Chimni, OBE, Quartermaster General
Standing: Major General T. Sheodatt Singh, Military Secretary; Major General S.N. Sharma, Director of Medical Services; Major General H. Williams, CBE, Engineer-in-Chief

After the capture of Hajipir Pass in Pakistan-occupied Kashmir on 28 August 1965 (subsequently returned to Pakistan under the 1966 Tashkent Agreement)

One-third of the US aid-Patton tanks of Pakistan's 1st Armoured Division ("Pattonnagar") destroyed in 1965, near Bhikkiwind in Punjab

Prime Minister Indira Gandhi visiting captured territories in December 1971 shortly after the ceasefire in the 1 Corps Sector, accompanied by Lt. Gen. K.P. Candeth, GOC-in-C Western Command (in peaked cap)

Sheikh Mujib-ur Rehman on arrival at Dhaka after his release by Pakistan. Also present Lt. Gen. J.S. Aurora, GOC-in-C Eastern Command and Major General B.F. Gonsalves, GOC 57 Division

Captain (later Lieutenant General) P.S. Bhagat, Bombay Sappers and Miners, invested with the VC at the Viceroy's House in 1941

Subedar Joginder Singh, The Sikh Regiment, posthumously awarded the PVC in 1962

Company Quartermaster Havildar Abdul Hamid, The Grenadiers, posthumously awarded the PVC in 1965

Lance Naik Albert Ekka, Brigade of the Guards, posthumously awarded the PVC in 1971

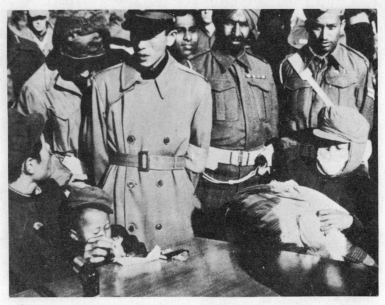

Custodian Force (India), Korea, 1953

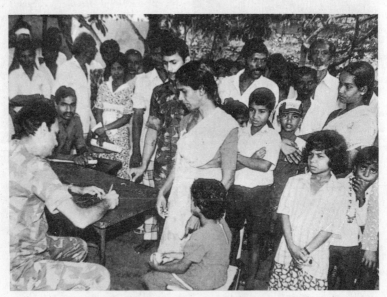

The Indian Peace-Keeping Force providing medical relief, Sri Lanka, 1988

A living bunker in a snow-bound area on the Line of Control in Kashmir

A Cheetah Light Observation Helicopter of the Army Aviation Corps lands on an ice-pillar near the Siachen Glacier

The three Service Chiefs, General S.F. Rodrigues, Admiral L. Ramdas, and Air Chief Marshal N.C. Suri, laying wreaths on 26 January 1992 at the Amar Jawan Jyoti (War Memorial)

arrested on 23 April 1930, leading to protests. The local authorities handled the situation ineptly; the bringing of armoured cars in to the narrow streets aggravated the people.[22] Fire was opened, killing many and wounding more, further infuriating the crowd. Two Garhwal Rifles platoons (Nos. 1 and 4) having been through the aid to civil power ordeal the previous day, and repeatedly embussed in the hot sun and stood down the next day, eventually declined to embus for the third time, and sought their discharge. Temporarily all troops were withdrawn from Peshawar city, it being days before control was regained. The tribesmen from across the border, thinking that British rule was collapsing, intruded into British-Indian territory, receiving assistance from the local tribesmen. They were dispersed, but the NWFP remained disturbed. In August, when a large number of Afridis made a major incursion into Peshawar district, martial law was declared and remained in force till January 1931.[23]

Reverting to the 2/18th Royal Garhwal Rifles, the battalion was unnecessarily disarmed on 24 April, and moved to Abbotabad, where a court of inquiry was held. The two allegedly disaffected platoons were sent to Kakul. The canard that the whole battalion was disaffected was totally unfounded, the court recording of the events of the first day, 23 April, 'The men concerned were called on to suffer very demoralizing and degrading treatment at the hands of a savage mob, in that they, for a period, between one and two hours, were subjected to treatment no soldier wearing the King's uniform should be asked to stand without retaliation. They were made to stand in closest contact with a raging mob, subjected to a hail of missiles and being struck with staves and iron-shod poles. Though their British officer and several comrades were wounded, yet no order to retaliate was received by these dumbfounded soldiers. They were acting on the strictest orders not to take offensive action without a direct order from a British officer or a magistrate. These orders had been instilled into them for the previous three or four days under instructions received from the civil authorities. Their provocation was long and great. They had their British officer severely

331

wounded, six men admitted to hospital, and ten who had to attend for treatment of their injuries. Not until Government property was in jeopardy, ie, a rifle was forcibly wrenched from them, did they fire on their initiative.'[24]

On 23 April an armoured car had been burnt, and a British despatch rider killed; an armoured car had fired ten rounds, and a British detachment had fired twenty-four rounds, but the two platoons of the Garhwal Rifles in contact (Nos. 2 and 3) had received no orders to fire. There was, thus, never any question of the battalion refusing to fire, as was disseminated at the time. As to Nos. 1 and 4 platoons which had ultimately refused to embus the next day, and sought their discharge, the court named two non-commissioned officers as the instigators of the trouble, and that they had been actuated by some influence outside the battalion, despite no evidence on the point, apart from imputing that the two had attended Arya Samaj prayer meetings, which was apparently not correct. All the non-commissioned officers of Nos. 1 and 4 platoons were tried, the sentences varying from penal servitude for life to three years' rigorous imprisonment. In fact the instigators were not the two senior non-commissioned officers, but the subedar commanding No.4 platoon, who was not then tried. Nos. 1 and 4 platoons had been in reserve on 23 April behind Nos. 2 and 3 platoons when the latter were under pressure. That afternoon he had his increment of pay withheld for six months by the commanding officer, for a delay in the distribution of rations of his platoon that day. He had earlier been told by the commanding officer to improve his performance. Getting Nos. 1 and 4 platoons not to embus and to ask for their discharge was his idea of retribution.

Lawrence James, is sceptical, and records, 'The refusal to perform crowd-control duties by a detachment of Garhwalis in 1930, was publicly explained as the consequence of regimental problems. Yet the Garhwali ringleader, on his release from jail, became an active Indian nationalist.'[25] Having read the court of inquiry and court-martial proceedings, I am more inclined to agree with the regimental history written by Lieutenant General R.B. Deedes. The regimental history records, 'Exhaustive enquiries by the CID, the army and the police in Peshawar, Abbotabad and elsewhere showed clearly that neither of the two NCOs of No.4 platoon (the instigators), nor any others in the battalion had any touch with any political body, nor had they been influenced by other outside subversive agents.'[26] The non-commissioned officer concerned, having been jailed by the British, obviously decided, on release, to go into politics in order to seek redress. He had no political connections while in service. The government, for its part, recorded on the official Peshawar Riots Committee Report: 'The situation in which troops were placed for some time...emphasises the difficulties and dangers, which are likely to occur through non-observance of the accepted principle that troops should not be brought in close physical contact with a violent and hostile mob.' General Sir James Willcocks, who had commanded the Indian Corps in France, looked back on forty years of commanding Indian troops including the then 39th Garhwalis, and concluded, 'Indians of all classes are of any people I know the easiest led when the leader understands their hearts, and the most difficult to manage when he does not.' In this case the commanding officer was changed.

At this juncture, the Report of the Statutory Commission on Indian Constitutional Advancement, presided over by Sir John Simon, was published in June 1930. Major C.R. Attlee, later to be the Prime Minister of Britain and in whose tenure India achieved independence, curiously signed this report which, *inter alia,* argued against handing over the responsibility for defending India to Indians, because military ability was not evenly distributed in the entire population, and the capacity to fight was confined to the martial races. In the recommendations, therefore, it was proposed that the task of defence on the grant of self-government should be "leased out" to Britain. The commission, in justification, produced the statistics that out of 158,200 combatants then in the Indian Army, 91,600 came from the Punjab and the NWFP, adding that Bengal, Assam and Orissa contributed nothing, and that the rest of the country contributed proportionately small numbers. The commission omitted to record that Bengal, Assam and Orissa had not been given the opportunity to contribute manpower-wise, and the other provinces' contributions were small because they were perforce limited by the exiguous quotas released by Army Headquarters. The commission, in relation to the eventual possibility of Dominion Status for India, echoing Cobbe, went on to recommend that that part of the Indian Army officered by British officers must be an Imperial Army, an Army of the Crown located in India, along with the British troops there under a Commander-in-Chief responsible to the Crown, through the Viceroy, and not to the Government of India. In addition there would be local troops (the "Indianized" units) welded, along with the ITF and the State forces, into one mobilization scheme for the defence of India (comparable to Cobbe's proposed Indian Dominion Army). Despite its incongruences, this was deemed a logical strategic perception. There might be some Staff College-qualified Indian officers in the Imperial Army, but the place for the employment of the majority of Indian officers was in the "local forces". The inappropriate analogy was made of the pre-1858 days of the East India Company, when the latter had two European forces under it, its own European forces and those of the Crown, for which it paid. Behind all the verbiage, the aim was obviously to ensure that the majority of British officers did not serve alongside Indian officers, and none under them. Partly prompted by this report, the Indian representatives, at the first session of the Round Table Conference with the British Government, insisted on the formal adoption of a resolution, as earlier mentioned, for the establishment of an Indian Military College. The Chetwode Committee was set up in 1931 to implement this. The intake was to be sixty for the Regular Army, and twenty for the ISF. Indians, thereafter, would not be admitted to Sandhurst. The suggestion that British Sandhurst cadets, opting for the Indian Army, complete their last term in the corresponding Indian institution, was not implemented. On the political plane, had the Indian request for Dominion Status been conceded at the Round Table Conference, the subcontinent may not have been partitioned subsequently, for, in 1929, the Viceroy, Lord Irwin, with the authority of the British Government, had affirmed that Dominion Status was implicit in the Montagu Declaration of 1917. However, in 1931, Ramsay MacDonald, now Prime Minister, retracted from the Irwin Declaration and averred at the Round Table Conference that the British Government did not contemplate equality of status between the (white) dominions and India.

Now, in 1930-32, various attacks and raids by Bengali revolutionaries occurred, the major one being on 18 April 1930, on the armoury of the Auxiliary Force (India) at Chittagong, killing a British sergeant. There had been assassinations by Bengali revolutionaries of Indian and British officials over the years since 1907, but this raid created a stir as it was an organized attack led by Ananta Singh, who was later murdered. However, the raiding party only carried off pistols; neither rifles, rifle ammunition, nor the Lewis machine-gun being taken. Further assassinations of British and Indian officials followed in various districts. Though the situation was within the capacity of the Bengal Police, for two years till the middle of 1932, two brigade headquarters and seven battalions were deployed in aid of the civil power.[27]

Earlier, in 1929, India had been asked to earmark some forces for overseas deployment in an emergency—two brigades for the Iranian oilfields, and a third for garrison duties in the Gulf. There was some correspondence with Whitehall as to the financial arrangements for this overseas deployment. For this and other outstanding financial issues the Garran Tribunal was appointed and gave its award in 1933. An annual grant of two million pounds was to be made by Britain for this purpose from 1 April 1939, it being one million pounds before that. By 1936 this overseas commitment had increased to two brigades for Egypt, and a brigade each for the Persian Gulf, the Red Sea, Burma and Singapore. In terms of the Tribunal's award, Britain accepted responsibility for any "major danger" on India's border, India being responsible for any "minor danger."

In February 1938, in the words of F.W. Perry, 'The position of the Indian Army was again brought to the fore in a paper on the

"Organization of the Army", by the War Secretary, Leslie (later Lord) Hore-Belisha. In it, while noting that the largest part of the British Army overseas was located in India, he advocated that part of the Imperial strategic reserve should be east of the Mediterranean. Reorganization of the Army in India was needed.'[28] A sub-committee was set up under Major General Henry Pownall to report on the current defence problems of India. This noted that India had a major contribution to make to Imperial defence, but recorded that India could not effect this contribution without assistance. 'A double-faceted movement was thus coming into view with a formalization of the Indian Army's role in Imperial defence on the one hand and a modernization of the Army on the other.'[29] A Modernization Sub-Committee under Major General Sir Claude Auchinleck reported in October 1938. His conclusions and those of Pownall were, by and large, embodied in those of the Expert Committee on the Defence of India, presided over by Admiral of the Fleet, Lord Alfred Chatfield, reporting in June 1939. The Chatfield Committee gracelessly opined that the Indian demand for ultimately a wholly Indian Army evidenced, 'either a striking ignorance of the true facts of the position, or a refusal to admit them.' It gratuitously added that India could not do without British troops, 'as a large number of responsible Muslims are seriously alarmed by the prospect of a Congress majority at the Centre gaining virtual control, whether by direct or indirect means, over defence policy.'

While the Chatfield Committee was deliberating, a multiple murder of four British officers (including the commanding officer) and three VCOs occurred in November 1938 in 4/2nd Punjab in the battalion training camp outside Nowshera. Two other British officers were severely wounded. While individual British officers had been sadly shot on different occasions by individual troops, such as in 5/8th Punjab in 1928 and 1929 (one assailant was refused leave, and the other failed in a promotion examination), this was the largest multiple killing of Britons since the mutiny of the 5th Light Infantry at Singapore in 1915. This unit had previously been the 74th Punjabis, "Punjabized" from the Madras Infantry in 1902. In 1905 the subedar major had been shot, in 1932 a murder had occurred in the unit, and in 1936 a VCO had been shot. On this occasion, while in training camp, the observance of Id had been postponed by a day on account of an Army/Air Cooperation demonstration for the brigade. The postponement of the observance was announced at 4.30 p.m. Though Id would normally have been observed the next day, the quarter guard was still manned by Muslims, despite there being Sikh and Dogra companies in the battalion.

During the night, a Punjabi Mussalman soldier, who was distressed by the postponement, ran amok, and killed and wounded officers and VCOs as already indicated. The surviving VCOs sought to indicate that the standard of recruits had gone down since 1928, whereafter recruits had been mainly obtained through the recruiting organization, as opposed to the earlier regimental recruiting parties. There were also interdistrict feuds among the Punjabi Mussalman companies. First, the commanding officer was killed while asleep in his tent, and the others when they came out of their tents on hearing the sound of firing. There was a "conspiracy of silence" as to how the "low-caste" assailant was able to get so much ammunition. There had also been total inaction on the part of the quarter guard. The battalion had "stood to" thinking it was under attack by Pathans, some troops had fired, and the assailant, who was hiding just outside the camp, was killed. The court of inquiry considered that the standard of the battalion was lower than that in the other battalions of the regiment, that it had a bad record for murder, and should be disbanded. The sanction of the King was obtained. In order to avoid publicity and as the Chatfield Committee was contemplating some reductions, this battalion was shown as being reduced in accordance with that committee's forthcoming recommendations. The Sikhs and Dogras were transferred to the new Crown or Central Reserve Police at Neemuch. All the Punjabi Mussalmans were either dismissed or discharged, including those on courses or on leave.[30] A similar outrage was contemplated in another battalion of the same regiment. Several personnel were discharged.

The Chatfield Committee, in its report of June 1939, endeavoured to produce a cost-effective modernization programme, with cost-offsetting reductions. There was a detailed allocation of troops for frontier defence, coast defence, internal security, and external defence with a general reserve. The Imperial Reserve Division from the Indian Army suggested by Pownall was redesignated "External Defence Troops", with the stipulations that they should be over and above India's requirements, and that they, 'need only be fit to operate in Asiatic theatres of war.'[31] Under the Chatfield reductions, three cavalry regiments and fourteen infantry battalions were to be disbanded over five years as offsetting measures for the modernization of the Indian Army, which according to the Auchinleck Sub-Committee, 'was showing signs of falling behind the forces of such states as Egypt, Iraq and Afghanistan.'[32] The Chatfield Report was accepted, and published on 5 September 1939, thirty-four million pounds being allotted for modernization (a grant of twenty- five million pounds and a loan of nine million pounds). By then the Second World War had commenced, with little or no modernization, the only reduction effected in terms of the Chatfield Report being, by circumstance, that of the 4/2nd Punjab. Whenever Britain was at war, the Indian Army was also at war, except when the British specifically did not wish to use non-white troops, as in the Boer War, or had a general sufficiency of troops along with their allies, as in the Crimean War. At this point, the "Indianizing" units were one-eighth of the army. As to the official attitude towards these "Indianizing" units, Stephen Cohen quotes a retired British officer, 'Chetwode's solution was to get...the very best British officers into the non-Indianizing units, segregating the Indians. At that time there was not the same feeling of equality as there was later; if you want to call it that, there was a definite colour bar, it was in people's blood.'[33] Auchinleck, for his part as prescient as ever, wrote to L.S. Amery, Secretary of State for India, since May 1939, 'In my opinion, we have been playing a losing hand from the start in this matter of "Indianization". The Indian has always thought, rightly or wrongly, that we never intended the scheme to

338

succeed and expected it to fail. Colour was lent to this view by the way in which each new step forward had to be wrested from us, instead of being freely given. Now that we have given a lot we get no credit because there was little grace in our giving.'

TWELVE

The War Years (1939-1945)

ON 3 SEPTEMBER 1939, Lord Victor Alexander Linlithgow, the Viceroy, proclaimed that a state of war emergency now existed. He did not consult the Central Legislature, it being constitutionally argued that, with Britain at war, India was concomitantly at war. He did, thereafter, invite Mahatma Gandhi to meet him, and they met on 5 September. Some Indian princes, individually, and the others, later, through the Chamber of Princes, promised the full support of their forces. The Viceroy then sought the cooperation of the political parties in the war effort. After much debate, the Congress declined cooperation, unless India was first, 'declared an independent nation, and present application must be given to this status to the largest extent possible.' One Congress view expressed, apart from the insult of not being consulted by the Viceroy, was that the way the British were going about construction in New Delhi, they seemed to be planning to stay a thousand years. The Viceroy's House had 340 rooms, was over three-quarters of a mile in circumference, and was bigger than the palace of Versailles. Jawaharlal Nehru indicated that he was personally fervently anti-Nazi, and Gandhi had told Linlithgow that he viewed the war, 'with an English heart,' and had even advised the Congress Working Committee (CWC) to extend its unconditional support. L.S. Amery wanted Linlithgow to be permitted to tell the Congress that India would get, 'full and immediate post-war Dominion status,' but Winston Churchill, according to the *Amery Diaries 1929-1945,* replied, 'The Hindu-Muslim feud is the bulwark of British rule in India.' Amery then sagely wrote in early 1940, 'There remains the alternative of letting things slide into something like civil war, after which a partition of India like the partition of Ireland, and just as fruitful of further trouble,'[1] but Churchill was apt to ignore both Amery and India.

Of this period, Khushwant Singh records, 'On the resignation of the Congress ministries, the governors took over the administration in seven provinces.... While the Muslim League eagerly filled the power vacuum, the Congress reaffirmed its decision to non-cooperate with the war effort, and went further into the wilderness. A group led by Subhas Chandra Bose and Sardul Singh Caveeshar broke away from the parent body to organize more active opposition to the British.'[2] By this time Gandhi had isolated Subhas Bose, promoting Nehru as the heir-apparent, urging that he could not accept Bose's ideas at the cost of non-violence. A few days later, the Muslim League, in a session at Lahore, formally resolved that its aim was an independent Muslim state. The League Working Committee had drafted the proposed resolution before the outbreak of war. On the occasion of the resignation of the Congress ministries, M.A. Jinnah declared a "Day of Deliverance". In contrast, Maulana Abul Kalam Azad, in his Presidential address of the Fifty-third Session of the Indian National Congress at Ramgarh in March 1940 iterated, 'I am proud of being an Indian. I am part of the indivisible unity that is Indian nationality....I can never surrender this claim!' In no province did the League itself have a majority, the Muslim League having won only 108 out of a total of 485 seats reserved for Muslims in the 1937 elections. (The only elections the League was to win in certain provinces were those of 1946, but even then the North West Frontier Province [NWFP], with a ninety-two per cent Muslim majority, had a Congress ministry.)

The 1940 Muslim League Lahore resolution did not use the word "Pakistan", but the intention was apparent from the wording, 'that no constitutional plan would be workable in this country or be acceptable to the Muslims, unless it is designed on the following basic principles, namely, that geographically contiguous units are demarcated into regions which should be so constituted, with such territorial adjustments as may be necessary, that the areas in which the Muslims are numerically in a majority as the northwestern and eastern zones of India should be grouped to constitute independent states, in which the constituent units should be autonomous and sovereign.' This was validly interpreted by non-Muslims at the time, and Lord Louis Mountbatten later, that the Muslim League in 1940 did not want the whole of the Punjab and Bengal, but was willing to exclude the eastern half of the Punjab and the western half of Bengal, which were predominantly non-Muslim. The original draft of the Muslim League resolution was sponsored by Sir Sikandar Hayat Khan, the Unionist Party Premier of the Punjab, who later deeply regretted his action. He was not a communalist. The Unionist Party of the Punjab—consisting of Hindus, Muslims and Sikhs—had a majority headed by him. He believed in a regional culture, not in communal culture. At the instance of the Viceroy, he had joined the Muslim League, though still heading the Unionist Party. But for his premature death in 1942, the course of events in the Punjab, thereafter, might have been different. Earlier he had been a member of V.D. Savarkar's revolutionary group in London. When, after his release from the Andamans, Savarkar (1883-1966) visited Lahore, he was welcomed by Sir Sikandar at the railway station, a brave act in British days. (Savarkar had been repeatedly incarcerated for his revolutionary activities from 1919 to 1937, later becoming a leader of the Hindu Mahasabha.)

In Bengal, Fazlul Huq, the leader of the Krishak Praja Party, also was no communalist. He had wanted to form a coalition with the Congress, but the Congress condition was that the revolutionaries in jail must first be released. Huq hesitated as he knew the Governor would baulk. An opportunity for a stable Hindu-Muslim coalition in

Bengal was missed. Huq too had joined the Muslim League at that time on the advice of the Viceroy, but he found Jinnah autocratic, more than "a Pharaoh of Egypt", and was to resign from the Muslim League in 1941. (In 1954, when he defeated the Muslim League, and became the Chief Minister of East Pakistan, he said in Calcutta, 'Those who divided the country were traitors.' For this he was dismissed.) In Sind, the Chief Minister, Khan Bahadur Allah Bux Soomro, had not followed the Viceroy's suggestion of joining the League, declaring, 'The Muslim League view of Muslims as a separate nation in India on the basis of their religion is un-Islamic and improper.' (In 1942 he was to resign from the National Defence Council, and return his title. He was sequentially dismissed from office, and later killed.) In Baluchistan, there was no assembly, but the political leader was Khan Samad Khan, the "Baluch Gandhi". Despite the above position, an early vignette of what some British military officers, not Sir Claude Auchinleck, thought of the concept of partition is recorded by Badr-ud-din Tyabji in his *Memoirs of an Egoist*. When he was posted in Delhi in 1939 as a young ICS officer, certain British officers were telling him that eventual partition along religious lines would be a good thing. The first Briton to talk to him on this was Colonel (later Major General) Eric Dorman-Smith. Tyabji recounts, 'I found somewhat to my surprise and discomfiture that Dorman-Smith was not alone in thinking on these lines. It was being actively debated among a most lively group of General Staff officers,' in the Army Headquarters. 'They thought of it not only as a possibility, but as something not altogether undesirable, certainly not a matter for alarm....The Muslim part was bound to join the Commonwealth, and the rest would then have no option but to follow suit.'[3] The officers concerned conversed with Tyabji on the subject because they knew him to be a Muslim, seemingly not being aware that there could be Muslims opposed to partition.

The strength of the Indian Army on 1 October 1939 was 194,373, including 34,515 non-combatants enrolled. There were ninety-six infantry battalions and eighteen cavalry regiments. In addition there were the four Class A Indian State Force (ISF) cavalry regiments and seven infantry battalions.[4] The Indian Territorial Force (ITF) numbered 19,000 and the ISF aggregated 53,000, including the eleven Class A units. There were also four Assam Rifles battalions in the North-East. The call up of reservists commenced in September 1939 itself. The number of VCOs had progressively been decreased in the "Indianized" battalions and regiments, since platoons were commanded by newly-commissioned ICOs, though a category of warrant officer had been sought to be introduced in order to offset, to the extent possible, the loss of promotion prospects for NCOs. One of the earliest decisions was to appoint the normal complement of VCOs again in such units, as all units were to be equally "Indianized", except the Gurkha Rifles, as also to discontinue the warrant officer category. British and Indian officers now served alongside each other in all units, the former later spontaneously serving under the latter where seniority so indicated. Officers, irrespective whether British or Indian, were posted in relation to units' needs and the individual officer's seniority. Apart from the introduction of emergency commissions for Indians (IECOs) also, first through Dehra Dun, then at Mhow and Bangalore, and latterly Belgaum, direct commissions as VCOs, as in the First World War, were reintroduced after a short platoon commanders' course at Faizabad.

As mentioned in the previous chapter, one brigade each was already in Egypt and Malaya from August 1939, apart from the garrison at Aden having been strengthened in April. When a second brigade reached Egypt in October, the two were grouped as the 4th Indian Division, a third brigade subsequently following. Chenevix Trench describes their deportment: 'In Cairo and the Delta they set an example which was to be followed by hundreds of thousands of Indian troops in the Middle East, of being the best behaved and best disciplined of all the Allied contingents.'[5] To replace the brigades despatched overseas, the seventeen provincial ITF battalions were embodied. Ten Nepalese battalions were inducted into India in March 1940, on the earlier pattern established in 1857 and 1914 (and which was to be adopted again in 1948), though this time there were some disciplinary problems in one of the battalions on the Frontier. ISF contingents were also deployed outside their states, in British-India. What has been described as a state of "phoney war" now prevailed for some months. In this period Linlithgow gauged the need to make India a great base, but neither he nor the then Commander-in-Chief, Robert Cassells, could obtain from Britain directions for recruiting and training more men, so not much could be done except to try and progress modernization. A British general officer has described to Stephen Cohen the mental posture prevailing at the outbreak of the war: 'There was an element among the senior British officers of the British and Indian Armies that (thought that) what was good enough for us in pre-1914 was good enough for us post-1914. I myself had very little confidence in most of the senior officers of the Indian Army in World War I and between the wars. "Yes men" were less nuisance than the "no men" and, though I may be biased in saying this, a succession of cavalry Cs-in-C over a long period resulted in a horse soldier with a high handicap at polo...being preferred to others who were generally much better officers. However, in all fairness that was a situation which was prevalent in other armies before the World War II.'[6] For many such officers in the Indian Army, re-orientation only occurred in 1943. (One Cavalry officer transferred to the Infantry in 1943 insisted that a colour presentation to his battalion must be his first priority, war or no war. He had his way.)

The Chatfield programme of modernization was reduced from five to two years, but this was in many ways notional, as Britain did not have much equipment to spare, and the major source was to be the US. India did not have the dollars to pay, and "Lend Lease" equipment was not yet available. (Two weeks before the "Lend Lease" Bill was eventually signed, Franklin Roosevelt was to send Averill Harriman to see Churchill with the message, 'Get out of India soon, or you may not get what you need now.' Shortly after Roosevelt wrote to Churchill that American public opinion just could not understand why Indians could not have self-government straight away. This was to lead later to the 1942 Cripps Mission to

India.) But in early 1940 there was no expansion so far in the Indian Army. Chenevix-Trench says of this period, 'The Indian Government was eager to help, but the received wisdom in Whitehall was that the war would be won by the naval blockade and the trusty French: there was little need for the British Army to exert itself, none for the Indian Army to do so.'[7] The wartime financial modalities were now embodied in a Defence Expenditure Agreement of November 1939, for which Linlithgow strove valiantly. The Government of India was committed to contributing to the total expenditure a sum equivalent to its normal peacetime expenditure on defence, plus the cost of measures undertaken in purely Indian interests and a share of measures taken jointly in the interests of Indian defence by Britain, while the British Government met everything over and above this. (The agreement was fair, but against which Churchill was later often to inveigh, as it resulted in Britain owing a war debt to India of over 1,000 million pounds.)

At the end of May 1940, a plan to assist Afghanistan against an attack by the Soviet Union was approved by Britain, entailing the raising by India of five infantry divisions (6th, 7th, 8th, 9th, and 10th), and one armoured division (31st), over the next twelve months. In the event, three of these divisions had later to be offered for Iraq, and one for Malaya, necessitating further expansion to replace them. The new divisions were expected to be ready only during May-December 1941, due to the equipment constraint.[8] Owing to an emerging threat from Japan, an improvized 11th Indian Division with two brigades was hastily despatched to Malaya, the third brigade for it already being located there. Montgomery was to say of his experience as a divisional commander in the British Expeditionary Force (BEF) in France in 1940, that, 'it was totally unfit to fight a first class war on the continent of Europe; we sent our army into that most modern war with weapons and equipment which were quite inadequate and had only ourselves to blame for the disaster which overtook us in 1940.' Sadly there was no one to voice similar exculpation at the time of the predictable impending reverses in Malaya, Singapore and Burma. As in the First Anglo-Afghan War,

346

scapegoats had to be found, and Indians were often convenient. The Indian Army was comparatively less ready in fact for a jungle war with Japan, than it had been in 1914 for a trench war with Germany. Of the pre-war Indian Army, General J.N. Chaudhuri was later to say, 'It was non-innovative. Army Headquarters at Delhi were content to let the War Office in Whitehall do their thinking for them.' Even the uniforms for a war in the jungle were the same khaki pattern as devised in the last century for the Frontier. Any contemporary idea that the field formations sent to Malaya and Burma were well-equipped would, at the best, be wishful thinking, and, at the worst, wilful deceit. Separately, the 5th Indian Division was despatched in September 1940 to Port Sudan for the operations in Italian East Africa.

Auchinleck was appointed the Allied land commander in northern Norway in May 1940, and the only contributions required from the Indian Army in the war against Germany in Europe in 1940 were, 'a few Frontier experts sent to Norway to persuade (British) Guards and Territorial battalions that the only way to prevail in mountain warfare was to walk to the tops of mountains; and four animal transport companies of the Royal Indian Army Service Corps (RIASC), with pack mules....They acquitted themselves well and during the chaos of the German breakthrough and the retreat to Dunkirk maintained the discipline, turnout and self-respect which many around them lost, greatly enhancing the reputation of the Indian Army.'[9] In mid-1940 there occurred an incident which had both political undertones and overtones. The Sikh squadron of the Central India Horse refused to embark when the regiment was proceeding to Egypt. One-hundred-and-eight were court-martialled in July 1940. Four were executed, and one hundred sentenced to transportation. The rest were imprisoned. Investigations had shown, according to Khushwant Singh, that, 'Communists, who had acquired influence in the central districts (of the Punjab) adhered to the party line of regarding the war in Europe as Imperialist; their agents busied themselves disseminating anti-war propaganda among Sikh soldiers. The Akalis, who mattered more than all the other parties put together, were the most confused. The leaders, most of whom had served terms of imprisonment during the gurdwara agitation, had little love for the British. They were equally hostile to the Muslim Leaguers and to the pro-British Unionists. But they wished to preserve the numerical strength of the Sikhs in the armed services so that when the day of reckoning came, the Khalsa would have an army of its own. The Akali Party agreed to help the government and pressed for more Sikh recruitment; at the same time...the unenthusiastic support of the Akalis and the antagonism of the Communists during the "imperialist" phase of the war was reflected in the reluctance of Sikh peasants to enlist and disaffection in some regiments.'[10]

Chenevix-Trench, an Indian Cavalry officer though of a different regiment, felt that, 'the Sikhs had been "got at" by persons warning them of a nefarious British plot to have them exterminated so that the Punjab would be ruled by Moslems.'[11] Actually, the trouble could have been anticipated, if Major (later Brigadier) A.E. Barstow's caution in the 1928 Government publication, *Handbooks for the Indian Army—Sikhs* had been acted on. He had then iterated, '...the "Kirti" movement recently organized by Sikh agitators in the Doaba tract should be carefully watched...the "Kirti" movement is a part of a conspiracy against the State which has been conducted since 1923...it was explicit in the expression of its revolutionary aims, and has persistently advocated the cause and ideals of the Indian Ghadrites and glorified the Babbar Akalis as martyrs and heroes. The Punjab "Kirti" party has been formally affiliated to the Communist party. The organization is undeniably a real danger. Given a...grievance, it could do great harm.'[12]

Apart from the mutiny in the Sikh squadron of the Central India Horse, Khushwant Singh links the same disaffection to two other incidents, 'Some Sikhs of the 31st (actually 3/1st) Punjab Regiment deserted. Sikhs of the RIASC serving in Africa refused to load stores on the plea that they were not coolies.'[13] The latter case occurred in the 4th Indian Division Ammunition Company, RIASC, in February 1940, where fifteen were court-martialled. (Though not mentioned by Khushwant Singh, eighty-four were also court-martialled in Hong Kong in January 1941, in the 12th Heavy Regiment of the Hong Kong and Singapore Royal Artillery. North Indians had been enrolled in the garrison artillery there since the previous century. Here, apart from any political influences that may have been at work, the aggravating cause was the Sikh troops being ordered to wear steel helmets, on the plea that the order was applicable to the whole Hong Kong garrison. A similar injudicious order had been given in France in 1914, but on the extent of the resentment becoming evident, had been rescinded. The carrying of steel helmets at all times would appear to have aggravated the abovementioned Ammunition Company mutiny.) Lawrence James also mentions the case of, 'the five Sikhs who had mutinied and murdered their officers when the Japanese invaded Christmas Island (in December 1941). They were taken prisoner after the war, but their death sentences were commuted to penal servitude for life in December 1946.'[14] (He, however, does not mention their unit;they possibly also belonged to the Hong Kong and Singapore Royal Artillery.) A temporary ban was then imposed in 1940 on the enrolment of Sikhs. A Committee of British officers acquainted with Sikhs, all from the Sikh Regiment, presided over by Brigadier Barstow, was appointed to go into the situation. It found evidence of "Kirti" and Communist infiltration, and a sense of uneasiness concerning the Unionist Party Ministry's alignment with the Muslim League, which had begun to talk of a Muslim state in the Punjab. The Sikh grievances were redressed— assurances were given that Sikh interests would not be sacrificed to appease the Muslims, and Sardar Baldev Singh (the future Defence Minister after independence) was appointed a Minister in the Unionist Party Ministry. The ban on the enrolment of Sikhs was lifted, and a Khalsa Defence of India League was organized under the chairmanship of the Maharaja of Patiala, to step up the resumed Sikh recruitment. The Sikh community quickly realized what a loss it would be if either the British continued to curtail recruitment, or if Sikh recruits were not forthcoming in response to the British call. Nevertheless, in 1943, a Sikh field company still mutinied.

Meanwhile, at the end of 1940, although units of the 31st Armoured Division were still without tanks, notwithstanding this perspective planning for a second armoured division (32nd) nevertheless commenced.[15] The 3rd Indian Motor Brigade from the 31st was, however, earmarked for the Middle East. It consisted of three cavalry regiments, mounted in unarmoured trucks without wireless, and moved in February 1941. A little earlier, a squadron commander in Hodson's Horse was asked by an eminent brass-hat how he communicated with his troop leaders; he replied sourly, 'Thought reading.'[16] While new battalions were being undoubtedly raised rapidly by "milking" existing units, the latter were being rendered less effective, depending how often they were "milked" for successive new raisings. Some of the pre-war battalions were "milked" at least thrice in twelve calendar months. According to F.W. Perry, the 2/12th Frontier Force had posted out thirty-seven officers and VCOs, and 385 other ranks, between July 1940 and March 1941, when it moved to Malaya. Many of the other units sent to Malaya and Burma were in the same situation. 'By December 1941 this battalion had only 121 other ranks with over a year of post recruit service...'[17]

In March 1941, the Defence of India plan still contemplated five infantry divisions for Frontier defence, but now envisaged an armoured brigade, instead of an armoured division. The 1941 expansion plan thus featured, 'five further infantry divisions (14th, 17th, 19th, 20th, and 34th), the second armoured divison (32nd),' mentioned earlier, and, 'the armoured brigade for Frontier defence (50th).' The 50th Tank Brigade was in the event first formed with British armoured regiments and an Indian motor battalion, but never deployed on the Frontier. Nor were any of the aforesaid infantry divisions. As F.W. Perry perceptively observes, 'In view of the later employment of these formations, it is interesting to observe how that employment came almost as an afterthought. The reason for their formation was the defence of the North-West Frontier, which continued to be a preoccupation even after Germany's invasion of Russia. The prospective enemy to be faced on the Frontier had, by then, become Germany itself—if they ever got so far.'[18] They did not get so far having been held at Stalingrad, but billions of rupees had already been spent on concrete fortifications in the NWFP on all possible thrust lines—a miniature Maginot or Siegfried Line, pill-boxes, bunkers, underground command posts, hospitals, gun positions, antitank obstacles (dragon's teeth) the complete array for some of the new formations then being raised for the Frontier, but in the event never to be deployed there. (When I last saw some of these defences in the spring of 1945, near Landikotal, they were occupied by the local Pathans and their goats.)

Archibald Percival Wavell's victories over the Italians in Cyrenaica, where the 4th Indian Division was part of his force, and the liquidation of Italian East Africa, where both the 4th and 5th Indian Divisions were part of the force, in the winter of 1940-41, brought some pride to the Indian Army. In January 1941, Auchinleck, who had detailed knowledge of the Indian Army and sympathy with Indians, took over as Commander-in-Chief from his British Army predecessor, though the War Office had instead sought to thrust on Amery and India, either General Lord Gort or General Lord Ironside, for whom no employment was found in Britain. He was not so fettered in his approach to the War Office as the latter had perforce been, and discarded the prevalent fixation that the so-called non-martial races could not be effective infantrymen, ordering the re-raising of the Madras Regiment, the Mahar Regiment and the Sikh Light Infantry, as also the raising of the Assam Regiment, the Bihar Regiment, and the Ajmer Regiment. Indian officers were posted over British officers, whenever the necessity arose. It was he who provided the understanding that expanded the Indian Army to over two million. Some fifty new battalions were needed under the 1941 expansion plan, for apart from the battalions for the five new divisions there were requirements on the lines of communication, and "garrison" duties like guarding large depots. A detachment from the 25/4th Bombay Grenadiers, a garrison battalion, was even sent as far as Diego Garcia in the Indian Ocean to secure the staging facilities there. Guarding the Italian prisoners of war alone, captured in the operations in Italian North and East Africa, needed fourteen battalions.[19] At the end of 1941, it was decided to convert the ITF battalions, already having been embodied for two years, into general service units, it being believed that ITF units could not be embodied for more than two years. Perry comments 'There is no confirmation of this in the ITF Act or in the Rules and Regulations, and it could be an example that what is believed to be true is sometimes stronger than truth itself.'[20] By and large, fifty per cent of the ITF personnel agreed to stay on. By the middle of 1943, there were forty-six garrison battalions, consisting often of elderly pensioners, by when some began being converted into general service battalions, as in the case of the Ajmer Regiment mentioned below, by introducing younger personnel.

Usually the ITF units reformed as battalions of their parent regiments, but the first two battalions of the Ajmer Regiment, however, were formed from ITF and garrison battalions of the Bombay Grenadiers. The opportunity was also taken to even out the manpower "burden" on regiments. An instance of this rationalization was the 11/14th Punjab, an ITF unit, becoming the 14/9th Jat Regiment. The Chamar Regiment, the Afridi and Lingayat Battalions were also raised variously in 1942-43. The Chamar Regiment was associated with the 2nd Punjab Regiment, and the Lingayat Battalion with the Mahratta Light Infantry. This necessitated recruiting classes not previously recruited, but this also led to other problems. 'In units formed from the new classes, recruits lacked the experience necessary to become NCOs and VCOs and these places had to be filled by members of the old classes, causing a lot of ill-feeling.'[21]

In the spring of 1941, the reverses in Cyrenaica, Greece and Crete occurred at the same time as a successful insurrection in Iraq by the pro-German Rashid Ali Gailani against the pro-British Regent, and threatened the whole British position in the Middle East. Linlithgow and Auchinleck promptly offered to divert to Basra an Indian brigade sailing to Malaya, and to reinforce it by another two Indian brigades. The offer was accepted, and the expeditious arrival of the Indian brigades in Iraq restored the situation for the British.

Rashid Ali fled to Iran in May, the Regent was restored, and the three Indian brigades were deployed in Iraq. The promptitude Auchinleck had shown in reacting to the threat in Iraq in June led to his replacing Wavell in the Middle East, and Wavell, in turn, replacing him in India. The Viceroy's Executive Council was now expanded, and the National Defence Council set up (the latter had initially been proposed as the War Advisory Council). In the expanded Executive Council, there were, besides the Viceroy and the Commander-in-Chief, three British members of Finance, Home and Communications, and eight Indians, all the latter non-officials. Thus, for the first time, the Viceroy's Executive Council had an Indian majority.

Additional armoured regiments were now required to complete formation organizations, while the conversion of the former horsed cavalry regiments was still in progress, limited mechanization having commenced in 1938 with the 14th Scinde Horse and the 13th DCO Lancers having taken over one squadron each of Vickers light tanks, in use since the 1920s, and Crossley armoured cars, from British units. The Crossley armoured cars were already unfit for further service, so the hulls were removed and mounted on a commercial Chevrolet chassis. An Armoured Fighting Vehicles' School had also been established at Ahmednagar from the assets of the Machine-Gun School at that station. The seven new regiments were referred to as "The Roaring Forties", since they were all numbered in the Forties (numbered from 42nd to 48th, they had existed in the latter part of the First World War as well, being disbanded in 1919). The three training regiments of 1937 (12th Cavalry, 15th Lancers, 20th Lancers) were converted into two Indian Cavalry Training Centres. As equipment was still a constraint in 1941, and the Mediterranean shipping route was closed, an Eastern Group Supply Council was formally set up in March 1941 to coordinate, manufacture and supply among the Commonwealth countries in the Indian and Pacific Ocean regions. Linlithgow, having anticipated that India must become a huge base, had already held an Eastern Group Supply Conference in New Delhi in October 1940, attended by representatives of Australia, New Zealand, South Africa, and all

British territories east of Suez. Though a stimulus was thereby given to Indian industrial production, Britain was still perforce the main source of supply for India. 'Allocations to what was then an inactive theatre held low priority, and, by October 1941, even to complete the 1940 programme India had received only thirty-six per cent of her needs for field artillery, nineteen per cent for Bren guns, and eleven per cent for mortars. On 11 September Wavell drew the attention of the Cabinet to India's deficiencies, warning against the political consequences if Indian troops now abroad suffered disaster through lack of equipment.'[22]

Before the 1940 expansion programme could be completed, events necessitated the despatch of some of these incomplete formations overseas. In March 1941, the 9th Division had been ordered to Malaya, but, as already narrated, a brigade had to be diverted to Iraq on account of the developments there. A little later Persia was also occupied, so that, by September, three infantry divisions and elements of the 31st Armoured Division were in Persia and Iraq ("Paiforce"). Earlier, in March, a brigade was sent to Burma, followed shortly by a further brigade, in relation to an envisaged Japanese threat. Concomitantly, there was now a German threat to Persia and Iraq through the Caucasus. A base for ten divisions in Iraq was conceived, and a supply route opened to Russia through Persia. 'The only people who can have got any satisfaction out of the job were the RIASC companies, 203 and 204, who carried supplies from Baluchistan to the Russians. In six-wheeled ten ton lorries (which in fact weighed twenty-one tons loaded), they drove 730 miles from Baluchistan to Tabriz and back, again and again and again...starting their journey in a temperature of 126 degrees and ending it in blizzards, snow and ice. Some of the roads were terrifying....The first convoy to arrive...with a load of artillery ammunition was met by a guard of honour....A subedar and a havildar were awarded the Order of the Red Star. At least the Russians appreciated their efforts.'[23] India suggested the force projection in Iraq be reduced to six infantry divisions and an armoured division, which hopefully would be in position by April 1942, if equipment was available. By then, however, all these demands for Indian formations had imposed disruptions even on the 1941 expansion programme.

With the 1941 expansion programme, though not complete, now in effect earmarked for Iraq, the Indian Army conceived a 1942 expansion programme of four further infantry divisions (23rd, 25th, 28th, and 36th), and even a third armoured division (43rd).[24] This programme was truncated by the Japanese successes from December 1941 onwards. The 28th and the earlier 34th Divisions were never raised, as the units earmarked were diverted to replace those shattered by the Japanese advance. Similarly the 36th then became a British division, the Indian units initially earmarked for it being also diverted like those for the 28th and 34th. The 26th Indian Division was, however, hastily put together for the defence of the approach to Calcutta through the Arakan in May 1942. The 1943 expansion programme envisaged an infantry division, an airborne division and an armoured brigade.'But in face of all the difficulties in reviving the 1942 programme this expansion was not undertaken.'[25] Though the 42nd (later known as the 2nd) Airborne Division was formed at Bilaspur, in the then Central Provinces, in 1944, it was not yet complete at the end of the war. The concept of two further armoured divisions, over and above the 31st, was also dropped in 1943. The various changes in perspective planning as to them are instructive.

An armoured division had been included in each of the three annual expansion plans, despite the known shortage of tanks. It was for this reason that the 31st originally was to have only one armoured brigade and two motor brigades. Then, towards the end of 1940, it was to be two armoured brigades and one motor brigade. When the 3rd Motor Brigade moved in early 1941 to Egypt, the organization was to be two armoured brigades and a support group. Thereafter, an armoured brigade without tanks took part in the occupation of Persia, the rest of the division joining up by the end of 1941. In June 1942 the British organization of one armoured brigade per division was decided on. The changes in operational perceptions, and the shortage of qualified personnel, led to the amalgamation of whatever was on the ground of the 32nd and 43rd as the Headquarters 44th Armoured

Division in March 1943.[26] Three of the armoured brigades would be independent tank brigades (50th, 254th, 255th), and other surplus brigade headquarters, like the 268th, would become normal infantry brigades. The March 1944 review confirmed this position, which should have been discernible two years earlier, thus avoiding infructuous raisings, reorganizations and disbandments.

At the time of the Japanese attack in December 1941 and thereafter, there was much adverse comment on the inadequate performance of certain Indian units in Malaya and Burma. Captain M.K. Durrani, of the Bahawalpur Infantry, who was later awarded the George Cross, had recounted some of his observations during the pre-hostilities period: 'The biased treatment of Indians by British officers and the general discontent of Indian troops...was universal in Malaya....We had occasionally seen some' rusty vehicles (armoured cars) creep over a metalled road...they failed suddenly even when moving on a good road, and it would be blocked until the arrival of a crane....To a new officer, the commanding officer humorously said, "Have you brought your running shoes?"'[27] Though the brigade had been there a year, digging of earthwork defences only commenced on the Siam-Malaya border three months before the commencement of hostilities. Some of the trenches collapsed in the tropical rainfall. There were no concrete defences. When Wavell visited these defences as Supreme Commander, he was of the view that, 'no hope can be pinned on them.'

There were problems of officer management as well, for example in the 4/19th Hyderabad Regiment at Singapore recounted by the then Captain (later General) K.S. Thimayya. A Lieutenant Zahir-ud-din was arrested, for keeping a German woman with him, while on detached duty. She had earlier been married to an Indian, and was suspected of being a German agent. (She was also arrested, and was found to be a British agent too.) Zahir's platoon, on his instigation, voiced their collective resentment. The commanding officer asked for a British battalion to move into the lines. Thimayya sought permission to speak to the platoon. The men returned to duty, and the British battalion left. Thimayya became suspect, and was posted

356

back to India, thereby fortuitously not becoming a prisoner of war. (In another battalion of the same regiment in Ceylon a little later, the British commanding officer was shot while sleeping under his mosquito net. An Indian officer, M.G. Jilani, was tried, but the charges were correctly dismissed for lack of evidence.) More problematic was the formation of the force known as the 'Indian National Army' (INA) from among the Indian prisoners of war, which is dealt with in the next chapter. Some of the "Indianized" battalions were involved. Auchinleck after the war was to write, on the completion of the de-briefing of the concerned officers, 'The policy of segregation of Indian officers into separate units, the differential treatment in respect to pay and terms of service as compared with British officers and the prejudice and the lack of manners by some, by no means all, British officers and their wives, all went to produce a very deep and bitter feeling of racial discrimination in the minds of the most intelligent and progressive of the Indian officers.' Separately, fifty years after the fall of Singapore, details have started emerging of British Commonwealth personnel working for the Japanese in Malaya prior to the hostilities. One such is believed to have been a New Zealander, an officer in the 16th Punjab Regiment, attached to an air intelligence unit, who apparently had a relationship with a Japanese woman.

It is generally believed that the Japanese attacked Pearl Harbour first. Allowing for the time zone differences, the attacks, in effect, were simultaneous. The Japanese pre-empted any British entry into Siam. The Indian troops' performance was as good or bad as that of the high command, in relation to the degree of British preparedness, or lack of it, as instanced in the sinking of the *Prince of Wales* and the *Repulse*. Most Indian units fought gallantly, for instance, 5/2nd Punjab, 3/17th Dogras, and many others. Underestimation of the potential enemy played a part in the disaster, a kind of racial contempt. Air Chief Marshal Robert Brooke Popham, Commander-in-Chief in Malaya and Singapore in 1940, had scorned both the Japanese and their aircraft. Extensive "milking", undoubtedly had eroded the effectiveness of most units, apart from the ostensible

Indian Cavalry there not even having any tanks. Stephen Cohen quoted an Indian officer who was captured by the Japanese but did not join the INA, 'I was in an old cavalry unit. We were made into mechanized cavalry, and sent to Malaya. We were mechanized to the extent that we had had our horses taken away from us. The Japanese had tanks and armour, they surrounded us three times, and we were caught the last time.'[28] Formations were often "patchwork" affairs. The 17th Indian Division, which was destined to suffer a reverse in the first battle of the Sittang River in Burma in 1942, only commenced raising in the 1941 expansion programme, and in the same year was ordered to move two brigades to Malaya, and divisional headquarters and one brigade to Burma. The training imparted to these new formations was all for open warfare, and not jungle warfare, for, arguably, the 17th Indian Division was intended for the NWFP. Perry opines, 'On the basis of the evidence "milking" would seem to be a hazardous procedure to use as a method of expansion. Certainly it would appear to be so when carried to the extremes it was in the Indian Army, where the number of battalions was more than doubled in a period of eighteen months....On the basis of the Indian Army experience of 1918, when large numbers of new battalions were produced in a very short time, the method was effective. It does, however, rely on the gamble that the army will not be required to face a first class enemy during the period of expansion. In the Indian Army experience of the first few months of the Japanese war the gamble was lost.'[29]

Here it is instructive to quote in relation to the fall of Malaya and Singapore, where so many Indians were taken prisoner, Brigadier Sir John Smyth, VC, a former Member of Parliament, who had commanded the 17th Indian Division in the reverse suffered in the first battle of the Sittang in Burma: 'By 1941 the British were becoming acutely anxious about the defence of Malaya and Singapore, which looked like being threatened with imminent invasion by the Japanese. Dill was now Chief of the Imperial General Staff, and he had no hesitation in promoting Percival to lieutenant general over the heads of all his contemporaries and sending him out as General

Officer Commanding in Malaya. In so doing Dill signed Percival's military death warrant—and then himself died before he could hold out a helping hand. The loss of Singapore to the Japanese came as no surprise to those British Chiefs of Staff who were fully informed of the situation....Now as the years have passed and people can study the Malayan Campaign...they have begun to wonder whether Percival was to blame at all. It is a somewhat ungenerous—but not unusual—characteristic of the British people that, having countenanced a state of military unpreparedness...in times of peace, they should have to salve their consciences by seeking scapegoats for the inevitable disasters which follow when war comes upon them, and a retreat from Mons is followed by a Dunkirk, a Singapore and a Rangoon....And when the Japanese war came we suffered disaster together, he in Malaya and I in Burma...in the circumstances which existed when the Japanese invaded Malaya, there was probably no general on earth—or indeed in history—who could have turned that grievous defeat into a British victory. The others were just lucky that they were not there...(In Europe) that wonderful ditch the English Channel gave the defeated British Army time to rearm and live to fight another day. Yet, despite the magnitude of their defeat, the BEF only started their advance into Belgium on 10 May and were all back in the Dunkirk salient some twenty days later—the British people gave them a great welcome home. It has always been considered an honour to have been at Dunkirk. Yet Singapore, where a much smaller force resisted very much longer, was considered a disgrace. Percival's army in Singapore, with no British Navy, no Air Force and no safe ditch behind which to take refuge when defeat came upon them, were forced to surrender. And they then suffered a hellish three years in Japanese hands, during which time ten thousand of them died. Wainwright's ordeal in the Philippines was much the same as Percival's. But the great difference between the two was that when it was all over, the United States gave Wainwright and his troops a returned heroes' welcome—whereas the British didn't give the survivors of Singapore any welcome at all.'[30] Nor did India.

Doubt as to the qualitative inferiority of the Indian Army was shortly to afflict Churchill. Singapore had fallen on 15 February 1942, Rangoon was evacuated on 7 March, and, thereafter, the Andaman and Nicobar Islands were captured, the Japanese executing Major A.G. Bird, the Secretary to the British Chief Commissioner there. Much shipping was sunk in the Bay of Bengal, and the Japanese could have landed on India's long eastern coast at a place of their choosing. It was only after the war that it was learnt from the Japanese that they had had no intention to invade India by sea, but only by land. The threat to India's eastern coast, however, was serious enough for Churchill to warn that Calcutta, Madras and Ceylon might also fall to the Japanese, after Singapore and Burma. This meant considerable movement of troops, including Indian formations, to Ceylon. On 6 April 1942 the first Japanese bombs fell on the east coast at Vizagapatam and Cocanada (now Kakinada), a Japanese signal at the time the Cripps Mission was visiting India. No planes or anti-aircraft guns were in a position to engage the intruding planes from the Andamans. Inevitably there was a large exodus from each of these cities. There were believed to be only eight heavy anti-aircraft guns in India at that time. Then a report that a large Japanese invasion fleet was heading for South India caused a considerable exodus from Madras, including the government offices.

Sir Stafford Cripps in March-April 1942, made the offer of independence immediately after the war ended, with a constitution to be framed by Indians, with provision for provinces opting out of the Indian Union if they desired to do so. After some deliberation, the Congress rejected this offer. The offer appeared to concede Pakistan, but, if constitution-making had gone forward, it is possible no province would have opted to stay out of the Union. The Cripps offer was designed to preserve the unity of India, and yet appeal to the Muslims. After the Cripps offer the Congress sought arrest, and the British made no further move to end the deadlock till after the war in Europe was over. (In the elections held soon after the war, the Muslim League, sequentially, was more successful than hitherto.)

Malaya and Burma having been lost, the defence of India's eastern frontier was the major concern. There was not much confidence in the ability of the British-Indian forces to do so. Linlithgow decided on increased association of Indian opinion, and expanded his Executive Council further. In July 1942 membership was raised from twelve to fifteen, bringing in three more Indians, thus increasing the number to eleven. The War Department was divided into the War Department under Wavell, the Commander-in-Chief, and a Defence Department under Sir Firoz Khan Noon. Two Indians, the Jam Saheb of Nawanagar, and Sir Ramaswami Mudaliar, a member of the Executive Council, were appointed to sit in the British War Cabinet and the Pacific War Council. All this did not lead to a reorientation in thinking in the Indian Army in India till after the abortive offensive of the improvised 14th Indian Division in October-December 1942 in the Arakan directed at Akyab, whereafter the Chief Psychiatrist of Eastern Command reportedly considered almost the whole division to be a "psychiatric case". Conjoined with all these problems, there were several others requiring the deployment of troops—from June 1942 onwards for several months, the "Hurs" terrorism in Sind required martial law and two brigades to put down, over and above the very considerable police forces deployed; from July onwards three brigades were required for operations in Waziristan against the Faqir of Ipi; the civil disturbances resulting in some areas from the 'Quit India' movement necessitated the deployment of fifty-seven battalions, with critical operational communications to Assam being cut for several days at a time; and in 1943 dealing with "locust invasions" in Sind and Baluchistan, and famine relief in Bengal, required several battalions.

The failure of the 14th Indian Division "offensive" in the Arakan, and its return to its starting point, after suffering losses, was sadly a foregone conclusion in the light of the improvisations after it was launched. There was considerable disappointment at the inability of the Indian Army to hit back successfully. It seemed unable to beat the Japanese, and doubts began to be felt again by Churchill as to its military value. On 9 September 1942, Churchill had petulantly remarked to L.S. Amery, 'I hate Indians. They are a beastly people...' Stephen Cohen comments on Churchill's ingrained attitude towards the Indian Army: 'One British (Army) officer posted earlier in the century to an obscure and desolate post in South India made good use of his time by reading and studying before he wangled his way out. He was Winston Churchill, whose later disparaging opinion of the Indian Army may have been formed at that time.'[31] In the summer of 1942 the British Treasury, supported by Churchill, complained of the huge expenditure that was being incurred by Britain in 'keeping the invader from Indian soil.' The Finance Member, Sir Jeremy Raisman, fully supported by Linlithgow and L.S. Amery, the Secretary of State, declined to agree to any alterations in the agreement of November 1939. Churchill, thereupon, in December 1942, asked whether reliance could be placed on the greatly expanded Indian Army. Linlithgow was confident it could be relied on. Churchill, on the other hand, depressed by the 14th Division's failed offensive, was far from satisfied. He talked of the inutility of maintaining so many Indian troops, and of the need for a drastic reduction. Subsequent developments justified Linlithgow's and Wavell's confidence, though Churchill, in order to convince Roosevelt of the pitfalls in distressing the Muslims by extending concessions to the Congress party, told Roosevelt that seventy-five per cent of the Indian Army was Muslim, though it was actually thirty-five per cent. When this was subsequently conveyed to him, he did not correct the percentage he had given Roosevelt, with the result that this inaccuracy became self-perpetuating, a myth handed down to posterity as historical fact.

The large-scale offensive operations ultimately envisaged against the Japanese by land, sea and air, necessitated a review of the operational command structure, and concomitantly affected the choice of Viceroy to succeed Linlithgow, who had held the appointment for over seven years. Wavell for his part, as Commander-in-Chief, was the overall commander of the abortive offensive in the Arakan, but was simultaneously the War Member of the Viceroy's Council. The sequential "post mortem" led to the decision that the conduct of the operations against the Japanese should no longer be with the India Command, which would now only be responsible for

Frontier defence and internal security, as also support to the new South-East Asia Command. The creation of the appointment of Supreme Commander was eventually announced in August 1943. Wavell was fitted by past appointments for this post, but neither Churchill nor Roosevelt was keen to appoint him on account of his "reasoned pessimism" as to any early offensive after that of the 14th Division, in view of the prevailing constraints. Admiral Lord Louis Mountbatten was appointed Supreme Commander, Wavell Viceroy, and Auchinleck re-appointed Commander-in-Chief. (Philip Ziegler, Mountbatten's biographer, viewed Mountbatten's appointment as a process of, in a way, successful, "upward failure"—the damage in action to HMS Javelin, the loss of HMS "Kelly", the failure of the Dieppe raid, and so on.) Churchill, however, considered that Wavell should only be a stopgap Viceroy, till the end of the war, when a political appointment would be made. Churchill thought that a professional soldier as Viceroy would keep India quiet till the end of the war, without getting immersed in politics. Wavell was to be a "law and order" Viceroy. In the event, Churchill got a shock, for Wavell was a soldier who quickly understood Indian politics. Wavell had views, for which he has not been given sufficient credit, as to the necessity for constitutional advancement, without waiting for the end of the war. Shortly after taking over as Viceroy, he wrote to London, 'Above all there is a question of credibility. We have lost the trust and confidence of Indians by promising so much and doing so little. He, however, sadly came up against Churchill's "passionate feelings about India". Separately, Churchill had been feeling some remorse for his shabby treatment of Auchinleck in North Africa. He had not accepted Auchinleck's date for the Alamein offensive of mid-September 1942, but later had accepted as timely Alexander's and Montgomery's date of 24 October 1942. Auchinleck, sequentially, had been without an appointment for ten months. In November 1942, Harold Nicolson, then the British Resident Minister in Cairo, had recorded in his diary a conversation he had had with Churchill as to Auchinleck being relieved of the Middle East Command: 'It is difficult to remove a bad general at the height of a campaign, but it is atrocious to remove a good one. We cannot afford to lose such a man from the fighting line....I sent for Montgomery and I gather that there was some confusion and difficulty between him and Auchinleck.' Robert Boothby, who had worked with Churchill in the 1920s, has said he never could take, 'the streak of cruelty in Churchill,' who he believed, 'sacked or broke people, sometimes with relish.' That Montgomery had the Alamein position to launch his offensive from, was due entirely to Auchinleck, who had relieved Neil Ritchie and taken over himself. Montgomery would continue to be Auchinleck's nemesis. He had applied at Sandhurst for the Indian Army, but had not passed out high enough in relation to the available vacancies. As a corps commander under Auchinleck in Britain in 1940, he used to go over Auchinleck's head to the War Office. Meanwhile, Churchill again felt that the then size of the Indian Army should be reduced. Alan Hartley, the Deputy Commander-in-Chief at GHQ(India) had ill-advisedly earlier countered that the Indian Army had been over-extended to meet Imperial needs, and had, thereby, become a "second class" army. Though Churchill was prevailed upon at the British Cabinet meeting of 20 May 1943 that the Indian Army should not be reduced, he kept on coming back to the point, in January 1944 recording that "the mass of low grade troops" must be reduced. Auchinleck's letter in September 1943 that the three operationally fit Indian divisions in the Mediterranean should be returned to enable them to be deployed against the Japanese was not taken well. They were not made available.

Meanwhile a committee to tone up the performance of Indian units and formations in July 1943 had recommended the following:

● The infantry should be given first claim on cadet officers and educated recruits. The quality of officers and NCOs should be improved. Pay should be increased. "Milking" should cease.

● Basic recruit training should be increased to nine months, and should be followed by two months of jungle warfare training.

• The reinforcement system should be improved, and drafts should include an adequate proportion of experienced NCOs.

• Brigades should include a British, Gurkha and an Indian battalion.[32]

'These proposals were accepted almost in their entirety, and by the end of 1943 India had developed a more comprehensive training organization than any other country at that time. The specific orientation ...was towards jungle warfare.'[33] Much of the credit for this general toning up must go to Auchinleck. In the period after his reappointment in June 1943, the 14th and 39th Indian Divisions were converted into Jungle Warfare Training Divisions outside Chhindwara, in the then Central Provinces, and Saharanpur in the UP respectively. The organization was that of an infantry division, except that the units were grounded and became training units, designed to give two months' post-basic recruit training in jungle warfare before the trained soldiers were drafted with non-commissioned officers to the 14th Army. As a result of such measures, the Army was qualitatively very different by February 1944, when the Japanese resumed their offensive. The mainly Indian 14th Army, under General William Slim, repulsed the Japanese, and then inflicted on them the biggest defeat that their ground forces suffered in the Second World War, the Japanese suffering much greater casualties than in the Pacific at the hands of the Americans. Separately, the Corps of Electrical and Mechanical Engineers had been created in May 1943, by separation of the concerned personnel from the Indian Army Ordnance Corps.

To comprehend the extent of the defeat of the Japanese in Burma at the second battle of the Sittang River, three years after the earlier British-Indian reverse, Louis Allen needs to be quoted, 'X Day is what the Japanese in Burma called it. In the calendar it was 20 July 1945, just over three weeks before the war in the Far East came to an end. On that day, thousands of Japanese troops belonging to 28th Army came out of the rain-sodden fastness of the hills of the Pegu Yomas and attempted to break through the cordon of British and Indian divisions which held the line of the long road that led from Mandalay to Rangoon. It was the very last battle which the British Army fought in the Second World War, the last battle of the Japanese forces in South-East Asia, the last battle of a united Indian Army before partition into India and Pakistan split up for ever one of the finest armies in the history of warfare. The battle involved some extraordinary coincidences and some fantastic disproportions in casualties. Yet, as far as the British official history is concerned, the drama of the breakout over the Sittang seems to have been missed. "No attempt will be made to describe in detail the fighting during the breakout," writes the official historian, "It is a story of interceptions on the main Pegu-Toungoo road with brief, hard-fought actions in darkness and pouring rain."...Of an initial force of at least 20,000 men, the Japanese finally managed to collect into camps in Tenasserim, at the time of the surrender, about 7,000 survivors. In other words, in a matter of three weeks, an entire Japanese army had lost over half its strength. During the same period, the combined British and Indian forces, including a Burmese guerrilla force, had lost precisely ninety-five men—a ratio of about a hundred to one. There was another difference too from most of the other battles the Japanese had fought in Burma. Their losses in prisoners were relatively high—only relatively, because their stern code excluded a soldier who became a prisoner of war from Japanese society should he ever attempt to return home. This ensured that men were captured, as a rule, only when unconscious, dying from fever or wounds, or unable to reach the pin of the hand-grenade that would allow them to commit suicide and so redeem their shame....740 prisoners were brought into the cages of 17 and 19 Indian Divisions in a couple of weeks, and these included the highest ranking officers ever taken in the Burma campaign—captains and lieutenants.'[34]

As indicated earlier, India was to be the support base for South-East Asia Command (SEAC). Prior to the separation, India Command was to have been the base for thirty-four divisions for operations against the Japanese, which included an amphibious operation through Rangoon. A re-examination by SEAC put the offensive force at twenty-five divisions, 'with three or four of the divisions for the offensive operations bypassing India, and with at least part of the operations, when launched, maintained from bases outside India.'[35] The repulse of the Japanese offensive in Manipur and the Arakan, indicated that Burma could be recaptured by the land route, and that there was no need for a major amphibious operation directed at Malaya and the Dutch East Indies. As described by Perry, in July 1945, 'before mounting the operation for the invasion of Malaya, divisions to be supported were reduced to fifteen and two-thirds, with a further seven and two-thirds to be reduced from Europe. Here again there were elements of fantasy....The war, however, was nearly over....'[36]

In June 1944, GHQ attempted to obtain 600 officers from Australia, but only 168 were seconded.[37] This attempt had come about because the wastage rates of Indian candidates in the selection process was high, and the British Army, as a source, was drying up in 1944, having latterly provided 200 officer cadets a month, against 160 Indian officer cadets available a month in the same period. Over half the Indian applicants did not get through the Provincial Selection Boards, and of the remainder the Services Selection Boards rejected seventy-five per cent.[38] At the end of the war there were approximately 32,750 British and 14,000 Indian officers in the Indian Army. 'When queried about the special merits and demerits of Indian officers, British commanders agreed almost unanimously on the superior ability of the Indian (officer) to handle his troops.'[39] By this time two million combatants had been enrolled in the Indian Army and half-a-million non-combatants. The ISF then aggregated 100,000, of whom over 41,000 were serving outside their states. Wavell, as Viceroy, was to record in September 1944, '...nothing will ever be said of all that India has done with the scanty resources allotted to it.'[40]

The 5th Indian Division had returned to India in 1943 for deployment against the Japanese, whereafter the 4th, 8th and 10th

Divisions had taken part in the Italian campaign, the 4th then moving to Greece. Alexander had asked for the 31st Armoured and the 6th Indian Divisions also for Italy, but this was not agreed to, though the 43rd Lorried Infantry Brigade was made available. With the end of the war in Europe, the 6th Indian Division in the Persian Gulf area had been broken up into independent brigades in November 1944, and, by 1945, the brigades in Persia and Iraq had a large number of ISF units. After the Japanese surrender, Indian divisions were the first into Siam and French Indochina, as well as into the western islands of the Dutch East Indies. An Indian brigade relieved Australian forces in Borneo in January 1946. Indian units remained in South-East Asia even for some period after independence. Here the tragic events of late 1945 in Soerabaya need mentioning for their pathos, with so many savagely killed in notional post-war peacetime conditions, after having survived the official ending of the war. 'On 25 October the 49th Indian Brigade (Brigadier A. W. Mallaby) arrived at Soerabaya, charged with succouring the Dutch internees, disarming and evacuating the Japanese, and keeping the peace. It was not at first clear whether this was internal security or war....On 28 October a 49th Brigade convoy, peacefully going about its routine business, was attacked: eleven officers and fifty other ranks were captured and shot out of hand. Another convoy, consisting of Dutch women and children being brought down to the docks, was also attacked; most of the lorries were burnt, the Dutch and their small Mahratta escort hacked to pieces. It was war, not internal security. Mallaby arranged a truce, but within hours the radio station and jail were attacked and their Mahratta and Rajputana Rifles guards, ammunition expended, were barbarically butchered. Mallaby, trying to negotiate another cease-fire, was murdered....In three days 49th Brigade had lost eighteen officers and 374 men. 5th Indian Division (Major General Mansergh) arrived to carry out the tasks which had proved beyond 49th Brigade...Many fine soldiers died in this quarrel which had nothing to do with them, men who had fought in East Africa, the Desert, the Arakan, Assam and Burma. Among these was one of the finest soldiers in the Indian Army, Lieutenant Colonel

Sarbjit Singh Kalha, DSO and Bar, 2/1st Punjab, just the sort of officer his country most needed.'[41]

One noteworthy development was the ending of the ostensible superiority of British troops vis-a-vis Indian troops. The junglecraft of the Indian and Gurkha soldier was better than that of the British soldier. By early 1944, Indian divisions were among the best in the world, and British divisional commanders on the Burma Front called for Indian rather than British battalions, according to Slim, an Indian Army officer, whom Mountbatten described, as recorded by Major General Geoffrey Evans, 'the finest general the Second World War produced.' Mountbatten commented, 'Besides his great qualities as a leader in the field, Slim was a master of strategy, tactics and logistics, the Meiktila/Mandalay operation being a classic example. It was a superb achievement by him and his 14th Army (mainly Indian). His plan was as brilliant in its conception as in its subsequent execution. It was a bold plan relying for its fulfilment on secrecy, on speed and taking great administrative risks. Throughout the many anxious months, his competence, the confidence, sympathy and understanding he exuded, and his imperturbality, whatever the situation, inspired all who came in contact with him, both in good times and bad.'[42] Auchinleck had hoped that, eventually, Slim would succeed him as Commander-in-Chief of the Indian Army. And yet, ironically, despite this encomium, Slim also was being "sacked", by his immediate British Army superior in Allied Land Forces, South-East Asia, General Sir Oliver Leese, inasmuch as Slim was not to command the 14th Army in the then prospective invasion of Malaya, but was being sidetracked to continue mopping up operations in Burma, and then to garrison Burma with the 12th Army to be raised. Slim wrote to Auchinleck as the senior officer of the Indian Army, that he could not continue to serve under an officer who did not have the fullest confidence in his capabilities, and that, therefore, he now wished to retire. Auchinleck happened to be in London in May 1945, and took up Slim's case with the Chief of the Imperial General Staff (CIGS), Lord Alanbrooke, and, in June, Mountbatten both discussed and corresponded with Auchinleck on the subject.

"If" is undoubtedly the central word in "Life". Leese was now relieved of his appointment, and Slim succeeded him, later to become CIGS. An actual case of the biter being bit.

The far-seeing Auchinleck, in early 1945, even before anyone knew when the war would be over, had convened an Army Reorganization Committee (India) under Lieutenant General Sir Henry Willcox, to recommend the post-war composition of the Indian Army. Class-wise, it was to be a "national" army, it being assumed by Auchinleck that India would receive some form of self-government after the war. The Willcox Committee recommended an Indian Army of approximately 280,000. The sequential composition table came to be known as Plan 280. In consonance with the concept of a "national" army, most of the wartime regiments were to be retained as they embodied more wide-based recruitment, and some of the pre-war regiments with more restricted recruitment were to be disbanded as an offsetting measure. Apart from certain infantry battalions to be disbanded from regiments that were to be retained, specific regiments then recommended for disbandment through no fault of theirs, but only on account of their comparative seniority of raising, were the 19th Lancers, the Central India Horse, the 16th Punjab Regiment and the 7th Gurkha Rifles. One facet that even then came up for discussion was a self-governing India being unlikely to need all the Gurkha Rifles regiments, and as to how many of these Gurkha regiments would Britain be prepared to take over when India was granted self-government. That decision was, by circumstance, taken in 1947, but it is evidence of Auchinleck's prescience. Separately, immediately after the Japanese surrender, Auchinleck convened a committee as to the future status of VCOs, presided over by Major General H.R. Briggs. The latter on 28 August 1945 sent a questionnaire on the subject to Pandit Nehru, who had just been released after three years in jail. Nehru did not favour a new category of officer being introduced in place of the VCO.

To conclude this chapter, one agrees with Perry's summation of the role of the Indian Army in the Second World War, in which it suffered 24,338 killed, 64,354 wounded, and 11,754 missing: 'At

370

least until the outbreak of war with Japan, from which time the defence of India became a major priority, the role of the Indian Army was to continue to be an Imperial Reserve. Indeed throughout the first half of the century this was the Army's role, however much it was denied publicly, a role required by Britain's possession of a colonial empire and by Britain's inability or unwillingness to accept the role. Even after the start of the Japanese war the role continued, in that Indian formations were retained in the Gulf and the Middle East to serve Imperial purposes even though they would have been invaluable for the defence of India's frontiers.'[43]

India was, in effect, given three African divisions in lieu. Perry adds, 'Without the Indian Army Britain would have been quite unable to meet her many commitments in the Middle East and Far East.' The doughty Auchinleck went even further, 'I think the English never cared; the English who lived in England, the politicians especially, I don't think they ever took any interest in India at all. I think they used it....They couldn't have come through both wars if they hadn't had the Indian Army...I think they never really understood it.'[44] Churchill ultimately paid tribute to, 'The unsurpassed bravery of Indian soldiers and officers.' The end of the Second World War not only saw the Dutch out of the Netherlands East Indies, but the commencement of the French departure from Indo-China. Wavell also discerned that the British could not hold on to the subcontinent. The eventual decision to grant independence to India sequentially affected Burma and Britain's African empire as well.

Sir John Longford-Holt, MP, was later to record: 'In 1948...when I was a very young MP in the Conservative Party then led by Sir Winston, I happened to be sitting alone with him....I asked Churchill who in his view was the greatest general the British produced in the war. The answer was immediate and definite—Auchinleck.'[45]

THIRTEEN

The 'Indian National Army' (INA) Or The Azad Hind Fauj

AN OFFICIAL summary of 6 November 1942 iterated, 'No one knew anything about the INA before the fall of Singapore. It came like a bombshell after the capitulation. It seemed that the Japanese had made some prearrangements to tamper with the loyalty of the Indian Army.'[1] Singapore fell on 15 February 1942, the anniversary of the mutiny in the 5th Light Infantry at Singapore in 1915. Some 85,000 men, the remainder of the British-Indian-Australian forces, surrendered. About 20,000 had already been killed or previously captured. The situation then has been described by Philip Mason, who was the Joint Secretary in the War Department in New Delhi in 1945-1946 (Sir Chandulal Trivedi was the Secretary) at the time of what were later referred to as the "INA trials". 'The final surrender was the culmination of a disaster as complete and dramatic as any that has befallen British arms anywhere in the world... Of the troops who fell into Japanese hands, more than half, nearly 60,000 altogether, were Indians; in the course of their captivity, rather less than half of them, about 25,000, threw off their allegiance and joined what was called the INA; this was the army of "Free India" a "provisional government" that claimed to be a national state under the Presidency of Subhas Chandra Bose...and to be allied with the Japanese. In military law, they thus committed the offences of mutiny, desertion and waging war against the King.'[2] There are several strands interwoven in the woof and warp of the INA's or the Azad Hind Fauj's history.

Rash Behari Bose had gained prominence as part of the group that made an attempt on the life of the Viceroy, Lord Charles Hardinge, in 1912. After the failure of the Ghadr Party's uprising on 19 February 1915, Rash Behari, via Shanghai, reached Japan, a centre for many Asian political refugees, even though Japan was allied with the British during the First World War. Rash Behari was a dedicated revolutionary, and, unlike many of his colleagues, totally secretive. He met other revolutionaries sheltering in Japan, like Sun Yat Sen. Rash Behari had been introduced to one of the most powerful men in Japan, the leader of the Black Dragon Society. He was, thus, safe from the British. In 1919 he married a Japanese woman, an extraordinary occurrence at that period in Japan. She sadly died six years later. Rash Behari became a Japanese citizen in 1923. He tilted with Mahatma Gandhi through correspondence. In 1926 he organized an All-Asia Conference at Nagasaki, and edited *The Voice of Asia*. In 1927 he became the President of the Japanese branch of the Indian Independence League (IIL).

Another Indian resident in Japan, in the words of Gerard Corr, was, 'the splendidly eccentric Raja Mahendra Pratap...his revolutionary credentials were impeccable...he did have some influence in the top overseas Indian councils.'[3] He has last been mentioned at Kabul in the First World War, as the President of the Provisional Government of Free India. He had travelled around the world after the First World War, visiting Japan thrice, and staying on after 1936 to found 'his World Federation Centre for the propagation of his personal thesis that peace and freedom for the whole human race would come only with the establishment of a federal world government.... The freedom of India...would follow automatically as Asia liberated itself step by step... he looked to the liberation of India coming about through the combined forces of Nepal, Iran and Afghanistan. In his biography, *My Life Story for Fifty Five Years*, Pratap defined his self-governing Asian Federation as one consisting of Aryan units. One unit would stretch from Assam to Iran; the other sectors were the Far East and West Asia. They would cooperate with a Europe federated under Hitler, Mussolini, America and Russia....His host country turned a deaf ear, but when Pratap openly disagreed with Japanese plans towards India after the fall of Malaya and Singapore, they silenced him', in March 1942.[4] He still had contacts and followers in Italy and Germany from his First World War and pre-Second World War sojourns; it is to these two countries that we now move.

Whereas, initially the British referred to the INA as "Jifs" (Japanese Indian forces), they had earlier commenced using the term "Hifs" (Hitler's Indian forces) for those Indian prisoners of war captured in North Africa in 1941, who were collaborating with their captors, before the fall of Singapore. The Indian prisoners had been moved from North Africa to Italy, by the time Subhas Chandra Bose arrived in Germany as "Mr Mazotta", having escaped in January 1941 from India, via Afghanistan. In Italy, an Indian revolutionary, Mohammed Shedai, was in residence, and was already in contact with these prisoners for getting them to collaborate with the Italians. Shedai and Bose came into conflict over control of any Indian prisoners of war willing to collaborate, Bose prevailing with the Germans. It was formally agreed between the Italian and German governments that the Germans would get the "cooperative" Indian prisoners. They were transported to nearby Dresden, and, on 19 December 1941, the Wehrmacht agreed to train those who joined Bose's force, and call them the Indian Legion. In Europe, no Indian officer agreed to collaborate. Major (later General) P.P. Kumaramangalam, DSO, MBE, was among those who refused.

Bose had been always been keen on a military wing for the Indian nationalist movement since his spell in the University Training Corps during the First World War, when he had also sought to enrol in the 49th Bengal Regiment, but had been rejected on account

374

of his weak eyesight. He had then adapted a verse:

> There is but one task for all,
> One life for each to give,
> Who stands if freedom fall?
> Who dies if India live?

He now iterated, 'Throughout my life it was my ambition to equip an army that will capture freedom from the enemy.' Leonard Gordon records, 'Bose stressed that the British would never leave India unless they were driven out by force. What was needed was a catalytic force from outside combined with a massive rebellion within India. He was trying to prepare the catalytic force...it was decided that the Germans would direct the entire training programmes and the Indians would be a contingent...within the German army. All men were started at the lowest rank, and the Germans were to decide who was fit to be an officer on the basis of merit.'[5]

Before the prisoners were brought to Germany, Bose had visited them in Italy. From among approximately 16,000 Indian prisoners, some 2,500 reportedly volunteered. The rest chose to remain prisoners. 'On the whole, this was disappointing to Bose, who expected a much larger...number of volunteers, who were being given, in his terms, the opportunity to move from a mercenary army to a nationalist one.'[6]

Bose insisted that men of different communities be mixed. Walter Harbich, the commander of the Indian Sonderkommando 'B', has written: 'In the beginning, Indian volunteers were divided into platoons according to their religion.... Bose wanted division into sections so that every platoon had a Hindu, a Sikh and a Muslim section. After a brief acclimatization to this arrangement His Excellency Bose desired a complete dissolution of the units based on religion so that the ideal which he had in mind was realised and the Indians were united in the smallest tactical unit, the section, regardless of their religious profession. Contrary to the original doubts, the result was surprisingly good.'[7]

There were problems later as to *jhatka* and *halal* meat when a regiment was raised, but were apparently got over by the Germans doing the slaughtering. The Indians wore the German type of uniform, and, 'on the left sleeve of the tunic was stitched a silken emblem in the Indian national colours with the picture of a springing tiger.'[8] The Swastika and German eagle were also worn. Abid Hasan, Bose's political secretary, has left a record of the limited success of his endeavors to win over prisoners to join in the Legion: 'Let us suppose there were some people so loyal to the British that they would never join. There were people like that....A few were hesitating to join because they had taken the oath very seriously....A major part of them were worried about their families....Another was that they had opposed and fought against the Germans. To join hands with the enemy, went against the thinking of a soldier.'[9]

Shedai now wrote to the Italian and German governments that Bose was incapable of communicating with ordinary soldiers: 'Firstly, he is not from the province of these soldiers. He does not understand them. Their mentality is quite different from that of his....Secondly, Mr. Mazotta belongs to a class which has nothing in common with the soldiers. He cannot understand their needs because he is not one of them.'[10] Leopold Fischer, who later converted and took the name Swami Aghenanda Bharati, was then a translator, and recorded Bose's speech to the Indian prisoners as: '...you have fought on the wrong side, the British are our enemies, this is the chance to use your skills to fight them and make India free. Hitler is your friend, a friend of the Aryans, and you will march to India as your Motherland's liberators, may be via the Caucasus and the Khyber Pass, may be by some other route.'[11] Bose decided that the best recourse would be to accept German officers. Indians would be part of the German Army, so that, if they were captured, they would be treated as prisoners of war. They, therefore, took a modified form of the German oath, 'I swear by God this holy oath, that I will obey the leader of the German State and People, Adolf Hitler, as commander of the German Armed Forces, in the fight for the freedom of India, in which fight the leader is Subhas Chandra Bose....'[12]

Meanwhile, in Japan in September 1941, Rash Behari, conscious that Burma could be used by the Japanese as a base for an attack on India, felt that the Japanese, in turn, could be used to gain India's freedom. He approached the head of the Black Dragon Society, and Rash Behari was asked by the Japanese General Staff to explain how Indian independence could be achieved. Rash Behari 'stressed that Japanese help was vital if the British were to be driven out of India....He requested the aid of the Japanese Army for the attainment of the objective of his life's work—a free homeland.'[13]

Rash Behari heard nothing, but on 18 September, the thirty-three year old Major (later Lieutenant General) Iwaichi Fujiwara had been summoned by General Sugiyama, the Chief of the General Staff, and given a written directive, 'to set up a small intelligence group to work in South Siam and Malaya. The group was to be known as the Fujiwara Kikan (agency) and would consist of some fifteen people, a mixture of army officers, intelligence school graduates and civilians.'[14] Sugiyama told Fujiwara to go to Bangkok and assist, 'in establishing a good working relationship with the Indian Independence movement and any other anti-British organizations, Malay and Chinese....The General went on: "Your duty in the event of the outbreak of war will be to facilitate the Japanese campaign in Malaya... From the point of view of the establishment of the Greater East Asia Co-Prosperity Sphere, it will be better if you pay some attention to Indian affairs and to the future relations between India and Japan."'[15]

Fujiwara's task was to suborn Indian soldiers, while developing good relations with such Indians as were favourably disposed to the Japanese. After the war, Fujiwara was to write that he had replied: 'In order to realize the great concept of a New Asia, we will encourage Indian Independence, and Japanese-Indian co-operation, beginning with operations in the Malayan sector.'[16] 'In mentioning Independence, Fujiwara had already gone a shade further than his orders allowed...but his superiors were never to share his breadth of vision.'[17] When Sugiyama gave Fujiwara his directive, the Japanese General Staff were not concerned about India, nor its liberation on the lines proposed by Rash Behari: nor was India included in the Co-

Prosperity Sphere. But, 'a successful southern expansion would result in substantial Indian communities being gathered into the empire's fold. Of more immediate importance were the large numbers of Indian troops in the British forces in Malaya, Singapore and Hong Kong. Some sort of Indian policy, therefore, had to be worked out: and the view began to develop that not only should India be included in the Co-Prosperity Sphere but that a military operation was viable.'[18]

A Japanese Army cell, the Minami Kikan, had already been planted in Rangoon in 1940, for such a purpose, and now the Fujiwara Kikan arrived in Bangkok in October 1941. This would not be the first time that Fujiwara would be working with Indian revolutionaries. 'In December 1940 Fujiwara had helped three Indian revolutionaries escape from a Hong Kong prison. He had got them away to Canton where they asked if they might be transported to Bangkok, which, once again, as in 1914-15, was fast becoming an important centre of nationalist activity.' Fujiwara had got them to Bangkok, where they were temporarily sheltered by the Japanese military attache. In April-May 1941, Fujiwara visited southern Siam and reported on the Indian Army in northern Malaya. The three Indian revolutionaries from Hong Kong had introduced the Japanese officer to Giani Pritam Singh, a Sikh priest who had arrived in Bangkok in 1939, and formed the Independence League of India. 'The League was the direct descendant of the Ghadr Party of Bangkok...and it numbered some old Ghadrites in its ranks. The chief one was Baba Amar Singh....'[19] Amar Singh had been part of the Ghadrite group that had sought to smuggle arms to India through Burma in 1915. Arrested by the Burma Police, the leader of the group, Sohan Lal, had been hanged after trial, and Amar Singh had been sentenced to transportation in the Andamans. Released after twenty-two years, he had rejoined his Ghadrite companions in Bangkok. On their own initiative, Pritam and Amar Singh had started anti-British propaganda among the Indian troops in Malaya, by the circulation of letters which stated that the Indian soldier 'is being misled by the English and made to fight for Rs. 14 per month.'[20]

On 28 November Fujiwara was informed that war was imminent. He had already deployed his operatives in all the important locations in Malaya. He and his 'F' Kikan would be under command of the Japanese 25th Army, part of Field Marshal Terauchi's Southern Expeditionary Force. On 4 December an agreement was signed between the Japanese and Pritam Singh. 'As the 25th Army progressed through Malaya the League would absorb all Indians...and would organize a volunteer force from among the officers of the Indian Army and other Indians in Malaya and Singapore. Further, the Japanese would not treat Indian soldiers and civilians as nationals of an enemy country....On the winning of Indian independence, the Japanese would refrain from demanding any kind of concession.'[21] On 8 December the Japanese landed in Malaya and southern Siam. The same day Rash Behari was summoned in Tokyo, and invited to organize the Indian population in the territory being occupied in Malaya. Meanwhile, on leave in Malaya, just before the onset of hostilities, Captain Mohan Singh, 1/14th Punjab Regiment, on the spur of the moment had announced to his friends that, 'in the event of war with the Japanese he did not intend to get himself killed. If they saw him coming down the country fighting the British he was supposed to defend, none of them should be surprised.'[22]

T.R. Sareen records, 'It is clear that the subversion of Indian troops was a carefully thought-out and integral part of the Japanese plan of campaign....Surrender leaflets were dropped by plane, and the fall of Penang, within ten days of the outbreak of war, was ascribed by Baba Amar Singh to the excellent work done by the Fifth Column.'[23] The campaign progressed favourably for the Japanese, and prisoners were being progressively taken. Among the early surrenders were Subedar Allah Ditta Khan, 22 Mountain Regiment, on 8 December (he was promoted to captain in January), and Captains Mohan Singh and Mohammed Akram on 15 December (the latter was later to be killed in March 1942 in an air crash, along with Pritam Singh, *en route* to Tokyo). Mohan Singh was accompanying his commanding officer at the time of his surrender. In the opinion of the Subedar Major of 1/14th Punjab Regiment: 'Mohan Singh was

379

conscientious and efficient, and enjoyed the trust, alike, of his CO, his fellow officers and his men....'[24] Stephen Cohen, who had interviewed the late Mohan Singh, has recorded, 'Mohan Singh claims that he was actively considering joining the Japanese before he was captured.... In an unpublished history of the INA he relates that...the ICOs were secretly celebrating Axis victories....'[25] (Mohan Singh subsequently published it in 1974 as *Soldiers' Contribution to Indian Independence*.)

After capture near Jitra on 15 December, 'he appears to have yielded to the mingled threats, blandishments and promises of position and prestige offered by Giani Pritam Singh and Fujiwara,' in the words of Sareen, who concludes, 'While there is little doubt that Indian officers were fully aware previous to the outbreak of war of the activities of Japanese-sponsored anti-British elements, there is no positive evidence that Mohan Singh or any other Indian officer had contact, before capture, with cells of disaffection in Siam or Malaya. Despite the strong pro-Sikh bias of the first INA and the suspicious circumstances of the meeting early in the campaign of Mohan Singh and Giani Pritam Singh, it is considered, in view of his strongly nationalist sympathies which became immediately evident, that, while Mohan Singh was probably ripe for subornation, his encounter with Giani Pritam Singh was purely fortuitous and not the result of a previous arrangement.'[26] This is confirmed by Mohan Singh. A British account said of him, 'He has got no weakness in the form of greed, lust, drink, women, etc as far as one can find out... right or wrong, one thing was certain, that Mohan Singh was sincere and not acting a part.'[27]

This is abundantly borne out by his transparently sincere autobiography. Some of the methods now adopted for suborning Indian troops were, 'to send Indians right to the front line and then shout to the Indian troops not to fire; the other method was to send the Indian prisoners back after treating and feeding them well, thus showing that the Japanese treat Indians very well.'[28] Following the battle of the Slim River on 7 January 1942, three Indian infantry brigades were dispersed, and up to 4,000 prisoners taken. They were 'immediately subjected to intensive propaganda by Mohan Singh and his men. This propaganda was almost completely successful, and the majority of the PW readily agreed to transfer their allegiance to the Japanese side. It was at this time that the plan was made of sending organized contact parties of PW to accompany the Japanese, not only to round up stragglers and wounded, but, if necessary, fight against the British forces.'[29] Command of these 230 volunteers, as part of 'F' Kikan, was given to Allah Ditta. From 29 January they commenced training for the assault on Singapore, one Japanese being attached to each of the six sections, and two Japanese officers accompanying Allah Ditta. The sections were formed and led by VCOs of 1/14th Punjab, 5/14th Punjab, 4/19th Hyderabad, 2/1st Gurkhas, and one of Sikhs of the Bombay Sappers. (Jemadar Puran Singh of the 2/1st Gurkha Rifles was later to become Inspector General of Police in Nepal.) The five sections deputed successfully infiltrated, and planted the Japanese flag on the island on 14 February, mingling with units still fighting, and thus effecting "large-scale surrenders". Of Lieutenant General A.E. Percival and the fall of Singapore, Mohan Singh, an eyewitness, later wrote, '...he had to scatter his resources, making the best of a bad bargain; he did whatever was earthly possible to defend the doomed island....He was a brave and efficient general. The circumstances and events were beyond his control. He could not do better. The final outcome of his campaign must have been clear to him long before.' Singapore had earlier been designed as a fortress, with guns facing out to sea. It had not then been expected that an attack could come down the Malayan Peninsula. Sareen observes that: 'With the fall of Singapore, the history of the "F" Kikan volunteers as an independent unit ends....For a few months they enjoyed a privileged position as members of Mohan Singh's bodyguard with the inauguration of the (first division of the) INA in September 1942 they became merged in the Nehru Brigade. Some later rose to high rank in the INA, while others quickly sank back into obscurity: following the collapse of Mohan Singh some became non-volunteers....The Fujiwara Kikan undoubtedly played a very large part in weakening the morale of

Indian troops in Malaya....'[30] Another similar group of volunteers had been sent to Burma in early February from Kuala Lumpur with the same tasks. Mohan Singh came to Singapore after the surrender. The 1942 British account continues, 'Captain Mohan Singh lectured to the 60,000 Indian troops assembled in Farrer Park (on 17 February), and 90 per cent of them went wild with the idea of Indian Independence, and the national Army....Major Fujiwara decided to keep the Indian soldiers who surrendered in the general capitulation as PW for some time.'[31] The bitterness of being ill-equipped had been conjoined with the feeling that they had been dedicated, and to have given them less than they deserved, was a betrayal of trust by the British.

In April 1942, Mohan Singh came back from a conference in Tokyo, called by the Japanese in the name of Rash Behari. By this time, inadequate food, lack of medicines, brutal treatment, including the beating of officers and soldiers alike, had made the idea of the INA less attractive to most of those who had ostensibly cheered it on 17 February. Lists were asked for whether personnel elected to volunteer for the INA, with implied threats by the Japanese that the non-volunteers would be ill-treated, and the leaders in any non-co-operation would be shot.

Captains H.C. Badhwar (later Major General) and K.P. Dhargalkar (later Lieutenant General) of the 3rd Cavalry, as described by the latter, 'were taken to the Japanese Gestapo Headquarters where we were locked in underground cages, which were about five feet long by five feet wide and seven feet high, and sometimes held as many as five or six prisoners of war. We were kept inside these cages for eighty-eight days during which time we saw nothing of the outside world. We had to answer all of nature's calls in the cage.'[32] VCOs of the same regiment were confined in latrines for eleven days as a punishment for refusal to collaborate. These threats had their effect, and many volunteered, some with the ostensible aim of ultimately escaping to India. Amongst the several, who did not join, were Captain (later Lieutenant General) Harbakhsh Singh, 5/11th Sikhs, and Captain (later Lieutenant General) A.C. Iyappa,

Signals. Mohan Singh won over the VCOs and senior non-commissioned officers by making them officers. The VCO designation was abolished. With the evacuation of Rangoon in March 1942, the Japanese Premier, General Tojo, made a broadcast to India on 4 April, in which, *inter alia,* he stated, 'Imperial Forces have previously occupied Rangoon, which is an important point in Burma, and the Andaman Islands, a strategically important point...and a place of exile for Indian independence patriots. And now advancing further, it has been arranged to strike a decisive blow against the British military power and military establishment in India....This was a golden opportunity for Indians to exert all their strength to create India for the Indians, and establish India's original form.'[33]

Though the Japanese had agreed to the setting up of the INA, they intended to control it, and only allotted it the roles of law and order in the occupied areas, and responsibility for the Indian prisoners of war, whereas Mohan Singh viewed it as an army of liberation, under his control. He sought to expand it. Rash Behari supported the Japanese against Mohan Singh. Meanwhile, Gordon records, 'Fujiwara heard repeatedly about a Bose in Berlin. Although Bose had not come out officially in Berlin, word of his work in Berlin seems to have been spreading....Fujiwara was forced to dampen Mohan Singh's eagerness to bring Subhas Bose to the scene....'[34] Owing to his continued differences with the Japanese, as to the role of the INA, and the arming and equipping of the first division, Mohan Singh decided to dissolve the INA. His dissolution order of 21 December 1942 has its own historicity, 'The INA will be dissolved shortly. It is with deep regret and great reluctance that this decision has been arrived at. Circumstances have arisen under which it is impossible for the INA to forge ahead to achieve its goal, i.e. the complete Independence of India without any foreign control, influence or interference....Though we have not been able to achieve our final object, the movement has not been in vain. It has inculcated in us a true national spirit. It has brought a degree of unity among us unknown in the past, and it has shown to us and the world at large what we are capable of, if only we are left to ourselves.... Let us never forget that we are not concerned with ourselves alone. We have at stake, that great and beautiful land of ours with its 400 millions—our brothers and sisters. To her freedom we are wedded.... A confirmatory order will be sent out as soon as arrangements with the Nipponese are complete. In the event of my being separated from you before such an order is issued, the dissolution will take place automatically and immediately. Also, at the same time, the resignation of all members of the INA and their release from all obligatiors and undertakings to me and the INA will be taken for granted.'[35] The INA oath had been to him personally.

Earlier Fujiwara's assignment had been changed, and he was no longer the liaison officer with the INA. Colonel Iwakuro was given a wider role—he was more senior and was involved in Japanese Army politics. 'Iwakuro was more concerned with the propaganda and espionage activities of the INA and shared the doubts of most high-ranking Japanese officers that this force could ever be of much military value. These officers wondered about troops who surrendered and also soldiers who would switch sides...(he) set up an espionage training centre on Penang Island and several teams were prepared and, on Japanese initiative, sent into India. Their missions were almost a complete failure.'[36] Mohan Singh was not consulted, even though some of them consisted of INA personnel. Most missions were landed from submarines, and some came overland, but at least one was parachuted in. The points of entry varied from Orissa to Sind. All these missions in 1942 and early 1943 were captured, and thirteen persons were executed. Separately, Mohan Singh had agreed to a Japanese request for a group from the INA to do intelligence work on the Burma front. Lieutenant Colonel Niranjan Singh Gill, who, though almost ten years senior to Mohan Singh, nevertheless worked closely with him, and Major Mahabir Singh Dhillon, both KCIOs, were among those deputed by Mohan Singh, in response to the Japanese request. Dhillon crossed over, and was awarded the MBE. (He retired as a Brigadier after independence. After retirement both he and his wife were murdered by a relative on account of a property dispute.) Gill hesitated, returned to Singapore, and was arrested and tried by the Japanese for his criticism of their attitude towards the INA. (After independence, he was appointed as an Ambassador.) Dhillon's crossing over weakened Mohan Singh's position, and hardened Iwakuro in his views as to the INA.

Meanwhile, in May 1942, Subhas Chandra Bose, who had had a meeting with Mussolini, had not yet been able to get the Axis powers to issue a declaration for a free India. He had been invited to come to South-East Asia by the Council of Action of the IIL, presided over by Rash Behari, but was not in a position to travel without German assistance. He, therefore, wrote to Joachim von Ribbentrop on both these matters. Bose was called to meet Hitler, who, 'lectured Bose on the world situation, the great distances from German advances to the Indian frontier, and his unwillingness to make any moves or issue any proclamations that could not have any practical effect.'[37] Hitler, however, said Bose would be assisted to go to Japan to take over the Indian independence movement. Transportation would be by submarine. Bose held a press conference on 12 June 1942 after his latter May meeting with Hitler, stating *inter alia:* 'I regard myself as a servant of the Indian nation and my present task is to lead the fight for India's independence....My own experience has now convinced me that, by the logic of history, the Tripartite Powers have become our natural friends and allies.'[38] His journey to Japan took several months. Of this phase in the INA story, Philip Mason observes, 'One must respect such a man as Subhas Chandra Bose, who resigned from the Indian Civil Service because he sincerely believed it his duty to India; that respect can hardly be extended to all who changed sides in adversity and who a second time chose the more comfortable path. But it would be wrong to imply that opportunism was the sole motive. The story of Mohan Singh...provides one example of an officer who made his choice from a genuine conviction and was prepared to suffer for his beliefs. And the personality of Bose must have been an overriding factor with many.'[39] At this juncture in 1943, Pandit Nehru threatened to oppose Subhas Chandra "with open sword in hand", if he arrived in

India, assisted by an Axis power.

Rash Behari, who was ailing with tuberculosis, came from Bangkok to meet Subhas Chandra in order to hand over to a younger man. He, among others, had been urging the Japanese to bring him from Europe. Subhas Chandra had a meeting with Tojo on 10 June 1943, and impressed the latter. Tojo supported Indian independence, but was noncommittal on an early offensive into India, in which Bose wanted the INA to participate. Bose was unaware that Orde Wingate's first Chindit expedition had entered Burma in February. Even though the 14th Indian Division offensive in Arakan had been aborted, the Japanese were still gauging British intentions in the context of Wingate's expedition. Bose held a press conference in Tokyo, where he stated, 'since the enemy fights with his sword, we too should fight with the sword....Only if a large number of Indians undergo this baptism of fire can they win the race, and get the reward of freedom.'[40] Bose spelt out the necessity for a violent revolutionary approach: 'Gandhi's way was valuable, but had proved insufficient.'[41] Moving to Singapore, he was met at the airfield by all those INA officers who had not agreed to Mohan Singh's dissolution of the INA. As one of these officers said, 'The INA was not the creature of Mohan Singh, but of the IIL...therefore Mohan Singh had no power to dissolve it.'[42]

Subhas Chandra, in his address of 5 July 1943, exhorted the INA officers and men, 'For the present, I can offer you nothing except hunger, thirst, privation, forced marches and death. But if you follow me in life and in death...I shall lead you to victory and freedom.' Tojo, in South-East Asia for governmental work, reviewed an INA parade. After the "dissolution" of December 1942, the strength of the INA had dropped to 12,000. Now another 10,000 prisoners of war answered Bose's appeal, and, by 1945, 18,000 civilians as well. The first division only had small arms, and was to be trained for guerrilla warfare, but more time was devoted to political indoctrination. Two further INA divisions were also sanctioned. Some officer cadets were sent to Japan for training. (After independence two of these were later commissioned in the Indian Army after cadet training at the Indian Military Academy, IMA.) Terauchi still viewed the INA as a "propaganda" force, to be deployed in detachments with Japanese units in contact, to encourage Indian defections, while Bose declared, 'they would lead the way in the reconquest of India from its foreign occupiers...(he) displayed great optimism that, once Indian national forces...entered India, there would be a great rising against the British.'[43] In July 1943 Bose met the Burmese nationalist leader, Ba Maw, who had agreed to head the Burmese administration under the Japanese. Some Burmese nationalists, like Aung San, had earlier operated with the Japanese in the conquest of Burma. Aung San in turn was now commanding the Burma National Army (BNA).

Bose separately received a suggestion from some INA personnel that he should meet Mohan Singh, and consider an appointment for him. The former had been ill for several months. Bose was not too sympathetic, and suggested Mohan Singh had not been tactful with the Japanese. Mohan Singh offered to serve under Bose, but the latter left the matter indeterminate, apparently to avoid giving the Japanese the impression that he, in any way, condoned Mohan Singh's "independent" posture of December 1942. In any case, 'Mohan Singh had a mind of his own; he would not fit easily...and might make trouble if restored to power. Bose had him moved to healthier surroundings in Sumatra and improved his amenities, but made no further contact.'[44] On 29 December 1943 he visited the Andamans, and received the freedom of Port Blair. The islands as such could not be handed over to the Indians, but some administrative departments could. Lieutenant Colonel A.D. Loganadan was appointed the Chief Commissioner.

In January 1944 the Japanese took the decision to launch an offensive into India to pre-empt any British offensive into Burma. The Japanese concern stemmed from the operations of the first Chindit expedition. The offensive would first be launched in the Arakan in February directed at Chittagong, followed by the capture of Imphal and Kohima in April. Thereafter, the monsoons would prevent the movement of British-Indian reinforcements, and the Japanese would firm in on a more defensible line. Apart from an INA propaganda and espionage group with each Japanese division, Bose desired that the Subhas Regiment be given a mission. The former had mostly already been deployed with the Japanese "firm base" divisions before Bose's arrival, but were now augmented, particularly in the Arakan. New groups were raised for the Japanese offensive divisions. The Japanese also wanted to break up the Subhas Regiment into battalion groups, but Bose wanted the INA to lead the advance into India, 'The first drop of blood to be shed on Indian soil should be that of a member of the INA.' 'Bose was pacing leagues ahead with the vision of one, then two whole divisions in action, and five more which he would raise from new Indian prisoners.'[45] Eventually, one battalion of the Subhas Regiment was to be deployed with the Japanese force opposite the West African Division in the Kaladan Valley, while the other two would guard routes through the Chin Hills. On 3 February, he addressed the regiment before its move, 'Blood is calling to blood. Arise.... The road to Delhi is the road to Freedom. On to Delhi.'[46]

In the Arakan in February, the 7th Indian Division was cut off; among the claimed reasons for the Japanese 'success was the reconnaissance and subversion of an Indian (Gwalior Lancers) outpost position by Major L.S. Misra, the INA Commander in Arakan....At about the same time messages were received from Master Chopra's party of spies despatched by submarine (to Orissa) in December (1943).'[47] The Japanese now withdrew their objections to the spy schools being under Bose, which they had not conceded to Mohan Singh. But at the end of March 1944 a party of agents from the disbanded spy school at Penang had surrendered in India, and broadcast from New Delhi. Trained by the Japanese, despatched by submarine, it would appear their intention had been to reach the British, and convey information. Captain M.K. Durrani was arrested, as the INA personnel concerned had been trainees under him, before being taken over by the Japanese; he had apparently been on leave in Penang just before their departure for India. Durrani was later to confirm the above in his post-war account, *The Sixth Column*. Durrani was interrogated for days by the Japanese, and, after an interview with Bose, by INA officers. (He was awarded the George Cross in 1946.)

Meanwhile, many Indian prisoners of war who had not joined the INA, continued dying in the labour camps in Borneo, the Celebes and Siam; in the latter, hundreds of Indian labourers and British prisoners died in the construction of the infamous "Death Railway". Separately, a group of Indian civilian agents, briefed by Bose, had landed in Orissa by submarine, made their way to Calcutta, and set up a transmitter in Behala. One member of the group, T. Mukherjee, disappeared, and was later an approver at the trial of four of the group, information also being supplied to the investigators by the Durrāni group. One member of the group, Americk Singh, escaped, after being sentenced to death, hid for over a year with Bose's contacts, and later returned to Malaya, where he wrote a book. According to Leonard Gordon, 'Though not a complete failure, the underground missions organized...by Bose with their (Japanese) help had very limited successes and many failures. On his side of the battlefield in 1945, Subhas Bose had to cope with the even larger failure of the Japanese invasion of India and its consequences for the INA, the Azad Hind movement, and himself.'

During March 1944, the 2nd and 3rd Regiments of the 1st INA Division were ready to enter India with the Japanese Imphal offensive. L.S. Misra from the Arakan addressed them at a parade, and was decorated. On 1 March Bose learnt that there would be no Japanese military administration of the Indian areas about to be occupied, and that some responsibility would devolve on him. Of this period, Hugh Toye, an Intelligence officer in the Second World War dealing with the INA, says, 'The Japanese respected courage, and courage they certainly found in Bose. They despised disloyalty, and this was a taint from which the INA, in their eyes, could never free itself. Hence their respect for the leader, and the contempt in which they were to hold the request and opinions of his military commanders. Bose showed no fear of them and sometimes little respect, indeed his readiness to quarrel with them over the slightest infringement of his rights was one of the pillars of his reputation.'[48]

It, however, has to be remembered that the position of the INA officers vis-a-vis the Japanese was not on all fours with that of Bose — legally still prisoners of war, they could be rearrested at any time, as happened to several.

About this time Major N.S. Bhagat was removed by Bose from command of the 2nd INA Division, under raising, for disloyalty and insubordination. From its inception, Bhagat had not been happy as to the INA. He had been sent by the Japanese to a labour camp in the Pacific. He had been with Mohan Singh in the IMA, Dehra Dun, who now sought his assistance, arranging his recall. Bhagat reluctantly agreed, hoping to be able to control Mohan Singh. He joined the second INA with the same expectation. Bose had him watched, and, after removing him, had him kept in custody till the war ended. (N.S. Bhagat retired as a Brigadier after independence. He is the brother of the late Lieutenant General P.S. Bhagat, the first Indian officer VC, as also the first Indian VC awardee of the Second World War.) N.S. Bhagat, who had stood first in the order of merit at the first course at the IMA, is described by Mohan Singh as, 'brilliant, upright and brave....' Meanwhile, the Legion in Europe was declared by Bose to be part of the INA, though the Germans continued to designate it the 950th Regiment of the German Army.

The Japanese and the INA entered India in the Imphal offensive on 19 March. The fall of Imphal was expected in three weeks. Some Manipuris joined the INA, among them were M. Koirang Singh, later to be a Chief Minister of Manipur. 'Tojo stated in the Diet that the Provisional (Indian) Government would administer occupied Indian territory. For his part, Bose issued a call to the Indian people to cooperate with the invaders, and prepared proclamations as Supreme Commander and as Head of State. Then, on March 24th ... he attended a full conference between the Provisional Government and the Japanese Army on the problems of the occupation. Discussion soon centred on the chairmanship of the joint Indo-Japanese labour and supplies boards through which the Japanese were to obtain their requirements after Bose's administration took over. It was a stormy meeting. Bose would not agree to Japanese chairmen and the point was never settled. In fact the Japanese certainly intended to control India as effectively as they controlled Burma.'[49] Lieutenant Colonel A.C. Chatterjee was appointed the Chief Civil Administrator. On 21 April, on information supplied by the Japanese, Bose announced the capture of Kohima by the "Indo-Nip-ponese" forces. At this time, M.Z. Kiani, commanding the 1st INA Division, thirty-five miles from Imphal, asked for the return of the Subhas Regiment, two battalions of which were in the Chin Hills under Shah Nawaz (after independence, a Minister in the Indian Central Government). The latter had reported, 'the hardships his men were suffering. The ground was difficult, rations were poor and scanty, there was much malaria and no medicine, there were no pack animals, and half the men were being used as porters.'[50] Now, 'Bose dealt personally with the case of a Tamil recruit at.... Rangoon...who had died after field punishment. There was clear evidence of high-handedness and cruelty. Bose presided at the court of inquiry...reprimanded and removed the commandant. The affair worried him.'[51]

On 22 April, K.P.K. Menon later the Chief Editor, *Matrabhumi*, Calicut, was arrested by the Japanese Security Police. He had resigned from the Council of Action in December 1942, about the same time as Mohan Singh. 'Menon's stalwart attitude towards the Japanese, whom he distrusted, and towards Bose...was well-known: the bitter remarks which he freely uttered about both had circulated widely. "You say Bose is a man of action," he once said, "man of action indeed, he acts first and thinks afterwards." He particularly abominated Bose's belief in dictatorship for India.... Such behaviour was intolerable both to the Japanese and to Bose. Menon, a man of sixty, was interrogated over a period of two months, and sentenced by a military court to six years' rigorous imprisonment for lack of faith in Japan and for calling Bose a Fascist dictator.'[52]

Bose now warned the 2nd INA Division to move from Malaya for operations in July-August, and the 3rd INA Division by the end of 1944. The Japanese Imphal campaign was purportedly going well in June, though slower than conceived '...the 1st Division had been in action and there was great optimism. Everyone had been thrilled to read about the bold action of the 2nd Guerrilla Regiment from April 24th to May 6th, (the attempted attack on Palel airfield). The Japanese, in Rangoon, spoke highly of the INA in battle, and there were other reports of Kiani's leadership and the wonderful work of his men.... Even on July 10th, when Bose was told that the Japanese were abandoning their Imphal campaign, he seems to have had no inkling of the magnitude of its disaster.... So, to begin with, everything in Rangoon was again triumphal.... A death sentence, imposed by an INA court martial, was commuted to imprisonment...an investiture in which Bose pinned his highest award for bravery on to the tunic of a disabled Sikh officer, an INA parade at the tomb of Bahadur Shah, last of the Mughals.... He despised Allied propaganda, scorned its two agents the "Bluff and Bluster Corporation" (BBC) and the "Anti-India Radio" (AIR).... (He announced) soldiers of the Indian Army would be received on the same terms, and their Indian Army service would be allowed to count for their INA pensions.'[53] On 10 July there was a public function for the "new comrades", fewer than a hundred Indian soldiers who had been recently captured.

On 26 July, the Japanese announced the abandonment of the Imphal campaign, Tojo separately resigning for reasons of internal Japanese Army politics. In his Special Order of the Day on 14 August, Bose referred to the temporary suspension of the campaign, necessitating a tactical withdrawal. On 28 August a new decoration was announced for those who killed or captured British soldiers. 21 September was fixed as "Martyrs' Day" in memory of the agents executed in India. Bose, by now, knew that there had been hundreds of desertions, not only among the forward INA regiments and propaganda groups, but also among those in Burma and even in Malaya. Earlier that month he had made a speech to all INA officers in Rangoon, indicating that it was 'the loose conduct, luxury and corruption of the officers that had been responsible for the state of morale in which desertions were possible. The disaster had been a clear failure of leadership.'[54] He upbraided them, 'for placing their own comfort before that of their men, for peculation and treachery,' demanding that any officer who did not want to fight should leave the INA at once. Bose should have realized that most of the "officers" had no training as officers, but had been promoted by Mohan Singh. Very few had been trained at the INA Officers' Training School.

Of the 6,000 INA personnel sent towards Imphal, just 3,600 returned, of whom 2,000 were admitted to hospital; 400 were killed in action, and 1,500 died of disease or starvation; 715 were captured, and about 800 surrendered.[55] Simultaneously, there were atrocities on captured soldiers by INA personnel on Japanese orders, as also Japanese atrocities on INA personnel. An example of the former was on 19 March 1944, when a prisoner was bayoneted and killed by INA personnel on orders from the Japanese. On at least one occasion the Japanese bayoneted some INA personnel on the charge that they were Indian spies. Fujiwara, then liaison officer with the Japanese headquarters, under which the 1st INA Division was operating in the Imphal campaign, recorded, 'As a revolutionary army its morale was high, and it was quite well-organized, but the standard of its tactics, training and leadership was low.... It lacked, in particular, offensive strength and tenacity.' Toye validly comments, 'He does not mention equipment, but it lacked that too. The INA in action had no wireless sets, no telephones, no transport, no weapons heavier than light machine guns. Its soldiers wore old British khaki uniforms in which they were easily distinguishable.... The Japanese and British Indians... wore inconspicuous jungle green. Nevertheless Fujiwara concedes something; the 2nd and 3rd INA Regiments did assist the Japanese to hold out on the Palel road at a time when its collapse would have been very serious.'[56] Bose's concept of mass Indian desertions to the INA did not, in the event, materialize.

Bose visited Japan in October 1944 at the invitation of the new Japanese Premier, General Koiso. They agreed to an INA strength of 35,000 under arms for whom they would pay, and to 15,000 under training, for whom the IIL would continue to pay. 'Before he left Tokyo Bose asked to be allowed to approach Soviet Russia. He believed that the alliance between Russia and the West would not outlast the war in Europe...and that Russia might, therefore, be willing to sponsor him next. To the Japanese he suggested that, as an unofficial intermediary with no face to lose, he might be able to improve their relations with Russia. The Japanese declined.'[57] He returned to Singapore in December 1944, and learnt that the only department handed over by the Japanese in the Andamans was Education. The Japanese had baulked at handing over anything else, and continued to persecute the islanders. Fifty-five Indians had been executed, and thirty-three imprisoned as spies since his visit up to September, and in October 200 more were under arrest and investigation.[58] Bose decided to write off the Andamans. Meanwhile, in Bangkok, dissension prevailed in the IIL. After a visit, Bose gave the Japanese Security Police a list of ten to be arrested, and eighty others for surveillance. The Japanese arrested the ten Indians listed.

By now most of the two INA divisions were to be deployed on a defensive line along the Irrawaddy. In the event only the 4th Regiment of the 2nd INA Division could be deployed. The 1st Division was too weak, and the rest of the 2nd Division was waiting in Rangoon for its heavy equipment, the ship carrying which from Malaya had been sunk. Even in the 4th Regiment, under G.S. Dhillon, 150 men had been sent to the rear as suspect, leaving him with 1,200 men to defend twelve miles of the river, in the area of Pagan, an impossible task. On 4 February, four officers were promoted to the rank of major-general, Shah Nawaz being one of them, in command of the 2nd INA Division. The crossing of the Irrawaddy by the 7th Indian Division commenced on 14 February 1945, and, despite initial setbacks, it began securing the far bank. Dhillon's regiment suffered several casualties, and about 240 surrendered. Dhillon was forced to withdraw, and received a message from Bose, 'I have heard with grief, pain and shame of the treachery shown by Lieutenant Hari Ram and others. I hope the men of the 4th Regiment will wash away the blot on the INA with their blood.'[59] Simultaneously Bose wrote to the INA Police at Mandalay, 'the men who recently deserted from Mandalay...are still in Mandalay area.... Please do everything possible to arrest them or to shoot them.'

Meanwhile, the 2nd INA Regiment, under P.K. Sahgal, established a defensive base on the western slopes of Mount Popa, where Shah Nawaz joined his new divisional headquarters. An 'X' Regiment was also raised from the remnants of the 1st INA Division on 27 February. This period in the INA story is portrayed in a GHQ (India) Intelligence Summary. 'A measure of courage cannot be denied to the leaders of INA front-line units in Burma in 1945 when...they faced up to British equipment, tanks, guns and aircraft with rifles and bullock carts and empty stomachs.' On 2 March Bose learnt that five staff officers of Headquarters 2nd INA Division had surrendered, leaflets signed by them had been dropped on INA positions, and that further surrenders were consequently likely. Bose had already authorized the death penalty for desertion. He now ordered the observance of "Traitors' Day", and ordered the INA Police to look for "undesirable officers", who might so far have not been detected. Several consequently were relieved of their appointments, and taken into custody.

Toye encapsulates the INA operations thereafter, based on his wartime interrogations: 'Dhillon's regiment suffered heavy casualties in actions near Taungzin on March 15th to 17th, in which it showed persistence and gallantry.... Late in March one of Dhillon's battalion commanders deserted.... The Indian Army was now ready to clear Mount Popa.... It was clear that a full-scale attack would develop next day (3 April). During the night three officers and some NCOs deserted. In the morning, said Sahgal ".... Everybody appeared to feel that the enemy had full information about our dispositions, and as he was in such overwhelming strength, our case was hopeless"...Sahgal ordered a counter-attack, but the two concerned platoons deserted. A second counter-attack after nightfall was successful, but Sahgal then heard that virtually the whole of his 1st Battalion, including the commander, all company commanders and about three hundred men, had deserted. The remainder could not face another attack. Sahgal withdrew.... Nothing was left but retreat and disintegration.... Not all gave in without a fight. A party of six hundred under a Captain Bagri was surprised by British tanks....

Bagri and about a hundred of his men perished in a last desperate charge with hand grenades and bottles of petrol. But it made no difference. At the end of April only fugitives remained at large: on May 13th Shah Nawaz, Dhillon and about fifty men surrendered at Pegu: the story of the 2nd INA Division was over.'[60]

Earlier Bose had refused to countenance the use of the INA against the BNA of Aung San, after its revolt from the Japanese on 25 March. As this action of Aung San had its own nuances, a digression from the INA story is necessary. The BNA, a Japanese creation, trained and equipped by them, now turned against them. As described by Louis Allen: 'The Burmese forces lined themselves up for a parade in Rangoon, supposedly before setting off for the front, and then calmly made their way out of the city and went over to the British,'[61] killing the Japanese officers with them. The BNA story had begun in 1940, when a Japanese Colonel (Suzuki) visited Burma as a journalist, and contacted some of the anti-British graduates of Rangoon University. He encouraged them in their ideas of independence from the British, but intended to use them to sabotage American supplies to Chiang Kai-shek through Rangoon. Thirty, including Aung San, their leader, were trained by the Japanese in Hainan in 1941. When war broke out in December 1941, they acted as guides for the Japanese and became the nucleus of the BNA. Aung San had been promised independence for Burma, and this was granted under Japanese suzerainty in 1943, with Dr Ba Maw as Premier. Ba Maw has described the BNA's role in the achievement of Burmese independence: 'Notwithstanding all the evil done by many in it, this spirit shone most fiercely in that ragtag army in the making. Nothing could wholly obliterate that army's role and significance in the revolutionary struggle which took place in Burma.'[62] Aung San, the commander of the BNA, secretly met General Slim. On 27 March, the whole of the BNA came out in open rebellion against the Japanese. Louis Allen concludes: 'So much for the vicissitudes of war....The fall of Rangoon finally convinced the Burmese officers of the BNA that they had made the right decision.'[63] (Aung San was assassinated in 1947. His daughter,

Aung San Suu Kyi, was awarded the 1991 Nobel Peace Prize.)

When one of Bose's ministers suggested that he also should turn on the Japanese, 'he replied simply that the Indians in Malaya would pay a heavy price if he did.'[64] On 4 May, the first brigade of the 26th Indian Division landed from assault craft at Rangoon. Toye, an Intelligence officer dealing with the INA, summarizes its end, 'So the Indian Independence Movement in Burma came peacefully to an end, its leaders behaving with dignity and giving what assistance they could to the British commanders. It was inevitable, nevertheless, that stern action would be taken. Seven hundred and fifty of the ex-Indian Army officers and men were shipped to India for investigation in May. They were followed, as the months passed, by many thousands more from Rangoon, and then from Malaya and Bangkok.' Shah Nawaz, who had delayed in joining the INA as he totally distrusted the Japanese, attributed most of the blame to the latter: '...with a clear conscience I can say that the Japanese did not give full aid and assistance to the Azad Hind Fauj....they let us down badly....The Japanese did not trust the INA. They had found out through their liaison officers that the INA would not accept Japanese domination in any way, and that they would fight the Japanese in case they attempted to replace the British.' Of some 15,500 INA personnel in Burma in 1945, 150 were killed in action; 1,500 died of starvation or disease; 5,000 surrendered or deserted; 7,000 were captured; 2,000 escaped towards Bangkok. Of some 40,000 Indian prisoners of war, who did not join the INA, 11,000 died in captivity, of disease, starvation or were murdered some even cannibalized by the Japanese.

The Indian Legion's fate now needs to be mentioned. After Bose's departure from Germany, it continued its training, and Sonderkommando 'B', the more elite group, was merged with the 950th Regiment, the main body. Bose had been promised that they would be used against the British, but this did not occur. First moved to Belgium, and then to the southwestern coast of France, in Gordon's words, 'some of the soldiers proved hard to control.' Another account describes them as "mutinous". Placed under the Waffen SS, they were ordered back to Germany, but *en route* some were killed by the French Maquis. As the Allies advanced, 'the Legion gradually disintegrated, and most were eventually captured by the Allies. They certainly did not fulfil the hopes that Bose had for them.'[65] An official summary of August 1945 describes them after repatriation and some incidents in their camp at Bahadurgarh, '950 Regiment were on the whole more hardened...they were never anti-German... the men of the Indian Legion are a particularly truculent, ill-disciplined lot...'[66]

Bose was killed on 18 August 1945, when a plane conveying him to Tokyo, and, thereafter, hopefully to Russia, crashed in Formosa. If he had survived the war, would he have become the Prime Minister of India after Pandit Nehru? On 19 August, Jawaharlal Nehru was interviewed as to his current views on Bose and the INA, in relation to what he had said in 1943. He stated, 'About 25,000 Indian soldiers, mostly Sikhs and Muslims joined the Japanese...and formed the INA....I was of the opinion and am still of the opinion that the leaders and others of this Army had been misguided in many ways, and had failed to appreciate the larger consequences of their unfortunate association with the Japanese. Three years ago I was asked in Calcutta what I would do if Subhas Bose led an army into India on the plea of liberating India. I replied that I would not hesitate to resist this invasion, even though I did not doubt that Subhas Bose and his Indian colleagues were motivated by the desire to free India, and were in no way tools of the Japanese. Nevertheless they had put themselves on the wrong side and were functioning under Japanese auspices. Therefore, whatever the motive of these people, they had to be resisted in India or outside.' The next day Nehru spoke again, 'Now a very large number of officers and soldiers of the INA...are prisoners and some, at least have been executed....At any time, it would have been wrong to treat them too harshly, but at this time—when it is said big changes are impending in India—it would be a very grave mistake leading to far-reaching consequences if they were treated just as ordinary rebels. The punishment given to them would, in effect, be a punishment on all

India and all Indians, and a deep wound would be created in millions of hearts.'[67] The executions referred to were nine, for espionage or sabotage, out of some thirty VCOs, NCOs and other ranks already tried by a court-martial in 1942-44 apart from the thirteen civilians hanged from the "secret" parties, after trial by special judges.

For the sequence of decisions as to the disposal of the former INA personnel, one needs to revert to Philip Mason, for he was the ICS official dealing with the subject, '...clearly the problem was a big one with political implications; it was not faced at the time— there was too much to do—and they were sent back to India.... The Indian public did not know at this stage of their existence. But when the war with Japan suddenly ended, the problem could not be postponed any longer.... All were guilty of an offence legally punishable with death but, of course, there could be no question of executing 25,000 men. It would have been cruel, impolitic and unjust. On the other hand, the offences of mutiny and desertion could not be condoned—and this in the interest not so much of abstract justice as of the future of the Indian Army. To the new India, that Army would be a valuable possession if it preserved its discipline; without it, a serious danger. It was decided that, in the first place, those who had joined the INA with the intention of deserting from it should be classed as White, and restored to their former privileges, while the Greys—those who had been misled—should be summarily tried, dismissed and released. The Blacks would remain; they were those who had been well aware of what they were doing and among them the Blackest were those...who had tortured, flogged or killed their comrades, either to make them join the INA or, after they joined, to punish them for attempted desertion. For a few of the Blackest, the law should take its course; for the other Blacks, the death penalty would be commuted to imprisonment of varying lengths, in most cases short.... It is difficult to believe that any body of humane and responsible men in that position at that time would have decided on a different course of action. I defended it in the Assembly in Delhi in 1946 and I would defend it again today. But events moved with extreme rapidity and in a way no one foresaw—and I concede at once that if the way things would go had been foreseen it would have been far wiser to adopt a different handling in regard to the Public.... The policy was right; the public handling—as it turned out—was seriously wrong....the policy was announced.... I drafted the communique myself—and it met, at first, with gratified approval...but in a few weeks all this was changed. In a wave of nationalist emotion the INA were acclaimed heroes who had fought for the freedom of India...and in the face of this storm of public feeling—at which Congress leaders were secretly as much perturbed as the British—the original policy was changed; India was very near Independence, and it was surely incongruous to punish men for casting off an allegiance which the State was, in any case, on the point of relinquishing.... A second decision was taken that, though all should be tried and found guilty, dismissal would be the punishment for waging war against the King. The INA's claim to have been fighting for patriotic motives would be taken at its face value, and its members would be treated as though prisoners of war; only those who had committed acts of brutality would be liable on conviction to death or imprisonment. This decision was felt by many Englishmen to be a betrayal, not only of the 35,000 prisoners who had stood firm, but also of the victorious Indian Army. And in a sense it was a betrayal. It shook the Indian Army; it disturbed the villages to which the INA men went back; it played a part in the naval mutinies of February 1946. All the same, I believe that, in the extraordinary circumstances of the time, it was the right choice between two bitter alternatives. To have persisted on the old line would have led to a betrayal of Britain's true purpose in India. A postscript must be added to this highly compressed—and highly controversial—outline. It concerns an error of judgment and a blunder. The first prisoner to have been tried in the original plan was a King's Commissioned Officer who, so the prosecution alleged—had ordered two would-be deserters to the British to be hung up by their extended arms and flogged by a whole battalion; one of them was dead when taken down. It, originally, had been proposed to hold the trials in a remote spot where they would not attract much attention; so sure was Field Marshal Auchinleck that this case would horrify public opinion that he gave orders that the trial should be in public and held in an accessible place. The Red Fort at Delhi was chosen.... The choice of scene was taken as a deliberate taunt.... That was the error of judgment. Then, at the last moment, a technical legal difficulty arose in the flogging case and it was postponed; in its place was put the trial of three other accused, who, it was said, were charged with behaviour no less brutal. But this was not so.... The men were released, rightly in view of the previous decision, and I believe that both Britain and India owe Field Marshal Auchinleck a debt for a hard decision. But the accused ought not to have come to trial at that stage and in that way...it was a blunder and I do not propose to say where I think the blame lay beyond saying that it did not adhere to the Commander-in-Chief.'[68]

Auchinleck issued a humane, memorable and evocative memorandum in February 1946, explaining his reasons for the commutation of the sentences of Shah Nawaz, G.S. Dhillon and P.K. Sahgal. Meanwhile, Nehru visited Singapore in March 1946 at the invitation of the IIL, and met Lord Louis Mountbatten, then still Supreme Commander. He mentioned that he thought that the INA was more national than the Indian Army, and that, in his view, the vast majority of the INA personnel should be taken back into the Indian Army. Mountbatten advised him that it was in independent India's own self-interest that the fabric of the Indian Army not be rent asunder, for any future government would have to rely on it. On his return, Nehru wrote to Maulana Abul Kalam Azad, the Congress President, on 28 March 1946, 'I pointed out in Malaya that we could not keep it (INA) going as an army there or in India....' In May, Nehru met Lord Archibald Wavell, and sought that ex-INA personnel be taken into the police as the latter had an "oppressive" image. Wavell said it would be "fatal" to do so. Burhanuddin, who was to have been tried first, was at this time sentenced to seven years' rigorous imprisonment. Fourteen other INA personnel—one officer (Abdur Rashid), four VCOs and nine other ranks—were also tried and sentenced to imprisonment for gross brutality, before Auchinleck decided, at the end of April, to discontinue all further proceedings. Abdur Rashid's defence was curious. He said he had joined the INA to safeguard the interests of his community against the non-Muslims, 'who were to invade India with the Japanese, and establish a Ram Raj.' (Mohan Singh was never brought to trial.) Nehru wrote a letter on 4 May 1946 to Auchinleck, thanking him for his decision. As John Connell recounts, 'who was the greater man in statesmanship or moral integrity—the writer of this letter or its recipient?'[69] Thereafter Lieutenant General Francis Tuker excoriated the Commander-in-Chief: 'The acumen of our military authorities had not won much admiration....From that time then dates the indifference of the British officer of the Indian Army towards his higher command,' and avers that the GHQ was displaying, 'Homiletics and suppliant posteriors seductive to the foot of insolence.'[70] Separately, in his last days as Viceroy, Wavell had to veto, with the approval of the British Cabinet, an all-party motion in the Legislative Assembly for the immediate release of Burhanuddin, Abdur Rashid and the others imprisoned. On Wavell's departure, it was tabled again. Nehru met Mountbatten on 1 April 1947 two days before the motion, and said he was aware that Auchinleck might resign if the veto was withdrawn, and of the irretrievable damage at the commencement of Mountbatten's Viceroyalty if the veto was renewed. As described by H.V.Hodson, 'Lord Mountbatten started with the advantage of having had a "preliminary round" with Pandit Nehru on the latter's visit to Singapore (in March 1946), when he persuaded the Indian leader to cancel his intention of laying a wreath on the INA memorial... He had then told Pandit Nehru, "The people who will serve you well in your national army of the future are those who are loyal to their oath; otherwise if you become unpopular, a disloyal army may turn against you."'[71] Mountbatten again went through what he had said in Singapore to Nehru, as to maintaining the fabric of the Indian Army. The motion was withdrawn, and they were, in the event, released in August 1947. From the point of view of hindsight, however, Bose was ultimately right, when, in 1943, he had said that the convulsive effects of the war with Indian participation would undermine the British Empire, even if the Axis lost.

FOURTEEN

Partition, Independence And The Accession Of States

FOR HIS times, Lord Macaulay had been perceptive in the 1830s, when he had looked forward to 'the proudest day in English history when a grateful India, moulded in a European pattern, would set up on her own as a free country.' Henry Lawrence, in 1844, had been even more prescient when he had said, 'We cannot hold India for ever.... Let us, so conduct ourselves, that when the connection ceases, it may do so, not in convulsions but with mutual esteem and affection, and England may have in India a noble ally, enlightened and brought into the scale of nations under our guidance and fostering care.' In December 1945, Lord Archibald Percival Wavell, in a way the Henry Lawrence of those years, had sent to London "a proposed programme of action." As Penderel Moon puts it, '...the most important feature of the plan was a proposal for dealing with Jinnah and the demand for Pakistan. If, at any stage, Jinnah caused a deadlock by persisting in this demand, he was to be told that HMG would have to make their own decision and this would be based on the principle that large non-Muslim populations could not be included in Pakistan against their will. This meant that he would get

403

only a "husk", "the maimed, mutilated and moth-eaten Pakistan" that he had rejected. Wavell thought that there was at least a chance that, confronted with this prospect, Jinnah would set to work to get the best possible terms for the Muslims within a united India. If he did not, then he would have to be allowed the truncated Pakistan. It is perhaps to be regretted that Wavell was not given the opportunity of carrying out this plan. Even if it had failed to overcome Jinnah's obduracy, it might at least have led to the adoption of a truncated Pakistan as the solution of the Indian problem by a quicker and less sanguinary path than the one that in the end was taken. But the Labour Government were still hopeful of preserving the unity of India and reluctant to commit themselves to bringing Pakistan into existence by a British decision.'[1]

Now in early 1946, serious cases of mutiny suddenly occurred in the Royal Indian Navy (RIN), less serious in the Royal Air Force (RAF) (wanting their early repatriation) and in the Royal Indian Air Force, and a lesser protest in the Indian Army, at Jubulpore in the Signal Training Centre. As to the latter, Pandit Jawaharlal Nehru said at a press conference on 3 March 1946,'...the men...have remained completely peaceful....The demands were for better treatment in regard to rations, amenities etc, and equality of treatment between Indian and British soldiers. There were also some political demands.... Such demands should not normally be made on the basis of a strike....We have seen recently strikes by American and British servicemen.'

The RIN mutiny took a more serious form at Bombay and Karachi, necessitating the deployment of troops. At some other ports and ships, there was indiscipline as well, but not as serious. Sardar Vallabhbhai Patel met the RIN mutineers' leaders and advised them to surrender, and seek redress in the proper way. Mahatma Gandhi upbraided them for 'setting a bad and unbecoming example,' and had a message for the country, 'Now that it seems we are coming into our own, indiscipline and hooliganism ought to go....'

A case of collective indiscipline also occurred in a Gurkha Rifles Centre. The men were going on demobilization, and their kits were being inspected, as is the practice, to see that they had no objectionable items. Certain items were found with some men, who were then remanded for disciplinary action. 'The rest objected, became insolent, violent, and refused to obey orders. The six ringleaders were arrested, tried by court-martial, and given sentences ranging from five years to six months.'[2] To add to the manifold problems, there was a gang of American deserters operating in Calcutta, indulging in thefts and murders requiring ferreting out by British and Indian Military Police, the American forces having left. In addition, when the Indian Army Ordnance Corps took over the American Ordnance Depots in Assam and Bengal, arms and ammunition of all types were found lying about, despite assurances, some exploded, some unexploded, some buried by the labourers. The civilian inhabitants had been helping themselves, thus aggravating the law and order problem for years to come, not only in these areas but elsewhere as well, wherever unaccounted Second World War arms and ammunition were sought, for instance, in Bengal, the Punjab, Telengana, Naga Hills, and the Chambal ravines. Apart from this, arms and ammunition from the battlefields of Burma were being brought into India, particularly the Punjab, by personnel coming on leave. The law and order situation was not improved by a Bihar Police "strike" in March, necessitating the deployment of troops, including on traffic duty in Patna. Forty policemen were dismissed in the "strike."

The British Cabinet Mission sent out to India in March 1946 produced a workable plan, which gave Muslim majority areas some autonomy, but preserved the unity of India. Gandhi described it as, 'the best document the British Government could have produced in the circumstances.' M.A. Jinnah set the tone of the Simla Conference with the Cabinet Mission by refusing to shake hands with the Congress President, Maulana Abul Kalam Azad. Both the Congress and the Muslim League appeared to accept the proposals, but then both resiled. The Mission could possibly have given out their plan as an award, to be implemented by the Viceroy, instead of inviting acceptance, but the British Government was not prepared to impose a solution on the two main political parties. Meanwhile Francis Tuker, a Gurkha Rifles officer, as the GOC-in-C, Eastern Command, had officially been frequently urging reconstitution of the Indian Army on a communal basis, 'Communalism was reality....With this in mind it was apparent that even in a united India, if the Army were to survive, then it would only survive if it were grouped into its communal classes.... The chasm was too deep and was daily widening.... It meant that the mixed regiments of Hindu and Muslim soldiers would some time or other break to pieces. The best would be desertion by the sepoys; the worst, fighting within the unit.... In the end, this shattered army would shatter India to smithereens....So it seemed...certain that whether India were united or divided the Army must, in any case, be grouped into communal units or formations. It was hoped, with little confidence, that (the country) would hang together and so keep our precious army integral, but it was expected that it would split in half and that the Army, would thus, in any case, be as a consequence, divided. That, it would seem, must be the end of our army; but no, we saw that there was even then a chance of saving it, and, in later days, rebuilding it....This one chance lay in handing out to each of the two parts a contingent of its own, and in keeping a third part under the management of all the three parties concerned, British, Muslim, and Hindu. If possible the third contingent should be built round one completely impartial body, the Gurkha Brigade under its British officers....'[3] Fifteen months later when the reconstitution had to take place, Tuker had to accept, 'that no Muslim residing in Hindustan could join the army of that dominion...was a source of grievance which was later removed.'

Tuker has been quoted at some length, as, by March 1946, he was disagreeing on most current issues, as his book *While Memory Serves* portrays, particularly, as brought out in the previous chapter, in relation to the moderate policy adopted towards the 'Indian National Army' (INA) personnel. He alleged the Muslim League considered General Headquarters (GHQ), under Sir Claude Auchinleck, as a "Hindu" Headquarters. Some British officers in GHQ threatened to resign if the Army was reconstituted, as suggested by

Tuker in advance of a formal decision as to the future constitutional set-up whether the country was to remain united, or was to be divided. Auchinleck was still hoping for a united India, so that the Army would not have to be reconstituted urging that if India and Pakistan were to have separate Defence forces, it would seem certain that the combined total of the forces must be greater than that of the Defence forces designed to serve a united India. With all these pressures, he was constrained to broadcast on 28 March 1946 to all officers: '...the magnificent divisions of the Indian Army are world-renowned. The Indian soldiers will go down to posterity as among the finest fighting soldiers of the world. Let the Indian Army guard its good name.... The great event of India's history is about to take place, viz, the transfer of power from Britain to India. It must be a peaceful transfer, with the least possible dislocation. The objects of the British is to hand over a peaceful India. The object of the Indians is to take over a peaceful India. Our objects are, therefore, identical.... The Army is the Anchor of the Country....In short, the Indian Army may well be the instrument which will ensure that this great period in India's history will pass peacefully and in a spirit of goodwill on all sides.... Indian officers, do not cut your own foot with your own mattock *(apne paon aap kulhari mat maro)*....British officers, serve the New India as loyally as in the past your Indian comrades have served the present India.' The Indian Army did not belie his expectations, though a year later Tuker was to say of Auchinleck's unenviable position, 'Bit by bit his influence had waned. His position was the unenjoyable one which invited kicks from all and sundry, and ha'pence from none.'

On 8 April 1946, as the War Member, Auchinleck, in replying to a resolution in the Council of State, *inter alia*, stated, 'It is the declared policy of the Government of India to nationalize the Armed Forces in the shortest possible time compatible with the maintenance of efficiency. The object is to create a completely national army....' Thereafter, in the same month, on his own initiative, the No. 1 Selection Board was courageously assembled, and with himself

presiding, was asked to make prospective promotion recommendations, including for an Indian Chief, in the context of possible
immediate nationalization, which the British Board did.[4]

On 31 May 1946, Auchinleck was promoted to Field Marshal,
much after certain British Army officers junior to him, like Bernard
Montgomery and H.M. ("Jumbo") Maitland-Wilson. The London
Times then validly commented: 'He is acknowledged on all hands to
have been one of the greatest Commanders-in-Chief in India in the
history of that office. His period of command in the field was one in
which the British forces were still inadequately equipped, but the
forces under his command, nevertheless, managed to snatch victory
at Sidi Rezegh, and, though defeated in the next campaign, succeeded in barring the road to Egypt against all expectation. It is
probable, however, that his greatest service in the course of the war
was performed in India, where the whole responsibility for the administrative background to the campaign in Burma lay upon his
shoulders. He won the confidence of the Indian Army.'

At this time Montgomery arrived in Delhi as Chief of the
Imperial General Staff (CIGS) designate. He continued his unjustified criticism of Auchinleck in his memoirs, 'It seemed to me that
Auchinleck was wrapped up entirely in the Indian Army, and
appeared to be paying little heed to the welfare of the British soldiers
in India.' Separately, he also had meetings with Maulana Azad and
Jinnah, as the respective presidents of their parties. The latter made
it clear that he would never tolerate Hindu rule over Muslims. When
Montgomery asked why, Jinnah replied, 'How can the two lie down
together; the Hindu worships the cow, I eat it.'[5]

On 22 July, Wavell formulated the plan to convert his Executive
Council into an Interim Government, until it became possible to
progress by agreement to something more permanent. It was to
consist of well-known Indian political figures selected by all parties,
in place of members hitherto chosen by the Viceroy himself. Jinnah
made it apparent that the Muslim League would not accept the
proportion of representation offered by the Viceroy. In the first week
of August, Wavell, thereupon, announced the installation of an

interim government under him with Nehru as the vice-president, and Jinnah, sequentially, announced that 16 August 1946 would be observed as "Direct Action Day" by Muslims all over India. (One of the three anti-partition Muslims in this first interim government, Sir Shafaat Ahmad, was murderously assaulted in Simla on 24 August; he fortunately escaped.) It was obvious that Jinnah's real concern was with his own power, and not concern *per se* for the Muslims who would remain in the residual India, in the event of partition. Meanwhile communal tension had been building up in Calcutta since February, as to which dominion it should be allotted to, some Muslims (not all) wanting it to be allotted to the notional East Pakistan. Tuker, still GOC-in-C, posits the prevailing situation, 'Direct action in India could only mean action by force as a protest against the decrees of the existing government.... It seemed that this really meant that since the Muslims could not get their Pakistan by negotiation, they were to get it by direct and forceful action. Most Muslims, the more simple and vigorous, certainly read that meaning into Direct Action Day.... It seemed that the Muslim League Ministry of Bengal had no intention of resigning as part of the Direct Action programme.'[6] On 9 August, the Congress had observed "Remembrance Day" in Calcutta to commemorate the 1942 'Quit India' movement martyrs. "Remembrance Day" passed off peacefully, but "Direct Action Day" did not, leading to "The Great Calcutta Killing", with the equivalent of two divisions' worth of troops being deployed, and, thereafter, causing a chain reaction all over North India, leading exponentially to further demands for the deployment of troops. Jinnah then declared, 'What we have done today is the most historic act in our history...this day we bid goodbye to constitutional methods.... Today we have also forged a pistol and are in a position to use it.' It is, therefore, dealt with in some detail, as the initial flames of a great conflagration. The undivided Army confounded sceptics like Tuker, who had never served with an Indian unit, and remained impartial right through the subsequent communal holocausts up to 14 August 1947.

The Bengal Muslim League leader, Khwaja Nazimuddin, later

Governor-General and then Prime Minister in Pakistan, speaking on 11 August, had said: '...the Interim Government, without the support of the Muslim League, would before long certainly bring about a very serious clash between the communities. Although final plans for direct action had not yet been settled, there were scores of ways well-known to Calcutta Muslims by which the League could make a thorough nuisance of themselves, not being bound to non-violence as was the Congress.'[7] On 16 August, an immense Muslim crowd in Calcutta was addressed by the Chief Minister, H.S. Suhrawardy, later Prime Minister in Pakistan. He orated that 'the Cabinet Mission was a bluff, and that he would see how the British would make Nehru rule Bengal. Direct Action Day would prove the first step towards the Muslim struggle for partition.'[8] Tuker adds, 'Our intelligence patrols noticed that the crowd included a large number of Muslim goondas, and that these slipped away from the meeting from time to time, their ranks being swelled as soon as the meeting was over. They made for the shopping centres of the town where they, at once, set to work to loot and burn Hindu shops and houses.'[9] By that evening, these goondas had killed and pillaged all over Calcutta. The Hindus and Sikhs ultimately retaliated. Tuker now describes Suhrawardy driving around Calcutta with the military commanders. He 'was eager to expose the depredations of Hindus against his co-religionists, pointing an accusing finger at peaceful men and charging them with laying in wait for Muslims...that Hindu and Muslim unity would not exist very much longer in the army.'[10]

Tuker continues, 'I do not know—no one knows—what the casualties were. On one night alone some 450 corpses were cleared from the streets by the three British battalions.... All one can say is that the toll of dead ran into thousands.... The Army had a grim time, the grimmest being the clearing of dead from the battlefield.... At last we were finding out where the rest of the stolen weapons of Burma had gone, for they were appearing in the hands of the worst elements of the goonda population of Calcutta and of other Bengal towns.'[11] A subsequent estimate put the carnage at 4,000 dead (3,467 bodies were actually cleared from the streets), and 10,000 wounded over four days. Suhrawardy decided to bring in some Punjab Police to stiffen the Calcutta Police, whose cohesion he himself had shattered with his communalism. Tuker narrates, 'With the Punjab Police behind them, Muslims were cock-a-hoop driving their trucks through Hindu areas and insulting all and sundry.... Suhrawardy...was, at that time, and, for many months after, a strong proponent of Muslim interests and antagonistic to every thing Hindu...with an irritating habit of saying things that he knows full well would get a rise out of the other man.... He is too prone to think that the other side will readily forget an injury that he wishes to be forgotten...much blame is to be attributed to the arrogant Punjabi Muslim police who were at the root of all the discreditable doings...in a Calcutta court some of them were acting as escorts, so they sat throughout the proceedings facing the Judge with their boots on the desk, refusing to put their feet down on the floor....'[12]

Variously, from the UP, Delhi and Bihar, there were reports of attempts by the Revolutionary Socialist Party and the Communist Party to tamper with military personnel, including Indian Emergency Commission officers not placed in acceptable grades for regular commissions. 'Efforts of political hotheads to get into unit lines were immediately resisted, and, on the whole, the men were very loyal in bringing to their commanders all subversive leaflets and pamphlets which were handed to them or sent to them by post...(the Army) was indifferent to all politicians, but it was strongly pro-Army, and it was its pride in itself that carried it through.'[13] A case occurred of an acting major donating the entire contents of the unit treasure chest to the party concerned, himself going underground till later apprehended and tried. The All India Gurkha League now announced that it would not countenance the continuance of Gurkha units in "Imperial" (British) service. About this time, the Tibet Revolutionary Party, based at Kalimpong, was expelled from British-India, one of the averments being that it had printed hundred rupee-notes, with Nehru's head in place of George VI's. Separately, in Assam, where there were certain wastelands which belonged to the Assam government, 'for some time indigent

Muslims from East Bengal had been squatting on these lands, and thus claiming right of possession. Muslim immigration had reached its peak during that period when the Japanese were advancing towards India through Burma....In time the migration of these Muslims into Assam would upset the balance of votes in favour of Muslims against Hindus....Probably it was this danger which spurred the Assam government to its policy of eviction.'[14]

On 2 September 1946, there were hopes that a better communal situation would prevail when the Muslim League decided to join the Interim Government. These expectations were soon to be belied in East Bengal, but first mention needs to be made of Nehru's letter of 12 September to Auchinleck as to the Indian Army*. Nehru postulates in this letter: 'The immediate questions before us are a change in the whole outlook of the Indian Army making it national in reality and more in accord with public sentiment; the withdrawal of the British forces from India; and the withdrawal of Indian troops from abroad, more specially from the Netherlands East Indies and Iraq.' At the time Indian troops were also in Japan, Hong Kong, Malaya, Siam, Burma, Borneo, Ceylon, Italy and the Middle East. The letter was to await the arrival of the new Defence Member, Sardar Baldev Singh, for its formal consideration. The latter, later, in his first broadcast to the Armed Forces on 9 October, stated that, 'Nationalization will be speeded up at an accelerated pace compatible with efficiency,' and announced the setting up of "The Armed Forces Nationalization Committee", with Sir N. Gopalaswami Ayyangar as chairman, Brigadier K.S. Thimayya as an Army member, and Lieutenant Colonel B.M. Kaul as secretary. One of the civilian members was the inestimable Pandit H.N. Kunzru. This was possibly the first time that Brigadier (later General) Thimayya and Lieutenant Colonel (later Lieutenant General) Kaul may have had to work together officially, but their subsequent official relationship was not cordial as we shall see in the Krishna Menon era. (Gopalaswami

---

* It is reproduced in full in Appendix 4, for its historicity, as it is an official formulation by the Vice-President of the Interim Government

Ayyangar, a former Prime Minister in Jammu and Kashmir State till 1945, was later to be a Defence Minister.) The partition decision and the date for independence were not then known, so this committee's recommendations were overtaken by events, but they did eventually provide some parameters for deciding the number of British personnel to be retained after independence, the committee having recommended nationalization by June 1948. (Forty-eight per cent of the British officers and ninety-four per cent of the non-commissioned officers sought employment under either Dominion after independence.)

Reverting now to East Bengal in October 1946, in order to study the anatomy of a communal disturbance. Here according to Tuker, 'the object of the uprising had been conversion to Islam, and not extermination of Hindus,' which set off as is known, the large-scale retaliatory killing of Muslims by Hindus in Bihar and the UP (Garh Mukhteshwar), which, in turn, kindled the violent attack by the Muslims on the Hindus and Sikhs near Rawalpindi, causing the equally violent counter-attack by the Sikhs, and the sequential civil war of communal reprisals. (The Muslim League had begun to build-up a stock of arms in the Punjab as early as December 1946, as came out in the subsequent 1949 trial in Pakistan of the Nawab of Mamdot.) Tuker, as GOC-in-C thought that, 'there was one favourable factor on our side in that area, and it was that the Muslim majority was so large that it had no need to fear the other community: thus, Muslims would only assault Hindus out of sheer villainy, and, in sheer villainy, only a limited number of their co-religionists would join....The possibility of disturbances organized by the Muslim leader, Ghulam Sarwar, had been foreshadowed some time ago by several sources. Unfortunately this information was regarded with suspicion and extra police were not moved into the area as early as they might have been....A certain number of ex-army personnel were reported to be his adherents....The mode of action was to demand tribute from Hindus in various villages on pain of forcible conversion or death. Many had paid, others had been converted, most had fled, and a number who resisted were killed.... It was not long before

the usual complaints started to come in about the biased action of troops, always false accusations by Muslims against Hindu troops....
All the accusations were investigated and proved to be false...the Army stood firm against it (communal virus) in the most wonderful way for many months. The traditional spirit of impartiality, the old spirit of pride in their regiment held them together for longer than any could have deemed possible. I believe that this is the greatest achievement of the British in India.'[15] Again, later, in October, 'in East Bengal our men were still out all over the countryside, bringing back confidence to the persecuted Hindus.... Of the many allegations of rape made against the Army not a single one, after the most careful and painstaking investigation, was ever proved by any evidence whatsoever, including medical evidence.'[16] And then, in Bihar: 'The record of Colonel Venning's 1 Madras supports everything that I have to say about the complete impartiality and soldierly behaviour of the Indian Army under this violent test. His men were nearly all Hindus, and they fought against great odds and with great determination.'[17]

It is said of Wavell, that as a military commander he always carried a file marked "The Worst Possible Case" (WPC) an exercise in contingency planning for an emergency. Such contingency plans had, by now, been prepared. Sand model exercises had been held *inter alia* for the security of Europeans and armouries (first named Operation "Asylum", an harking back to the fears of 1857, and later "Gondola"), in the event of a sudden breakdown of law and order. Mountbatten was later to say that all he had got from Wavell was a file on Operation "Madhouse". The General Staff, with many British Army staff officers in it, being more pessimistic than Auchinleck, had, under instructions from Britain through the Viceroy also prepared two paper plans, "Madhouse" in the event of the Indian Army becoming unreliable, and "Bedlam" in the event of it becoming hostile. Then, admittedly based on the premise that Britain's day in India was drawing to a close, during a visit Wavell personally re-presented London with his plan in December 1946, an earlier modified version of the Cabinet Mission's "Breakdown Plan", for a progressive withdrawal, stage by stage, of the British administration and British troops northwards, handing over the Hindu-majority provinces (the southern ones), and the British administration establishing itself in the northern provinces (described by Leonard Mosley as Operation "Ebbtide"[18]).Auchinleck was opposed to the plan; the British had a duty to perform, and must not be panicked into any withdrawal, even stage-wise, despite the communal killings. Wavell suggested March 1948 as the terminal month for the final transfer of power, by when he hoped a *modus vivendi* could be evolved with the concerned Indian political leaders. During the period of the implementation of his plan, he expected 30,000 communal killings. Alternatively, the British should decide to stay for ten years, and position four to five British divisions in India for that period. With the demand for British demobilization already precipitating mutinies, such as the RAF in India and the Parachute Regiment in Malaya, the British Government was in no position to find four to five divisions for ten years. Though the Labour Party, in its election manifesto, had included independence for India, nevertheless Operation "Ebbtide" seemed to them to be a scuttle, which it was not. (The figure of 30,000 lives seemed mind-boggling at the time, though it was modest to what transpired under Mountbatten.) It was, therefore, decided in January 1947 to replace Wavell by Mountbatten, though Clement Attlee did not tell Wavell at the time. King George VI recorded in his diary on 17 December, 'Attlee told me that Lord Wavell's plan for our leaving India savours too much of a military retreat and does not realize it is a political problem and not a military one.' The King approved Mountbatten's appointment, but sagely added, 'Lord Mountbatten must have concrete orders as to what he is to do. Is he to lead the retreat out of India, or is he to work for the reconciliation of Hindus and Muslims?'[19] This is all that Wavell had been seeking for over two years. The time-frame of fifteen months that he posited for the British withdrawal from India, was, in effect, the same as was to be given to Mountbatten. Three years later, Wavell was dead, aged sixty-seven, his efforts to keep India undivided unappreciated.

415

What was the law and order position in March 1947 when Mountbatten arrived? There had been communal riots in Lahore, Amritsar, Attock, Murree, Rawalpindi and Multan. Over 2,000 had been killed. In the Punjab, the Unionist Party Ministry had resigned, and the Governor administered the province, as the Muslim League was unable to form a ministry. In the UP there had been serious riots at Khurja and Bareilly. (The figures of communal incidents in the UP alone are 1,127 in 1939, 374 in 1946, 467 in 1947, and 468 in 1950.) Tuker reviews the situation in his Command: 'Partitionitis was spreading. In the UP Muslims were drawing up plans for an autonomous Muslim unit in the NW part of the province contiguous to the Punjab. Muslim opinion opposed the division of Bengal, hoping that undivided Bengal would continue under a Muslim government.... Above all, Muslims ardently desired Calcutta....'[20] At this time some 150 men of a Gwalior Infantry battalion refused to go on parade, complaining about the reduced scale of the *atta* ration. They demonstrated on the streets of Gwalior city. A few days later, they were joined in their demonstration by men of another Gwalior Infantry battalion. The demonstrating State troops had to be rounded up, tried and dismissed. In Calcutta there was firing almost daily, resulting in over 800 casualties, including ninety-six killed. Then the Gurkha Armed Police mutinied in reaction to the imported Punjabi Muslim police, urging, 'If the (imported) Punjabi Muslim police are allowed to shoot Hindus, Sikhs and Gurkhas, then why should we not kill Muslims? If the present preferential treatment goes on, then we cannot serve any longer.' The imported Punjabi Muslim police, given superior treatment, were regarded as, 'Mr. Suhrawardy's personal bodyguard, to be forward in all things.' Tuker opines, 'In short, the Bengal Ministry, by unfair treatment and taking a communal line, was fast ruining the one reliable police force that Calcutta possessed.'[21]

In the Naga Hills, there was a serious recrudescence of headhunting; extremist Nagas were writing to Winston Churchill to seek independence from India, while some moderates were in correspondence with Nehru. In Assam, there were riots at Barpeta,

Tuker iterating, 'the determination of the Bengal Muslim League to fill Western Assam with Muslims, and, thereby, so to alter the balance of population that there would be a Muslim majority in the area and so a good chance in days to come of Western Assam being a part of a Muslim province.'[22] And what of the Indian Army, 'In the ranks the absence of communal feeling was most marked, even at this provoking time....They were worried about their relatives in the riot areas....The sense of duty shown by our leave men was an example to all armies. These men would go on leave, find their whole property destroyed and looted, their families scattered, indigent, or even murdered, and yet, somehow, they would return punctually, report for duty. But this army had to be divided...'[23] 'The Bihar Police mutiny (of March/April 1947) would appear to have been a very futile and strange occurrence, were it not understood that it was a rebellion prodded on by Communists.'[24] The Bihar Police at Patna, Gaya, Monghyr and Jamalpur were affected, armoured cars being used in at least one instance to regain control of the concerned police armouries. About this time, a senior Indian UP ICS officer wrote to the press, 'In the last six months I have been watching with great apprehension the deterioration that has been going on not only in the quality of the work of officers, but also a deterioration in the standards and morals of officers themselves.... Officers are so concerned with pushing their own interests, fighting for this or that job...that discipline and efficiency have been impaired.... Lobbying for posts is frequent.... The common procedure now is for an officer to go to Delhi.'[25]

Lord Mountbatten arrived on 22 March 1947, and stated, 'This is not a normal Viceroyalty in which I am embarking....His Majesty's Government are resolved to transfer power by June 1948.... This means a solution must be reached within the next few months.' The instructions to him from the British Prime Minister *inter alia* directed, 'In the first place you will impress upon the Indian leaders the great importance of avoiding any breach in the continuity of the Indian Army and of maintaining the organization of defence on an all India basis.' Mountbatten came not to govern India, but to find a political solution. His charter was to work for a unitary Government of India on the basis of the Cabinet Mission Plan. This, insofar as Jinnah was concerned, was wishful thinking. The eventual political solution was the painful partition of India into two countries, and flowing from that flawed surgery, after 1971 three countries. The question whether partition was inevitable will always remain a matter for debate. Some think it became inevitable when Jinnah resorted to direct action in August 1946; others when Nehru failed to realize the strength of Jinnah and the Muslim League in 1946 at the time of the Cabinet Mission's proposals, however incongruous Jinnah's claim to be the sole leader of undivided India's millions of Muslims. It was the core of his power game. (Few outside India realize that there are more Muslims in India today than in Pakistan, and more Muslims proportionately from the territory of the present Union of India in the Indian Army today, than there correspondingly were in August 1947. Most Britons, who were then in India, certainly do not. What is pertinent now is not what caused the partition, but that it exercises a malevolent influence in the post-independence histories of, first, the two, and then, the three, successor states of the subcontinent. The painful surgery of partition has not excised the cancer.)

Any plan for the partition of India would appear to have involved the partition of the Indian Army, even though Mountbatten, on 8 April 1947, told Liaquat Ali, as recorded by Campbell Johnson in *Mission with Mountbatten,* that there will be no splitting of the Indian Army: 'The mechanics won't permit it, and I won't.' After it had been decided to split it, Mountbatten's Chief of Staff, Hastings Ismay, a former Indian Army officer, was later to say, of the division of the Indian Army, 'the biggest crime and the biggest headache.'[26] Before this, in 1946 a position paper had been prepared by the War Office on the assumption that independent India would remain undivided, but may opt out of the Commonwealth. Titled, "The Strategic Value of India to the British Empire", the thrust was that India should preferably remain in the Commonwealth. The British paper contained, among many interesting facets as to independent

India's perceptions from a Russophobe's viewpoint, the recommendation, 'we should not give up the Andaman and Nicobar Islands, but should hold and develop them as outposts to Burma and Malaya.' This point was to come up pointedly later at the time of the draft Indian Independence Bill in June 1947. Sequentially, Mountbatten, pondering partition, asked Auchinleck for a position paper on the "Strategic implications of the setting up of an independent Pakistan"*. Here, on 24 April 1947, Auchinleck opined, 'Any idea of a "corridor", such as the Polish corridor, can be discarded as quite impracticable.' Jinnah was later still to explore the possibility of one.[27] Meanwhile, Liaquat Ali, after his conversation with Mountbatten, had immediately forwarded a paper for the "Partition of the Indian Armed Forces", though no formal partition decision had yet been taken, acting on the rationale that if the division of the armed forces was conceded, then Pakistan was conceded. After Jinnah, who was from Bombay, Liaquat Ali, from the UP, created Pakistan. Both Baldev Singh and Auchinleck disagreed with Liaquat Ali, Auchinleck stating, 'The Armed Forces of India, as they now stand, cannot be split up into two parts each of which will form a self-contained Armed Force.' Mountbatten decided to discuss Liaquat Ali's paper at a meeting on 26 April.

The impression bruited at the time was that Auchinleck was anti-Pakistan, Malik Sir Feroz Khan Noon, till recently the Defence Member of the Viceroy's Executive Council, publicly declaiming that, 'while the partition (of the Army) was being organized there must be none of the old anti-Pakistan British clique at the head of the Army.' Tuker incorrectly added, 'Beginning with the days of influence wielded at GHQ by Hindu politicians during the fatal days of the INA trials, Muslim leaders had more than once privately voiced their distrust of what they considered to be the pro-Congress tendencies of our Delhi headquarters. The Malik now gave public expression of these doubts.'[28] By now there had also been communal

---

* For details, see Appendix 5. The author of the main part of the paper was reportedly Lieutenant General Sir Arthur Smith, the Chief of the General Staff.

riots in Agra and Cawnpore in the UP, followed by Budaun. Tuker was constrained to comment, 'The UP police had lapsed into such a state of communal cleavage...the civil police were the worst...the armed police better...the Special Armed Constabulary hardly at all affected.... The behaviour of our Indian soldiers was almost beyond praise. They showed...an Indian soldier had no communal feeling in the execution of his duty,'[29] as they had similarly shown over a century earlier at Benares and Bareilly.

On 23 May the British Cabinet approved, in principle, a draft Partition Plan which, in the event of failure to secure a final compromise on the basis of the unitary Cabinet Mission Plan, Mountbatten was authorized to lay before the Indian leaders on 2 June. Gandhi was currently voicing strong objections at his prayer meetings in Delhi to 'the vivisection of the motherland.' Distressing communal incidents were, at the time, occurring in the Punjab and Gurgaon district, with troops being called out in both extensively. A British officer, Major A.V. Ousby of 1st Sikh, was later killed by rioters as an offshoot of the latter disturbances. (Two more British officers were to be killed, during these disturbances, Lieutenant W. Morley, Artillery, near Amritsar in September, and Captain H.M. Ayris, Indian Grenadiers, at Rewari station in October. The heroic Lieutenant Colonel W.H.M. Fawcett's killing at Multan by an other rank was unconnected with the disturbances *per se*. He sought to protect an Indian officer, of the Para Marathas, who had refused to grant the concerned other rank some leave.) Here it needs to be mentioned that the British personnel toiled loyally till their departure, even when such toiling led to their "extinction". According to the publication "The Transfer of Power", at the meeting on 2 June, Mountbatten said the unitary Cabinet Mission Plan was still 'the best solution,' but realized, 'the convergence of opinion as to Partition,' conscious that it was contrary to Congress principles, and that the Muslim League did not agree to the partition of provinces. Insofar as he himself was concerned, there was, 'the impossibility of fully accepting the principles of one side and not of the other.' He covered the problems of the position of the Sikhs, and the future of Calcutta, as also the Indian preference for the immediate transfer of power as opposed to June 1948 (the successor countries were to be offered Dominion status[30]).

The then Congress President, Acharya J.B. Kripalani, in accepting partition, pending ratification by the All-India Congress Committee (AICC), replied, 'We believe, as fully as ever in a united India. The unity we aim at is not that of compulsion, but of friendship and cooperation. We earnestly trust that when present passions have subsided, our problems will be viewed in their proper perspective, and a willing union of all parts of India will result therefrom.'[31] Sardar Baldev Singh stated, 'My Sikh friends and I accept the principle of division...with the hope...that care will be taken...when framing the terms of reference for the Boundary Commission.'[32] Jinnah agreed verbally, pending the meeting of the League Working Committee. Transfer of power was to be not later than 15 August 1947, according to Mountbatten, for tactical reasons, as he wished the concerned parties to 'realize that they must move quickly.' It would also be another epochal event for him on 15 August, though he did not say so at the time, his being appointed Supreme Commander, South-East Asia, on 15 August 1943, and the Japanese surrender being on 15 August 1945. In the "Conclusions" he appended in September 1948 to his "Report on the Last Viceroyalty" submitted to the British Government, he was to say, 'If the implementation was to take place at all, speed seemed essential; delay might have plunged the whole Indian sub-continent and not the Punjab only, into disruption and chaos; the only possible alternative to a quick transfer of power was to reopen recruitment of British officials to the Indian Civil Service and Indian Police, and to bring in a large number of British Army Divisions.' The League Council accepted the Partition Plan as a compromise, being unable to agree to the partition of the Punjab and Bengal. The Congress Committee accepted partition, 'in the circumstances now prevailing,' while regretting, 'the secession of some parts of the country from India.' (On his deathbed, on 11 September 1948 Jinnah described Pakistan as the biggest blunder of his life; according to his physician, Colonel

Ilahi Bakhsh, as recounted in the Peshawar *Frontier Post* in November 1987.)

In Bengal and the Punjab the legislative assemblies sat and decided on partition, paving the way for the appointment of a Boundary Commission. To meet the "exceptional position" of the North-West Frontier Province (NWFP), a referendum was to be held there. There was also the issue of the predominantly Muslim district of Sylhet in the predominantly non-Muslim province of Assam. Separately, the British Government accepted Nehru's view, 'that Hindustan will succeed to the position of India as an international entity,' Liaquat Ali stating that he did not wish, 'to waste time arguing whether Hindustan should take the title of India,' as recorded in "The Transfer of Power". (India, before independence, had been made a founder member of the United Nations in 1946. After the formation of Pakistan, India was accepted as the successor state by the UN, and had to make no fresh application. Pakistan was asked to apply, and its application was sponsored by India.) Sequentially, a Partition Committee was also set up, with, among other expert committees, an Armed Forces Reconstitution Committee (AFRC). Auchinleck, who had hitherto been "gloomy" about the effects of division on discipline, was now, as a result of the lead given by the political leaders, 'confident he could produce at the earliest reasonable moment two Armies, each of which would be as efficient as the existing one, provided the advice of the experts on the question of division was given due consideration.' Sir Chandulal Trivedi, who had been Secretary of the War Department for three years during the Second World War, was invited to serve on the AFRC.

The last plea to preserve the unity of the Army, according to Major General S.F. Irwin, then Deputy Chief of the General Staff, 'came from the Indian officers, whose most senior members, the brigadiers, earnestly represented the case for a combined army, serving both Dominions.'[33] I.M. Muthanna, Cariappa's biographer, records, 'Cariappa's subsequent activities and utterances prove that he was one of those who held the above view.'[34] What they would appear to have had in mind was that each dominion would furnish the recruits, but there would have been unified command and training to deal with the defence of the subcontinent as a single problem common to the two dominions. By this time, however, events had already made it impossible of acceptance by the two prospective dominions' political leaders.[35]

Thus, by happenstance, the Army's image had been subjected to some exacerbation in the eyes of Nehru and others by the then senior Indian officers themselves. Interestingly, on 25 April 1947 (the partition decision had not yet been taken), Cariappa had written from London to Nehru urging that the Army be kept intact "at any cost". Suddenly, on 10 May 1947, as recorded in "The Transfer of Power", Ismay had reported to Mountbatten, 'Cariappa (then on the Imperial Defence College Course in London) came to see me yesterday and volunteered the amazing suggestion that the Indian Army, with either Nehru or Jinnah as Commander-in-Chief, should take over power when we left in June 1948. I at once said that the proposal was not only wholly impracticable, but highly dangerous, that throughout history the rule of an army had always proved tyrannical and incompetent, and that the army must always be servants and not masters. I added that the Indian Army, by remaining united and refusing to take sides, could wield a tremendous influence for good in the disturbed days that lie ahead, but that they must always be subservient to civil power. I concluded by begging him to put the idea right out of his mind, and never to mention it again even in the strictest secrecy.' Ismay added, 'It is hard to know whether Cariappa in putting forward this idea is ingenuous and ignorant, or ingenuous and dangerous.' On his return to India in June 1947, after the partition decision had been announced, Cariappa modified his proposal, to, as outlined above by Irwin, now suggesting a combined operational Indo-Pakistan Army. Before that, Mountbatten, after meeting Jinnah on 7 April 1947, had met C. Rajagopalachari, 'I told him that Brigadier Cariappa, the most senior Indian officer had given a most courageous lead in his statement to the Indian press in London that it would take five years before they could do without British officers.... Mr Rajagopalachari was glad to think that Brigadier

Cariappa had the courage to make this statement, particularly since, he said, that "it was due to the senior Indian officers themselves that the politicians had been misled...all Indian officers had combined together to give the impression that the sooner the British were pushed out the better."'

According to "The Transfer of Power", there was now extreme secrecy as to the clause relating to the Andamans in the draft Indian Independence Bill received by Mountbatten on 14 June which islands the British Government proposed to make into a British settlement, as they were of vital importance in the scheme of Commonwealth Defence, and were not to be regarded as a part of British-India. Mountbatten informed London that any attempt, 'to claim the Andaman Islands as colonies, to be treated in the same way as Aden, will cause an absolute flare-up throughout the length and breadth of India.'[36] The British Chiefs of Staff still argued cogently for the islands to be retained by Britain as earlier urged but in the context of the Viceroy's opinion, the British Government decided that it would not be politic to pursue their Chiefs of Staff's suggestion of separating the islands from India. Then, on 2 July, the Muslim League pressured Mountbatten, urging that the islands should be included in Pakistan, 'for geographical and strategic reasons,' and on 5 July Jinnah urged that, 'they are not part of India historically or geographically.... Pakistan's claim to these islands is very strong since the only channel of communication between eastern and western Pakistan is by sea, and the islands occupy an important strategic position on the sea route, and provide refuelling bases. The Dominion of India have no such claim.'[37] Had these islands also been "partitioned", there would have been major subsequent disputes in this archipelago as well.

On 15 June the Governor of the Punjab reported that the partition announcement of 3 June had made no discernible improvement in communal relations, commenting, 'It was ordained from the first that the communities would massacre and loot one another.' On 23 June, the Provincial Legislative Assembly voted for partition, 'with a large section of Lahore and scores of villages throughout the province in fire-blackened ruins,' Liaquat Ali on 17 June complaining of, 'the full-scale war of extermination,' being waged in Gurgaon. On 24 June, Jinnah asked for utter ruthlessness to suppress disorder in Lahore and Amritsar, while Nehru sought that martial law be declared in the two cities. The Governor, in consultation with the military commanders, did not think there was a case yet for the declaration of martial law. On 26 June the Sind Assembly voted for partition. But here the Muslim League had won a majority of seats in the 1946 elections, due to the faulty electoral system—thirty per cent had voted for the Congress, thirty per cent for Nationalist Muslims, and only forty per cent for the League. As to the NWFP, the 3 June statement required a referendum as to which of the new dominions the province should join. On 5 June, the Congress party Premier, Khan Abdul Ghaffar Khan's brother, Dr Khan Sahib, later to be assassinated in 1958, suggested a third course, an independent Pathanistan, which Mountbatten ruled out. Simultaneously, the Premier asked that the Governor, Sir Olaf Caroe, be replaced; Lieutenant General Rob Lockhart was appointed as the Governor. On 28 June, Khan Abdul Ghaffar Khan and his Red Shirts decided to abstain from the referendum to be held from 6 to 17 July, since there was to be no option for a free Pathanistan. In the event, the referendum was held as scheduled. With the Khudai Khidmatgars abstaining, as there was no third option for Pathanistan, the result was a foregone conclusion. My company and I were then deployed in aid of the civil authority between Thal and Hangu in Kurram. The result for the whole of the NWFP was 289,244 for Pakistan, and 2,874 for India. As the votes for Pakistan were assessed to be 50.49 per cent of the total electorate, the Viceroy viewed the result as in favour of Pakistan. In the area of Thal, attacks on the few who were suspected of having voted for India commenced on 14 August itself. Ghaffar Khan was later to title his book, *Thrown to the Wolves*. This lion of a man spent most of the rest of his life in jail or exile. (On 22 August, the elected NWFP Ministry, headed by Dr Khan Sahib, was dismissed, and arbitrarily replaced by a Muslim League Ministry. The brothers were arrested in June and September 1948 respectively.)

In the month of June, the Congress, 'were determined to oppose any move towards an independent but united Bengal,' as sought by Suhrawardy. The Governor was simultaneously of the view that it was too late to declare Calcutta a free city, or under joint control, a possibility which Jinnah was reported as favouring, and which was also being propounded by Suhrawardy, in the event of partition. On 20 June, the Bengal Assembly voted in favour of partition, with the amalgamation of Sylhet with East Bengal. A referendum was thus also held in Sylhet on the question of joining East Bengal or remaining in Assam, showing a majority of 55,578 in favour of East Bengal. The result may have been different if the Assam Congress had been as active as the Muslim League. Tuker recounts, 'The well-organized Muslim League being to the fore in all these electioneering activities. They had brought into Sylhet hosts of their friends. All were, alike, a nuisance to us, but thoroughly terrified the more moderate Nationalist Muslims into voting for the League in the interests of their future skins.'[38] Separately, in the Punjab, there was a report on the willingness of the Sikh leader, Giani Kartar Singh, to try to come to an agreement with Jinnah for the inclusion of a Sikh "Khalistan" in Pakistan, but this was opposed by Baldev Singh, who had earlier on 3 June already stated that the Sikhs were unable to contemplate being forced into a state founded on Islamic principles against their will, and that the Boundary Commission should be instructed to ensure that as large as possible a percentage of the Sikh population should be included in East Punjab. Mountbatten declined to influence the commission. (Later, on 13 September, Auchinleck was to write to Mountbatten, 'The Sikh plans are ... to make Simla the capital of a Sikh State in which there will be ... possibly not many Hindus ... to concentrate the Sikhs in the Eastern Punjab ... to have concentrated power there.')

Meanwhile, Montgomery, from 24 June onwards, had visited India and Nepal. He reached an outline agreement for British-Gurkha troops transiting through India, the ten Gurkha regiments not forming part of the planning for the partition of the army between India and Pakistan, though there was reportedly a move by some of the British officers of the 5th Gurkha Rifles (Frontier Force) Centre, then at Abbotabad, that the regiment should continue to be part of the "Piffers", allotted to Pakistan. Instead, the division was between India and Britain, with tripartite negotiations being conducted with Nepal. Six regiments were eventually allotted to India, and four to Britain. The War Office expressed a preference for the 2nd, 7th and 10th Gurkha Rifles for reasons of sentiment, as also being desirous, in the choice of the four regiments, of diversifying recruitment throughout the length of Nepal. An example of the sentimental association invoked was that of the 2nd Gurkha Rifles and the British 60th Rifles in the siege of Delhi in 1857. Allowing for the recruiting parameter mentioned earlier, the choice of the fourth regiment was left to GHQ (India). The regiment chosen was the 6th Gurkha Rifles, one of whose battalions was, by circumstance, then on duty at the Viceroy's House. For the personnel of the regiments allotted to Britain, there was a concomitant option, whether they preferred to serve in the Indian Army rather than join the British forces overseas, and vice-versa for the personnel of the Indian regiments. This option process was later deemed, by the concerned British commanding officer of a 7th Gurkha Rifles battalion, to have resulted in a "mutiny" at Ahmedabad. It was in no way a mutiny, but, unfortunately, was viewed as such by the authorities concerned. The majority of the men had merely declined to be photographed for the new British documentation, since they intended to opt for the Indian Army. To accommodate the numerous optees for India, not only did existing regiments like the 5th Gurkha Rifles have to raise new battalions, but a new regiment had to be raised, the 11th Gurkha Rifles. (The success of this arrangement with Nepal is evidenced by the circumstance that there are now many more Gurkha battalions than the original nineteen allotted on 15 August 1947. The phonetically more correct spelling "Gorkha" has since been adopted in the Indian Army as opposed to the continued usage of "Gurkha" by the British.) On 27 June the retention of British officers in a limited number and with a restricted role was agreed, with British troops commencing withdrawal on 15 August and completing by

28 February. During Montgomery's visit Nehru reportedly welcomed the prospect of Slim being the Commander-in-Chief of the Indian Army from 15 August, in place of Auchinleck, but Mountbatten did not agree to any change at that juncture. This apparently was a ploy in order not to make Slim CIGS, Montgomery arguing that an officer with an Indian Army background was not acceptable as CIGS. (Mountbatten prevailed on Clement Attlee subsequently to bring Slim back from retirement as the CIGS. Montgomery protested to Attlee that he had already told General Sir John Crocker that he was to be the CIGS. 'Well, untell him,' replied Attlee.)

The modalities of the partition of the armed forces were approved on 30 June by Mountbatten, he paying tribute to Sir Chandulal Trivedi's contribution, and observing that, 'Auchinleck is delighted beyond measure.' A Joint Defence Council was sequentially set up to monitor the partition of the armed forces and of Defence assets. In relation to the dimensions of the task, previous estimates by GHQ had varied from three to five years. It now had to be done in less than two months. The parameters were that, by 15 August, as far as possible, all units should be located within their own dominion, and personnel to be shed by one dominion should be moved to units of the other dominion. With exceptions such as the Madras Regiment, the Maratha Light Infantry, the Dogra Regiment, the Garhwal Rifles, the Sikh Light Infantry, the Kumaon Regiment, the Assam Regiment, the Mahar Regiment and the Gurkha Rifles, each unit contained men of different classes and religions, including battalions of regiments like the Rajput Regiment, the Jat Regiment, and the Sikh Regiment. Under the final Army Partition scheme a Muslim soldier domiciled in Pakistan and a non-Muslim domiciled in the rest of India had no choice but to serve his respective dominion, or be discharged. But a Muslim from India or a non-Muslim from Pakistan could elect which dominion he would serve (this meant a questionnaire to be filled in), with a subsequent entitlement to reoption. There was later a problem whether those Indian Muslims, who had initially opted for Pakistan, could finally reopt for India. In the sphere of Indian Muslim sub-units, however, mistakes were made by the Army Sub-committee of the AFRC, even though it had two Indian members and one Indian secretary. The Army Sub-committee had assumed for planning purposes on the suggestion of the Pakistani members that the majority of Indian Muslim personnel would opt for Pakistan, and had already allotted Indian Muslim sub-units to Pakistan even before the concerned Record offices could process the individual options. The task was, undoubtedly, gigantic, but the mistake was avoidable. In the event the majority of the personnel of many Indian Muslim sub-units had opted for India, but because the sub-units had been erroneously allotted to Pakistan under a misconception, and who had taken it into their reckoning in their organization tables, the concerned Indian Muslim sub-units, with the majority of personnel who had opted for India, continued to be allotted to Pakistan by the AFRC, despite representations, except later for one Kaimkhani squadron.

This tragic mistake could have been avoided. I can vouch for such contretemps, as I was commanding one such Indian Muslim rifle company at Thal in Kurram (NWFP). To compound our confusion, before we left Thal in September for India, two Dogra companies from regiments allotted to Pakistan reported to replace one Indian Muslim company which had opted for India but had been allotted to Pakistan. *En route* our Indian Muslim company was forcibly taken off our train at Lahore, and during a halt at Jalandhar we were given a third Dogra company in lieu of the same Muslim company. We eventually reached our destination in India in late October, and in due course had a fourth Dogra company allotted from a different regiment to the other three, who were then re-allotted to another regiment. This example is not being given in order to carp, but to illustrate the difficulties of the period. The movement of about half-a-million personnel was entailed, since demobilization to the Willcox Committee post-war strength of 280,000 was very much in progress (on 14 August the undivided strength was over 400,000), some of the concerned units still in the process of returning from overseas, from as far apart as Iraq and Japan. The staff work required for putting all this into effect was complex, and much of it was carried out in what were wartime conditions. Owing to the disturbed conditions in the Punjab, Plan "Rail Cross" was now augmented by "Sea Cross" from Bombay to Karachi.

Already for much of 1947, units of the undivided Army had been dispersed in an all-out effort to keep the peace. While it was not possible to stop the mutual killing, the soldiers of the respective communities, who had fought side by side in the Second World War, prevented the slaughter from being much worse. As internal unrest spread in the Punjab, millions left their homes and set out with their livestock and belongings for their new dominion. They constituted the largest permanent migration of people in human history. Jinnah had never imagined an upheaval of this magnitude, as a result of the partition decision. Moving in two opposite directions, in the Punjab, they covered all roads, railways and bridges. They introduced gigantic problems of control, shelter and feeding. A Military Evacuation Organization was set up by each dominion in September 1947 for a few months to help them. Major Ram Singh of the Rajput Regiment and some of his company were killed on this duty in Lyallpur district. 'Could any army suffer such surgery and survive?' There was the oft-expressed fear that control of some of these moving sub-units might be lost, and so unleash bands of armed men taking sides in the inter-communal strife. It says a great deal for the discipline of the undivided Army that this did not happen. It is astonishing that this movement was carried out in such a short time, not only because of the numbers involved, but because the railways were choked with refugees, and even some military specials were subjected to attack and sabotage, as my battalion was twice, resulting in twenty-six killed and seventy-two wounded (including seven officers) in this one battalion alone. Certain evacuee camps, like Kurukshetra, were also run by the Indian Army.

In the meantime, the British Prime Minister, presumably on Montgomery's advice, decided that it would be most untimely to discuss Britain's longterm strategic requirements in the region with Indian leaders. A hint of this attitude of Montgomery had been discernible when Auchinleck had sought to take two brigadiers, Cariappa and M.S. Rajendrasinhji, with him to an exercise in Britain in March 1947, and had asked for the exercise papers for them to study. Montgomery did not agree, as they were not yet Major Generals, but added, 'We are much concerned in London about Nehru's latest statement about an Indian Republic.'[39] Thereafter, on 11 July, Nehru wrote to Mountbatten, urging more rapid nationalization of the armed forces, by June 1948, with Indian officers promoted to the highest ranks more quickly, than the then GHQ thought practicable at a time when the armed forces were being reconstituted. In the process of reconstitution, feeling had hardened against Auchinleck. Up to 14 August, the role of Auchinleck's GHQ had been to "break down" the undivided Army, whereas, from 15 August, the role of Army Headquarters (India) would be to "build up" the reconstituted Indian Army. In his next progress report to London, according to "The Transfer of Power", Mountbatten sequentially wrote: 'Recently I have been very worried about the attitude of the Congress in general, and Baldev Singh, in particular, towards Auchinleck. They had got it firmly in their heads that he had become definitely anti-Congress, and it almost reached a point when they were going to refuse to have him as Supreme Commander on the 15th. Auchinleck, for his part, told me Baldev Singh was so impossible that he could scarcely carry on with him, and was prepared to resign if it would help me.... I pointed out to Nehru that Auchinleck had only a few weeks ago been criticized by Jinnah and Liaquat as being anti-League, and further that he had also been subjected to a good deal of criticism by his own countrymen on the grounds of his alleged partiality towards the Indians as a whole at the expense of the British officers. I added that I was absolutely positive as to Auchinleck's integrity and military competence. I got the invaluable Trivedi down from Orissa.... Trivedi saw Nehru and Patel, and impressed Auchinleck's sterling qualities on them.... He (Baldev Singh) had on his own initiative been to see Auchinleck that very afternoon and then he had told him that he was extremely sorry if he was responsible for the present state of their relationship; further that he admired Auchinleck very much and that he would have no wish to be Defence Member unless he felt that he had his (Auchinleck's) confidence. Apparently Auchinleck was very touched by this generous approach.... The truth is that I had already told Nehru that Baldev Singh was not a very good Defence Member, and ought not to have that portfolio in the new Cabinet...fortified by the reconciliation between Auchinleck and Baldev Singh, I had no hesitation in eating my words about the latter. It now seems certain that Baldev Singh will be the Defence Minister. He seems slow in the uptake, but he has had a hard row to hoe, and I am inclined to think he means well.'[40] Before going firm on Sardar Baldev Singh as the Defence Minister in the new Cabinet on 15 August, Nehru had considered making Dr Shyama Prasad Mookerjee the Defence Minister in view of Mountbatten's earlier criticism of Baldev Singh.

On 11 July, the Viceroy described the Punjab as "most unsettled" thereafter, at its meeting on 17 July, the Central Partition Council approved a plan prepared by Auchinleck to deal with clashes and disturbances along the boundaries of the two dominions on and after 15 August, and before that, from 1 to 15 August, in the undivided Punjab. The Joint Defence Council would have the authority of India and Pakistan to declare affected districts "disturbed", and the Supreme Commander would have the authority to appoint a military commander with a sufficiency of forces to restore order. Major General T.W. Rees was appointed the Joint Commander of this force of two divisions minus, that came to be known as the "Punjab Boundary Force", which was to be operative from 1 August, and be responsible for 37,500 square miles of territory astride the prospective boundary. On 12 August the Governor reported that the Boundary Force was, 'not adequate to present and future tasks,' and that the police in Lahore and Amritsar were now unreliable. Auchinleck decided to visit these two cities, and, thereafter, augmented the Boundary Force.

As to the merger of the princely states, at a meeting on 13 June, there had been differences of opinion on whether any princely state could claim independence, Nehru maintaining this was precluded, and Jinnah that it was not. On 12 June the Nizam had already announced his intention to become sovereign on the departure of the paramount power, with any relationship to the successor states to be decided later,but separately seeking treaty access to an Indian port. On 17 June, Jinnah reaffirmed his views on the states' sovereignty, and the Maharaja of Travancore decided upon a declaration of independence, on the lapse of paramountcy. On 19 June, Nehru countered that it was bad enough for India to be partitioned, without being "Balkanized". Before reviewing the position as to the states on the Indian side of the prospective border, the position on the Pakistani side needs mentioning. All the three states—Khairpur, Bahawalpur and Kalat—were initially reluctant to accede to Pakistan. Taking Bahawalpur as an illustration, the Muslim League in Simla came to know of the Nawab's initial unwillingness, and besieged him in his house in Simla, preventing him from meeting Sardar Patel.

On 1 August, Mountbatten listed the Indian states that, so far, had been holding out in relation to accession—Travancore, Hyderabad, Dholpur, Indore and Bhopal—Kashmir and Junagadh being dealt with separately. Travancore gave in under pressure of the States' People's Movement, after an assault on the Dewan, Sir C.P. Ramaswami Iyer. The Maharaja of Dholpur, convinced of the divine right of kings, suggested a treaty relationship as an alternative to accession. Only on 14 August, the last day, did he sign. The Maharaja of Indore, delivered the Instrument of Accession on 15 August, backdated to 14 August. As to Bhopal, on 10 August, contemplating abdication, the Nawab asked for an extension of ten days from 15 August, to enable him to see what decisions were taken by Hyderabad and Kashmir. Hyderabad was given an extension of two months for the purposes of negotiation, later extended to a year. In Kashmir in August, the Maharaja appeared to have decided to dismiss his Dewan, Pandit R.C. Kak, and was, according to the Viceroy, said to be contemplating a referendum. Unknown to the Maharaja, while he wavered, the tribesmen in the NWFP were about to organize themselves for a brutal invasion of Kashmir, in which, according to Tuker, 'a leading part was taken by the Muslim officers of the INA,'[41] amongst others. (On 22 August, GHQ (Pakistan) had issued instructions to Pakistani Army formation headquarters for each of the six Pathan tribes to organize "lashkars" of 1,000 each by the first week of September, to be equipped, and led by a major.)

As 14 and 15 August approached, the pressures became more intense. Reconstitution of the units formed only one part of the partition of the undivided Army. There were, after the Second World War, large reserves of weapons, ammunition and equipment. With the exception of the seventeen ordnance factories, agreement was reached on how these assets should be divided, and an agreed percentage (66:34) was devised. This plan, initially, postulated the existence of the Supreme Commander's Headquarters, who would order the movement of these military assets, and who would, notionally, have the power to see that these move orders were carried out. But, after 15 August, that power no longer remained with the British. The subsequent partition of the assets of the armed forces had to depend on the cooperation of the two dominions. A Committee of Defence Secretaries was appointed for the purpose, and six crore rupees later paid to Pakistan as her share of the ordnance factories.

On 14 August a Pakistani complaint was received by the Viceroy as to the purported allocation of a large part of Gurdaspur district to East Punjab by "a political decision", and protests by Sardar Patel about the inclusion of the tribal Chittagong Hill Tracts in East Pakistan. Mountbatten replied that he was in no position to influence the Boundary Commission's decisions. Auchinleck had returned on 15 August after visiting the Boundary Force. Rees had reported, in relation to the habitual complaints against the troops in such situations: 'Their action has been completely impartial.' Auchinleck, in turn, informed Mountbatten: 'So far the troops have been completely impartial and extremely well-disciplined, in spite of baseless and mischievous stories to the contrary....' Mountbatten summed up at the Joint Defence Council meeting on 16 August: '...the soldiers are doing everything that is humanly possible to try and hold the situation...the situation is long past military action and requires political leadership of a high order.'

The American commentator, Walter Lippmann, had written on 7 June 1947 in the *Washington Post*: '...with an elegance and style that will compel and receive an instinctive response throughout the civilized world, Attlee and Mountbatten have done a service to all mankind by showing what statesmen can do, not with force and money, but with lucidity, resolution and sincerity.' He should have included Wavell and Auchinleck as well in the ambit of his commentary, for they also did a service to all mankind by showing what soldiers can do with even greater lucidity, resolution and sincerity. Shortly after a decision was taken to wind up the Boundary Force, on the Boundary Commission's awards having been published on 17 August, each dominion taking over responsibility for its side of the border, but a Military Evacuation Organization of each dominion to operate. It was now found necessary to establish Headquarters Delhi and East Punjab Command (later to be redesignated as Headquarters Western Command), with Lieutenant General Sir Dudley Russell as the GOC-in-C, since Headquarters Eastern Command was already stretched responsibility-wise, and the new Army Headquarters (India) was finding it inconvenient to administer Delhi Area direct which GHQ had latterly been doing. During August and September a quarter-of-a-million people lost their lives, and some fourteen million in all migrated. Separately, C. Rajagopalachari, who was eventually to succeed Mountbatten as Governor-General, recorded, 'If the Viceroy had not transferred power when he did, there could well have been no power to transfer.' Sadly, thereafter in chronological sequence, Gandhi was assassinated on 30 January 1948, Jinnah was to die of cancer in September 1948, and thereafter in 1951 Liaquat Ali was to be assassinated. Meanwhile at the "break-up" party at the Staff College, Quetta, Major Yahya Khan, later to be the President of Pakistan, was stating to Colonel (later Lieutenant General) S.D. Verma, the Chief Instructor: 'Sir, what are we celebrating? This should be a day of mourning. As a united country, we could have been a strong and powerful nation. Now we will be fighting one another.'

On 1 September Montgomery chose to write to Mountbatten, 'It is my opinion that Auchinleck's usefulness in India has finished. He is 63; he has spent all his life in India under a previous regime; he is too old to readjust himself to new ideas which he dislikes in his heart. He is viewed with suspicion by the senior officers of the Indian Army.... I personally consider, if you want military matters to run smoothly and effectively in India, you will have to remove Auchinleck; I further consider if you do not do so you will have trouble.... I would tell Auchinleck to retire and recommend him for a GCSI, nothing more....'[42] As it so happened, Auchinleck received a letter by hand from Mountbatten on 26 September: 'This is probably the most difficult letter I have ever had to write in my life.... I am well aware that you did not ask for the title of Supreme Commander.... It is not, however, only the title to which exception is taken. There is no doubt in my mind that Indian Ministers resent the fact that at the head of Supreme Headquarters there should be a man of your very high rank and great personal prestige and reputation—so immeasurably superior in these respects to their own Commander-in-Chief.... It is only fair to add that Pandit Nehru himself has no personal bias in the matter and sympathizes with the difficulties of your position.... The point has now been reached when I can no longer prevent them from putting up an official proposal to the Joint Defence Council that the Supreme Commander's Headquarters should be abolished and replaced by an organization with a less high-sounding title and headed by less high-ranking officers. The discussion of a proposal of this kind in the Joint Defence Council could be absolutely deplorable. It is possible that the Pakistan representatives would oppose the proposal out of cussedness, but not, I fear, out of any sincere desire to support you. It is only a short while ago that they were pressing for your removal, on the grounds of your alleged anti-Muslim sentiments.... You have often told me, with your characteristic unselfishness, that you would willingly and indeed gladly fade out of the picture—I do not need to assure you that I...told the Cabinet in London that I regarded you as the greatest

Commander-in-Chief that India has ever had.... My original intention was that your peerage, if you decided to accept it, would appear in the next New Year Honours List since...I imagined that you would be at your post until the spring of next year....'[43]

Auchinleck declined the peerage, and it was decided he would leave India on 1 December. He undoubtedly did more for broad-basing recruitment and nationalizing the officer cadre than any of his predecessors or contemporaries. The decision to downgrade the Supreme Commander's Headquarters was undoubtedly the correct one, but it was resented by Pakistan, which protested. Some military commanders have to chase luck; others luck chases. Auchinleck fell in the former category, and Montgomery in the latter. Had Auchinleck opted for the British Army, he would have surely become the CIGS. Would Montgomery, if he had passed out high enough from Sandhurst and got the sought-for vacancy in the Indian Army, have made it to Commander-in-Chief in India?

Meanwhile, much before Auchinleck's departure, as the Maharaja of Jammu and Kashmir wavered, 5,000 Pakistani tribesmen and soldiers on leave, led by regular officers also on leave, apart from ex-officers of the INA, brutally invaded the State on 22 October in about 300 civilian lorries, and headed for Srinagar. Most of the Muslims in the State Force and some from the police, deserted, many joined the raiders, and guided them. On hearing of these desertions, the Chief of Staff of the State Force, Brigadier Rajinder Singh, with an ad-hoc force of 150 men, moved to Uri, delayed the raiders for two days and destroyed the Uri bridge. He and his gallant force were overwhelmed and killed. (When the 'Maha Vir Chakra' award was later instituted, equivalent to the Distinguished Service Order [DSO], the first award, posthumously, was to this hero.) Even before this, Pakistan had cut off the supply of food, petrol and other essential commodities to the State, thus breaking the Standstill Agreement, and military pressure was being applied from Pakistani bases in the form of hit-and-run border raids, particularly in the area of Poonch, thereby dispersing the State Force over a wider area with no reserves. The railway service from Sialkot to Jammu had also been discontinued, and the free transit of travellers hindered.

On 15 October the State appealed to the British Prime Minister, but no reply was received. Had the raiders not paused at Baramula to indulge in an orgy of pillage and rapine, Srinagar, which they had planned to reach on 26 October and whose electric supply had been already cut, would have fallen. (The girls then abducted were sold in hundreds for Rs 150 each.) A British couple, Colonel and Mrs D.O.T. Dykes, were killed. He was the Commandant of the Sikh Regimental Centre, and they had gone to the Baramula Convent Hospital, along with their children, for his wife's confinement (she had been there for a previous confinement as well). When the raiders tried to rape Mrs Dykes, who had just had her delivery, Colonel Dykes sought to save her. Both were killed. The newborn baby was thrown into a well. Some nuns were raped and four killed. On the Maharaja acceding to India on 26 October, the 1st Battlion, The Sikh Regiment, then deployed on internal security, in the neighbourhood of Gurgaon near Delhi, was flown in on 27 October, just in time to save Srinagar, Pakistan described this emergent fly-in, mainly using civil airlines aircraft, after a legal accession, on the basis of general modalities earlier agreed to by Pakistan, as an invasion. (Organizationally, Mountbatten said this short-notice fly-in of the 1st Sikhs surpassed anything similarly achieved in South-East Asia Command in the Second World War.) As to the Pakistani complaint that there had been planning over a long period for such a fly-in to have taken place, the three British Commanders-in-Chief in New Delhi recorded, 'No plans were made for sending these forces, nor were such plans even considered, before 25th October, three days after the tribal incursion began,' when the Maharaja requested military aid from India. The fly-in to Srinagar would not have been possible if the raiders had not paused at Baramula for two days for their nefarious reasons.

The Indian Army, which needed some period for consolidation, after the trauma of the "surgery" of partition, has, by circumstance, sequentially remained operationally extended ever since. Even at that time some attendant problems immediately surfaced; two occurrences were alleged to be "mutinies". Both, in their way, were avoidable, and were not mutinies. The first occurred in the 6th Animal Transport (AT) Regiment at Allahabad. Reinforcements were required for a similar regiment inducted into Kashmir, almost immediately after its arrival from Pakistan, having shed its Muslim personnel there. The decision seems to have been taken amidst the turbulence of the period to post all the Mazhabi Sikhs from the 6th AT Regiment to the other regiment. This *en masse* transfer was inevitably deemed discriminatory by the class in question, which protested peacefully. In the second case, for reasons that did not seem very intelligible after the occurrence, a Muslim Kaimkhani squadron that had opted for India was proposed to be transferred from one Indian armoured regiment, then in Malaya to another in India. From the latter, a Rajput squadron, upset as to a promotion, was contemplated to be transferred to the first armoured regiment, on the plea of rationalization. The Rajput squadron protested peacefully, questioning the necessity of the so-called rationalization. The latter regiment was hastily put into suspended animation, with the result that, when later it was allotted for the possible Hyderabad "Police action", it only had one of its original troops. Greater circumspection has obviously got to be exercised before taking such hasty class composition decisions.

Pakistan, which might have had, initially, a difficult frontier tribal problem, was now rid of it for some months, as the attention of all the tribesmen, down to as far south as Waziristan, was focused on loot and rape in Kashmir. Some of these self-same tribesmen had attacked my battalion's trains on the Frontier twice in September. They were, even then, organized into platoons, with civilian transport, and armed with light and medium machine-guns and Boyes' anti-tank rifles. These were obviously the tribal "lashkars" ordered on 22 August to be concentrated and equipped by the Pakistan Army Headquarters by the first week of September 1947 in accordance with Operation "Gulmarg", and to be led into Kashmir by Pakistan Army personnel, shown on leave. V.P. Menon has recorded, in *The Story of the Integration of the Indian States*: 'I must admit that Sir

439

George Cunningham, who had relieved General Sir Rob Lockhart as Governor of the NWFP, sent warnings of the move of these tribesmen to General Lockhart, who had now become Commander-in-Chief of the Indian Army; but these warnings were vague, probably because Cunningham himself was not being kept fully in the picture by his own government. In any case, these reports failed at the time to excite any feeling of undue alarm or concern in the Government of India.'[44] While my battalion's special train was delayed for two weeks at Lalamusa in October for lack of a locomotive, it was well-known locally that these tribesmen were establishing bases in Pakistan near the border with Jammu and Kashmir.

When contacted by 1st Sikhs on the outskirts of Baramula, the raiders also had mortars and flame-throwers. They could not have come by all this fortuitously, including their rations, and petrol for their transport. Though Pakistan averred that the tribal eruption into Kashmir was spontaneous and uncontrollable, they had undoubtedly been equipped under some guidance and direction, and were led, apart from former INA officers like I.J. Kiani and Burhanuddin, by a "General Tariq", later revealed to be Major General Akbar Khan of the Pakistan Army Headquarters, subsequently to be convicted for the coup attempt in 1951 dubbed the "Rawalpindi Conspiracy Case", and later to be a Minister in the Zulfikar Ali Bhutto government. Pakistan had also effected a large-scale drawal of maps of Kashmir from the Survey of India before independence, Akbar Khan having apparently commenced to plan the invasion of Kashmir while still posted at GHQ (India), on his own initiative. Furthermore, after Lockhart rang up his officiating counterpart, Douglas Gracey, in Rawalpindi, the Dykes children were fortunately recovered and sent to Britain. This rescue could not have been so promptly effected, unless there had been an affective Pakistan Army link with the so-called "raiders". In his memoirs, *Raiders in Kashmir*, published in 1970, Akbar Khan made no secret of official Pakistani involvement, '...after Partition, I was asked by Mian Iftikharuddin on behalf of Liaquat Ali Khan to prepare a plan for action in Kashmir.... I was called to a meeting with Liaquat Ali Khan at Lahore, where the plan was adopted, responsibilities allotted, and orders issued.' Later in 1985, in an interview published in the Pakistan "Defence Journal" (Karachi, June-July 1985) he reconfirmed this.

Separately, Jinnah's private secretary, Khurshid Ahmad, who had been in Srinagar to keep Jinnah informed, was returned to Pakistan after the arrival of the Indian troops. On learning of the fly-in, Jinnah ordered Gracey to induct the Pakistan Army into Kashmir. Gracey said he could not do so without reference to the Supreme Commander. Auchinleck flew to Lahore on 28 October, and explained to Jinnah that, since the State was now legally part of India, the entry of Pakistani troops into the State would entail the withdrawal of all British officers serving in the Pakistan Army. He had much earlier conveyed his undeserved "distrust" of Auchinleck to Montgomery. Jinnah, thereupon, withdrew his instructions to Gracey, but invited Mountbatten and Nehru to Lahore to discuss the matter. Nehru was too ill to travel, but Mountbatten and Ismay met Jinnah on 1 November, who suggested that both sides withdraw simultaneously. When Mountbatten sought to know how Jinnah could effect the withdrawal of the tribesmen, with Pakistan having already described their invasion as uncontrollable, Jinnah said, 'If you do this I will call the whole thing off.' The officer commanding the 1st Sikhs, Lieutenant Colonel Dewan Ranjit Rai, was sadly killed between Baramula and Pattan, and was posthumously awarded the Maha Vir Chakra. (He should more appropriately have been awarded the Param Vir Chakra, equivalent to the Victoria Cross.) Actually he should have gone to Washington as our military attache, but had been replaced by Colonel (later Lieutenant General) B.M. Kaul. The latter, on hearing of Rai's death, which would presumably not have occurred if Kaul had not displaced him in the Washington posting, thereupon sought return to India for employment in Kashmir.

Meanwhile, Pakistan had accepted the accession by the Nawab of Junagadh, even though it was not contiguous and was eighty-five per cent Hindu. (Earlier, Jinnah had encouraged the accession of the contiguous, predominantly Hindu states of Jodhpur and Jaisalmer, but had not ultimately succeeded in this endeavour.) The Sheikh of

Mangrol and the Raja of Babariawad, adjoining Junagadh, had acceded to India. The pro-Indian Dewan, Nabi Bakhsh, was replaced. The Nawab's new Dewan was Sir Shah Nawaz Bhutto, the father of Prime Minister Zulfikar Ali Bhutto, later hanged in Pakistan. Urging overlordship, they ordered Junagadh troops into Mangrol and Babariawad. Asked to withdraw these troops, they refused. The 7th Indian Infantry Brigade and some armour were moved to Rajkot. The people of Junagadh protested against the accession to Pakistan, and elected a "Provisional Government". The Nawab fled to Pakistan with all the money and securities in the treasury, and, in early November, the Dewan and the senior State Council member, Captain Harvey Jones, asked the Government of India to take over the administration of Junagadh. Here mention needs to be made of Brigadier Gurdial Singh, the brigade commander, as he is not at all remembered today. V.P. Menon recounts, 'When Brigadier Gurdial Singh was asked to take over charge of the Kathiawar Defence Force, Lord Mountbatten had advised him, in my presence, to "hold the scales even" between the two communities. I had not felt too happy over his homily. Brigadier Gurdial Singh was an evacuee from West Punjab. He had lost his entire family and property in the communal holocaust. During the Junagadh crisis, however, he not only displayed cool judgment and great resourcefulness, but, above all, he behaved in a manner singularly free from communal rancour or bitterness. A deputation of Junagadh Muslims assured me later that they had nothing to complain of either during or after the occupation,'[45] on 9 November 1947. The new Dewan had also fled to Pakistan the day before.

By this time, in Kashmir, a headquarters had been established, named the Jammu and Kashmir Force, with Major General Kalwant Singh as the General Officer Commanding. Baramula was occupied on 8 November, its population reduced from 14,000 to 1,000. Pakistan, for its part, from early on, was referring to the "Azad Kashmir" government in contradistinction to the legal Jammu and Kashmir Government headed by Sheikh Abdullah, the latter being attacked in very offensive terms, even though it was the first responsible democratic government the State had ever had. On 31 December the Government of India formally appealed to the United Nations, on Mountbatten's suggestion to Gandhi and Nehru, though several ministers had qualms as to the desirability of doing so. Thus 1947, the year of independence, closed, V.P. Menon, then Secretary in the States' Ministry, validly recording, 'We had no territorial ambitions in Kashmir. If the invasion by the raiders had not taken place, I can say in the face of any contradiction that the Government of India would have left Kashmir alone. Indeed Lord Mountbatten on his return to England publicly stated (at the East India Association) that he had, on the authority of the Government of India, informed the Maharaja that he was perfectly free to accede to Pakistan if he chose to do so.'[46]

As to the partition decision, the great Pakistani poet, Faiz Ahmad Faiz, poignantly recorded before he sadly died:

This is not the Dawn we waited for so long,
This is not the Dawn whose birth was sired,
By so many lives, so much blood.

Ayesha Jalal has since wryly commented in her book, *The Sole Spokesman: Jinnah, the Muslim League and the Demand for Pakistan,* 'In the making of Pakistan, religion appears to have been the determinant of nationality.'[47] Today, we should spare a thought for the very many like Maulana Azad, Khan Abdul Ghaffar Khan, Shah Nawaz Khan, Sir Shafaat Ahmed, Badruddin Tyabji, and Brigadier Mohammed Usman, more numerous than the protagonists of the "two-nation" theory.

FIFTEEN

Post-independence—The Nehru Years

ON 21 APRIL 1946, Mahatma Gandhi had written in the *Harijan:* 'If Swaraj is round the bend, we can now look upon the military as ours and need have no hesitation in taking all the constructive work we can from them. Up till now they have only been employed in indiscriminate firing on us. Today they must plough the land, dig wells, clean latrines, and do every other constructive work that they can, and thus turn the people's hatred of them into love.'

Articles had also been written at that time with a similar thrust. These feelings had developed in the British period, whilst the Army had remained aloof from politics, and correctly continues to do so. This did not, however, mean that the personnel in the Indian Army under the British were not nationalists. They were, but the political leadership then had been indifferent to the concerns of the Army, its personnel being resented as mercenaries. K.M.Cariappa called on the Mahatma on a couple of occasions after independence before the latter's death, the latter stating, as recorded in Cariappa's biography by I.M. Muthanna: 'I have always had the greatest admiration for the discipline in the Army, and also for the importance you army people pay to sanitation and hygiene.'[1]

444

Post-independence—The Nehru Years

Nonetheless, some resentment towards the Army continued even almost till after the 1965 conflict with Pakistan, it becoming the practice in these post-independence years for some to magnify the shortcomings of the Indian Army through a microscope, and to use a telescope to examine their own. And this despite the superb performance of the Army during the civil disturbances in 1946 and 1947, and its continued employment in 1948 on internal security duties, apart from the magnificent response of the 90,000 troops progressively inducted into Jammu and Kashmir, many of whom had either lost their families or had not yet been resettled, or had just returned after a long spell overseas. In addition, excessive demands began being made on the Army for the maintenance of essential services, under the Armed Forces (Emergency Duties) Act, 1947, necessitating Prime Minister Jawaharlal Nehru having to write to all provincial premiers that the passing of the act did not mean that the maintenance of essential services in the country had become the responsibility of the Army.

At this juncture, the implementation of what was termed the New Pay Code for ICOs, as distinct from KCIOs, shortly after independence, was to cause concern at the extent of the consequent reduction in emoluments in each officer rank. Even allowing that the reduction was graduated over a period of time, the progressive reduction in take-home pay caused considerable deprivation and anguish, the representations going on for several months, particularly in the light of the increased pay differential with KCIOs. It is this differential that had caused much heart-burning during the Second World War when the British officer and ICO, alongside each other, were fighting the same enemy. It is true that when the emoluments were correlated during the Second World War, it was with the Finance Department's proviso that the matter would be reviewed after the war. It was, nevertheless, ironical that this post-war pay review for officers was progressed by the then Financial Adviser (Defence Services), Chaudhuri Mohammed Ali, during the tenure of the Interim Government, when Liaquat Ali was the Finance Member, Mohammed Ali himself becoming the

445

Pakistan Secretary-General in August 1947 and later Prime Minister. Now, again ICOs were fighting an enemy alongside KCIOs in Jammu and Kashmir, but a pay differential, nevertheless, was allowed to subsist. Eventually ICOs were told that those who did not wish to serve on the New Pay Code could resign. Next was the prospective implementation of reduction in the size of the Army. The Willcox Committee had envisaged in 1945 an eventual post-war undivided Army of 280,000 (Plan 280). In August 1947, the undivided Army was above 400,000. On partition, India's share was 280,000 (excluding the forces of the integrated states), and Pakistan's about 150,000. On 16 September 1947, the Prime Minister directed that the strength of the Army should be preferably 150,000, but in no case beyond 175,000, with a 'trained militia behind it.' He added, 'It is true partition does not make India more secure. It might be said to add to her insecurity.' Thereupon, in September itself, General Sir Rob Lockhart sought the government's specific threat assessment, in a meeting with the Prime Minister. Nehru told Lockhart, 'We foresee no military threats....' The sanguine political assessment, thereafter, was that the Army's commitment in Jammu and Kashmir was not expected to be of any extended duration, as the government had complained to the United Nations in December 1947; a governmental direction was even given in June 1948 to the forces in Jammu and Kashmir stalling any offensive action, in view of the forthcoming July visit of the United Nations Commission for India and Pakistan (UNCIP). As is now known, this naive expectation was to be belied. The Jammu and Kashmir military operations were at the time, even referred to as a "Police Action". Notwithstanding that these operations were still very much on, and that Hyderabad's position had not yet been resolved, under Finance Ministry pressure in the light of the Prime Minister's direction, a planning exercise was carried out by Brigadier (later General) J.N. Chaudhuri for reducing the Army to a level of 200,000, once the Jammu and Kashmir operations and the Hyderabad problem were over (Plan 200), the then Finance Minister conceding in February 1948 that pending the return of "normal conditions" the

Army was expected to be maintained at the existing level (approximately 280,000, of whom 90,000 were eventually to be inducted into the Jammu and Kashmir operations during 1948). The 1948 figure of 200,000 was to encompass any State Force units that were eventually merged, but would sequentially entail the corresponding disbandment of Indian Army battalions, as also of corps like the Military Police and the Pioneer Corps, as well as the East Punjab Militia or Defence battalions raised in 1947 for a particular limited purpose, enrolling a fair number of ex-'Indian National Army' (INA) personnel, apart from ex-servicemen.

At this point, on 1 January 1948, Lockhart retired on grounds of ill-health, and was succeeded by Lieutenant General (later Sir) F.R.R. Bucher. In anticipation of prospective changes when India was to become a republic, his appointment was, in May 1948, formally designated as the "Chief of the Army Staff and Commander-in-Chief". India having become a republic in 1950, the term "Commander-in-Chief" ceased to be in use from 1955, as the President of India was now the Supreme Commander*. Sequentially, the King's colours were progressively replaced by the President's colours, and the badges of rank changed, the Crown being replaced by the Ashoka lions and the four-pointed star by the five-pointed star of India.

Though it has never been more than an exaggerated fear that a military coup could occur in India, no Army chief ever having had the slightest such ambition, the para-military forces began to be increased by Sardar Vallabhbhai Patel, as a counterpoise to the Army, on the analogy of the British troops in India having been the counterpoise to the Indian Army pre-independence. It was not the Army under a British Chief that was posited, but some notional future Indian Chief. His personal relationship, as also Nehru's, with Bucher, was extremely cordial, in fact better than with Lockhart. As to Bucher, Mountbatten recorded, 'I told him (Nehru, on 30 March 1948) that whereas General Gracey (in Pakistan) was apt to fancy

---

* For a complete list of all the Army Chiefs since 1947, see Appendix 1.

himself as having some political knowledge and was less likely to keep the necessary close touch with his own Prime Minister, he could rest assured that General Bucher would never attempt to take any political action, and would keep close touch with his Prime Minister. Nehru entirely agreed.'[2] (Later, in January 1961, K.S. Thimayya was to be totally wrongly suspected of harbouring such ambitions, B.M. Kaul, on becoming Chief of the General Staff, getting the Intelligence Bureau [IB] to institute a secret inquiry against him for some indiscreet remarks by him while in service.) Bucher's appointment was essentially an interim one while the concerned officers acquired some experience as GOsC-in-C, for the Interim Government had been desirous of complete nationalization of the Army by June 1948. Some in the government were tentatively thinking of appointing Lieutenant General M.S. Rajendrasinhji, DSO, as the first Indian Chief. When this was orally mooted to him, he correctly advised that, at that juncture, the decision should be by seniority, and that he himself, by age, was still available to be the Army Chief, if the government was then so desirous. (He succeeded General K.M. Cariappa in January 1953.) The Defence Minister, in an answer to a sequential question in the Assembly announced that the choice of an Indian as the first Army Chief would be by seniority.

Now the question of new provincial and class regiments began to be raised by various provincial chief ministers and political leaders. None were agreed to, as, at this time, the State Forces were not yet merged, and whose screening modalities and mustering out concessions, as applicable, were still being worked out by the Military Adviser-in-Chief, Indian State Forces (ISF), Major General K.S. Himmatsinhji. Nehru's reply to Premier R.S. Shukla of the Central Provinces in August 1948 needs to be quoted as it reflected the Central Government's general policy in this regard: '...you suggest the formation of provincial units in the regular Indian Army....The Defence Ministry's reply, with which I entirely agree, is that such a practice would be opposed to the policy of Government and would disturb the present organization of the Army. It would be wholly inadvisable under present conditions. The policy of Government has been to endeavour to maintain a homogeneous Indian Army. Recruitment is on a zonal, and not a provincial, basis. Many of the men from the C.P. are being recruited into the regular armed forces and militia, and will be later recruited into the Territorial Army. To give provincial names to Army units would be to come in the way, slightly, of a homogeneous Indian Army which thinks in terms of India rather than in terms of a province. Any other policy would, rather, encourage a provincial spirit which is unfortunately so strong today.'[3] Similar replies were sent to some other chief ministers, like West Bengal's, and to class organizations representing for redesignating an existing regiment with a class title, or raising new class regiments, like an Ahir Regiment, the latter being informed that Ahirs were already sufficiently represented in the Army and no new class regiments were being contemplated for the future. (Dr B.C. Roy was to reopen the matter of a Bengal Regiment in 1949 when Cariappa became Chief. The raising of a new provincial regiment was again not conceded, Cariappa, however, agreeing to an initial Bengali company in the 2nd Battalion, The Rajput Regiment, his own regiment, to be followed later by some further recruitment of Bengalis in the same infantry regiment, apart from existing recruitment in other arms and services.) (Another representation later was for the Madras Regiment to be redesignated, when the states of Andhra Pradesh, Tamil Nadu, Karnataka and Kerala were created, and for mention to be included in the title of the regiment of all these states, since the regiment recruited from all of them. This also was not agreed to.)

Then, by September, the matter of alcohol consumption in the Army had become a vexed issue, with the possibility of the introduction of prohibition. Two letters on the subject are reproduced, as the matter became quite controversial after Bombay introduced prohibition and the odd serviceman carrying liquor on leave was arrested, including officers, necessitating the matter to be moved before the Supreme Court, with the Central Government's approval. The Prime Minister then wrote to Bucher on 21 September 1948, 'You know that it is the Government of India's general policy to encourage prohibition. In some provinces this has already been adopted....I have no desire, at this stage, to interfere with the practice prevalent in the Defence Forces, but I have little doubt that this general policy will gradually have to be introduced in the Defence Forces also...'[4] Though Nehru did not emphasize the matter in this letter, there had already been an audit objection as to V.K. Krishna Menon, then our High Commissioner in London, having procured earlier, in 1948, 4,275 cases of Scotch whisky towards the then annual requirement of the Defence Services canteens, including for British officers in India, at a price higher than warranted. (It is no longer so imported.) The resultant outcry in the Constituent Assembly on 8 February 1949 was directed towards some preferring Scotch whisky, when Indian-manufactured whisky was available, apart from the higher price Krishna Menon bought it at. A further letter on 22 September 1948 from the Prime Minister to Bucher, *inter alia,* stated, 'Too much public consumption of alcohol is naturally not quite in keeping with the general temper of the public. So, while there is no ban, a certain consideration might be shown to the public viewpoint in public.'[5]

When Bombay introduced prohibition, all mess and canteen liquor stocks had been frozen. The Supreme Court now exempted Defence Services personnel from provincial prohibition on account of their all-India liability. Toasts with liquor, at regimental dinner nights, were later correctly to be with water. Meanwhile, the operations in Jammu and Kashmir continued, with many notable successes, despite units still reorganizing after "partition", and the difficult communications, like the reliefs of Leh and Poonch, and the capture of Rajauri, Tithwal, Kargil, and the Pir Kanthi feature, but also a few reverses, the latter due in some cases to Pakistan's duplicity, like the withdrawal necessitated from the Pandu feature near Uri, when the UN Commission had asked both sides to desist from offensive operations. (The brigade then moving towards Domel and Muzaffarabad was instead ordered by the Prime Minister to relieve Poonch first.) The failure, either to relieve the State Force garrison at Skardu, beleaguered with their families, due to the difficult terrain, or to give them permission to withdraw, was a command failure. The garrison was ultimately overwhelmed in August 1948[6], the women raped and abducted, and their children killed, the Pakistani commander reporting back, 'All Sikhs killed; all women raped.' That there would be a Pakistani advance from Gilgit on Skardu was obvious *ab initio*. Soon after the announcement of the transfer of power, the British had retroceded the Gilgit Agency to the Maharaja. Nevertheless, all the British officers in Gilgit had opted for Pakistan, and none for the State. On 4 November 1947, Major W. Brown, the British commandant of the Gilgit Scouts, had ceremonially hoisted the Pakistani flag at Gilgit, after, on 1 November, the Muslim personnel of the Jammu and Kashmir Infantry at Bunji, thirty-four miles from Gilgit, had liquidated the non-Muslim personnel, and then deserted. The non-Muslims who escaped fled to Skardu from Bunji. Thereafter, the Pakistanis in January 1948 commenced the siege of Skardu. The details of these operations are embodied in the official history published in 1987.

These operations witnessed the raising of the Jammu and Kashmir Militia, by Colonel B.M. Kaul, who had returned from Washington in March 1948. He reported directly to the Chief Minister, Sheikh Mohammed Abdullah, who had ratified the Instrument of Accession in October 1947 before India accepted it, and who, before the Pakistani invasion, had earlier rejected two approaches by M.A. Jinnah to accede to Pakistan. The militia was then a State Government force, created from the volunteers—students, shopkeepers, farmers and National Conference politicians—who had come forward spontaneously to resist the Pakistani invaders, even before the arrival of the Indian Army. First, armed only with 'lathis', or, in some cases, with their own private arms, they were later issued weapons from the Jammu and Kashmir State armoury. These highly-motivated volunteers were, thus, the forerunners of the Jammu and Kashmir Militia, today's Jammu and Kashmir Light Infantry, half-Muslim, half-non-Muslim. Despite organizational problems, these militia battalions were immediately deployed against the invaders. (They have fought in four successive conflicts since their raising.) Their performance was exemplary. (For his part, Kaul had some differences with Sheikh Abdullah, reverted to the Indian Army, and five years later, according to his own account, was deputed in 1953 by the Prime Minister, in Kaul's "personal capacity", to "oversee" the arrest of Sheikh Abdullah.)

Major General Kalwant Singh left Jammu and Kashmir on 1 May 1948 to become the Chief of the General Staff at Army Headquarters, while two divisional headquarters were simultaneously created there, Srinagar Division (Major General K.S. Thimayya, DSO) and Jammu Division (Major General Atma Singh). This was the time, in May, that Pakistan much later stated that its army had been inducted into Jammu and Kashmir, as the Indian Army was threatening the Pakistani heartland from Jammu and Kashmir, citing the conclusion of Douglas Gracey's alleged appreciation, purportedly of late April 1948, to this effect: 'If India is not to be allowed to sit on the doorsteps of Pakistan to the rear and on the flank, at liberty to enter at her will and pleasure; if civilian and military morale is not to be affected to a dangerous extent; and if subversive political forces are not to be encouraged and let loose within Pakistan itself, it is imperative that the Indian Army is not allowed to advance beyond the general line Uri-Poonch—Naushahra.' Here one must mention the heroic Brigadier Mohammed Usman, scarcely remembered today, killed in Pakistani shelling, and who was given a mammoth funeral at New Delhi, as also the earlier epic bravery of a machine-gun platoon of the 1st Battalion The Mahar Regiment at the first battle of Jhangar which fought on to the last man and the last round, though the battalion under whose command it was had withdrawn. After their machine-gun positions had been overrun, these stalwart, ostensibly non-martial, Mahars were decapitated by the Pakistanis.

Meanwhile, as jeeps were urgently required for these operations, Krishna Menon approved a contract with a little-known firm in London for 2,000 jeeps. An advance of over 143,000 pounds was paid, 155 unserviceable jeeps were supplied and the firm went into liquidation, the Public Accounts Committee later recording: 'It is not possible to hold that the lapses were merely procedural or due to defects in the rules.' (The confusion was to be worse confounded when, in 1951, he approved a further contract for 1,007 jeeps at, twice the previous price, with a comparable advance. This firm, also little-known, agreed to absorb the government's losses on the previous contract. Only forty-nine jeeps were delivered, this firm defaulting as well on the plea that the contract for jeep spare parts had not been given to it as promised. A claim for 254,498 pounds was filed by the government against the firm. In 1961, while Krishna Menon was the Defence Minister, the entire claim was waived. This documented case is mentioned in passing to illustrate how certain procurements for the Defence Services have led to innuendo.) Considerable friction also developed at the time between the Indian missions in Paris and London, Sardar H.S. Malik and Krishna Menon respectively, over the attempted procurement of arms and ammunition for the Jammu and Kashmir operations in France without London keeping Paris informed.

Eventually, in the last week of December 1948, UNCIP, in consonance with the Security Council resolution of 9 November 1948, during further visits to New Delhi and Karachi, in the context of India's complaint a year earlier, put forward certain modified proposals. Both governments having accepted them, the Government of India saw no reason why hostilities should not cease at once, that is, without waiting for the commission's formal announcement. The government, accordingly, on its initiative, directed Bucher to inform Gracey that the Indian troops would cease-fire, provided Gracey could give an effective reciprocal assurance, which he did. The cease-fire was ordered by India and Pakistan with effect from midnight, 1 January 1949, at a time when the initiative was with the Indian Army and a spring offensive had been planned. In its earlier first report No S/1000, the UNCIP had recorded as to Pakistan's belated admission that the regular Pakistan Army had been fighting in Jammu and Kashmir: 'The presence of Pakistan troops in J&K, however, constitutes a material change in the situation inasmuch as the Security Council did not contemplate the presence of such troops in that State, nor was it apprised thereafter by the Government of

Pakistan.' At this point, on 1 January 1949, 57,000 square miles were under Indian control, and about 32,200 had been seized by Pakistan. (Of the Indian 57,000 square miles, 12,000 square miles were later seized by China; of the 32,200 square miles seized by Pakistan, 27,000 were constituted to form the Northern Areas—Gilgit, Astor, Skardu, Hunza and others—administered by Islamabad, and 5,236 square miles administered by the so-called "Azad Kashmir" government.) Pakistan later ceded some territory to China which the latter recorded as "disputed". Nehru, *ab initio*, and not the UN had suggested to hold a plebiscite in Jammu and Kashmir, which consisted of the Muslim-majority Kashmir Valley, the Hindu-majority Jammu, and the Buddhist-majority Ladakh. Even before the accession, the Ladakh Buddhist Association had submitted to the Maharaja that he should either, 'govern Ladakh directly, or merge it with the Hindu-majority Jammu province, or allow it to join East Punjab.'[7]

There were eight conditions attached to the subsequent UN resolutions, the most important being that the Pakistani troops had first to withdraw completely from all areas occupied by them, and that the Jammu and Kashmir Government was to be recognized as the only legitimate government of the State. Pakistan never fulfilled these pre-conditions. Eventually, after waiting for Pakistan to fulfil these pre-conditions, the Jammu and Kashmir Assembly decided to join the Indian Union. (As early as 13 August 1948, the UNCIP had assured India that it did not recognize the right of Pakistan to have any say in the affairs of the State and that it recognized the right of India to defend the State from external aggression.)

Of these 1947-48 Jammu and Kashmir operations, Major General (later Lieutenant General) S.K. Sinha, who, as a Major, was a staff officer dealing with these operations at the time, says in his book, *Operation Rescue: Military Operations in J&K, 1947-48*: 'One often hears conflicting views regarding the operations in Kashmir. Some talk of them in terms of a police action whereas others regard them as a major campaign. In actual fact they were neither, and those who consider them in terms of one or the other, have not correctly evaluated these operations....These operations ultimately involved the employment of nearly 90,000 Indian troops, on a terrain unprecedented for modern warfare. The enemy opposing us was no less strong.... He had heavy anti-aircraft and medium guns, in addition to the normal field and mountain artillery, all of which he used with skill and precision. We were up against regular forces, similarly organized and trained, who only a little while earlier, formed part of the same undivided Indian Army. And in this fighting lasting over a year, we lost 1,500 precious lives. Our other casualties were 3,500 wounded and 1,000 missing/prisoners, making a total of 6,000. The enemy on the other hand is estimated to have suffered 20,000 casualties, of whom about 6,000 were killed...a large portion of the enemy comprised irregular troops, who often adopted guerrilla tactics.'[8] On 29 January 1949, the Prime Minister was to record, 'we could well proceed on the assumption that the truce in Kashmir will continue and will lead to a future settlement....The present Army (strength) continues say for the next six months in any event.'

Separately, the Hyderabad 'Police Action' had been launched on 13 September 1948, and using mainly the 1st Armoured Division. (Before this, in July 1948 there had been a contingency induction of ten Nepal Army battalions for internal security, if, on account of lakhs of Hindus fleeing from persecution by the Razakars in Hyderabad, there were communal disturbances elsewhere in India. Fortunately there were none.) If, in August 1947, the Nizam had acceded and had introduced responsible government, this 'Police Action' would not have been necessary. He had retained, in 1947, Sir (later Lord) Walter Monckton as his adviser. Philip Ziegler, Lord Louis Mountbatten's biographer, describes the position in a review of Monckton's biography: 'Extravagantly rich, spectacularly mean, resolutely doleful, this Indian Getty, Muslim ruler of a Hindu state, was from the start destined for eventual disaster. Monckton did what he could to avert it, but the Nizam listened to the truth only if he found it congenial, and even Monckton could not make his version palatable. In 1948, when India...was growing impatient with the continuing intransigence of Hyderabad, Monckton almost brought off a deal that would have assured the Nizam of far greater autonomy than he had any reason to expect. At the end, however, he was defeated by the enfeebled obstinacy of his client. "Lost", he cabled laconically to Mountbatten. "I often wonder whether that silly old Nizam had any idea what a superlative genius (Monckton) was conducting the negotiations," Mountbatten wrote to Monckton's widow.'[9]

The situation in the State, in early September 1948, as reported by India to the UN was, 'people stricken with fear, administration completely disorganized and State finances depleted. Hundreds of thousands of Hyderabad Hindu citizens had sought refuge in neighbouring Indian provinces having been victims of Razakar terrorist atrocities. Large numbers of non-Hyderabadi Muslims had been imported. Nearly one hundred thousand of these newcomers were employed in army, police and other State services. There were 11,000 political prisoners in jails. Thousands of illicit imported firearms including high velocity weapons were in the hands of irresponsible armed irregulars.'[10] The military appreciation was that the operation would not last more than three weeks. To restore tranquillity within the State and prevent grave reactions outside it within adjacent Indian territory, orders had been issued to Army Headquarters on 9 September to carry out the 'Police Action'. Major General J.N. Chaudhuri, the General Officer Commanding (GOC), was given 13 September as D-Day by Headquarters Southern Command, though there was apparently a last minute suggestion for a postponement till 15 September. On the evening of 17 September, the Hyderabad Army surrendered. The 'Police Action' had lasted 108 hours. Here, V.P. Menon, who was still Secretary in the States' Ministry records, 'On our side the total casualties were slight but on the other side, owing to scrappy operations and lack of discipline, the Irregulars and the Razakars suffered comparatively more casualties. The number of dead was a little over 800. It is unfortunate that so many should have died in this action, though the number is insignificant when weighed against the killings, rape and loot inflicted by the Razakars on the Hindus of the State....On the very first day the advancing Indian troops captured Lieutenant T.T. Moore, an ex-British Army Commando and Special Services officer, who had been employed by the Hyderabad army since August 1947, and who was driving in a loaded jeep in the direction of Naldrug. It was discovered that his jeep was full of explosives, while his personal papers showed that he had been given the responsibility for arranging demolitions. He had been sent at top speed by the Hyderabad army headquarters to demolish the Naldrug and other bridges. He had been told that the Indian Army advance would take place on 15 September. If the Indian Army had marched in on the 15th, and not on the 13th, they would have found all the important bridges blown up.'[11] After the successful conclusion of this 'Police Action', the Prime Minister recorded, 'There is a certain artistry about such planning....I should like to express again our satisfaction at the behaviour of our troops, which, according to all reports, was beyond reproach, and which showed a sustained discipline and restraint.'

On 23 September, the Nizam informed the Security Council that he had withdrawn the case that he had earlier submitted. Though some members of the Security Council pressed for a discussion, it was ultimately dropped. Pakistan, nevertheless, made a series of allegations against the Indian Military Government at the UN. The Nizam expressed surprise at Pakistan's allegations and recorded, 'The situation is considerably better than it was some months ago, and the subjects of my state are living peacefully. There is no doubt that the administration had broken down during the latter part of the last (Laik Ali) Ministry's regime, but at present the Military Government has achieved success not only in restoring but improving the administrative machinery.'[12] The usual complaints against the Army when so employed began coming in. The Prime Minister replied to some of them. A reply to a Congressman is reproduced, 'I have been taking a great deal of interest in Hyderabad affairs. I find that unfortunate occurrences took place in some rural areas some time back. But it is completely wrong to imagine that our soldiers were guilty of these. In fact I have received, from almost every source, praise of our Army's behaviour. We have been asked on behalf of many

Muslims in Hyderabad not to remove our Army.'[13] The 1948 situation had, in fact, been succinctly predicted in 1926 by the then British Resident, Sir William Barton: 'There can be no doubt that it (Hyderabad) owes its very existence to the British connection.... Left entirely to himself it is doubtful if the present Nizam would be able to maintain himself for any length of time. Three strong currents of political activity converge on Hyderabad: the Maratha, the Andhra and the Kanara movements.... Good government is the only antidote to this poison, and it must be regretfully observed that the Nizam's attitude for the past five years leaves but a faint hope that he would, if he realized his dreams of unchecked absolutism, consider the welfare of his people in the least degree.'[14] It was the same Nizam in 1926 as in 1948. The Army, for some time, continued to be employed thereafter for about a year in aid to the civil power against the Communist insurgency in Telengana, inflicting about 300 casualties, when the troops had to move out for a precautionary concentration on the international border in 1950. (The Communist Party had issued a call for the workers to seize power, describing the Government of India, in February 1948, as anti-people. This Maoist insurgency still subsists in Andhra Pradesh, today as the banned People's War Group [PWG].) A startling incident of Leftist violence now occurred at Dum Dum on 26 February 1949. An armed gang simultaneously attacked the Ordnance factory, the airport and the Jessop factory. Three Britons and an Anglo-Indian were flung into a furnace at the latter, an aircraft set on fire, and some revolvers stolen. The then West Bengal Premier said the gang belonged to the Revolutionary Communist Party.

A proposal for taking back all ex-INA personnel, who had formerly served in the Indian Army, was now made to Army Headquarters. (Those who had been classified "white" had been reinstated before independence.) Stephen Cohen quotes a retired Indian lieutenant general in 1963 as saying, 'The INA! They should all have been court-martialled in the field and shot. (Q: All of them?) Yes, all that were guilty, it was stupid bringing them back. It should have been handled as a military matter; it was very bad to let them off with little or no punishment, they were soldiers and had taken an oath....What kind of precedent was the INA? To let a group rebel and not punish them.'[15] This extreme viewpoint, however, was not then a majority one, for very many serving personnel had brothers who had joined the INA. After discussions over a period in 1948, the Army Headquarters' viewpoint was accepted by the government—those who had not committed atrocities (the "greys") would be offered re-employment in the Army, but would not count seniority for the period they spent in the INA. Some accepted this offer, but many did not as they may have had to serve under those who had been junior to them. Some of the latter were absorbed in services like the Indian Foreign Service (IFS) and the Indian Police Service (IPS). Lieutenant Colonels N.S. Gill and A.D. Loganadan were made Ambassadors. Captain Shah Nawaz Khan joined the Congress and became a deputy minister. Other ex-INA officers, like Captain Mohan Singh, also joined the Congress; he became an MP (Rajya Sabha). The latter was a supporter of Chief Minister Pratap Singh Kairon. Separately, the Prime Minister wrote in July 1948 to the chief ministers concerned on behalf of the ex-INA personnel who were not desirous of seeking re-employment in the Army, or whom Army Headquarters were not desirous of taking back: 'You know that we have been anxious to help ex-INA personnel to find employment. We have undertaken this responsibility as a Government and we hope that provincial governments will cooperate in this process.'[16]

A new Territorial Army (TA) Act was now passed in 1948, in place of the earlier 1920 Indian Territorial Force (ITF) legislation. The first units were raised in August 1949, the formal inauguration being done by the then Governor-General C. Rajagopalachari in October 1949. It consists of non-departmental and departmental units. The former are the infantry battalions drawn from the whole country, affiliated to various regiments, and comprising able-bodied personnel between the ages of eighteen to forty-two. The urban units carry out training on weekends spread throughout the year. The provincial (rural) units are embodied continuously for two months in a year. Embodied TA units have been employed creditably during the operations against Pakistan and China, in aid to the civil power in Punjab and Assam, and in peacekeeping operations in Sri Lanka. The departmental units were created from 1956, and are entirely financed by the concerned ministries, such as Railways, and Gas and Petroleum. There are also TA General Hospitals in some states. (The ecological units latterly raised under the Ministry of Forests and Environment have been designed for re-afforestation and the maintenance of the environmental balance, and consist of ex-servicemen commanded by regular or TA officers. These ecological units are always kept mobilized, as they are concerned with time-bound projects extending over five to ten years.) Separately, Nehru had always been keen on the concept of a "trained militia" supporting a small compact regular army in war. This was first started by the Punjab Government as the National Volunteer Corps, Mohan Singh separately starting his Desh Sewak Sena, the two differing seriously in August 1948. Revived by B.M. Kaul, in the 1950s, as the Lok Sahayak Sena (National Volunteer Force), it was later given up as a waste of resources. A National Cadet Corps (NCC), officered by regular and NCC officers, was also constituted in 1948 for both boys and girls with senior and junior divisions, the former replacing the University Training Corps of 1920. The current strength of all cadets is over one million. There is no service liability.

In December 1948, the Prime Minister sent a message of thanks to the King of Nepal for the loan of the Nepalese Contingent, which is reproduced not only in the context of the continued friendly relationship between the two Armies, but also because it encompasses the internal security situation in the country at the time: 'In July 1948 Your Highness' Government readily agreed to help India by placing at her disposal ten battalions of the Nepal Army. Government of India are extremely grateful for this help. The loan of the Nepalese Contingent made it possible for the Government of India to take away Indian Army troops employed on internal security duties for Hyderabad action, and, thereby, helped the Government of India in maintaining peace and tranquillity throughout the country.

Since the conclusion of the Hyderabad action the Government of India have been considering to what extent troops employed in connection with Hyderabad could revert to their internal security duties and thereby permit the return of the Nepalese Contingent whom you were so kind enough to lend. We now consider that from about the middle of January 1949 it should be possible for the Nepalese Contingent to return to Nepal...which proved once again the very close friendship which binds the two countries.'[17] (At Nepal's request, an Indian military training team was thereafter sent in 1950, remaining there for ten years. Separately, an agreement was signed in 1965 to modernize the Nepalese Army. Assistance in modernization has again been sought by Nepal in October 1992.) India and Nepal are closely linked by geography, history, culture, trade and family ties.

On 14 December 1948, it was announced that Lieutenant General K.M. Cariappa would be the next Army Chief with effect from 15 January 1949, observed ever since as Army Day annually. Two of the decisions in his tenure were to create the Parachute Regiment from the existing parachute-trained battalions of the (2nd) Punjab Regiment, the Maratha Light Infantry and the Kumaon Regiment; as also the Brigade of the Guards, then of four battalions, each the seniormost battalion, as applicable, of the Punjab Regiment, the then Indian Grenadiers, the Rajputana Rifles and the Rajput Regiment, on the lines of the British Guards Brigade (he himself had been attached to the Coldstream Guards in London for a spell in the early 1930s). Classes were to be mixed in consonance with the government's policy already announced that all classes in the country were eligible to be enrolled in the Army. (The recruitable male population of each district was sequentially worked out.) Each Guards battalion would do a tenure by rotation at the present Rashtrapati Bhawan (President's House); the other three would conform to the normal parameters for peace and field tenures. There was no problem about the Parachute Regiment, for it was a long-mooted proposal as the battalions in question had been parachute-trained in the Second World War, and 50 Independent Parachute Brigade was

461

to continue. It was, therefore, a necessary organizational decision. The creation of the Brigade of the Guards, however, was not a necessary requirement, organizationally or operationally. Thereafter, for instance, the 1st Battalion The Punjab Regiment became the 1st Battalion The Parachute Regiment, and the 2nd Battalion of the same regiment became the 1st Guards (Punjab). From the point of view of hindsight, little operational purpose had been served in creating this new regiment from the then existing battalions, a viewpoint even then urged. (Not that it has not done very well. It has, but so have other regiments equally.) The mixing of classes could have been achieved in any other regiment, without creating a new one, as has been successfully effected in the Mahar Regiment. Predictably, other infantry battalions began representing as to why should they also not have an opportunity of duty at the residence of the head of the country. All battalions are now eligible for duty at the Rashtrapati Bhawan.

Meanwhile, 'the Shiromani Akali Dal had also made the demand (in 1948) for communal electorates and reservation of seats for Sikhs in the Legislatures as well as in the Army. The Special Sub-Committee of the Advisory Committee on Minorities under the chairmanship of Vallabhbhai Patel came to the conclusion that the acceptance of the demand of the Shiromani Akali Dal would be a fundamental departure. The Sub-Committee felt that the Sikhs did not suffer from any handicaps; they were a highly educated and virile community with great gifts as soldiers, farmers and artisans, and most remarkable spirit of enterprise.... On 25th May 1949, Sardar Patel moved for consideration of this Report of the Advisory Committee in the Constituent Assembly. He emphasized that...in the long run, it would be in the interest of all to forget that there is anything like majority or minority in this country and that, in India there is only one community.'[18] With the cease-fire in Jammu and Kashmir, as also the Hyderabad situation resolved, the government could again turn its attention to the size of the Army. As a first step the merger of the ISF had to be attended to. As on 15 August 1947, forty-four states were maintaining units under the ISF scheme, aggregating 75,311 personnel. In addition, there were a large number of state units outside the ISF scheme. These non-ISF scheme units were mainly ceremonial and armed police units, and, as in the case of Hyderabad, often out of proportion to the ceremonial or armed police requirement. The pay of the latter was lower than the pay of the ISF scheme units, and nor had they, sequentially, been inspected by the British military advisers. The ISF scheme units, and their Imperial Service Troops predecessors, had a long record of military service in various campaigns, ninety-eight units serving outside their states in the Second World War alone, some as far afield as Italy earning numerous decorations in all campaigns. For the Jammu and Kashmir operations and the Hyderabad 'Police Action', an appeal had to be made to the rulers for ISF scheme units, as under the Instrument of Accession the authority over these units vested in the rulers, unless they were already attached to the Indian Army. They very readily responded.

The ISF scheme units were now viewed in four groups:

- those of states to be merged into the neighbouring province, like Rampur;
- those of states to be administered as Chief Commis-sioner's provinces, like Manipur;
- those of Hyderabad and Mysore;
- those of states formed into unions, other than the Union of Travancore and Cochin.

In the case of units in the first and second categories, after being taken over by the Government of India, they were allowed initially to remain in their original locations, and on the same terms till they had been screened for absorption, and those not absorbed were given mustering out concessions. Hyderabad had the largest number of units, and these, by circumstance, came under Indian Army control from 1 April 1950, as also those of Mysore, and the Union of Travancore-Cochin. In the case of the other unions, like Madhya Bharat, the authority to administer and maintain their ISF units was vested in the Rajpramukh. The expenditure was to be met from the particular union's revenues. The merger of the forces of these unions in the last category was thus more complex. An officer of the Indian Army was lent to the concerned Rajpramukh to command the forces of the particular union, their strength and role being integrated into the defence of India, and being reconstituted on the pattern of the corresponding Indian Army units, including their officer cadres. As a result of financial integration, these units were, eventually, completely taken over by the Indian Army with effect from 1 April 1951. There was anguish for several years as to the way the merger of the ISF had been carried out. Much of it was inevitable, as all changes are painful, but here each solution adopted to resolve a problem, itself became a problem. Even if such a micro-Indian Army as the ISF could not be wholly accommodated in the macro-Indian Army after independence due to financial constraints, they deserved, in view of their long history, to have been better understood in their new regiments and formations after merger, as they were not all ceremonial. The famous cavalry charge at Haifa was by the Jodhpur, Hyderabad and Mysore Lancers. The only transport unit to win a battle honour in the history of the Indian Army was the Jaipur Transport Corps at Shaiba in Mesopotamia. As Sir Claude Auchinleck validly recorded in 1961: 'In my early days in India, fifty years ago, there was a tendency among some, who should have known better, to deride these soldiers of the Indian States as "ragtime" soldiers or "stage-supers", dressed up in brilliant uniforms to please a Ruler's fancy. This, of course, was quite untrue. It is true that units varied in efficiency, but this holds good for all armies...there can be no question of their bravery, loyalty, patience in adversity and steadfastness under stress...they deserve to be remembered as such with honour....'[19]

They were often more efficient than has been acknowledged at the time of the merger processing. Some of the ISF units, like the 1st Mewar Infantry, today's 9th Battalion The Grenadiers, were proud inheritors of an ancient history from 1303, very much older than that of the Indian Army. (It was initially affiliated to the Rajputana

Rifles, but on the Jam Saheb wanting the Nawanagar—Saurashtra—Infantry to be affiliated with the Rajputana Rifles, with which he had served, and not with the Grenadiers, this change was made.) Against the Mughals, they were unrivalled in gallantry. The Sawai Man Guards (today's 17th Battalion The Rajputana Rifles), dating from the sixteenth century, in its day gave Jaipur a splendour that can never recur, and yet the request to include it in the new Brigade of the Guards was not conceded. Apart from the North-West Frontier and the First World War, the contribution of the ISF scheme units on recent battlefields, both pre-independence in the Second World War like the 1st Jind Infantry in Malaya (not one person joined the INA), and the 1st Jaipur Infantry and the Jodhpur Sardar Infantry in Italy, and post-independence like the Sawai Man Guards, the 1st Patiala Rajendra Sikh Infantry, and the battalions of the Jammu and Kashmir Infantry in Jammu and Kashmir, has not been fully acknowledged. In some of these units, the same families had served for four centuries and more. It is not only the units of the larger states that had served with distinction, but also of small states, like Suket, in the Jammu and Kashmir operations. The late Maharaja of Jaipur has poignantly recorded in his book, *The Indian State Forces:* 'That this should have happened in our Republic under the first Indian Commander-in-Chief, General K.M. Cariappa, is indeed a sad story. Whatever may have been the political reasons—perhaps it would not be fair to put all the blame on General Cariappa....'[20]

Part of the government's thrust in seeking a reduction in the Army was in order to augment the Navy and the Air Force. President Rajendra Prasad informed Parliament on 31 January 1950 that it was the government's intention to reduce Defence expenditure, 'as a measure of economy as well as a gesture of peace,' but concomitantly emphasizing, 'The first essential of freedom is the strength to preserve it.' Nevertheless, warning orders were issued for the disbandment of certain infantry battalions under Plan 200, but shortly after a precautionary concentration of troops became necessary on both the East and West Pakistan borders in February and March 1950, following a Hindu exodus from East Bengal, and a

Muslim exodus from Bihar and West Bengal to East Pakistan, and sequential anti-Hindu riots there. The situation was then defused by talks in New Delhi between Nehru and Liaquat Ali in April. Chronologically, the North Korean invasion of South Korea now occurred in June, then, thereafter, the Chinese entry into Tibet, followed by the massive Chinese intervention in North Korea in October-November as a reaction to the US threat towards the Yalu, MacArthur having just predicted an imminent end to the hostilities. India contributed the 60th (Parachute) Field Ambulance to the UN force, it arriving in Korea on 20 November. Jeffrey Grey recounts, 'The Indian Field Ambulance was one of the outstanding successes of the Commonwealth involvement, earning an extraordinarily high reputation among all the other Commonwealth forces. Initially, however, their arrival was viewed as something of a mixed blessing. The British Army's Director of Medical Services...wrote in such a vein.... "I have served a good deal in India and I know how well the Indians react if they get a pat on the back and are told what good fellows they are. But if they are not employed in what they would regard as a satisfactory role they might be inclined to be offended....Perhaps they could be employed to cover Base troops in some convenient port or area. I am sure that would satisfy their ambitions." Perhaps because he too was a "colonial" (Australian), Robertson (the Commonwealth force commander) did not follow this patronising advice. Dealing with... Indian soldiers was not new ground for Robertson. As pointed out, he had had 12,000 of them under his command in 1946-47 in Japan....'[21]

Despite the Chinese entry into Tibet, the government proceeded with its "economy" exercise in relation to defence expenditure, *The Statesman* reporting on 13 October 1950 that defence capital expenditure was to be kept constant at an annual thirty-five crore rupees a year, and revenue expenditure progressively reduced: financial year 1951-52, Rs 165 crores; 1952-53, Rs 160 crores; and, thereafter, an annual Rs 140 crores. This was confirmed by the Prime Minister in Parliament on 17 November, that he had ordered such an exercise, that the Korean war would not become a world war, and that the

Indian Army should be a compact, mobile army, not based on
numbers. (This had again been envisaged when an Indian Defence
Ministry delegation to Canada in May 1949 had reported that it had
been "profoundly impressed" by the Canadian system of a compact
defence force, capable of rapid expansion, forgetting that the geopo-
litical situation on the Indian subcontinent was not on all fours with
that prevailing for over a century on the North American continent.)
As to the Chinese entry into Tibet, and India's acquiescence in
relation to it, Sardar Patel, the then Home Minister, wrote on 7
November 1950 to the Prime Minister*. *Inter alia*, he recorded, 'It
looks as though it is not a friend speaking...but a political enemy....'
He urged, 'if necessary, reconsideration of our retrenchment plans
for the Army....' The ensuing relationship with China would have
been different, had Nehru heeded Patel, but the latter shortly passed
away. Nehru, however, countered, 'There are limits beyond which
we cannot go at least for some years, and spreading out of our army
on distant frontiers would be bad from every military or strategic
point of view.... If we fall out completely with China, Pakistan will
undoubtedly try to take advantage of this.... We cannot have all the
time two possible enemies on either side of India....' Thereafter, on
21 December, the Prime Minister stated that the government preferred a highly mechanized and relatively small army to a large and
ill-equipped "foot" force, and intended to reduce the size of the
Army for economy reasons.[22] This was much the same as what the
then Brigadier J.N. Chaudhuri had formulated in the draft Plan 200
in early 1948, in the context of the Prime Minister's directive of 16
September 1947. (The former had to think differently as to the size
of the Army, when he became the Army Chief after the 1962 conflict
with China.) 50,000 Army personnel (excluding ISF personnel) were
accordingly reduced in the financial year 1950-51. Separately, in
1951, as a sequel to the Chinese occupation of Tibet, the
Himmatsinhji Committee had been appointed to go into the
responsibility for border and external intelligence, over and above

---

* For more details, see Appendix 6.

that for internal intelligence, which was already vested in the Intelligence Bureau. The committee inexplicably recommended that the border and external intelligence gathering responsibility should solely be vested in the IB, omitting the Director of Military Intelligence.

Meanwhile, in September 1950, a mutiny had occurred in Srinagar in the 4th Battalion The 11th Gorkha Rifles. This mutiny has lessons even today, for, notwithstanding, a similar mutiny was to occur also in Srinagar in 1961 in the 2nd Battalion The Assam Regiment. First, a few words on the history of the 11th Gorkha Rifles (11 GR). Towards the latter part of the First World War, "composite" Indian Army battalions had been created by taking companies from existing battalions in order to expedite the process of "Indianizing" British formations in the Middle East, so that British battalions could be made available for France (inevitably, the precise end of the war could not then be foreseen). Though the 11 GR as a regiment was not raised, four of the composite Indian Army battalions were designated 1/11 GR, 2/11 GR, 3/11 GR and 4/11 GR. To illustrate how these composite battalions were then raised, 2/11 GR can be taken as an example. It was put together with companies from 1/2 GR, 1/3 GR, 2/4 GR, and 1/7 GR. All these composite battalions were disbanded in 1919. After the formal signing in November 1947 of the Tripartite Agreement between Nepal, India and Britain, all Gorkha personnel had the choice of opting either for India or Britain. Most of the personnel of 7 GR and 10 GR, Limbus and Rais, opted for India, and were, by May 1948, formed into three battalions of a new regiment, 11 GR. It being incorrectly assumed that in 1918 only 1/11 GR and 2/11 GR existed, in 1947-48 it was decided that 3/11 GR, 4/11 GR and 5/11 GR would be the designation of these three new battalions (the many Magar, Gurung and other optees for India from 2 GR and 6 GR were put into new battalions of the Gorkha regiments, allotted to India, with the requisite class connection).

4/11 GR, less one company, had just been de-inducted from a high altitude area to Srinagar (the fourth company was to follow). On 15 September a mobile cinema show had been arranged. The men were in a merry mood after their recent high altitude hardships. The commanding officer and other officers and their families were present. The singing in the film exhilarated the men, leading to whistling. The commanding officer did not appreciate the latter occurring in front of the officers' families, and told the men not to behave like *kabutars* (pigeons), and used other similar epithets. This was, naturally, not liked by the men, who continued their whistling in the excitement of seeing their first film show after over a year. The commanding officer repeated the same indecorous language, cancelled the film show at 10 p.m., and ordered the battalion to parade immediately in field service marching order with full equipment. The men demonstrated near the officers' mess, and chased the officers, though there was no attempt to kill or seriously injure them. The commanding officer had himself admitted to hospital with minor injuries. The battalion continued to carry out all normal duties thereafter, including extensive flood relief. After a court of inquiry, the commanding officer was brought down in rank and posted back to another regiment; two officers who had displayed dereliction of duty were tried and dismissed; the subedar major was prematurely retired; fourteen junior commissioned officers and other ranks were tried and awarded varying sentences; nearly 300 men, who were present, were released with mustering out concessions being shown as part of the 1950-51 rundown of 50,000 personnel in the Army; seventeen junior commissioned officers and 478 other ranks, who were not present, were accommodated in other battalions of the 11 GR, in the Regiment of Artillery, in the Military Police, the Border Scouts and the Assam Rifles. 4/11 GR was formally disbanded on 31 January 1951.[23] Curiously a Gorkha other rank of another regiment had killed an officer in the transit camp at Srinagar in 1948 with his *kukri* for using similar indecorous language. But the lesson had not been learnt by the then commanding officer, 4/11 GR, and had still not been learnt by the commanding officer, 2nd Assam, in 1961, or the commanding officer, 4/3 GR, in 1979. In the latter case the offensive language used by the commanding officer was *chura* and *chamar*. Thirteen were brought to trial for mutiny. Another mutiny had also occurred in 1961 in the 15th Battalion The Rajput Regiment, a class-company battalion. The collective indiscipline was confined to a particular class, in relation to alleged class problems. The 2nd Assam case was much more complex. There was groupism amongst the officers, the commanding officer's tent having earlier been burnt on the apparent instigation of an officer not in the commanding officer's group. The mutiny itself was instigated by another officer, who had taken leave at the time. Sixty-three were brought to trial, and the unit disbanded. A unit with the same number was later raised, in 1963, as part of the post-1962 augmentation. The disaffection was solely the creation of the officers, and the junior commissioned officers and other ranks were used by these officers as a means of inflicting retribution on a commanding officer and adjutant that they disliked. Whereas in the case of 2nd Assam better officer-management was necessary, in the case of 15th Rajput, 4/11 GR and 4/3 GR better man-management was necessary.

Separately, the peace talks at Panmunjom had led to a cease-fire in the Korean war on 27 July 1953. The main problem concerning India now was the supervision of the exchange of prisoners of war, including the difficulties implicit in the UN decision not to repatriate forcibly prisoners of war who did not wish to return to their own country. India withdrew the 60th Field Ambulance, as India was to provide the Custodian Force (India) (CFI) supervising the exchange of prisoners of war, as well as chairing the UN Neutral Nations Repatriation Commission (NNRC). Over 22,000 Chinese and North Koreans refused repatriation, as also 359 from the UN Command. The latter consisted, among others, of 325 South Koreans, twenty-three Americans, and one Briton, but first all these prisoners of war had to be taken over by the CFI, each one explained why he should return to his own country, despatch the willing prisoners of war, if any, to his country, and report to the UN those who were unwilling. This difficult task had to be completed in four months. Lieutenant General Thimayya was the Chairman, NNRC, Brigadier B.M. Kaul his Chief of Staff, and Major General S.P.P. Thorat, DSO, was the commander of the 5,000-strong CFI. The CFI did its work with acknowledged restraint, but many prisoners of war refused to cooperate during the period from November 1953 to January 1954. In February the NNRC was wound up, and the CFI returned to India, but before that Thimayya and Kaul had had serious working disagreements, Kaul tendering his resignation. Thimayya did not forward it, and instead, sent Kaul on leave to India. Later, in 1959, Thimayya, from the point of view of hindsight, was to express the view that he should then have recommended acceptance of Kaul's resignation. The US President, General Dwight Eisenhower, wrote to the Prime Minister commending the CFI, which from the wording would appear to be condescending, but, undoubtedly, was not meant to be so: 'The practical wisdom, understanding, courtesy and firmness shown by your officers and men would do credit to any first-rate fighting force.'

At the time the Indian Army had an approximate strength of 325,000; another precautionary concentration on the borders of West and East Pakistan had become necessary in the period 1952-53, on account of Pakistan's "war propaganda". Then, in April 1954, the UN requested India, Canada and Poland, with India presiding, to constitute the International Armistice Supervisory Commission to monitor the cease-fire in French Indo-China. The commission opened four offices in Hanoi, Saigon, Vientiane and Pnom Penh. Most of the personnel and communications were provided by the Indian Army. Twenty-six permanent and twenty-six mobile teams were organized by the three-member countries to monitor the deployment on both sides, to arbitrate in cease-fire violations, to supervise the return of prisoners of war, and to ensure no movement of warlike stores. This work continued till 1970, when international developments overtook the working of this commission. (In 1992, the Indian Army has again provided teams and one battalion at the request of the UN in Kampuchea.)

1956 witnessed a skirmish in Kutch at Chhad Bet, following a Pakistani intrusion, a forerunner of events in 1965. Thereafter, in November 1956, the UN asked India along with nine other neutral nations to constitute the United Nations Emergency Force (UNEF) to supervise the Egyptian-Israeli cease-fire in the Sinai. One battalion and some staff officers were sent, by rotation, on a year's tenure till June 1967 when the Third Arab-Israeli War took place. In 1960, command of the UNEF was assumed by Major General (later Lieutenant General) P.S. Gyani, and sometime thereafter by Major General I.J. Rikhye. While the Gaza commitment was still current, a brigade group under Brigadier K.A.S. Raja was sent to the former Belgian Congo (today's Zaire), in July 1961, at the request of the UN. On the completion of his tour of duty, he was replaced by Brigadier R.S. Noronha, MC, in July 1962. All units carried out their UN tasks superbly. (During the 1962 conflict with China the return of this brigade was not sought.) Major General D. Premchand then assumed command of Katanga Area, with 16,000 UN troops (including the Indian Brigade). (Thereafter in the 1960s India provided the UN Force Commander in Cyprus, then in Namibia, and today in the former Yugoslavia.)

Meanwhile, for the first time, as a consequence of US aid to Pakistan from 1954, a comprehensive five-year assessment of the Army's equipment needs had been forwarded to the government in 1956, which encompassed a "discard" or overhaul policy for all Second World War equipments, according to their respective life. There had been individual equipment projections after independence—for example, armoured vehicles—but the totality of the financial crunch over five years had not been readily discernible. Now it was, and aggregated over Rs 500 crores, comprising, *inter alia*, the introduction of a self-loading rifle; replacement of the 4.2-inch mortar and the 25-pounder-gun, and the introduction of a new pack howitzer; re-equipment of the armoured regiments; and replacement and/or overhaul of the vehicle fleet.[24] The Prime Minister was later to concede in 1963 in the Rajya Sabha that the Defence Committee of the Cabinet, 'possibly agreed to one-tenth of what they had asked.' But even as to the introduction of the self-loading rifle, there was avoidable delay. The events, after the Army was offered the Indian self-loading rifle (ISLR) in 1956, are best described by Lieutenant General S.D. Verma, first the Master General of the Ordnance

(MGO), and later in 1957, the Chief of the General Staff (CGS), in his book, *To Serve with Honour:* 'On taking over as the MGO, I had got the Technical Directorate moving to develop an ISLR. About a dozen prototype rifles had been produced, and as the CGS, I sent them for user trials to selected units located in different climatic conditions from the snowbound Himalayas to the damp marshy areas of Kutch and the dry sandy deserts of Rajasthan. On getting favourable reports, I put up a paper for the approval of the Chiefs of Staff Committee. The Naval and the Air Force chiefs (Admiral Carlisle and Air Marshal Mukerjee) said that if the rifle was all right for the major user, the Army, they would accept it for their services also. Armed with the agreement that all the three services were in favour of adopting the ISLR, I sponsored a paper for the Defence Minister's Production Board. I presented it personally at the meeting in March 1958, with Mr. Krishna Menon in the chair. The major points of the plan were: the rifle was acceptable to the Army, Navy and Air Force; the rifle could be produced at the existing ordnance factories controlled by the Defence Ministry without any foreign exchange requirement or assistance from outside sources; and the field army would be re-equipped in four years.

'The only doubt raised at the meeting was about the claimed muzzle velocity of the rifle. I submitted that the Defence Science Organization had been involved with the development of the rifle from the beginning, and if there was any doubt about its muzzle velocity, it could again be checked and rectified. The Finance Member on the committee raised the question of disposal of the existing stocks of the .303 Lee-Enfield rifles. I said the government of Burma had recently asked for a large number of these weapons, and we could sell them their requirement. There was also a proposal to arm Home Guards and villagers living near the Pakistan border. By the time these commitments were met, there would not be much left to worry about. No decision was taken at that meeting, nor was any communicated to the General Staff subsequently. To this day I do not know what happened to that proposal, put forward as a Joint Chiefs of Staff paper, the highest military authority in the services.

'The sequel is rather a sad commentary. If sanction had been given for the production of the ISLR at that time in March 1958, the Army would have been equipped and trained in the use of it by early 1962, and would have been in a position to face the Chinese aggression. When the Chinese attacked in October 1962, one of the first items we asked for from the British and American governments was a large stock of self-loading rifles. These were flown in by the planeload, and rushed up to the troops located at various high altitude pickets. Units had been sent up to 17,000 to 18,000-foot high passes in a hurry, many of them still clad in olive green summer uniforms and wearing canvas P.T. shoes. They had not even seen these weapons, let alone become familiar with their use. One can only speculate and say "If only...." The reverses and the humiliation suffered by the Army could have been avoided. But the ordnance factories had been kept busy producing coffee percolators instead of ISLRs.'[25]

Turning now to the events preceding the 1962 conflict with China. There were portents from 1950 onwards. Krishna Menon was not then the Defence Minister, nor was B.M. Kaul as powerful as he was later to be. Cariappa had met Nehru in 1951 to discuss the defence of the North-East Frontier Agency (NEFA), and was told, 'You mind only Kashmir and Pakistan.' It is true that, during the five years (1957-62) that Menon was the Defence Minister, Nehru acted as his defender, but, nevertheless, Menon was not entirely to blame for the reverses, even though he resigned eighteen days after the Chinese onslaught of 20 October 1962. As to B.M. Kaul, he was already being built up by the Prime Minister much before Menon became the Defence Minister. Kaul had even been invited by the Chinese in 1954. All three, then, did not realize that whatever soft words were spoken in Beijing, the Chinese have always regarded all others as inferiors. Howsoever the Chinese may have flattered B.M. Kaul during his 1954 visit, the Chinese military delegation that visited India in 1956 and had witnessed a firepower demonstration arranged by him at Chandigarh, had reportedly commented, during a halt at Rangoon to the Burmese, that the then senior officers of the

Indian Army were "chair-borne" soldiers. On different planes, Menon and Kaul were Nehru's "eminences grises". But as Major General D.K. Palit puts it in his book, *War in High Himalaya:* 'It was not Krishna Menon who was primarily culpable for the practice of general officers establishing direct access to politicians.... It was Nehru who, many years previously, first established this irregularity. He had come across Kaul in the years just before independence.... A strong rapport had sprung up between the two distant kinsmen.'[26]
The Sino-Indian Treaty of 1954 was based on non-interference, with India relinquishing, in 1955, the military detachments at Gyantse and Yatung, and the postal and telegraph facilities to Lhasa, which went back to Francis Younghusband's 1904 expedition, Nehru stating: 'Free India had no wish to continue with any imperialistic rights or privileges.' The question of border delineation was not brought up, yet it would appear that the Chinese had probably occupied the 17,000-foot-high Aksaichin and patrolled other areas claimed in Ladakh from July 1951 onwards. The first official Chinese claim was made in 1954. Ten alignments of the Aksaichin highway were reconnoitred in 1954-55, and it was announced as completed in September 1957. Two Indian patrols were sent to the area in 1958, one returned, and one, under Major G.K.K. Iyyengar of the Madras Sappers, was seized by the Chinese. In October 1958, an Indian protest was ultimately lodged regarding the opening of the highway and the non-return of the patrol. In early 1959 Chou En-lai was to claim 14,000 square miles in Ladakh and 36,000 in today's Arunachal Pradesh. September witnessed the Chinese attack on the Assam Rifles post at Longju in NEFA, and, in October, fifty miles within Indian territory, nine members of a police patrol were killed and ten taken prisoner. Nehru and Menon had, till then, viewed the border with China on par with the one between the US and Canada, the Aksaichin being described as, 'where not even a blade of grass grows.' Nehru later asserted in Parliament in 1959 after the occurrence of the clashes: 'I saw no reason to discuss the frontier with the Chinese government, because, probably, if you like, I thought there was nothing to discuss.' For his part, Krishna Menon still caustically

stated at Agra on 10 September 1961: 'I am not aware of any aggression, incursion, encroachment or intrusion by the Chinese.' Even the publication of a training pamphlet on Chinese tactics was disallowed in the late 1950s.

In August 1959, the then Army Chief, General K.S. Thimayya, was constrained to resign in view of the interference in promotions by Menon, later commenting that, '....The whole thing was about Kaul.'[27] Nehru talked him into withdrawing his resignation. Thimayya described his subsequent working relationship with Menon as, 'things were very bad after that.' Palit records, 'He suffered undeserved humiliation at Krishna Menon's hands, following his sensational but injudicious resignation, and subsequent retraction.'[28] I, having personally attended some of Krishna Menon's talks and briefings, had observed that he displayed a perverse kind of enjoyment at believing that he was hated. Questioned genuinely, he would threaten to have the questioner court-martialled. Conflict was the *leit-motif* of his life. Lieutenant General S.P.P. Thorat recounted in his autobiography, *From Reveille to Retreat:* '(In 1959) When I (as GOC-in-C, Eastern Command) met Mr Menon in Delhi, I opened the subject (defence against the Chinese) with him. In his usual sarcastic style he said that there would be no war between India and China, and (if there was) he was quite capable of fighting it himself at the diplomatic level.'[29] Frank Moraes, the journalist and editor, wrote of him that, 'he suffers neither fools nor wise men gladly.'[30] (Despite the above auguries, in relation to Chinese intentions, the government had directed the Chiefs of Staff in 1960, 'to be prepared for and resist external aggression, mainly by Pakistan.') In early 1961, some anonymous alleged army officers wrote to the Prime Minister: 'The Defence Minister....seems to wield some black magic over....the Prime Minister.'[31] After that, in April, in Parliament, Acharya J.B. Kripalani had stated, 'I charge him with wasting the money of a poor and starving nation. I charge him with having created cliques in the Army. I charge him with having lowered the morale of our armed forces. I charge him with the neglect of the defence of the country against the aggression of Communist China.' Welles Hangen, thereafter, narrated, 'Indian officers actually approached a Western attache in New Delhi for help in arranging to have Menon assassinated.'[32] I am personally totally sceptical, not of Hangen, for he is a recorder, but of the attache's account. When, according to Hangen, General P.N. Thapar took over as Army Chief in May 1961, Menon told him that the Service Chiefs could not expect to understand everything that he, as Defence Minister, was doing, but they should not worry, because it was "for the best".[33] The plot against the then Major General (later Field Marshal) S.H.F.J. Manekshaw, in order to prevent his possible promotion in due course as Army Chief, was evolved by Kaul and the subsequent inquiry ordered by Menon. The presiding officer, Lieutenant General Daulet Singh, after due recording, advised dismissal of the allegations, and action against the accusers. Of the two, Menon and Kaul, Thimayya was to say that Kaul was 'smarter and more dangerous,'[34] and also, 'I doubted that there is any ideological or emotional affinity between the two.' In December 1961, the Portuguese enclave of Goa was liberated, using the 17th Infantry Division and the 50th Parachute Brigade (in a ground role). Here, too, many of the troops employed had no boots, but were shod in canvas shoes. Adequate notice was not taken then of the equipment deficiencies revealed, even though Kaul marched in with the advanced guard battalion. The subsequent "Forward Policy" of putting an air-maintained Indian post next to a road-maintained Chinese post in Indian Chinese-claimed territory was the External Affairs Ministry's concept, not Menon's, but approved by Nehru. In 1960, Thorat held an exercise at Lucknow to assess Chinese intentions. The conclusions arrived at correctly portrayed what the Chinese actually did in 1962. Earlier on 8 October 1959, Thorat had already sent to Army Headquarters his appreciation of the situation, who put it up to Menon. He chose to ignore it. Nehru later said it had never been shown to him. When Daulet Singh, a forthright officer and then GOC-in-C Western Command responsible for Ladakh, wrote to Thapar on 16 August 1962 that a conflict was imminent with China, spelling out his reasons at considerable length, a reply was received back, within four days, that the government at the highest level was of the view that no conflict was likely in the near future. *Inter alia,* Daulet Singh also represented as to the probable disastrous repercussions flowing from the "Forward Policy". In the event, the developments from 20 October 1962 onwards, the date of the massive Chinese onslaught, are well-known. Nehru was to ask Thapar to submit his resignation on grounds of poor health. He was succeeded by Lieutenant General J.N. Chaudhuri. (After retirement, Thimayya had written in the July 1962 issue of *Seminar:* 'I cannot, even as a soldier, envisage India taking on China in an open conflict on its own.... We could never hope to match China in the foreseeable future. It must be left to the politicians and diplomats to ensure our security.') In 1967 Kaul was to write *The Untold Story,* seeking to exculpate himself, heaping the blame on Menon, and portraying Nehru as being in Menon's pocket. Only after vacating his appointment as the Chief of the General Staff at New Delhi, and taking over as General Officer Commanding the newly-constituted Headquarters 4 Corps, did enlightenment dawn: 'Frankly speaking, I had now fully understood all the implications.... I thought we should reconsider the whole of our position in this theatre.'[35] That apparently was not to be. Yet Chester Bowles, who was twice US Ambassador in India, recounts in his book, *Promises to Keep,* 'when I stopped in India in March 1962 for a brief visit...Kaul...whom I did not know...told me that he expected an attack by Communist China between July and October of that year, and asked what the US could be expected to do to assist. When I expressed my scepticism about such an attack...Kaul insisted...' (Later, when Bowles was back again as the US Ambassador in 1963, he informed Nehru of this incident, Nehru commented, 'I wish he had told me too.') The subsequent decisions not to permit ground attacks into Tibet from Ladakh, nor air attacks on the attacking Chinese, were, undoubtedly, Menon's. Some later tried to draw the inference that the Army fought better against the Chinese in the West compared to the East. The distinction sought to be drawn is both incorrect and invidious. It must be remembered that the Chinese only engaged approximately 24,000 in both Ladakh and NEFA, out of a then Indian Army of 4,00,000, as most of the latter were still deployed against Pakistan, in accordance with the government's 1960 directions. In Ladakh, only a brigade-plus had been inducted; in NEFA, it was a division-minus initially, for 400 miles of border and 33,000 square miles of difficult terrain. Depending on the circumstances, the troops fought equally well or worse, bearing in mind that most of the troops in Ladakh were deployed on our side of the Chinese claim line, whereas, in NEFA, they were all deployed north of the claim line right up to the border. Sequentially, the comparative casualties are informative:

	Killed	Wounded	Missing	Total
• NEFA	1,150	500	1,600	3,250
• Ladakh	230	50	60	340

Insofar as the long-suffering Indian soldier is concerned, one quotes their commander on the Namka Chu, the late Brigadier J.P. Dalvi, who was taken prisoner by the Chinese, 'The Gorkhas, the Rajputs, the Sikhs, the Dogras, the Bengalis, the Mussalmans of the Grenadiers, the Ahirs, the South Indian Signallers and all others from the four corners of India had nothing to sustain them but their regimental pride and traditions. They had done what they had done, because they were soldiers. For no man can do more than give his life for his country.'[36] Insofar as the causes of the failure are concerned, the late Brigadier Dalvi is most succinct, '1962 was a national failure of which every Indian is guilty. It was a failure of the Higher Direction of War, a failure of the Opposition, a failure of the General Staff (myself included); it was a failure of responsible public opinion and the press. For the Government of India, it was a Himalayan blunder at all levels....'[37] Of Dalvi's book, *Himalayan Blunder*, Neville Maxwell has recorded, 'This may come to be regarded as a classic of military literature, epitomizing the predicament of the officer under orders which he knows must lead to the destruction of his command.'[38]

Fidelity & Honour

By way of an epitaph on the Namka Chu action in October 1962, one invokes the poem published in *The Hindustan Times* on 18 November 1962:

As the brutal rock shatters the
placid glass
Into a thousand irreparable
fragments,
A bitter grief is hurled at
normalcy and peace.
Never will they be quite complete
again;
The Cracks of pain and death
Will always show. The weeping
Of wives bereft, of the
anguished old,
Will echo down the years of
history.

The wasted unspent lives, the
loss of years
Too many to be counted,
Too precious to be valued;
A generation unborn, men's
immortality—
There lies the bitterness
So violent, the heart revolts
and weeps
Unceasing, arid, unshed tears.
The sense of shame, of
betrayal unforgiveable
Never to be redeemed,
Of Sacrifice avoidable,
insensate,
That is the guilt we share.

The valley is silent,
Shrouded in death's
immobility,
Final and absolute,
But the soundless cry from the
mountains
Beats upon our ears
Pitiless, undeniable—
"We died—unsuccoured,
helpless;

We were your soldiers.
Men of bravery and pride,
Yet we died like animals
Trapped in a cage with no
escape,
Massacred at will,
Denied the dignity of battle.

With the cold burning flame
of anger and resolution,
With the courage, both of the
living and dead
Avenge our unplayed lives,
Redeem the unredeemable
Sacrifice
In freedom and integrity.
Let this be your inheritance
And our unwritten epitaph".

Prince Klemens von Metternich had said that, 'Men who make history have not the time to write it.' In retrospect, all that can be said in defence of Menon and Kaul, is, to invoke Metternich, that they suffered from "an excess of zeal". Their fortunate exit ensured the Army remained apolitical.

Thereafter, the Prime Minister, in the Rajya Sabha, stated in early 1963, 'If Honorable Members will try to think of the whole background in which we developed in the past, they will see that we were anxious to save money on defence. We had been criticising for long—the Congress and every public man in India had been criticising—heavy expenditure on defence and on the Army. We were anxious to use all the resources we had for economic betterment, for industrialization and all that. We were anxious not to spend too much on the Army—I am talking of about 10 or 12 years ago. We realise that the real strength of the country, even from the defence point of view, was the industrial apparatus behind it, the industrial background. In times of crisis, we cannot depend on getting arms, etc, from abroad. We have to produce it ourselves. If, in a crisis, you have to rely on everything to come from outside then even if things go wrong in small details, you cannot use these tools, because you have to get spare parts from outside. Therefore, we thought that even from the point of view of the defence of the country, we should industrialise. No country that is not industrialised is militarily strong today. Therefore, we decided then to save money on defence and apply it to the schemes of development and industrialisation, including, of course, plants essential for defence, and on becoming scientifically advanced. There was no other way of making India strong, politically or in defence matters.

'...Right from the day the Chinese came into Tibet, we felt that a new danger threatened us, though not immediately. The fact that a great and powerful country had come right up to our borders which had been, more or less, dead and peaceful, was a great change. We realised this possible danger and we thought that we should gradually prepare for it, in the main, by building roads. Roads are essential for reaching our border. Then many things happened. They came to Tibet in a bigger way and later, two or three years later, there was the Tibetan revolution and the Dalai Lama came here (in 1959). All these were warnings to us that things were happening there, and we took that warning; but that warning did not and could not lead us to assume a bellicose attitude towards China, because that would not have helped us at all. To threaten China or to have a pugnacious attitude towards China was merely not to our advantage at all from any practical point of view. It would have created the very situation which we are trying to avoid or postpone. Today, we have got to face, as we had to face, first, Pakistan's threat to us and its bellicose attitude, and then the Chinese. We have to face both of them, possibly together. There was a certain compulsion of events and no Government, however much it may have differed from our ways of thinking, could have functioned very differently from what we did, always keeping in view the fact that the real thing before us was to strengthen India industrially and not superficially, by getting an odd gun or an odd aircraft.'

Apart from Dalvi's poignant book, the first to appear, there have subsequently been several personal accounts of the 1962 reverses in NEFA. In the sequence of the operations some of these books were, *The Fall of Tawang* by the first Divisional Commander, Major General Niranjan Prasad; *The Untold Story* by the Corps Commander, Lieutenant General B.M. Kaul; and *The Unfought War* by Lieutenant Colonel (then Major) J.R. Saigal, the latter portraying events after the withdrawal from Sela. These have now been followed by *War in High Himalaya—The Indian Army in Crisis 1962*, by Major General D.K. Palit, Director of Military Operations at that time. The latter is the most detached and objective account, so one concludes this chapter by quoting him—'The truth is that we were planning and operating in a doctrinal vacuum.'[39] '...the Army, its senior commanders and staff inexplicably allowed themselves to be cajoled or browbeaten into futile and implausible deployments along the Karakoram and Himalayan Ranges.'[40] 'Nor did the Army High Command live upto expectations. Its strategic perceptions were unsound: it failed to understand or moderate ministerial directions that patently foreboded disaster, and it abjectly accepted political overreach in operational supervision.'[41] 'Their failure to impress on the politicians the impossibility of the operational tasks demanded of them, and above all for the insensitivity to the plight of the officers and men in the battalions witlessly rushed up into the high mountains insufficiently armed, clothed or provisioned—at the mercy of an enemy well-prepared for war.'[42] 'Our forces could not have stopped the Chinese at the Namka Chu, or at the Chip Chap (Ladakh) or at Walong (on the eastern flank of NEFA) and should never have been sent there for that purpose. But the fact remains that, at all these places, the Army did its best and made the enemy pay a price for its gains. Only at Sela have we betrayed our trust. There, where we could have stopped them, we ran away without fighting, and the tragedy is that the betrayal came not from the troops but from the generals in command.... I think that all three Generals, A.S. Pathania (the second Divisional Commander), Kaul, and Sen (the GOC-in-C) should be deemed remiss in battle.'[43] Had Niranjan Prasad been told to officiate as Corps Commander when Kaul was medically evacuated on 17 October, and had Lieutenant General Harbakhsh Singh been allowed to continue as Corps Commander after he had taken over on 22 October, it is possible the Sela debacle would not have occurred. Harbakhsh Singh had told Lal Bahadur Shastri on 22 October, when he visited Tezpur as Home Minister, that he was confident of stopping the Chinese at Sela. Unfortunately, Kaul, with the Prime Minister's support, returned to re-assume command of 4 Corps on 27 October, and as a result the Sela debacle occurred. The Brigade Commander, Hoshiar Singh, had initially wanted to stay and fight, but the new Divisional Commander (A.S. Pathania) wanted Hoshiar Singh to withdraw, and Kaul was indecisive in not ordering the Divisional Commander to stay and fight the Sela battle. Palit's encapsulation of Kaul's personality is apposite, 'he seemed to spend a large part of his life in disguise, even from himself.'[44]

The last word in this chapter rests with Lieutenant General T.Henderson-Brooks, who presided over the 1962 Operations Review Committee, and whose report is still classified. In March 1989 he recounted, 'In my opinion, it was not really a war. One Indian division had to cover a front of 500 miles. To have a section in position, it was necessary to use the remainder of the platoon to maintain them. The section was only flag flying. When the clash occurred, the unfortunate reinforcements were not properly clothed or armed and without supporting weapons. They were not acclimatized.... On the other hand, the Chinese soldier was... attacking downhill.'[45] On the political plane, one can agree with K. Subramanyam's postulation, 'If we take into account the magnitude of the crisis that India faced, it would seem that Nehru pulled her through it at a relatively low cost.'[46]

SIXTEEN

The Post-Nehru Years

JAWAHARLAL NEHRU, THE idealist, sadly passed away on 27 May 1964, a commentator then observing that, 'Nehru died the day when the Chinese committed the massive aggression into India.' In 1963 in the Rajya Sabha he had admitted, 'I remember many a time when our senior generals came to us, and wrote to the Defence Ministry saying that they wanted certain things....If we had foresight, known exactly what would happen, we would have done something else...what India had learnt from the Chinese invasion was that in the world of today there was no place for weak nations....We have been living in an unreal world of our own creation. It is possible that our peaceful ways were responsible for our unpreparedness to meet such a wanton and massive onslaught from a nation we mistook to be socialist.'[1] As to the too brilliant and paranoid V.K. Krishna Menon, the prescient Maulana Abul Kalam Azad, recorded, in his autobiography, 'Sardar Patel and I did not always see eye to eye, but we were agreed in our judgment about him.'

The then Director of Military Operations, Major General D.K. Palit, was later to elaborate, 'The decision-making system during 1959-62 was starkly ad hoc and designed primarily to suit the personality of the Prime Minister—who preferred to deal with these matters personally—even Krishna Menon seldom took a stand on any point or even made any contribution when the Prime Minister was in the chair...in the Army Headquarters, it was General Kaul who had caught the Prime Minister's eye....'[2]

Of B.M. Kaul it can verily be said, that it was his fate to outsmart himself. His account, *The Untold Story,* is but the half-told story. The late Durga Das, the eminent journalist and former editor of *The Hindustan Times,* was, thereafter, to record in 1969 after Nehru's death: 'The fact of the matter is that Nehru felt gnawings of conscience throughout this episode. He knew that the blame for the disaster was more his than that of his loyal friend.' In fact, he had told Y.B. Chavan, then Chief Minister of Bombay, in October 1962: 'You see they want Menon's blood. If I agree, tomorrow they will ask for my blood.' The reverses, however, had a salutary effect for the country, inasmuch as President S. Radhakrishnan was constrained to insist on the acceptance of Menon's resignation; to turn down Nehru's suggestion to make Kaul the Army Chief; not to bring back any retired officers for the appointment; to insist on the seniormost serving general officer, J.N. Chaudhuri, even though he had received his retirement orders, succeeding P.N. Thapar; and to iterate, 'War or no war, invasion or no invasion, attack or no attack, we must not be caught napping again. We must increase our strength....Military weakness has been a temptation; a little military strength may be a deterrent.'[3] Accordingly, the new Defence Minister, Y.B. Chavan, placed before Parliament in June 1964 a Rs 5,000 crore Five-Year Defence Plan for the three Defence Services, the Army's manpower ceiling being increased to 825,000. This plan and the increased manpower ceiling were still in the process of implementation when the conflict with Pakistan was inflicted on India in 1965.

The new Prime Minister was Lal Bahadur Shastri, and with him both the nation's political will and military confidence were to be revitalized. Earlier, Krishna Menon, in a public speech in Bombay in 1963, after the acceptance of his resignation, had admitted, 'There were considerable divisions of the Chinese army in Tibet, and it is no breach of security to say that even at that time China had more forces in Tibet than the whole of the Indian Army, or at least as much.'[4] Much before Nehru's sudden death, Welles Hangen had clairvoyantly recorded of Shastri in 1963 in his book, *After Nehru Who?*: 'The mouse might well roar.'[5]

To the surprise of Pakistan, in 1965, he proved to be no mouse, and was to roar, but in 1964 it appeared to Pakistan that Shastri had been chosen to be the Prime Minister by the Congress party as he was thought to be the least controversial successor to Nehru, and that he would thus naturally need time to consolidate his position, as also revivify the country after the 1962 trauma. In fact, Zulfikar Ali Bhutto, the Pakistani Foreign Minister said, 'India is in disarray.' In April 1965, therefore, Pakistan decided to administer a phased *coup de grace* to India, deemed to be reeling under the effects of famine, and language riots in the south, necessitating the extensive deployment of troops. K. Kamaraj had, about this time, already cautioned all political parties, particularly the Congress and the Communist, in relation to the seeming policy of the former to call on the Army recurringly to counter disturbances created by the latter. Presumably, with mainly Pakistan in mind, Kamaraj stated, without any justification, that one day the Indian Army would refuse to go back to the barracks, and that the Communists would then find themselves worse off under military rule, than they had ever been under Congress rule. This postulation got, subconsciously, conjoined with the political thinking at the time that led to the Chiefs of Staff Committee's proposal for the creation of the appointment of a Chief of the Defence Staff being turned down. (In early 1961, when Nehru had asked for Lord Louis Mountbatten's opinion of K.S. Thimayya in the context of the "coup" canard, Mountbatten was so convinced of the falsity of the allegation, that he had suggested that the appointment of the Chief of the Defence Staff be created for Thimayya before he retired. Nehru did not act on the suggestion.) At the time of Nehru's funeral while Gulzari Lal Nanda was still officiating as Prime Minister before Shastri's selection, J.N. Chaudhuri had made elaborate arrangements for security, by bringing troops into Delhi, recalling the confusion that prevailed at Mahatma Gandhi's funeral, when Mountbatten had feared for Nehru's life. Chaudhuri was later to recount that his telephone had then been tapped as the fear had circulated that a military takeover was imminent.

The Rann of Kutch appeared an unlikely sector for Pakistan to start a conflict with India, but the April 1965 military intrusion there by Pakistan was part of the larger game plan to draw off the Indian Army 1,200 kilometres to the south, before infiltrating, and then attacking, Jammu and Kashmir, in August and September that year. In April, Pakistan also threatened Indian road communications to Ladakh. Other aims were to test in the desert Pakistan's US-supplied armour and equipment. By then Pakistan had received 900 million dollars of US armaments and ammunition. In 1954, a day before announcing the American decision to give military aid to Pakistan, President Dwight Eisenhower had sent a personal letter to Prime Minister Nehru assuring him that aid to Pakistan was in no way directed against India, and in the event of misuse of American military aid in the form of aggression, the USA would undertake immediately appropriate action to thwart such aggression. This, in the event, was not to be so in 1965. A Central Reserve Police (CRP) battalion, commanded by an ex-Army officer, was the first to arrive in the area, and performed creditably. Earlier, Pakistan had tried to establish a post in Chhad Bet in 1956, but had been foiled by the 7th Battalion, The Grenadiers, then a camel-borne unit, but today mechanized, raised from former Indian State Force (ISF) units. To meet the 1965 situation, Army Headquarters decided to conduct a holding action in Kutch with two brigades moved for the purpose, and to concentrate the main forces instead along the border in the north against a possible Pakistani threat. There was much criticism then of the Army for adopting such a "negative" strategy, the word "cowardice" even being frequently invoked. The Kutch situation was shortly resolved by arbitration in July by the British Prime Minister, Harold Wilson. The sequential perception of the Pakistani "hawks", like Zulfikar Ali Bhutto, but not of their Commander-in-

Chief, General Mohammed Musa, who sought more time to prepare
for a war, was one of an all-pervasive, 'Indian pusillanimity and poor
performance,' in Kutch. When war with India in Jammu and Kashmir was being discussed, the then Governor of the West Punjab,
the Nawab of Kalabagh, told President Ayub Khan: '...do not listen
to Bhutto. His father or grandfather did not handle a sword or a gun.
I warn you that if you attack India, you will face reverse.' He was
subsequently removed from the governorship for this, and later shot
dead by his son.[6]

Curiously, in February 1965, the Institute of Defence Analysis
in Washington had conducted a "crisis game" based on the Kashmir
scenario. The "game" enacted in Washington concluded that, 'Pakistan
was likely to gain Kashmir or a large part of it,' in 1965. Operation
"Gibraltar"—Pakistan sending 7,000 military and para-military personnel in civilian clothes into Kashmir, led again by selected army
officers as in 1947—was launched in early August scarcely a week
after signing the agreement in London to end the hostilities in Kutch,
the Indian formations having commenced their withdrawal from the
international border in accordance with the London agreement. Very
much earlier, on 15 September 1950, the United Nations' Representative in India and Pakistan, Sir Owen Dixon, had categorically said
in his Report No. S 1791, '...when the frontier of the State of Jammu
and Kashmir was crossed on, I believe, 20 October 1947, it was
contrary to international laws, and that when in May 1948, as I
believe, units of the regular Pakistani forces moved into the territory
of the State, that too was inconsistent with international law.' Bhutto
and his coterie now again in May 1965 prevailed on the Pakistani
President, Ayub Khan, counter to the advice of General Musa,
formulating that India, if pressed in Kashmir, would not resort to a
general war by crossing the international border. This line of action
had been rendered very attractive by the contrived "Hazratbal" (the
revered hair of the esteemed Prophet) agitation and disorder in 1963
in Srinagar. While simultaneously dealing with the Pakistani intruders, the Indian forces crossed the cease-fire line to cut off the ingress
of the Pakistanis, and captured the Hajipir Pass, after the UN

Observer Group had officially reported that Pakistan had violated the cease-fire line extensively, 'The series of violations that began on August 5 were to a considerable extent in subsequent days in the form of armed men, generally not in uniform, crossing the Cease Fire Line from the Pakistani side for the purpose of armed action on the Indian side....' (No. S 6651). Despite the invasion of Kashmir by this Pakistani force, India had not crossed the international border in retaliation so far.

Then, on 1 September, Pakistan launched Operation "Grand Slam", thus further escalating the conflict, attacking Akhnur in the Chhamb-Jaurian sector in order to sever the Jammu-Srinagar highway, and the Jammu-Poonch road. On 3 September, U Thant, the UN Secretary-General reported to the Security Council, 'I have not obtained from the Government of Pakistan any assurance that the cease-fire line will be respected henceforth or that efforts would be extended to restore conditions to normal along that line. I did receive assurance from the Government of India...that India would act with restraint with regard to any retaliatory acts and will respect the cease-fire agreement and the cease-fire line if Pakistan does likewise.' The sequential Indian ripostes of 6 September were in the Lahore and Sialkot sectors. The third component of the Pakistani grand strategy was now launched in the Kasur-Khemkaran (Asal Uttar) sector directed at Beas, in order to cut the Indian communications to Amritsar, and Jammu and Kashmir, the road to Delhi thereafter being open whereby India would be brought to her knees. (The name of the Indian village in question was apt, "Asal Uttar"—ultimate reply.)

Separately, in September 1965, the Chinese Foreign Minister had visited Pakistan by invitation, and after a fortnight China gave an ultimatum on 17 September to India, to remove its posts from "Chinese" territory, or face the consequences; China concomitantly concentrated its troops along the Indian border, and, thereby, pinned down six Indian divisions. Shastri, thereupon, replied that the Chinese were at liberty to remove the Indian posts if there were, in fact, any on "Chinese" territory, thus enhancing his increasing image as a courageous leader. The ultimatum was first extended, and, thereafter, China remained silent, though continuing its operational deployment till the cease-fire with Pakistan. The US, however, had twice cautioned China to "stay out of it", but despite these US cautions China, notwithstanding, had issued its ultimatum. This conflict with Pakistan, not in any way of India's making, in effect ended in only a limited victory, whereas it could have been a major victory for India, had hostilities continued, or had not so many opportunities been missed, Lieutenant General Harbakhsh Singh, GOC-in-C Western Command, validly recording, 'I have heard it said, on the conclusion of hostilities, that our concept of operations lacked offensive dash and dimensions, forgetting the elementary wisdom that, unless the ends, are balanced against the means available, a campaign is foredoomed to failure. In actual fact,...we were in no position to go in for an all-out war with Pakistan, but were compelled to do so. In view of this, each stage of the offensive had to be carefully analysed to ensure that it was within the bounds of practicability. And although we never threw caution to the winds, calculated risks were accepted.'[7]

Palit has thereafter recorded that when the UN sponsored a cease-fire and was pressing India and Pakistan to accept it, the Prime Minister consulted the Army Chief, that if he held out against UN pressure for a few days whether the Army would be able to achieve significant results on the ground. The Chief of the Army Staff's reported advice, according to those present in the Emergency Cabinet Committee meeting, was that we were running low on ammunition, and, hence, it would be better to accept the cease-fire. On the basis of this advice, the then Prime Minister accepted the cease-fire. When a complete review of our ammunition expenditure in the 1965 war was made, it was found that on an average only fourteen to twenty per cent of our ammunition stocks had been used. What would have happened if the Army Chief had pressed on with the war, with the Pakistan Army scraping the bottom of its ammunition barrel.[8] As in 1948, by Roy Bucher, the cease-fire was reportedly agreed to by Chaudhuri in 1965, just when the Indian Army had successfully countered all possible Pakistani initiatives, and the latter had no further arrows in its quiver, including no ammunition. On 13 and 15 September, Pakistan had turned down earlier international appeals for a cease-fire, spelling out its curious terms—prior agreement for the withdrawal of all troops by both sides including in Jammu and Kashmir, the induction of an Afro-Asian peacekeeping force, and a commitment by India to hold a plebiscite within three months. There has been a spate of books from the Pakistani viewpoint on this conflict virtually from its very conclusion; by Altaf Gauhar, Ayub Khan's confidant; by General Musa; and Air Marshal Asghar Khan, their former Air Chief. The latter bluntly records in his introduction to his book, *The First Round, Indo-Pakistan War, 1965,* 'A war which appears now to have been fought for no purpose.'

By contrast, Lieutenant General Harbakhsh Singh's *War Despatches* have only been published twenty-five years later. Before reverting to the latter, mention needs to be made that this conflict, in effect, set in motion the break-up of Pakistan, for East Pakistan, already feeling economically deprived, thereafter felt militarily defenceless. It was an ingenious part of the Indian Army's counter-strategy at the time not to attack East Pakistan. The Soviet-sponsored 1966 Tashkent Agreement formally concluded the 1965 hostilities, but undoubtedly caused Prime Minister Lal Bahadur Shastri's massive heart-attack (his second), and sequential death. He had committed himself in Parliament not to return the Hajipir Pass to Pakistan, but, at Tashkent, had had to do just that. (This agreement and its ripple effects were, in the event, ultimately to lead to Ayub Khan's ouster in 1969.) Lal Bahadur Shastri had proved to be a good Prime Minister. He had bravely faced up to the welter of problems confronting him, and was overcoming them, till his health eventually failed him, as it had been feared it may. He had convincingly established that he did not take counsel of his fears, and had earlier urged that he should be judged by his own performance, and not by the yardstick of Nehru's policies. At the time of his untimely death, he was constantly growing in the public's image as a positive Prime Minister. Had he lived, he was to have had a dialogue with Sheikh

Mohammed Abdullah for a political solution, involving the Kashmiri opposition as well. Had he been able to do so, the situation may have been different today. There is no gainsaying that thanks to Shastri and Chavan, civil-military relations improved exponentially.

As to these civil-military relations, V.K. Krishna Menon had earlier postulated an unexceptionable formulation, when he was the Defence Minister, quoted by Michael Brecher, though its assertion was unnecessary as it was already unequivocally being acted on by the Army, both before and after independence: 'It is wrong for the Army to try to make policy; their business is to be concerned with military tactics. Military planning and arrangements and things of that kind must remain in the hands of the Government, and even inside the Government, these questions are largely conditioned by finance....The Government is not going to say that it wants one company here or two companies there, but the Government will certainly say, "we should attack Pakistan" or "we should not attack Pakistan"...or things of the kind; these are all matters of policy...of course, military matters are merely questions of expertise; strategy includes considerations related to our political orientation.'[9] Yet, in 1962, there had been constant interference by Nehru and Krishna Menon before the operations as to the deployment even of companies and platoons and also after their commencement in relation to the deployment of brigades and battalions. In 1962 the Indian Army had ventured into a conflict, as to the timing of which it did not generally agree, and as to the result of which it was not sanguine, whereas in August/September 1965, it was both agreeable to, on account of the necessity, as well as confident of countering Pakistan. The relationship between the Prime Minister and the Army Chief was sound right through 1965 (as it was to be even more so in 1971). Any decisions taken by the political leadership were left to the military leadership to carry out unfettered. Thus, in the event, it was Shastri and Chavan who adhered to Menon's formulation, not Nehru and Menon.

Before moving on from the 1965 conflict with Pakistan, one

must mention some of the missed opportunities as reflected in his *War Despatches* by Lieutenant General Harbakhsh Singh. First, one needs to take one of the missed opportunities in this conflict in the 11 Corps Zone in the Punjab, the case of the 3rd Battalion The Jat Regiment in the Amritsar Sector. '3 Jat under the inspiring leadership of their Commanding Officer, Lt Col (later Brig) D.E. Hayde, raced for the (Ichhogil) Canal and captured its east bank....The gallant unit then swung south and captured the bridge on the Grand Trunk axis....The leading elements of the battalion crossed the Ichhogil Canal and reached the Bata Shoe Factory (in the Lahore suburb of Batapur) which was to be the limit of the Bridgehead. Having scored a sensational success, 3 Jat then started looking over their shoulders for the logistical support to hold on to their objective....This unfortunately was not forthcoming. It was a crucial moment that required the touch of determined leadership to push through urgent requirements to the unit....Commander 54 Infantry Brigade, unfortunately, did not rise to the occasion. It is admitted that enemy air action had strafed the administrative convoy...that morning and some vehicles were destroyed....The opportunity, however, went abegging—a brilliant success was allowed to slip away unexploited. But worse was to follow. The brigade commander had lost touch with 3 Jat since the morning (an inexcusable lapse, for he should have been treading on the heels of this epoch-making thrust) and was probably unaware of the momentous success achieved by this unit. Assuming that he could neither replenish nor reinforce 3 Jat, he decided to go on the defensive....3 Jat were ordered to vacate their gains and withdraw....It is at this stage a purely academic argument as to where the fault lay—the fact remains however that a cheap victory had been thrown to the winds for want of aggressive and enterprising leadership.'[10] It is an irony that the Pakistani battalion 3 Jat defeated, and whose commanding officer was captured, received more and higher awards.

In relation to the Sialkot sector, Harbakhsh Singh objectively records: 'But when the dust settled down, and the achievements of 1 Corps were viewed in their correct perspective, stripped of the aura of sensation the initial feeling of exaltation gradually gave way to one of disillusionment. For, with the exception of a few minor successes, the formation's record of operational performance was virtually a catalogue of lost victories. It is admitted that we dealt a telling blow to the enemy, but we must concede the fact that it fell far short of a decisive defeat when it was within our capacity to do so and for which the circumstances were so favourable. In consequence the enemy armour was only mauled instead of being crippled beyond recovery—our primary aim. The 'Patton' met its Waterloo mainly because of its complicated gadgetry beyond the comprehension of the average Pakistani soldier and the excellent gunnery of our own armour—not through any tactical ingenuity at higher level of command. We penetrated only 11 miles into enemy territory beyond the bridgehead at our deepest stretch, when, but for the mishandling of forces, especially armour, the completion of our mission appeared well within our grasp. As the truth of these shortfalls in achievements dawned on us, there came the gnawing feeling of unfulfilment—a painful realization that we were capable of doing so much, but had done so little. The sense of disillusionment deepened to chagrin when, on further investigation, it was revealed that a decisive victory slipped out of our hands due to poor leadership on the battlefield....The Armoured Division fought a good action at Phillora, where the skill of junior leadership combined with excellent gunnery badly mauled the enemy armour. But, unfortunately, this was the only bright spot in the otherwise dismal performance of the formation, consistently dogged by want of competent direction at Divisional and Brigade level. The imagination, enterprise and audacity normally associated with armoured thrusts were conspicuously absent....A regrettable lack of understanding between certain commanders often thwarted cohesive action so essential in the achievement of a common goal. There were misunderstandings galore between the infantry and armour commanders in the second battle of Chawinda. A lack of rapport appears to be the only explanation.... It was fortunate, too, that Pakistan failed in her grand design in the Khemkaran Sector. A blitzkrieg deep into our territory towards the Grand Trunk Road or the Beas Bridge would have found us in the helpless position of a commander paralysed into inaction for want of readily available reserves while the enemy was inexorably pushing deep into our vitals. It is a nightmarish feeling even when considered in retrospect at this stage.'[11]

Of the latter, the London *Times* was to report, 'a graveyard (the "Pattonnagar" of September 1965) of about 50 Pakistan tanks, mostly M48s, collected simply from one engagement.... At least 18 M48s were recovered in full working order.' Pakistan, after launching this thrust in the Punjab by its 1st Armoured Division and the 11th Infantry Division, had even vaingloriously invoked the slogan of "Marching to Delhi".

Here the Pakistani paratrooper operations directed at the airfields in Punjab need mentioning, not because they failed, but on account of the heroic way the peasants, mainly Sikh, rallied, despite the extensive Pakistani propaganda directed at them. 'Information pieced together from interrogation of captured personnel revealed that the paratroop effort was mainly confined to the dropping of three groups of this force, one each on the airfields at Pathankot, Halwara and Adampur. The strength of each batch was approximately three officers, one junior commissioned officer and sixty other ranks, selected from Pakistan's crack "Special Service Group". Their mission was to destroy the aircraft and vital installations on the airfields mentioned above.... In dealing with these paratroopers, the villagers took a major part in first informing the military of their presence and then chasing and surrounding them, with nothing more than "lathis" until the ad hoc forces...could arrive at the scene. In certain cases the villagers overpowered armed paratroopers and handed them over to the military authorities. In all cases the peasantry showed great patriotism, courage and determination.'[12]

India's gains from this conflict, initiated by Pakistan, were manifold. The Army and the country both regained the self-respect lost in 1962. As Durga Das earlier recorded, 'If the Army gave India Kashmir, Kashmir gave India its Army.' Officer casualties in this conflict were proportionately higher than they should normally have been. (This was again to be so in 1971. A Pakistani Major captured in the Western Sector in the 1971 conflict was to say that if only they had had the same kind of officers as in the Indian Army, the Pakistan Army would not have been worsted.)

Pran Chopra has pithily encapsulated the impact of this war on the country: 'When the lists of casualties and awards began to come out, many people understood, for the first time, not with the help of statistics, but with their hearts, what an assembly of races and faiths India is; how closely its parts are knit with the whole. Of the men who died or won the awards in the extreme north-west corner of the country, as many were from Madras and Bengal as from the nearby States. There were Hindus among them, Muslims, Parsis, Christians, Anglo-Indians, Jews, and tribals. And more Sikhs per thousand of their population than any other community—and it was the Sikhs whom Pakistan had made the special target of subversive propaganda. More than anything else this showed how badly Pakistan had misunderstood the depth of the fissures in Indian society. Pakistan's mistake was understandable. The cacophony of discord in India over the past years, especially in the few months following the skirmish in Kutch, had been deafening. But these were the trees, not the wood, which Pakistan mistook them to be. The wood showed itself in the first few days of the fighting by India's multi-religious, multi-racial armed forces, and by the political system of the country which suspended for the time being all its internal feuding. Here and there were signs of jingoistic exuberance, the exaggerated assertiveness of those who are unable to digest their patriotism. But, generally, there was mature and steady self-confidence, much more than Pakistan, and possibly India, expected; and it was particularly marked in areas closest to the battle, the western districts of the Punjab.'[13] (This was again to be so in 1971 as well.) This 1965 conflict has some lessons for us today, not only at the micro-level, a similar gamut as in 1962, though, fortunately, less in the negative facets of blunder, and bluster; but also at the macro-level in the country, of unity amidst the disunity, of integration amidst the diversity, and of sobriety amidst the jingoism. In fact, the deliberations of the National Integration

Council were postponed, it being deemed that there was no necessity as there were no problems of national integration after the Pakistani attack of 1965 (and the earlier Chinese attack of 1962). The nation had been thereby integrated.

Every war has a political cost and consequence, and this time round, after the 1965 conflict by circumstance for Pakistan. Within six years Pakistan and India were in armed conflict again, after ten million refugees had entered India from East Pakistan by September 1971, and this time eventuating in the independence of Bangladesh, establishing that the same religion was not a sufficiently cementing force binding East and West Pakistan. The so-called Agartala (Tripura) Conspiracy Case was undoubtedly an important event in the history of the autonomy movement of East Pakistan, which eventually led to the break-up of the unity of Pakistan in 1971, and, apart from the overwhelming fact of geographical discontiguity, brought about an independent Bangladesh. The *coup d'etat* by Ayub Khan in October 1958, had already entailed martial law. (In the years 1951-58, whereas there had been seven Prime Ministers and one Army Chief in Pakistan, in India there had been one Prime Minister and several Army Chiefs.) The alleged Agartala Conspiracy was formally announced in January 1968. Over a period of time, thirty-five persons had been arrested in all in this case, including Sheikh Mujib-ur Rehman, two members of the Civil Service of Pakistan, and others from the Pakistan Army, Navy and Air Force. Not only was India supposed to be involved, but incredulously, the US also. Mujib had already been arrested on several occasions before, including under the martial law regulations, for seeking greater autonomy for East Pakistan, urging that the conjoined entity of Pakistan could only be strong if the Centre was weak, the latter only being responsible for defence and foreign affairs. Ayub, in West Pakistan, argued that a strong Centre was necessary if Pakistan was to be strong. As to the alleged conspiracy, Richard Sisson and Leo E. Rose have commented: 'No solid evidence of a Mujib-Indian Conspiracy that had an independent Bangladesh as its objective has yet emerged, even in the post-1971 period, during which Pakistan could have produced such proof, without any serious political consequences, domestic or international.'[14] In fact, the dismay with Ayub was so extensive, that, in the Presidential elections of 1965, the Combined Opposition Parties' candidate against Ayub was Fatima Jinnah, the sister of Pakistan's founder. She had only been narrowly defeated by the use of the official machinery. The death of Sergeant Zahur-ul-Huq in custody in 1968 led to a mass upsurge, and strengthened the separatist movement, basically aggravated by the economic disparity felt by the fifty-six per cent of Pakistan's population in the Eastern wing, and the concomitant inequity in appointments and promotions. For instance, in the rank of major generals and above in 1965, there was only one Bengali major general out of sixteen Pakistanis holding general officer rank, that is the East Pakistani percentage in this rank was 5.8 per cent. Ayub, thereafter, dropped the case in the light of the magnitude and duration of the protest. For his part, though Mujib would appear to have visited Agartala, he had been arrested by the Indian authorities, his request for assistance refused, and, thereafter, he had returned to East Pakistan. The result of the 1970 Pakistani general election was, in effect, the penultimate phase of the break-up of Pakistan. The Awami League, under the leadership of Mujib, won an absolute majority. The resultant political tussle with the General Yahya Khan-Bhutto combine, which had ousted Ayub in 1969, led to Mujib's arrest, and the ultimate emancipation of Bangladesh. At this juncture, the percentage of East Pakistani major generals and above was even worse, 2.8 per cent, that is one out of thirty-four.

The announcement, on 1 March 1971, of a further postponement of the convening of the Pakistan National Assembly, led to a general strike in the whole of East Pakistan, the martial law authorities imposing a curfew and resorting to firing. Pakistan Army reinforcements were flown in, and, on 7 March, Lieutenant General Tikka Khan took over as the Governor and Martial Law Administrator. On 15 March, General Yahya Khan arrived at Dhaka, ostensibly to negotiate with the Awami League, but, on 23 March, authorized military action against the populace, which Tikka Khan commenced at midnight, 25-26 March, and the Pakistan Army cleared major towns with the support of artillery. Major Zia-ur-Rehman, who was commanding an East Bengal Regiment (EBR) battalion at Chittagong and was later to be the President of Bangladesh, gave a call to arms against Pakistan over Chittagong Radio. Five other EBR battalions responded, as did the 14,000-strong paramilitary East Pakistan Rifles (EPR). As a result of the continued crackdown by Pakistan, these EBR and EPR personnel and millions of refugees streamed into India. By September the latter figure had reached ten million. Two officials now took over the functions in Dhaka of Tikka Khan, who had carried out the crackdown—Lieutenant General A.A.K. Niazi took command of the troops in East Pakistan, and Dr A.M. Malik was appointed the Governor. In November Pakistan sent a delegation to China to seek assistance, and had also sought US aid. India, for her part, as a safeguard, signed a pact of peace and friendship with the Soviet Union against outside interference. The strategy now adopted by Pakistan lay in West Pakistan, and, accordingly, resorted to pre-emptive air and ground attacks in the west. India, thereafter, sought a quick victory in the east, while holding the Pakistani thrusts in the west, with counter-thrusts. In the east all, eventually, went India's way, while in the west the situation was, on occasion, inconclusive, despite the superb planning by Lieutenant General K.P. Candeth, GOC-in-C Western Command. He rightly records in *The Western Front: 1971:* 'One thing stands out—the Indian soldier with his courage, loyalty and tenacity, given proper leadership, is second to none. Time and again he has stood as a bulwark against aggression....How well the Army has succeeded in integrating the diverse communities and creeds that make up India...' Overall, it could well be said that the Indian Army's reverses of 1962 had been wiped out by the successes of 1965 and 1971, and, also, just as the Indian and British Armies had suffered reverses in 1942, the defeat of the Pakistan Army in the east in 1971 was comparable to the defeat of the Japanese 28th Army in Burma in 1945. Or as Professor Hugh Tinker has put it in *The Indo-British Review,* 'We may say in cricketing terms, that one was lost (1962), one was drawn (1965), and one (1971) was won by an innings. In many ways, 1962 was a re-run of 1942.'[15]

In 1971 General (now Field Marshal) S.H.F.J. Manekshaw received full support from Prime Minister Indira Gandhi for his conceptualization. However, once again the Indian Army could not take its own time. Whereas, in the Security Council, the Soviet Union could look after India's interests, this was not so in the General Assembly where a resolution against India had been moved. After Pakistan had launched its pre-emptive strikes in the west, the Indian advance into East Pakistan had begun, the Pakistanis holding strong points, and the Indian Army generally bypassing them. On 9 December, Niazi informed Bhutto in New York that resistance was purposeless, and, on 16 December, Niazi surrendered, Richard Sisson and Leo E. Rose describing it aptly:'General Niazi, Commander of the Forces of Muslim Pakistan, surrendered his arms to three generals of "Hindu" India—one a Parsi (General S.H.F.J. Manekshaw), another a Sikh (Lieutenant General J.S. Aurora), and the third a Jew (Major General J.F.R. Jacob).' Thereafter, on the conclusion of the Simla Agreement, India returned the remainder of the over 90,000 Pakistani prisoners, and vacated the territory occupied in the west. Candeth was, thereupon, constrained to observe, 'It is odd that the Pakistani, who prides himself as a warrior, should lose to India every time in war, and that the Indian, whom the world considers clever, subtle and devious, should have been worsted at the conference table.'[16] In July 1972, Pakistan convened an inquiry, under its Chief Justice Hamoodur Rehman, into its reverses. His November 1974 report deemed several senior army officers culpable: 'Through successive years of Martial Law Administration, these commanders had become depraved, morally corrupt and professionally incompetent. They had lost the will, the determination and the competence to fight. These commanders have brought disgrace and defeat....'[17] For over twenty years now a conflict has been avoided, though they cannot be called twenty years of peace on account of Pakistan's interference in Kashmir and Punjab. It is, therefore, appropriate now to turn to the various insurgencies that the Indian Army has been confronted with.

Telengana, in 1948, has already been mentioned. This was an ideological Communist insurgency, in which, approximately, 300 guerrillas were killed during the Army's first post-independence counter-insurgency operations in 1949. The movement abated after the creation of the State of Andhra Pradesh, but various Communist splinter groups, like the People's War Group (PWG), recently banned, an element of the Communist Party of India (Marxist Leninist) have caused a recrudescence, dealt with in the main by the State armed police without recourse to the Army. (An integrated regional strategy has had to be prepared by the Central Government to deal with Left extremist violence, which is now current, not only in Andhra, but also parts of Karnataka, Maharashtra, Madhya Pradesh, Bihar and Orissa. This Leftist violence resulted in 413 deaths in 1990 alone, mainly in Bihar and Andhra Pradesh.) Next, in chronological sequence for the Army, was the protonationalist insurgency in the Naga Hills, today's Nagaland. The Nagas had sought to be different from the rest of India, even in a representation to the Simon Commission in 1928. A.Z. Phizo could be said to be the architect of present-day Nagaland, though he never accepted it, seeking its independence. The then Major (later Field Marshal) Ayub Khan had served in the 1st Battalion The Assam Regiment in 1944, which battalion also had Nagas serving in it. In 1948, when the now Major General Ayub Khan was GOC East Pakistan, Phizo, who had served in the 'Indian National Army' (INA,) sent some of these demobilized Naga ex-servicemen to meet Ayub Khan. Thereafter, East Pakistan's aid to the insurgencies in the North-East can be said to have commenced in the 1950s, from the development of this initial East Pakistani contact, later followed by support from China. Phizo left the then Naga Hills District in December 1957 for Britain, never to return till after his death in 1990, even though every other member of his family had accommodated themselves in India, including his daughter, Adino, who eventually became a leader of his Naga National Council (NNC) party. He had vowed that he would only return to a sovereign Nagaland. In June 1956, Phizo had planned the capture of Kohima, but the Semas and Phizo fell out on the very outskirts of Kohima town, the Semas marching away. The irony of his life was that when he died in Britain on 30 April 1990, the Government of India paid for his body to be brought back to Nagaland. The Nagas desired that he should not be buried according to custom in his ancestral village of Khonoma, but in Kohima beside the State Secretariat, the symbol of the government of the State of Nagaland. (Dimapur airfield has been renamed after him.) Only a moderate trace of Phizoism remains in Nagaland today, as represented by the Khodao Yanthan faction of the NNC party (he accompanied Phizo to Britain), a tribute to the counter-insurgency operations of the Army, and the Assam Rifles; but it must be said that when the Army was called out in aid of the civil authority in Tuensang in December 1955, it was with too little. The 17th Battalion The Rajput Regiment, less two companies, moved from Shillong, where it was on a peace tenure, to Tuensang, cleared the hostiles' hide-out and returned to Shillong as ordered. Martial law was rightly never contemplated, but, by circumstance, the requisitioning of aid by the civil authorities in Nagaland on a piecemeal basis continued for several months. In this early phase, as recounted by S.P.P. Thorat, a Gorkha Rifles battalion reported fourteen rifles and 4,000 rounds of ammunition as "lost". A subedar and some others had actually sold them to the hostiles. The arms were never recovered. No view of the insurgency was taken in totality, jointly by the Army and the civil administration, till a GOC was sanctioned in 1956 for the Naga Hills and Tuensang Agency, eventually culminating in the sixteenth state of the Indian Union. This marginalized Phizo, but the activities and occasional ambushes of the banned anti-Phizo National Socialist Council of Nagaland (NSCN) in its various factions nevertheless continue in Assam, Manipur and Nagaland from hideouts in Myanmar and Bangladesh. The State of Nagaland is in its way a monument not only to the success of the Indian Army's and Assam Rifles' operations in aid of the civil power, but also to Phizo, inasmuch as the Naga tribes, after generations of hostility, have now a larger identity, though the occasional violent clash involving head-hunting still occurs, apart from tribalism in its parliamentary form of party defections.

Shortly after Phizo, the architect of the Mizo (Lushai) insurgency, Laldenga, also died in July 1990 in London, where he had gone from India for medical treatment. In this insurgency also, the Army was deployed for several years, the insurgents getting much of their weaponry from East Pakistan, and some from China. But Laldenga, a former clerk in the Army in the Second World War, was clearer in his long-term aim, to use insurgency to seize political power in Mizoram, the home of the Mizos, within the Indian Union. He eventually signed an accord at New Delhi in 1986, which Phizo, earlier, had declined to do. But while Phizo had ceased to have any influence in mainstream Naga politics from the 1970s, Laldenga always did. He called upon his Mizo insurgents to come overground, participated in elections, and became the Chief Minister of Mizoram in 1988. His Mizo National Front (MNF) was originally the Mizo National Famine Front, formed during the rat-induced famine of the 1950s. Social work alone would not have brought him political power ultimately, hence the MNF insurgency, augmented in numbers by some dismissed/discharged personnel from the 2nd Battalion The Assam Regiment, disbanded in 1961. The MNF insurgency had been named "Operation Jericho" by Laldenga, all opposition confronting him being expected to crumble. This insurgency reached its peak in 1966. (One of the bonuses of the 1971 conflict was the then elimination of the Naga and Mizo "underground" camps in East Pakistan, and the "pipeline" for them to China. By 1978, the latter halted aid to these insurgents, as part of the endeavour to "normalize" relations with India.) From the underground, Laldenga went into voluntary exile abroad via Pakistan during the 1970s, in order to obtain support for his cause. But even while abroad, he, over the next ten years, participated in three political dialogues, while his MNF insurgents conducted protracted operations against the Army during this period. The June 1986 accord was, eventually, signed. A year after becoming the Chief Minister of Mizoram, he was out of office in 1989, being defeated in the Assembly elections, his party split on charges of corruption against him. His return to power was to be through the ballot box but death supervened. Some Hmar ethnic tribals of northern Mizoram, however, supported by the NSCN, have now commenced a violent agitation, demanding an autonomous district council. Insurgencies in Manipur had also to be dealt with, as well as in Tripura. In the former, it was not only the NSCN, but also the People's Liberation Army (PLA) which had sent personnel to Tibet, and more recently the United Liberation Front of Manipur. In Tripura, the insurgents had bases in Bangladesh. After operations by the Army and the Assam Rifles, the Tripura National Volunteers (TNV) signed a tripartite accord in 1988, but other militant groupings have now surfaced, like the All Tripura Tribal Force (ATTF) and the United National Liberation Front (UNLF).

Next, chronologically, in this narration of major aid to the civil authority, is "Operation Blue Star" at Amritsar on 3 June 1984. The necessity for ordering the Army into the Golden Temple, and about forty other gurdwaras ("Operation Woodrose") would not have occurred if Sant Jarnail Singh Bhindranwale had not been built up. (In the event, as is known, overcoming Bhindranwale and his band of 200 extremists, including a couple of ex-Army officers, in the Golden Temple complex, did not resolve terrorism in Punjab. A political solution has to be eventually arrived at in any insurgency even though the terrorists seek to thwart such an endeavour, the recent 1992 elections being a step in that direction.) In a subsequent interview, after he had become the Army Chief, General K. Sundarji, the GOC-in-C Western Command in 1984, when "Operation Blue Star" was carried out, iterated, 'From the outset it was a very sad thing. All of us hoped it would never come to this. But, when I was finally charged with the mission, I was convinced at that time that there was no other option. None. It was a duty to be performed.'[18] By the time he made this statement, Indira Gandhi had been, sadly, assassinated, and General A.S. Vaidya, Sundarji's predecessor, who had been Army Chief at the time of "Operation Blue Star" was also, shortly, and equally sadly, to be assassinated. In the immediate aftermath of "Operation Blue Star", mutinies and mass desertions, aggregating 2,337 persons, mostly recruits and young soldiers, had taken place, the Commandant of the Sikh Regimental Centre being killed. The units concerned were (the number of personnel tried by court-martial in 1985 being indicated in brackets) the 14th Battalion The Punjab Regiment (eleven), the Sikh Regimental Centre (115), the 3rd Battalion The Sikh Regiment (twenty-five), the 9th Battalion (fifty-one), and the 18th Battalion (twenty-four) of the same regiment. (The 9th Sikh was also disbanded.) In this context, Sundarji commented in the same interview: 'The very first battalion to enter the Golden Temple was the 10th Guards—half of its members are Jat Sikhs from Amritsar District. The fact that they went in and did such a magnificent job, notwithstanding the emotional turmoil within themselves, is the best indication of what Army morale was like.'

The court of inquiry into the mutiny in the Sikh Regimental Centre brought out that there was no evidence of any attempt to subvert Sikh troops by outside agencies, recording, however, 'The emergence of religious fundamentalism and linguistic chauvinism in many states, particularly in the Punjab, would no doubt have its effect on troops hailing from that region, even when they are emotionally integrated particularly in an organization like the Army.' The mutinies among the Jat Sikhs, and not among the Mazhabi Sikhs, resulted, as recounted by the court of inquiry, from incomplete information, and inadequate communication with their officers, thereby leading to a temporary emotional upsurge, rather than a deliberate premeditated act. These mutinies have had no impact on the relationship with the Jat Sikhs in the Army. In the same interview, Sundarji rightly observed, 'I don't think any other class of soldiers has passed through such a traumatic experience. Some people in the country—and in the Service—speak loosely about Sikh loyalty and their need to re-establish their credibility. But the Sikhs have been through fire and have come out flying high. What hurts them are these kinds of patently unjustified doubts. The Sikhs don't need to make any further demonstrations (of loyalty).' Sundarji was then questioned at this interview in relation to Vaidya having introduced certain other class companies into twelve battalions raised in his residual tenure—into a Rajputana Rifles battalion, Garhwalis and South Indian classes over and above the existing Rajputs and Jats; into a Sikh Regiment battalion, Dogra, Garhwali and South Indian class companies, plus a Sikh company; into a Dogra Regiment battalion, Rajput, Jat, and South Indian class companies, plus a Dogra company; into an Assam Regiment battalion, Dogra, Garhwali and South Indian class companies, plus a company of the existing classes; and a further Assam Regiment battalion with Dogra, Gorkha and South Indian class companies plus a company of the existing classes. In this context, Sundarji, in this February 1986 interview, stated that no sudden restructuring of the Army was being undertaken as a result of the desertions after "Operation Blue Star", rightly going on record to say, 'Government policy is to have totally integrated all-caste units gradually.' He should also have brought on record that certain battalions, which became class battalions after independence, were actually class company battalions with some Muslims before independence, the latter being allotted to Pakistan.

Thereafter, in 1987, the government was required to send an Indian Peace-keeping Force (IPKF) to Sri Lanka in accordance with the Indo-Sri Lankan Accord ("Operation Pawan"). This was not the first time that Indian troops had been sent to Sri Lanka, at the latter government's request. An infantry battalion, less two companies, was flown in to secure Colombo airport in relation to a "Maoist" uprising, in early 1971. Some, unaware of the constraints of the 1987 situation, have unfairly sought to depict the IPKF's performance as a "fiasco". The figure of 1,155 Indian Army dead, till the withdrawal of the IPKF, is often quoted, but, in effect, the IPKF fought with one arm tied behind its back, on account of the inherent political restrictions imposed in this peace-keeping situation. The despatch of the IPKF to Sri Lanka was a political decision, not a military one—to guarantee the integrity of Sri Lanka. The Indo-Sri Lankan Accord, one element of which was the IPKF, had been necessitated by the continued flow of Tamil refugees into India on account of the reported genocide of Tamils in Sri Lanka, following on from the

operations of the Sri Lankan army against the Tamil militants
fighting for Eelam, a Tamil homeland in Sri Lanka. These 200,000
Sri Lankan Tamil refugees were becoming an increasing burden on
India and for the State of Tamil Nadu, with attendant problems of
law and order, even though a few had been relocated in Orissa. It was
the subsequent political failure to carry the Tamil Tigers along with
the accord, they having originally given indications that they would
comply and surrender their arms, that led to the tragic stalemate
between the IPKF and them. Since then there have been disclosures
in the defeated Sri Lankan opposition motion for his impeachment—
that President R. Premdasa had supplied sophisticated arms and ammunition to the Liberation Tigers of Tamil Eelam (LTTE), ostensibly not intended for use against the IPKF, but which, in fact, were,
including anti-aircraft guns, and now in use against the Sri Lankan
Army.

The Indian Army, after suffering 4,000 casualties, including
wounded, in this ostensible low-intensity conflict, will not easily
forget the experience, till it was eventually withdrawn in 1990 from
Sri Lanka, on the change of presidents in that country, and prime
ministers in India. Of the casualties suffered in Sri Lanka (both dead
and wounded), twenty per cent were among officers, twelve per cent
junior commissioned officers, and eight per cent other ranks. The unfortunate casualties establish that all ranks did well, particularly the
younger officers as always. Organizationally, the LTTE do not
drink, smoke, womanize or embezzle. Their postulation is, 'You
deviate, you die.' It is no longer a revolutionary movement, but more
of a "Pol-Potist" mafia. The LTTE's expertise with explosives was
the first lesson learnt by the Indian Army in this peace-keeping role,
an expertise apparently taught to the LTTE by the Israelis. Another
was the LTTE's proficiency in picking off IPKF officers; the LTTE
proved to be more vicious than any Naga or Mizo insurgent. Apart
from Rajiv Gandhi's assassin having been a Sri Lankan Tamil
woman, an early instance of this viciousness was when a Tamil-
speaking IPKF officer went to comfort a group of stranded Tamil
women, and was promptly shot dead by one of them. The cult of the

LTTE, of course, would never have been established but for the earlier callousness of the Sri Lankan government towards the Tamils. (Women cadres of the LTTE have also led attacks against the Sri Lankan Army camps, as, for instance, in July 1992 at Katupotha.) For their part, instead of a settlement, the internal dynamics of the LTTE do not permit now of compromise. They are governed by a deathwish for the Sri Lankan Tamils of today, and thinking of Eelam for the Tamils of the next generation, and not for those of the present one.

This is apparent from the way former Prime Minister Rajiv Gandhi was assassinated in 1991 while on an election tour in South India. It was, moreover, not the first assassination attempt on Rajiv Gandhi on account of the Sri Lankan Tamil problem. During his State visit to Sri Lanka in 1987 as Prime Minister, he had inspected a guard of honour at Colombo. One of the guards, a Sinhala naval rating, swung his rifle at him, catching him on the shoulder as he ducked. The Sri Lankan armed forces were not happy about the Indo-Sri Lankan Accord and the induction of the IPKF, because they had lost many compatriots in the operations against the Tamil militants. It was for this reason that the concerned Indian security agencies had, then, insisted on rifles being exchanged between alternate men, just before the formal ceremony. Prime Minister V.P. Singh withdrew the IPKF in 1990, and, thereafter, in late 1990, Prime Minister Chandra Shekhar dismissed the Dravida Munnetra Kazhagam (DMK) government in the State of Tamil Nadu, after it was established that the LTTE operated a terror network against Sri Lankan Tamil refugees throughout Tamil Nadu. This was to be, tragically, re-confirmed when it was manifest how easily Rajiv Gandhi's assassins had rehearsed and operated in Tamil Nadu, even videos being made of the "dry runs". Deeming that Rajiv Gandhi might be re-elected as Prime Minister, feeling slighted by him, the LTTE supremo alleg-edly had passed the order for a woman "human bomb" to assassinate Rajiv Gandhi, with what tragic results the world knows. In a discussion with a Sri Lankan Tamil resident in London, Rajiv Gandhi, on 15 March 1991, had stated that he himself was clear as to what should be done to resolve the Sri Lankan problem, but he was not sure if the LTTE were similarly clear in their perception. For his part, V. Piribhakaran, the LTTE supremo, thereafter, told the British Broadcasting Corporation (BBC), 'We have been conducting a guerrilla type of warfare. Now we are transforming ourselves into a conventional type of military structure.' The LTTE has lost too many of its cadres and spilt too much blood to now settle for a compromise.

Separately, in 1988, the Indian Army successfully rescued the Maldives government, under mercenary attack. The prompt despatch of Indian paratroops to the Maldives, at the request of the latter's government to avert a coup, earned India, and the Indian Army, accolades.

The Kashmir story continues; legally, it is a domestic problem, but since 1947 it has been distorted by Pakistan. At the time of its legal accession to India, Kashmir was secular. It was India, which, even before accession, had first postulated that the will of the Kashmiri people be ascertained. It was M.A. Jinnah, by now Governor-General of Pakistan, who had hedged the modalities for this, in his discussion of 1 November 1947 with Lord Louis Mountbatten and Hastings Ismay. Mountbatten's official account records Jinnah's suggestion that both sides should, 'withdraw at once and simultaneously.'[19] This is of importance, as Pakistan, for the record, still insisted that it had nothing to do with the ostensible tribal invasion, though Campbell-Johnson recounts, 'When Mountbatten asked him (Jinnah) to explain how the tribesmen could be induced to remove themselves, his reply was, "If you do this, I will call the whole thing off," which at least suggests that the public propaganda line that the tribal invasion was wholly beyond Pakistan's control will not be pursued too far in private discussion. On inquiry, Mountbatten found that Jinnah's attitude to a plebiscite was conditioned by his belief that the combination of Indian troops in occupation and Sheikh Abdullah in power meant that the average Moslem would be far too frightened to vote for Pakistan.'[20] Mountbatten then suggested a plebiscite under United Nations auspices. It was Jinnah who turned it down, suggesting instead a joint plebiscite under the two Governors-General, at which suggestion Mountbatten backed off as he was only a constitutional Governor-General for a few months, whereas Jinnah was a permanent executive one.

Pakistan has latterly renewed its demand for the implementation of a 1949 UN resolution asking for a plebiscite in Kashmir, but it has not found US support, the latter's State Department spokesman stating, in July 1991, that the 1949 resolution was not only about the plebiscite, but had seven other clauses, including all Pakistani forces first withdrawing from Kashmir, which made it, 'not the most practical way to solve the problem. As it turned out it didn't work,' and that the 1972 bilateral Simla Agreement offered "a constructive way". The US considers any continuing support by Pakistan to over 150 militant groups in Kashmir as "dangerous and destabilizing", branding the kidnappings of foreign visitors by the militants as "terrorist tactics". Meanwhile, the US State Department's annual report on "Patterns of Global Terrorism, 1991", released in April 1992, notes: 'There were continuing credible reports throughout 1991 of official Pakistani support for Kashmiri militant groups engaged in terrorism in Indian-controlled Kashmir, as well as support to Sikh militant groups....This support allegedly included provision of weapons and training.' The US informed Pakistan in May 1992 that it could be included among states sponsoring terrorism. All the militant groups are working to a strategy, prepared by their Pakistani minders, being trained in over one hundred training camps in Pakistan-Occupied Kashmir (POK), and also in Pakistan itself, some with the Afghan mujahidin, of a high-intensity proxy war, equipped with modern armaments, the universal machine-gun, Israeli Uzi and the Chinese rocket-propelled grenade launcher (RPG), with night-firing capability. Firing along the 640 kilometre Line of Actual Control is almost a daily occurrence, to provide diversions or covering fire for the 20,000 Pakistani-trained terrorists to infiltrate. The future of the Kashmir Valley is, however, ensured by the ultimate success of the Indian Army and the other security forces. In 1991 alone, the Army had arrested over 2,500 militants, while nearly 1,000 had been killed or died due to adverse weather, but there is no mistaking the determination of the terrorists to create situations in which innocents get caught in the crossfire. (Over 4,000 Kalashnikovs have been recovered.) The terrorists' aim is to widen the gulf between the people and the government, arising from the past ineptitude of both New Delhi and Srinagar particularly when the Kashmiri leadership latterly was in charge of governance. It is also clear that the secessionists are bent on preventing any dialogue with the recognized leaders of the Kashmiri community, as brought out by their pre-emptive killing among many others, of Mufti Mirwaiz, Maulana Masoodi, and Mir Mustafa, apart from the killing of Vice-Chancellor Mushir-ul-Haq. Earlier, the Indian Consul-General in Birmingham, Ravindra Mhatre, had been killed in February 1984. As the former Chief Minister, Dr Farooq Abdullah, has put it, 'Pakistan believes that as long as India has problems...Pakistan will be at peace.' The same Pakistani rationale applies to Punjab also. The Pakistanis do not want "Khalistan" *per se* to come into being, as that would eventually lead to claims on Pakistani territory for the Sikh shrines there, and, eventually, for Maharaja Ranjit Singh's kingdom.

But stoked by Pakistan, Punjab as well drifts from terrorism to insurgency, with the blatant encouragement of a "Kalashnikov culture" by Islamabad. It can also be said that secessionism has its own illogic, such as the bizarre alliance between the Sikh separatists and Pakistan, ignoring the gory events of Partition. The terrorists in Punjab have been provided with sophisticated weapons, including AK-47s and shoulder-fired missiles. Eight years since "Operation Blue Star", ten people on an average have been killed daily by the terrorists. Terrorism in Punjab, and latterly in the UP Terai, has acquired a momentum of its own, quite unrelated to real or perceived Sikh grievances, like the mindless killing of nearly 300 people on board the Air India Jumbo *Kanishka* in 1985, and more recently the senseless beheading of an All India Radio (AIR) official, and the murder of seven Punjab Health Department officials, including the Director, for progressing the family planning programme. There were till recently, 1,400 gangs of terrorists and mercenaries. In these circumstances, it is unrealistic to expect that depredations of the killer gangs of secessionists and terrorists in Punjab can be put to an end totally, recourse also being had to narco-terrorism. There is another aspect of the Punjab situation. It is a part of the strategy of the Sikh terrorists to bring about Hindu-Sikh riots in and outside Punjab, to force Hindus to migrate from Punjab, and for Sikhs to migrate to Punjab. The nefarious purpose of the terrorists in Punjab is thus the creation of a "Khalistan", either directly through the establishment of a separate State, or the snapping of links between society in Punjab and society elsewhere in the country. The latter now seems to be the immediate aim, after fourteen years of violence. Though the anti-terrorist operations in Punjab are still in the main conducted by the police, Army back-up has had to be provided, as, for instance, deployment in all the districts of Punjab for a few months before the 1992 elections, and for a while thereafter in addition to the Army blocking the terrorists' ingresses from Pakistan ("Operation Rakshak"). The Punjab police, with Army back-up ("Operation Rakshak II") is now admirably on top of the situation. The militants' degeneration into criminality has facilitated infiltration by the Punjab police. In 1992, till September, 1,300 militants have been killed.

Taking an overview of the Kashmir and Punjab situations, it would appear that, while Kashmir continues to be a *casus belli* for Pakistan, and the Punjab insurgency a seeming *quid pro quo* for the creation of Bangladesh, Pakistan has opted for an indefinite proxy war in these states, as conflict escalation in these sectors is not an affordable option today, because a decisive military outcome is even more unlikely now for Pakistan than it was in 1947-48, 1965 and 1971. Or as Christina Lamb pithily puts it in *Waiting for Allah*, 'Since 1982, the US had assisted Pakistan in a massive military build-up...more than 5.5 billion dollars of mostly military assistance, as well as forty F16 fighter jets. On top of this was a considerable cut, estimated at least as 40 per cent, from those arms destined for the Afghan resistance. By 1990, then, the Pakistan Army was extremely well-equipped....Pakistan has already lost three wars against India, prompting a senior level State Department official to warn, "If I were a Pakistani military planner, I'd take a lesson from history."'[21] The nature of conflict on the subcontinent *vis-a-vis* Pakistan is thus changing. An Indian Army prepared only for a conventional conflict with Pakistan will be adding to its own problems, and will not be contributing to conflict resolution. The challenge will not only be directly from the neighbouring state, but from the anti-systemic forces fostered and encouraged by it in India against India. The transfer of expertise and armaments by the anti-systemic forces within the country is also a significant development. The Indian Army is thus becoming the world's largest operational laboratory subjected to the complexities of various external and internal security pressures. What is separately perplexing is that all those human rights groups, which are so vocal over the minimal deaths and destruction during the Army's operations, are silent as to the terrorists' atrocities. This suggests that the concern for human rights is not free from political prejudices.

As to the numerous internal security duties given to the Army in 1946 and 1947, Francis Tuker had recorded in 1950 after his departure from India, 'We should recollect that to give such duties to an army is to misuse that army...policing should be done by those who are adapted to its requirements;...quasi-military bodies, well-armed, and yet trained and authorised for the most exacting policing duties. An army can only exert its powers when it has an enemy and when it is permitted to use its weapons to the full, and freely against that enemy. To tie it about with restrictions, and still to force it to operate is to ruin it for war.... To a lesser extent, due to its exclusive attention to the western frontier of India, this has also happened to the Indian Army.'[22] Though the times have changed, over forty years after Tuker, that is still the Indian Army's dilemma, called out for 475 communal disturbances in the two decades 1951-70, and 369 in the five years 1981-85; it must, therefore, evolve its own *modus vivendi* of being ready to defend the country in a conventional conflict, yet coping with multiple low intensity conflicts, and, along with the

515

latter, numerous internal security commitments. Some of these internal security commitments are often without any justification, but with the emotive state of the country difficult to counter. Instead of the Army being the last option, it is often the first recourse. The commitment has increased progressively since independence. This is a piquant commentary, but incontrovertible. For instance, 1988 witnessed, among other calls for the use of troops, the strike of the armed constabulary in Gujarat, which necessitated use of the equivalent of almost two infantry divisions to resolve it. (In 1946-47, it had been the Bihar Police that had to be disarmed by the Army and 2,000 Gorkha ex-servicemen were, thereafter, recruited into the Bihar Military Police. In 1973, the UP Provincial Armed Constabulary [PAC] had to be disarmed by the Army, on government instructions. There were casualties on both sides—twenty-two PAC personnel killed, and fifty-six injured; Army thirteen killed, including a major, and forty-five injured. Whereas some PAC battalions were disbanded, after six years of trials only forty-three PAC personnel were sentenced. Separately, the UP Congress Ministry resigned, as it felt that the indiscipline of the PAC was a reflection on the Ministry. In 1979, the Central Reserve Police Force [CRPF] had to be disarmed, as well as some elements of the Central Industrial Security Force [CISF] also on government instructions, as far apart as Orissa, South India and near Delhi.) In 1989, the Army was called out for months amid the horrendous communal carnage in Bihar, the Buddhist-Muslim conflict in Leh, and the Bodo troubles in Assam, apart from the Meham mayhem in Haryana. In 1990, it was widespread deployment in Himachal Pradesh, apart from Bihar and Assam again. In 1990 alone, there were 1,404 communal incidents, the highest in recent years, resulting in 1,248 killed and 6,627 injured. According to the Defence Ministry Annual Report for 1991-1992, apart from assistance, in natural calamities and maintenance of essential services, the Army was called out in Uttar Pradesh,Tamil Nadu, Punjab, Andhra Pradesh, Rajasthan, Himachal Pradesh, Jammu and Kashmir, Bihar, Arunachal Pradesh, Assam, Nagaland, Manipur and the Union Territories of Delhi and Dadra Haveli. Admittedly the

Army was not called out for the minor incidents, but nevertheless to continue to burden the Army with quelling the more widespread urban violence, can only be catastrophic in its long-term effects, and will make it, inefficiency-wise, a para-police force, one more aggregation to the already existing para-military and armed police proliferation, thus serving our neighbour's strategic aims of destabilizing the country. Protracted use of the Army in aid to the civil power only blunts its efficiency. Consequently, from selected CRPF personnel of all communities, the government has now created a Rapid Action Force (RAF) of ten battalions, each to be located adjacent to recurrent scenes of communal violence. Scarcely was the first battalion ready, when it was rushed to Sitamarhi in Bihar in October 1992.

In 1990 another counter-insurgency task ("Operation Bajrang") was given to the Army by the Central Government to deal with the United Liberation Front of "Asom" (ULFA). As has happened at the commencement in all such "aid to the civil" commitments in the North-East or elsewhere, the Army was initially engaged in an unequal battle, again with one arm tied behind its back, being subjected to some ambushes, as it lacked intelligence, the intention to call out the Army having been "leaked" a week earlier to the ULFA, by some officials of the Assam government. The ULFA was familiar with the terrain, and could surprise any adversary. The Army also had to contend with some indifference from the population, and hostility from the unemployed youth. The ULFA, as in the case of the other insurgencies, started with the psychological advantage of having allies in the police and the lower bureaucracy. The ULFA's rise was due to the problem of stagnation in Assam, and the feeling of sequential marginalization. Many Assamese were apt to see discrimination and bias, where none existed, and to feel a quasi-colonial relationship with the rest of India. This perception was heightened during the anti-foreigner (non-Assamese speaking) agitation of 1979-85. The ULFA was then the violent face of this agitation, the Army having found the mass graves of those killed by it. Though comparatively small, it is very well-funded through extor-

517

tion, and equipped, there being some recent evidence of narco-terrorism. It is disciplined and controlled, and modelled on the LTTE, with which it is alleged to have had some contacts. It commands fear, though it has only a one-point ideology, independence from India, in stark contrast to the average Assamese psyche. Despite all the difficulties, and after taking some casualties, the Army succeeded in capturing some 2,000 ULFA activists, when a stop was called to the Army's operations in April 1991 with the 1991 elections impending, just when the Army was painstakingly getting on top of the situation. The Army's overall balance sheet had been entirely positive. To have wished for instant dividends was wishful thinking. There were notable successes, as well as some failures. Political experimentation for its own sake sent the wrong signals to the ULFA, for short-term expediency has no place in the North-East.

The ULFA maintained a low profile right through the elections, but made the headlines again in June 1991 when six of its top leaders masterminded two daring jailbreaks at Dibrugarh and Tezpur, apparently with the tacit connivance of a section of the concerned jail staff. This was followed by the coordinated abduction of several officials including a Soviet engineer (subsequently killed). The July 1991 kidnappings by the ULFA were manifestly a State-wide plan to express disapproval of the installation of a Congress government, a political party the militants are averse to. The subsequent decision by the newly-elected State Congress government, to declare a general amnesty for the ULFA, could only be viewed with dismay, in view of the Army's extended operations to apprehend 2,000 of them, on the basic premise that there can be no compromise with terrorism. In August 1991, the Army was called out again ("Operation Rhino"), this time by the State government, with a much better response from the public, the police and the bureaucracy. The results were encouraging by way of surrenders, bringing a faction of the ULFA hierarchy to the conference table. In view of the ULFA making alliances with groups like the Bodos, the restriction on operations has again been lifted. A long-term solution in the North-East is only possible when those concerned recognize the dangerous consequences of ethnic politics, and learn to be even-handed in dealing with sub-nationalism, instead of playing one off against another, as previous Assam governments had been prone to do, leading earlier to the inception of the Naga and Mizo insurgencies, and the sequential increasing exponential deployment of the Army. At the same time, the administration must address the causes of Assam's malaise, which has to be simultaneously predicated with toning up the bureaucratic machinery. In the case of all the insurgents the demand of independence is constitutionally unacceptable. Training camps have been pinpointed in Bangladesh, apart from the arming facilities provided by the Kachin Independence Organization (KIO) in northern Myanmar to the insurgents from North-East India apart from some aid also from Pakistan. Even when the Army's operations strive to be blemishless, the insurgents "create" atrocities. If, as it is said, revolution devours its own children, in a way it can be said extremism destroys its parents. The ULFA's latest 1992 line of wooing the Bangladeshi migrants overturns the entire recent history of Assam. Separately, the NSCN, ULFA and the United Liberation Front of Manipur have formed the Indo-Burma Revolutionary Force (IBRF).

One of the many other agitations of the 1980s, which was for the time being resolved in 1988, was that for "Gorkhaland", led by Subhas Ghising, the ex-serviceman President of the Gorkha National Liberation Front (GNLF). He then evidenced statesmanship in accepting the creation instead of the Darjeeling Gorkha Hill Council, of which he became the Chairman. In the memorandum signed by him in August 1988 with the Government of India, he had insisted on the inclusion of a provision for Indian Gorkhas to be eligible to join any regiment/corps of their choice, according to the district recruiting quota. This was, in effect, already so, as Indian Gorkhas had been eligible, according to their caste/tribe, to join any of the seven Indian Gorkha Rifles regiments, as per the percentage prescribed for Indian Gorkhas vis-a-vis Nepalese Gorkhas, as also other arms and services. He had initially sought the raising of a separate regiment for

Indian Gorkhas, to avoid their being viewed as "foreigners" and 'mercenaries' by some critics, by having to serve along with the Nepalese Gorkhas. A new class regiment was not conceded in conformity with the declared policy of the government in this regard, but their eligibility for any regiment/corps in the Army was re-confirmed. As stated, this already subsisted as there were Indian Gorkhas in, for instance, the Artillery, Military Police, Army Service Corps, the Brigade of the Guards, the Mahar Regiment, and so on. Ghising ostensibly sought self-esteem for the Indian Gorkhas as Indian citizens, in contradistinction to those who were Nepalese citizens, though the Nepalese government rightly does not desire its citizens to be viewed as "mercenaries" either. By circumstance of the post-"Operation Blue Star" 1985 infantry raisings, Indian Gorkhas were also eligible for enrolment in addition in the Assam Regiment. As is known, Ghising had also sought the expulsion of Nepalese citizens, after a cut-off date, from the Darjeeling Hills in the greater interest of the "unity and sovereignty" of India, that is, according to his pronouncement, in order allegedly to foil the "Greater Nepal Conspiracy" by those who still claim to be Nepalese and not Indians. As a further step to foil the alleged "Greater Nepal Conspiracy" for the inclusion of Darjeeling in Nepal, Ghising has reiterated his demand for the constitutional recognition by India of the Gorkhali language and not Nepali, for the ten million people of Nepalese origin residing in India, seeking to draw a distinction between Gorkhali and Nepali. Ghising has also now renewed his demand for the Darjeeling Hills being made a Union Territory.

Separately, in June 1987, a shooting incident occurred in the 8th Battalion The Jat Regiment during a training exercise, wherein four officers were killed, including the commanding officer, by two of their own troops. One officer, two junior commissioned officers (including the subedar major), and the two assailants were tried by a court-martial. The commanding officer and the second-in-command were the actual intended victims, and the other two officers were killed incidentally. All four deceased were non-Jat, and all five accused were Jat. The accused officer was cashiered and sentenced to life imprisonment; the subedar major was acquitted; the subedar dismissed and sentenced to life imprisonment; and the two other ranks sentenced to death but have appealed. The deceased commanding officer, during his two tenures in command, had repeatedly admonished the accused officer for inefficiency, and he had told the subedar major that his integrity was suspect. In the 1938 case of the 4/2nd Punjab, it was not a conspiracy to kill the commanding officer; it was an individual aberration. In the case of the 8th Jats, it was a deliberate conspiracy to kill the non-Jat commanding officer, and second-in-command.

To conclude this chapter on the post-Nehru years, Prime Minister Lal Bahadur Shastri had too short a term of office (1964-66), dying prematurely from a heart attack. His successor, Indira Gandhi, after winning the 1971 elections, declared an Emergency (1975-77), and was thereafter defeated in the subsequent 1977 elections. Morarji Desai, in a way, witnessed the de-construction of his government (1977-79). Charan Singh followed for a few months. In 1984, when Indira Gandhi was assassinated by her Sikh body-guards after having come back to power in 1980, the country had wondered as to who would take over. The nation turned to her son, Rajiv Gandhi, in the 1984 elections. Thereafter, Rajiv Gandhi would not have lost the 1989 elections, if it had not been for the innuendoes attaching to the Bofors 155 mm howitzer procurement for the Indian Army; while the disclosure of the holders of the secret Swiss bank accounts is being considered by the Swiss courts, the former Bofors President, Martin Ardbo, had said the secret of the pay-offs would be buried with him. After the limited durations of the V.P. Singh and Chandra Shekhar governments, the selection of P.V. Narasimha Rao, after the 1991 elections, as the Prime Minister, has established after four-and-a-half decades, that it is not necessary in Indian democracy to be a Nehru or Gandhi for the Congress party to form a government at the Centre.

All the political parties since independence have, so far, not been able to, resolve the socio-economic problems of the country entailing increased aid to civil power commitments for the Army. The present government is trying. Running a large country of 870 million like India is, of course, no easy matter. With dynamism and dedication very much more could have been achieved, particularly if the countrywide bureaucracy shook off its inertia and lethargy.

Dr Bimal Jalan, then Chairman of the Economic Advisory Council to the Prime Minister, thereafter an executive director at the World Bank, and now Governor of the Reserve Bank of India, has forthrightly gone on record, 'As far as the bureaucracy is concerned, one aspect is inertia. Most bureaucrats, including myself, do not care about the outcome of what we are doing. We are doing it because it is the way it had been done.' In the Indian Army, too, on the one hand, while there is undoubtedly much increased professionalism in many, there is also the irrelevance of tokenism in several.

EPILOGUE

THE PROLOGUE inevitably encapsulated the years before independence and the partition of the British-Indian Army. This Epilogue overviews the subsequent period. The oft-quoted Marc Bloch, in *The Historian's Craft,* has appositely emphasized: 'Misunderstanding of the present is the inevitable consequence of the ignorance of the past. But a man may wear himself out just as fruitlessly seeking to understand the past, if he is totally ignorant of the present.'[1]

By any parameter, the irreversible partition of the subcontinent has solved nothing, but only created new problems, like Kashmir. Mahatma Gandhi had just said on 30 January 1948 that he was ready to go to Pakistan, when he was assassinated by Nathuram Godse. A few days before M.A. Jinnah died on 11 September 1948 while he lay on his deathbed he had expostulated to Liaquat Ali, in the presence of Fatima Jinnah, his sister, and Colonel Ilahi Baksh, his physician, according to the Peshawar *Frontier Post* account published on 26 November 1987: 'If now I get an opportunity, I will go to Delhi and tell Jawaharlal to forget about the follies of the past and become friends again.' About the same time, he reportedly said, according to Alan Campbell-Johnson, 'The only man I have ever been impressed with in all my life was Lord Mountbatten.'²

By 1951, Liaquat Ali had also been assassinated, his killers in Pakistan not yet having been traced. Then an attempt was made on Jawaharlal Nehru's life in the 1950s. Is assassination, political murder or otherwise, more endemic in the subcontinent than elsewhere? 1958, Dr Khan Sahib killed in Pakistan; 1959, S.W.R.D. Bandaranaike killed in Sri Lanka; 1975, Mujib-ur Rehman killed in Bangladesh; 1979, Zulfikar Ali Bhutto hanged in Pakistan; 1981, Zia-ur-Rehman eventually assassinated in Bangladesh after putting down twenty-two coup attempts in five years; 1984, Indira Gandhi; 1985, Sant Harchand Singh Longowal, co-signatory of the Punjab Accord with Rajiv Gandhi; 1986, General A.S. Vaidya; 1988, Zia-ul-Haq killed in Pakistan; 1991, Rajiv Gandhi killed by the Liberation Tigers of Tamil Eelam (LTTE), as also Sri Lankan Defence Minister Ranjan Wijeratne; and Lieutenant General Fazle Haq, former Governor of the North West Frontier Province (NWFP), in Pakistan.

The dichotomous image of the undivided Indian Army that existed before independence has been alluded to in the Prologue. The inimitable Winston Churchill made his usual contribution on this subject on 12 December 1946 in the House of Commons: 'We must not allow British troops or British officers in the Indian Army to become agencies and instruments of enforcing caste Hindu domination.' Yet, for almost two decades after independence, this dichotomous image, curiously, for certain inexplicable reasons, still subsisted as to the nationalist Indian Army, though, by circumstance, to a lesser extent. In his *Autobiography* (1936), Nehru had observed that the Indian infantry are of, 'as much use today as the Roman phalanx,' and the rifle, 'as little better than a bow and arrow.' He added, 'No doubt their trainers and mentors realize this.' In *The Discovery of India* (1946), he commented: 'The policy of balance and counterpoise...deliberately furthered in the Indian Army. Various groups were so arranged as to prevent any sentiment of national unity growing up amongst them, and tribal and communal loyalties and slogans were encouraged.' Nehru bestowed his early praise on the 'Indian National Army' (INA). Yet it was the derided undivided Indian Army that did so much to reduce the flow of blood in 1946 and 1947. Archibald Wavell had been insightful when he said in March 1947 before his departure, 'I believe that the stability of the Indian Army may perhaps be a deciding factor in the future of India. It has shown how all communities may work together to meet a common danger with comradeship and devotion.' After Wavell's departure, Lord Louis Mountbatten, on 24 March 1947, recorded a discussion, 'I asked Nehru if he agreed that the Army was the final guarantor of law and order, and that the morale and discipline of the Army was of the highest importance. He agreed.' Francis Tuker was to refer, before his departure in October 1947 from Eastern Command, to the divided Indian Army as, 'an oasis in a desert of chaos,' particularly in relation to the then disturbances in Assam, Bengal, Bihar, the UP, Punjab, Delhi and Gurgaon.

In retrospect then, the years since independence have been, in a sense, both the best of times and the worst of times for the Indian Army. The best of times, for the Army became completely nationalized after independence. Undoubtedly, also the worst of times, due to the various operational setbacks in 1962.

Otto von Bismarck, in the last century, had described what the army officer class should be, 'Poor, frugal, but pursuing honour with feudal fidelity; its whole existence devoted to King and Country; no Rule of Life but Duty; no Ambition but the greatness of the Nation.' Nearer home, sixty years ago, General (later Field Marshal) Sir Philip Chetwode, then Commander-in-Chief in India, had iterated succinctly on 10 December 1932 at the inauguration of the Indian Military Academy (IMA), Dehra Dun, the evocative exhortation still rightly emblazoned in Chetwode Hall, 'The Safety, Honour and Welfare of your Country come first, always and every time. The Honour, Welfare and Comfort of the Men you command come next. Your own Ease, Comfort and Safety come last always and every time.'

General K. Sundarji, on taking over as the Chief of the Army Staff on 1 February 1986, was sufficiently concerned, in the light of his experience hitherto, to write to all officers. A few extracts are reproduced, quoted then in *India Abroad* of 7 March 1986: 'It is imperative that we have a totally combat effective Army to support the revitalised India of tomorrow in her rightful place in the world. This involves getting the "man-machine-mix" just right, improving the quality of both and placing them in a structure which will be effective in the battlefield milieu of the Nineties and the early decades of 2000....

'However, no amount of modernization of arms, equipment, tactics and organizations can produce results unless we have the right kind of man in the right state of mind, manning the system. And that is what this letter of mine is about....

'The fact that the Army is one of the national institutions which has, comparatively speaking, weathered the post-Independence years and yet remains effective, should not make us complacent....We should, therefore, look at ourselves first and be not only frank but hypercritical....Paradoxically, all this is happening while in the narrow sense, professional competence has been going up at all levels since 1947. Broad-based though our intake has become, our young officers have proved in every action which they have fought, that they are brave and lead from the front—our officer casualty ratio in every action testifies to this. Where then, are we going wrong?

'First, let us look at ourselves—in the practice of our profession, we have not insisted on standards being maintained and turn our eyes away from irregularities (living in a glass house?); we have not been tolerant of dissent during discussion and encourage sycophancy (a result of our having "switched off" professionally?). We have not been accepting any mistakes (due to hankering after personal advancement?), thus encouraging our juniors to either do nothing worthwhile or to over-supervise their juniors, who in turn are not allowed to develop professionally or mature as men. This leads to frustration. Finally, some have perhaps unthinkingly developed a yen for five-star culture and ostentation which flows from new-rich values in our society, where money is the prime indicator of success and social position. This adoption of mercenary values in an organization like the Army which depends for its elan on values like honour, duty and country above self, is disastrous for its elan and for the self-esteem of the individual in it. And once we start thinking of ourselves as third-class citizens, it is not long before our civilian brethren take us at our own valuation, and some of them perhaps not without a touch of glee!

'All of us talk about "officer-like qualities" and about being officers and gentlemen. I am not sure whether to many of us these terms mean the same thing. It refers to the "Sharafat" that is ingrained in the best of Indian culture; of honour and integrity; of putting the interests of the Country, the Army, the unit and one's subordinates before one's own; of doggedness in defeat; of magnanimity in victory; of sympathy for the underdog; of a certain standard of behaviour and personal conduct in all circumstances; of behaving correctly towards one's seniors, juniors and equals. I am very concerned about the increasing sycophancy towards seniors which unless checked will corrode the entire system...

'In dealing with peers and juniors also, courtesy, consideration and good manners are equally essential. There is none so disgusting as a person who boot-licks the senior, boots the junior and cuts the throats of his peers. I also notice that, of late, there has been a regrettable communication gap developing between officers and men. I attribute this primarily to selfishness on the part of the officers, and not caring enough about the men. This must be corrected. At all levels, we must insist that we live up to the Chetwodean motto...

'While on the quality of life, I must mention that, by custom and usage of service, some privileges do go with added responsibility and senior rank, and I am sure that none would grudge these if used sensibly. However, in some cases senior officers tend to get delusions of grandeur and overdo their privileges on a Moghul style.' Remedial measures have been initiated by Sundarji and his successors as to this "Mughalization".

All that this really amounts to is that our promotion Selection Boards, have made, over the decades, errors of judgement, resulting, in both war and peace, certain commanders doing the worst they could do—making the worst of a good job as evidenced in Lieutenant General Harbakhsh Singh's 1965 *War Despatches*. Philip Ziegler, Mountbatten's biographer, cannot conceal his feeling that, in the British Navy, Mountbatten, a great man, was an outstanding example of successful "upward failure" (Dieppe raid etc). The Indian Army too has had its quota of "upward failures", both pre and post-independence, in no way as distinguished as Mountbatten. The late Lieutenant General Daulet Singh often said before the onset of the 1962 conflict with China, that the then Indian Army was heading the way of the South Vietnamese army, before its defeat by the Viet Cong. Sequentially, in the words of Hugh Tinker, 'In the long term, the effect of the Himalayan defeat was salutary.' The most objective overall account of the 1962 conflict is by the Director of Military Operations of that period, Major General D.K. Palit, who has validly titled his book, *War in High Himalaya—The Indian Army in Crisis, 1962.* The Indian Army being equipped with the .303 bolt action rifle was not the main reason for the debacle, as many made out. Some stirring successes in the 1965 and 1971 conflicts with Pakistan arrested this decline.

The Indian Army's internal future is entirely in its own hands. Individual chiefs have shown the capacity to put ills right. If all the chiefs over the next few decades consistently continue to take remedial action, as is being done today, whenever it is necessary, we can hopefully get out of this slough. Organizations do not stand still, and, in the process of evolution, problems tend to get compounded over time, sometimes to the point where solutions are no longer feasible, for there are inherent absurdities in any hierarchical organization, and the Indian Army is no exception. As I have said in the Prologue, the Indian Army is still a paradigm for its times*. In 1962, it could have been said "Paradigm Lost". Today it is "Paradigm Regained". On the plus side, unlike the known coups in Pakistan and Bangladesh, and the perfunctory ones in Sri Lanka, the Indian Army

---

* For the Indian Army's approximate order of battle, see Appendix 7.

has consistently remained brilliantly apolitical. A Pakistani writer had chosen to rationalize in 1974: '...both India and Pakistan began their independent life in 1947, and inherited the British military traditions and institutions. In twenty-six years, Pakistan has undergone one minor and two major martial laws, whereas in India, the military has not been able to play such a vital political role.'[3]

And this *obiter dicta* after twenty-one Pakistan Army officers (including one retired Brigadier), along with fourteen Pakistan Air Force officers, had been arrested in 1973 for seeking to capture power from the civilian government apart from the 1951 "Rawalpindi Conspiracy". Whether during the Emergency 1975-77, or the aftermath of Indira Gandhi's assassination, the Indian Army officers have lived up to Chetwode's further prescient exhortation of 10 December 1932: 'May I urge you to remember that politics do not and cannot find any place in army life. An Army can have no politics. It is the paid servant of the people, and is at the disposal of the government of the day, whatever may be the political complexion of that government. Once there is any suspicion that an army, or any part of it is biased politically, from that moment that army has lost the full confidence of the nation who pays for it. It is no longer impartial, and that way leads to chaos and civil war.' Fortunately for the country, no serving officer has thought differently.

Stephen Cohen has summed up the position correctly in *The Indian Army—Its Contribution to the Development of a Nation* (1990): 'De Tocqueville and other theorists argued that democracy and a large standing army were incompatible, but India has managed both.'[4] There can be no doubt that the paradigmatic Indian Army has gloriously served the nation during the difficult decades since independence. Not a day passes in the calendar year when some unit of the Indian Army is not observing its battle honour day, mostly post-independence honours.

It has been said that each writer tends to interpret the past in his own light, for history is an argument without end. However, I have sought to avoid mythification of the Indian Army, and kept in mind Karl Marx's commentary in *The Eighteenth Brumaire of Louis*

Napoleon that all great events in world history reappear in one fashion or another—the first time as tragedy, the second time as farce. While Marx was paraphrasing and elaborating on Hegel, aphorisms do not always work out precisely in real life. So while events and even personalities do come twice, but as we have seen in this story the likely sequence can be reversed, first as farce, then as tragedy. Moreover, the problem for any army, as this story of the Indian Army shows, is that burlesque is not only full of bathos, but also pathos, as in 1915 in Mesopotamia, or in 1962 in the North East Frontier Agency (NEFA).

Thus this last century of the millenium has been for the Indian Army, both dazzling in its achievements, as well as tragic in its failure. Failure is always an orphan as in 1962, though success has many fathers as in 1971. As to Indian society and the Indian Army in the next century, one needs only to dwell on Professor Hugh Tinker's postulation: 'Gandhi's mentor, John Ruskin, observed in "Unto This Last", "...the soldier's trade, verily and essentially is not slaying but being slain....He holds his life at the service of the State....He will keep his face to the front, and he knows that this choice may be put to him at any moment, and...does in reality die daily....Truly the man who does not know when to die does not know how to live." This was certainly Gandhi's creed; and however improbable, it links the Indian soldier with the Mahatma.'[5]

To conclude, 'What you run away from, runs after you,' is an old Romanian proverb. Time has a tendency to conquer memory, but the past catches up with us from time to time. Bernard Malamud had said, 'Without heroes, we are all plain people and do not know how far we can go'; Tarun J. Tejpal has added, 'A nation needs heroes....To invent them can be hazardous....a nation whose heroes have feet of clay can find itself mired in ankledeep mulch.' With the Indian soldier present, India does not need to invent heroes, nor will the nation be mired in mulch, for one cannot but be profoundly moved by his dignity, magnanimity and spirit. What one discerns most of all is his inner strength, born out of endurance and tribulation over the centuries.

As for myself, I am one with Walter Allen, the English critic, who once said, 'Every writer knows that he puts pen to paper at the risk of continual misunderstanding on the part of the majority of his readers.' My reason for writing this history is as posited by Liddell Hart, 'History is a catalogue of mistakes. It is our duty to profit by them.'

POSTSCRIPT (1993–2000)

Wars begin when you will, but they do not end when you please.

Machiavelli

This is the devilish thing about foreign affairs: they are foreign, and will not always conform to our whims.

James Reston

THREE MAJOR issues affecting national defence, and concomitantly the Indian Army, awaited decision by the new Central government in March 1998. The first was the need for a national security organization to monitor the external, and increasing internal, threats from or via our neighbours; the second was whether there should be a tested Indian nuclear deterrent, in view of Pakistan impliedly threatening to use it's nuclear capability in 1984, 1987 and 1990, and China's nuclear missile modernizing programme, the latter aiming to achieve a range of 12,000 km; and the third was a deferred governmental decision on the 1990 Arun Singh (former Minister of State for Defence) Committee report recommending the integration of the Armed Forces' Headquarters with the Ministry of Defence, for optimization in Defence decision-making. (In no other major democracy have the armed forces' headquarters been excluded from the government.) In addition, solutions were required for the long-standing problems

532

Postscript

of insurgency and narco-terrorism in Jammu and Kashmir, Punjab and the North-East, which continued in varying degrees, the Army being extensively deployed in Jammu and Kashmir, and the North-East. (In the Kashmir Valley alone, the equivalent of nearly one hundred battalions, including the counter-insurgency Rashtriya Rifles and para-military forces, is currently deployed in this ostensibly low-intensity conflict, as opposed to only 13 in the seemingly high-intensity conflict of 1947–48.)

For the first issue, a task force was set up in April 1998. In relation to the second, the Cabinet decided that India should become an overt nuclear power in May 1998 (Pokhran II). This became inevitable when a series of proposals by India, made over four decades, were successively ignored in the UN General Assembly—in 1954, the first to call for a ban on all nuclear testing; in 1965, for a non-discriminatory treaty on non-proliferation; in 1978, for a treaty on the non-use of nuclear weapons; in 1982, for a nuclear freeze; and in 1988, for a phased programme for complete nuclear elimination. Had India been heeded, India would have had no need for a nuclear bomb. Nuclear weaponry had been discussed in India since 1964, when China became a nuclear-weapon state, conducting 44 further tests before eventually accepting the Nuclear Non-Proliferation Treaty (NPT) of 1970. Work on the May 1974 Indian peaceful underground nuclear explosion (PNE) (Pokhran I) had been given the governmental go-ahead 18 months earlier in 1972, after an Indian mission's failure to get a joint assurance from the five nuclear-weapons powers[1], as well as President Nixon moving a nuclear-armed task force against India in 1971. Furthermore, from early 1973 onwards Pakistan had begun receiving funds from some members of the Organisation of Petroleum-Exporting Countries (OPEC) for its nuclear programme, authorized by the late Z.A. Bhutto in January 1972, and for which there had been contacts with China since 1965. An Indian nuclear capability did not exist at that time. This Pakistan–China nuclear technology collaboration went ahead even though in 1978 Prime Minister Morarji Desai publicly abjured nuclear weapons. There were, progressively, clandestine imports of nuclear technology, as also of actual sensitive items like nuclear trigger mechanisms, by Pakistan, Dr A.Q. Khan, the 'father' of the Pakistani bomb, being involved in the Netherlands in a controversy over the alleged removal of documentation on nuclear centrifuge technology. (After the imposition of sanctions in May 1998 against Pakistan, some OPEC countries have again helped out—one, for instance, with free oil worth some Rs 8,500 crores.) The Pokhran I PNE was a mere statement of capability by India.

Pakistan's Indocentric, if not Indophobic, posture had been accentuated after its defeat in the 1971 conflict, its view being that a nuclear-weapon capability would neutralize India's conventional superiority, and enable covert operations in Kashmir, short of a conventional conflict. Simultaneously, there had been advocacy that US nuclear safeguards should be accepted by India. Earlier, in 1965, the US had not even been able to prevent Pakistan from using some 900 million dollars worth of US-aid weapons against India in a conflict solely initiated by Pakistan, and despite written assurances to India by President Eisenhower in 1954, the US decision as to military assistance to Pakistan, as part of the US 'containment' strategy, having been taken as early as July 1951. This US policy of aiding Pakistan militarily had taken on a life of its own. (By repeated programmes of arms aid to Pakistan since 1954, the US made an arms race in the subcontinent inevitable.) Moreover, in June 1978 at the UN Special Session on Disarmament, India had rightly argued that a nuclear weapon-free zone did not provide security to non-nuclear weapon states, as long as nuclear-weapon states continued to possess nuclear weapons. In 1979, the US Administration was compelled to invoke the Symington Amendment against military aid to Pakistan on account of its advanced nuclear-weapons programme, but only imposed limited sanctions for a limited period, for thereafter the US looked away virtually throughout most of the 1980s as Pakistan built its nuclear weapons with the help of China, since it wanted Pakistani support in Afghanistan, having earlier received Pakistani support for the U2 flights over the then USSR. General Alexander

Haig, the US Secretary of State, even assured Pakistan in 1981 that the US would not interfere with its nuclear programme. Then there were reports that China had tested a nuclear device for Pakistan, and in 1985, US Senators John Glenn and Alan Cranston sought legislation to stop all aid to countries, like Pakistan, with proven programmes, also concomitantly imposing sanctions (the Glenn Amendment). Thereafter there was the Pressler Amendment, seemingly a stringent nuclear non-proliferation law, which recognized that Pakistan's main preoccupation was not to be the lynchpin from any conviction in the US' containment policy, but as a device for acquiring the military means to wage war against India; in its passage, however, it was predicated with annual certification that Pakistan had not reached explosive capability, to enable aid to continue. This the US Administration readily gave till the Soviet withdrawal from Afghanistan in 1989. Thereafter the passage in the US House of the half-truth annual certification became more difficult, with consequent delays in aid. The Pressler Amendment was then reversed, in October 1995, by the Brown Amendment, prompted by the US military-industrial complex, which once again freely allowed military aid to Pakistan. If the basic Pressler Amendment was logical, which it substantively had been, then the Brown Amendment defied all logic.

In the light of Henry Kissinger's precept, 'A power can survive only if it is willing to fight for its interpretation of justice and its conception of vital interests,' in 1983 an integrated Indian guided-missile programme for the three Defence Services had perforce to be started, in the context of Pakistan's and China's continuing nuclear-weapons programmes, as a step towards possibly developing a nuclear option, but simultaneously emphasizing nuclear disarmament. (Insofar as the Army was concerned, the missiles for its use were to be mainly the 'Nag' anti-tank missile, the short-range 'Trishul' surface-to-air missile, and the 'Prithvi' tactical battlefield missile.) In 1995, India, in the context of the apparently continuing China-Pakistan nexus, latterly also with North Korea, and China's expanding modernized nuclear-weapon capability, decided to go in for nuclear weaponization in self-defence. (China had, after 1962, sought to contain India through the transfer initially of conventional, and later of nuclear, military capability to Pakistan. Today, 80 per cent of Pakistan's heavy armaments are of Chinese origin or design.) As global political power today rests on the salience of nuclear weapons, India sequentially opted to break-out of the non-proliferation regime before September 1999, by when it was expected to sign the Comprehensive Test Ban Treaty (CTBT), being disillusioned with the lack of progress in nuclear disarmament among the nuclear-weapon states. India expressed its determination to go ahead with the 2,000-km Agni II ballistic missile, test-fired in April 1999, on account of Pakistan having commenced production of the 2,000 km 'Ghauri' missile, based on the North Korean 'Nodong', thus changing the military equation in South Asia. A test of the Agni III, with a range of over 3,000 km, is now envisaged. (The firing by the North Koreans of their even longer-range 'Taepo-Dong-I' in August 1998 created a degree of concern in the US, which was not displayed when Pakistan test-fired the 'Ghauri' in April 1998. This can only be interpreted as tacit US permissiveness for Pakistan fulfilling its role as a surrogate frontline state in US interests, having been given since 1982 a further 5.5 billion dollars of mostly military assistance.) The affordable minimum nuclear capability for India to deter nuclear blackmail and a possible threat of use against India over the next decade is certainly less than one hundred warheads, as against some 20,000 in the world today (earlier some 60,000 before the commencement of scaling down), China having some 500. India rightly rejected the US suggestion that it should specify in concrete terms its minimum requirements for nuclear deterrence, positing that it is difficult to have fixity in number or range of nuclear missiles in a fluctuating environment.

The US has pressed India the hardest to dismantle its strategic programme, thereby indirectly ensuring nuclear superiority in the region for China. While this does not signify any US bias for China, the US biding its time hopefully for the Chinese Communist regime to erode from within as elsewhere, the US should nevertheless realise that the Indian polity has greater congruence with it, than have Pakistan and China. The US can trust China to possess nuclear weapons, but not India. Even in the matter of easing sanctions, the US had been more accommodating towards Pakistan, for example, in supporting further International Monetary Fund/World Bank loans to Pakistan, but not as promptly for India, black-listing some 200 Indian public-sector and private-sector enterprises, as well as their subsidiaries and affiliates, and denying certain technologies to India for 40 years, the US semantics being that Pakistan's economy was dysfunctional, and therefore needed immediate help, whereas India's economy was stronger. Nevertheless, the withholding of infrastructural loans for new power plants, etc, meant that the Indian economy had been weakened. The US pressure on them had challenged the very independence of the multilateral financial institutions, whose charter forbade their politicisation by member countries. (World Bank loans, worth two billion US dollars of infrastructural lending to India alone, apart from those of other multilateral aid agencies, had been selectively delayed by the US, but not to Pakistan; while latterly the US has been easing after President Clinton's visit in the expectation that India will sign the CTBT, though the US itself had not ratified, it still wants India to sign the NPT.) The selective lifting of sanctions by the US obtusely ignored that the bulk of Pakistani spending is on defence and debt servicing, resulting in a 1.8 billion US dollars deficit, as also on its misadventures in Kashmir and Afghanistan, assisted certainly, as a US frontline state, in the latter till 1989, and even beyond, by the CIA. (An imperious US has replaced an imperial Britain in playing the Great Game in Afghanistan. Whereas, after two Anglo-Afghan wars in the 19th century, Britain had learnt that all foreigners come to grief in Afghanistan, the irony is that the US had forgotten this fact, despite so educating the Russians in the decade 1979–89. The geo-political games by the US and Pakistan continued.) The Soviet Union having disintegrated, Pakistan has disproportionately large forces for its population and genuine defence commitments. Defence expenditure and debt servicing together exceed Pakistan's revenue budget.

There was thus no rationale in the Indo-Pakistan equation hitherto adopted by the US, as there was none in 1951. (The roots of the anti-Indian bias in US policy goes back to India's independent foreign policy during the Cold War.) After three CIA personnel were murdered at Langley in the USA in 1993 by a Pakistani, the attempt to blow up the World Trade Centre in New York also being the endeavour of at least one Pakistani, and a further four US officials murdered in Karachi, as well as the Egyptian embassy in Islamabad being partially blown up, the US should concern itself more in stopping the export of terrorism from Pakistan—Pakistan's Inter-Service Intelligence (ISI)-trained militants and foreign mercenaries being behind the 1995 Chrar-e-Sharief conflagration in Kashmir (their leader, Mast Gul later being lionised on Pakistani TV), as well as the murder of five foreign tourists taken hostage in Kashmir; Pakistan's renewed blatant intervention in Afghanistan in the form of the mainly Pakistani-funded and trained Taliban, medieval and misogynist in its outlook, ostensibly in order to keep the trade routes to the Central Asian republics open, but also purportedly to provide Pakistan with strategic depth and earlier to enable the United Oil Company of California (UNOCAL) to lay a gas and oil pipeline from Turkmenistan to Karachi; Pakistan's ISI's collusion with the CIA and the Taliban in the forays into Tajikistan, thus widening the Pashtun-Tajik divide in Afghanistan, the ISI then receiving financial support from the CIA, of several hundred million dollars annually; its hitherto virtual indifference to the narcotics traffic from the border area with Taliban-controlled Afghanistan, Pakistani drug traffickers funding the Taliban, resulting in the heroin-Kalashnikov culture (a Pakistani media term) in Karachi, till this border area was declared in February 1999 to be a bigger source of drugs than the Golden Triangle of Myanmar by the US Anti-Narcotics Bureau and the International Drug Control Agency (Pakistan had on 27 February 1999 announced an all-out drive against drug cultivation and trafficking, costing 56 million US dollars, but blames Afghanistan); as also the diversion by the ISI of some three million US-supplied weapons, some 40 per cent of all those intended for the Afghan 'resistance', costing 150 million US dollars. In a country where much of the terrorism against India had been conducted with Pakistani state support, it had become difficult to discern which terrorist activity may not have been sanctioned by the Pakistani government. Despite the US condemnation of terrorism world-wide, Pakistan still received what may be termed most favoured nation (MFN) status, though the US State Department had realistically indicated in its annual reports on global terrorism from 1991 to 1995 that Pakistan was aiding terrorism in Kashmir and Punjab. The US had soft-pedalled as to formally declaring Pakistan a terrorist state (apart from terming the 'Harkat-ul-Ansar' a terrorist organisation in 1997, and in 2000 that Pakistan was 'harbouring and aiding known terrorists'), notwithstanding Farooq Abdullah, the Chief Minister of Jammu and Kashmir, repeatedly urging this, and full documentation being available to the US in Yossef Bodansky's 1995 work, 'Pakistan, Kashmir and the Trans-Asian Axis' (the author headed a US Congressional Task Force on terrorism). In its turn, the Taliban is waging a terrorist campaign of assassination against Afghan refugees in Peshawar who do not toe its line. Created by its own misadventurism, Pakistan is now compelled to try to ride the rogue Taliban tiger, in order to endeavour to control it. Thus, while the US had spelt out in December 1998, in an article in Indian newspapers, its policy towards South Asia, it did not take into consideration the causes of the corrosive problems in the subcontinent. One consistent mental block with the US had been its failure to address the manifold defence concerns of India, protestations notwithstanding. The US' apparent show of impartiality, designed to give solace more to Pakistan, where the desire for parity with India in all matters is supreme, was rightly viewed as obtuseness in India. India had repeatedly iterated that its nuclear policy, as also foreign policy, is not Pakistan-centric, whereas Indophobia has hitherto been at the very basis of Pakistan's relations. India cannot ignore its 14,000 km land border, 7,000 km maritime boundary, and some 500 islands, as also the existence of the China factor, eg, the sale of two billion US dollars worth of arms to, and the Chinese naval tie-up with Myanmar, giving it a toehold in the Bay of Bengal, and the ratification of the 1914 McMahon Line with Myanmar, but not so far with India. Nor does the US text admit that India's record as a responsible nuclear power, particularly as to export controls, has been faultless, whereas that of Pakistan, and even of some of the P5 powers, has not been so. It is also curious, but nevertheless true, that nuclear weapons in reality are not weapons of actual use in the nature of war today. They are weapons of deterrence, and are the currency of power. An illustration of this is the nuclear P5 nations, who, despite there being no Soviet Union or Warsaw Pact now, still wish to preserve this nuclear-power currency[2]. They are only for the retention of nuclear weapons for themselves, and consider that any other nation acquiring nuclear weapons will be destabilising, for, as Quentin Reynolds has aptly put it, 'Scientists split the atom, now the atom is splitting us.' India, a nation of one billion, cannot be denied this currency of power, when it has consistently emphasised nuclear disarmament, world-wide, on a non-discriminatory basis. All nuclear-weapon states, P5 or otherwise, must subscribe to no-first-use and to non-use against non-nuclear weapons states. India had offered a no-first-use agreement to Pakistan, but this had been rejected by the latter, the Pakistani Foreign Secretary stating in November 1998, that 'nuclear roll-back is not in our dictionary, NPT not in our vocabulary,' Pakistan reasoning that nuclearization counters India's superiority in conventional forces.

Earlier, in October 1998, India had proposed certain confidence-building measures (CBMs). Eventually at the historic meeting of the two Prime Ministers at Lahore in February 1999, some of these were substantively agreed to, and a Memorandum of Understanding (MOU) was signed by the two Foreign Secretaries. Firstly, both nations agreed to provide each other with advance notification in respect of ballistic missile flight tests; secondly, both will undertake national measures to reduce the risks of accidental or unauthorised use of nuclear weapons (hitherto Pakistan has been the only country where the armed forces had control over nuclear weapons, and not the civilian government:

this by circumstance continues); thirdly, in the event of an accidental or unauthorised incident that could create the risk of nuclear fallout for both, or precipitate the outbreak of a nuclear war, the two sides undertook to notify each other about the development; fourthly, appropriate communication mechanisms for these purposes will now be identified/established; fifthly, while they agreed to abide by the respective unilateral moratoria on conducting further nuclear tests, there will be a qualifying clause, 'Unless either side, in exercise of its national sovereignty decides that extraordinary events have jeopardised its supreme interests.' (China has independently accepted no-first-use, but not the US, which maintains a maximalist approach.) Separately, Henry Kissinger, who in 1971 had pressed China to intervene against India, now rightly regards India as one of the six great powers of the post-Cold War 'polycentric' world, along with the US, Russia, China, Japan and the European Union, led by Germany, but this does not seem to have been so far fully understood by the US Administration, as to India's permanent membership of the Security Council.

In November 1998, there had been also been reports of Pakistan having earlier commissioned a plutonium-production reactor at Khushab, vestiges of plutonium having been discerned by the US at the May 1998 explosions site in the Chagai Hills. This was no surprise to India, the reactor being set up by China, but the reports again highlight the hitherto Pakistan-China nuclear proliferation linkage. The commissioning of this reactor had been hastened, even as negotiations for the Fissile Materials Cut-off Treaty (FMCT) were underway in Geneva, as a possible cover for future supplies of Chinese plutonium-weapons to Pakistan. Whereas India had announced a moratorium on nuclear-weapon testing, Pakistan would have had to test again, as plutonium-weapons require more testing than uranium-weapons, and hence possible recourse by Pakistan to the qualifying clause in the MOU mentioned above. As an alternative, it could get some ready-made weapons from China, just as it has already received 34 complete 296-km M-11 missiles, and help in setting up an M-11 ballistic missile factory at Fatehjung. India is thus the only non-NPT nuclear nation without an external benefactor. The US also seeks a moratorium by India on fissile material production, when Pakistan and China have not yet declared such a moratorium.

While all these considerations are relevant in negotiating the FMCT, it is clear that the NPT has been breached by China, since it has helped Pakistan to become a nuclear-weapons state, the commissioning of the plutonium-production reactor being proof of the continuing violation of China's obligations under the NPT. (China is helping Pakistan in order to ensure that Pakistan does not stir up the already restive Muslims in China's neighbouring Xinjiang province.) Even as the US is calling on India publicly to suspend production of fissile material, the US does not similarly talk about nuclear restraint to China, nor is the US transparent about what it is doing about the ongoing Chinese proliferation activities. The US has been adopting a soft line vis-à-vis China to enlist its cooperation for US policies, mutual relations having cooled. The result is an acceleration in the growth of Chinese authoritarianism, over issues like Taiwan. Whether or when China will stop proliferating is a question nobody in the US can answer. So, while China shares with India a continuing civilization that dates back four millennia, China, unlike India, is never off the cuff in any of its responses. Each utterance represents a calculated consensus. Thus whereas it is true that China has hitherto continued to arm Pakistan, however, with the progression of Pakistan into a fundamentalist state, and China again having law and order problems with the Uighurs of Xinjiang, where numerous Wahabi Sunni 'mujahideen' from Afghanistan have reached, at least one Pakistani being beheaded, and the development of India's own strategic capability, the arithmetic for China, hopefully, may shift slowly in favour of a China-India linkage. This presently notional tie-up will have the added advantage of close relations with Russia, still a technological superpower with separate existing treaties respectively with India and China, and thus scope for an emerging trilateral diplomacy, as earlier suggested by the Russian Prime Minister, though not presently agreeable to China. China has currently opposed any retention by India of a minimum nuclear deterrent, even if it signs the CTBT, and, along with the US, insisting India signs the NPT, forgetting that India opted for nuclear weapons only because others had them. (A Sino-Indian post-nuclear dialogue has resumed since February 1999, the Indian viewpoint on all relevant issues having been progressively conveyed to the Chinese.) If and when the nuclear-weapon states give up their nuclear arsenals, as for biological and chemical weapons, then India, nuclear-weapon-wise, would do so immediately. In the Indian view, which it has maintained for over four decades, nuclear disarmament should be effected immediately. Nuclear wars are not winnable or fightable, as correctly postulated by Presidents Gorbachev and Reagan in November 1985.

As to a national security organization, the non-violence through which India attained her independence had inhibited the development of a national strategic culture. Post-independence, the void in institutionalised strategic thinking continued, despite the Indian Army having to fight four conflicts and to take part in a number of UN peacekeeping, as also strategic power-projection, missions. Any strategic thought that sequentially developed was due only to reactive compulsions; the totality of a national security culture was not understood, that ongoing national security strategy was an integral part of the national polity, India being legitimately entitled to a permanent seat in the UN Security Council as the largest democracy in the world. Nevertheless, as the world moves towards a multi-polar dispensation, India must be one of the poles. Undoubtedly earlier Central governments had felt the need for some form of a National Security Council (NSC) that would maximize efficiency and minimize wastage through systemic planning. In 1962, in the wake of Chinese aggression, a National Defence Council, in 1985 a Policy Planning Committee on National Security, and in 1990 a semblance of an NSC, actually a National Security Advisory Council, had been constituted. These concepts did not progress much owing to the changes in prime ministers and Central governments. (In the event, these bodies were more for public consumption, than expert bodies.) Then followed, for a short while, a Strategic Policy Group in 1995. Thereafter, the United Front government was too short-lived to enable it to establish its pattern of an NSC. The country's need for an institutionalized mechanism for long-term national strategic planning had in November 1998 resulted in the latest NSC.

Thus, while a consensus already existed for an NSC, there has nevertheless been criticism of the staffing of the organization created in November 1998, this criticism being encapsulated in expressions like 'The mountain in labour has produced a dead mouse' (*Times of India*, 20 November 1998) and 'NSC may add red-tapism to policy-making' (*Hindustan Times*, 20 November 1998). A six-member NSC, headed by the Prime Minister, now reviews facets pertaining to national security management, vis-à-vis national development. Essentially, the new NSC would appear to be the Cabinet Committee for Political Affairs (CCPA), augmented by the Deputy Chairman of the Planning Commission. The official announcement made the Principal Secretary to the Prime Minister the National Security Adviser, and thereby the main conduit for servicing the NSC. The Ministers for Home Affairs, Defence, External Affairs and Finance, and the Deputy Chairman of the Planning Commission are the members of a panel that has a three-tiered structure. The formal constitution of an NSC is thus significant, with India going nuclear in May 1998, and the continuing proxy war by Pakistan in Jammu and Kashmir having an increasingly direct bearing also on the whole country's internal security situation, for example, in Punjab and most other states, involving both subversion and narco-terrorism, ISI-supplied arms, fake currency and drugs now being in the possession of mafias and other criminal gangs, country-wide.

The hostile reactions of some of the nuclear powers and their allies to India's five May 1998 tests, the resultant economic sanctions, the sequential pressures to sign the CTBT and to cap the Indian missile programme, all required perceptive study. The new NSC's tasks, therefore, include conducting the country's first-ever strategic defence review encompassing the next 10 to 15 years, and formulating command and control systems for the country's nuclear weapons. The support for the NSC has three elements: instead of a new NSC secretariat, its secretariat is the existing Joint Intelligence Committee (JIC) augmented for its new role; the Strategic Policy Group has been strengthened, comprising the Cabinet Secretary, three Service Chiefs, the Union Secretaries from the ministries concerned, including External Affairs, Home, Defence, Finance, Revenue and Defence Production, the Governor of the Reserve Bank of India, the Director of the Intelligence Bureau, the Scientific Adviser to the Defence Minister, and the Space and Atomic Energy Chiefs, thus providing inter-ministerial co-ordination for the NSC; the third element is a National Security Advisory Board, comprising some 30 non-political persons of eminence, from outside the Central government. By and large, the 26 June 1998 report of the NSC Task Force, set up in April 1998 for the purpose, had not been acted upon. The task force had recommended an independent secretariat with expert back-up. The present structure combines the two posts of the Principal Secretary to the Prime Minister, and the National Security Adviser. Both are full-time commitments. Combining the two results in either or both not being managed effectively. Since the Principal Secretary is involved in the day-to-day work of the Central government, perspective planning of national security management by the same official is bound to be affected. Centralization of decision-making in the Prime Minister's Office (PMO) has severely clogged governance for several decades.

As for the Strategic Policy Group, it is, in effect, an expanded Secretaries' Committee. It can only make generalist comments on others' papers. To carry out a strategic defence review, there should be experts to produce a draft on which the Secretaries could comment. Also, by making the JIC the NSC Secretariat, any long-term intelligence assessment will be neglected, and the strategic defence review will not have any structured foundation. The aim of setting-up an NSC is to eradicate ad hocism in national security decision-making. This aim will be defeated by the bureaucratic ambivalence of the NSC as now constituted. Earlier, the

JIC had been moved from the jurisdiction of the Chiefs of Staff Committee in 1965, and made an autonomous assessment body in the Cabinet Secretariat, after it was manifest that the 1962 reverse was the result not of the absence of intelligence, but of the failure to assess it in an holistic manner. However, the tendency of intelligence agencies to withhold information from the JIC in a game of one-upmanship, as to who can reach the Prime Minister first, and the inability of ministries and senior bureaucrats to understand that long-term intelligence assessments are essential inputs for policy-making, undermined the effectiveness of the JIC. The operations in Sri Lanka against the LTTE in 1987–90, the outbreak of insurgency in Kashmir in 1989, the continued sectarian violence in various parts of the country, continuing militancy in the North-East, and the implications of the China–Pakistan proliferation linkage, with seeming US acquiescence, and latterly the North Korean–Pakistani connection in the form of the Pakistani 'Ghauri' missile, all point to the failure to establish an expertise-based intelligence system. (The then Pakistani Foreign Minister, in 1998, had publicly claimed that its missiles in production were superior in performance to the corresponding Indian missiles, and that all major Indian cities are within range of the Shaheen - II.) In national security decision-making, it is thus pivotal not to mix-up the responsibilities for intelligence assessment and policy-making.

Further, despite the ongoing information age, our politicians and senior bureaucrats have so far failed to realise the importance of assessed intelligence. This reluctance is rooted in the authoritarian style of half a century of Central governmental functioning, marked by an inept preference for ad hocism. This is apparent in the conversion of the JIC into the NSC Secretariat. Overall, therefore, the NSC set-up announced encompasses already existing arrangements in a refashioned form, with bureaucrats as the main personae. Instead of cutting red tape, the ostensible new set-up has ended up adding to the existing red tape. The Central government should still think of having a wholetime National Security Adviser as the effective head of the NSC. The person should be a political appointee of Cabinet rank, with bipartisan acceptance.

After the above encapsulation of the events of Pokhran II in May 1998, and the setting-up of the NSC in November 1998, it remains to be said that the latter should have been done first; thereafter Pokhran II could have been conducted after a comprehensive strategic review within a strategic gameplan, taking all possible economic sanctions and technology controls into account.

In relation to the integration of the Defence Headquarters, it would appear that in seeking to create an NSC as an essential pillar of optimal policy-making, the Prime Minister was confronted with the bureaucracy's reluctance to surrender some of its prerogatives assumed since 1952, when the then Defence Secretary made the three Armed Forces' Chiefs report directly to the bureaucracy instead of to a political authority, 'military intelligence' apparently being deemed an oxymoron, by an ostensibly 'uncivil' civil service. The then Prime Minister, while not agreeing with a written representation by General K.M. Cariappa, had undertaken to form a 'Defence Council', that was to be at the core of the integrated Ministry of Defence, as in Britain, where the professional opinion of the Service Chiefs, and even possibly a Chief of the Defence Staff, or a permanent Chairman of the Chiefs of Staff, would have weightage over generalist administrators. Eventually, the then Prime Minister did not set up this council, thus in effect making the Service Chiefs subordinate to a civilian official, instead of to a political authority, but thereafter set up a Defence Committee of the Cabinet. Even this committee gradually went into disuse, the three Service Chiefs progressively ceasing to be invited after 1980. Had it still been functional, there would not have been political blunders like sending the Army headlong into Operation 'Bluestar' in Amritsar in 1984, or the Indian Peace-keeping Force (IPKF) into Sri Lanka in 1987 at the invitation of the then Sri Lankan government, ostensibly treating the Army as a force available at the beck and call of the political authority, but kept outside the integrated structure of the Central government, our leaders preferring to react to events, rather than to anticipate them.

Senior bureaucrats apparently also succeeded in avoiding making policy-making changes, while establishing the NSC, despite these being recommended by the Task Force set up for the purpose, for as Louis Thiess had perceptively said, 'Working with the government is like spinning your wheels in the sand,' This was not good news at a time when the military was being sidelined from the policy-making hierarchy, as, for instance, in the reported 1998 differences between the then Defence Secretary and the three Service Chiefs. An exercise resumed in January 1999, in the context of the 1990 Arun Singh Committee report and the recommendations of the Estimates Committee (1992–93) of the 10th Lok Sabha, after the transfer of the then Defence Secretary, and the removal of the Naval Chief. When the Arun Singh Committee made its proposals, they were opposed by the bureaucracy, which thought civilian control would be reduced, and the powers of the three Service Chiefs enhanced. This was also noted in March 1996 by the Parliamentary Standing Committee, that the Ministry was categorically opposed to its integration with the Armed Forces' Headquarters. Actually, the proposals were designed to make civilian control more efficient, and for the three Chiefs to become more effective professional advisers to the Defence Minister. Sequentially, 'Civilian control' over the Armed Forces came to mean 'Civil service control', with control not being exercised by elected political functionaries accountable to Parliament, but by bureaucrats answerable only to other bureaucrats. (Earlier in 1969, the Administrative Reforms Commission [ARC], chaired by Morarji Desai, had also favoured an integrated Defence Ministry, in order to redress the imbalance between generalist and professional opinion in what should be a specialist ministry. Prime Minister Indira Gandhi shelved this ARC recommendation in the run-up to the 1971 Conflict.) The new NSC structure which relegates the Service Chiefs to the Strategic Policy Group, full of senior bureaucrats, can only result in chagrin, especially since the Central government, installed in March 1998, had promised earlier to reverse the marginalization of the Armed Forces. Hitherto, the lack of not only inter-ministerial coordination but also of intra-ministerial co-ordination in the Defence Headquarters, had stood out as a pivotal weakness in Defence policy-making. Political and economic realities all over the world make the armed forces the basic instrumentality of the state. Unfortunately, this concept had not been understood by successive Prime Ministers, often resulting in inadequate perception of security imperatives, and insensitivity to the needs of the Armed Forces. There is now ostensibly to be an integrated Defence Headquarters, as recommended in 1969 by the ARC, and in 1990 by the Arun Singh Committee, with the Armed Forces' Headquarters being merged with the Ministry of Defence, thus bringing Defence Services officers closer to the decision-making process. This merger, if effected, is to be welcomed, as long as it ensures that the mechanism of selection and promotion is protected from political patronage. The gravest threat Indian democracy can face today is the politicization of the Armed Forces. Our democracy has been safe because of the Armed Forces being apolitical.

As to Kashmir, the problem is still festering. Kashmir has been Pakistan's obsession, being described as 'the core issue' by the latter. Pakistan acquired by force what are known as 'Pakistan-occupied Kashmir' (POK) and 'the Federally Controlled Northern Areas' (FCNA), and has not withdrawn from them despite the UNCIP resolutions of 13 August 1948, requiring it do so. Since it failed to do so, all responsibility for the stalemate lies on Pakistan. India has been regularly holding elections in Kashmir since 1953; the same cannot be said for Pakistan as to POK. All this notwithstanding, on 23 March 1997, Pakistan's then President declared that 'Kashmir is a matter of Pakistan's survival,' and Pakistani political parties have since then referred to it as 'the unfinished agenda of Partition.'[3] It is political perversity to still invoke the 'two-nation' theory, and to make Kashmir the unfinished agenda of Partition, when the Kashmir dispute did not arise from the actual Partition process of British India, and the Muslim population of India is more than the total population of Pakistan. Rather, the unfinished agenda of Partition is the integration in Pakistan, in Sindh for instance, of the Muslim migrants (Mohajirs) to Pakistan. Pakistan always has some desperate compulsion to keep the Kashmir issue alive, for as Chief Minister Farooq Abdullah has often said, Pakistan thinks that by creating problems for India, it will have no problems of its own. India's diplomacy has thus been reactive, rather than setting the agenda—right from the ill-advised concept in 1947 of self-determination in Kashmir, to the continuing active support by Pakistan, in September 1947 by arming raiders in advance, largely ex-Servicemen, euphemistically referred to as tribesmen, backed up initially by regular personnel as commanders, and later by regular units and formations, and over the past decade, 1989–1999, by the training and equipping of terrorists and religious fanatics with equipment even more sophisticated than those in the possession of the Indian security forces, such as satellite telephones and the 'Stinger' surface-to-air missile. Pakistan's low-cost, low-intensity conflict with India, now a decade old, has revealed declining local support for the militants, and a corresponding rise in the number of foreign mercenaries, mostly Taliban, trained and armed by Pakistan, an increase from 15 to 80 per cent of the aggregate, and who have already served not only in Afghanistan, but also in Chechnya and Bosnia. (A Taliban-type code of dress and behaviour is now being enforced in Kashmir by these foreign mercenaries, with young girls being shot in the legs for wearing jeans and death threats to cable TV operators.) This unchecked religious fanaticism can only lead to the eventual 'Talibanization' of Pakistan, a boomerang effect. A government which has permitted religious extremist groups to traffic in arms in order to extend support to Kashmiri militants is inviting a backlash. Already in 1995 there had been an attempted coup by 35 Islamic extremists in the Pakistan Army, led by Major General Abbasi. Apart from over 20 years of martial law, there had also been earlier attempted coups in 1951 and 1973, before the coup of October 1999. In Kashmir in 1999 alone, more than 1000 militants, mostly foreigners, were killed. Earlier in 1998 alone, an unprecedented seven Pakistani attempts were foiled to

Postscript

dislodge Indian troops from the Saltoro ridge, west of the Siachen glacier. The years 1998 and 1999 witnessed further Pakistani provocations, even as the then political leadership sought to talk in Dhaka, Durban, New York and Lahore. The tempo in the mini-artillery war rose each time the leaders met. Bearing the brunt were innocent civilians in the Kargil and Uri sectors. Thus, over 20,000 Kashmiri civilians have been killed by Pakistani firing and terrorists from 1990, apart from the five Western hostages. In this period the Indian Army has lost some 1500 soldiers, apart from further casualties among the para-military forces. Even as the two Prime Ministers were talking about Kashmir at Lahore on 20/21 February 1999, ISI-trained foreign terrorists were murdering 31 innocent Hindu civilians in the area of Rajauri and Udhampur, sending a signal of sorts to the then Pakistani Prime Minister. On 27 February, he thereafter stated, 'In case the (Kashmir) issue is not resolved within a given timeframe, Pakistan would adopt other means to break the deadlock.' The Pakistan Army/ISI tiger is beyond control as revealed in the contrasting faces of the Lahore Declaration of February 1999, and the massive intrusions across the Line of Control in May 1999 in the Kargil Sector. See Appendix 8 and Map. In fact, Nawaz Sharif's election campaign, and that of his allies, was funded by the ISI in 1990, to the extent of 1.6 million pounds sterling, as ordered by the then Pakistan Army Chief, General Mirza Aslam Beg, thus leaving no doubt about the Pakistan Army dominating Pakistan's polity.

Today, the outcome of very few conflicts is decided on the battlefield, the outcome being decided at the negotiating table. Force is only one component of national security; the other elements include diplomacy, and psychological and economic pressures. Pakistan earlier fought an unsuccessful war in 1965 to wrest the Kashmir Valley from India, and yet India had to return, at the 1966 Tashkent Conference, the Hajipir Pass, the main infiltration route which it had captured. So while we give up territory that we rightfully claim to be ours, Israel, in contrast, continues to hold on to the Golan Heights and the security zone in southern Lebanon. Thus in our case victory does not by itself bring peace. The 1971

Indo–Pakistan conflict is a further example. Seemingly, vis-à-vis Pakistan, while the Indian Army wins the battles, and the country wins the war, the nation loses the peace. India once again gave away its military gains, such as over 90,000 Pakistani prisoners-of-war, at the negotiating table at Simla in 1972. The price for failing to resolve the Kashmir issue at Simla has been incalculable. The late Z.A. Bhutto had then said at Simla that he was convinced by the events of 1971 that Pakistan could not acquire Kashmir by war, and that the emergence of Bangladesh had struck a deadly blow to the two-nation theory and to Pakistan's claim to speak for the Muslims of the subcontinent, but he had actually already approved the commencement of Pakistan's nuclear programme. There has sequentially been Pakistan-aided internal subversion not only in Kashmir, but also in other states of India, with the aim of destabilizing the whole country. Unlike Pakistan, in India's case romanticism prevailed over realism. A personality-oriented culture had been postulated as a strategic culture. In the absence of institutionalized national security thinking, we have been conned into making concessions, or we have on our own made concessions in a vainglorious pursuit of international encomia. We should have heeded Martin Buxbaume's dictum, when meeting the late Z.A. Bhutto at Simla in 1972, 'If you think you have someone eating out of your hand, it's a good idea to count your fingers.' Continuous military sacrifice without political negotiating wisdom cannot bring security. Instead, the question that needs to be asked is for how long can this bloodletting by Pakistan of Indian lives continue? The Lahore meeting of 20/21 February 1999 held out some hope, till the Pakistani Prime Minister's statement of 27 February that Pakistan would continue support for the Kashmiris fighting against Indian rule. Effective national security depends as much on efficient diplomacy as on military prowess. Diplomacy, however, can only deliver results if it is backed, in the long run, by a firm political will. In its half-century as an independent state, India has often lacked this, nor has it hitherto consistently sought to structure this. In 1947, we had rushed to the UN deeming it an international policing agency. It was to become, in relation to the Kashmir issue, no more than an arena for superpower politics, despite Warren Austin, the then US representative at the UN Security Council, categorically stating on 4 February 1948, 'With the accession of Jammu and Kashmir to India, the sovereignty went over to India and is exercised by India, and that is why India happens to be here as a petitioner.' After 1951, in order to win over Pakistan as its surrogate, the US shifted its stance on the Kashmir issue. Juridically, Pakistan has no *locus standi* in relation to the territory of Jammu and Kashmir. Separately, Ms Bhutto, no longer in power, has belatedly made the suggestion that insurgency is not the way out in Kashmir, and that a non-insurgent solution should be found. The Chinese President, Jiang Zemin, has also advised Pakistan that Kashmir should be separated from other issues. The tradition of Islam should make Pakistan re-think, for the holy Prophet had said, 'He who believes in Allah and the last day must not put his neighbour to inconvenience.' The Prophet's wife asked him, 'I have two neighbours. To which of them should I send a present?' The Prophet replied, 'To the one whose door is nearer to you'. The only way ahead, when cross-border terrorism ends, is an alliance as part of SAARC, or a confederation of the two countries, which once were one, and which should have continued as one.

Concomitantly, terrorism in India today has been described in a Home Ministry report as 'a multinational systemic crime' involving 'various kinds of organizations that operate across national boundaries from one or more countries simultaneously.' A bad case pertaining to lax internal security was the 1995 Purulia armsdrop by a foreign plane. In its September 1998 presentation to its Parliamentary Consultative Committee, the same ministry stated that the emerging contours of the challenges to the country from subversion and terrorism point to the Pakistani ISI, which has now encircled the country, with ISI operatives even functioning from Kathmandu, eg, the IC-814 hijacking, and also from Dhaka. At one time, the ISI had been active mainly in Punjab, and then Jammu and Kashmir. Now it has spread itself to Western Uttar Pradesh and the Terai, the North-East, Calcutta, Chennai,

Coimbatore, Mumbai and Delhi, employing narco-terrorism and causing serial bomb blasts, apart from sedulously distributing seditious publications encouraging a communal divide, and making videos of military installations, et al. Reportedly, Osama Bin Laden, the Saudi national and terrorist, sheltered by the Taliban in Afghanistan, also secretly visited Mumbai, Hyderabad and Delhi, before the US Cruise missile attacks in August 1998 on his camps near Khost, in order to unleash terrorism in India. These self-same camps had earlier been set up by the CIA and ISI in the decade 1979–89. Some 200 Indian operatives, variously from Kerala, Andhra and UP, inter alia, have reportedly been trained in his camps. (In one of the camps attacked, Pakistan was training individuals for infiltration into Kashmir. This should embarrass both the US and Pakistan, but it does not.) It is an irony of history that the US bears a considerable measure of responsibility for spawning Frankenstein's monsters like Bin Laden in Afghanistan, and who is now targeting US installations world-wide, the US being the source of all evil in his eyes, followed by India.

As for Punjab, from 1982 onwards, Khalistani militants had been trained in Pakistan by the ISI, and even abroad, by ex-CIA operatives. While the post-1992 anti-militancy drive, anchored with an Army deployment of almost 120,000 troops (seven divisions), has, by and large, crushed the India-based militants, under the direction of the ISI, militants based abroad still have considerable threat potential. The assassination of the Punjab Chief Minister, Beant Singh, in a 'human bomb' attack in August 1995, gave a boost to these foreign-based militants. Thereafter, much has been achieved by the Punjab Police through undercover operations, for example, aborting a plan by ISI-trained terrorists in January 1999 to assassinate the Central Home Minister. So, while a groundswell against militancy in the Punjab countryside, from where it once got sustenance, as also unrelenting Police pressure as well as some extraditions from abroad, have reduced the number of horrendous incidents, vigilance, including by the Army, is still important to maintain the hard-won normalcy, for the sporadic striking potential of these foreign-based militants is high, as evidenced by the numerous weapons like the AK-47, and considerable tonnage of explosives and drugs, still being seized from them, when they infiltrate into India from Pakistan through various routes, via Rajasthan, Gujarat and the Konkan coast. In the decade to-date, some 5,000 Sikh youths have also been recruited abroad, and trained in Pakistan or overseas, Punjab continuing to be a priority in the ISI-sponsored secessionist plots and international narco-terrorist syndicates.

As for the North-East, which is a mosaic of ethnic, cultural and linguistic groups, if only deploying further Central security forces, including the Army, could have solved the problem of militancy and strife there, then the region would have been free of insurgency long ago. Forty-eight out of 69 districts of the North-East are affected. While the people suffer from the lack of employment facilities, and neglect by the politicians, the change from a largely tribal to a modern society has added to the unrest. As a January 1999 Home Ministry paper iterated, the need is for far better governance, and much less corruption, for as Justice Felix Frankfurter said, 'Government is the art of making men live together in peace and with reasonable happiness.' An issue which needs particular attention is the increasingly militant assertion by the 'have-nots' of their social and legal rights. This unsettled condition, however, is not peculiar to India alone. The entire tribal region up to the western border of Thailand is unsettled. Development funds poured into the North-East by the Centre have provided the militants with an additional source of funding. With large outlays but little to show by way of development, it is clear much of the money is going to politicians, and then to the various insurgent groups. Several politicians have now acquired a vested interest in perpetuating insurgency. In Tripura, for example, where a demographic imbalance has been created by the influx of outsiders reducing the ethnic tribals to a mere 24 per cent, resulting in anti-foreigner killings and the situation necessitating a joint command of the Army and the para-military forces, the main groups of insurgents are reportedly courted respectively by the Marxist party-in-power (eg, the All Tripura Tribal Force) and the opposition Congress (eg, the National Liberation Front of Tripura). Thus, grand larceny from a 'colonial' India is often made out to be regional or tribal 'patriotism'. Political solutions must be found for these insurgencies, by not patronizing and promoting corrupt politicians. As the militant groups must count on the sympathy of the local population, the imperative is to tackle the problems of the people, so as to wean them away from the militants. The anguish of deprivation is so marked that as to who is an outsider, and who is not, gets accentuated, but undoubtedly, as an example that stands out in the region, peace has given Mizoram a chance to develop in the past decade, proportionately much more than the other states, since its insurgency was resolved by bringing the insurgents, led by the late Laldenga, 'overground' in 1986, and then into governance, though Army deployment needs must continue. The State government elected in 1998 had been courageous in accepting that the Chakmas residing in Mizoram for decades are not outsiders, and had given them District Council status. Felicitously, the Bangladesh government and the leaders of the tribal insurgency in the Chittagong Hill Tracts (CHT) have also shown realism in signing the significant agreement to end hostilities in the CHT. This has enabled thousands of refugees housed in camps in Tripura to return to the CHT. The humane handling of the Chakma issue by the Mizoram government will hopefully have a salutary impact on the Arunachal Pradesh government, where the All-Arunachal Pradesh Students' Union has revived its campaign against the Chakmas, Hajongs and Tibetans who were settled there by the Central authorities. The students' 'Operation Clean' may create an ugly situation in Arunachal Pradesh, if action is not successful to defuse it, by emulating the understanding shown by the Mizoram government. One other North-eastern state in which the Centre has achieved a measure of success, after a second protracted insurgency, is Nagaland, by negotiation of a one-year extension of the cease-fire with the well-trained, well-armed Isak-Muivah faction of the National Socialist Council of Nagaland (NSCN-IM), as also the Khaplang faction (NSCN-K) declaring a cease-fire, though one cannot be optimistic about an early formal accord. In the interim, the extensive deployment of the Army and para-military forces perforce continues in Nagaland and Manipur.

In Assam and the remaining states of the North-East, the law and order situation continues to be a matter for concern. The banned United Liberation Front of 'Asom' (ULFA) and other militant organizations continue to be disruptive, though less so over the past decade since 1990, as a result of the endeavours of the Army and other security forces. (The ULFA was helped to be set up in 1978 by the NSCN-IM. Today both still have links in procuring and selling drugs, wherewith to buy further arms.) The ULFA, reduced to a hard core of 1,600 as a result of concerted Army and political action, had earlier taken advantage of the present Assam Chief Minister's initial reluctance to use the Army to reassert the dominance of the security forces. As a consequence, on the occasion of the annual Republic Day celebrations in January, the ULFA and other organizations still call for a boycott of the observance. ULFA has succeeded in blowing up an oil pipeline, as on some earlier 'protest' occasions in previous years since November 1990, when the Army was first called out against ULFA. In Manipur, the complexity of the relationships between the Meiteis, Kukis and Nagas continues to subsist. A comparatively new element in the insurgencies in Manipur is the Kuki insurgency. Whereas the aspirations of the NSCN are predicated with the disintegration of the present geographical Manipur, no other insurgency in Manipur can wholly support this concept. Also, over the past decade, ULFA, which has some Rs 500 crores, collected through protection levies, salted away abroad, has apparently been playing host to and educating the children of Kachin (Myanmarese) militants as a kind of partial pay-back for safe havens provided by the Kachin Independence Army (KIA), and training of new ULFA members, for each of whom Rs 50,000 is paid to the KIA. (When earlier under Army pressure hundreds of 'underground' ULFA cadres surrendered, dubbed 'SULFA', during the tenure of the late Chief Minister, Hiteshwar Saikia, he mistakenly allowed them to retain their arms. 'SULFA' have consequently become an 'overground' law and order problem. Both ULFA and SULFA claim to be Robin Hoods, but actually are robbing hoods.) Separately, the hopes after the 1993 Bodo Accord had diminished, due to non-implementation by the government, for various reasons. The banned National Democratic Front of Bodoland (NDFB), and the 300-strong hard-line Bodoland Tigers Liberation Force (BTLF), earlier engaged in a fratricidal war with other Bodo groups, still seek a 'Bodoland', or Udayachal, previously independent but now autonomous, on the north bank of the Brahmaputra, plus two autonomous districts on the south bank, by attacking non-Bodos, even though Bodos are no longer in the majority in the areas sought to be 'Bodoland', being reduced to 18 per cent due to influx from outside. The BTLF has now agreed to a cease-fire. (The influx into Assam continues, Assam having a population density of 287 per sq km, and Bangladesh 800. Sequentially, the Home Ministry note of January 1999 records the ominous emergence in Assam of several Muslim militant organizations such as the Muslim Liberation Front, the Muslim United Liberation Front, the Muslim Liberation Tigers, the Muslim Volunteer Force, and the Islamic Liberation Army.) The Bodo insurgent groups have also cautioned the Royal government of Bhutan against the recently concluded anti-insurgency agreement with India for the removal of Bodo bases from the foothills in Bhutan, but have denied any Bodo hand in the deaths of one Bhutanese major and two soldiers. Simultaneously, cooperating militant organizations are providing fellow insurgents with safe conduits and havens along the Indo-Bangla and Indo-Myanmar borders. In return for such assistance, in a new-found commonality of purpose, the ULFA is assisting the others in their battles with the security forces. To take one recent consequence, as the barbed-wire boundary fence has not made progress, a night curfew has been imposed since August 1998 along the entire 423 km stretch of Meghalaya's border with Bangladesh, to stop the movement of militants and ISI-supplied arms from camps in Bangladesh. The present friendly government in Bangladesh has done much to reduce this militant movement in forested areas, the

Bodos and ULFA, for example, as a result of Bangladeshi pressure, having moved their camps to Bhutan. In January 1999, the Governor of Assam made an appeal for the construction of the barbed-wire fence to be put on a war-footing, in order to curb illegal migration, failing which Assam will become a Muslim-majority state, intelligence reports putting the number of illegal migrants in Assam alone today at four million. Meghalaya's nascent militant organization, the Hynniewtrep National Liberation Council, is not elaborated on, as it is on the run.

To conclude, 1999 ended on a positive note for the Army, after the successful Kargil counteraction, being assured of the weapons systems needed to meet its short and long-term requirements, under 'a strategic partnership' with Russia. The Army will initially receive some 100 of the latest Russian T90 tanks to replace some of the over 30-years old Russian T55 and indigenously-manufactured Vickers 'Vijayanta' tanks, these two types aggregating some one thousand. (Pakistan had earlier in 1999 deployed some 300 Ukrainian tanks.) Some 200 T90 will also be produced indigenously, along with the upgrading of the T72 assembly line, the air defence systems and infantry combat vehicles. Some weapon-locating radars will also be imported. This reassurance on equipment comes after several years of equipment 'famine'. The Army continued to be called out as before for internal security, and also in aid to the civil power in environmental tragedies, like the cyclone in Orissa. Lastly, human rights criticism continues to be of concern to the Army, constantly required to engage insurgents and terrorists. The Indian Army is the largest military laboratory in the world, always in a crucible, whether in war or peace. Indian soldiers are not only the best in the world as the dedication to this book makes clear, but also possibly the most humane, as well-described by Defence Minister George Fernandes. '... in training and motivation, they're second to none ... men and women beyond the narrow divide of caste, region and language—a microcosm of what India should be if it is to achieve the greatness that beckons it.' Yet, social activists miss no opportunity to criticise the Army. Such criticism should be premised on the recognition that there is no armed force in the world, when deployed in aid of the civil authority, where human rights violations have ever been entirely eliminated. Mistakes there will inevitably be. The irony is that the Army is required almost daily to perform the last rites of one or more of its personnel, who die while ensuring the human rights of insurgents and terrorists, the latter in the main targeting civilians, who incur 95 per cent of the casualties in this strife. The Army's efforts, in defence of the country, to restrain terrorists, trained and armed across the border, have on occasions been branded as human rights violations. Country-wide, 30,000 civilians have lost their lives over the past four decades since the onset of the various insurgencies, but often as not this is the result of actions by militants. Conversely, 5,000 personnel of the security forces have lost their lives. Human rights activists adopt a legal formalism that prevents them from discerning the perils the security forces have to face, day in and day out, at the risk of their lives. What of the rights of the personnel of the security forces who have been killed doing their duty? Unfortunately the entire human rights debate is in an adversarial mode, with the social activists deeming themselves as selfless, but viewing the totality of security forces as brutal. At this juncture, when the normal structures of governance in 210 out of 535 districts in the country are under various degrees of pressure, the Prime Minister has in April 2000 asked a group of Cabinet ministers, headed by the Home Minister, 'to review the national security system in its entirety' and to finalise its report within six months. This group also will formulate specific proposals for the implementation of the Kargil Review Committee Report (see the Executive Summary at Appendix 8).

May 2000

Appendices

Appendix 1

Army Chiefs in India

Name	Assumed Command
1. Major Stringer Lawrence	1752
2. Colonel John Adlercron	1754
3. Colonel Robert Clive	December 1756 (And Governor)
4. Major John Caillaud	25 February 1760
5. Major John Carnac	31 December 1760
6. Lieut-Colonel Eyre Coote	April 1761
7. Major Thomas Adams	1763
8. Major John Carnac	January 1764
9. Major Hector Munro	July 1764
10. Brigadier-General John Carnac	January 1765
11. Major-General Robert Lord Clive	April 1765 (And Governor)
12. Colonel Richard Smith	29 January 1767
13. Brigadier-General Sir Robert Barker	24 March 1770
14. Colonel Alexander Chapman	18 January 1774
15. Lieut-General Sir John Clavering, K.B.	2 November 1774
16. Lieut-General Sir Eyre Coote, K.B.	25 March 1779
17. Lieut-General Robert Sloper	21 July 1785
18. Lieut-General Charles Earl Cornwallis, K.G.	12 September 1786 And Governor-General)

19. Major-General Sir Robert
    Abercromby, K.B.   28 October 1793

20. Lieut-General Sir Alured Clarke,
    K.B.   16 March 1797

21. Lieut-General Gerard Lake
    (afterwards Lord Lake)   13 March 1801

22. General Charles
    Marquis Cornwallis,K.G.   30 July 1805 (And
                                                        Governor-General)

23. General Gerard Lord Lake   5 October 1805

24. Lieut-General George Hewitt   17 October 1807

25. Lieut-General Sir George
    Nugent   14 January 1812

26. General Francis, Earl of Moira
    (afterwards Marquis of Hastings)   4 October 1813(And
                                                        Governor- General)

27. Lieut-General the Hon'ble
    Sir Edward Paget, G.C.B.   13 January 1823

28. General Stapleton, Lord
    Combermere, G.C.B.   7 October 1825

29. General George, Earl of Dalhousie,
    G.C.B.   1 January 1830

30. General Sir Edward Barnes,
    G.C.B.   10 January 1832

31. General Lord William H.C. Bentinck,   15 October 1833(And
    G.C.B.   Governor-General)

32. Lieut-General the Hon'ble
    Sir Henry Fane, G.C.B.   5 September 1835

33. Major-General Sir Jasper Nicolls,
    K.C.B.   7 December 1839

34. General Sir Hugh Gough, Bart,
    G.C.B. (afterwards Lord Gough)   8 August 1843

35. General Sir Charles James Napier,
    G.C.B.   7 May 1849

36. General Sir William Maynard Gomm,
    K.C.B.   6 December 1850

37. General the Hon'ble George
    Anson   23 January 1856
38. Lieut-General Sir Patrick Grant,
    K.C.B.   17 June 1857
    (Officiating)
39. General Sir Colin Campbell, G.C.B.
    (afterwards Lord Clyde)   13 August 1857
40. General Sir Hugh H. Rose,
    G.C.B.   4 June 1860
41. General Sir William Rose Mansfield,
    K.C.B.   23 March 1865
42. General Lord Napier of Magdala,
    G.C.B., G.C.S.I.   9 April 1870
43. General Sir Fred. P. Haines,
    K.C.B.   10 April 1876
44. General Sir Donald M. Stewart,
    G.C.B., C.I.E.   8 April 1881
45. General Sir Fred. S. Roberts,
    V.C., G.C.B., C.I.E.   28 November 1885
46. General Sir Geo. S. White,
    V.C., G.C.I.E., K.C.B.   8 April 1893
47. Lieut.-General Sir Charles Edward
    Nairne, K.C.B.   20 March 1898
    (Provisional)
48. General Sir W.S.A. Lockhart,
    G.C.B., K.C.S.I.   4 November 1898
49. General Sir A.P. Palmer, K.C.B.   19 March 1900
50. General Viscount Kitchener of
    Khartoum, G.C.B., O.M., G.C.M.G. 28 November 1902
51. General Sir O'Moore Creagh,
    V.C., G.C.B.   10 September 1909
52. General Sir B. Duff, G.C.B., G.C.S.I.,
    K.C.V.O., C.I.E.   8 March 1914
53. General Sir C.C. Monro, G.C.S.I.,
    G.C.M.G., K.C.B.   1 October 1916

54. General Lord Rawlinson of Trent,
    G.C.B., G.C.V.O., K.C.M.G.,
    A.D.C.   21 November 1920
55. Field Marshal Sir William Birdwood,
    G.C.B., G.C.S.I., K.C.M.G., D.S.O.   6 August 1925
56. Field Marshal Sir Philip Chetwode,
    G.C.B., G.C.S.I., K.C.M.G., D.S.O.   30 November 1930
57. General Sir Robert Cassells,
    G.C.B., G.C.S.I., D.S.O.   29 November 1935
58. General Sir Claude Auchinleck, G.C.I.E.,
    C.B., C.S.I., D.S.O., O.B.E.   27 January 1941
59. General Sir Archibald Wavell, G.C.B.,
    C.M.G., M.C.   11 July 1941
60. General Sir Alan Hartley, G.C.I.E.,
    G.C.B., D.S.O.   17 January 1942
61. Field Marshal Sir Archibald Wavell,
    G.C.B., C.M.G., M.C.
    (Second term)   7 March 1942
62. Field Marshal Sir Claude
    Auchinleck, G.C.I.E., G.C.B.,
    C.S.I., D.S.O., O.B.E.
    (Second term)   20 June 1943 to
                                             14 August 1947

63. General Sir Rob Lockhart, K.C.B,
    C.I.E, M.C   15 August 1947 to
                                             31 December 1947

64. General Sir Roy Bucher, K.B.E,
    C.B, M.C   01 January 1948 to
                                             14 January 1949

65. General (later Field Marshal)
    K.M. Cariappa, O.B.E.   15 January 1949 to
                                             14 January 1953
66. General Maharaj Rajendra Sinhji,   15 January 1953 to
    D.S.O.   14 May 1955
67. General S.M. Shrinagesh   15 May 1955 to
                                             07 May 1957

Appendices

68. General K.S. Thimayya, D.S.O.   08 May 1957 to
                                           07 May 1961
69. General P.N. Thapar   08 May 1961 to
                                           19 November 1962
70. General J.N. Chaudhuri   20 November 1962
                                           to 07 June 1966
71. General P.P. Kumaramangalam,   08 June 1966 to
    D.S.O.   07 June 1969
72. General S.H.F.J. Manekshaw, M.C.   08 June 1969 to
                                           31 December 1972

    Field Marshal S.H.F.J. Manekshaw,
    M.C.   01 January 1973 to
                                           14 January 1973
73. General G.G. Bewoor, P.V.S.M.   15 January 1973 to
                                           31 May 1975
74. General T.N. Raina, M.V.C.   01 June 1975 to
                                           31 May 1978
75. General O.P. Malhotra, P.V.S.M.   01 June 1978 to
                                           31 May 1981
76. General K.V. Krishna Rao, P.V.S.M.   01 June 1981 to
                                           31 July 1983
77. General A.S. Vaidya, P.V.S.M.,   01 August 1983 to
    M.V.C.**, A.V.S.M   31 January 1986
78. General K. Sundarji, P.V.S.M.,   01 February 1986 to
    A.D.C.   30 April 1988
79. General V.N. Sharma, P.V.S.M.,   01 May 1988 to
    A.V.S.M., A.D.C.   30 June 1990
80. General S.F. Rodrigues, P.V.S.M.,   01 July 1990 to
    V.S.M., A.D.C.   30 June 1993
81. General B.C. Joshi, P.V.S.M.,   01 July 1993 to
    A.V.S.M., A.D.C.   18 November 1994
82. General S. Roychowdhury,   22 November 1994 to
    P.V.S.M., A.D.C.   30 September 1997
83. General V.P. Malik, P.V.S.M.,   01 October 1997
    A.V.S.M., A.D.C.

Appendix 2

Division Head Quarters Peshawar 3 June 1857

Sir,

I have the honor to report for the information of the Chief Commissioner of the Punjab that I have this day before a General Parade ordered for the purpose caused the extreme penalty of the Law to be carried out by hanging in the cases of 2 Havildars, 2 Naiks, and 8 Sepoys of the 51st Regiment N.I. convicted by a General Court Martial of Desertion.

One Havildar and two Sepoys were also sentenced to death, I have considered it expedient to commute the sentence of the Havildar to one year's imprisonment with hard labor, and that of the Sepoys to transportation for Life.

A nominal Roll of the above mentioned individuals together with the English translation of an address to the Native Troops on Parade prior to the Execution, is forwarded for submission to the Chief Commissioner.

I have etc.
Sd. Sydney Cotton (Brig)
Comdg the Peshawar Division

Appendices

To

Capt H.R. James
Offg. Sec. to the Chief Commr. Punjab.

English Translation

Address to the Native Regiments assembled on Parade for the purpose of witnessing the Execution of 12 Sepoys of 51st Regiment N.I. delivered by order of Brigadier Sydney Cotton Commanding Peshawar Division.

Soldiers, for upwards of a hundred years, the Native Army had served the Government with devotion and fidelity wherever and whenever there has been War. Sepoys have fought side by side with their Officers. In the Deccan, Afghanistan, Burmah and Punjaub, their gallantry has been conspicuous. The Government to Reward such services has extended its kindness and liberality to the native Soldier—Pay, Extra Pay, Hutting Batta, Pensions, Family Pensions, Good Conduct Pay, have one after another added for their benefit, and paid punctually, without exception, to those deserving such boons.

Notwithstanding in the last few months, Regiments having attended to the falsehoods of evil disposed men, have abandoned their allegiance to Government, and openly mutinied, on the pretext only, that Government has intended to convert them forcibly from their religions. But what an infamous falsehood! what a gross misrepresentation! who dares to impute to the Government such an intention? Such never has been, nor will be, all well know that during the period of the English rule, in this Country, from generation to generation the Mussulman sounds his call to prayers, and the Hindoo worships according to his religion. Every individual pursues his devotions without molestation in accordance with the tenets of his religion.

But these deluded fools, these unfortunate wretches without consulting their own interest, having listened to the falsehoods and fabrications of base villains have become Guilty of the most heinous Crimes.

567

At the Stations of Meerut, Delhi, Umballa and Ferozepore, Regiments have mutinied and have committed Murder, Plunder and Arson, Sepoys have deserted, have been insolent to their Officers and have openly defied authority.

Government has heard of these Outrages Committed by the Soldiers so liberally paid by it and has determined upon retributions, such atrocious crimes shall henceforth be put down by a strong hand and adequate punishments shall be dealt out without mercy.

In the 51st Regiment N.I. 250 Sepoys with the Subadar Major of the Corps deserted into the District and towards the Hills. Many of these have been killed, and the remainder in confinement, the Subadar Major was executed before you the other day for the great crime of Desertion and now you will witness the extreme penalty of the law carried out in the case of 12 more sepoys of this Regiment for the same offence, are these men who have forsaken their allegiance better off for their misdeed?

The 55th Regiment N.I. Mutinied at Murdan and deserted towards the Hills, behold their reward! Many Hindoos have been forcibly converted to Mahomedanism, many are wandering about trembling for their lives, and dying from starvation, the remainder are now in Confinement awaiting the penalties of their Mutinous and Treacherous conduct.

So long as Sepoys serve obediently and faithfully and behave themselves properly, the Government will always look to their interest and welfare, but if they commit crimes of Mutiny and desertion, such as have lately taken place in the Native Army, the severest penalties of the law shall most certainly in all cases be inflicted to the fullest extent.

True translation

Peshawar
3rd June 1857

Sd. J. Wright, Captain
Dy Asst. Adj. Genl.

Appendix 3

NAI, Foreign Political Consultations, No. 3022, 31 December 1858

PROCLAMATION ISSUED BY THE BEGUM IN BIRJIS QADR'S NAME

At this time certain weak-minded foolish people have spread a report that the English have forgiven the faults and crimes of the people of Hindoostan; this appears very astonishing, for it is the unvarying custom of the English never to forgive a fault, be it great or small; so much so, that if a small offence be committed through ignorance or negligence, they never forgive it.

The Proclamation of the 10th November 1858, which has come before us, is perfectly clear, and as some foolish people, not understanding the real object of the Proclamation, have been carried away, therefore, we, the ever abiding Government, Parents of the people of Oudh, with great consideration put forth the present Proclamation, in order that the real object of the chief points may be exposed, and our subjects be placed on their guard.

First. It is written in the Proclamation, that the country of Hindoostan which was held in trust by the Company, has been resumed by the Queen, and that for the future, the Queen's Laws shall be obeyed. This is not to be trusted by our religious subjects; for the Laws of the Company, the Settlement of the Company, the English Servants of the Company, the Governor General, and the Judicial administration of the Company, are all unchanged; what then is there new which can benefit the people or on which they can rely?

Second. In the Proclamation, it is written that all contracts and agreements entered into by the Company will be accepted by the Queen. Let the people carefully observe this artifice. The Company has seized on the whole of Hindoostan, and if this arrangement be accepted, what is then new in it? The Company professed to treat the Chief of Bhurtpoor as a son, and then took his Territory; the Chief of Lahore was carried off to London, and it has not fallen to his lot to return; the Nawab Shumshooddeen Khan on one side they hanged, and on the other side they took off their hats and salaamed to him; the Peishwa they expelled from Poonah Sitara, and imprisoned for life in Bithoor; their breach of faith with Sultan Tippoo, is well known, the Rajah of Banares they imprisoned in Agra. Under pretence of administering the Country of the Chief of Gwalior, they introduced English customs; they have left no name or traces of the Chiefs of Behar, Orissa and Bengal; they gave the Raes of   Furruckabad a small monthly allowance, and took his territory, Shahjehanpoor, Bareilly, Azimgarh, Jounpoor, Goruckpoor, Etawa, Allahabad, Futtehpoor &c. our ancient possessions, they took from us on pretence of distributing pay; and in the 7th Article of the Treaty, they wrote on Oath, that they would take no more from us, if then the arrangements made by the Company are to be accepted, what is the difference between the former and the present state of things? These are old affairs; but recently in defiance of treaties and oaths and notwithstanding that they owed us millions of rupees, without reason, and on the pretence of the mis-Government and discontent of our people, they took our country and property worth millions of rupees. If our people were discontented with our Royal predecessor Wajid Ally Shah, how come it they are content with us? And no ruler ever experienced such loyalty and devotion of life and goods as we have done! What then is wanting that they do not restore our country.

Further, it is written in the Proclamation, that they want no increase of Territory, but yet they cannot refrain from annexation. If the Queen has assumed the Government why does Her Majesty not restore our Country to us, when our people wish it? It is well known that no King or Queen ever punished a whole Army and people for rebellion; all were forgiven; and the wise cannot approve of punishing the whole Army and people of Hindoostan; for so long as the word 'punishment' remains, the disturbances will not be suppressed. There is a well known proverb 'a dying man is desperate' (Murta, Kya na Kurta) it is impossible that a thousand should attack a million, and the thousand escape.

Third. In the Proclamation it is written that the Christian religion is true, but no other creed will suffer oppression, and that the Laws will be observed towards all. What has the administration of Justice to do with the truth, or falsehood of a religion? That religion is true which acknowledges one God, and knows no other; when there are three Gods in a religion, neither Mussulmans nor Hindoos, nay—not even Jews, Sun worshippers, or fire worshippers, can believe it true. To eat pigs, and drink wine, to bite greased cartridges, and to mix pigs' fat with flour and sweet-meats, to destroy Hindoo & Mussulman temples on pretence of making roads, to build Churches, to send clergymen into the streets and alleys to preach the Christian religion, to institute English schools, and pay people a monthly stipend for learning the English Services, while the places of worship of Hindoos & Mussulmans are to this day entirely neglected; with all this, how can the people believe that religion will not be interfered with? The rebellion began with religion, and for it millions of men have been killed. Let not our subjects be deceived; thousands were deprived of their religion in the North West, and thousands were hanged rather than abandon their religion.

Fourth. It is written in the Proclamation that they who harboured rebels, or who were leaders of rebels, or who caused men to rebel, shall have their lives, but that punishment shall be awarded after deliberation, and that murderers and abettors of murderers, shall have no mercy shown them; while all others shall be forgiven, any foolish person can see, that under this Proclamation, no one, be he guilty or innocent, can escape; everything is written and yet nothing is written but they have clearly written that they will not let off any one implicated; and in whatever Village or Estate the army may have halted, the inhabitants of that place cannot escape. We are deeply concerned for the condition of our people on reading this Proclamation, which palpably teems with enmity. We now issue a distinct order, and one that may be trusted that all subjects who may have foolishly presented themselves as heads of Villages to the English, shall before the 1st of January must present themselves in our camp, without doubt their faults shall be forgiven them, and they shall be treated according to their merits. To believe in this Proclamation it is only necessary to remember, that Hindoostanee rulers are

571

altogether kind and merciful. Thousands have seen this, Millions have heard it. No one has ever seen in a dream that the English forgave an offence.

Fifthly. In this Proclamation it is written that when peace is restored Public Works, such as roads and canals will be made in order to improve the condition of the people. It is worthy of a little reflection that they have promised no better employment for Hindoostanies than making roads and digging canals. If people cannot see clearly what this means, there is no help for them. Let no subject be deceived by the Proclamation.

Appendix 4

Dear Sir Claude,   12 September 1946

As you know, I am greatly interested in problems of defence, more specially in relation to foreign policy. I have today drafted a note for the Secretary of the Defence Department mentioning some matters in my mind. I shall put this up before the Cabinet after the Defence Member arrives here and has given consideration to my note. I am sending you a copy of this note (reproduced below) as, being head of the Army in India, you are naturally very intimately concerned with its future.

Yours sincerely,
Jawaharlal Nehru

H.E.Field Marshal Sir Claude Auchinleck,
GCIE., GCB., CSI., DSO., OBE., ADC.,
Commander-in-Chief in India,
New Delhi

There are several important matters which will have to be considered very soon by the full Cabinet. Some of these involve considerations of foreign policy, others concern the future of the Indian Army. I suppose all these matters will have to be reviewed at an early date by the various Committees of the Defence Department, the Defence Committee of India and ultimately by the Cabinet, and policies will be laid down of the future. We have been waiting for the arrival of the new Defence Member because obviously it is desirable for all these matters to be considered in his presence. It is unfortunate that there has been some delay already in dealing with them. I suggest that the War Department and the other Departments concerned should prepare themselves with all the necessary papers, notes, etc. for this formal consideration of future policy, so that everything should be ready by the time the Defence Member comes. I take it that he will be here within a week at the most. At the first Cabinet meeting after his arrival these matters can be considered.

It is obvious that one of our first tasks, as a national Government based on popular approval, is to attempt to transform the whole background of the Indian Army and make it feel that it is a national army of India. It was impossible for this to be done in the past because the whole conception of the Indian Army was different and the average soldier fought far more in terms of an external allegiance than of allegiance to his own country.

The Indian Army, as is well known and recognised throughout the world, consists of a very fine body of men of whom any country can be proud. That is a great asset for us and we should preserve this asset and not allow it to deteriorate in any way. It would be a great pity if communal feelings spread in the Indian Army because these would inevitably lead to a weakening of the structure as well as a deterioration in morale. Our policy must therefore be aimed at keeping the Army away from such communal feelings as far as possible. While we have necessarily to pay attention to fair representation in the Army of the different communities in India, it should be made perfectly clear that the ultimate criteria are merit and capacity. It is now I think well recognised that we should give up the idea of some people of India belonging to martial races and therefore being particularly suited for the Army, and others belonging to non-martial races. This distinction must disappear and we must deal with the whole of India on the same basis.

I have mentioned above the necessity for making the Army feel that it is a national army of India. This means that a deliberate attempt should be made to make them feel so and to make them realise that their service and their allegiance is primarily due to their own country. They must be made to feel proud of their country and to believe in its great future. They must realise that it is their onerous and honourable duty to guard this country from aggression and foreign intrusion so that the country may develop rapidly and take its proper place in the world.

While it is therefore necessary to infuse a new nationalist spirit in the ranks of the Indian Army, it is equally necessary to make the Indian public feel that the army is theirs and is not some kind of hostile force imposed on them. They should be proud of their army and it should be an honour for any Indian to belong to that army. Fortunately some change has been visible in the attitude of the Indian public generally towards the Indian Army. This should be encouraged in every way. Thus the Indian Army and the public generally will come closer to each other and the barriers which have divided them in the past will disappear. The army as such of course should remain apart from politics.

If we are to develop, as we must, a national army in India (and army of course includes here navy and airforce) that army must be manned by Indian nationals from top to bottom. A national army has no place for non-nationals except as experts and advisers. Generally speaking this policy has been accepted but the process of change has been remarkably slow. This has to be speeded up and in future where foreign help is necessary this should be as far as possible in the nature of expert and advisory help.

The army carries out the policy of the Government. During the past that policy has been largely controlled from London. In future the foreign policy of India and of course the domestic policy also will be progressively an independent policy controlled by the Indian National Government. That policy will endeavour to co-operate wherever possible with British policy, but it may not be dictated to by British foreign policy. Its sole aim must be the good of India and of the Indian people and the maintenance of peace in India and abroad.

Unfortunately the army has to be used sometimes for quelling domestic disorders. All soldiers hate this kind of work. It is against their self-respect and is bad for the morale of the army. Nevertheless sometimes this becomes an essential duty of the army, when disorders cannot be controlled by the Police whose normal duty this is. It would be desirable, wherever necessary, to increase the Police force or to form special peace preservation corps for this particular purpose so as to relieve the army as far as possible of this distasteful duty.

The Indian Army has often been used against the tribesmen of the North West Frontier. Only recently the air arm has been used for this purpose in Waziristan. Fortunately human casualties were very few and I am very happy to learn that these operations have ended and some kind of settlement is on the point of being reached. This matter raises broad questions of policy. Bombing of civilians or backward people who have no protection against this form of attack is peculiarly objectionable. For many years past bombing of the Frontier has been bitterly criticised in India and even abroad. There is a strong military case for this form of action as it is rapid, far less expensive and usually does not involve many casualties. Nevertheless, it is extraordinarily difficult for public opinion in India or elsewhere to approve of it and it has become an urgent matter to consider this policy as a whole and to revise it. Some other way will have to be found to deal with recalcitrant tribesmen. It is obvious that murder cannot be tolerated nor can kidnapping or ransom. This kind of thing has to be met firmly and put down. At the same time the approach has to be a friendly one. In an attempt to gain the co-operation of the tribes quick results may not be obtained but I have little doubt that the foundation will be laid thereby for future co-operation and this problem of a hundred years old standing will be far nearer solution. However that may be, it must be recognised that bombing of these areas or of any civilians is abhorrent to public opinion and no national government can indulge in it except possibly in cases of extreme crisis and danger.

When we talk of a National Army in India it naturally follows that the British Army in India should no longer remain here for any purpose, including Frontier defence. India must make her own arrangements for her defence and the British Army has to leave India as rapidly as possible. This need not wait for the deliberations of the Constituent Assembly. It is recognised by all concerned, including the British Government, that we are all aiming at the independence of India. Independence with foreign troops on the soil of India would be a travesty and a farce. Therefore all foreign troops have to be withdrawn though a certain number of British officers may remain here by agreement for a period.

All questions of defence are today in a fluid state because of rapid developments in the science of warfare. It is quite conceivable that our present methods of warfare may become completely out of date within 10 years or so owing to scientific research. The coming of atomic energy and the possibility of our using cosmic rays are revolutionizing the whole conception of life as it is lived today and will have the most powerful effects on the whole structure of modern civilization. Those effects will be specially notable in regard to war. It may be that war itself may become an impossible way of handling human problems. However that may be, it is obvious that any effective war machine must have behind it a high stage of industrialization and scientific research both extensive and intensive. No country which is not industrialized can carry on war for long, however good the army might be. No country which has not got its scientific research in all its forms and of the highest standing, can compete in industry or in war with another. This leads to the conclusion that scientific research must be organised on the broadest scale.

A very important matter which will have to be considered soon is the employment of Indian troops overseas. I gather that they are spread out at present in the following places: Japan, Hong Kong, Malaya, Siam, Netherlands East Indies, Burma, Borneo, Ceylon, Iraq, Middle East and Italy. It is not obvious to me why Indian troops should do

577

the policeman's job in various countries. It may be that for the moment they may be necessary in the period of transition from war to peace conditions in some places. I think it is highly undesirable for Indian troops to be employed outside the frontiers of India. The fine body of men that comprise the Indian Army have been admired abroad but at the same time they have been disliked often enough as representing foreign domination. We seek to dominate no foreign country, we want to be friends with other peoples. It may be that on occasions of crisis we may have to take some abnormal step but the general policy must be one of withdrawal of Indian troops from overseas.

In particular this question arises in regard to the Netherlands East Indies and Iraq. In both these cases public opinion has vigorously objected and many months ago it was stated that Indian troops would be withdrawn from the Netherlands East Indies. It is well known that Indian sympathies are with the Indonesian Republic and when the occasion comes for it this Republic will be formally recognised by the Indian Government. If this is so, then it is an offence against our national policy and public opinion in India to keep any Indian troops in the Netherlands East Indies. I understand they are being withdrawn but apparently this is being done to suit the convenience of the Dutch authorities. Why we should accommodate the Dutch who are playing the role of an aggressor and dominating power in Indonesia, I do not understand. We have no sympathy with the Dutch there and we think that they are wholly in the wrong. We should help them in no way at all. Therefore the withdrawal of Indian troops from the Netherlands East Indies must be expedited. During this brief interval while they are there, it must be made perfectly clear that they are to be used in no way against the people of Indonesia or to the embarrassment of the Indonesian Republic. This should be made perfectly clear both to the Dutch and the Indonesian Republic.

In Iraq Indian troops have been recently sent ostensibly to protect the oilfields there which supply oil and petrol to India. It is certainly desirable to protect our oil supplies but it appears to me dangerous policy to give small and inadequate protection and at the same time to gain the ill will of other countries. Thus Iran, on the borders of Iraq, has protested against our sending troops to Basra. Obviously the presence of Indian troops there may be considered as a continuous provocation in the international field. We are not concerned with the internal politics of Iran or with those of any other country. We are not in a position to police other countries, and we should not get embroiled in international conflicts and manoeuvres. Therefore this business of sending or keeping troops in Iraq for use in Iran should be ended.

In this note I have referred to many aspects of our army, army policy and foreign affairs. They touch each other. There are many other matters concerning the Indian Army in which the Government is interested and in regard to which it desires changes. But I do not wish to burden this note any further. The immediate questions before us are a change in the whole outlook of the Indian Army making it national in reality and more in accord with public sentiment, the withdrawal of the British forces from India, and the withdrawal of Indian troops from abroad, more specially from the Netherlands East Indies and Iraq.

All these matters will have to be considered by the Cabinet finally, but before that is done the various other Committees and Departments involved should consider them and be ready with their notes and papers. The Defence Member will, I hope, also give his earnest consideration to these important problems.

Defence Secretary   *12.9.46*
                                                            (J. Nehru)

Appendix 5

The Military Implications of Pakistan

24th April, 1947

You asked me the other day to give you my opinion on the strategic implications of the setting up of an independent Pakistan. I enclose a note which sets out the situation as I see it, taking a long-term view of the problem.

I also enclose a note written by my Deputy Chief of the General Staff setting out a view which might well be taken by the advocates of Pakistan. In my opinion, this view is really a short-term one and does not take into account the potentialities of the future...

His Excellency Rear Admiral The Rt Hon'ble Auchinleck
Viscount Mountbatten of Burma, KG, GMSI,
GMIE, GCVO, KCB, DSO

*

THE MILITARY IMPLICATIONS OF PAKISTAN

This paper is based on the following assumptions:
a)That India is split into two sovereign independent States—Pakistan and Hindustan, with boundaries as shown in the attached map.

b)That neither Pakistan nor Hindustan remain within the British Commonwealth of Nations, though either or both may be in close treaty relationship with it.

As will be seen from the map, the two regions of Pakistan, that is the western region and the eastern region, are separated from each other by some 1500 miles.

It is true that this gap is traversed by reasonably adequate rail and road communications, but these would be completely controlled by Hindustan and available for the use of Pakistan only by the goodwill of Hindustan, who could close them at any time if she so desired. The same conditions would apply to the passage of fighting aircraft wishing to pass between the two regions, as the use of facilities such as airfield, refuelling stations, and radar would depend entirely on the goodwill of Hindustan.

Any idea of a 'corridor' such as the Polish corridor can be discarded as quite impracticable.

By sea, the movement of Pakistan forces between the two regions would be an extremely dangerous operation if Hindustan were hostile.

Any strategic co-operation, except to a limited extent by aircraft between the two regions, would be most difficult, if not impossible, in the event of strained relations between Pakistan and Hindustan.

*

EASTERN PAKISTAN

a)It would seem that at the most the Eastern region of Pakistan cannot include a greater area than that comprised of Bengal east of the Brahmaputra and Assam, and this is the area shown on the map. This would have practically no resources of any strategical value, and its Muslim inhabitants have few war-like traditions, though they enlisted in considerable strength in the last war in transport and pioneer units. Their officer-producing potential appears to be negligible at present. Rail and road communications in the region are poor and ill-adapted for purposes of defence against aggression. There is one port, Chittagong, which, though of small capacity, reached a high standard of efficiency under British military direction during the last war. There are no mineral resources, factories, repair shops or any establishments which could contribute to the upkeep of Armed Forces. There are, however, a number of airfields constructed during the last war for the Allied Air Forces operating over Burma but the upkeep of any airfield would involve a considerable expenditure.

b) The region would be open to attack by land from the North, though communications are not highly developed, and also from the West though a land attack on this front would entail crossing the Brahmaputra—not an easy operation. A serious land attack from the East can be ruled out owing to the lack of roads through the Lushai hills, though an enemy advance against Chittagong from the South, as attempted by the Japanese in the last war, is a possibility.

c) By air the region could be attacked from hostile air bases to the North-East and West, and its defence would need air forces and anti-aircraft defences out of all proportion to its size or importance.

d) Attack from the sea would always be a possibility and could be given reasonably close support from short-based aircraft. A combined operation by an enemy against Chittagong would have to be guarded against, and this would entail the provision of seaward and anti-aircraft defences on a considerable scale.

e)Altogether, the effort involved in providing adequate defence against aggression for this region would seem to be out of all proportion to its economic or strategic value, and certainly could not be provided from the resources available in the region itself. Help would have to be sought from the Western region of Pakistan on a large scale.

*

WESTERN PAKISTAN

a)The Western region of Pakistan, as will be seen from the map, would consist of a long narrow stretch of country lying between the high tablelands and mountains of Baluchistan and Afghanistan and the plains of the Eastern Punjab. In fact it comprises the valley of the Indus and its Westernmost tributaries: the Jhelum, the Chenab and the Ravi.

The region being all length without breadth is basically difficult to defend from the strategic point of view. Whether attack should come from the West or the East, there is a lack of depth so essential in modern war to success of any defensive plan.

The average width of the region is about 300 miles only, except in the extreme South, while the distance from Karachi to Rawalpindi is about 700 miles.

If Kashmir is to be included in the region, the distance from Karachi to the Northern frontier where it meets the Pamirs would be about 1100 miles.

The region is well provided with rail communications, especially in the Northern part but the general trend of these communications, as will be seen from the map, is North and South, whereas any large scale attack by land is bound to come from the West or the East.

Moreover these communications all converge into a bottle-neck on the lower Indus about Sukkur and Hyderabad (Sind) before running into Karachi.

Karachi is the only channel through which supplies and munitions can come direct by sea from the outside world, so that if the main North and South communications are severed about Hyderabad or Sukkur, the northern part of the region will be entirely cut off from all direct overseas sources of supply. Should the neighbouring States to the West and East be hostile, or even if one were hostile and the other not, the procurement of munitions and supplies overland across the Western or Eastern frontiers would be a long and most uncertain business, dependent entirely on the goodwill of the neighbouring State—Afghanistan or Hindustan—to provide the necessary transit facilities.

b)The region would be particularly vulnerable to attack from the air, either from the West or the East, and the lack of depth on which stress has already been laid would make a really efficient defence against such attack almost impossible under modern conditions. The advantage would all be on the side of the aggressor.

c)The general trend of the four big rivers from North to South, though it may be held to provide successive lines of defence against attacks by land from the West or the East, is really more of a disadvantage than an advantage, owing to the handicap it would place on the free movement of troops and stores within the region, bridges over these rivers being few and far between and vulnerable to air attack or sabotage.

d)The region contains practically none of the natural resources on which a country must depend for success in war, except wheat and cotton and a little oil near Attock. There is the possibility of more oil being found, but so far no definite proof of this.

There are no minerals and practically no industrial plants except at Karachi where there is ship repair industry. There are certain railway workshops which might in war be turned over to make munitions but their capacity is infinitesimal by modern standards.

e)Attack by land forces across the Northern sector of the Eastern frontier, that is on the general front Jullundur-Bhatinda, would present no serious difficulty to an aggressor. In fact an advance on this front would be well served by rail and road communications leading directly to the main supply bases in the interior of Hindustan and could be well supported from the air.

Large scale attack by land on the Southern part of the Eastern frontier, that is from Bhatinda South-West-wards to Jodhpur, is not so likely, but there is nothing to prevent small hard hitting and mobile motorized enemy forces from striking across the frontier towards Multan, and the main line of railway connecting

Lahore with Karachi. In fact this form of enemy activity based on the Rajputana railway system would be almost certain to eventuate.

f)From the West, the most serious threat by land is likely to be against Quetta and then down the Bolan Pass against the communications bottle-neck at Sukkur, the capture of which by an attacker would go far to paralyse the defence.

In these days of fast-moving and hard-hitting armies, which can be supplied from the air, a serious land offensive along the Makran Coast through Kalat and Las Bela against Karachi is by no means an impossibility, and adequate provision would have to be made against it. Should an aggressor attain complete superiority in the air which is quite possible in certain circumstances, a hostile land advance would also be possible through the Khyber Pass directly against Peshawar, but this is unlikely to be attempted so long as some vestige of air power is left in the defence.

g)A combined operation by the enemy for the direct capture of Karachi is always a possibility, and such an operation could be easily supported by shore-based aircraft from airfields in Kathiawar and South Western Rajputana. Seaward and anti-aircraft defences, including Radar warning system, would be needed on a large scale for the defence of Karachi.

h)The sea routes leading to Karachi would be open to continuous seaborne and airborne attacks from enemy bases in the Persian Gulf and on the West Coast of India, and there is little doubt that this line of supply would be most unreliable if the enemy knows his business.

i)To sum up, it may be said that the Western region of Pakistan would be strategically and economically most unfitted, at least for a long time to come, to withstand attack by any power possessing even relatively small modern armed forces and that its isolation from the outside world would be almost a certainty in a comparatively short period after the outbreak of hostilities.

The only sources of supply to which Pakistan can look for the procurement of the munitions and supplies essential in war lie in the great industrial areas of Europe, Russia, or the United States, all of which are separated from both regions of Pakistan by thousands of miles of sea or by long land routes practically devoid of any means of transit.

From the purely military and strategical aspect, which is the only angle from which the problem has been viewed in this paper, it must be concluded that the provision of adequate insurance in the shape of reasonably good defensive arrangements for Pakistan would be a most difficult and expensive business, and that no guarantee of success could be given.

*

NOTE BY DCGS(A) ON THE PAPER "MILITARY IMPLICATIONS OF PAKISTAN"

(Written from the point of view of Pakistan)

The paper appreciates the defence of Pakistan from the military and strategical aspect, and very clearly and adequately states the weakness of Pakistan in the event of aggression across her several frontiers.

In my view, however, a Muslim League appreciation of the defence problem facing Pakistan would take account of certain other factors, mainly political, not referred to in this paper.

I have therefore written in the following paragraphs what I think such an appreciation would contain. A consideration of these points may be of some help to the C-in-C should the appreciation have to be argued out with the politicians.

The possible enemies of Pakistan can be conveniently considered in three groups -
      a)   Russia.
      b)   Afghanistan, Persia, Burma.
      c)   The Independent Frontier tribes and Hindustan.

Russia

Neither a united nor a divided India can defend herself against Russia. Any such defence can only be done politically through the UNO of which Pakistan will be a member. The successful political defence by Persia against Russian aggression in Azerbaijan is an example.
The provision of Armed Forces designed to defend Pakistan against Russia is therefore not contemplated.

a) Afghanistan

Pakistan would expect to have a mutual non-aggression treaty with Afghanistan. Even so, she must be prepared to deal with an Afghan incursion into Pakistan territory should this pact be broken. The routes by which such incursion can take place are few, and there is no reason to suppose that a Pakistan army, with all the advantages in experience and training which their officers and men would have, could not defeat such aggression if they were kept concentrated and well handled.

It is, however, considered that hostile action by Afghanistan is more likely to be confined to stirring up tribal trouble in Independent territory.

b) Persia

Short of an attempt to capture the port Karachi, an attack by Persia would serve little purpose. The Persian Army is considered quite incapable of sustaining any offensive that would bring her within reach of the River Indus. Persian armour is of little or no military value and they could not support any such offensive by air. Pakistan is, on its South-Western front, very well protected by the Baluchistan desert, and in this respect the vital port of Karachi is very favourably situated.

c) Burma

For many years to come there will be no Burmese Army capable of carrying out any large offensive against Eastern Pakistan. Burma will require all her military resources for competing with her own internal problems. While a minor operation against Chittagong is possible, Chittagong is much easier to defend than attack. The approaches to Chittagong are bad, and the military garrison of Eastern Pakistan should be well able to defeat the small forces that could be brought against it.

Reinforcement from Western Pakistan would indeed be long and difficult, and Eastern Pakistan would have to rely on its permanent garrison provided from Western Pakistan plus a certain number of infantry battalions that could be raised from the tribes in the hill tracts south of Assam.

The NWF and Hindustan

None of the above appear to constitute the main problem that will confront Pakistan during those difficult first years when she is finding her feet and organizing her slender resources. The real problem lies in controlling the frontier tribes in the NW and in defeating any aggression by Hindustan.

There is good reason to believe that these two would not take place together, forcing Pakistan to fight on two fronts. Any Hindustan aggression into Pakistan would call for a Jehad to which our co-religionists on the frontier may be expected to respond at least with neutrality, leaving the Pakistan forces free to deal with Hindustan.

But even when these threats are considered separately, neither will be easy for Pakistan to counter. Pakistan can ill afford to pay and employ the tribesmen as the British have done, and it would be no exaggeration to say that any serious frontier trouble would fully occupy all the armed forces that Pakistan could maintain, and leave her incapable of resisting any simultaneous attack from Hindustan. Therefore, even though an attack by Hindustan might well result in the stopping of any frontier disturbances, it might then be too late for Pakistan to turn to protect herself against Hindustan.

The main enemy of Pakistan will be Hindustan, but we think that a concerted attack on Pakistan, sponsored by a Hindustan Government, is unlikely. A Hindustan Government as a member of the UNO would be unwilling to face the UNO as an aggressor. What is far more likely is that parts of Hindustan, e.g. the Sikhs, might become inflamed over some question of the treatment of minorities and take independent action.

If this is so, then it is probably unlikely that the Pakistan forces, in countering this threat, would be called upon to fight on all her frontiers with Hindustan.

It will be agreed that Pakistan is economically a poor country, and that her resources are small. But it can be argued that she will be no poorer than Afghanistan or Persia, who have successfully retained their independence and preserved their nationality through two World Wars.

At the worst, Pakistan can have an army equal to the armies of Afghanistan, Persia, or Burma. Within the whole international set-up, why then should she be in a worse position to defend herself? I suggest that the above is, in outline, the sort of view of the situation that the advocates of Pakistan will take. They will refuse to consider the situation in terms of any threat from a first-class power or in terms of armoured forces or air offensives. They will regard their defence problem in terms of some local third-class war which will be settled one way or another with infantry and artillery.

Appendix 6

Sardar Patel's Letter to the Prime Minister
November 7, 1950

My dear Jawaharlal,

Ever since my return from Ahmedabad and after the Cabinet meeting the same day which I had to attend at practically fifteen minutes' notice and for which I regret I was not able to read all the papers, I have been anxiously thinking over the problem of Tibet and I thought I should share with you what is passing through my mind.

I have carefully gone through the correspondence between the External Affairs Ministry and our Ambassador in Peking and through him the Chinese Government. I have tried to pursue this correspondence as favourably to our Ambassador and the Chinese Government as possible, but I regret to say that neither of them comes out well as a result of this study.

The Chinese Government have tried to delude us by professions of peaceful intentions. My own feeling is that at a crucial period they managed to instil into our Ambassador a false sense of confidence in their so-called desire to settle the Tibetan problem by peaceful means.

There can be no doubt that, during the period covered by this correspondence, the Chinese must have been concentrating for an onslaught on Tibet. The final action of the Chinese, in my judgement, is little short of perfidy.

The tragedy of it is that the Tibetans put faith in us; they chose to be guided by us; and we have been unable to get them out of the meshes of Chinese diplomacy or Chinese malevolence. From the latest position, it appears that we shall not be able to rescue the Dalai Lama.

Our Ambassador has been at great pains to find an explanation or justification for Chinese policy and actions. As the External Affairs Ministry remarked in one of their telegrams, there was a lack of firmness and unnecessary apology in one or two representations that he made to the Chinese Government on our behalf. It is impossible to imagine any sensible person believing in the so-called threat to China from Anglo-American machinations in Tibet. Therefore, if the Chinese put faith in this, they must have distrusted us so completely as to have taken us as tools or stooges of Anglo-American diplomacy or strategy. This feeling, if genuinely entertained by the Chinese in spite of your direct approaches to them, indicates that, even though we regard ourselves as the friends of China, the Chinese do not regard us as their friends. With the Communist mentality of "Whoever is not with them being against them", this is a significant pointer, of which we have to take due note.

During the last several months, outside the Russian camp, we have practically been alone in championing the cause of Chinese entry into the UNO and in securing from the Americans assurances on the question of Formosa. We have done everything we could to assuage Chinese feelings, to allay their apprehensions and to defend their legitimate claims, in our discussions and correspondence with America and Britain and in the UNO. In spite of this, China is not convinced about our disinterestedness; it continues to regard us with suspicion and the whole psychology is one at least outwardly, of scepticism perhaps mixed with a little hostility.

I doubt if we can go any further than we have done already to convince China of our good intentions, friendliness and good-will. In Peking we have an Ambassador who is eminently suitable for putting across the friendly point of view. Even he seems to have failed to convert the Chinese. Their last telegram to us is an act of gross discourtesy not only in the summary way it disposes of our protest against the entry of Chinese forces into Tibet but also in the wild insinuation that our attitude is determined by foreign influences.

It looks as though it is not a friend speaking in that language but a potential enemy.

In the background of this, we have to consider what new situation now faces us as a result of the disappearance of Tibet, as we know it, and the expansion of China almost up to our gates. Throughout history, we have seldom been worried about our north-east frontier. The Himalayas have been regarded as an impenetrable barrier against any threat from the north. We had a friendly Tibet which gave us no trouble. The Chinese were divided. They had their own domestic problems and never bothered us about our frontiers.

In 1914, we entered into a convention with Tibet which was not endorsed by the Chinese. We seem to have regarded Tibetan autonomy as extending to independent treaty relationship. Presumably, all that we required was Chinese countersignature. The Chinese interpretation of suzerainty seems to be different. We can, therefore, safely assume that very soon they will disown all the stipulations which Tibet has entered into with us in the past. That throws into the melting pot all frontier and commercial settlements with Tibet on which we have been functioning and acting during the last half a century.

China is no longer divided. It is united and strong. All along the Himalayas in the north and north-east, we have, on our side of the frontier, a population ethnologically and culturally not different from Tibetans or Mongoloids.

The undefined state of the frontier and the existence on our side of a population with its affinities to Tibetans or Chinese have all the elements of potential trouble between China and ourselves. Recent and bitter history also tells us that Communism is no shield against imperialism and that Communists are as good or as bad imperialists as any other. Chinese ambitions in this respect not only cover the

Himalayan slopes on our side but also include important parts of Assam.

They have their ambitions in Burma also. Burma has the added difficulty that it has no McMahon Line round which to build up even the semblance of an agreement.

Chinese irredentism and Communist imperialism are different from the expansionism or imperialism of the Western powers. The former has a clock of ideology which makes it ten times more dangerous. In the guise of ideological expansion lie concealed racial, national and historical claims.

The danger from the north and north-east, therefore, becomes both Communist and imperialist. While our western and north-western threats to security are still as prominent as before, a new threat had developed from the north and north-east. Thus, for the first time after centuries, India's defence has to concentrate itself on two fronts simultaneously. Our defence measures have so far been based on the calculations of a superiority over Pakistan.

In our calculations we shall now have to reckon with Communist China in the north and north-east—a Communist China which has definite ambitions and aims and which does not, in any way, seem friendly disposed towards us.

Let me also consider the political considerations on this potentially troublesome frontier. Our northern or north-eastern approaches consist of Nepal, Bhutan, Sikkim, Darjeeling and the tribal areas in Assam. From the point of view of communications they are weak spots. Continuous defensive lines do not exist. There is almost an unlimited scope for infiltration. Police protection is limited to a very small number of passes. There, too, our out-posts do not seem to be fully manned.

The contact of these areas with us is, by no means, close and intimate. The people inhabiting these portions have no established loyalty or devotion to India. Even Darjeeling and Kalimpong areas are not free from pro-Mongoloid prejudices. During the last three years, we have not been able to make any appreciable approaches to the Nagas and other hill tribes in Assam. European missionaries and other visitors had been in touch with them, but their influence was, in no way, friendly to India or Indians. In Sikkim, there was political ferment some time ago. It is quite possible that discontent is smouldering there. Bhutan is comparatively quiet, but its affinity with Tibetans would be a handicap. Nepal has a weak oligarchic regime based almost entirely on force; it is in conflict with a turbulent element of the population as well as with enlightened ideas of the modern age.

In these circumstances, to make people alive to the new danger or to make them defensively strong is a very difficult task indeed and that difficulty can be got over only by enlightened firmness, strength and clear line of policy. I am sure the Chinese and their source of inspiration, Soviet Russia, would not miss any opportunity of exploiting these weak spots, partly in support of their ideology and partly in support of their ambitions.

In my judgement, therefore, the situation is one in which we cannot afford either to be complacent or to be vacillating. We must have a clear idea of what we wish to achieve and, also of the methods by which we should achieve it. Any faltering or lack of decisiveness in formulating our objectives or in pursuing our policy to attain those objectives is bound to weaken us and increase the threats which are so evident.

Side by side with these external dangers we shall now have to face serious internal problems as well. I have already asked Iengar to send to the External Affairs Ministry a copy of the Intelligence Bureau's appreciation of these matters. Hitherto, the Communist Party of India has found some difficulty in contacting Communists abroad, or in getting supplies of arms, literature, etc., from them. They had to contend with difficult Burmese and Pakistan frontiers on the east or with the long seaboard.

They will now have a comparatively easy means of access to Chinese Communists and through them to other foreign Communists. Infiltration of spies, fifth columnists and Communists would be easier. Instead of having to deal with isolated Communist pockets in Telengana and Warangal we may have to deal with Communist threats to our northern and north-eastern frontier where, for supplies of arms and ammunition, they can safely depend on Communist arsenals in China.

The whole situation thus raises a number of problems on which we must come to an early decision so that we can, as said earlier, formulate the objectives of our policy and decide the methods by which those actions will have to be fairly comprehensive involving not only our defence strategy and state of preparation but also problems of internal security to deal with which we have not a moment to lose. We shall also have to deal with administrative and political problems in the weak spots along the frontier to which I have already referred.

It is, of course, impossible for me to be exhaustive in setting out all these problems. I am, however, giving below some of the problems, which, in my opinion, require early solution and round which we have to build our administrative or military policies and measures to implement them.

> (a) A military and intelligence appreciation of the Chinese threat to India but both on the frontier and to internal security.
> (b) An examination of our military position and such redisposition of our forces as might be necessary, particularly with the idea of guarding important routes

or areas which are likely to be the subject of dispute.
(c) An appraisement of the strength of our forces and, if necessary, reconsideration of our retrenchment plans for the Army in the light of these new threats.

(d) A long-term consideration of our defence needs. My own feeling is that unless we assure our supplies of arms, ammunition and armour, we would be making our defence perpetually weak and we would not be able to stand up to the double threat of difficulties both from the west and north-west and north and north-east.

(e) The question of Chinese entry into the UNO. In view of the rebuff which China has given us and the method which it has followed in dealing with Tibet, I am doubtful whether we can advocate its claims any longer. There would probably be a threat in the UNO virtually to outlaw China, in view of its active participation in the Korean war. We must determine our attitude on this question also.

(f) The political and administrative steps which we should take to strengthen our northern and north-eastern frontiers. This would include the whole of the border, i.e., Nepal, Bhutan, Sikkim, Darjeeling and the tribal territory in Assam.

(g) Measures of internal security in the border areas as well as the States flanking those areas such as Uttar Pradesh, Bihar, Bengal and Assam.

(h) Improvement of our communications, road, rail, air and wireless, in these areas and with the frontier outposts.

(i) Policing and intelligence of frontier posts.

(j) The future of our mission at Lhasa and the trade posts at Gyangtse and Yatung and the forces which we have in operation in Tibet to guard the trade routes.

(k) The policy in regard to the MacMahon Line.

There are some of the questions which occur to my mind. It is possible that a consideration of these matters may lead us into wider questions of our relationship with China, Russia, America, Britain and Burma. This, however, would be of a general nature, though some might be basically very important, e.g., we might have to consider whether we should not enter into closer association with Burma in order to strengthen the latter in the dealings with China. I do not rule out the possibility that, before applying pressure on us, China might apply pressure on Burma. With Burma, the frontier is entirely undefined and the Chinese territorial claims are more substantial. In its present position, Burma might offer an easier problem for China and, therefore, might claim its first attention.

I suggest that we meet early to have a general discussion on these problems and decide on such steps as we might think to be immediately necessary and direct quick examination of other problems with a view to taking early measures to deal with them.

Vallabhbhai Patel
7th November 1950

Appendix 7

An Approximate Outline Order of Battle of the Indian Army—1992*

Manpower (including Territorial Army)—1,100,000.

Five regional Commands (Northern, Western, Central, Eastern, Southern).

Eleven Corps headquarters.

Two armoured divisions.

One mechanized division.

Twenty-two infantry divisions.

Ten mountain divisions.

Fourteen independent brigades, including one parachute brigade.

Three independent artillery brigades.

Six independent air defence brigades.

Four engineer brigades.

An aviation corps of seventeen squadrons of helicopters.

Territorial Army of 160,000 volunteers, mainly thirty infantry battalions.

* Extracted from *The Military Balance—1992-93* (London).

Appendix 8

Report of the Kargil Review Committee
Executive Summary

INTRODUCTION

Against the backdrop of an animated public discussion on Pakistan's aggression in Kargil, the Union Government vide its order dated July 29, 1999 constituted a Committee to look into the episode with the following Terms of Reference:

  i) To review the events leading up to the Pakistani aggression in the Kargil District of Ladakh in Jammu & Kashmir; and

 ii) To recommend such measures as are considered necessary to safeguard national security against such armed intrusions.

The Committee comprised four members namely K. Subrahmanyam (Chairman), Lieutenant General (Retd.) K.K. Hazari, B.G. Verghese, and Satish Chandra, Secretary, National Security Council Secretariat (NSCS) who was also designated as Member-Secretary.

Given its open-ended terms of reference, the time constraint and, most importantly, the need for clarity in setting about its task, the Committee found it necessary to define its scope of work precisely. To deal with the Kargil episode in isolation would have been too simplistic; hence the Report briefly recounts the important facets of developments in J&K and the evolution of the Line of Control (LoC), Indo–Pak relations since 1947, the proxy war in Kashmir and the nuclear factor. However, the Committee's 'review' commences essentially from 1997 onwards coinciding with Nawaz Sharif's return to office as Prime Minister of Pakistan. This has enabled the Committee to look at developments immediately preceding the intrusions more intensively. The Committee has sought to analyse whether the kind of Pakistani aggression that took place could have been assessed from the available intelligence inputs and, if so, what were the shortcomings and failures which led to the nation being caught by surprise. However, the actual conduct of military operations has not been evaluated by the Committee as this lay outside the Committee's mandate and would have called for a different type of expertise. The Committee's recommendati ˙ for preventing future recurrence of Kargil-like episodes are confined to the country's land borders. Since some of these are generic in nature, they would have a bearing on future threats to the country whether on its land borders or otherwise.

The Committee approached its task in a spirit of openness and transparency with its focus on establishing the facts. It viewed its task as a cooperative venture with the concerned Ministries, Defence Services, Intelligence Agencies and other concerned organisations and avoided getting into adversarial relationship with the officials and non-officials with whom it was required to interact. Given this approach it was able to enlist the willing cooperation of all concerned.

Although the Committee was not statutory in nature, as a result of Cabinet Secretary's directions it was able to secure the widest possible access to all relevant documents, including those with the highest classification and to officials of the Union and J&K Governments. In the pursuit of its task the Committee sought presentations from the concerned organisations and agencies. It held meetings with those who in its judgement were in a position to throw light on the subject. In this process, it met former President R. Venkataraman, Prime Minister A.B. Vajpayee, ex-Prime Ministers V.P. Singh, P.V. Narasimha Rao and I.K. Gujral, the Home Minister, External Affairs Minister, Defence Minister, the Deputy Chairman, Planning Commission, the Governor and the Chief Minister of Jammu and Kashmir, the National Security Adviser, the Cabinet Secretary, the Defence Secretary, the Foreign Secretary, the Home Secretary and a host of other officials and non-officials, including media persons. The Committee held over a hundred meetings, the records of which are appended to the Report. Detailed questionnaires were prepared by the Committee to elicit information. It made four visits to various parts of J&K to hold discussions with local officials and non-officials, and to get a better sense of the terrain and the prevailing field conditions. It undertook a visit to Bangalore to obtain a first-hand knowledge of certain Defence research and development facilities and for discussions with experts regarding technological options. The Committee invited reliable information from the public pertaining to events leading up to the Pakistani aggression in Kargil through a press note in the national dailies and the regional media. It scanned a large number of news items and commentaries published in the national dailies, journals and magazines. Apart from this, it perused several books published in recent months on the Kargil episode.

The Committee's Findings are based primarily on official documents, authenticated records and copies of documents, while other parts of the Report draw on materials received by the Committee and views of experts and knowledgeable persons who were invited to interact with it.

The Committee's Report comprises 14 Chapters in addition to a Prologue and an Epilogue. Important documents referred to by the Committee are enclosed as annexures with the main Report. Other relevant documents, Records of Discussions and source materials have been put together in 15 volumes and appended to the Report. The Findings and Recommendations of the Committee are set out in the succeeding sections of this summary.

FINDINGS

I. Developments Leading to the Pakistani Aggression at Kargil

The Review Committee had before it overwhelming evidence that the Pakistani armed intrusion in the Kargil sector came as a complete and total surprise to the Indian Government, Army and intelligence agencies as well as to the J&K State Government and its agencies. The Committee did not come across any agency or individual who was able clearly to assess before the event the possibility of a large-scale Pakistani military intrusion across the Kargil heights. What was conceived of was the limited possibility of infiltrations and enhanced artillery exchanges in this Sector.

A number of former Army Chiefs of Staff and Director Generals of Military Operations were near unanimous in their opinion that a military intrusion on the scale attempted was totally unsustainable because of the lack of supportive infrastructure and was militarily irrational. In the 1948, 1965 and 1971 conflicts, the Indian Army was able to dominate the Pakistani forces on these heights. This area has been the scene of fierce artillery exchanges but minimal cross-LoC military activity. These factors, together with the nature of the terrain and extreme weather conditions in the area, had generated an under-standable Indian military mindset about the nature and extent of the Pakistani threat in this sector.

The developments of 1998 as reported in various intelligence inputs, notably the increased shelling of Kargil, the reported in-creased presence of militants in the Force Commander Northern Area (FCNA) region and their training were assessed as indicative of a likely high level of militant activity in Kargil in the summer of 1999 and the consequent possibility of increased infiltration in this area. The Pakistani reconnaissance mission in August 1997 in Gharkun village was noted and a patrol base established in Yaldor. An opera-tion was also planned to apprehend the infiltrators if they returned in the summer of 1998. They apparently did not do so.

The nearest approximation to the events of May 1999 was a 15 Corps war-game in 1993 which envisaged a Pakistani long range penetration group positioning itself south of National Highway (NH) 1A and bringing the Srinagar–Leh highway under fire from both sides. Even that assessment did not visualise an intrusion to hold ground by hundreds of Pakistan Army regulars.

Intrusions across the LoC are not uncommon. Pakistan had in the past intruded into the Indian side of the LoC and the Indian Army had responded adequately. There had, however, been no intrusions since 1990. An attempt to capture a post or two on the LoC was, however, anticipated as revealed in the press briefing of the acting GOC 15

Corps on January 11, 1999. Even this was not the kind of intrusion that actually took place in the Mashkoh, Dras, Kaksar and Batalik areas.

The terrain here is so inhospitable that the intruders could not have survived above 4000 metres for long without comprehensive and sustained re-supply operations. They were even running short of water at these heights towards the end of the operations. Though heavily armed, the intruders did not have rations for more than two or three days in many forward 'sangars'. Re-supply could have taken place only if there was no air threat and the supply lines could not be targeted by Indian artillery. In other words, it would appear that the Pakistani intruders operated on the assumption that the intrusions would be under counterattack for only a few days and thereafter some sort of ceasefire would enable them to stay on the heights and be re-supplied.

Such an assumption would be totally unsustainable in purely military terms. It would only be logical on the expectation, based upon political considerations, that Pakistan would be able to engineer international intervention to impose an early ceasefire that would allow its troops to stay in possession of the territory captured by them. Such an assumption could not have been made without close consultation with the Pakistani political leadership at the highest level. General Musharraf has disclosed that the operations were discussed in November 1998 with the political leadership and there are indications of discussions on two subsequent occasions in early 1999. The tapes of conversations between General Musharraf and Lieutenant General Aziz, Chief of General Staff, also revealed their expectation of early international intervention, the likelihood of a ceasefire and the knowledge and support of the (Pakistani) Foreign Office.

In retrospect, such an expectation was unreal. The Pakistani establishment has a long and consistent history of misreading India's will and world opinion. In 1947, it did not anticipate the swift Indian military intervention in Kashmir when it planned its raid with a mix of army personnel, ex-servicemen and tribals under the command of Major General Akbar Khan. In 1965, it took Zulfikar Ali Bhutto's advice that India would not cross the international border to deal with Pakistan's offensive in the Akhnur sector. In 1971, it developed high but totally unwarranted expectations about the likelihood of US–Chinese intervention on its behalf. The same pattern of behaviour was evident this time too. This is presumably the price the Pakistani leadership has paid for its inability to come to terms with military realities. It has obviously been a victim of its own propaganda.

It is evident from Pakistani pronouncements and the writings of those with access to the highest decision-making levels, that at least from 1987 onwards, when Dr A.Q. Khan conveyed a nuclear threat to India in a Press interview to an Indian journalist, Pakistan was convinced that its nuclear weapons capability would deter India's superior conventional forces. Written accounts of foreign observers have highlighted that since 1980, the Pakistani military establishment had entertained ideas of deterring Indian nuclear and conventional capabilities with its nuclear weapons and of carrying out a brash, bold strike to liberate Kashmir which would go unchallenged if the Indian leadership was weak or indecisive.

Successive Indian Chiefs of Army Staff and Director Generals of Military Operations told the Committee that bringing to bear India's assumed conventional superiority was not a serious option in the last ten years for a variety of reasons: commitments in Sri Lanka, subsequent deployments in Punjab, the North-East and Kashmir, and a drastic reduction in Defence outlay. Pakistani writings over the years have highlighted the Indian Army's involvement in counter-insurgency in Kashmir and its perceived degradation as an effective fighting force.

Several Pakistani writers agree that the 'Kargil plan' was formulated in the eighties in the last years of General Zia-ul-Haq. There are different versions on whether it was sought to be operationalised during the tenures of Benazir Bhutto and General Jehangir Karamat, Chief of Army Staff. General Musharraf's disclosure that it was discussed with the political leadership in November 1998 soon after he assumed office has been referred to in the Report. It is difficult to say whether the initiative for this move came from the Army or was politically driven. There was a heady combination of circumstances and personalities. Nawaz Sharif, the Prime Minister, had successfully removed from office the President, the Chief Justice and the then Army Chief, General Karamat, in whose place he appointed General Musharraf who superseded two others. General Musharraf himself served in Afghanistan and had ties with Osama Bin Laden and other extremists. He is a Mohajir and an ambitious, hard-driving man. He had served in the Northern Areas for several years and had been associated with the crackdown on the Shias. He had commanded the Special Services Group (SSG) which launched an attack on Bilafond La in Siachen but was frustrated.

Some Pakistani columnists claim that Nawaz Sharif thought that if he succeeded in seizing a slice of Indian territory in Kashmir, he would be hailed as a 'Liberator' and thereby enabled to gain absolute power through amendment of the Shariah law. There is no clear evidence on the basis of which to assess the nature and extent of Nawaz Sharif's involvement in the Kargil adventure. The balance of probability suggests that he was fully in the picture. This is borne out by the tapes referred to earlier and the repeated assertions of General Musharraf. Those who know Nawaz Sharif personally believe that he has a limited attention span and is impatient with detail. Accordingly, it is reasonable to assume that Nawaz Sharif was at least aware of the broad thrust of the Kargil plan when he so warmly welcomed the Indian Prime Minister in Lahore.

Influential sections of the Indian political class and media have been outraged at the duplicity of the Pakistani leadership. Some argue that Nawaz Sharif could not have been so duplicitous and therefore tend to absolve him and lay all blame on General Musharraf. However, having a declaratory policy different from that actually pursued is not unknown in international realpolitik and diplomacy. This existentialist divergence between the two necessitates diplomatic interaction, continuous political analysis, Track-II diplomacy and intelligence collection, collation and assessment.

The Committee has not come across any assessment at operational levels that would justify the conclusion that the Lahore summit had caused the Indian decision-makers to lower their guard. This has been confirmed by the discussions the Committee had with a number of concerned officials. Nonetheless, there was euphoria in some political quarters, among leaders in and out of office, though some others saw serious pitfalls in the Lahore process.

The Committee has attempted a partial reconstruction of Operation BADR based on diaries and notebooks recovered from Pakistani personnel during the operation as well as intercepts. It would appear that reconnaissance parties comprising officers started crossing the LoC in late January/early February 1999. They established a first line of administrative bases within a limited distance across the LoC in February. March saw heavy snowfall and so they could move further forward only in April. At that stage, more men joined them and perhaps the bulk of the intruders entered Indian territory in late April. This sequence of events appears logical as earlier induction of larger numbers would have added to logistic problems and increased the risk of detection. Care was exercised by the intruders to move only in the gaps between the Indian winter posts and to avoid detection by Winter Air Surveillance Operations (WASO). They were equipped for extreme cold and snow conditions. In the initial advance, they used Igloo snow tents and constructed 'sangars' of loose rock. Perhaps late in April, they moved up a further two to three kilometres. WASO helicopters and operational reconnaissance flights repeatedly flew over them as is evident from one of the diaries captured in Mashkoh Valley. A combination of factors prevented their detection: camouflage clothing; helicopter vibrations which hampered observation; opportunity for concealment on hearing the sound of approaching helicopters; and peacetime safety requirements of maintaining a certain height above the ground and a given distance from the LoC. Since the effort was largely to detect infiltration, most flights flew along valleys and not across the ridges. All these factors made the WASO patrols of negligible value as is also evident from the records of previous years.

After a lull in the winter from late December 1998, there was very heavy snowfall in March 1999 which compelled 121 Infantry Brigade to vacate one of its 25 winter posts in the South-West Spur of Point 5299 in the Kaksar sector, popularly known as Bajrang post. Winter patrols sent out in early April 1999 were unable to carry out their task due to adverse snow conditions. The Pakistanis creeping forward also suffered avalanche casualties in the month of March 1999 as revealed by a diary captured in the Mashkoh Valley. All the Indian military commanders the Committee met emphasised the point that while it would have been possible for patrolling to be carried out even under these conditions, it would have required the troops to be specially equipped to withstand glacial conditions, as in Siachen, and a willingness to accept possible casualties. Until now, this had not been considered necessary or acceptable.

It would appear from the locations of 'sangars' [...]* that the plan was to avoid initially confronting the Indian forces by moving stealthily along the unheld gaps. The Pakistani intruders were meant to disclose themselves in the later part of May 1999 and demonstrate that they were in possession of the Kargil heights along a "new LoC" before the normal opening of the Zojila pass when regular patrolling by the Indian Army would commence. Presumably they felt that with the advantage of the commanding heights, their better acclimatisation and by now their more secure logistics, the situation would be distinctly in their favour. The Indians would need time to assemble their forces, acclimatise their troops and build up their logistics which would be difficult before Zojila opened. They would also have to suffer unacceptable casualties in attacking the heights. This would ensure time enough for an internationally arranged ceasefire.

This was probably Pakistan's expectation. In fact, however, the intrusion was detected on May 3, 1999, by "shepherds" who are occasionally retained by the Brigade Intelligence Team for forward information gathering. The patrols sent out in the next few days confirmed the presence of intruders on May 7. The Indian Army's response was very rapid and by May 9, two well-acclimatised battalions returning from Siachen had been concentrated in the Batalik

---

* Government Security Deletion.

sector to contain the intrusion. In the next few days, three more battalions were moved from the Valley into the Kargil sector to counter known and possible intrusions in other sub-sectors. By May 24, two additional Brigades had moved into the area and the Indian Air Force was committed on May 26. By the end of May an additional divisional headquarters had been inducted to take over command of a portion of the Kargil Sector from 3 Infantry Division. This rapid and strong Indian reaction was obviously not expected by the Pakistanis. It was now their turn to be totally surprised [...].* Simultaneously, Pakistan tried to lobby with the international community for a ceasefire, which would leave it with some Indian territory and thereby justify its misadventure. Initially, there was support for a ceasefire but once Tololing fell and the Indian Government and Army exhibited their determination to clear the entire intrusion, the international community called on Pakistan to withdraw from and respect the sanctity of the LoC.

The sitrep issued by 15 Corps on May 11, 1999 was explicit on eight identified intrusions in the Batalik sector involving 160 to 240 intruders. The Northern Command had already made a request for the use of helicopter gunships on May 8. The Northern Command issued orders on May 12 that the whole J&K theatre be put on alert and additional troops be inducted into the Kargil sector. There are obvious discrepancies between the documented responses of 15 Corps and the Northern Command and the information regarding the nature and extent of intrusions at that stage, then available in the Ministries of Defence and Home in Delhi, as is evident from the statements of concerned officials.

Movement of forces within a corps is entirely within the competence of the corps commander and does not require clearance from any other authority. For the 15 Corps, an operation on a single brigade front was a 'localised' action. The record establishes that the 15 Corps Commander carried out his deployment with commendable expedition and competence providing adequate margins for all possible contingencies.

* Government Security Deletion.

The Committee found that though the Corps Commander had moved adequate forces to contain the intrusion in the Batalik sector and followed it up with a similar deployment of forces in the Kaksar, Dras and Mashkoh valley sectors, there was still no clarity in the assessment of the magnitude of the intrusions and the composition of the intruders. This is evident from the statement of the Corps Commander on May 19 [...].*

Pakistan insists on projecting most of the intruders as Mujahideen, with the Northern Light Infantry (NLI) troops in a supporting role. The assessment of the nature and composition of the intruders was hampered by a number of factors. Pakistan deliberately violated the normal rules of war by sending in servicemen as Mujahideen and obfuscating their service identities. Secondly, as pointed out elsewhere, there was inadequate coordination at the ground level among Army intelligence and other agencies. This was lacking even at the Joint Intelligence Committee (JIC) because of the low level of representation by the Director General of Military Intelligence (DGMI) at the assessment process and the DGMI representative not coming fully briefed on the latest situation. It is also apparent that the assessment was conditioned by the two decade old mindset that Kargil was unsuitable for cross-LoC military action.

There are reports in the media, some of which are said to have originated from young officers, JOOs and other ranks, that in the initial stages, the Indian Army suffered avoidable casualties, taken as it was by surprise. However, the progressive data of Indian casualties from May to July 1999 obtained by the Committee does not entirely support this hypothesis. The Committee did not go into the matter further as its terms of reference do not require it to do so.

There were also comments in the media that Army jawans were inadequately equipped for the extreme cold and hazardous conditions when ordered to assault the Kargil heights. Their weapons and equipment compared unfavourably with those of the Pakistani intruders. The Army had prescribed extra-cold clothing meant for

---

* Government Security Deletion.

heights between 9000–13,000 feet in this sector for use in normal times, and special (glacial) clothing for heights above that. Special clothing is issued for use in the Siachen area and certain limited reserves were held in stock. When hostilities commenced, this reserve clothing was issued to the men. Troops returning from Siachen duty discard their special clothing which is then usually disposed of by auction. However, in the previous year, the Corps Commander had ordered that part-worn serviceable (PWS) Siachen clothing be preserved. This PWS stock was also issued to the troops during the Kargil action. Despite this, there was still an overall shortage. This warrants a review of standards of provisioning for reserves as well as a policy of holding special clothing for a certain proportion of other troops in the Kargil and other high altitude sectors.

Though the new light rifle (5.56 mm) has been inducted into service, most troops are yet to be equipped with light rifles. Adequate attention has not been paid to lightening the load on infantry soldiers deployed at high altitudes. In broader terms, increasing the firepower and combat efficiency of infantrymen has also suffered as has the modernisation process as a whole. This needs to be speedily rectified.

[...]* The Air Chief further maintained that if air power was to be used, the country should be prepared for a Pakistani response. Therefore, the relevant Air Commands and units were activated. The Cabinet Committee on Security (CCS) finally authorised the use of air power on May 25. [...]*

In order to ensure that Pakistan would be deterred from any adventurous escalation, the Indian Armed Forces progressively moved to deploy in a deterrent posture. These measures sent out a clear message to Pakistan and the rest of the world that India was determined to oust the invader by military means. The Western and Eastern fleets of the Indian Navy were concentrated in the North Arabian Sea. From intercepted signals, it would appear that these steps had a healthy restraining effect on the Pakistani Armed Forces. This was impliedly admitted by Nawaz Sharif in his address to the nation on July 12, 1999.

* Government Security Deletion.

The Kargil action saw the deployment of a limited number of troops and aircraft on a restricted front in response to a shallow Pakistani penetration across the LoC of no more than eight to nine kilometres at most. Nevertheless, given the terrain and political implications were a "new LoC" to be created, and in the background of nuclear capability on both sides, this was not a minor skirmish but a short, sharp war in which the Indian Army and Air Force suffered 474 killed and 1109 wounded (as of July 26, 1999). To regard it as anything less would be mistaken. The consequences of its failure for Pakistan are there for all to see.

II. Intelligence

It is not widely appreciated in India that the primary responsibility for collecting external intelligence, including that relating to a potential adversary's military deployment, is vested in the Research and Analysis Wing (R&AW). The DGMI's capability for intelligence collection is limited. It is essentially restricted to the collection of tactical military intelligence and some amount of signal intelligence and its main role is to make strategic and tactical military assessments and disseminate them within the Army. Many countries have established separate Defence Intelligence Agencies and generously provided them with resources and equipment to play a substantive role in intelligence collection. For historical reasons, the Indian Armed Forces are not so mandated. Therefore, it is primarily R&AW which must provide intelligence about a likely attack, whether across a broad or narrow front. Unfortunately the R&AW facility in the Kargil area did not receive adequate attention in terms of staff or technological capability. The station was under Srinagar but reported to Leh which was not focussed on Kargil but elsewhere. Hence intelligence collection, coordination and follow-up were weak.

The Intelligence Bureau (IB) is meant to collect intelligence within the country and is the premier agency for counter-intelligence. This agency got certain inputs on activities in the FCNA region which were considered important enough by the Director, IB to be communicated over his signature on June 2, 1998 to the Prime Minister, Home

Minister, Cabinet Secretary, Home Secretary and Director-General Military Operations. This communication was not addressed to the three officials most concerned with this information, namely Secretary (R&AW), who is responsible for external intelligence and had the resources to follow up the leads in the IB report; Chairman JIC, who would have taken such information into account in JIC assessments; and Director-General Military Intelligence. Director, IB stated that he expected the information to filter down to these officials through the official hierarchy. This did not happen in respect of Secretary (R&AW) who at that time was also holding additional charge as Chairman, JIC. The Committee feels that a communication of this nature should have been directly addressed to all the officials concerned.

Such lapses, committed at one time or the other by all agencies, came to the notice of the Committee. These illustrate a number of deficiencies in the system. There is need for greater appreciation of the role of intelligence and who needs it most and also more understanding with regard to who must pursue any given lead. It further highlights the need for closer coordination among the intelligence agencies.

There were many bits and pieces of information about activities within the FCNA region. Very few of these could be considered actionable intelligence. Most of them tended to indicate that Kargil was becoming a growing focus of Pakistani attention which had been clearly demonstrated by the marked increase in cross-LoC shelling in 1998. The reports on ammunition dumping, induction of additional guns and the construction of bunkers and helipads all fitted into an assessment of likely large-scale militant infiltration and yet more intensive shelling in the summer of 1999. The enhanced threat perception of Commander 121 Infantry Brigade, Brigadier Surinder Singh also related to increased infiltration. R&AW assessed the possibility of "a limited swift offensive threat with possible support of alliance partners" in its half-yearly assessment ending September 1998 but no indicators substantiating this assessment were provided. Moreover, in its next six monthly report ending March 1999, this assessment was dropped. In fact, its March 1999 report emphasised the financial constraints that would inhibit Pakistan from launching on any such adventure.

No specific indicators of a likely major attack in the Kargil sector such as significant improvements in logistics and communications or a substantial force build-up or forward deployment of forces were reported by any of the agencies. Information on training of additional militants with a view to infiltrating them across the LoC was not sector-specific. There was an increase in shelling in 1998 both in the Neelam Valley (in POK) and Kargil (India). The Indian side resorted to heavy firing since it was necessary to suppress Pakistani fire aimed at disrupting the traffic on NH-1A from Srinagar to Leh. While the intelligence agencies focussed on ammunition dumping on the other side, they appeared to lack adequate knowledge about the heavy damage inflicted by Indian Artillery which would have required the Pakistani Army to undertake considerable repairs and re-stocking. That would partly explain the larger vehicular movements reported on the other side. The Indian Army did not share information about the intensity and effect of its past firing with others. In the absence of this information, R&AW could not correctly assess the significance of enemy activity in terms of ammunition storage or construction of underground bunkers. This provides another illustration of lack of inter-agency coordination as well as lack of coordination between the Army and the agencies.

The critical failure in intelligence was related to the absence of any information on the induction and de-induction of battalions and the lack of accurate data on the identity of battalions in the area opposite Kargil during 1998. Prisoners of War have disclosed the presence of 5, 6 and 13 NLI Battalions and 24 SIND Battalion in the FCNA region from October 1998 onwards. The Indian Army has also assessed that elements of 5, 6 and 13 NLI were amongst the units that were initially used by Pakistan to launch the intrusions in April/May 1999. These units did not figure in the Order of Battle (ORBAT) supplied by R&AW to the DGMI dated April 1998. Since then, and until Indian troops came into contact with these battalions in May–June

1999, there was no information of their presence in the area. R&AW issued another ORBAT on June 1, 1999 which also did not show any changes in the area opposite Kargil between April 1998 and May 1999. An analysis carried out by the Committee on the basis of information now available shows that there were in fact a number of changes in the ORBAT of Pakistani forces in the FCNA region during 1998/early 1999. These changes included the turnover of some units, induction of two additional battalions over and above the 13 already in the Sector as reported by R&AW in April 1998 and the forward deployment of two battalions from Gilgit to Gultari and from Skardu to Hamzigund (near Olthingthang) respectively. In other words, if no de-inductions took place, for which the Committee lacks evidence, there was a net increase of two battalions in the FCNA region over and above R&AW's projections as well as a forward deployment of two battalions within the sector during the period April 1998 to February 1999. The responsibility for obtaining information on them was primarily that of R&AW and, to a much lesser extent, that of DGMI and the Division or Brigade using their Intelligence and Field Surveillance Unit (IFSU) and Brigade Intelligence Team (BIT) capabilities.

It could be argued that given the nature of the terrain, the climatic conditions and the unheld gaps in existence since 1972, there was no way of anticipating the intrusion during the winter provided Pakistan accepted the risk of incurring casualties in avalanches, which it did. However, since Pakistan was focussing upon Kargil, information regarding the induction of two additional battalions in the FCNA region and the forward deployment of two battalions could have proved to be an indicator of the likely nature of Pakistani activity in this sector. In that event, perhaps greater risks in patrolling in snow conditions might have been found acceptable. More focussed intelligence about the activities of Pakistan in the FCNA region would have followed. In the Committee's view, a significant gap in information prior to the detection of the Kargil intrusion was the inability of R&AW to accurately monitor and report changes in the Pakistani ORBAT in the FCNA region during 1998 and early 1999 and to a lesser extent that of DGMI, the BITs and IFSUs to notice the additional forward deployment of troops in the vicinity of the LoC.

The Kargil intrusion was essentially a limited Pakistani military exercise designed to internationalise the Kashmir issue which was tending to recede from the radar screen of the international community. It was, therefore, mainly a move for political and diplomatic gain. The armed forces play their war games essentially within military parameters. Unlike other countries, India has no tradition of undertaking politico-military games with the participation of those having political and diplomatic expertise. If such games had been practised, then the possibility of limited military intrusions to internationalise the Kashmir issue might have been visualised.

One of the most realistic assessments of Kashmir developments as they unfolded during Pakistan's proxy war was Operation TOPAC, a war game written by a team of retired Indian Army officers in 1989. It is interesting to note that Operation TOPAC has since been mistakenly attributed even by high-placed Indian officials and agencies to Gen Zia-ul-Haq. This shows how close the authors of Operation TOPAC were able to get into the mind of the Pakistani establishment in relation to their aims in J&K.

As mentioned earlier, WASO did not provide intelligence input of significant value. Those of the Aviation Research Centre (ARC) of R&AW were no doubt extremely valuable. The Army makes six-monthly indents and, wherever necessary, special indents on the ARC. These indents and their prioritisation depend on the nature of the threat perception which, in turn, is shaped by inputs from R&AW. This circular process entails the Army having to depend upon inputs from R&AW for its own threat assessment. In other words, the Indian threat assessment is largely a single-track process dominated by R&AW. In most advanced countries, the Armed Forces have a Defence Intelligence Agency with a significant intelligence collection capability. This ensures that there are two streams of intelligence which enable governments to check one against the other.

The Indian Intelligence structure is flawed since there is little back-up or redundancy to rectify failures and shortcomings in intelligence collection and reporting that goes to build up the external threat perception by the one agency, namely, R&AW which has a virtual monopoly in this regard. It is neither healthy nor prudent to endow that one agency alone with multifarious capabilities for human, communication, imagery and electronic intelligence. Had R&AW and DGMI spotted the additional battalions in the FCNA region that were missing from the ORBAT, there might have been requests for ARC flights in winter and these might have been undertaken, weather permitting. As it happened, the last flight was in October 1998, long before the intrusion, and the next in May 1999, after the intrusions had commenced. The intruders had by then come out into the open.

The present structure and processes in intelligence gathering and reporting led to an overload of background and unconfirmed information and inadequately assessed intelligence which requires to be further pursued. There is no institutionalised process whereby R&AW, IB, BSF (Border Security Force) and Army intelligence officials interact periodically at levels below the JIC. This lacuna is perhaps responsible for R&AW reporting the presence of one additional unit in Gultari in September 1998 but not following it up with ARC flights on its own initiative. Nor did the Army press R&AW specifically for more information on this report. The Army never shared its intelligence with the other agencies or with the JIC. There was no system of Army authorities at different levels from DGMI downwards providing feedback to the Agencies.

There is a general lack of awareness of the critical importance of and the need for assessed intelligence at all levels. JIC reports do not receive the attention they deserve at the political and higher bureaucratic levels. The assessment process has been downgraded in importance and consequently various agencies send very junior officials to JIC meetings. The DGMI did not send any regular inputs to the JIC for two years preceding the Kargil crisis. The JIC was not accorded the importance it deserved either by the Intelligence Agencies or the Government. The Chairmanship of JIC had become the preserve of an Indian Police Service (IPS) officer who was generally a runner-up of the post of Secretary (R&AW) or DIB. The post was in fact left unfilled for 18 months until December 1998. During this period, Secretary (R&AW) doubled as Chairman, JIC.

There are no checks and balances in the Indian intelligence system to ensure that the consumer gets all the intelligence that is available and is his due. There is no system of regular, periodic and comprehensive intelligence briefings at the political level and to the Committee of Secretaries. In the absence of an overall, operational national security framework and objective, each intelligence agency is diligent in preserving its own turf and departmental prerogatives. There is no evidence that the intelligence agencies have reviewed their role after India became a nuclear weapon state or in the context of the increasing problems posed by insurgencies and ethno-nationalist turbulences backed with sophisticated hi-tech equipment and external support. Nor has the Government felt the need to initiate any such move.

III. The Nuclear Factor

A lot has been written both at home and abroad about Pakistan being able to commit limited aggression in Kashmir because of the mutual nuclear deterrence deemed to have been established as a result of the Indian and Pakistan nuclear tests in May 1998. The Committee examined this proposition in detail. It studied the Indian perception of the Pakistani nuclear threat as well as the sequence of developments of the Indian and Pakistani nuclear weapons programme. The Committee's findings are based on published literature, classified reports, statements by some of the main actors in the Indian nuclear weapons programme, former Intelligence Chiefs, former Foreign Secretaries and former Prime Ministers. These are summarised below.

President Zulfikar Ali Bhutto committed Pakistan to acquiring nuclear weapons at a meeting held in Multan on January 24, 1972 in the wake of the country's defeat in the Bangladesh war. As has been highlighted by a number of eminent Pakistani writers, the primary motivation for this effort was to deter India's conventional arms superiority. According to Pakistani perceptions, it was able to do so on three occasions. This was well before the Pokhran and Chagai tests in May 1998.

According to a statement made before the Committee, R&AW had assessed that by 1981–82, Pakistan had enough weapons-grade enriched uranium to make one or two uranium weapon cores. Former President Venkataraman and the then Scientific Adviser, Dr V.S. Arunachalam, both said that Indira Gandhi agreed to a nuclear weapons test in 1983 but called it off under US pressure.

A report published in 1984 indicated that Pakistan had obtained from the Chinese the design of its fourth nuclear weapon tested in 1966. It was therefore a proven design. By the early 1980s, Indian intelligence was aware of the China–Pakistan nuclear weapons deal. So also the US, as evident from a declassified document of 1983.

In 1987, Pakistan conveyed a nuclear threat to India at the time of (the training exercise) BRASSTACKS. This was officially communicated by Pakistan's Minister of State for Foreign Affairs, Zain Noorani to the Indian Ambassador in Islamabad, S.K. Singh. It was also communicated by the Pakistani nuclear scientist, Dr A.Q. Khan to the Indian journalist Kuldip Nayyar.

In January 1990, Pakistan's Foreign Minister, Sahibzada Yakub Khan, visited Delhi and spoke to the Indian Foreign Minister, I.K. Gujral and the Prime Minister V.P. Singh in terms which they regarded as verging on an ultimatum. Some time later, the Indian Air Force was placed on alert following the Pakistan Air Force being similarly ordered. The Indian Prime Minister inquired of the then Air Chief whether it was possible for the IAF to intercept hostile Pakistani aircraft carrying nuclear weapons. Air Chief Marshal S.K. Mehra replied that no such guarantee could be given and that the only logical answer for India was to acquire a nuclear deterrent of its own. American accounts describe Robert Gates' visit to Islamabad in May 1990 and his warning to President Ghulam Ishaq Khan and General Aslam Beg against any rash action against India. The Pakistanis describe this as one more instance when their nuclear deterrent prevented Indian aggression. During this crisis, the Kahuta establishment was evacuated, a fact that the Indian mission in Islamabad communicated to Delhi. On the 1990 events referred to above, there are varying perceptions among Indian officials. The majority view is that there was an implied threat.

In August 1990, information was received from a sensitive intelligence source that in any future confrontation, Pakistan might use nuclear weapons as a first resort. V.P. Singh and I.K. Gujral have a vivid recollection of this report. In October 1990, the US imposed sanctions on Pakistan under the Pressler Amendment, implicitly confirming to the world that Pakistan possessed nuclear explosive capability.

The Committee was informed by Air Chief Marshal S.K. Mehra, the former Air Chief, that flight trials for delivery of Indian nuclear weapons were conducted in 1990 and that efforts to adapt the delivery system to the weapon commenced even earlier. V.P. Singh said that he inherited the programme from Rajiv Gandhi and pursued it further. Gujral added that every Indian Prime Minister sustained the nuclear weapons programme. While all Indian Prime Ministers treated this programme as strictly confidential, they reassured the public that the country's nuclear option was being kept open. On the other hand, Pakistan's Prime Ministers, Benazir Bhutto and Nawaz Sharif and its Chief of Army Staff General Aslam Beg openly talked of Pakistan having acquired nuclear weapons.

It would not be unreasonable for Pakistan to have concluded by 1990 that it had achieved the nuclear deterrence it had set out to establish in 1980. Otherwise, it is inconceivable that it could sustain its proxy war against India, inflicting thousands of casualties, without being unduly concerned about India's "conventional superiority". Even as late as May 1998, when both sides conducted their nuclear tests, India had not used its conventional superiority during the preceding nine years of sustained proxy war by Pakistan in Kashmir. Successive Indian Army Chiefs and Director Generals of Military Operations told the Committee that the idea of using India's conventional superiority did not arise for various reasons other than the nuclear factor.

The 1998 Pokhran tests were the outcome of a policy of consensus on nuclear weapons development among Prime Ministers belonging to the Congress, Janata Dal, United Democratic Front and BJP. For reasons of security, none of these Prime Ministers took any one other than Chairman of the Atomic Energy Commission (not all), and the Scientific Adviser to the Defence Minister into confidence. The Chiefs of Staff, senior Cabinet Ministers and senior civil servants were kept out of the loop.

The nuclear posture adopted by successive Prime Ministers thus put the Indian Army at a disadvantage vis-à-vis its Pakistani counterpart. While the former was in the dark about India's nuclear capability, the latter as the custodian of Pakistani nuclear weaponry was fully aware of its own capability. Three former Indian Chiefs of Army Staff expressed unhappiness about this asymmetric situation.

Successive Indian Prime Ministers failed to take their own colleagues, the major political parties, the Chiefs of Staff and the Foreign Secretaries into confidence on the nature of Pakistan's nuclear threat and the China–Pakistan nuclear axis. The Prime Ministers, even while supporting the weapons programme, kept the intelligence and nuclear weapons establishments in two watertight compartments. Foreign policy was being conducted without Foreign Ministers and Indian diplomats being apprised of the nature of the threat to the country or of India's own nuclear capability. It is quite likely that this secretiveness on the part of the Indian Prime Ministers and the country's inability to exercise its conventional superiority could have confirmed Pakistan in its belief that its nuclear deterrent had indeed been effective in Kashmir since 1990 and it could therefore pursue the proxy war and the Kargil adventure with impunity on the basis of its own prescribed rules of the game.

Pakistan fully understands that nuclear deterrence can work both to its advantage and detriment. In a speech on April 12, 1999, General Musharraf stated that though the possibility of large-scale conventional war between India and Pakistan was virtually zero, proxy wars were not only possible but very likely. At the height of the cold war, when mutual deterrence was in operation between the superpowers, it used to be argued by strategists that 'salami slicing' of small pieces of territory which the adversary would not consider worth escalating to nuclear levels was always feasible. To counter the risk, the US developed a strategy of flexible response. What Pakistan attempted at Kargil was a typical case of salami slicing. [...]* Since India did not cross LoC and reacted strictly within its own territory, the effort to conjure up escalation of a kind that could lead to nuclear war did not succeed. Despite its best efforts, Pakistan was unable to link its Kargil caper with a nuclear flashpoint, though some foreign observers believe it was a near thing. The international community does not favour alteration of the status quo through nuclear blackmail as this would not be in the interest of the five major nuclear powers. Pakistan obviously overlooked this factor.

The P-5 statement of June 4, 1998 and the Security Council Resolution 1172 of June 6, 1998 condemned the Indian and Pakistani nuclear tests. It exhorted both countries to sign the CTBT and NPT, and referred to Kashmir as a root cause of tension between them. This could have encouraged Pakistan to conclude that what its caretaker Prime Minister in 1993, Moeen Qureshi, claimed as the objective of linking Kashmir with the nuclear issue had been achieved and that Pakistan was in a position to implement a strategy outlined as far back as 1980, namely, to seize Kashmir in a bold, brash move when the Indian leadership appeared weak and indecisive.

President Clinton's statement in China assigning a role to that country in South Asia must have further encouraged Pakistan. The US also tilted in favour of Pakistan in imposing sanctions following the nuclear tests, on the ground that its economy was weaker. At the same time, Pakistan would have realised that the impact of sanctions on India was only marginal and should the Foreign Minister Jaswant Singh–US Deputy Secretary of State Strobe Talbot talks make progress, the nuclear card might not be available for too long. With the passage of time, "crying nuclear wolf", even if linked to Kashmir, would progressively lose credibility.

Further, Pakistan's image was damaged by its association with

---

* Government Security Deletion.

the Taliban, Osama Bin Laden and increasing Islamisation. Within Kashmir, the Indian Security Forces were steadily gaining ascendancy over militancy. It is possible that Pakistan's political and military leadership concluded that the window of opportunity for internationalising the Kashmir issue by projecting it as a nuclear flashpoint was fast closing. Pakistan, therefore, needed to act in 1999. This conclusion is borne out by the veiled nuclear threats held out by Pakistan's political leaders and officials at the time of the Kargil crisis. Except for one irresponsible editorial in an Indian party paper, there were no analogous pronouncements in this country.

Some accounts claim that the Kargil intrusion was planned in 1997 and that preliminary reconnaissance and training of personnel commenced that year. If this is accepted, while Pakistan's reliance on its nuclear deterrence to prevent India from escalating would still be important, the actual nuclear tests conducted in May 1998 would not in themselves be all that significant as nuclear deterrence between the two was in place as far back as 1990.

IV. Counter-Insurgency (CI) Operations, Kargil and Integrated Manpower Policy

In going on alert to deter any Pakistani escalation and then focussing on eliminating the intrusion at Kargil, the Army had to withdraw [...]* battalions deployed in J&K from their counter-insurgency role. This caused consternation in the State Government and some worry even to the para-military forces which were largely reliant on the Army in this regard. The heavy involvement of the Army in counter-insurgency operations cannot but affect its preparedness for its primary role, which is to defend the country against external aggression. This point has often been emphasised by Pakistani analysts. Such a situation has arisen because successive Governments have not developed a long-term strategy to deal with insurgency. The Army's prolonged deployment in a counter-insurgency role, adversely affects its training programme, leads to fatigue and the development of a mindset that detracts from its primary role. However, the Ministry of

---

* Government Security Deletion.

Home Affairs, State Governments and para-military forces tend to assume that the Army will always be there to combat insurgency. This was vividly demonstrated when the Committee was referred to the Union Home Ministry's "Action Plan" for fighting militancy and the proxy war in J&K prepared in May 1998. This defined the role of the Army as being to ensure "zero infiltration" across the LoC.

The para-military and Central Police Forces are not trained, raised and equipped to deal with trans-border terrorism by well-trained mercenaries armed with sophisticated equipment who are continuously infiltrating across the border/LoC. Over the years, the quality of these forces has not been appropriately upgraded effectively to deal with the challenge of the times, and this has led to the increased dependence on the Army to fight insurgency. The net result has been to reduce the role of the Indian Army to the level of a para-military force and the para-military forces, in turn, to the level of an ordinary police force. Pakistan has ruthlessly employed terrorism in Punjab, J&K and the North-East to involve the Indian Army in counter-insurgency operations and neutralise its conventional superiority. Having partially achieved this objective, it has also persuaded itself that nuclear blackmail against India has succeeded on three occasions. A coherent counter-strategy to deal with Pakistan's terrorist-nuclear blackmail and the conventional threat has to be thought through.

The committee believes that a comprehensive manpower policy is required to deal with this problem. In the present international security environment, proxy war and terrorism have become preferred means of hurting a neighbour's social, political and economic well-being. Given Pakistan's unrelenting hostility towards this country, it is necessary to evolve a long-term strategy to reduce the involvement of the Army in counter-insurgency and devise more cost-effective means of dealing with the problem.

There has also been criticism that redeployment of military units from CI duty in the Valley to the Kargil sector resulted in providing easy passage for a large number of hardened militants who were infiltrated by Pakistan across the Shamsabari Range into the Kupwara–Uri area and even south of the Pir Panjal.

Fidelity & Honour

The Unified Command was also reorganised with the Director General Rashtriya Rifles (DGRR) being brought in from Delhi to replace GOC 15 Corps. The latter was relieved of this responsibility to enable him to devote full attention to his principal national defence task. However, within weeks of the conclusion of Operation VIJAY, the status quo ante was restored. DGRR returned to Delhi and GOC 15 Corps resumed his place in the Unified Command. The Committee also found Unified Command HQ's intelligence structure lacking in timely and continuous analysis and assessment of intelligence, which is critical for the success of CI operations.

More thought must be given to all these issues. Unified Command HQs have also been set up in Assam from time to time under different circumstances and with a somewhat different structure. But whether in J&K or Assam, there has sometimes been tension both between the Army and para-military/Central Police Organisations/Police formations and between the civil and military authorities. This is an unhappy state of affairs and should not be allowed to linger. The kind of manpower reorganisation the Committee proposes could provide a partial answer, but would still leave untouched the question of how best to structure Unified Command HQs in the future, wherever they might be required.

The decision taken two years ago to reduce the Indian Army's strength by 50,000 men, and reinvest the savings on establishment costs in force modernisation, was a wise one. This reduction in numbers had no bearing on the Kargil crisis and it would be a gross misunderstanding of military realities to believe otherwise.

In spite of continuing counter-insurgency operations over the past many years, there has been no integrated equipment policy in respect of the Army, para-military and Central police forces. The manpower integration proposed would also ensure compatibility of equipment and render it easier for the Army and the other forces to operate side by side effectively when required to do so.

There is an equally pressing need to fashion an effective border management policy which covers not only terrorist infiltration, but illegal migration, smuggling and the flow of narcotics. These are all

626

matters of national concern but are being looked at compartmentally. The inevitable result has been sub-optimal border management at a time when the narcotics trade has been playing a crucial role in Pakistan's promotion of cross-border terrorism.

V. The Technological Dimension

Technology has added significantly to the potential of armies and terrorists. The AK 47 has transformed the lethal potential of the terrorist who has often outgunned the country's security forces in Punjab and J&K. The terrorist comes equipped with rapid fire, stand-off weapons, high explosives, wads of currency (real and fake) and sophisticated communications equipment. He can act alone and also as a member of an integrated team. He is highly motivated and often a person conditioned by years of fundamentalist schooling. Despite the challenge of terrorism over the past many years, the Indian Army and other security forces have lagged behind in the quality of their surveillance and communication equipment, although technologically superior equipment is readily available the world over. Only after the Kargil intrusion was direction-finding equipment acquired in increasing numbers. Helicopters employed for air surveillance patrolling do not have sophisticated monitoring and sensing devices. The Kargil battle was fought with less than optimum communications capability. While self-reliance and indigenisation are sound principles, the availability of critical equipment in time of combat is the supreme consideration that must govern acquisition policy. This does not appear to be the case at present, and there is no mechanism to monitor that the process of equipment acquisition serves the best interests of the country.

The Defence Research and Development Organisation (DRDO) and the chain of Defence laboratories under its jurisdiction is responsible for indigenising and constantly upgrading the country's weapons and equipment inventory and related supplies. The dilemma has always been to determine the correct balance between "make or buy". There are obvious constraints such as of foreign exchange and the non-availability of state-of-the-art technology from advanced nations which are at best only prepared to share these with their military allies. As a non-aligned power, India has not had access to some of the Western technologies that have flowed to Pakistan. Dual-use technology-denial regimes have also operated against India. These considerations demand that the country develop a degree of self-reliance in Defence-related technology and military hardware. Considerable progress has been made in this direction. The achievements in this field can neither be denied nor denigrated. Nevertheless, a number of instances were brought to the notice of the Committee in respect of which there have been significant cost and time overruns in the development and induction of indigenous weapons and equipment for the three Armed Services. While extenuating circumstances can be cited, the fact is that the Services have had to do without such items whereas Pakistan has not been similarly handicapped. Some of these issues were in fact examined in detail by the Committee on Defence Expenditure (1990–91). This report has unfortunately not been made public, and, the Committee understands, many of its more substantial recommendations await implementation.

VI. Media Relations and Information

If the media served the country well, much of the credit goes to the initiative it itself took and to some individuals within the Government and the Armed Forces. Information is power, especially in this Information Age. The media moulds national and international opinion and can be a potent force multiplier. This was evident at Kargil—India's first television war. All things considered, coverage by the print and electronic media was by and large satisfactory. Yet it was apparent that, with some exceptions, media personnel lacked training in military affairs and war reporting and that the Armed Services lacked training and preparedness to facilitate the task of the media and counter disinformation.

Defence Public Relations is routinely handled by the Ministry of Defence through regular Information Service cadres. This establishment is not equipped to handle media relations during war or even proxy war. The briefing function during the Kargil crisis was taken over by a triad of senior military and civil spokesmen. Army Head-quarters set up an Information and Psychological Warfare Cell under an officer of the rank of Major General with direct access to the Army Chief. This enabled Army Headquarters both to monitor and dissemi-nate information in a better calibrated manner than would have been the case otherwise.

Reporting on the campaign revealed a lack of public information about the command structure of the Armed Forces and how respon-sibilities are distributed within the national intelligence framework. While arrangements were made for official briefings at Delhi, there were inadequate arrangements at the Corps, Division and Brigade levels. Nor were there arrangements to brief officers and men at the ground level on daily developments, nor to interface with the civil authorities. The result was generation of a lot of inaccurate informa-tion such as the reported capture of a number of Indian Army bunkers (whereas the enemy only occupied one permanent patrol post which had earlier been vacated on account of extreme weather conditions), the existence of three-storeyed enemy bunkers equipped with televi-sion sets, and the purchase by the intruders of cement from the Dras–Kargil market.

A number of simple misperceptions became apparent in newspa-per reports questioning the absence of the Army Chief in Poland during the early part of May 1999 and the Northern Army Com-mander going to Pune about the same time. The early military appreciation was of limited infiltration in Kargil. Nevertheless, the Corps Commander, in whose area of responsibility the intrusion (as it was subsequently discovered to be) occurred, had acted promptly and vigorously to deal with even larger eventualities. There was no need to cancel the Army Chief's visit which had been long planned and was of some political significance. The COAS remained in touch with developments at home and there was no vacuum in the higher military leadership because of his absence abroad during the early phase of Kargil developments. The Army Commander, in turn, went to Pune for a briefing from his predecessor, Lieutenant General S. Padmanabhan, now Southern Army Commander. He too was in constant touch with his Command and HQ 15 Corps, and had already set in motion various precautionary measures.

Some of all this is inevitable in the fog of war. But efforts have to be made to review information handling procedures within the Armed Forces and their public dissemination. The Army needs such improved public relations capability even otherwise when deployed on counter-insurgency duties. Public relations are presently managed by the Ministry of Defence, and at the formation level by military officers who have no media background.

A comprehensive account of the Kargil operations remains to be brought out. Pakistani political and military leaders have repeatedly highlighted their nuclear capability and their will to use it. Accounts have also appeared in Pakistan of how India was thrice deterred by its nuclear capability. India's reticence in setting the record straight about the earlier conflicts and the developments in the nuclear field appear to have influenced the Pakistani mindset, and led to the adventurous miscalculation over Kargil.

The first overall briefing on the Kargil situation in the Military Operations Room was given to the Defence and External Affairs Ministers on May 17 with the Chiefs of Staff Committee (COSC) in attendance. This was followed by a meeting of the CCS chaired by the Prime Minister on May 18, and a briefing of the Prime Minister and Defence Minister on May 24, with the COSC in attendance, by when the magnitude of the Kargil intrusion had been more or less fully assessed. The Army Chief had returned from Poland by May 20 when the CCS met again on May 25,* with the COSC in attendance, and the use of air power was cleared.

War and proxy war do not leave the civil population untouched. Human rights violations, civilian casualties, destruction or commandeering of property, refugee movements and the disruption of infrastructure and livelihoods must be expected. This calls for the creation of a civil military interface at various levels to deal with a whole

---

* CCS met formally only on 25-5-99; earlier meetings of May 99 were briefing sessions.

range of problems on an emergency basis. Such liaison was lacking during the Kargil action and points to a deficiency that must be made good.

The outcome of the Kargil operation was both a military and diplomatic triumph for India. The Pakistani intruders were evicted with heavier casualties than those suffered by India. The sanctity of the LoC received international recognition and Pakistan was isolated in the comity of nations. While attending to such shortcomings as have been brought to light, the nation can be proud of the manner in which the Armed Forces and the people as a whole acquitted themselves.

VII. Was Kargil Avoidable?

A Kargil-type situation could perhaps have been avoided had the Indian Army followed a policy of "Siachenisation" to plug unheld gaps along the 168 km stretch from Kaobal Gali to Chorbat La. This would have entailed establishing a series of winter cut-off posts with communications and other logistic support and specially equipped and trained troops to hold these positions, and undertake winter patrolling despite risk of cold injuries and avalanche casualties which would have had to be accepted. Such a dispersal of forces to hold uninhabited territory of no strategic value, would have dissipated considerable military strength and effort and would not have been at all cost-effective. If, however, it has had to be done now, such a policy can only be regarded as no more than a temporary expedient. The alternative should be a credible declaratory policy of swiftly punishing wanton and wilful violations of the sanctity of the LoC. This should be supplemented by a comprehensive space and aerial-based surveillance system.

RECOMMENDATIONS

The Findings bring out many grave deficiencies in India's security management system. The framework Lord Ismay formulated and Lord Mountbatten recommended was accepted by a national leadership unfamiliar with the intricacies of national security management.

There has been very little change over the past 52 years despite the 1962 debacle, the 1965 stalemate and the 1971 victory, the growing nuclear threat, end of the cold war, continuance of proxy war in Kashmir for over a decade and the revolution in military affairs. The political, bureaucratic, military and intelligence establishments appear to have developed a vested interest in the status quo. National security management recedes into the background in time of peace and is considered too delicate to be tampered with in time of war and proxy war. The Committee strongly feels that the Kargil experience, the continuing proxy war and the prevailing nuclearised security environment justify a thorough review of the national security system in its entirety.

Such a review cannot be undertaken by an over-burdened bureaucracy. An independent body of credible experts, whether a national commission, or one or more task forces or otherwise as expedient, is required to conduct such studies which must be undertaken expeditiously. The specific issues that require to be looked into are set out below.

NATIONAL SECURITY COUNCIL

The National Security Council (NSC), formally constituted in April 1999, is still evolving and its procedures will take time to mature. Whatever its merits, having a National Security Adviser, who also happens to be Principal Secretary to the Prime Minister, can only be an interim arrangement. The Committee believes that there must be a full-time National Security Adviser and it would suggest that a second line of personnel be inducted into the system as early as possible and groomed for higher responsibility.

Members of the National Security Council, the senior bureaucracy servicing it, and the Service Chiefs need to be continually sensitised to assessed intelligence pertaining to national, regional and international issues. This can be done through periodic intelligence briefings of the CCS with all supporting staff in attendance.

INTELLIGENCE

Kargil highlighted the gross inadequacies in the nation's surveillance capability, particularly through satellite imagery. The Committee notes with satisfaction that steps have been initiated to acquire this capability. Every effort must be made and adequate funds provided to ensure that a capability of world standards is developed indigenously and put in place in the shortest possible time. It is for consideration whether a two-stream approach—civil and military— in regard to the downloading and interpretation of the imagery may not be a better alternative than depending on a single agency. Some countries have created a national surveillance command. Since the Indian system is still in the initial stages, decisions taken at this juncture will have long-term implications.

Unmanned Aerial Vehicles (UAVs), also known as Remotely Piloted Vehicles (RPVs), are extremely useful and effective in surveillance, especially if they have night vision and thermal imaging capabilities. UAVs have just been inducted and are operating in the plains under the charge of the Army. Similar efforts should be made for the acquisition of high altitude UAVs. Institutionalised arrangements should be made to ensure that the UAV imagery generated is disseminated to the concerned intelligence agencies as quickly as possible. UAVs could also prove effective in counter-insurgency operations. They may replace WASO patrols in the long run. However, in the interim, the possibility of using more stable WASO platforms than Cheetah helicopters and equipping them with thermal imaging sensors should be explored.

The most spectacular intelligence coup of the Kargil operations was the interception of a series of high level Islamabad–Beijing telephone conversations. This highlights the capabilities of communication intelligence which in India is fragmented among a number of agencies and is not adequately funded. The equipment needs to be modernised in keeping with the advances made by Pakistan in inducting advanced communication technologies. There has also been a gross shortage of direction-finding equipment which could contribute significantly to counter-insurgency operations.

The United States has grouped all its communication and electronic intelligence efforts within a single organisation, the National Security Agency (NSA). The desirability of setting up a similar organisation in India with adequate resources for this extremely important and non-intrusive method of gathering technological intelligence calls for examination. Adequate attention has not been paid to developing encryption and decryption skills. The centralised communication and electronic intelligence agency should feed all the information it generates to the country's premier national intelligence agency which should in turn disseminate this material to all concerned users. The problems and purposes of monitoring communications within the country and the effort devoted to listen in on external communications are different. Increasingly, organised crime and anti-national elements are using encrypted communications. While the effort to build up adequate communication and electronic intelligence capability should be tailored to suit India's particular needs, parochial departmental interests should be effectively countered.

In many advanced countries, technological intelligence collection is undertaken by an integrated Defence Intelligence Agency with adequate resources. In India, the Defence intelligence effort is limited in relation to the role assigned to the external intelligence agency (R&AW) except for limited tactical and signal intelligence. The resources made available to the Defence Services for intelligence collection are not commensurate with the responsibility assigned to them. There are distinct advantages in having two lines of intelligence collection and reporting, with a rational division of functions, responsibilities and areas of specialisation. The Committee is of the view that the issue of setting up an integrated Defence intelligence agency needs examination.

The Committee has drawn attention to deficiencies in the present system of collection, reporting, collation and assessment of intelligence. There is no institutionalised mechanism for coordination or objective-oriented interaction between the agencies and consumers at different levels. Similarly, there is no mechanism for tasking the agencies, monitoring their performance and reviewing their records to evaluate their quality. Nor is there any oversight of the overall functioning of the agencies. These are all standard features elsewhere in the world. In the absence of such procedures, the Government and the nation do not know whether they are getting value for money. While taking note of recent steps to entrust the NSCS with some of these responsibilities the Committee recommends a thorough examination of the working of the intelligence system with a view to remedying these deficiencies.

All major countries have a mechanism at national and often at lower levels to assess the intelligence inputs received from different agencies and sources. After the 1962 debacle, the then existing JIC under the Chiefs of Staff Committee was upgraded and transferred to the Cabinet Secretariat. It was further upgraded in 1985 with the Chairman being raised to the rank of Secretary to the Government. The Committee finds that for various reasons cited in the Report, the JIC was devalued. Its efficacy has increased since it became part of the National Security Council Secretariat. However, its role and place in the national intelligence framework should be evaluated in the context of overall reform of the system.

Pakistan's action at Kargil was not rational. Its behaviour patterns require to be carefully studied in order to gain a better understanding of the psyche of its leadership. In other countries, intelligence agencies have developed large 'White Wings' of high quality analysts for in-house analysis. They also contract studies with university departments and think tanks with area specialisation. This is sadly neglected in India. The development of such country/region specialisation along with associated language skills is a time-consuming process and should not be further delayed. A generalist administration culture would appear to permeate the intelligence field. It is necessary to establish think tanks, encourage country specialisation in university departments and to organise regular exchanges of personnel between them and the intelligence community.

Counter-Terrorist Operations

There is general agreement that in the light of the new situation of proxy war and large-scale terrorism that the country faces, the role and the tasks of the para-military forces have to be restructured particularly with reference to command and control and leadership functions. They need to be trained to much higher standards of performance and better equipped to deal with terrorist threats. The possibility of adopting an integrated manpower policy for the Armed Forces, para-military forces and the Central Police Forces merits examination.

The Army must be young and fit at all times. Therefore, instead of the present practice of having 17 years of colour service (as has been the policy since 1976), it would be advisable to reduce the colour service to a period of seven to ten years and, thereafter, release these officers and men for service in the country's para-military formations. After an appropriate period of service here, older cadres might be further streamed into the regular police forces or absorbed in a National Service Corps (or a National Conservation Corps), as provided for under Article 51A(d) of the Constitution, to spearhead a range of land and water conservation and physical and social infrastructure development on the model of some eco-development battalions that have been raised with a fair measure of success. This would reduce the age profile of the Army and the para-military forces, and also reduce pension costs and other entitlements such as married quarters and educational facilities. The Army pension bill has risen exponentially since the 1960s and is becoming an increasing burden on the national exchequer. Army pensions rose from Rs 1568 crores in 1990–91 to Rs 6932 crores (budgeted) in 1999–2000, the equivalent of almost two-thirds of the current Army salary bill.

The para-military and police forces have their own ethos and traditions and might well be chary of such lateral induction as has been proposed. This objection might be overcome were the para-military forces to undertake recruitment on the basis of certain common national military standards, and then send those selected for training and absorption in the Army for a period of colour service before reverting to their parent para-military formations. The Committee is aware of the complexities and sensitivities involved in any such security manpower reorganisation. Nevertheless, national security dictates certain imperatives which the country may ignore only at its peril. The proposed reorganisation would make a career in the armed forces attractive on the basis of the lifetime employment offered by the two or three-tiered secondment formula.

BORDER MANAGEMENT

Border management has become immensely more complex over the years. It is now handled by the Assam Rifles, the Border Security Forces and the Indo-Tibetan Border Police. Border fencing in Punjab has produced positive results. Elsewhere, vested interests have come in the way of effective border management. The smuggling of narcotics, man-portable arms and explosives, illegal migration and the infiltration of trained mercenaries have all exacerbated border management. Narcotics is dealt with by the Finance Ministry while other aspects are handled by the Home Ministry. If the country is to acquire increased capabilities for area surveillance and electronic fencing, the present structure and procedures for border patrolling must be reviewed. The Committee is therefore of the view that the entire issue needs detailed study in order to evolve force structures and procedures that ensure improved border management and a reduction, if not the elimination, in the inflow of narcotics, illegal migrants, terrorists and arms.

DEFENCE BUDGET AND MODERNISATION

A number of experts have at various times suggested the need to enhance India's Defence outlays as budgetary constraints have affected the process of modernisation and created certain operational voids. The Committee would not like to advocate any percentage share of GDP that should be assigned to Defence. This must be left to the Government to determine in consultation with the concerned Departments and the Defence Services.

Among aspects of modernisation to which priority should be given is that of equipping infantrymen with superior light weight weapons, equipment and clothing suited to the threats they are required to face in alpine conditions.

NATIONAL SECURITY MANAGEMENT AND APEX DECISION-MAKING

India is perhaps the only major democracy where the Armed Forces Headquarters are outside the apex government structure. The Chiefs of Staff have assumed the role of operational commander of their respective forces rather than that of Chiefs of Staff to the Prime Minister and Defence Minister. They simultaneously discharge the roles of operational commanders and national security planners/ managers, especially in relation to future equipment and force postures. Most of their time, is, however, devoted to the operational role, as is bound to happen. This has led to a number of negative results. Future-oriented long-term planning suffers. Army Headquarters has developed a command rather than a staff culture. Higher decisions on equipment, force levels and strategy are not collegiate but command-oriented. The Prime Minister and Defence Minister do not have the benefit of the views and expertise of the Army Commanders and their equivalents in the Navy and Air Force so that higher level defence management decisions are more consensual and broadbased. The present obsolete system has perpetuated the continuation of the culture of the British Imperial theatre system of an India Command whereas what is required is a National Defence Headquarters. Most opposition to change comes from inadequate knowledge of the national security decision-making process elsewhere in the world and a reluctance to change the status quo and move away from considerations of parochial interest. The status quo is often mistakenly defended as embodying civilian ascendancy over the Armed Forces, which is not a real issue. In fact, locating the Services' Headquarters in the Government will further enhance civilian supremacy.

Structural reforms could bring about a much closer and more constructive interaction between the Civil Government and the Services. The Committee is of the view that the present obsolete system, bequeathed to India by Lord Ismay, merits re-examination. An effective and appropriate national security planning and decision-making structure for India in the nuclear age is overdue, taking account of the revolution in military affairs and threats of proxy war and terrorism and the imperative of modernising the Armed Forces. An objective assessment of the last 52 years will show that the country is lucky to have scraped through various national security threats without too much damage, except in 1962. The country can no longer afford such ad hoc functioning. The Committee therefore recommends that the entire gamut of national security management and apex decision-making and the structure and interface between the Ministry of Defence and the Armed Forces Headquarters be comprehensively studied and reorganised.

INDIA'S NUCLEAR POLICY

The Report clearly brings out that, beginning with Indira Gandhi, successive Prime Ministers displayed extreme sensitivity towards the nuclear issue and consistently supported an Indian nuclear weapons programme. They judged it necessary to envelop it in the utmost secrecy and consequently did not take their own party colleagues, the Armed Forces and senior civil servants into confidence. This has caused many in the country to believe that India's nuclear weaponisation programme is a departure from the traditional policy of merely keeping the nuclear option open indefinitely. The record must be set straight. The contribution of Indira Gandhi, Rajiv Gandhi, V.P. Singh, Chandra Shekhar, Narasimha Rao, Deve Gowda and Inder Kumar Gujral to India's emergence as a nuclear weapon state, and the compulsions on them to ensure this, should be made known. The record clearly establishes that the Indian nuclear weapons

programme had a much wider consensus than is generally believed. The Committee therefore recommends the publication of a
White Paper on the Indian nuclear weapons programme. This will
also bring out the stark facts of the evolution of Pakistan's nuclear capability with assistance from countries who tirelessly decry
proliferation, and the threats posed to India through nuclear blackmail.

MEDIA RELATIONS AND INFORMATION

Kargil was the first war which Indian correspondents covered by
going to the front in significant numbers. It was also the country's
first television war and one in which the Indian Army had to handle
the media right on the battlefront. This has been a learning experience
for the Government, the Armed Forces and the media. Neither the
Northern Army Command nor HQ 15 Corps nor the lower field
formations had media cells which could cater to the requirements of
the press corps. This reveals an obvious lacuna which must be
plugged. The Army has decided to revive and upgrade its war correspondents' course at the College of Combat, Mhow. The media
should avail of this opportunity so that there is a cadre of trained war
correspondents at any time. Simultaneously, media relations and the
techniques and implications of information war and perception management must form a distinct and important module at all levels of
military training. It must also be recognised that the media has to be
serviced at many levels—national, local and international. None is
less important than the other.

While dealing with the information issue, the Committee would
also like to draw attention to the fact that Indian security forces are
deployed year round in very difficult and inhospitable terrain ranging
from high mountains to dense forests and sandy deserts. The US
Armed Forces usually operate dedicated radio and TV channels to
entertain and inform their armed forces when deployed overseas. The
Government should seriously consider similar dedicated facilities for
the Indian Armed Forces. If such facilities had been available at the

time of Kargil, some of the misleading reports and rumours that gained currency could have been effectively countered.

This Report brings out the vast gap between the actual policies pursued by the Government and developments on the ground on the one hand and popular perceptions derived from public pronouncements on the other. In a democracy, it is incumbent on the Government to reduce any such gap. While the country's nuclear programme must remain confidential, there was a failure on the part of successive Prime Ministers to educate the people on the realities of nuclear security confronting the country. In the case of Defence policy and insurgency situations, sufficient public information is not available. There is no single, comprehensive official publication containing details of the Kashmir question, the UN resolutions and why they could not be implemented, as well as of more recent developments in Kashmir through the years of proxy war, terrorism and ethnic cleansing together with Pakistan's involvement in all of these. The Government must review its information policy and develop structures and processes to keep the public informed on vital national issues.

It would appear that one of the major factors influencing Pakistan's aggressive behaviour in 1947, 1965, 1971 and 1999 has been its self-image of martial superiority and a deliberately cultivated perception of an ineffectual Indian Army and a weak and vacillating Indian Government. Though Pakistan was discomfited in all the four military adventures it undertook, it has attempted to portray each of them as a narrowly-missed victory. Even the 1971 defeat is blamed on the Soviet Union. Developments in Afghanistan and its final denouement have been portrayed as projecting Pakistani military prowess in defeating the Soviet super-power, India has not published authoritative histories of the 1965 and 1971 wars. It is necessary to publish authentic accounts of the 1965 and 1971 wars and to establish the facts. While this Report appends, with appropriate security deletions, the three Service Headquarters' presentations of Operation VIJAY, Operation SAFED SAGAR and Operation TALWAR; that were made before the Committee, we recommend that an authoritative account of this unique high altitude war be published at an early date. Further to these, communicating the scope, extent and history of India's nuclear weapons programme should be an essential part of the exercise of deterrence. The record needs to be set right, not through strident propaganda, but by a cold-marshalling of the facts regarding contemporary events and past history.

TECHNOLOGY

The longstanding controversy between the Services and the DRDO on drawing the line between "make" or "buy" resulted in the formulation of a new Procurement Policy in 1995. This liberalised the procedures for the import of equipment as against its indigenous development. However, this policy needs periodic review in the light of changing circumstances. Experience would suggest that such a review is presently overdue. One problem the DRDO faces is that the armed forces borrow unique features from weapons and equipment on offer from advanced military suppliers around the world and marry these in their "General Staff Requirements" to make "impossible" demands. There is an element of truth in this assertion but none can be faulted for desiring the best. A true partnership must be established between the Services and the DRDO to ensure that the latter gets full backing and funding from the Services and the former, in turn, get the indented equipment they require without undue delay.

The design and development of special materials as well as Defence stores and equipment often entails working at the frontiers of technology. It is therefore possible and desirable to harness national talent wherever it lies—in the Universities and Indian Institutes of Technology, and in the private and public sectors—and not only within the DRDO and designated Defence undertakings. Casting the net wider would be advantageous and would ensure a greater degree of competition and technological spin-off into the civil sector. This would also facilitate Defence exports, the better utilisation of highly sophisticated industrial capacity and related manpower and enable

Defence laboratories and Defence undertakings to concentrate on those areas which cannot be hived off to the civil sector, public or private, on grounds of high security or limited applicability of end use for civilian purposes. There is a whole gamut of issues here which merits consideration.

CIVIL MILITARY LIAISON

The establishment of a civil-military liaison mechanism at various levels, from the ranking Command HQ to the operational formations on the ground, Division, Brigade or Battalion, is most necessary to smoothen relationships during times of emergency and stress, like war and proxy war, and to ensure that there is no room for friction and alienation of the local population. Situations of no-war-no-peace call for norms and procedures that avoid delay and endless red tape. Relocating villages behind the Army's forward defence line in J&K can best be done through an initially limited experimental move and further action on the basis of policies evolved as a result of that learning experience. Likewise, steps should be taken to issue ID Cards to border villagers in certain vulnerable areas on a priority basis, pending its extension to other or all parts of the State. Such a policy would also be relevant in the North-East, Sikkim and part of West Bengal.

The Kargil Sector and other areas along the LoC have suffered loss and damage on account of war and shelling. A rehabilitation programme for Kargil must be put in place as a precursor to a longer term development package that includes the completion of by-pass roads for strategic movements between Zojila and Leh. This will render NH-1A an exclusively civilian highway and not a military target, skirting as it does a part of the LoC in this sector.

The dedication and valour of the Ladakh Scouts and J&K Light Infantry merits recognition through the raising of additional units of these regiments with a higher component of men from Kargil being inducted into the Ladakh Scouts.

DECLARATORY POLICY FOR LoC

More attention should be given to monitoring and analysing developments and trends in "Azad J&K" and the Northern Areas which are in ferment and whose fate and future cannot be divorced from any consideration of the Kashmir Question. Likewise, the Kashmiri diaspora overseas must be kept better informed about the situation in J&K and what happened in Kargil.

Misperceptions and ambiguities about the Siachen/AGPL sector need to be dispelled and the facts of "cartographic aggression" here made known. There is no warrant for departing from the logic of extending the LoC from NJ 9842 and "thence north to the glaciers" as set out in the delineation of the Ceasefire Line under the Karachi agreement of July 29, 1949 which was subsequently converted into the Line of Control by the Simla Agreement in 1972. This broadly upholds the current Actual Ground Position Line (AGPL). The Pakistani fallacy of showing the LoC as running northeast to the Karakoram Pass must be exposed.

The country must not fall into the trap of "Siachenisation" of the Kargil heights and similar unheld unpopulated "gaps" in the High Himalaya along the entire length of the Northern border. The proper response would be a declaratory policy that deliberate infringement of the sanctity of the LoC and wanton cross-border terrorism in furtherance of proxy war will meet with prompt retaliation in a manner, time and place of India's choosing. Pakistan and the world must know that India's defence of the integrity of its own territory, including that within its own side of the LoC, is not and cannot be held to be escalatory and that the aggressor and his victim cannot be bracketed and placed on par.

Such a declaratory policy must be backed with credible measures in J&K to win back alienated sections of the population, attend to genuine discontents, political and economic, and enable the victims of ethnic cleansing to return the their homes in the Valley or elsewhere in the State with security and honour. To this end, the Union and State Governments must jointly initiate a twin policy of reform and devolution to and within J&K and a dialogue with Pakistan. India's commitment to maintaining the sanctity of the LoC/AGPL and the international endorsement of this position won during the Kargil crises has within it the seeds of a larger, long-term settlement that can bring enduring peace and tranquillity to J&K and stable and cooperative Indo–Pakistan relations on the basis of the Simla–Lahore process within the framework of SAARC.

CONCLUSION

The Committee's review brings out many lessons that the Armed Forces, Intelligence agencies, Parliament, Government, media and the nation as a whole have to learn. These have been set out in the preceding findings. These should stimulate introspection and reflection, leading to purposeful action. The Committee trusts that its Recommendations will be widely discussed and acted upon expeditiously so that the sacrifices made will not have been in vain. The best tribute to the dedication of those killed and wounded will be to ensure that "Kargils" of any description are never repeated.

There is both comfort and danger in clinging to any long-established status quo. There will be many who suggest the most careful deliberation on the report. Procrastination has cost nations dear. Others will no doubt advocate incremental change. Half-measures will not do; synergy will be lost. The Committee has after very wide interaction sign-posted directions along the path to peace, ensuring progress, development and stability of the nation. How exactly the country should proceed to refashion its Security-Intelligence-Development shield to meet the challenge of the 21st Century is for the Government, Parliament, and public opinion to determine. There is no turning away from that responsibility.

15 December 1999

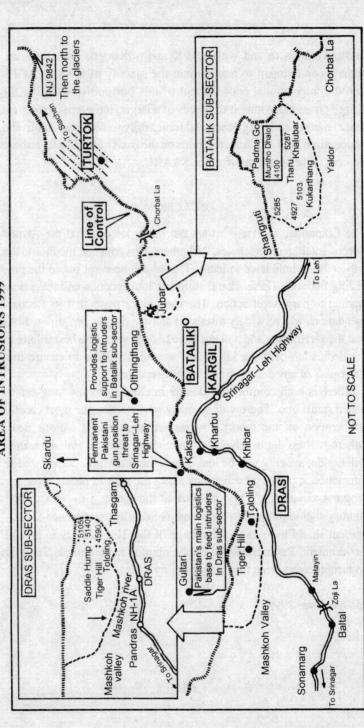

AREA OF INTRUSIONS 1999

NOT TO SCALE

DRAS SUB-SECTOR

BATALIK SUB-SECTOR

Line of Control

NJ 9842
Then north to the glaciers

TURTOK

To Siachen

Chorbat La

Chorbat La

Padma Go
Muntho Dhalo 4100
Tharu 5287
Khalubar
5103 Kukarthang
4927
Yaldor
Shangruti
5285

To Leh

Provides logistic support to intruders in Batalik sub-sector

Olthingthang

Jubar

BATALIK

KARGIL

Srinagar–Leh Highway

Kharbu

Kaksar

Khibar

Permanent Pakistani gun position threat to Srinagar–Leh Highway

Skardu

Thasgam

Saddle Hump 5105
Tiger Hill 5140
Tololing 4590

Mashkoh river

DRAS

NH-1A
Pandras

Mashkoh valley

To Srinagar

Gultari

Pakistan's main logistics base to feed intruders in Dras sub-sector

Tiger Hill

Tololing

DRAS

Mashkoh Valley

Matayin

Zoji La

Baltal

Sonamarg

To Srinagar

Notes And References

Chapter One

This chapter is largely based on Martin Moir's *A General Guide to the India Office Records* (British Library, London, 1988); *The Imperial Gazetteer of India, The Indian Empire* (Oxford, 1909) Volume IV; and the Government of India publication, *The Army in India and its Evolution* (Calcutta, 1924). Specific references are given below:

1. Thorpe, B., ed., *The Anglo-Saxon Chronicle*, London: 1861, Vol. II, p. 66.
2. Prasad, R.C., *Early English Travellers in India*, Delhi: Motilal Banarsidas, 1980, pp. 4-5.
3. Shaw, J., *Charters relating to the East India Company*, Madras: 1887, p. 2.
4. Moir, M., *A General Guide to the India Office Records*, London: 1988, p. 3.
5. Moir, op. cit., pp.5-6.
6. Thompson, E.J., & Garratt, G.T., *Rise and Fulfilment of British Rule in India*, London: 1934, p. 12.
7. Moir, op. cit., p. 6.
8. Cadell, P., *History of the Bombay Army*, London: 1938, p. 8; and *The Army in India and its Evolution*, Calcutta: 1924, p. 4.
9. Lenman, Bruce, *The East India Company and the Emperor Aurangzeb, History Today*, 1987, Vol. 37, p. 29.
10. Moir, op. cit., p. 7.
11. Moir, op. cit., p. 14.
12. Moir, op. cit., p. 17.
13. Moon, Penderel, *The British Conquest and Dominion of India*, London: Duckworth, 1989, p. 11.
14. Moir, op. cit., p. 18.
15. Williams, J., *An Historical Account of the Rise and Progress of the Bengal Infantry from 1757 to 1796*, London: 1817, p. 23.
16. Rice Holmes, T., *A History of the Indian Mutiny*, London:

Macmillan, 1898, p.48.
17. Orme, R., *Mss India*, British Library (Oriental and India Office Collections), henceforth (BL[OIC]), Vol. I.
18. Fuller, J.F.C., ed., Terraine, J., *The Decisive Battles of the Western World*, London: 1970.
19. Edwardes, M., *Clive*, Introduction by Terraine, J., London: 1977, p.viii.
20. Moir, op. cit., p.18.
21. Malleson, G.B., *Essays and Lectures on Indian Historical Subjects*, Calcutta: 1866, pp. 60-61.
22. Lake's Despatches, (BL[IOC]).
23. Rice Holmes, op. cit., pp.49-50.
24. Moir, op. cit., p.18.
25. Moir, op. cit., p.19.
26. Howitt, W., *A Popular History of the Treatment of the Natives by the Europeans in all their Colonies*, London: 1838, pp.212-213.

Chapter Two

This chapter is largely based on Sir Penderel Moon's *The British Conquest and Dominion of India* (London, 1989); Colonel G.B. Malleson's *The Decisive Battles of India* (London, 1885); Amiya Barat's *The Bengal Native Infantry, It's Organisation and Discipline, 1796-1852* (Calcutta, 1962); and P. Macrory's *Signal Catastrophe* (London, 1966). Specific references are given below:

1. Wilson, W.J., *History of the Madras Army*, Madras: 1882, Vol. I, p. 72.
2. Broome, A., *History of the Rise and Progress of the Bengal Army*, London: 1850, p. 274.
3. Barat, Amiya, *The Bengal Native Infantry, It's Organisation and Discipline, 1796-1852*, Calcutta: 1962, p. xi.
4. Barat, op. cit., p. 7.
5. Mason, P., *A Matter of Honour*, Harmondsworth: Penguin Books, 1974, p. 90.

6. Broome, op. cit., p. 250.7.
7. Malleson, G.B., *The Decisive Battles of India,* London: W.H. Allen, 1885, p. 125.
8. Malleson, op. cit., pp. 111 & 122.
9. Broome, op. cit., p. 263.
10. Dodwell, H.H., *Dupleix and Clive,* London: 1920, p. 270.
11. Williams, J., *An Historical Account of the Rise and Progress of the Bengal Infantry from 1757 to 1796,* London: 1817, pp. 4-5.
12. Moon, Penderel, *The British Conquest and Dominion of India,* London: Duckworth, 1989, p. 7.
13. Letter to Bengal, 23 March 1759, (Despatches to Bengal), Vol.I, No.898 (BL [OIC]).
14. Auber, P., *Rise and Progress of the British Power in India,* London: 1837, Vol.I, pp. 71-72.
15. Malleson, op. cit., p. 110.
16. Malleson, op. cit., pp. 128-129.
17. Malleson, op. cit., p. 133.
18. Malleson, op. cit., pp. 143 & 150.
19. Malleson, op. cit., p. 181.
20. Malleson, op. cit., p. 185.
21. Malleson, op. cit., p. 186.
22. Malleson, op. cit., p. 193.
23. Malleson, op. cit., p. 208.
24. Datta, K.K., *Anti-British Plots and Movements before 1857,* Meerut: Meenakshi Prakashan, 1970, p. 1.
25. Moon, op. cit., p. 124.
26. Roberts, P.E., *History of British India under the Company and the Crown,* Oxford: 1939, p. 158.
27. Ninth Report of the Committee of Secrecy, 1773, House of Commons (BL [OIC]), p. 550.
28. Orme *Mss,* Vol.17, p. 13 (BL [OIC]).
29. Letter to Bengal, 16 March 1768 (Despatches to Bengal), Vol.4, (BL [OIC]).
30. Ninth Report, op. cit., p. 549.
31. Long, J., *Selections from the unpublished records of Government, 1748-1767,* Calcutta: 1809, p. 151.

32. Letter to Bengal, 28 April 1782 (Despatches to Bengal), Vol.12, (BL [OIC]).

33. Moon, op. cit., p. 202.

34. Rennell, J., *The Marches of the British Army in the Peninsula of India*, London: 1792, p. 33.

35. Mill, James, *The History of British India*, London: 1858, Vol.VI, pp. 270-271.

36. Tuker, F.S., *Gorkha—The Story of the Gurkhas of Nepal*, London: 1954, p. 83.

37. Tuker, op. cit., p. 80.

38. Moon, op. cit., p. 379.

39. Tuker, op. cit., p. 81.

40. Stranks, C.J., ed., *The Path of Glory, being the Memoirs of John Shipp*, London: 1969, p. 112.

41. Macrory, P., *Signal Catastrophe*, London: Curtis Brown,1966, p. 220.

42. Macrory, op. cit., pp. 204 & 210.

43. Macrory, op. cit., p. 244.

44. Macrory, op. cit., p. 258.

45. English, B., *John Company's Last War*, London: Harper Collins,1971, pp. 63 & 98.

46. English, B., op. cit., p. 6.

Chapter Three

This chapter is largely based on Sir Penderel Moon's *The British Conquest and Dominion of India;* Amiya Barat's *The Bengal Native Infantry, It's Organisation and Discipline, 1796-1852*; Lieutenant Colonel W.J. Wilson's *The History of the Madras Army* (Madras, 1892); Philip Mason's *A Matter of Honour* (London, 1974); and Burton Stein's *Thomas Munro* (New Delhi, 1989). Specific references are given below:

1. Barat, Amiya, *The Bengal Native Infantry, It's Organisation and Discipline, 1796-1852*, Calcutta: 1962, p. vii.

2. Barat, op. cit., p. xi.

3. Mason, Philip, *A Matter of Honour,* London: Harmondsworth, 1974, pp. 236-37.
4. Cohen, S.P., *The Indian Army,* Delhi: OUP, 1990, p. 5.
5. Keigwin to King Charles II, (BL[OIC]) Home Misc. Series, Vol. 52, No.1, pp. 206-09.
6. Strachey, R. and O., *Keigwin's Rebellion 1683-84,* Oxford: 1916, pp. 82-83, 132, 166-67.
7. Council of Fort St. David to Directors, 6 August 1751, (BL[OIC]) Home Misc. Series, Vol. 93, No.7, pp. 18-19.
8. Wilson, W.J., *The History of the Madras Army,* Madras: 1892, Vol. I, p. 38.
9. Moon, Penderel, *The British Conquest and Dominion of India,* London: Duckworth, 1989, p. 57.
10. Mason, op. cit., p. 85.
11. Phythian-Adams, E.G., *The Madras Soldier,* Wellington: India, 1958, pp. 27-30.
12. Malleson, G.B., *The Decisive Battles of India,* London: W.H.Allen, 1885, p. 175.
13. Malleson, op. cit., p. 195.
14. Moon, op. cit., pp. 128-30.
15. Moon, op. cit., p. 187.
16. Moon, op. cit., p. 135.
17. Moon, op. cit., p. 188.
18. Moon, op. cit., p. 190.
19. Moon, op. cit., p. 208.
20. Moon, op. cit., pp. 166 & 178.
21. Wilson, W.J., op. cit., p. 18.
22. Wilson, op. cit., Vol. II, p. 151.
23. Wilson, op. cit., Vol. II, pp. 137-39.
24. Moon, op. cit., p. 262.
25. Moon, op. cit., p. 268.
26. Moon, op. cit., p. 269.
27. Wilson, op. cit., Vol. II, p. 303.
28. Moon, op. cit., pp. 349-52.
29. (BL[OIC]) Political and Secret Department L/P & S/3/3, 18 May 1807.
30. Stein, Burton, *Thomas Munro,* Delhi: OUP, 1989, p. 147.

31. Stein, op. cit., p. 148.
32. Stein, op. cit., p. 148.
33. Cardew, A., *The White Mutiny, A Forgotten Episode in the History of the Indian Army,* London: 1929, pp. 142-44.
34. Badenach, W., *Inquiry into the State of the Indian Army,* London: 1826, p. 144.
35. Carey, P.B.R., *Sepoy Rebellion in Java in 1815,* Leyden: 1977, pp. 294-322.
36. Pemble, J., *The Invasion of Nepal,* Oxford: 1971, p. 96.
37. Mason, op. cit., p. 246.
38. Badenach, op. cit., p. vi.
39. Badenach, op. cit., p. 141.
40. Majumdar, R.C., *The Sepoy Mutiny and the Revolt of 1857,* Calcutta: Firma KLM, 1957, p. 37.
41. (BL[OIC]), L/Mil/5/428.
42. Mason, op. cit., p. 226.
43. Sen, S.N., *Eighteen Fifty Seven,* Delhi: Government of India, 1957, p. 18.
44. Barat, op. cit., p. 276.
45. Lawrence, H., *Essays on the Indian Army and Oudh,* London: 1859, p. 157.
46. Barat, op. cit., p. 280.
47. Moon, op. cit., p. 632.
48. A Retired Officer, *Mutiny in the Bengal Army,* London: 1857, p.4.
49. A Retired Officer, op. cit., p. 25.
50. A Retired Officer, op. cit., p. 6.
51. Rice Holmes, T., *A History of the Indian Mutiny,* London: 1898, p. 57.
52. Malcolm, J., *The Political History of India,* London: 1826, Vol. 2, p. 243.
53. Barat, op. cit., pp. 296-97.

Chapter Four

This chapter is largely based on S. B. Chaudhuri's *Civil Disturbances*

During the British Rule in India 1765-1857 (Calcutta 1955); K.K. Datta's *Anti-British Plots and Movements before 1857 (Meerut, 1970);* R.C. Majumdar's *The Sepoy Mutiny and the Revolt of 1857* (Calcutta, 1957); Penderel Moon's *The British Conquest and Dominion of India:*, and G. Pandey's *The Construction of Communalism in Colonial North India* (Delhi, 1990). Specific references are given below:

1. Smith, V. , *The Oxford History of India* ,Oxford: 1920, p. 713.
2. Chaudhuri,S.B., *Civil Disturbances During the British Rule in India 1765-1857,* Calcutta: 1955, p. xxii.
3. Majumdar, R.C., *The Sepoy Mutiny and the Revolt of 1857,* Calcutta: 1957, p. 57.
4. Smith, V., op. cit., p. 515.
5. Smith, V., op. cit., p. 515.
6. Moon, Penderel, *The British Conquest and Dominion of India,* London: Duckworth, 1989, pp. 211-213.
7. MacMunn, G., *The Martial Races of India* , London:1932, p. 151.
8. Datta, K.K., *Anti-British Plots and Movements before 1857,* Meerut: Meenakshi Prakashan,1970, p. 5.
9. Chaudhuri, S.B., op.cit., p. 57.
10. Datta, K.K., op.cit., pp. 14-20.
11. Chaudhuri, S.B. , op.cit., pp. 74-76.
12. Chaudhuri, S.B., op.cit., pp. 119.
13. Moon, Penderel, op.cit., p. 295.
14. Mill, J., *History of British India,* London:1858, Vol. VII, pp. 127-132.
15. Mill, J., op.cit., Vol VII, p. 184.
16. Wilson, H.H., *The History of British India from 1805 to1835,* London: Vol VII, p. 184.
17. Nevill, H.R.,*Benares:A Gazetteer* ,Lucknow: 1929,Vol. XXVI of the District Gazetteers of UP, *see* Preface, 1907, pp.207-209.
18. (BL[OIC]), Bengal Criminal Judicial Proceedings, Vol. 22, (Consultation No 46), p. 130.

19. Mill, J., op.cit., Vol VII, p. 334.
20. Pandey, G., *The Construction of Communalism in Colonial North India,* Delhi: OUP, 1990, p. 480.
21. Pandey, G., op.cit., p. 40.
22. Majumdar, R.C., op.cit., p. 53.
23. Majumdar, R.C., op.cit., p. 55.
24. Majumdar, R.C., op.cit., pp. 54-55.
25. Majumdar, R.C., op.cit., p. 58.
26. Majumdar, R.C., op.cit., p. 59.
27. Moon, Penderel, op.cit., p. 473.
28. Moon, Penderel, op.cit., 479.
29. Moon, Penderel, op.cit., 475.
30. Moon, Penderel, op.cit., p. 582.
31. Moon, Penderel, op.cit., p. 581.
32. Majumdar, R.C., op.cit., p. 65.
33. Chaudhuri,S.B., op.cit., p. xviii.

Chapter Five

This chapter is largely based on T. Rice Holmes' *A History of the Indian Mutiny* (London,1898); and G.H.D. Gimlette's *Postscript to the Records of the Indian Mutiny* (London, 1913). Specific references are given below:

1. Hodson, H.V., *The Great Divide* , Karachi: OUP, 1985, p. 23.
2. Moon, Penderel, *The British Conquest and Dominion of India,* London: Duckworth,1989, p. 9.
3. Moon, Penderel, op.cit., p. 7.
4. Jacob, J., *Tracts on the Native Army of India* , London: 1858, p. 106.
5. Hodson, H.V., op.cit., p. 23.
6. Baird, J.G.A., *The Private Letters of the Marquess of Dalhousie,* Shannon: 1972, p. 369.

Notes and References

Notes and References

7. Pemble, J., *The Raj, the Indian Mutiny and the Kingdom of Oudh,* Hassocks: 1977, pp 100-01.
8. Hervey, A., *Ten Years in India, or The Life of a Young Officer,* London: 1850.
9. Russell, William Howard, *My Indian Mutiny Diary*, ed. Edwardes Michael, London: 1957, p. xiii.
10. Mohammed, Shan, *The Writings and Speeches of Sir Syed Ahmed Khan,* Bombay: 1972, p. 15.
11. Gimlette, G.H.D., *Postscript to the Records of the Indian Mutiny,* London: 1913, p. 46.
12. Gimlette, G.H.D., op.cit., p. 47.
13. Gimlette, G.H.D., op.cit., p. 48.
14. Gimlette, G.H.D., op.cit., p. 41.
15. Gimlette, G.H.D., op.cit., p. 42.
16. Gimlette, G.H.D., op.cit., p. 86.
17. Russell, W.H., op. cit., p. vii.
18. Gimlette, G.H.D., op.cit., p. 45.
19. Rice Holmes, T., op.cit., p. 63.
20. Brown, Judith M., *Modern India ,The Origins of An Asian Democracy,* Delhi: OUP, 1984, p. 84.
21. Chand, Tara, *History of the Freedom Movement in India.*, Delhi: Government of India,1972, pp. 43 & 100.
22. Gimlette, G.H.D., op.cit., p. 40.
23. Gimlette, G.H.D., op.cit., p. 12.
24. Taylor, P.J.O.,in *The Statesman,* New Delhi, 31 August 1990.
25. Gimlette, G.H.D., op.cit., p. 127.
26. Gimlette, G.H.D., op.cit., p. 199.
27. Gimlette, G.H.D., op.cit., p. 131.
28. Taylor, P.J.O., *in The Statesman,* New Delhi, 30 March 1990.
29. Coghill, K., *Coghill Papers,* Cambridge: Centre of South Asian Studies, p. 7.
30. Rice Holmes, T., op.cit., pp. 116-17.
31. Tuker, F.S., *Gorkha —The Story of the Gurkhas in Nepal,* London: 1954, p. 158.
32. Rice Holmes, T., p. 462.

33. Rice Holmes, T., p. 467.
34. Rice Holmes, T., p. 467.
35. Rice Holmes, T., p. 470.
36. Rice Holmes, T., p. 470.
37. Rice Holmes, T., p. 471.
38. Rice Holmes, T., p. 498.
39. Rice Holmes, T., op.cit., p. 501.
40. Rice Holmes, T., op.cit., p. 577.
41. Anonymous, *The Thoughts of a Native of Northern India on the Rebellion, Its Causes and Remedies*, London: Macmillan,1858, p.16.
42. Roberts, F.S., *Forty-One Years in India,* London: 1914, pp. 241-42.
43. Rice Holmes, T., op.cit., p. 635.
44. Kaye, J. W., *History of the Sepoy War,* London: 1875, Vol. I, p. 519.
45. Knollys, H., *Life of General Sir Hope Grant,* Edinburgh: 1894, Vol. 1, pp. 178-80.
46. Rice Holmes, T., op.cit., p. 636.
47. Kaye, J.W., op.cit., Vol 1, p. 516, *see* Notes, p. 519.
48. Sen, S.N., *Eighteen Fifty Seven,* Delhi: Government of India, 1957,C.402.
49. MacMunn, G., *Turmoil in 1914 and After,* London: Jarrold, 1935, p. 25.
50. Woodyatt, N.G., *The Regimental History of the 3rd Gorkha Rifles,* London: 1929, p. 19.
51. Azad, M.A.K., Foreword to Sen, S.N.'s *Eighteen Fifty Seven* , Delhi: Government of India,1957, p. xiii.
52. Azad, M.A.K., op.cit., p. xv.
53. Chattopadhyaya, H., *The Sepoy Mutiny, 1857,* Brooklands: Calcutta: Brooklands, 1957, p. 202.

Chapter Six

This chapter is largely based on *The Imperial Gazetteer of India, The Indian Empire,* Volume IV (Oxford, 1909); the Government of India publication, *The Army in India and its Evolution* (Calcutta, 1924); Pierce G. Fredericks' *The Sepoy and the Cossack* (London, 1971); Dr W. Trousdale's *War in Afghanistan, 1879-80* (Detroit, 1985); and Brian Robson's *The Eden Commission and the Reform of the Indian Army, 1879-95,* (London, 1982). Specific references are given below:

1. Parliamentary Papers Relating to "Bootan", House of Commons, 1865, p. 153.
2. Army Headquarters, India, Intelligence Branch, *The Second Afghan War,* pp. 17-18.
3. Trousdale, Dr W., *War in Afghanistan 1879- 80,* Detroit:1985, p. 51.
4. Robson, Brian, *The Eden Commission and the Reform of the Indian Army, 1875-95,* London: *Journal of the Society of Army Historical Research,* 1982, Vol. LX, No. 241.
5. Trousdale, W., op.cit., p. 51.
6. Hanna, H.B., *The Second Afghan War,* London: 1889, Vol. 3, p. 139.
7. Trousdale, Dr W., op.cit., p. 113.
8. Fredericks, Pierce G., *The Sepoy and the Cossack,* London: 1971, pp. 195-98.
9. Macgregor, C., *Diary of the 3rd Afghan War in 1879-80* , ed. Dr W. Trousdale, Detroit: Virgin Publishing, 1985.
10. Fredericks, Pierce G., op.cit., p. 220.
11. Villiers, F., *Peaceful Personalities and Warriors Bold* , London: 1907, p. 148.
12. Fredericks, Pierce G., op.cit., pp. 232-34.
13. Brown, Judith M., *Modern India, The Origins of an Asian Democracy,* Delhi: OUP, 1984, p. 95.
14. King, Peter, *The Viceroy's Fall—How Kitchener Destroyed Curzon,* London: Pan Macmillan,1986, p. 27.

Chapter Seven

This chapter is largely based on Sir Philip Magnus' *Kitchener: Portrait of an Imperialist* (London, 1958); and Peter King's *The Viceroy's Fall—How Kitchener Destroyed Curzon* (London, 1986). Specific references are given below :

1. Philips, C.H., ed., *The Correspondence of Lord William Cavendish Bentinck*, London: 1977, Vol. II., Letter 690, pp.1064-65.
2. Kitchener Papers, Roll I, National Archives of India.
3. Kitchener Papers, Roll I, National Archives of India.
4. Dilks, David, *Curzon in India,* Lor.don:1970,Vol. I, p. 206.
5. E.C. Dugdale, Blanche, *Arthur James Balfour,* London: 1956, p.403.
6. Quoted in Magnus, Philip, *Kitchener : Portrait of an Imperialist,* London : John Murray, 1958, p. 176.
7. Magnus, Philip, op. cit., p. 196.
8. King, Peter, *The Viceroy's Fall—How Kitchener Destroyed Curzon,* London: Pan Macmillan,1986, p. 51.
9. Dilks, David, op. cit., Vol. I, pp. 211-212.
10. Kitchener Papers, Roll II, National Archives of India.
11. Lawrence, Walter Roper, *The India We Served,* London: 1928, p. 248.
12. Kitchener Papers, Roll II, National Archives of India.
13. Dilks, David, *Curzon in India,* Vol. II, p. 30.
14. Kitchener Papers, Roll II, National Archives of India.
15. Kitchener Papers, Roll II, National Archives of India.
16. E.C. Dugdale, Blanche, op. cit., p. 405.
17. E.C. Dugdale, Blanche, op. cit., pp. 406-408.
18. Quoted in Magnus, Philip, op. cit., pp. 214-215.
19. King, Peter, op. cit., p. 84.
20. Quoted in Magnus, Philip, op. cit., p. 217.
21. Earl of Ronaldshay, *The Life of Lord Curzon,* London: 1928,

Vol. II, p. 383.
22. Quoted in Magnus, Philip, op. cit., p. 219.
23. Quoted in Magnus, Philip, op. cit., p. 220.
24. Edwardes, Michael, *High Noon of Empire*, London: 1965, p. 236.
25. Magnus, Philip, op. cit., p. 223.
26. Quoted in Magnus, Philip, op. cit., p. 224.
27. Quoted in Magnus, Philip, op. cit., p. 233
28. Quoted in Magnus, Philip, op. cit., p. 349.
29. Leslie, Shane, *Studies in Sublime Failure*, Banaras: 1932, p. 215.
30. Welldon, J.E.C., *Recollections and Reflections*, London: 1915, p. 226.
31. Ronaldshay, op. cit., p. 390.
32. Pal, B.C., *Memories of my Life and Times,* Calcutta: 1973, p. 502.
33. Lawrence, Walter Roper, op. cit., p. 247.
34. (BL [IOC]), Add MSS 50, 074.
35. *The Indo-British Review*, Madras, Vol. II, No. 2, pp. 49-54.

Chapter Eight

This chapter is largely based on F.W. Perry's *The Commonwealth Armies: Manpower and Organisation in two World Wars* (Manchester, 1988); F.J. Moberley's *The Campaign in Mesopotamia* (HMSO, London, 1927); Norman Dixon's *On the Psychology of Military Incompetence* (London: 1976); and Russell Braddon's *The Siege* (London, 1969). Specific references are given below:

1. King, Peter, *The Viceroy's Fall—How Kitchener Destroyed Curzon,* London: Pan Macmillan, 1986, p. 240.
2. King, Peter, op. cit., p. 240.
3. Curzon Papers, (BL [IOC]), 23 October 1913.
4. Moberley, F.J., *The Campaign in Mesopotamia,* London: HMSO,

1927, p. 59.

5. Perry, F.W., *The Commonwealth Armies: Manpower and Organisation in two World Wars,* Manchester: 1988, p. 90.
6. Perry, F.W., op. cit, p. 89.
7. Perry, F.W., op. cit., p. 92.
8. Perry, F.W., op. cit., p. 93.
9. Perry, F.W., op. cit., p. 94.
10. Dixon, Norman, *On the Psychology of Military Incompetence,* London: Random Century, 1976.
11. Braddon, Russell, *The Siege,* London: Random Century, 1969, p. 61.
12. Dixon, N., op. cit., p. 98.
13. Braddon, R., op. cit., p. 65.
14. Braddon, R., op. cit., pp. 79-80
15. Barker, A.J., *Townshend of Kut* , London: 1967, p. 173.
16. Dixon, N., op. cit., p. 99.
17. Dixon, N., op. cit., p. 100.
18. Braddon, R., op. cit., p. 129.
19. Braddon, R., op. cit., p. 289.
20. Dixon, N., op. cit., p. 107.
21. Dixon, N., op. cit., p. 109.
22. Braddon, R., op. cit., pp. 333-34.
23. Braddon, R., op. cit., p. 13.
24. Perry, F.W., op. cit., p. 94.
25. Perry, F.W., op. cit., p. 95.
26. Perry, F.W., op. cit., p. 96.
27. Saxena, S.N., *Role of Indian Army in First World War,* Delhi: 1987, pp. 117-18.
28. Perry, F.W., op. cit., p. 96.
29. Perry, F.W., op. cit., p. 228.
30. Perry, F.W., op. cit., pp. 97-98.
31. Dixon, N., op. cit., pp. 239-40.
32. British Public Record Office, Kew (WO 95/3924).
33. Greenwood, A., *Field Marshal Auchinleck,* Durham: Pentland Press,1990, p. 36.
34. Greenwood, A., op. cit., p. 45.

Chapter Nine

This chapter is largely based on F.C. Isemonger and J. Slattery's *An Account of The Ghadr Conspiracy* (Lahore: 1919); De Witt C. Ellinwood and S.D. Pradhan's (ed.) *India and World War I* (Columbia, 1978); Dr Gopal Singh's *History of the Sikh People* (Delhi, 1988); Khushwant Singh's *History of the Sikhs* (London, 1922); Sir Michael O'Dwyer's *India as I Knew it* (London, 1922); G. MacMunn's *Turmoil and Tragedy in India in 1914 and After* (London, 1935); and Army Headquarters Simla's *Report in Connection with the Mutiny of the 5th Light Infantry at Singapore* (BL[OIC]) L/Mil/7/7191. Specific references are given below:

1. Wolpert, Stanley, "Congress Leadership in Transition",essay in Ellinwood, De Witt C. and Pradhan, S.D., ed., *India and World War I*, Columbia: 1978, pp. 127-28.
2. Dua, R.P., *The Impact of the Russo-Japanese War on Indian Politics,* Delhi: 1966, p. 1.
3. Cohen, S.P., *The Indian Army—Its Contribution to the Development of a Nation,* Delhi: OUP, 1990, p. 91.
4. Singh, Dr Gopal, *History of the Sikh People,* Delhi: World Book Centre,1988, p. 633.
5. Nanda, B.R., *Gokhale,* Delhi: 1960, p. 271.
6. Wolpert, Stanley, *Tilak and Gokhale* , Berkeley: 1962, p. 280.
7. Nanda, B.R., op. cit., p. 277.
8. Singh, Dr Gopal, op. cit., p. 634.
9. Singh, Dr Gopal, op. cit., p. 635.
10. Bose, A.C., "Aims and Weaknesses of Indian Revolutionaries", essay in *India and World War I*, p. 119.
11. Isemonger, F.C. and Slattery, J., *An Account of the Ghadr Conspiracy 1913—1915*, Lahore: 1919, pp. 76-80.
12. Singh, Khushwant, *The History of the Sikhs,* Delhi: OUP, 1991, Vol. II, p. 182.
13. Singh, Khushwant, op. cit., Vol. II, p. 183.

14. O'Dwyer, Michael, *India as I knew it,* London: 1922, p. 200.
15. Isemonger, F.C. and Slattery, J., op. cit., *see* p. 141.
16. MacMunn, G., *Turmoil and Tragedy in India in 1914 and After* London: Jarrold, 1935, p. 105.
17. O'Dwyer, Michael, op. cit., pp. 205-06.
18. National Archives of India, File Home Pol., 13 November 1916, pp. 452-53.
19. O'Dwyer, Michael, op. cit., p. 208.
20. Singh, Dr Gopal., op. cit., p. 640.
21. Bose, A.C., op. cit., p. 120.
22. Sir Louis Dane Papers, (BL[OIC]), MSS Eur D 659/7.
23. Chenevix-Trench, C., *The Indian Army, 1900-47*, London: Thames & Hudson,1988, p. 42.
24. O'Dwyer, M., op. cit., p. 178.
25. O'Dwyer, M., op. cit., p. 182.
26. Kemp, P.K., *History of the 4th Battalion, King's Shropshire Light Infantry*, Shrewsbury: 1955, pp. 18-21.
27. War Office, London, *Statistics of the British Military Effort in the Great War,* London: HMSO 1922, pp. 68-69.
28. Moore, W., *The Thin Yellow Line,* London: Leo Cooper, 1974, p. 217.
29. Imperial War Museum, MSS of A.H. Dickinson, London; MSS of E.A. Brown; MSS of R. Pears; MSS of W. Lowther Kemp, Royal Commonwealth Society, London; MSS of R.W. Mosbergen;MSS of M.B. Shelley; MSS of Major Arthur Thompson; Beckett, Ian, "The Singapore Mutiny"*(Journal of the Society for Army Historical Research,* London, 1982) pp. 132-53; James, L., *Mutiny in the British and Commonwealth Forces* (London, 1987) pp. 219-227; MacMunn, G., op. cit., pp. 105-113.
30. Tilak, B.G., *His Writings and Speeches,* Madras: 1918, p. 365.
31. Proceedings of the 32nd Indian National Congress, Calcutta: 1917.
32. Brown, Judith M., "British India and the War of 1914-18", essay in *India and World War I*, pp. 20—21.

33. Wolpert, Stanley, "Congress Leadership in Transition", essay in *India and World War I* , pp. 127-130.

Chapter Ten

This chapter is largely based on Edmund Candler's *The Sepoy* (London, 1919); and De Witt C. Ellinwood and S.D. Pradhan's (ed.) *India and World War I,* as well as files in the (BL[OIC]). Specific references are given below:

1. Hervey, Capt. A., *Ten Years in India or The Life of a Young Officer,* London: 1850, pp. v-vii.
2. Field Marshal Earl Roberts, *Forty-One Years in India*, London: 1914, pp. 499-500.
3. Field Marshal Earl Roberts, op. cit., pp. 531-32.
4. (BL [OIC]), File No. L/MIL/7/7268.
5. (BL [OIC]), File No. L/MIL/7/7270.
6. Candler, Edmund, *The Sepoy*, London: 1919, p. 1.
7. Candler, E., op. cit., p. ix.
8. Chenevix-Trench, C., *The Indian Army and the King's Enemies 1900-47,* London: Thames and Hudson, 1988, p. 85.
9. (BL [OIC]), File No. L/MIL/7/7273.
10. Heathcote, T.A., *The Indian Army, 1822-1922,* London: David & Charles, 1974.
11. Stein, Burton,*Thomas Munro,* Delhi: OUP,1989, p. 259.
12. Stein, Burton, op. cit., p. 259-60.
13. Auchinleck, Field Marshal Sir C.J., in his Foreword to Phythian-Adams, Col. E.G., *The Madras Soldier,* Madras: Government Press, 1945, p. v.
14. Hope, Sir Arthur, in his Foreword to Phythian-Adams, Col E.G., *The Madras Soldier*, pp. vii-viii.
15. Maxwell, Leigh, *My God Maiwand,* London: Leo Cooper, 1979, pp. 179.

16. Army HQ (India), *Recruiting in India before and during the War of 1914-18,* Calcutta: Government Press, 1919.
17. Pradhan, S.D., ed., *India and World War I,* Columbia: 1978, pp. 51-58.
18. Navalkar, H.N., *The Life of Shivaram Janba Kamble,* Pune: 1930, pp. 142-157.
19. Cohen, S., *The Indian Army, Its Contribution to the Development of a Nation,* Delhi: OUP, 1990, p. 61.
20. (BL [OIC]), File No. L/MIL/7/7274-5.
21. Candler, E., op. cit., p. 104.
22. (BL [OIC]), File No. L/MIL/7/7277.
23. Candler, E., op. cit., p. ix.
24. MacMunn, G., *Martial Races of India,* London: Sampson Low, 1932, p. v.
25. Pradhan, S.D., op. cit., pp. 51-58.

Chapter Eleven

This chapter is largely based on various files and committee reports in the (BL[OIC]); and in the Ministry of Defence Historical Section (MDHS), Delhi; as also Sir Penderel Moon's *The British Conquest and Dominion of India* . Specific references are given below:

1. Government of India (GOI), *India's Contribution to the Great War:* 1923, pp. 260-63.
2. GOI, op. cit., pp. 236-38.
3. Field Marshal Earl Roberts, *Forty-One Years in India* ,London: 1914, Vol. 2, p. 444.
4. Morrison, Sir Theodore, *Imperial Rule In India,* London: 1899, pp. 142-45.
5. Curzon, Lord, *Memorandum on Commissions for Indians,* (BL [OIC]), 4 June 1900.
6. Creagh, General Sir O'Moore, *Indian Studies,* London: 1918, p.

273.

7. O'Dwyer, Sir Michael, *War Speeches,* Lahore: 1919, speech of 4 May 1918.

8. GOI, op. cit., p. 237.

9. (BL[OIC]), Files 7/13394-423, 19006-182.

10. GOI, op. cit., p. 237.

11. HMSO, "Report of the Committee to inquire into the Administration and Organisation of the Army in India", (1920) (943) (Esher Committee).

12. (BL[OIC]), "Sedition (Rowlatt) Committee, Report" (1918), and Moon, Penderel , *The British Conquest and Dominion of India,* London: Duckworth, 1989, p. 987.

13. Moon, Penderel, op. cit.

14. James, L., *Mutiny in the British and Commonwealth Forces,1797-1956,* London: Ashford, Buchan and Enright, 1987, p. 19.

15. Montagu Papers, (BL[OIC]).

16. Wolpert, Stanley, "Congress Leadership in Transition", essay in Ellinwood, D.C. and Pradhan, S.D, eds., *India and World War I,* Columbia: 1978, p. 139.

17. Wilkinson, T.C., *Two Monsoons,* London: 1991, p. 211.

18. MDHS, New Delhi, "Military Requirements Committee Report" (1921), and "Shea Committee Report" (1922).

19. MDHS, New Delhi, "Jacob Committee Report" (1923).

20. Singh, Jewan, in the *Army Quarterly,* London: 1931, p. 360.

21. MDHS, New Delhi, "Skeen Committee Report" (1926).

22. (BL[OIC]), "Mutiny of the 2/18th Royal Garhwal Rifles", File No. 5/861.

23. (BL[OIC]), "Report of the Peshawar Disturbances Enquiry Committee" 17/13/98.

24. (BL[OIC]), File No. 159/17.

25. James, L., op. cit., p. 21.

26. Deedes, Lt. Gen. R.B., *Historical Record of the Royal Garhwal Rifles,* Dehra Dun: 1962, Vol. 2, p. 21.

27. Moon, P., op. cit., p. 1041.

28. Perry, F.W., *The Commonwealth Armies: Manpower and*

Organisation in Two World Wars, Manchester: 1988, p. 101.
29. Perry, F.W., op. cit.
30. (BL[OIC]), L/MIL/7/7284, Collection 159.
31. MDHS, New Delhi, "Chatfield Committee Report", (1939), File No. 601/12808/H.
32. MDHS, New Delhi, "Auchinleck Modernisation Sub-Committee Report", (1938).
33. Cohen, S., *The Indian Army: Its Contribution to the Development of a Nation,* New Delhi: OUP, 1990, pp. 115-117.

Chapter Twelve

This chapter is largely based on F.W. Perry's *The Commonwealth Armies : Manpower and Organisation in Two World Wars* (London, 1988); and C. Chenevix-Trench's *The Indian Army and the King's Enemies 1900-47* (London, 1988). Specific references are given below:

1. Amery, L.S., *The Empire at Bay: The Leo Amery Diaries,* ed., Barnes, J., London: Hutchinson, 1988. pp. 609, 676&679.
2. Singh, Khushwant, *The History of the Sikhs,* Delhi: OUP,1991, Vol. 2, p. 241.
3. Tyabji, B., *Memoirs of an Egoist, 1907-1956,* Delhi: Roli, Vol. 1,1988, pp. 91-92.
4. Perry, F.W., *The Commonwealth Armies : Manpower and Organisation in Two World Wars,* Manchester: 1988, p. 102.
5. Chenevix-Trench, C., *The Indian Army and the King's Enemies, 1900-1947,* London: Thames and Hudson, 1988,p. 138.
6. Cohen, S., *The Indian Army:Its Contribution to the Development of a Nation,* Delhi: OUP, 1990, pp. 115-16.
7. Chenevix-Trench, C., op. cit., p. 137.
8. Perry, F.W., op. cit., p. 103.
9. Chenevix-Trench, C., op. cit., p. 138.
10. Singh, Khushwant, op. cit., p. 240.

11. Chenevix-Trench, C., op. cit., p. 137.
12. Barstow, A.E., *Handbooks for the Indian Army—Sikhs,* Calcutta: Government Press, 1928, p. 55.
13. Singh, Khushwant, op. cit., p. 240.
14. James, L., *Mutiny in the Commonwealth and British Armies—1797-1956,* London: Ashford, Buchan and Enright, 1987, p. 10.
15. Perry, F.W., op. cit., p. 104.
16. Chenevix-Trench, C., op. cit., p. 138.
17. Perry, F.W., op. cit., p. 105.
18. Perry, F.W., op. cit., p. 104.
19. Perry, F.W., op. cit., p. 105.
20. Perry, F.W., op. cit., p. 106.
21. Perry, F.W., op. cit., p. 107.
22. Perry, F.W., op. cit., p. 107.
23. Chenevix-Trench, C., op. cit., p. 159.
24. Perry, F.W., op. cit., p. 108.
25. Perry, F.W., op. cit., p. 108.
26. Perry, F.W., op. cit., p. 114.
27. Durrani, M.K., *The Sixth Column,* London: Cassell,1954, pp. 3, 6-7.
28. Cohen, S., op. cit., pp. 131-32.
29. Perry, F.W., op. cit., p. 109.
30. Smyth, J., *Percival and the Tragedy of Singapore,* London: Macdonald,1971, p. 19-20.
31. Cohen, S., op. cit., p. 47.
32. Perry, F.W., p. 111.
33. Perry, F.W., p. 111.
34. Allen, L., *Sittang, The Last Battle,* London: Macdonald, 1937, pp. ix-x.
35. Perry, F.W., op. cit., p. 113.
36. Perry, F.W., op. cit., p. 113.
37. Perry, F.W., op. cit., p. 111.
38. Perry, F.W., op. cit., p. 115.
39. Cohen, S., op. cit., p. 145.
40. Moon, Penderel, ed. *Wavell, The Viceroy's Journal,* London:

OUP, 1973, p. 89.

41. Chenevix-Trench, C., op. cit., p. 292.
42. Evans, Geoffrey, *Slim*, London: Batsford, 1964, pp. 214-15.
43. Perry, F.W., op. cit., p. 119.
44. (BL [OIC]), Oral Archives, No. 2/6.
45. Indian Army Association, UK, Newsletter, 1991.

Chapter Thirteen

This chapter is largely based on Leonard Gordon's *Brothers Against the Raj* (Delhi, 1989): Mohan Singh's *Soldiers' Contribution to Indian Independence* (Delhi, 1974); T.R. Sareen's *Japan and the Indian National Army* (Delhi, 1986) and *Select Documents on Indian National Army* (Delhi, 1988); Hugh Toye's *The Springing Tiger* (London, 1956); and G.H. Corr's *The War of the Springing Tigers* (London, 1975). Specific references are given below:

1. Sareen, T.R., *Select Documents on Indian National Army*, Delhi: 1988, p. 94.
2. Mason, Philip, in his Foreword to Toye, Hugh, *The Springing Tiger,* London: Cassell,1959, p. v.
3. Corr, G.H., *The War of the Springing Tigers,* London: Osprey, 1975, p. 54.
4. Corr, G.H., op. cit., p. 55.
5. Gordon, Leonard A., *Brothers Against the Raj*, Delhi: Penguin India, 1989, p. 456.
6. Gordon, L., op. cit., p. 457.
7. Gordon, L., op. cit., p. 456.
8. Gordon, L., op. cit., 457.
9. Gordon, L., op. cit., p. 457.
10. Gordon, L., op. cit., p. 458.
11. Gordon, L., op. cit., p. 458.
12. Gordon, L., op. cit., p. 459.

13. Corr, G.H., op. cit., p. 56.
14. Corr, G.H., op. cit., p. 56.
15. Corr, G.H., op. cit., p. 57.
16. Corr, G.H., op. cit., p. 57.
17. Corr, G.H., op. cit., p. 57.
18. Corr, G.H., op. cit., p. 58.
19. Corr, G.H., op. cit., p. 60.
20. Corr, G.H., op. cit., p. 61.
21. Corr, G.H., op. cit., p. 64.
22. Corr, G.H., op. cit., p. 67.
23. Sareen, T.R., op. cit., p. 25.
24. Sareen, T.R., op. cit., p. 25.
25. Cohen, S., *The Indian Army : Its Contribution to the Development of a Nation*, Delhi: OUP, 1990, p. 149.
26. Sareen, T.R., op. cit., p. 27.
27. Sareen, T.R., op. cit., p. 95.
28. Sareen, T.R., op. cit., p. 28.
29. Sareen, T.R., op. cit., p. 28.
30. Sareen, T.R., op. cit., p. 31.
31. Sareen, T.R., op. cit., p. 95.
32. Cohen, S., op. cit., pp. 155-156.
33. Sareen, T.R., op. cit., p. 43.
34. Gordon, L., op. cit., p. 468.
35. Sareen, T.R., op. cit., pp. 151-153.
36. Gordon, L., op. cit., pp. 533-34.
37. Gordon, L., op. cit., p. 484.
38. Gordon, L., op. cit., p. 485.
39. Mason, P., op. cit., p. viii.
40. Gordon, L., op. cit., p. 493.
41. Gordon, L., op. cit., p. 493.
42. Gordon, L., op. cit., p. 495.
43. Gordon, L., op. cit., p. 498.
44. Toye, H., op. cit., p. 100.
45. Toye, H., op. cit., p. 103.
46. Toye, H., op. cit., p. 103.

47. Toye, H., op. cit., pp. 103-4.
48. Toye, H., op. cit., pp. 106-7.
49. Toye, H., op. cit., p. 107.
50. Toye, H., op. cit., p. 110.
51. Toye, H., op. cit., p. 111.
52. Toye, H., op. cit., p. 113.
53. Toye, H., op. cit. pp. 115-116.
54. Toye, H., op. cit., p. 120.
55. Toye, H., op. cit., p. 125.
56. Toye, H., op. cit., p. 126.
57. Toye, H., op. cit., p. 130.
58. Toye, H., op. cit., p. 131.
59. Toye, H., op. cit., p. 139.
60. Toye, H., op. cit., p. 144.
61. Allen, L., *Sittang, The Last Battle,* London: Macdonald,1973, p. 24.
62. Allen, L., op. cit., p. 23.
63. Allen, L., op. cit., p. 25.
64. Toye, H., op. cit., p. 147.
65. Gordon, L., op. cit., p. 524.
66. Sareen, T.R., op. cit., p. 235.
67. Nehru's Press Conference of 19 August 1945 in the*Tribune,* 20 August 1945.
68. Mason, P., op. cit., pp. viii-xi.
69. Connell, J., *Auchinleck,* London: 1959, p. 819.
70. Tuker, F.S.,*While Memory Serves,* London: Cassell,1950, p. 59.
71. Hodson, H.V., *The Great Divide, Britain-India-Pakistan,* Karachi: OUP, 1985, p. 205.

Chapter Fourteen

This chapter is largely based on N. Mansergh's and Penderel Moon's *The Transfer of Power* (London, 1982); *Wavell: The Viceroy's*

Journal (London, 1973); H.V. Hodson's *The Great Divide, Britain-India-Pakistan* (Karachi, 1985); A. Campbell-Johnson's *Mission with Mountbatten* (London, 1951); F.S. Tuker's *While Memory Serves* (London, 1950); and V.P. Menon's *The Story of the Integration of the Indian States* (London, 1956). Specific references are given below:

1. Moon, Penderel, *The British Conquest and Dominion of India*, London: Duckworth, 1989, p. 1145.
2. Tuker, F.S., *While Memory Serves,* London: Cassell, 1950, p. 58.
3. Tuker, F.S., op. cit., p. 267.
4. Greenwood, A., *Field Marshal Auchinleck,* Durham: Pentland Press, 1990, p. 269.
5. Greenwood, A., op. cit., p. 267.
6. Tuker, F.S., op. cit., p. 153.
7. Tuker, F.S., op. cit., p. 154.
8. Tuker, F.S., op. cit., p. 158.
9. Tuker, F.S., op. cit., p. 158.
10. Tuker, F.S., op. cit., p. 162.
11. Tuker, F.S., op. cit., p. 165.
12. Tuker, F.S., op. cit., pp. 121-279.
13. Tuker, F.S., op. cit., p. 120.
14. Tuker, F.S., op. cit., p. 191.
15. Tuker, F.S., op. cit., pp. 170-8.
16. Tuker, F.S., op. cit., p. 194.
17. Tuker, F.S., op. cit., p. 190.
18. Mosley, L., *The Last Days of the British Raj,* London: Weidenfeld & Nicolson, 1961, pp. 50-51.
19. Wheeler-Bennett, J.W.,*King George VI,* London, 1960, pp. 709-11.
20. Tuker, F.S., op. cit., pp. 256-8.
21. Tuker, F.S., op. cit., pp. 234-5.
22. Tuker, F.S., op. cit., p. 232.
23. Tuker, F.S., op. cit., p. 260.
24. Tuker, F.S., op. cit., p. 250.

25. Tuker, F.S., op. cit., p. 254.
26. Campbell-Johnson, A., *Mission with Mountbatten,* London: Robert Hale, 1951, pp. 58, 137.
27. Tuker, F.S., op. cit., p. 280.
28. Tuker, F.S., op. cit., p. 278.
29. Tuker, F.S., op. cit., pp. 326-7.
30. Mansergh, N., and Moon, Penderel, *The Transfer of Power,* London: HMSO, 1982, Vol XI, p. xi.
31. Mansergh, N., and Moon, Penderel, op. cit., pp. 66-68.
32. Mansergh, N., and Moon, Penderel, op. cit., pp. 69-71.
33. Irwin, S.F., *The Indian Army in Partition,* Army Quarterly, London, July 1948, p. 152.
34. Muthanna, I.M., *General Cariappa,* Mysore: 1964, p. 36.
35. Irwin, S.F., op. cit., p. 152.
36. Mansergh, N., and Moon, P., op. cit., p. 306.
37. Mansergh, N., and Moon, P., op. cit., p. 830.
38. Tuker, F.S., op. cit., p. 382.
39. Greenwood, A., op. cit., p. 270.
40. Mansergh, N., and Moon, P., op. cit., Vol. XII, p. 600.
41. Tuker, F.S., op. cit., p. 72.
42. Greenwood, A., op. cit., p. 284.
43. Greenwood, A., op. cit., p. 279-82.
44. Menon, V.P., *The Story of the Integration of the Indian States,* London: Longmans, 1956, p. 414.
45. Menon, V.P., op. cit., p. 145.
46. Menon, V.P., op. cit., p. 413-4.
47. Jalal, Ayesha, *The Sole Spokesman: Jinnah, the Muslim League and the Demand for Pakistan,* Cambridge: Cambridge University Press, 1985, p. 1.

Chapter Fifteen

This chapter is largely based on my personal observations at the time. Specific references are given below:

1. Muthanna, I.M., *General Cariappa*, Mysore: 1964, p. 6.
2. Mountbatten Papers, Broadlands, England.
3. Nehru Memorial Museum and Library (NMML), New Delhi.
4. Bucher Papers, National Army Museum (NAM),London.
5. Bucher Papers, NAM, London.
6. Sinha, S.K., *Operation Rescue—Military Operations in Jammu and Kashmir, 1947-48,* Delhi: Vision Books,1977, pp. 82-83.
7. Madhok, B.R., *Jammu, Kashmir and Ladakh,* Delhi: Reliance, 1987, pp. 36, 68-71.
8. Sinha, S.K., op. cit., p. xiv.
9. Ziegler, P., *Daily Telegraph,* London, 1 June 1991.
10. NMML, New Delhi.
11. Menon, V.P., *The Story of the Integration of the Indian States,* London: Longmans,1956, pp. 376-377.
12. NMML, New Delhi.
13. NMML, New Delhi.
14. Menon, V.P., op. cit., p. 388.
15. Cohen, S., *The Indian Army: Its Contribution to the Development of a Nation,* Delhi: OUP, 1990, p. 156.
16. NMML, New Delhi.
17. NMML, New Delhi.
18. Singhvi, L.M., *Freedom on Trial,* Delhi: Vikas, 1990, p.112.
19. Foreword to the Maharaja of Jaipur's *Indian State Forces,* London: Leo Cooper, 1961, p. vi.
20. Maharaja of Jaipur, op. cit., p. xx.
21. Grey, J., *Commonwealth Armies and the Korean War:* Manchester University, 1988, pp. 96-97.
22. NMML, New Delhi.

23. Sharma, G., *Path of Glory—Exploits of 11 GR,* Delhi: Allied, 1988, pp. 23-24.

24. Verma, S.D., *To Serve with Honour,* Dehra Dun: Natraj, 1988, pp. 82-85.

25. Verma, S.D., op. cit., p. 104-105.

26. Palit, D.K., *War in High Himalaya: The Indian Army in Crisis, 1962,* Delhi: Lancer, 1991, p. 74.

27. Hangen, W., *After Nehru, Who?,* London: Rupert Hart Davis, 1963, p. 256.

28. Palit, D.K., op. cit., p. 72.

29. Thorat, S.P., *From Reveille to Retreat,* Delhi: Allied, 1986, p. 191.

30. Moraes, F., *India Today,* New York: Macmillan, 1960, p. 231.

31. Hangen, W., op. cit., p. 103.

32. Hangen, W., op. cit., p. 65.

33. Hangen, W., op. cit., p. 104.

34. Hangen, W., op. cit, p. 247.

35. Kaul, B.M., *The Untold Story,* Delhi: Allied, 1967, p. 383.

36. Dalvi, J.P., *Himalayan Blunder,* Bombay: Thacker,1969, p. 372.

37. Dalvi, J.P., op. cit., p. xv.

38. Maxwell, N., *India's China War,* London: Jonathan Cape, 1970, p. 427.

39. Palit, D.K., op. cit., p. 51.

40. Palit, D.K., op. cit., p. 2.

41. Palit, D.K., op. cit., p. 1.

42. Palit, D.K., op. cit, p. 355.

43. Palit, D.K., op. cit., p. 331.

44. Palit, D.K., op. cit., p. 77.

45. Henderson-Brooks, T., *Indo-British Review,* Madras: March, 1989, p. 38.

46. Subramanyam, K., *Indian Foreign Policy: The Nehru Years,* ed. B.R. Nanda, Delhi: Radiant Publishers, 1980, p. 130.

Chapter Sixteen

This chapter is largely based on my personal observations at the time. Specific references are given below:

1. Nehru, Jawaharlal, *Speeches and Writings, May 1963-May 1964*, Delhi: Government of India, Vol. V, pp. 76-80.
2. Palit, D.K., *The Hindustan Times*, New Delhi, 11 April 1971.
3. Radhakrishnan, S., *Speeches and Writings, May 1962-May 1964*, Delhi: Government of India, 1965, pp. 28, 83-84, 88-92, 97.
4. Menon, V.K.K., *India and the Chinese Invasion*, Bombay: Contemporary, 1963, p. 30.
5. Hangen, W., *After Nehru, Who?*, London: Rupert Hart Davis, 1963, p. 110.
6. Das, Durga, *India from Curzon to Nehru*, London: Collins, 1969, p. 399.
7. Singh, Harbakhsh, *War Despatches, Indo-Pak Conflict, 1965*, Delhi: Lancer, 1991, p. 7.
8. Palit, D.K., *War in High Himalaya: The Indian Army in Crisis, 1962*, Delhi: Lancer, 1991, p. 427.
9. Brecher, M., *India and World Politics*, London: OUP, 1968, p. 260.
10. Singh, Harbakhsh, op. cit., pp. 90-91.
11. Singh, Harbakhsh, op. cit., pp. 159-161.
12. Singh, Harbakhsh, op. cit., pp. 178-180.
13. Chopra, Pran, *Uncertain India*, Delhi: 1968, pp. 317-318.
14. Sisson, Richard, and Rose, Leo E., *War and Secession: Pakistan, India and the Creation of Bangladesh*, Berkeley: University of California Press, 1991, p. 42.
15. Tinker, Hugh, *Indo-British Review*, Vol XVI, No 1, Madras: 1989, p. 13.
16. Candeth, K.P., *The Western Front: Indo-Pakistan War 1971*, Delhi: 1984, p. xiv.

17. *The Times of India*, Delhi, 2 October 1988.
18. Sundarji, K., *India Today*, Delhi, 15 February, 1986.
19. Governor-General's Personal Report to the King, No. 5 of 7 November 1947 (Mountbatten Papers, Broadlands, England).
20. Campbell-Johnson, A., *Mission with Mountbatten*, London: Robert Hale, 1951, p. 229.
21. Lamb, Christina, *Waiting for Allah*, Delhi: Penguin Books India, 1991, p. 268.
22. Tuker, F.S., *While Memory Serves*, London: Cassell, 1950, p. 138.

Epilogue

1. Bloch, Marc, *The Historian's Craft*, Manchester University Press, 1954, p. 43.
2. Campbell-Johnson, A., *Mission with Mountbatten*, London: Robert Hale, 1951, p. 230 *fn*.
3. Rizvi, H.A., *The Military and Politics in Pakistan*, Lahore: 1974, p. xv.
4. Cohen, Stephen, *The Indian Army: Its Contribution to the Development of a Nation*, Delhi: OUP, 1990, p. 230.
5. Tinker, Hugh, *Indo-British Review*, Vol. XVI, No. 1, Madras, 1989, p. 11.

Postscript

1. Singh, Jaswant, *Defending India*, London: Macmillan Press, 1999, p. 312.
2. Op cit, p. 327.
3. Krishan, Y., *Journal of the Royal Society for Asian Affairs*, October 1998, p. 278.

Select Bibliography

Abdullah, Sheikh Mohammed, *Attish-e-Chinar*, Lahore: Chaudhury, 1981.

Ahmed, Sir Syed, *The Causes of the Indian Revolt*, Benaras: 1873.

Akbar, M.J., *Nehru, The Making of India*, Harmondsworth: Penguin, 1988; *Riot after Riot*, Delhi: Penguin Books India, 1988; *Kashmir Behind the Vale*, Delhi: Penguin Books India, 1991.

Ali, Chaudhri Mohammed, *The Emergence of Pakistan*, New York: Columbia University Press, 1973.

Allen, L, *Sittang, the Last Battle*, London: Macdonald, 1973.

Army Headquarters (India), *Recruiting in India Before and During the War of 1914-1918*, Calcutta: Government Press, 1919. Wellington's *Campaigns in India*, Calcutta: 1908. *Frontier and Overseas Expeditions from India*, Government Press, 1911. *The Third Afghan War, 1919*, Government Press, 1926.

Auber, P., *Rise and Progress of the British Power in India*, London, 1837.

Azad, M.A.K., *India Wins Freedom*, Madras: Orient Longman, 1988.

Babington, A., *The Devil To Pay: The Mutiny of the Connaught Rangers, India, July, 1920*, London: Leo Cooper, 1991.

Badenach, W., *Inquiry Into the State of the Indian Army*, London, 1826.

Baird, J.G.A., *The Private Letters of the Marquess of Dalhousie*, London: William Blackwood, 1919.

Barat, A., *The Bengal Native Infantry, Its Organisation and Discipline 1796-1852*, Calcutta: Firma KLM, 1962.

Barker, A.J., *The Neglected War*, London: Faber and Faber, 1967.

Barnes, J., ed., *The Empire at Bay: The Leo Amery Diaries, 1929-1945*, London: Hutchinson, 1988.

Barstow, A.E., *Sikhs (Handbooks of the Indian Army)*, Calcutta: Government of India, 1928.

Basu, P., *Oudh and the East India Company*, Lucknow: Maxwell,

1943.

Bhargava, M.L., *Saga of 1857,* Delhi: Reliance, 1992.

Bhullar, P., *The Sikh Mutiny,* Delhi: Siddharth, 1987.

Bolitho, H., *Jinnah, Creator of Pakistan,* London: John Murray, 1954.

Bowles, C., *Promises to Keep,* Delhi: B.I. Publications, 1972.

Braddon, R., *The Siege,* London: Jonathan Cape, 1969.

Brecher, M., *India and World Politics: Krishna Menon's View of the World,* London: OUP, 1968.

Broome, A., *History of the Rise and Progress of the Bengal Army,* London: 1850.

Brown, Judith M., *Modern India, the Origins of an Asian Democracy,* Delhi: OUP,1984.

Cadell, P., *History of the Bombay Army,* London: Longmans, 1938.

Callard, K., *Pakistan,* London: Allen & Unwin, 1957.

Campbell-Johnson, A., *Mission with Mountbatten,* London: Robert Hale, 1953.

Candeth, K.P., *The Western Front: Indo-Pakistan War 1971,* Delhi: Allied, 1984.

Cardew, A., *The White Mutiny,* London: Constable, 1929.

Cardew, F.G.A., *A Sketch of the Services of the Bengal Native Army,* Calcutta: 1803.

Carey, P.B.R., *The Sepoy Conspiracy of 1815 in Java :*University of Leyden, 1977.

Carthill, Al, *The Lost Dominion,* London: 1924.

Chagla, M.C., *Kashmir 1947-1965,* Delhi: Government of India, 1965.

Chakraborty, B., *The Congo Operation,* Delhi: Government of India, 1976.

Chakravarty, Suhas, *The Raj Syndrome: A Study in Imperial Perceptions,* Delhi: Penguin Books India, 1991.

Chand, Tara, *History of the Freedom Movement in India,* Delhi: Government of India, 1967.

Chandra, Bipan, *India's Struggle for Independence,* Delhi: Penguin

Books India, 1989.

Chaudhuri, N.C., *Clive of India,* London: Barrie and Jenkins,1975.

Chaudhuri, S.B., *Civil Disturbances during the British Rule, 1765-1857,* Calcutta: 1955.

Chattopadhyaya, H., *The Sepoy Mutiny, 1857,* Calcutta: Brooklands, 1957.

Cheema, P.I., *Pakistan's Defence Policy, 1947-58,* London: Macmillan Press, 1990.

Chenevix-Trench, C., *The Indian Army and the King's Enemies, 1900-1947,* London: Thames and Hudson, 1988; *The Frontier Scouts,* London: 1985.

Chopra, P., *Uncertain India,* Bombay: Asia, 1968.

Churchill, Winston, *The Story of the Malakand Field Force,* London: Longmans, 1898.

Connell, J., *Auchinleck,* London: Cassell, 1959.

Cohen, S., *The Indian Army: Its Contribution to the Development of a Nation,* Delhi: OUP, 1990.

Cook, H., *The Sikh Wars, 1845-1849,* London: Leo Cooper, 1975.

Cooper, F., *The Crisis in the Punjab,* London: Smith Elder, 1858.

Corr, G.H., *The War of the Springing Tigers,* London: Osprey, 1975.

Creagh, O'Moore, *Indian Studies,* London: Hutchinson, 1918.

Dalvi, J.P., *Himalayan Blunder,* Bombay: Thacker, 1969.

Das, Durga, *India from Curzon to Nehru and After,* London: Collins, 1969.

Das, S., *Communal Riots in Bengal,* Delhi: OUP, 1991.

Datta, K.K., *Anti-British Plots and Movements before 1857,* Meerut: Meenakshi Prakashan, 1970.

Datta, V.N., *Maulana Azad,* Delhi: Manohar, 1990.

Deedes, R.B., *Historical Record of the Royal Garhwal Rifles,* Dehradun: Army Press, Vol. 2, 1962.

Dilks, D., *Curzon in India,* London: Rupert Hart Davis, 1970.

Dixon, N., *On the Psychology of Military Incompetence,* London: Jonathan Cape, 1976.

Dodwell, H.H., *Dupleix and Clive,* London: 1920.

Draper, A., *Amritsar, The Massacre that ended the Raj,* London: Cassell, 1981.

Duff, J.C. Grant, *History of the Mahrattas,* London: 1826.

Dugdale, E.C., *Arthur James Balfour, First Earl of Balfour,* London: 1936.

Durrani, M.K., *The Sixth Column,* London: Cassell, 1955.

Edwardes, H.B., & H., Merivale, *Life of Sir Henry Lawrence,* London: Macmillan, 1872.

Ellenborough, E., *India under Lord Ellenborough,* London: J. Murray, 1926.

Edwardes, M., *Clive the Heaven-Born General,* Introduction by John Terraine, London: 1977; *High Noon of Empire,* Eyre and Spottiswoode, 1965.

Edwardes, M., *Red Year*: Hamish Hamilton, 1973.

Ellinwood, D.C., and Pradhan, S.D., ed., *India and World War I,* Columbia: South Asia Books, 1978.

English, B., *John Company's Last War,* London: Collins, 1971.

Evans, G., *Slim,* London: Batsford, 1969.

Eyre, Vincent, *Military Operations at Cabul,* London: J. Murray, 1843.

Falcon, R., *Handbook on Sikhs for Regimental Officers,* Allahabad: Pioneer, 1896.

Fane, H.E., *Five Years in India,* London: H. Colbert, 1842.

Fortescue, J.W., *History of the British Army,* London: Macmillan, 1910-30.

Fuller, J.F.C., *The Decisive Battles of the Western World,* edited by John Terraine, London, 1970.

Fraser, L., *India/Curzon and After*, London: William Heinemann, 1911.

Fredericks, Pierce G., *The Sepoy and the Cossack,* London: W.H. Allen, 1972.

Garratt, G.T. & Thompson, E.J., *Rise and Fulfilment of British Rule in India,* London: Macmillan, 1934.

Ghulam Hossein Khan, Saiyed, *Seir-ul-Mutaqherin,* Calcutta, 1789.

Ghosh, K.K., *The Indian National Army—Second Front of the Indian Independence Movement* , Meerut: Meenakshi Prakashan, 1969.

Gordon, L., *Brothers against the Raj,* Delhi: Penguin Books, 1989.

Government of India, *Communal Disorders Report,* Delhi, 1928.

Government of India, *The Army in India and Its Evolution,* Calcutta, 1924.

Government of India, *India's Contribution to the Great War,* Calcutta, 1923.

Greacem, L., *Chink—A Biography of Major General Eric Dorman Smith,* London: 1989.

Gimlette, G.H.D., *A Postscript to the Records of the Indian Mutiny,* London: Witherby, 1927.

Graham, C.A.L., *The History of the Indian Mountain Artillery,* Aldershot: Gale and Polden, 1957.

Greenwood, A., *Field Marshal Auchinleck,* Durham: Pentland Press, 1990.

Grey, J., *Commonwealth Armies and the Korean War,* Manchester University, 1988.

Gubbins, M.R., *An Account of the Mutinies in Oudh,* London: Richard Bentley, 1858.

Gupta, H.R., *The Life and Work of Mohan Lal,* Lahore: Minerva, 1943.

Hamilton, I., *Gallipoli Diary,* London, 1920.

Hangen, W., *After Nehru, Who?,* London: Rupert Hart Davis, 1963.

Hanna, H.B., *The Second Afghan War, 1878-79-80,* London: Constable, 1899-1910.

Hardinge, Rt Hon Lord, *My Indian Years,* London, 1948.

Harfield, A., *British and Indian Armies in the East Indies 1685-1935,* London, 1986; *British and Indian Armies on the China Coast, 1785-1985,* London, 1990.

Hayde, D.E., *The Battle of Dograi,* Dehradun: Natraj, 1991.

Heathcote, T.A., *The Indian Army, 1822-1922,* London: David and

Charles, 1974.

Hervey, A., *Ten Years in India, or The Life of a Young Officer*, London, 1850.

Hibbert, C., *The Great Mutiny—India 1857*, London: Allen Lane, 1978.

Hill, S.C., *Bengal in 1756-57*, London, 1905.

Hodson, H.V., *The Great Divide Britain-India-Pakistan*, Karachi: OUP, 1985.

Hopkirk, P., *The Great Game—On Secret Service in High Asia*, London: John Murray, 1990.

Hunter, W.W., *The Indian Mussalmans*, London, 1871.

Hutchinson, L., *Conspiracy in Meerut*, London: Allen and Unwin, 1935.

Howitt, W., *A Popular History of the Treatment of the Natives*, London, 1838.

Imperial Gazetteer of India, *The Indian Empire*, Oxford: Clarendon Press, Vol. IV, 1909.

Irwine, W., *The Army of the Indian Moghuls*, London, 1903.

Isemonger, F.C. & Slattery, J., *An Account of the Ghadr Conspiracy, 1913-15*, Lahore: Government Press, 1919.

Ismay, H., *The Memoirs of General Lord Ismay*, London: Heinemann, 1960.

Jackson, D., *India's Army*, London: Sampson Low, 1942.

Jacob, J., *Tracts on the Native Army of India : Its Organisation and Discipline*, London, 1858; *The Views and Opinions of Brigadier General John Jacob*, London, 1858.

Jaipur, Maharaja of, *The Indian State Forces*, London: Leo Cooper, 1961.

Jalal, Ayesha, *The State of Martial Rule—The Origins of Pakistan's Political Economy of Defence*, Cambridge, 1990.

James, L., *Mutiny in the British and Commonwealth Forces, 1757-1956*, London: Buchan and Enright, 1987.

Kaul, B.M., *Untold Story,* Delhi: Allied, 1967.

Kaur, Harminder, *Blue Star Over Amritsar,* Delhi: Ajanta, 1990.

Kaye, J.W., *History of the Sepoy War in India,* London: W.H. Allen, 1870-1876; *History of the War in Afghanistan,* London: Richard Bentley, 1851.

Khan, Akbar, *Raiders in Kashmir,* Karachi: National Book Foundation, 1970.

Khan, Ayub, *Friends Not Masters,* London: OUP, 1967.

Khan, F.M., *Story of the Pakistan Army,* Oxford: OUP, 1963.

Khan, M. Asghar, *The First Round, Indo-Pakistan War, 1965,* Delhi: Vikas, 1979; *General in Politics: Pakistan 1958-82,* Delhi: Vikas, 1983.

Khan, Shah Nawaz, *My Memories of the INA and Its Netaji,* Bombay: Rajkamal Publications, 1946.

Khan, S.G.H., *Seir-ul-Mutaqherin,* Calcutta: 4 Vols, 1789.

Khera, S.S., *India's Defence Problems,* Bombay: Longmans, 1968.

King, P., *The Viceroy's Fall—How Kitchener Destroyed Curzon,* London: Sidgwick and Jackson, 1986.

Kolff, D.H.A., *Naukar, Rajput and Sepoy,* Cambridge: Cambridge University Press, 1990.

Korbel, Josef, *Danger in Kashmir,* Princeton: Princeton University Press, 1954.

Lal, Mohan, *The Life of Dost Mohammed Khan,* London: Longman, Brown, 1846.

Lamb, C., *Waiting for Allah—Pakistan's Struggle for Democracy,* Delhi: Penguin Books India, 1991.

Lawrence, H., *Essays, Military and Political, on the Indian Army and Oudh,* London: Heny Colburn, 1859.

Lawrence, W.R., *The India We Served,* London: Cassell, 1928.

Lecky, E., *Fictions connected with the Indian Outbreak of 1857 Exposed,* Bombay, 1859.

Leslie, S., *Studies in Sublime Failure,* Benares, 1932.

Long, J., *Selections from the Unpublished Records of Government, 1748-1767,* Calcutta, 1809.

Longer, V., *Red Coats to Olive Green,* Bombay: Allied, 1974.

MacGregor, C.M., *The Defence of India,* Simla: Government of India, 1884.

Maclagan, M., *Clemency Canning,* London: Macmillan, 1962.

MacMunn, G., *Turmoil and Tragedy in India, 1914 and After,* London: Jarrold, 1935; *Martial Races of India,* London: Sampson Low, 1932; *The Armies of India,* London: A&C Black, 1911.

Macrory, P., *Signal Catastrophe,* London: Curtis Brown, 1966.

Madhok, B., *Jammu, Kashmir and Ladakh,* Delhi: Reliance, 1987.

Magnus, Philip, *Kitchener—Portrait of an Imperialist,* London: John Murray, 1958.

Mahajan, M.C., *Looking Back,* Bombay: Asia, 1963.

Majumdar, R.C., *The Sepoy Mutiny and the Revolt of 1857,* Calcutta: Firma KLM, 1974.

Malcolm, J., *Political History of India,* London, 1826.

Malleson, G.B., *The Decisive Battles of India,* London: W.H. Allen, 1885.

Malleson, G.B., *Essays and Lectures on Indian Historical Subjects,* London, 1866.

Malleson, G.B., *History of the Indian Mutiny,* London, 1878-80.

Mangat, G.S., *The Tiger Strikes,* Ludhiana: Gagan, 1986.

Mansergh, N. and Moon, P., *The Transfer of Power Vols X to XII,* London: HMSO, 1981-83.

Mason, P., *A Matter of Honour,* Harmondsworth: Penguin Books, 1974.

Maude, F.C., *Memories of the Mutiny,* London, 1894.

Maurice, F., *The Life of General Lord Rawlinson of Trent,* New York: Houghton Mifflin, 1928.

Maxwell, L., *My God—Maiwand,* London: Leo Cooper, 1979.

Maxwell, N., *India's China War,* London: Jonathan Cape, 1970.

Meinertzhagen, R., *Army Diary, 1899-1926,* London, 1960.

Menon, V.K. Krishna, *India and the Chinese Invasion,* Bombay: Contemporary, 1963.

Menon, V.P., *The Story of the Integration of the Indian States,*

London: Longmans, 1956.

Merewether, J.W.B. and Smith, F., *The Indian Corps in France,* London: John Murray, 1917.

Metcalfe, C.T., *Two Native Narratives of the Mutiny in Delhi,* London, 1890.

Michel, A.A., *The Indus Rivers,* Yale University Press, 1967.

Mill, J. and Wilson, H.H., *The History of the British in India from 1784 to 1835,* London: James Madden, Ten Vols., 1858.

Moberley, F.J., *The Campaign in Mesopotamia,* London, 1923.

Mohammed, Shan, *The Writings and Speeches of Sir Syed Ahmed Khan,* Bombay: Nachiketan, 1974.

Moir, M., *A General Guide to the India Office Records,* London: British Library, 1988.

Montgomery, Field Marshal Viscount, *Memoirs,* London: Collins, 1958.

Moore, R.J., *The Crisis of Indian Unity 1917-40,* Oxford: OUP, 1974; *End Games of Empire,* Delhi: OUP, 1968.

Moore, W., *The Thin Yellow Line,* London: Leo Cooper, 1956.

Montagu, E.S., *An Indian Diary,* London, 1930.

Montagu-Chelmsford: *"Report on Indian Constitutional Reforms",* London, 1918.

Moon, Penderel, *British Conquest and Dominion of India,* London: Duckworth, 1989; *Wavell: The Viceroy's Journal,* London: OUP, 1973; *Divide and Quit,* London, 1981.

Moraes, F., *India Today,* New York: Macmillan, 1960.

Moosa, M., *My Version, India-Pakistan War, 1965,* Lahore, 1983.

Mosely, L., *The Last Days of the British Raj,* London: Weidenfeld and Nicolson, 1961.

Mountbatten, Lord Louis, *Time Only to Look Forward,* London: Nicholas Kaye, 1949.

Muir, W., ed., W. Coldstream, *Records of the Intelligence Department of the Government of North Western Provinces during the Mutiny of 1857,* Allahabad: Government Press, Vols. I&II, 1902.

Muthanna, I.M., *General Cariappa,* Mysore, 1964.

Nanda, B.R., *Gokhale,* Delhi, 1960.

Narayan, B.K., *General J.N. Chaudhuri,* Delhi: Vikas, 1978.

Nevill, H.R., *Benares, A Gazetteer,* Allahabad: Government Press, 1909; *Bareilly, A Gazetteer,* Allahabad: Government Press, 1911.

Nehru, J.,*Autobiography,* London, 1936; *Glimpses of World History,* London: Drummond, 1949; *The Discovery of India,* Calcutta: Signet, 1945.

Noon, F.K., *From Memory,* Lahore, 1966.

O'Dwyer, M., *India as I knew it,* London: Constable, 1925.

Orme, R., *History of the Military Transactions of the British Nation in Indostan,* Madras, 1803.

Pal, B.C., *Memories of my Life and Times,* Calcutta, 1973.

Palit, D.K., *War in High Himalaya, The Indian Army in Crisis, 1962,* Delhi: Lancer, 1991.

Palmer, J.A.B., *The Mutiny Outbreak at Meerut,* Cambridge, 1966.

Pandey, G., *The Construction of Communalism in Colonial North India,* Delhi: OUP, 1990.

Parratt, I. and S.N.A., *The Anglo-Manipuri Conflict of 1891,* Delhi: Vikas, 1992.

Pearse, H., *Memoirs of Alexander Gardner,* London: Blackwood, 1898.

Pemble, J., *The Raj, the Indian Mutiny and the Kingdon of Oudh, 1801-1859,* Sussex: Harvester Press, Hassocks, 1977; *The Invasion of Nepal,* Oxford: Clarendon Press, 1971.

Percival, J., *For Valour—The Victoria Cross,* London, 1985.

Perry, F.W., *The Commonwealth Armies: Manpower and Organisation in Two World Wars,* Manchester University, 1988.

Philips, C.H., *The Evolution of India and Pakistan 1858-1947, Select Documents,* London, 1967.

Phythian-Adams, E.G., *The Madras Soldier,* Nilgiris: Wellington, 1958.

Pradhan, S.D., *The Indian Army in East Africa,* Delhi, 1990.

Prasad, N., *The Fall of Tawang,* Delhi, 1984.

Prasad, R.C., *Early English Travellers in India,* Delhi, 1980.

Prasad, Rajeshwar, *Days with Lal Bahadur Shastri,* Delhi: Allied, 1991.

Prasad, S.N., *History of the Custodian Force (India) in Korea, 1953-54,* New Delhi: Government of India, 1976.

Pratap, Mahendra, *My Life Story of Fifty Five Years (1886-1941),* Dehra Dun: World Federation Centre, 1947.

Praval, K.C., *Indian Army After Independence,* Delhi: Lancer, 1990.

Rahman, Amir Abdur, *The Life of Amir Abdur Rahman,* London: J. Murray, 1900.

Rai, Lajpat, *England's Debt to India,* New York, 1917; *Autobiographical Writings,* ed., V.C. Joshi, Delhi: University Publishers, 1965.

Reading, Marquess of, *Rufus Isaacs, First Marquess of Reading,* London, 1945.

Rennell, J., *Marches of the British Army in the Peninsula of India,* London, 1792.

"Report on East India Company Affairs from the Select Committee of the House of Commons," London, 1832.

Retired Officer, *The Mutiny in the Bengal Army,* London: Bosworth and Harrison, 1857.

Rice Holmes, T., *A History of the Indian Mutiny,* London: W.H. Allen, 1898.

Richards, F., *Old Soldier Sahib,* London: Faber and Faber, 1936.

Rizvi, H.A., *The Military and Politics in Pakistan,* Lahore: Progressive, 1976.

Roberts, Field Marshal Earl, *Forty-One Years in India,* London: Macmillan, 1914.

Roberts, P.E., *History of British India under the Company and the Crown,* Oxford, 1938.

Ronaldshay, Earl of, *The Life of Lord Curzon,* London, 1928.

Rose, Kenneth, *Curzon: A Most Superior Person,* London, 1965.

Rose, L.E. and Sisson, R., *War & Secession—Pakistan, India and the Creation of Bangladesh,* University of California Press, 1990.

Rowlatt, Justice Sidney, *Sedition Committee Report*, Calcutta: Government Press, 1918.

Russell, W.H., *My Diary in India in the Year 1857-58*, London, 1860; Calcutta, 1905.

Sadullah, M.M., *The Partition of the Punjab*, Lahore, 1983.

Saigal, J.R., *The Unfought War of 1962*, New Delhi, 1979.

Sanders, Lloyd, *Life of Lord Palmerston*, London: W.H. Allen, 1895.

Sain, Kanwar, *Reminiscences of an Engineer*, New Delhi, 1978.

Saksena, N.S., *Communal Riots in India*, Delhi: Trishul, 1990.

Sareen, T.R., *Japan and the Indian National Army*, Delhi: Agam Prakashan, 1986; *Select Documents on the Indian National Army*, Delhi: Agam Prakashan, 1988.

Saxena, K.M.L., *Military System of India, 1850-1900*, Delhi, 1974.

Saxena, S.N., *Role of Indian Army in First World War*, Delhi, 1987.

Sen, L.P., *Slender is the Thread*, Delhi: Sangam, 1973.

Sen. S.N., *Eighteen Fifty Seven*, Delhi: Government of India, 1957.

Sharma, Gautam, *Valour and Sacrifice—Famous Regiments of the Indian Army*, Delhi: Reliance, 1989; *The Path of Glory: The Exploits of the 11th Gorkha Rifles*, Delhi: Alliance, 1988.

Shaw, J., *Charters relating to the East India Company*, Madras, 1887.

Sheppard, E.W., *A Short History of the British Army*, Aldershot: Gale and Polden, 1959.

Shore, F.J., *Notes on Indian Affairs*, London, 1837.

Simon, Sir John, *Statutory Commission Report*, Calcutta: Government Press, 1930.

Singh, Amar Kaur Jasbir, *Himalaya Triangle*, London: British Library, 1983.

Singh, Gopal, *History of the Sikh People*, Delhi: World Book Centre, 1988.

Singh, Khushwant, *History of the Sikhs*, Delhi: OUP, 1991.

Singh, Mohan, *Soldiers' Contribution to Indian Independence*, Delhi: Army Educational Stores, 1974.

Sinha, S.K., *Operation Rescue—Military Operations in J&K 1947-48*, Delhi: Vision, 1977.

Sisson, R., and Rose, L.E., *War and Secession: Pakistan, India and the Creation of Bangladesh*, Delhi: OUP,1990.

Sitaramayya, P., *History of the Indian National Congress*, ed., J.C. Johri, Delhi: S.Chand, 1988.

Sleeman, W.H., *Rambles and Recollections of an Indian Official*, London: J. Hatchard, 1944.

Slim, Field Marshal W., *Defeat into Victory*, London: Cassell, 1956.

Smith, F., and Merewether, J.W.B., *The Indian Corps in France*, London: John Murray, 1919.

Smith, V.A., *The Oxford History of India*, London: OUP, 1920 and 1958.

Smyth, J., *Percival and the Tragedy of Singapore*, London: Macdonald, 1971.

Spear, T.G.P., *The Nabobs : A Study of the Social Life of the English in 18th Century India*, London: OUP, 1932.

Stein, B., *Thomas Munro*, Delhi: OUP, 1989.

Strachey, H., *Narrative of the Mutiny of the Officers of Army in Bengal in 1766*, London: T. Beckett, 1773.

Strachey, R. and O., *Keigwin's Rebellion, 1683-84*, Oxford: Clarendon Press, 1916.

Stranks, C.J.(d), *The Path of Glory, Being the Memoirs of John Shipp*, London: Chatto and Windus, 1969.

Thompson, E., and Garratt, G.T., *Rise and Fulfilment of British Rule in India*, London: Macmillan, 1934.

Thorat, S.P.P., *From Reveille to Retreat*, Delhi: Allied, 1986.

Thorpe, B., (ed.), *The Anglo-Saxon Chronicle*, London, 1861.

Toye, Hugh, *The Springing Tiger*, London: Cassell, 1955.

Tinker, Hugh, (ed.), *Indian Armed Forces*, Madras: *Indo-British Review*, 1989.

Tyabji, B., *Memoirs of an Egoist, 1907-1956*, Delhi: Roli, Vol. I, 1988.

Trousdale, W., (ed.), *War in Afghanistan, 1879-89: The Personal Diary of Major General Sir Charles Metcalfe MacGregor*, Detroit: Wayne University Press, 1985.

Tuker, F.S., *While Memory Serves,* London: Cassell, 1950; *Gorkha, The Story of the Gurkhas of Nepal,* London: Constable, 1957.

Venkateswaran, A.L., *Defence Organisation in India,* Delhi: Government of India, 1967.
Verma, S.D., *To Serve with Honour,* Dehra Dun: Natraj, 1989.
Von Bernhardi, F., *Germany and the Next War,* Berlin, 1911.

Waller, N.H., *Beyond the Khyber Pass,* New York: Random House, 1990.
Wavell, A.P., *The Palestine Campaign,* London: Constable, 1928.
Welldon, J.E.C., *Recollections and Reflections,* London, 1915.
Wheeler, Bennett, J.W., *King George VI,* London: Macmillan, 1956.
Wilkinson, T.C., *Two Monsoons,* London: Duckworth, 1976.
Willcocks, J., *With the Indian Corps in France,* London, 1920.
Wilcox, W.A., *Pakistan,* Columbia, 1963.
Williams, J., *An Historical Account of the Rise and Progress of the Bengal Infantry, from its formation in 1757 to 1796,* London: John Murray, 1817.
Wilson, H.H., and Mill, J., *The History of British India,* London: James Madden, 1858.
Wilson, W.J., *History of the Madras Army,* (Four Vols), Madras: Government Press, 1882-1889.
Woodman, D., *Himalayan Frontiers,* London: Barrie and Rockcliff, 1969.
Woodyat, N.G., *History of the 3rd Queen Alexandra's Own Gorkha Rifles,* London: Philip Allan, 1927.

Young, H.A., *The East India Company's Arsenals and Manufactories,* Oxford: Clarendon Press, 1937.

Ziegler, P., *Mountbatten,* London: Collins, 1958.

Select Bibliography

Manuscripts/Papers

Auchinleck Papers, University of Manchester, Ryland Library.

Bucher Papers, NAM, London.

Canning Papers, Sheepscar Library, Leeds.

Curzon Papers, (BL[OIC]), London F 111/112.

Dalhousie Papers, Scottish Record Office, Edinburgh.

Elphinstone Papers (1853-60), (BL[OIC]), London, MSS Eur F 87.

Gokhale Papers, NAI, New Delhi.

Hardinge of Penshurst Papers, Cambridge University Library.

John Jacob Papers, (BL[OIC]), London.

Lake Papers, (BL[OIC]), London.

Lockhart Papers, NAM, London.

Lytton Papers, (BL[OIC]), London.

Mayo Papers, Cambridge University Library.

Morley Papers, (BL[OIC]), London.

Outram Papers, NAM, London.

Rawlinson Papers, NAM, London.

Salisbury Papers, Christ Church College, Oxford.

Indo-British Review, Madras, Vol XVI, No. 1, March 1989; Vol II, No. 2.

History Today, Vol 37, February 1987.

Journal of the Society for Army Historical Research, Vol IX, No. 241, Spring 1982; Vol XII, No. 251, Autumn 1984.

Index

A

Abdullah, Sheikh Mohammed, 442, 451
Abdullah, Farooq, 513
Abdur Rashid, Capt, 401
Abdur Rahman, Amir of Afghanistan, 197, 203, 205, 208
Abercromby, Gen Sir Robert, 44, 97-9
Abbot, Col Augustus, 183-4
Adams, Maj Thomas, 33-4, 86
Afghan Wars: First (1839-42), 54-66; Second (1878-80), 198-204, 206; Third (1919), 204, 317-9
Afridi Battalion, 352
Agartala Conspiracy Case, 499-500
Aid to the civil authority, 124-143, 516-9
Aiyer, Sir P.S. Sivaswamy, 322
Ajit Singh, 265
Ajmer Regiment, 305, 351-2
Akalis, 321, 347-8
Akbar Khan, Maj Gen (Gen "Tariq"), 440
Alanbrooke, Field Marshal Viscount, 369
Alexander, Field Marshal Earl Harold, 363
Ali Brothers, Mohammed and Shaukat, 319
Ali, Chaudhuri Mohammed, 445
Allen, Louis (quoted), 365-6, 396
Amanullah, King of Afghanistan, 206, 317-9
Amar Singh, Baba, 378
Ambedkar, Dr B.R., 300
Amery, L.S., 338, 341, 361
Amherst, Earl William, Viceroy (1823-28), 109, 111, 137-8
Ampthill, Lord Oliver, 230, 236
Andaman Islands, 195, 360, 383, 387, 394
Anderson, Lt William, 72
Annexations, 147-51
Anson, Gen George, 159-61
Arakan, 20, 52-3, 78, 361-2, 387-8
Armed Forces Nationalization Committee, 412
Artillery, Indianization, 325
Asghar Khan, Air Marshal (quoted), 493
Asquith, H.H. (later Lord Oxford and Asquith), 239
Assam, 20, 52, 519
Assam Regiment, 305, 351
Assam Rifles, 344, 475, 504, 506
Atma Singh, Maj Gen, 452
Attlee, Clement, 1st Earl, 333
Auchinleck, Field Marshal Sir Claude, (xviii), (xix), 297, 336, 338, 339, 347, 351, 357, 363-5, 369, 400, 406, 434-7

Auckland, Lord George, Governor-General (1836-42), 54-9, 63, 140, 148
Aung San, Maj Gen, 387, 396
Aurora, Lt Gen J.S., 502
Aylmer, Lt Gen Fenton, 255
Ayris, Capt H.M., 420
Ayub Khan, President of Pakistan, 490-3, 499-500
Ayyangar, Sir N. Gopalaswami, 412
Azad, Maulana Abul Kalam, 341, 405, 486

B

Badenach, Capt Walter (quoted), 97, 105, 110
Badhwar, Capt H.C. (later Maj Gen), 382
Bahadur Shah II, last Mughal Emperor (1837-58), 149, 162, 392
Baillie, Col William, 42-3
Baji Rao II, Peshwa, 48, 149
Bakht Khan, 168
Baldev Singh, Sardar, (xviii), 349, 419, 432
Balfour, A.J., 224, 230
Baluch, 130th, 250, 275
Bangladesh, 499, 519, 528
Baramula, 438, 442
Barat, Amiya (quoted), 29, 81, 123
Barkatullah, 265-6
Barker, A.J. (quoted), 254
Barker, Sir Robert, 90
Barlow, Sir George, 102-4
Barnes, Gen Sir Edward, 220
Barrackpore mutinies: (1824), 106-10; (1852), 119; (1857), 157-9
Barrow, Gen Sir Edmund, 235, 243, 251
Barton, Sir William, 458
Barstow, A.E., Maj (later Brig), 348
Bearer Corps, 218
Beckett, Ian (quoted), 277
Bengal, 2, 5, 10, 13-4, 20, 37, 422, 426
Bengal Infantry, 29, 31-4, 40-3, 70
Bengal Regiment, 250, 281, 302, 449
Bentinck, Lord William, Governor-General (1828-35), 100-1, 103, 111, 154
Bhagat, Maj (later Brig) N.S., 390
Bhagat, Lt Gen P.S., 390
Bharatpur, Battle of (1805), 137; (1826), 137-8
Bhindranwale, Sant J.S., 506
Bhonsle, Raja of Berar and Nagpur, 48-9, 148
Bhutto, Z.A., 488, 500, 524
Bhutan, 194-5
Bihar Regiment, 305, 351

692

Menon, K.P.K., 391
Menon, V.K. Krishna, 450, 452, 473-8, 481, 486-7
Menon, V.P. (quoted), 439, 456
Metcalfe, Sir Charles (later Lord), 111
Metternich, Prince Klemens von (quoted), 481
Miani, Battle of (1843), 68
Military Accounts Department, 207
Military Evacuation Organization, 430
Military Requirements (Rawlinson) Committee, 323
Military Works Department, 212
Mill, James (quoted), 32, 49, 129-32
Minto, Lord Gilbert, Viceroy (1905-10), 235-9, 264
Mir Dast, Jemadar, 273
Mir Jafar, Nawab of Bengal, 30-5, 38, 87-90, 125
Mir Kasim, Nawab of Bengal, 15, 32-6, 87-8, 125
Mir Mast, Jemadar, 273
Mitchell, Lt Col M.W., 158
Mizos, 505, 519
Moberley, F.J. (quoted), 244
Mohammed Ali, Nawab of Arcot (also of the Carnatic), 42, 86, 91, 93
Mohammad Usman, Brig, 452
Mohammad Yusuf Khan, Indian Commandant, 24, 33, 85-6
Mohan Singh, Capt (General, INA), 379-385, 459
Moir, Martin (quoted), 1, 2, 5, 19
Monckton, Walter, 1st Viscount, 455
Monro, Gen Sir Charles, 257, 313
Monson, Col George, 94, 126
Montagu, Edwin, 282, 312-3
Montgomery, Field Marshal Viscount Bernard, 260, 363, 408, 426, 436
Moon, Sir Penderel (quoted), 31, 38, 51, 91, 94, 97, 98, 127, 134, 145, 156, 166, 403
Moorcroft, William, 67
Moplahs, 141-2, 320
Moraes, Frank (quoted), 476
Morley, Lord John, 236-40, 265
Morley, Lt W., 420
Morrison, Sir Theodore, 308
Mosley, Leonard (quoted), 415
Mountbatten, Lord Louis (Earl Mountbatten of Burma), 342, 363, 401, 415, 488, 511-12, 524, 525, 528
Mudaliar, Sir Ramaswami, 361
Muir, Sir William (quoted), 185
Mujib-ur-Rehman, Sheikh, 499, 524

Mulraj, Dewan, 72-3
Munro, Sir Hector, 36-7, 42-3, 88-9
Munro, Sir Thomas (quoted), 24, 101, 153, 297
Musa, Gen Mohammed, 329, 490
Muslim League, 341, 360, 403-4
Muthanna, I.M. (quoted), 444
Myanmar, 504, 519
Mysore Wars: First (1767-9), 39; Second (1780-84), 40, 42: Third (1790-92), 45; Fourth (1799), 47

N

Nagas, 139, 416, 503-5, 519
Namka Chu, Battle of (1962), 478-9
Nana Phadnavis, 41, 48
Nana Sahib (Dhondu Pant), 149, 164-5
Napier, Gen Sir Charles, 66-8, 73-5, 118, 146, 154
Narasimha Rao, P.V. Prime Minister (from 1991), 521
Narayan Rao, Peshwa, 41
Nasiri battalions, 51, 177, 183
Native commandants, 85, 307
Native Indian Land Forces, 224
Nawanagar, Jam Saheb of, 361, 465
Nazimuddin, K., 409
Nehru, Jawaharlal, Prime Minister (1947-64), 80, 340, 370, 385, 398, 401, 402, 474-8, 486, 524, 525
Nehru, Motilal, 328
Neill, Col James, 76, 173
Nepal, 50-2, 165, 178
Nepal Army, 246, 344, 460
Netherlands East Indies, 368, 371
Neutral Nations Repatriation Commission, 470
Niazi, Lt Gen A.A.K., 501-2
Nicolson, Harold (quoted), 363
Nicholson, Brig Gen John, 162, 169
Nicholson, Field Marshal Lord William, 242-3, 299
Nicolls, Gen Sir Jasper, 62-3, 65
Nixon, Lt Gen Sir John, 252-5
Noon, Sir Firoz Khan, 361, 419
Noronha, Brig (later Lt Gen) R.S., 472
North-East Frontier Agency (NEFA), 474-9, 530
North-West Frontier Province, 330, 425
Nott, Maj Gen Sir William, 59, 64-5
Nursing Service, 218

O

Ochterlony, Maj Gen Sir David, 50-2, 109, 137-8